"Frank Thielman's book on Paul does for a new generation what F. F. Bruce's *Paul: Apostle of the Heart Set Free* did in his day: provide an overview of the apostle's ministry based on the testimony of Acts and all thirteen letters traditionally ascribed to Paul. Without sacrificing depth, the book is impressively broad in scope, combining careful historical description with brief interpretations of each of Paul's letters. This is the book on Paul I would recommend to anyone who is looking for an overview of the apostle of grace."

—DOUGLAS J. MOO
Wheaton College

"Frank Thielman's *Paul, Apostle of Grace* is an amazing achievement. We needed an up-to-date work on Paul's life and letters, and Thielman has provided us with a work well-versed in the Greco-Roman and Jewish worlds that Paul inhabited. He also situates and explains the letters in the context of Paul's life.... Scholars, pastors, and students of Paul will find this work invaluable and will want to consult it again and again."

—THOMAS R. SCHREINER
Southern Baptist Theological Seminary

"At long last we have a worthy successor to F. F. Bruce's famous biography of Paul. Drawing on all relevant Jewish and Greco-Roman sources and giving the book of Acts its full weight as a historical witness, Thielman paints a remarkably vivid picture of the apostle in his historical context. He offers a satisfactory solution to the old riddle of how to situate the pastoral epistles, and he gives a compelling account of Paul's theology in the light in which it should be understood: his missional and pastoral ministry."

—SIGURD GRINDHEIM
Western Norway University of Applied Sciences

"Frank Thielman's sure-handed guide allows readers of Paul's thirteen letters and the book of Acts to accompany the apostle on his journeys through the Greco-Roman world. Thielman breathtakingly assesses what made Paul tick and drove him across land and sea to tell of the Messiah, sent by God, to save *all* people from the enormity of sin and humanity's rebellion against God."

—A. ANDREW DAS
Elmhurst University

"This meticulous study judiciously integrates Paul's canonical letters, Acts, Greco-Roman writings, ancient Jewish sources including the Old Testament, and a vast range of scholarship. Thielman is creative, impressively comprehensive, and deeply contemplative in his reconstructions of Paul's convictions, travels, companions, and concerns. This book will stand for decades as the preferred starting point for orientation into what the historical sources reveal regarding the apostle Paul's life and times and his testimony to the messianic Savior he called Lord."

—**ROBERT W. YARBROUGH**
Covenant Theological Seminary

"What Frank Thielman offers in this book is nothing less than the now-definitive biography of the apostle Paul, written with customary clarity, caution, and commitment to historical investigation and theological elucidation. Students, pastors, and scholars will equally benefit from this immensely valuable study."

—**ECKHARD J. SCHNABEL**
Gordon-Conwell Theological Seminary

"In a volume reminiscent of F. F. Bruce's classic *Paul: Apostle of the Heart Set Free*, Frank Thielman offers a wonderfully written portrait of Paul that is profound, insightful, and deeply rooted in good scholarship. . . . Anyone wanting to know the apostle Paul and his writings better will need to read and reflect on this masterful work."

—**CLINTON E. ARNOLD**
Talbot School of Theology, Biola University

"Thielman's reconstruction of Paul's life from Acts and the canonical letters is both readable and stimulating. His description of Paul's travels is especially evocative. Utilizing the latest scholarship on roads and transport in the Roman Empire, he presents the apostle's journeys in a way that makes geographical and hodological sense."

—**MARK WILSON**
Stellenbosch University

"For those who are looking for an inviting and very readable biography of this extraordinary man, the Lord's apostle of grace, this is it. Based on wide-ranging primary research in the book of Acts, the Pauline writings, and contemporary extra-biblical writings, and combined with a thorough grasp of modern scholarship on Paul, Thielman has produced a magnificent volume."

—**DANIEL I. BLOCK**
Wheaton College

PAUL
APOSTLE *of* GRACE

FRANK THIELMAN

WILLIAM B. EERDMANS PUBLISHING COMPANY
GRAND RAPIDS, MICHIGAN

Wm. B. Eerdmans Publishing Co.
2006 44th Street SE, Grand Rapids, MI 49508
www.eerdmans.com

© 2025 Frank Thielman
All rights reserved
Published 2025

Book design by Lydia Hall

Printed in the United States of America

31 30 29 28 27 26 25   1 2 3 4 5 6 7

ISBN 978-0-8028-7629-4

Library of Congress Cataloging-in-Publication Data

A catalog record for this book is available from the Library of Congress.

Unless otherwise indicated, all Scripture quotations are from the ESV Catholic Edition with Deuterocanonical Books, copyright © 2017 by Crossway, a publishing ministry of Good News Publishers.

For Abby

Contents

	List of Maps	ix
	Preface	xi
	List of Abbreviations	xiv
1.	Paul before His Encounter with Christ	1
2.	A Revelation from God	17
3.	Following Christ in Damascus and Arabia	27
4.	Return to Jerusalem	38
5.	Ministry in Syria and Cilicia	53
6.	Forming and Expanding the Multiethnic Church of God	67
7.	Advancement and Opposition in Southern Galatia	79
8.	Resistance to the Multiethnic Church	88
9.	Advancing Westward with the Gospel	104
10.	Church Planting and Suffering in Macedonia	114
11.	A Cool Reception in Athens and Laying a Foundation in Corinth	128
12.	An Urgent Letter from Corinth to Christians in Galatia	143
13.	Urgent Letters to Thessalonica and Overcoming Opposition in Corinth	155

CONTENTS

14.	A Visit to Jerusalem, a Collection for Its Needy Christians, and a New Beginning in Ephesus	167
15.	Ministry in Ephesus and a Letter to Christians in Corinth	178
16.	Trouble in Corinth and Strange Teaching in Ephesus	193
17.	"Fighting Without and Fear Within"	206
18.	A Turning Point	220
19.	Back to Jerusalem with the Collection Delegation	233
20.	Violence and Arrest in the Jerusalem Temple	247
21.	A Taste of Roman Justice in Caesarea-by-the-Sea	263
22.	A Turbulent Journey West and Respite on Malta	271
23.	House Arrest in Rome	286
24.	Visitors from Philippi and the Lycus River Valley	299
25.	Fighting from Prison against Discouragement in Ephesus	314
26.	Paul Finishes the Race	323
	Appendix 1: The Evidence for Paul	337
	Appendix 2: The Historical Setting of Paul's Imprisonment Letters	353
	Appendix 3: The Place, Manner, and Time of Paul's Death	363
	Notes	371
	Bibliography	461
	Index of Authors	487
	Index of Subjects	498
	Index of Scripture and Other Ancient Sources	510

Maps

MAP 1:	The Roman World in the First Century AD	xviii
MAP 2:	From Syrian Antioch to Cyprus to Southern Galatia and Back to Syrian Antioch	72
MAP 3:	From Syrian Antioch to Southern Galatia to the Aegean Region to Jerusalem and Back to Syrian Antioch	105
MAP 4:	From Jerusalem to Syrian Antioch to Southern Galatia to Ephesus to Macedonia, Illyricum, Achaia, and Back to Jerusalem	173
MAP 5:	The Temple	253
MAP 6:	From Caesarea to Rome	272

Preface

Writing a book about Paul's life is like putting together a puzzle of a thousand pieces, but a puzzle whose pieces can fit together in different ways. The best one can hope for, perhaps, is a picture that is reasonable and that, at least in some cases, is probable. In the following pages I have tried to produce such a picture of Paul. I hope that those who take the time to look at it carefully, even though they may disagree on the placement of some pieces, will nevertheless come away from the experience with a deeper understanding of the complex period of history and fascinating cultures in which Paul worked.

I hope, too, that all readers of this book will come away from it with an understanding of what motivated this remarkable human being. What drove him to endure often treacherous journeys of hundreds of miles to establish like-minded communities around the world as he knew it? What spurred him to recruit a network of coworkers who were willing to help him in this vast project? What kept him at the task even when it landed him in prison? What prompted him to produce a body of lengthy letters to these communities of such depth that millions of people still read them with profit today? If this book helps to clarify for the reader what made Paul tick, it will have accomplished its purpose.

It may be useful to describe at the beginning some of the assumptions that undergird this account of Paul's life and some of the ways in which it differs from most other similar accounts. First, I have used as sources for Paul's life primarily the canonical evidence for it, which seems to me to provide the earliest and most reliable information on the apostle. Especially as the book approaches the end of Paul's life, noncanonical sources such as 1 Clement, the Acts of Paul, and even the archaeological record also become important. I have tried to outline in the first appendix my reasons for trusting the account of Paul in Acts and for accepting all thirteen Pauline epistles as genuine.

Second, I argue for several positions on the course of Paul's life that are outliers among books on the apostle. Unlike many fine scholars who believe that Acts gives a reliable account of Paul's ministry, I think that the Jerusalem Council in Acts 15 corresponds to the Jerusalem meeting Paul describes in Galatians 2:1–10. Like most scholars who do not identify the two meetings, however, I also believe that Galatians is Paul's earliest letter and that it went to churches in the southern part of the Roman province of Galatia. I also argue that Paul wrote 1 Timothy, Titus, and 2 Timothy within the span of his life that Acts describes and not after a theoretical release from the Roman imprisonment that ends the Acts narrative. It seems historically likely to me that Paul did not survive that imprisonment and that he wrote 2 Timothy near the end of it. I try to give the main reasons for these positions when they come up in the book and to provide more detailed argumentation for them in appendices 2 and 3. I hope that even those who cannot agree with my reasoning will nevertheless enjoy thinking through the evidence again.

I have tried to produce a book that will be helpful to a wide range of readers. Those with some knowledge of ancient Roman history and geography and a bit of Greek will probably benefit most from it, but I hope the book will be interesting and intelligible to anyone who wants to know more about Paul, his letters, and early Christianity. When I discuss a Greek term, I have usually put it in the lexical form to make looking it up easier for those whose Greek is limited. When referring to the Greek while quoting a translation, however, I have usually left the Greek as it is in the original. I felt free to deviate from both these rules when doing so seemed to facilitate comparison or ease of understanding. Abbreviations of ancient texts follow the conventions in the *SBL Handbook of Style* and, if they are missing from there, the *Oxford Classical Dictionary*. Other abbreviations (of journals, scholarly monograph series, and collections of papyri and inscriptions) appear below in the list of abbreviations.

I am grateful to Deans Timothy George and Douglas Sweeney of Beeson Divinity School, and to the Samford University Board of Trustees, for their support of my request for two sabbatical leaves during which I did much of the research and writing for the book. I am also deeply grateful to an anonymous donor whose generous gift made it possible for me to do invaluable research for the book in Cambridge, Massachusetts, and Rome, Italy. The Beeson Divinity School faculty dialogue group read parts of the book and provided helpful feedback. My friend and colleague of many years, Gerald Bray, kindly read through the entire manuscript and provided thoughtful, insightful comments for its improvement.

I am thankful to the editorial team at Eerdmans for inviting me to write this book and shepherding it to completion. Michael Thomson, James Ernest, Trevor Thompson, Jenny Hoffman, and Lydia Hall, along with copyeditor Erika Harman, provided encouragement, reminders, and precise editorial skills that made the work more accurate and readable than it ever could have been without their involvement.

I also am deeply grateful to my three children and their wonderful families for their love, generosity, and practical support: I wrote parts of the book during happy visits to each of their homes. Humanly speaking, though, my greatest debt of gratitude is to my wife, Abby, who after forty years of marriage is still my very best friend and whose kindness, patience, love, and encouragement have made my labor on projects like this possible and our common labor in God's service a joy.

Abbreviations

AB	Anchor Bible
ABD	Freedman, David Noel, ed. *The Anchor Bible Dictionary*. 6 vols. New York: Doubleday, 1992
ABR	*Australian Biblical Review*
AcT	*Acta Theologica*
AGJU	Arbeiten zur Geschichte des antiken Judentums und des Urchristentums
AJEC	Ancient Judaism and Early Christianity
AmJT	*American Journal of Theology*
AnBib	Analecta Biblica
ANF	Roberts, Alexander, James Donaldson, and A. Cleveland Coxe, eds. *Ante-Nicene Fathers: The Writings of the Fathers Down to A.D. 325*. Peabody, MA: Hendrickson, 1994
ANRW	Temporini, H., and W. Haase, eds. *Aufstieg und Niedergang der römischen Welt*. Berlin: de Gruyter, 1971–
BBR	*Bulletin for Biblical Research*
BDAG	Danker, F. W., W. Bauer, W. F. Arndt, and F. W. Gingrich, eds. *A Greek-English Lexicon of the New Testament and Other Christian Literature*. 3rd ed. Chicago: University of Chicago Press, 2000
BDF	Blass, Friedrich, Albert Debrunner, and Robert W. Funk. *A Greek Grammar of the New Testament and Other Early Christian Literature*. Chicago: University of Chicago Press, 1961
BECNT	Baker Exegetical Commentary on the New Testament
BETL	Bibliotheca Ephemeridum Theologicarum Lovaniensium
BNTC	Black's New Testament Commentaries
BTB	*Biblical Theology Bulletin*
BZ	*Biblische Zeitschrift*
BZNW	Beihefte zur Zeitschrift für neutestamentliche Wissenschaft
CBQ	*Catholic Biblical Quarterly*

Abbreviations

CEB	Common English Bible
CEJL	Commentaries on Early Jewish Literature
CGL	Diggle, J., B. L. Fraser, P. James, O. B. Simkin, A. A. Thompson, and S. J. Westripp, eds. *The Cambridge Greek Lexicon*. 2 vols. Cambridge: Cambridge University Press, 2021
CGTSC	Cambridge Greek Testament for Schools and Colleges
CSB	Christian Standard Bible
Ebib	*Études bibliques*
EC	*Early Christianity*
ECAM	Early Christianity in Asia Minor
EDEJ	Collins, John J., and Daniel C. Harlow, eds. *The Eerdmans Dictionary of Early Judaism*. Grand Rapids: Eerdmans, 2010
EJT	*Evangelical Journal of Theology*
EKK	Evangelisch-katholischer Kommentar
ESV	English Standard Version
ExpTim	*Expository Times*
FF	Foundations and Facets
FOC	Fathers of the Church
FRLANT	Forschungen zur Religion und Literatur des Alten und Neuen Testaments
HTA	Historisch Theologische Auslegung
HTR	*Harvard Theological Review*
HTS	Harvard Theological Studies
HUT	Hermeneutische Untersuchungen zur Theologie
ICC	International Critical Commentary
IEJ	*Israel Exploration Journal*
IG	*Inscriptiones Graecae. Editio Minor*. Berlin: de Gruyter, 1924–
ILS	Dessau, Hermann. *Inscriptiones Latinae Selectae*. 3 vols. Berlin, 1892–1916
JAAR	*Journal of the American Academy of Religion*
JBL	*Journal of Biblical Literature*
JETS	*Journal of the Evangelical Theological Society*
JHS	*Journal of Hellenic Studies*
JNES	*Journal of Near Eastern Studies*
JQR	*Jewish Quarterly Review*
JRH	*Journal of Religious History*
JRS	*Journal of Roman Studies*
JSJ	*Journal for the Study of Judaism in the Persian, Hellenistic, and Roman Periods*
JSNT	*Journal for the Study of the New Testament*
JSNTSup	Journal for the Study of the New Testament Supplement Series
JSP	*Journal for the Study of the Pseudepigrapha*

ABBREVIATIONS

JSPSup	Journal for the Study of the Pseudepigrapha Supplement Series
JTS	Journal of Theological Studies
KEK	Kritisch-exegetischer Kommentar über das Neue Testament (Meyer-Kommentar)
KJV	King James Version
LCL	Loeb Classical Library
LNTS	The Library of New Testament Studies
LSJ	Liddell, Henry George, Robert Scott, and Henry Stuart Jones. *A Greek-English Lexicon*. 9th ed. with revised supplement. Oxford: Clarendon, 1996
MGS	Montanari, Franco, Madeleine Goh, and Chad Schroeder. *The Brill Dictionary of Ancient Greek*. Leiden: Brill, 2015
MM	Moulton, James H., and George Milligan. *The Vocabulary of the Greek Testament*. Grand Rapids: Eerdmans, 1959
MNTC	Moffatt New Testament Commentary
NASB	New American Standard Bible
NCB	New Century Bible
Neot	Neotestamentica
NETS	Pietersma, Albert, and Benjamin G. Wright, eds., *A New English Translation of the Septuagint*. New York: Oxford University Press, 2007
NICNT	New International Commentary on the New Testament
NICOT	New International Commentary on the Old Testament
NIGTC	New International Greek Testament Commentary
NIV	New International Version
NovT	Novum Testamentum
NRSV	New Revised Standard Version
NTL	New Testament Library
NTS	New Testament Studies
OCD^3	Hornblower, Simon, and Antony Spawforth, eds. *The Oxford Classical Dictionary*, 3rd ed., rev. Oxford: Oxford University Press, 2003
OCD^4	Hornblower, Simon, Antony Spawforth, and Esther Eidinow, eds. *The Oxford Classical Dictionary*, 4th ed. Oxford: Oxford University Press, 2012
OGIS	Dittenberger, Wilhelm, ed. *Orientis Graeci Inscriptiones Selectae*. 2 vols. Leipzig: Hirzel, 1903–1905
OTP	Charlesworth, James H., ed. *Old Testament Pseudepigrapha*. 2 vols. New York: Doubleday, 1983, 1985
PECS	Stillwell, Richard, William L. MacDonald, and Marian Holland McAllister, eds. *The Princeton Encyclopedia of Classical Sites*. Princeton, NJ: Princeton University Press, 1976
PEQ	Palestine Exploration Quarterly

Abbreviations

PNTC	Pillar New Testament Commentary
P.Oxy.	Grenfell, Bernard P., et al., eds. *The Oxyrhynchus Papyri*. London: Egypt Exploration Fund, 1898–
P.Tebt.	Grenfell, Bernard P., et al., eds. *The Tebtunis Papyri*, vols. 1–2. London: Henry Frowde, 1902, 1907
RB	*Revue biblique*
REB	Revised English Bible
ResQ	*Restoration Quarterly*
RHR	*Revue de l'histoire des religions*
RPC	Burnett, Andrew, et al., eds. *Roman Provincial Coinage*. 9 vols. London: British Museum Press, 1992–2016
RSV	Revised Standard Version
RTR	*Reformed Theological Review*
SNTSMS	Society for New Testament Studies Monograph Series
SP	Sacra Pagina
TAPA	*Transactions of the American Philological Association*
TDNT	*Theological Dictionary of the New Testament*. Edited by Gerhard Kittel and Gerhard Friedrich. Translated by Geoffrey W. Bromiley. 10 vols. Grand Rapids: Eerdmans, 1964–1976
THKNT	Theologischer Handkommentar zum Neuen Testament
TLZ	*Theologische Literaturzeitung*
TOB	Traduction Œcuménique de la Bible
TOTC	Tyndale Old Testament Commentary
TynBul	*Tyndale Bulletin*
VigChr	*Vigiliae Christianae*
WAWSup	Writings from the Ancient World Supplement Series
WBC	Word Biblical Commentary
WGRW	Writings from the Greco-Roman World
WUNT	Wissenschaftliche Untersuchungen zum Neuen Testament
ZAC	*Zeitschrift für Antikes Christentum/Journal of Ancient Christianity*
ZECNT	Zondervan Exegetical Commentary on the New Testament
ZNW	*Zeitschrift für die neutestamentliche Wissenschaft und die Kunde der älteren Kirche*
ZPE	*Zeitschrift für Papyrologie und Epigraphik*
ZTK	*Zeitschrift für Theologie und Kirche*

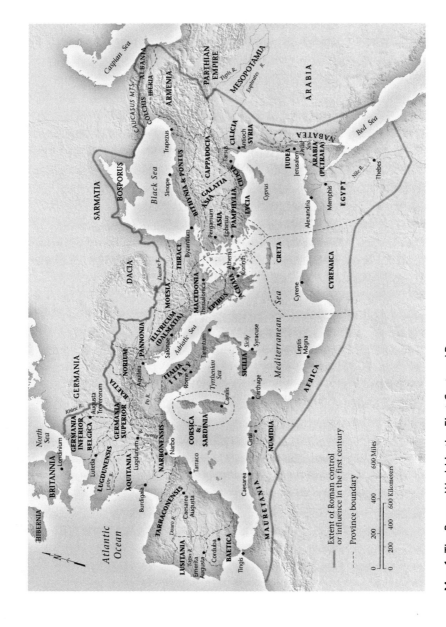

Map 1: The Roman World in the First Century AD

1

Paul before His Encounter with Christ

When, toward the end of his life, an angry mob accused Paul of defiling the temple in Jerusalem, he began his defense with a compact summary of his early life. "I am a Jew," he said, "born in Tarsus in Cilicia, but brought up in this city, educated at the feet of Gamaliel according to the strict manner of the law of our fathers, being zealous for God as all of you are to this day" (Acts 22:3). This brief comment raises a fascinating series of questions. If Paul was born in Tarsus, a center of Hellenistic philosophy and learning far to the northwest of Jerusalem, how did he eventually become a student of the famous Rabbi Gamaliel in Jerusalem?[1] If he learned his strict form of Judaism under Gamaliel, who was reasonable and no advocate of violence, why did he become so "zealous for God" that he tried to kill people, just as the zealous crowd to whom he was speaking were trying to kill him? If he and they were both consumed with this same kind of zeal, what brought them to this moment when they found themselves on opposite sides of the violence?

Born in Tarsus

The date of Paul's birth and his age at various crucial points in his life are not clear, but a few hints point to his birth about a decade after Christ's own birth and to his violent opposition to the Jesus movement sometime in his twenties. Luke describes Paul as "a young man" (νεανίας) when the Sanhedrin executed Stephen and the witnesses against him laid their garments at Paul's feet to prepare for Stephen's stoning (Acts 7:58). Philo of Alexandria could use a similar expression (νεανίσκος) to mean someone between twenty-one and twenty-eight years old (*Opif.* 105).² This meaning fits with the way both the Greek Scriptures of Paul's time and Luke himself, in the rest of Acts, use Luke's term. It could refer to young men of marriageable age (Ruth 3:10), to David as a young man during the period of his friendship with Jonathan (1 Sam 20:31), and to vigorous young soldiers (e.g., 1 Kgs 12:21; 1 Chr 19:10).

According to Luke, Paul's nephew was "a young man" (νεανίας/ νεανίσκος) when he sniffed out a plot on his uncle's life, gained entrance to the barracks where Paul was detained, and told Paul what he had overheard (Acts 23:17–18). Paul's nephew was young enough that the tribune to whom Paul sent him "took him by the hand" and spoke to him privately (23:19). But he was old enough that he delivered to the tribune a clear account of what happened in impeccable Greek (23:19–22).

So, when Luke says that Paul was "a young man" at the time of Stephen's death, it seems reasonable to imagine a twenty-something man with great zeal, a good education, and too little experience of life to empathize with people who disagreed with him on points of doctrine.

When did Stephen die? Luke gives the impression that a short period elapsed between the death of Jesus and the death of Stephen, since, in this part of his narrative, he measures time mainly in daily increments (Acts 1:3; 2:47; 4:3, 5; 5:42; 6:1). If Jesus died in the spring of AD 30, as seems likely, then it is reasonable to think of Stephen's death happening in AD 31 or 32.³ If Paul was in his early twenties when he presided over Stephen's lynching, that would put his birth slightly later than Jesus's birth, say between AD 5 and 10.

Luke says not only that Paul was born in Tarsus, in the Roman province of Cilicia, but that he held citizenship in that city (Acts 9:11; 21:39; 22:3). It is true that he moved to Jerusalem at an early age (22:3), but Tarsus still held significance for him as an adult. When some Greek-speaking Jews in Jerusalem began to hunt Paul down after his conversion, "the brothers . . . sent him off to Tarsus" to escape (9:30). He could identify himself to a military tribune as "a Jew, from Tarsus in Cilicia" (21:39), and others could identify him as "a man of Tarsus named Saul" (9:11). He seems to have considered Tarsus in some sense his home, and perhaps he still had relatives there.

The ancient geographer Strabo, who wrote his extensive *Geography* when Paul was a youngster, says that Cilicia has two parts, a "Rough" (τραχεῖα) area and a "Level" (πεδιάς) area (14.5.1).⁴ The western, rough part was an inhospitable, mountainous region famous for its pirates, but Tarsus was in the eastern, flat section on a fertile plain about ten miles inland. The cold, fresh water of the Cydnus River coursed from the Taurus Mountains right through the city center (14.5.12).[5]

Tarsus began to rise to prominence in the Roman Empire after Pompey gained control of the pirates in the rugged western area in 67 BC and all of Cilicia came under Rome's control.[6] By the fifties, the famous Roman statesman Cicero lived in the city while he served as governor of Cilicia and heard legal cases there (*Fam.* 3.8).[7] Later, the city supported Julius Caesar against Cassius in the civil war, and when Cassius gained control of the city, he saddled the Tarsians with economic burdens, taking "away all their money, private and public" (Cassius Dio, *Hist. Rom.* 47.31.3 [Cary, LCL]). When Caesar's avengers, Mark Antony and Augustus, took the city, however, they rewarded its loyalty to Caesar with freedom.[8] Speaking in the early second century AD, Dio Chrysostom could tell the Tarsians that "everything a man might bestow upon those who were truly friends and allies and had displayed such eagerness in his behalf [Augustus] has bestowed on you: land, laws, honour, control of the river and of the sea in your quarter of the world" (*Or.* 34.8 [Cohoon and Crosby, LCL]). As inhabitants of a free city, many people born there would be citizens, and Jewish people, such as Paul, could at least have a status that was something like citizenship (Acts 21:39).[9]

Strabo says that the city was famous in his own time, and thus in Paul's youth, for its schools of philosophy and rhetoric. He also claims, however, that it was rare for people to travel to Tarsus to take advantage of its educational opportunities. Instead, Tarsians tended to go abroad to finish their education (*Geogr.* 14.5.13). The city was especially rich in Stoic philosophers, and its citizens could "improvise unceasingly on the spot about any topic" (*Geogr.* 14.5.14). It seems to have been the kind of place where a Jewish child from a family well connected enough to have Roman citizenship (Acts 22:28; cf. 16:37–38; 22:25) might have access to a good education in the fundamentals of Greek reading, composition, and rhetoric. In Tarsus, people "were so eager about philosophy and everything else in terms of general education that they ... surpassed Athens and Alexandria" (*Geogr.* 14.5.13). Perhaps it was here that Paul began the basics of "the great learning" King Agrippa recognized in the speech Paul gave before him (Acts 26:24) and that is on display in the fluent Greek of Paul's letters.

It is unlikely, however, that Paul's early education in Tarsus would have involved study of the classics of Greek literature or exposure to the theater.[10] Although his family lived outside the land of Israel, they were observant Jews who followed the teachings of the Pharisees about how to keep the law.[11] According to Luke, Paul told the Jewish ruling council in Jerusalem, "I am a Pharisee, a son of Pharisees" (Acts 23:6), a point that Paul confirms in his letter to Christians in Philippi. His family spoke Aramaic, the native language of Palestine, knew they belonged to the lineage of the Jewish patriarch Benjamin, and were so concerned about observing the Mosaic law that they made sure to circumcise Paul on the eighth day (Phil 3:5–6; cf. Rom 11:1; 2 Cor 11:22).

The Pharisees were "the strictest party of our religion," as Paul reminded Herod Agrippa (Acts 26:5), but their strictness did not typically translate into harshness and violence. If Josephus is believable on this point, the common people tended to appreciate their help in understanding how to live in ways that were pleasing to God. Somehow for the young Paul, however, "accuracy" in the Pharisees' approach to the law laid the foundation for conflict with the Jesus movement, and, eventually, for violence against it.

Brought Up in Jerusalem as a Pharisee

It is understandable that Paul's family, as Pharisees, might make a move during his youth to Jerusalem where he was "brought up" and where he eventually received a more formal education from the famous first-century rabbi Gamaliel (Acts 22:3; 26:4; cf. 5:34). The land of Israel, and especially Jerusalem, was where the Pharisees flourished.[12] Theirs was a lay movement whose purpose was to encourage faithfulness to the Mosaic law, and since so much of the Mosaic law regulated the temple ritual, their approach to the law worked best in places near enough to the temple to visit it consistently.

The Pharisees were probably descended ideologically from the scribe Ezra who, according to Nehemiah 8, organized reading and instruction in the law for the people of Israel after their return to the land from exile and was himself both a scribe (8:1, 4, 13) and a priest (8:2, 9).[13] Nehemiah 9–10 paints a portrait of a people relieved to be living in the land of Israel, and especially in Jerusalem, after years of exile. They are both repentant for the sins of their ancestors that led them into exile and thankful to God who in his "great mercies... did not make an end of them or forsake them" (9:31). Neglect and violation of God's law had led to their exile from their own land and most recently to an existence under the domination of foreign powers even in the land of Israel. So, the scribe Ezra, the Levites, and the priests wanted to lead the people into a knowledge of the law and a strategy for obeying it under these new conditions (9:38–10:39).[14]

What would keeping the Sabbath look like in the Israel of the late fifth century BC with its many surrounding non-Israelite people groups wanting to buy and sell there? "If the peoples of the land bring in goods or any grain on the Sabbath day to sell, we will not buy from them on the Sabbath or on a holy day" (Neh 10:31). Buying from a non-Israelite on the Sabbath was not explicitly forbidden in the Mosaic law, but it is easy to see how the Mosaic legislation on the Sabbath could be extended in this way (cf. Neh 13:15–18).[15]

How would the complex operations of the temple be financed? "We also take on ourselves the obligation to give yearly a third part of a shekel for the service of the house of our God: for the showbread, the regular grain offering, the regular burnt offering, the Sabbaths, the new moons, the appointed feasts, the holy things, and the sin offerings to make atonement for Israel, and for all the work of the house of our God" (Neh 10:32–33). Specifically, how would the temple obtain enough wood to fuel the sacrificial fires that were a constant feature of its operation (Lev 6:8–9, 12–13)? "We, the priests, the Levites, and the people, have likewise cast lots for the wood offering, to bring it into the house of our God, according to our fathers' houses, at times appointed, year by year, to burn on the altar of the Lord our God, as it is written in the Law" (Neh 10:34). The Mosaic law contains no mandate to finance the temple's ongoing operations with an annual tax nor a system for providing wood for its sacrificial fires.[16] A new law to this effect, however, could be sensibly derived from the important place of the temple ritual in the Mosaic law.

There is an effort here to move beyond the Mosaic law's actual language and to figure out how to apply it in Israel's new existence under foreign domination. As the decades passed and Persian overlords gave way to a series of Hellenistic rulers, whether Macedonian, Egyptian, Syrian, Hasmonean, Idumean, or Roman, the need to figure out how the law should be obeyed in new situations only increased. At some point, scribes and priests divided into two separate classes, with scribes focusing on the scholarly study and interpretation of the law, and priests focusing on ruling the nation in negotiation with the more powerful non-Israelite nations that had a political stake in Israel. To speak in very broad categories, some within the scribal class seem to have evolved into the Pharisees and some within the priestly class into the Sadducees.

The Pharisees were mainly interested in encouraging all Israelites to follow the Mosaic law faithfully in the give-and-take of everyday life, and in changing social conditions. They were popular with most people since they interpreted the Mosaic law in ways that made it easier for most people to obey it. This stood in contrast to the aristocratic, Saducean ruling class.[17] By the first century, the Sadducees had a reputation for uncompromising readings of what the Mosaic law required and harsh interpretations of its penalties. They were, says Josephus, "more heartless than any of the other Jews" (*A.J.* 20.199 [Feldman, LCL]). The Pharisees were known for the "accuracy" (ἀκρίβεια) with which they interpreted the Mosaic law (Josephus, *B.J.* 1.110; 2.162; *Vita* 191; Acts 26:5; cf. Josephus, *A.J.* 17.41). This seems to mean that they studied the law thoroughly and had a systematic way of applying it to everyday life.

The Pharisees' interpretations of how the common Israelite should obey the law were handed down from generation to generation in a body of teaching variously called "the paternal tradition" (Josephus, *A.J.* 13.297, 408, my trans.) or "the tradition of the elders" (Mark 7:3, 5). Josephus describes this extrabiblical body of teaching as "regulations handed down by former generations and not recorded in the Laws of Moses" (*A.J.* 13.297 [Marcus, LCL]). He makes it clear that the Pharisees developed it "for the people" (*A.J.* 13.296) and "passed" it "on to the people" (*A.J.* 13.297), and that the people gladly received it (*A.J.* 13.288, 296, 298; 18.15; cf. 13.401–402 [Marcus, LCL]), performing "all prayers and sacred rites of divine worship . . . according to their exposition" (*A.J.* 18.15 [Feldman, LCL]).

The common people apparently appreciated the Pharisees' attempt to teach them how to obey the law, and to do so in a way that was practical and lenient (cf. Josephus, *A.J.* 13.294). Josephus describes them as "affectionate to each other" and eager to "cultivate harmonious relations with the community" (*B.J.* 2.166 [Thackeray, LCL]). This description of the Pharisees may receive confirmation in Mark's Gospel when the evangelist explains why the Pharisees objected to Jesus's disciples' practice of eating with unwashed hands: "The Pharisees and all the Jews do not eat unless they wash their hands properly, holding to the tradition of the elders, and when they come from the marketplace, they do not eat unless they wash" (Mark 7:3–4). Mark may be saying nothing more than that the Pharisees do what all Jews do, but there may also be a hint here that the Pharisees have encouraged the observance of these customs among the common people, and the common people have complied.[18]

Similarly, Luke describes Gamaliel (who, later in the narrative, will turn out to have been Paul's teacher) as "a teacher of the law held in honor by all the people" (Acts 5:34). Most Jews, in other words, held this great Pharisaic scholar in high regard. In Luke's narrative, Gamaliel was a sensible, nonextremist whose advice to the Jewish governing council about the new Christian movement was eminently reasonable: "If this plan or this undertaking is of man, it will fail; but if it is of God, you will not be able to overthrow them. You might even be found opposing God!" (Acts 5:38–39).[19]

In the gospels and Acts, the Pharisees seem particularly concerned about ritual purity at meals (including tithing food), avoiding association with known sinners, and observing the Sabbath. They come into conflict with Jesus because he eats with "tax collectors and sinners" (Mark 2:16; Matt 9:11; Luke 5:30). Jesus criticizes the relative importance they place on washing before eating (Mark 7:3–4a, 7) and of immersing utensils that contact food (Matt 23:25–26; Luke 11:39; cf. Mark 7:4b). In Matthew and Luke, Jesus describes the care they took in tithing the smallest amounts of food (Matt 23:23; Luke 11:42).

This matches the evidence from the Mishnah for their relationships with people who followed their rules on one hand ("Associates") and those that did not follow their rules on the other hand (the *Am-haaretz* or "people of the land"): "He that undertakes to be an Associate may not sell to an *Am-haaretz* [foodstuff that is] wet or dry, or buy from him [foodstuff that is] wet; and he may not be the guest of an *Am-haaretz* nor may he receive him as a guest in his own raiment" (m. Demai 2:3a [Danby]). The concern here is simply to avoid eating food in a way that causes one to contract impurity. Wet food and clothing could easily be ritually impure and could communicate that impurity to others, so the Pharisees, who wanted to avoid contracting impurity, had to be careful about eating meals with those who did not share their concerns.[20]

Why the worry?[21] The Pharisees wanted Israel, and especially Jerusalem and the temple, to be holy in accord with the teaching of Scripture. They therefore derived from the requirements of holiness for the priests in the temple ways that they could sanctify themselves, although they were mainly a lay movement. They also wanted to be sure to keep impurity away from the temple and its priests so that the rituals performed there would be performed in the holiness that God required. They were strict about tithing (Matt 23:23; Luke 11:42) since the Mosaic law stipulated that tithes belonged to the Levites and the priests, and this system helped to ensure the priests' sanctity.

An entire tractate of the Mishnah, much of it probably predating AD 70, regulated the problem of purchasing and using food that may not have been properly tithed (m. Demai).[22] Mishnah Hagigah 2:7 illustrates these concerns: "For the Pharisees the clothes of an *Am-haaretz* count as suffering *midras*-uncleanness; for them that eat Heave-offering [i.e., the temple priests] the clothes of Pharisees count as suffering *midras*-uncleanness; for them that eat of Hallowed Things [the priests actually officiating in the temple] the clothes of them that eat Heave-offering count as suffering *midras*-uncleanness; for them that occupy themselves with the Sin-offering water the clothes of them that eat of Hallowed Things count as suffering *midras*-uncleanness" (trans. Danby). Here, the Pharisees are not priests but observe a level of purity analogous to the purity of the priests in the temple and that separates them from the people of the land (the *Am-haaretz*). Those who handle the purification water in the temple are most holy, the priests who are presently officiating in the temple are the next most holy, any temple priest is the next most holy, and the Pharisees themselves occupy a level of holiness between the temple priests and the people. Perhaps they saw themselves as forming a kind of buffer between the people of the land, who were ignorant of the fine points of ritual purity, and the temple ritual.

It is reasonably clear from the gospels that Jesus appreciated some of the Pharisees' concerns. Jesus taught both the crowds and his own disciples that the Pharisees occupied "Moses's seat" (Matt 23:2).[23] Since authoritative teaching was done from a sitting position (e.g., Mark 9:35; 12:41–43; Matt 5:1; Luke 4:20–21; 5:3), this probably means that the Pharisees faithfully taught what Moses taught. Jesus goes on to say, "So do and observe whatever they tell you" (Matt 23:3). Later in the same discourse, Jesus mentions that the Pharisees "tithe mint and dill and cumin" (Matt 23:23a). He is critical of them for ignoring the law's more important teaching on justice, mercy, and faithfulness, in order to focus on tithing small amounts of food, but the problem was a matter of balance, not of practicing the tithe: "These [tithes] you ought to have done," he says, "without neglecting the others [justice, mercy, and faithfulness]" (Matt 23:23b).

It is also reasonably clear that not all Pharisees were Jesus's enemies.[24] Some Pharisees were interested enough in Jesus's teaching that they invited him to meals (Luke 7:36; 11:37; 14:1). The Pharisee Nicodemus sought Jesus out to learn from him because he believed that Jesus had come from God (John 3:1–2). He later defended Jesus when his colleagues unfairly maligned him (John 7:50–52) and sought to give Jesus an honorable burial (John 19:39). Some Pharisees warned Jesus that Herod Antipas wanted to kill him (Luke 13:31) and others became Christians after Jesus's death (Acts 15:5). Paul continued to consider himself a Pharisee after his conversion (Acts 23:6), and after he identified himself with them, some Pharisees came to the Christian Paul's defense before the Jewish ruling council, taking a position not unlike that of Gamaliel in the early days of the church. "We find nothing wrong in this man," they argued. "What if a spirit or an angel spoke to him?" (Acts 23:9; cf. Acts 5:34–39).[25]

There were, however, several sources of conflict between Jesus and the Pharisees. The Pharisees did not approve of Jesus's cavalier approach to eating with "tax collectors and sinners," as the gospels refer to them. For Jesus, these were not merely "the people of the land," who were ignorant of the details of ritual purity, but people who were "sick" and in need of a doctor—people who were unrighteous (Mark 2:17).[26] Nevertheless, the reason the Pharisees gave for being unhappy with Jesus's association with them was that he ate with them. Those who were unrighteous in obvious ways—the sexually immoral, thieves, murderers, adulterers, etc. (Mark 7:21–22)—were unlikely to be punctilious about tithing their food.[27] It is possible that at least some Pharisees had no problem with Jesus calling such people to repentance (Luke 5:32) but balked at Jesus's lax attitude toward ritual purity. Why did he need to call them to repentance in the context of a meal in their houses (Mark 2:15; Luke 5:29; 15:2)?

Jesus, for his part, did not approve of the Pharisaic tendency to elevate "the tradition of the fathers" over the central concerns of the Mosaic law itself. Some Pharisees seemed more concerned about observing the rules of ritual holiness than about tending to the much more basic concern of the Mosaic law with the moral holiness of God's people: honoring one's parents (Mark 7:9–13), giving alms (Luke 11:41), justice, mercy, faithfulness, and love for God (Matt 23:23; Luke 11:42). They seemed far too unconcerned about reaching out to the sinful who wanted to repent and welcoming them into the kingdom (Luke 15:1–32). This was the same criticism that the writing prophets had of the priestly class in their own time (Isa 29:13–14; Mark 7:6–7), and some Pharisees would have appreciated Jesus's point, but Jesus must have seemed to them to be taking this idea too far. "There is nothing outside a person that by going into him can defile him. . . . Do you not see that whatever goes into a person from outside cannot defile him?" (Mark 7:15, 18).

Such a view of the dietary regulations both of the Mosaic law and of "the traditions of the elders" was matched by Jesus's approach to the Sabbath. Jesus's Sabbath healings seemed to the Pharisees to be a clear violation of the Sabbath command. The Mishnah forbids the use of any curative for healing on the Sabbath that did not also have a normal use (m. Shabbat 14:3–4). The Sabbath was not a day for effecting a permanent change in anything: building, chopping wood, plowing, harvesting, writing (unless it was impermanent, or unreadable doodling), and certainly not healing.[28] As one synagogue ruler (who is not, however, identified as a Pharisee) put it to the crowds who came to Jesus on the Sabbath for healing, "There are six days in which work ought to be done. Come on those days and be healed, and not on the Sabbath day" (Luke 13:14). Jesus's insistence on healing on the Sabbath seemed to the Pharisees (and probably many other Jews) to be an egregious breach of the Sabbath command. Mark portrays Jesus's conflict with the Pharisees as growing gradually more serious until, after he heals a man with a withered hand on the Sabbath, they "went out and immediately held counsel with the Herodians against him, how to destroy him" (Mark 3:6; cf. John 5:18).

In addition to Jesus's approach to ritual purity and the Sabbath, the Pharisees found his teaching on the temple offensive, although this point of conflict is more allusive in the gospel narratives. It comes out most clearly in John's Gospel where John bookends Jesus's teaching ministry with references to conflict between Jesus and a combination of the temple authorities and the Pharisees over Jesus's relationship to the temple.

Near the beginning of his gospel, John describes Jesus's dramatic action of driving those who sold sacrificial animals and changed money in the temple out of its precincts with the command, "Do not make my Father's house a house of trade" (John 2:16). "The Jews" then ask Jesus for a sign that proves he has the authority to engage in such a provocation, and Jesus responds, "Destroy this temple, and in three days I will raise it up" (2:19). "The Jews" take this statement literally and respond in a way that points out the ridiculous nature of Jesus's claim to authority over the temple (2:20). A few paragraphs before this narrative, John has used the expression "the Jews" interchangeably with the expression "the Pharisees" (1:19, 24).

Near the end of his gospel, similarly, "the chief priests and the Pharisees" express the fear that the popularity of Jesus among the common people will lead the Roman authorities to "take away both our place and our nation" (John 11:47–48). "Our place" is probably the temple itself (cf. 2 Macc 5:17–20; Acts 6:14).[29] The expression might also contain a secondary reference to the "place" of authority that the chief priests and the particularly powerful Pharisees on the Jewish ruling council occupied with respect to the temple's affairs.[30] Their concern seemed to be that if they displayed an inability to control a populist movement creating disturbances in Jerusalem and the temple area itself, the Romans might feel the need to reorganize the way they ruled the temple, Jerusalem, and even Judea. The fear was not merely that the temple's power structure would be reorganized, however, but that the Romans would take the temple away.

Somewhere in the background here seems to lie the charge against Jesus that he would "destroy" the temple (John 2:19). This charge was probably based on a mixture of several elements of Jesus's teaching about the temple. He had claimed to be greater than the temple (Matt 12:6). He had engaged in a provocative action in the temple that seemed to portend its destruction (Mark 11:15–18; Matt 21:12–13; Luke 19:45–46; John 2:13–16). He had justified this action with a statement about the temple's destruction and then made the mysterious claim that he would himself rebuild the temple in three days (John 2:19). He had also prophesied that the gentiles would destroy the temple (Luke 21:6, 24; Mark 13:2; Matt 24:2).

The Jewish ruling council, at Jesus's trial before them, seems to have twisted all this into the false charge that Jesus had claimed, "I will destroy this temple that is made with hands, and in three days I will build another, not made with hands" (Mark 14:58; Matt 26:61; cf. Mark 15:29; Matt 27:40). Considering the Pharisees' concern to protect the sanctity of the temple, it is easy to see why at least some of the powerful members of their group who served on the Jewish ruling council would be disturbed by Jesus's teaching on the temple, or at least by the various misunderstandings of it.

A Persecutor of the Church

Jesus's approach to the law and the temple probably also stood behind the opposition of the pre-Christian Paul to the movement Jesus had started among the Jewish people.[31] Paul first appears in Luke's narrative as an attendant at Stephen's death where the "witnesses" against Stephen laid their clothing at "Saul's" feet before participating in his stoning (Acts 7:58), "and," Luke says, "Saul approved of his execution" (Acts 8:1; 22:20). A group from "the synagogue of the Freedmen" in Jerusalem had accosted Stephen and dragged him before the Jewish ruling council. Then, in a scene reminiscent of Jesus's trial before the council (Mark 14:57–58; Matt 26:60–61), false witnesses came forward and accused Stephen of saying that "this Jesus of Nazareth will destroy this place and will change the customs that Moses delivered to us" (Acts 6:14). "This place" was the temple, and Moses's customs were the traditions that preceding generations had handed down about how to observe the law of Moses, what Paul calls "the traditions of my fathers" (Gal 1:14).[32] These were precisely the traditions that Paul was zealous to keep and have kept, and he was willing to resort to violence to protect these customs (Gal 1:13–14; Phil 3:5–6).

Although most Pharisees in the early first century seem to have been peaceful—more in Gamaliel's school of thought than Paul's—the violent nature of Paul's zeal was not unprecedented. Writing in the early first century and around the time of Paul's pre-Christian persecuting activity, Philo opines that "it is well that all who have a zeal [ζῆλον] for virtue should be permitted to exact the penalties offhand and with no delay, without bringing the offender before jury or council or any kind of magistrate at all, and give full scope to the feelings which possess them, that hatred of evil and love of God which urges them to inflict punishment without mercy on the impious" (*Spec.* 1.55 [Colson, LCL]). Philo goes on to justify this violent zeal with a reference to Phinehas in Numbers 25, who, in Philo's retelling, suddenly and violently killed an Israelite man and his Midianite female companion as they were offering pagan sacrifices in disregard of the traditions of the fathers (ἀλογοῦντας ... τῶν πατρίων) (*Spec.* 1.56; cf. 1 Macc 2:24–27, 50, 54).³³ All this sounds a lot like an attempt to justify a lynching, exactly the kind of lynching that killed Stephen.

Later in the same treatise, moreover, Philo makes clear that he was not speaking merely theoretically but that there were in his own time thousands who were willing to stone to death anyone foolish enough to use God's name in an oath sworn falsely.³⁴ Using terms that are reminiscent of the descriptions of Pharisees in both Acts and Paul's letters, he says that these "thousands" are "full of zeal [ζηλωταί] for the laws, strictest [ἀκριβέστατοι] guardians of the ancestral institutions [τῶν πατρίων], merciless to those who do anything to subvert them" (Philo, *Spec.* 2.253 [Colson, LCL]).³⁵

The similarity of these terms to the expressions that Paul and Luke use to describe both the Pharisees and the basis of Paul's persecution of Christians is remarkable. "Zeal" is reminiscent of Paul's claim that "as to the law" he was a "Pharisee; as to zeal, a persecutor of the church" (Phil 3:5–6). "Strictest" is reminiscent of Paul's comment in Acts that he once lived as a Pharisee, "the strictest party of our religion" (Acts 26:5), and the expression "ancestral institutions" recalls Paul's claim that prior to his transforming encounter with Christ he was "extremely zealous ... for the traditions of my fathers" (Gal 1:14).³⁶

Josephus, writing several decades after Philo, but about events during roughly the same period, claimed that a movement came into existence in Judea in AD 6 that resisted the efforts of the Romans to conduct a census in Judea for taxing the people. As Josephus describes it, this "philosophy" seems to have had mainly economic and political goals for the liberation of Judea from Roman domination. Josephus comments, however, that one of its cofounders was a Pharisee (*A.J.* 18.4) and that, apart from their commitment to freedom and to calling God alone either governor or ruler, this "philosophy" agreed in everything with the Pharisees (*A.J.* 18.23). Josephus claims the movement led to sedition and murder, and that young people were particularly enthusiastic for it (*A.J.* 18.8).

It is clear from these references in Philo and Josephus that during the period of Paul's own youth, violent religious zeal was increasing in Judea. Some of this zeal centered on "the traditions of the fathers" and had a connection to the Pharisees' particular understanding of how the Mosaic law should be observed. It seems reasonable to think of Paul's "zeal" for persecuting Christians as part of this general trend (Phil 3:6; cf. Acts 22:3; Gal 1:13–14). He must have seen the followers of "the Way" as a movement within Judaism that undermined Pharisaic teaching on ritual purity, the Sabbath, and the centrality of the temple.

He probably considered Jesus's own death as the justified killing of someone who was leading the people astray by encouraging them to break the Sabbath, ignore the food laws, and neglect matters of ritual purity. He may well have heard that Jesus taught all this with "authority, and not as the scribes" (Mark 1:22), and that he claimed to speak with the authority of God himself. If Paul was an acquaintance of the high priest and the Judean ruling council (Acts 9:1; 22:5; 26:10), then he probably knew that the charge on which Jesus was executed was blasphemy because he claimed to be both the Son of God and the Son of Man, and to share God's glory at God's right hand (Mark 14:61–64; Matt 26:63–66; Luke 22:67–71; John 19:7). Stephen's vision of Jesus "standing at the right hand of God" (Acts 7:55–56) precipitated his stoning, "and Saul approved of his execution" (Acts 8:1).

The high priest Caiaphas, his powerful father-in-law Annas (who continued to carry the title of high priest), and other members of the Jerusalem nobility were, like Paul, eager to suppress the new movement (John 11:47–50; Matt 27:62–66; Acts 4:5–6, 16–17; 5:28; 6:12–7:1). Although Paul's reasons for this were more religious and their reasons more political, it is understandable that Paul would make common cause with them. The alliance was perhaps not unlike the partnership of the Pharisees and the "Herodians" in plotting Jesus's death (Mark 3:6).

From several angles, then, Paul's enthusiastic persecution of Jesus's followers makes sense. Religious zeal was on the rise among people with Pharisee-like convictions. Jesus and his followers held views that conflicted with the views of the Pharisees at various points. The powerful Jerusalem nobility was eager to rid itself of this troublesome new movement and therefore supported Paul's desire to do his part in stamping it out.

Paul before His Encounter with Christ

Even so, there remains something unusual about Paul's zeal. Both Paul and Luke hint that there was an irrational element to the level of violence Paul was willing to exercise against Christians. Paul himself does not say simply that he persecuted the church, but that he "savagely persecuted" and "tried to destroy it" (Gal 1:13 REB). He was a "violent, insolent person" (ὑβριστής) (1 Tim 1:13).[37]

In Luke's narrative, the post-conversion Paul reflects on his pre-Christian persecution of the church in a speech of defense before a raucous mob trying to kill him for defiling the temple (Acts 22:1–21). He begins his defense by referring to his education "according to the strict manner of the law of our fathers, being zealous for God as all of you are this day" (22:3). Like the mob he faced, the pre-Christian Paul's zeal led him to persecute Christians "to the death" (22:4) before he really understood what they believed. Similarly, in his speech before King Agrippa, he says that there was a maniacal character to the fury with which he persecuted Christians (26:11).[38] "It is hard for you to kick against the goads" (26:14), the Lord tells him at the time of his conversion, using a proverbial expression that often referred to resisting the gods or fate, but sometimes with the nuance that such resistance was nonsensical.[39]

Perhaps Paul's statement that he was "unworthy to be called an apostle because [he] persecuted the church of God" (1 Cor 15:9) arose out of a recognition of just how inexcusable his violent rampage against the church was. Like the unbelieving Jews he had in mind in Romans 10:2, he had "a zeal [ζῆλον] for God, but not according to knowledge" (cf. 1 Tim 1:13).

So, when Paul approached the high priest for letters of introduction to synagogues in Damascus asking them to permit him to arrest and conduct to Jerusalem anyone who belonged to the Way (Acts 9:2; 22:5), the high priest must have been happy to comply. These letters would not have constituted a formal command to the synagogues in Damascus—the high priest in Jerusalem probably had no jurisdiction over them—but a request to aid Paul in his effort to convey religious troublemakers to Jerusalem where they would face first a hearing before Judaism's most important religious authorities and then punishment, just as with Stephen. As with Stephen and, several decades later, James the brother of Jesus, this would be an inner-Jewish affair, conducted outside the boundaries of Roman authority.[40] Such a scenario is far from "inconceivable."[41]

CHAPTER 1

The journey from Jerusalem to Damascus was somewhere between 160 and 175 miles and took about nine days by foot, or five days by horseback.⁴² It was a large city with a Jewish population of many thousands, and it is easy to imagine newly baptized believers making their way back to Damascus from Jerusalem after attending one of the pilgrimage festivals where they heard the gospel from followers of "the Way" (Acts 9:2).⁴³ Luke gives the impression that the Christian community there was small and well integrated into the synagogues of the city. There seems to be some uncertainty that Paul would actually find "any belonging to the Way" in Damascus, and, after his conversion, Paul was "with the disciples" there, a phrase that implies he knew everyone in the group. The Jesus-follower Ananias, who instructed Paul immediately after his conversion, had a good reputation among "all the Jews who lived in Damascus" (22:12), and "synagogues" in the city allowed Paul, after his conversion, to proclaim Jesus within their assemblies as the Son of God (9:20).

"The Jews" who plotted to kill Paul in Damascus three years later (Acts 9:23–25; cf. Gal 1:17–18) seem to have been the aristocratic leadership at the top of the Jewish community with close ties to the city's government (2 Cor 11:32).⁴⁴ It is reasonable to speculate that this group had strong connections to the ruling priests and other members of the Jewish ruling council in Jerusalem, and to the Greek-speaking Jewish community of which Paul himself was a part (Acts 6:9–14; 7:1; 7:58; 8:1). That community, too, would eventually try to kill Paul, whom they must have viewed as a dangerous turncoat (Acts 9:29).

For now, however, Paul, a group of zealous Greek-speaking Jews in Jerusalem, and the Jewish aristocracy in Jerusalem made common cause. The need to preserve their places of wealth and privilege may have been the chief motivation for the aristocrats. The need to preserve the sanctity of God's people and the temple may have been the main goal of Paul and the Hellenists. Both parties agreed, however, that "the Way" of Jesus was a threat to their own ways of life and that if it was making inroads into synagogues in Damascus, Paul needed to travel there and snuff out its influence.

2

A Revelation from God

Both Paul and Luke agree that, suddenly, a stunning experience on the way to Damascus stopped Paul in his tracks. More than that, it transformed him from a fuming anti-Christian zealot into an enthusiastic proclaimer and defender of the Christian faith. In the words of "the churches of Judea" after they heard what had happened to Paul, "He who used to persecute us is now preaching the faith he once tried to destroy" (Gal 1:23). Paul and Luke agree that Paul's conversion was surprising, that it was like both a prophetic call and an apocalyptic vision, and that it resulted in Paul's conviction that God had called him to take the good news about Jesus to the non-Jewish world.

Paul's Conversion Was Surprising

The earliest sources on Paul agree that his experience on the road from Jerusalem to Damascus took him by surprise. Luke's dramatic account of Paul's encounter with Jesus puts special emphasis on this aspect of his conversion. Luke tells the story three times and begins each narrative with the detail that it happened amid Paul's fervent opposition to the Jesus movement. Paul was "still breathing threats and murder against the disciples of the Lord" (Acts 9:1), or he was on his way to Damascus to take Christians prisoner (22:5–6), or he was journeying to Damascus "in . . . connection" with his violent intentions against Christians (26:12) when "suddenly" (9:3; 22:6) a light flashed from heaven and surrounded him (9:3; 22:6; cf. 26:13).

Neither Paul nor Luke says anything about suppressed feelings of guilt or hidden misgivings about his anti-Christian fervor. Nothing resembling a Romans 7–style struggle to obey the law seems to have been torturing Paul. Instead, when he reflects on his pre-Christian past, Paul says he considered himself blamelessly righteous by the standards of the Mosaic law (Phil 3:6). Similarly, when Paul reminds the Galatians of the story of his conversion, his language hints at the lack of any preparation for it. He uses three imperfect-tense verbs to describe his violent persecuting activity and his own zeal-filled advancement in "the traditions of the fathers" (Gal 1:14). He "was persecuting [ἐδίωκον]" and "trying to destroy [ἐπόρθουν]" the church and "was advancing [προέκοπτον] in Judaism" (Gal 1:13–14). The present participle that follows these verbs picks up the nuance of continuous, unrelenting activity: "Being [ὑπάρχων] an extreme zealot for the traditions of my fathers" (Gal 1:14).[1] The picture is of someone moving full tilt in a single, focused direction and then, in Paul's words, "He who set me apart before I was born, and who called me by his grace, was pleased to reveal his Son to me, in order that I might preach him among the Gentiles" (Gal 1:15–16). Paul tells the Philippians he was "seized [κατελήμφθην] by Christ Jesus," using a verb that in the passive voice (as it is here) can mean "taken by surprise" (Phil 3:12).[2]

He tells the Corinthians that he is the least of the apostles and not even worthy to be called an apostle because he persecuted the church of God (1 Cor 15:9) and then leaps directly to his conversion, "But by the grace of God I am what I am, and his grace toward me was not in vain" (1 Cor 15:10). He describes his conversion to his coworker Timothy as a change from "blasphemer, persecutor, and insolent opponent" of Christ Jesus, who was acting in ignorance and unbelief, to a faithful servant of this same Christ Jesus (1 Tim 1:12–17). There is no reference in either of these passages to a period of transition from one set of convictions to the other. Here, just as in Luke and in the other, longer passages in his letters, Paul speaks of his conversion in binary terms as a switch from persecutor to proclaimer of the gospel. He became a proclaimer of the gospel not willingly but under compulsion (1 Cor 9:16–17).[3]

Is Luke's Story of Paul's Conversion an Edifying Fiction?

Some scholars have compared the story of Paul's conversion as Luke tells it to the story of Aseneth's conversion in the ancient historical novel Joseph and Aseneth.⁴ Aseneth was Joseph's Egyptian wife, and this story fills in the details of how a pious Israelite like Joseph could marry the daughter of an Egyptian priest (Gen 41:45, 50; 46:20). According to the story, Aseneth experienced a dramatic conversion to Judaism. Like Paul, she saw a magnificent heavenly light, collapsed, heard a man from heaven call her name twice ("Aseneth, Aseneth"), and said to the man, "Behold, [here] I [am], Lord. Who are you, tell me?" (Jos. Asen. 14:2–7). This heavenly man then identified himself as the chief of the Most High's house and commander of his army and urged Aseneth, "Rise and stand on your feet, and I will tell you what I have to say" (Jos. Asen. 14:8 [Burchard, *OTP* 2:225]).

There is a clear similarity between the pattern of Luke's three accounts (Acts 9:3–6; 22:6–10; 26:12–18) and this delightful tale. The similarity does not mean, however, that Luke's account is also an edifying tale following a common pattern for such stories. Although many scholars date it earlier and consider it a Jewish text, Joseph and Aseneth could be a Christian composition and may have been written as late as the early fourth century AD.⁵ If there is any literary connection between this text and Acts, then, the dependence likely runs from Acts to Joseph and Aseneth.⁶ Moreover, in addition to a number of smaller differences between the two stories, one major difference stands out: Aseneth's heavenly light and visitor appeared to her only after she had met Joseph and experienced a long period of inner conflict, anguish, and repentance (Jos. Asen. 6–13). Paul's conversion came out of the blue.

On this point, Luke's three accounts have more similarity to the story of Heliodorus in 2 Maccabees 3. According to this story, King Seleucus IV of Syria sent one of his high-ranking officials, Heliodorus, to confiscate the funds deposited in the temple in Jerusalem.⁷ Onias III, the godly priest in charge of the temple, was horrified and said "that it would be totally impossible to treat unjustly those who had placed their trust in the sanctity of the Place and in the augustness and immunity of the temple which is honored throughout the entire world" (2 Macc 3:12 [Schwartz]). Heliodorus, undeterred, pressed on to the temple treasury, but, as he was about to enter, there appeared in front of him a magnificently armored horse with a terrifying rider carrying armor and weapons of gold. He was in the company of two strong, gloriously dressed young men, also armed. The horse reared and attacked Heliodorus with its front hooves, and the young men "flogged him incessantly and rained blows upon him.". Heliodorus collapsed, was enveloped in darkness, recovered through the intercession of a pious man, and received a commission, which he obeyed, to "recount to all the greatness and power of God" (3:25–36).

There is no question that Acts postdates 2 Maccabees, and this story certainly describes the surprising conversion of one of God's enemies in a way that is like Paul's conversion. Just as with Heliodorus, Paul is trying to harm God's people (Acts 9:1–2; 22:4–5; 26:9–11) when a heavenly vision stops him in his tracks (9:4–5; 22:6–7; 26:13–15) and disables him (9:8–9; 22:11). He recovers through the intercession of a pious man (9:10–19; 22:12–16) and receives a heavenly commission to bear witness to the God who saved him (9:6, 15; 22:10, 15; 26:16–18).

Still, it is unlikely that the Heliodorus legend provided the pattern for the story of Paul's conversion in Acts.[8] Many of the details of the stories are different. Heliodorus sees no light from heaven. He comes under violent attack from angelic beings rather than having a conversation with the Lord. Instead of experiencing blindness after this encounter, moreover, Heliodorus drifts into unconsciousness from the aggressive physical beating he has endured.[9]

Most importantly, Paul's own account of his conversion in Galatians parallels most of the elements that the Acts narratives and the Heliodorus narrative have in common (Gal 1:11–17). By Paul's own testimony, he sought to harm God's people (1:13), was suddenly stopped by a "revelation of Jesus Christ" (1:12; cf. 1:16), and received a heavenly commission to proclaim a message from God (1:16). The element of heavenly light is missing from Paul's account, but if many scholars are right in seeing an allusion to the story of Paul's conversion in 2 Corinthians 4:5–6, then Paul too speaks of his experience as seeing a light from heaven: "For what we proclaim is not ourselves, but Jesus Christ as Lord, with ourselves as your servants for Jesus's sake. For God, who said, 'Let light shine out of darkness,' has shone in our hearts to give the light of the knowledge of the glory of God in the face of Jesus Christ."[10]

Luke, then, did not shape the story of Paul's conversion to fit a pattern of conversion legends he already knew, but he most likely received this way of telling the story from Paul himself. Both Paul and Luke agree that Paul's conversion came as a surprise to the apostle with no previous preparation.

A Revelation from God

It turned him from an enemy of God's people into someone called to widen its boundaries to include not only Jews but non-Jews also.

A Prophetic Call

When Paul describes his conversion in Galatians (1:13–17), he uses language reminiscent of the call narratives of the prophets. Paul is explaining to the Galatian churches that the gospel he preached among them came from God himself, and that his authority to preach it did not originate with the apostles in Jerusalem. To make this point, he reminds them of his conversion story, something he assumes they know: "For you have heard of my former manner of life in Judaism, how I used to persecute the church of God beyond measure" (Gal 1:13). His goal is to emphasize his lack of dependence on the Jerusalem apostles, so the reference to his conversion occurs in a long subordinate clause that leads to this main point: "But when He who had set me apart [ἀφορίσας με], *even* from my mother's womb, and called me [καλέσας] through His grace, was pleased to reveal His Son in me, that I might preach Him among the Gentiles [ἐν τοῖς ἔθνεσιν], I did not immediately consult with flesh and blood, nor did I go up to Jerusalem to those who were apostles before me; but I went away to Arabia, and returned once more to Damascus" (Gal 1:15–17 NASB).

Paul's use of the phrase "from my mother's womb" (ἐκ κοιλίας μητρός μου) in conjunction with the expression "called me" (με ... καλέσας), and his reference to reaching out to the gentiles (ἔθνη), are reminiscent of the call of the Lord's servant in Isaiah 49:1–6. In the Greek translation of the Hebrew Scriptures, that passage begins by urging the "islands" and "nations" (ἔθνη) to listen to what the servant has to say.[11] Referring to the Lord, the servant then says, "From my mother's womb [ἐκ κοιλίας μητρός μου] he called [ἐκάλεσεν] my name" (Isa 49:1). The servant next describes how the Lord commissioned him to serve and glorify the Lord through work that would at times seem futile but, in the end, would bring Israel back to the Lord and bring light and salvation to the nations of the whole earth (Isa 49:2–6). The parallels seem too close to be accidental, and so it is reasonably clear that Paul thought of the moment of his conversion as the moment when, like the servant, God called him to be "a light for the nations" so that God's "salvation may reach to the end of the earth" (Isa 49:6; cf. Acts 13:47).

CHAPTER 2

The identity of the servant in Isaiah 49:1–6 is famously ambiguous, and although Isaiah himself might be the one speaking in the passage, this is not clear (cf. 49:3).[12] Paul's language is also close, however, to God's summons to Jeremiah to prophesy to the nations: "Before I formed you in the belly [κοιλία, as in Paul], I knew you, and before you came forth from the womb [μήτρα, cf. Paul's μήτηρ, "mother"], I had consecrated [ἁγιάζω; Paul has ἀφορίζω, "separated"] you; a prophet to nations I had made you" (Jer 1:5 LXX). Paul's Greek is closer to Isaiah 49:1, but he seems to have also incorporated elements of this passage from Jeremiah. Here, God clearly addresses the prophet himself and, just as in Galatians, brings the thought of the prophet's consecration from his mother's womb into close connection with his call to prophesy to the nations. Probably, when Paul described his conversion in Galatians 1:15–16, he had both Isaiah 49:1–6 and Jeremiah 1:5 somewhere in the back of his mind and intended his readers to understand his conversion as not only a dramatic change but a prophetic call to take God's message to the gentiles.[13]

A Conversion

Paul's change, however, is too radical to account for it strictly in prophetic terms. It is true that the call narratives in the Old Testament prophetic literature sometimes emphasize a change from human inadequacy to God's empowerment for the prophetic task, but they do not describe the transformation of someone who opposes God's will into an enthusiastic proponent of it. Isaiah seems to have known that he was "a man of unclean lips" before he experienced his heavenly vision and the cleansing touch of the altar's burning coal (Isa 6:5–6). Similarly, Jeremiah's problem was not resistance to the Lord who appointed him a prophet but fear that he did "not know how to speak" because of his youthfulness (Jer 1:6). Amos, too, comments on his humble background as a shepherd when the Lord laid a compulsion on him to prophesy (Amos 7:14–15; cf. 3:7–8), but there is no indication that Amos was unwilling to do what the Lord had called him to do.

Paul's change, however, was qualitatively different. It certainly entailed a compulsion to preach the gospel (1 Cor 9:16), but it also entailed a transformation in his thinking so radical that what he considered "gain" before his conversion he now considered "loss" (Phil 3:7–9). Paul reports that from the first, others understood his conversion in the same way: "He who used to persecute us," said the Jesus followers of Judea, "is now preaching the faith he once tried to destroy" (Gal 1:23).[14]

The content of the message that God called Paul to preach to the gentiles, moreover, was more personal than verbal.[15] It was less a body of information than an encounter with a living human being who was also, somehow, the Lord. Paul says that the gospel came to him at the time of his conversion "through a revelation of Jesus Christ" (Gal 1:12) and describes his conversion as the moment at which God "was pleased to reveal his Son to me" (Gal 1:16). Paul "counted" as "gain" at his conversion not a particular message about God or from God but "Christ Jesus my Lord," as he puts it (Phil 3:8). What unbelievers failed to see when they refused to believe the gospel was its illumination "of the glory of Christ, who is the image of God" (2 Cor 4:4). At his conversion, Paul received "the light of the knowledge of the glory of God in the face of Jesus Christ" (2 Cor 4:6).

Paul's conversion, then, was primarily an encounter with Jesus, whom, as the encounter demonstrated, God had raised from the dead. His understanding of Christ's identity was radically reformed, and this had equally radical consequences for him personally. He tells the Corinthians, "Even though we once regarded Christ according to the flesh, we regard him thus no longer" (2 Cor 5:16). It is just possible this implies that Paul, prior to his conversion, had seen the earthly Jesus and heard him teach.[16] Even if it only refers to Paul's pre-Christian understanding of someone he had never met, however, it implies that at his conversion his view of Jesus's identity radically shifted. Prior to this point, he saw Christ as a threat to living the way God had laid down for his people in the Mosaic law and "the traditions of [his] fathers" (Gal 1:14). Now, he realized, the claims of Jesus and his followers must be right: Jesus was the Messiah, the promised Son of David of traditional Jewish expectation (2 Sam 7:12–13; Isa 9:6–7; 11:1–10; Jer 23:5–6; Psalms of Solomon 17:21; Mark 12:35–36).

If Paul describes his conversion in 2 Corinthians 4:6, then the divine glory that shone from Jesus the Messiah's face would imply that Stephen's dying vision had been a vision of something real. Paul, who was there when Stephen died, must have heard him say, "I see the heavens opened and the Son of Man standing at the right hand of God" (Acts 7:56). God had not only raised Jesus from the dead but also enthroned him at God's right hand where he shared the divine glory in accord with a traditional exegesis of Psalm 110:1. Perhaps Paul knew that Jesus had taught on this text in the temple a few days before his trial and death (Mark 12:35–37; Matt 22:41–46; Luke 20:41–44) and that he had made reference to it in the Sanhedrin trial where he was sentenced to death for blasphemy (Mark 14:62–64; Matt 26:64–66; Luke 22:69–71). In any case, in Romans 1:1–6 Paul seems to couple the view that Jesus was the Davidic Messiah and Son of God both with Jesus's resurrection and with his own conversion when he was "set apart [ἀφωρισμένος] for the gospel of God" (Rom 1:1; cf. Gal 1:15).

This radical shift away from knowing Jesus only according to the flesh to viewing him through the eyes of God and therefore as he really was (2 Cor 5:17; cf. 5:12) led to a radical shift in Paul's understanding of himself and others. It was as if he too had died and come to life (2 Cor 5:14; Gal 2:20; Rom 6:4–11) or been re-created by God (2 Cor 5:17; Gal 6:15). The life of the "I" that once was Paul gave way to an "I" whom Paul could describe as Christ living in him (Gal 2:20). "For me to live," he told the Philippians, "is Christ" (Phil 1:21).

Luke, too, presents Paul's conversion as an event reminiscent of a prophetic call, but also as an event that breaks the boundaries of such a call. Allusions to Ezekiel are especially prominent in Luke's three accounts of Paul's conversion.[17] The bright light (Acts 9:3; 22:6; 26:13) recalls the "brightness" surrounding God that Ezekiel saw in the vision preceding his call (Ezek 1:27–28). Paul falls to the ground and then hears a voice speaking (Acts 9:4; 22:7; 26:14) just as Ezekiel falls to the ground and hears the voice of someone speaking (Ezek 1:28 LXX).[18] At least in the Acts 26 account of Paul's conversion, the Lord then tells Paul, "stand on your feet" (στῆθι ἐπὶ τοὺς πόδας σου), using precisely the same words that the Greek translation of Ezekiel 2:1 uses when the Lord tells Ezekiel to stand up after his collapse at the sight of the Lord's glory (Acts 26:16).

Luke's focus, however, is not on the parallels between Ezekiel's mission and Paul's mission but on the identification of "the Lord" whom Ezekiel saw with Jesus.[19] "Jesus of Nazareth" (Acts 22:8) was not only the Davidic king of ancient expectation, now exalted to God's right hand (Ps 110:1; cf. Rom 8:34; Eph 1:20; Col 3:1), but he was identical with the enthroned "Lord" who appeared to Ezekiel in the form of a heavenly man bathed in brightness (Ezek 1:28; cf. 1 Cor 15:47; Phil 3:21).[20]

A Revelation from God

If Paul became suddenly convinced that the Jesus of Nazareth whom he had opposed and whose followers he persecuted was none other than the Lord in his glory, it is easy to see how it would change everything for him. Perhaps the question, "Saul, Saul, why are you persecuting me?" (Acts 9:4; 22:7; 26:14) was formulated to lead Paul to this realization. It may well have implied that he was opposing the now gloriously exalted Messiah in the same way that the biblical Saul, Paul's namesake, irrationally persecuted David, the Messiah's ancestor (1 Sam 22–26; cf. Rom 1:3).[21]

A Call to Preach the Gospel to the Gentiles

Luke also portrays Paul's conversion as the point at which God called him to proclaim the gospel to the gentiles and did so in a way that recalled the vocations of Jeremiah and of the servant in Isaiah's prophecy. These allusions are especially strong in Luke's third account of Paul's conversion. There, instead of instructing Paul to go ahead to Damascus where he would receive further instructions, Jesus gives those further instructions directly to Paul:

> "Now get up and stand on your feet. I have appeared to you to appoint you [προχειρίσασθαί σε] as a servant [ὑπηρέτην] and as a witness of what you have seen and will see of me. I will rescue you [ἐξαιρούμενός σε] from your own people and from the Gentiles. I am sending you to them to open their eyes [ἀνοῖξαι ὀφθαλμοὺς αὐτῶν] and turn them from darkness to light [σκότους εἰς φῶς], and from the power of Satan to God, so that they may receive forgiveness of sins and a place among those who are sanctified by faith in me." (Acts 26:16–18 NIV)

This recalls God's words to Jeremiah, "I appointed you [τέθεικά σε LXX] a prophet to the nations" (Jer 1:5). It also recalls his promise to the prophet to help him overcome the obstacles he would face in fulfilling this vocation: "I am with you to deliver you [ἐξαιρεῖσθαί σε], declares the Lord" (Jer 1:8; cf. 1:19). It echoes the Lord's summons to his "servant" (παῖς), whom God has made "a light [φῶς] for the nations [ἔθνεσιν], to open the eyes of the blind [ἀνοῖξαι ὀφθαλμοὺς τυφλῶν]" (Isa 42:6–7). In addition, it is reminiscent of God's promise two paragraphs later that he would turn darkness into light (σκότος εἰς φῶς) for the blind (Isa 42:16).

All this also sounds like God's commissioning of his servant (δοῦλος) in Isaiah 49:1–7 (LXX), "I have made you [τέθεικά σε] a light of nations [εἰς φῶς ἐθνῶν], that you may be for salvation to the end of the earth" (cf. Acts 13:47). The Greek does not match perfectly, but some of the terms are the same, and thematically these passages are all close to one another and to Acts 26:17–18.

This may mean, as several scholars have suggested, that this third telling of Luke's conversion is especially close to the story as Paul himself told it.[22] Its connections with Ezekiel 1–3, Jeremiah 1, and Isaiah 42 and 49 link it to Paul's own account of his conversion in Galatians 1:15–17 and 2 Corinthians 4:4–6. This account's unique preservation of Christ's apostolic commission to the gentiles ("I am sending [ἀποστέλλω] you"), moreover, meshes well with Paul's own insistence in Galatians that his apostolic commission to preach Christ among the gentiles came at the time of Christ's appearance to him and was free of any human involvement.[23]

Ananias's role in the Acts 9 and 22 accounts of Paul's conversion does not contradict this. When Ananias resists the Lord's instructions in Acts 9 to go to Paul and lay hands on him so that he might receive his sight back, the Lord encourages Ananias with the startling news that he has turned the persecutor Paul into his chosen instrument to take the Lord's name to the gentiles (9:15). In the Acts 9 account, however, Ananias never tells this to Paul but only heals him and speaks to him about the Holy Spirit (9:17–19). In Acts 22, Ananias tells Paul that he "will be a witness" for Jesus "to everyone" (22:15) but there is no mention of a mission to the gentiles.

Both Paul and Luke agree, therefore, that Paul's commission to preach Christ to the gentiles came to him as part of the "revelation of Jesus Christ" (Gal 1:12; cf. 1:16) he received at his conversion.[24] That revelation is probably what kept him in Damascus and Arabia for three years before he returned to Jerusalem (Gal 1:17–18; Acts 9:19b, 26; 26:20).

3

Following Christ in Damascus and Arabia

Paul's stunning encounter with the risen Christ seems to have led first to a period of repentance, then to a time of instruction among the small group of Jewish Christians in Damascus, and then to a period of proclaiming Jesus to both Jews and non-Jews in the Nabatean Kingdom east and south of Syria and Judea. Paul's preaching and teaching in this region led to trouble with the government authorities under Nabatea's King Aretas IV. It is reasonable to speculate that Paul's proclamation of one new people of God, comprised of both Jews and non-Jews who received forgiveness for their sins, threatened to upset a delicate political balance in the region. Paul likely preached that reverencing the local Nabatean deities was among his audience's sins, something that from a Nabatean perspective could easily anger the gods and lead to increased social problems. As a result of his preaching, Paul narrowly escaped arrest, fleeing over the city wall of Damascus during a brief period in which King Aretas IV, rather than the Romans, controlled the city.

THE IMMEDIATE AFTERMATH OF PAUL'S CONVERSION

Although Luke says that there were people around Paul at the time of his conversion, he also makes clear that only Paul felt the full weight of what had happened. In Luke's first account, he says that Paul fell to the ground (Acts 9:4; cf. 22:7) and that the men traveling with him heard a voice that surprised them so much they went speechless (9:7). Much later in the narrative, when Luke describes Paul's own telling of the story, he says that the people with Paul saw a bright light but did not hear the voice that spoke to him (22:9). Later still, when Paul tells the story again, he says that those around him fell to the ground and that he heard the voice, perhaps implying that only he understood it (26:14). The discrepancies in the three accounts have generated much discussion (and may simply reflect variations in the way Paul told the story), but the critical element is that the people with Paul knew that something highly unusual had happened. They saw a sudden, bright light and were stunned by it. They did not, however, see anyone and, although they may have heard a voice, they did not understand that anyone had identified himself as "Jesus, whom you are persecuting" (9:5, 26:15; cf. 22:8).

Luke says that the bright light Paul saw blinded him, and that the people with him guided him to Damascus (Acts 9:8; 22:11). They seem to have taken him to a house belonging to someone named Judas on "the street called Straight" (9:11), the main east–west thoroughfare. Judas's house may have simply been a place where one could rent a temporary room.[1] It is not likely that the Jesus followers Paul was intent on persecuting, some of whom had heard of his purpose for coming to Damascus (9:13–14), would have been eager to show him hospitality.[2] We can perhaps imagine that the people who were with Paul at the time of his conversion, and presumably supporting his effort to find and arrest Christians in Damascus, rented rooms on one of the city's main thoroughfares while they all regrouped and tried to decide their next step.

Paul's Period of Repentance

For Paul, the basic direction of his next step immediately became clear. He had to repent. Luke says that Paul neither ate nor drank anything for three days (Acts 9:9), and it is much more likely that this is a reference to Paul's repentance for opposing Jesus and his followers than that he was too shocked by his experience to eat or drink or that Luke is alluding here to the practice of fasting before baptism.[3]

Fasting seems to have been a common way of demonstrating repentance for sin in ancient Judaism, particularly when sin had led to some physical manifestation of God's judgment, such as Paul's blindness.[4] After David's adulterous liaison with Bathsheba, "the Lord afflicted the child that Uriah's wife bore to David, and he became sick," and "David therefore sought God on behalf of the child." As part of his appeal to God, he "fasted and went in and lay all night on the ground" (2 Sam 12:15–16). Similarly, Joel calls on Israel to fast in view of the judgment from God they have already experienced for their sin (Joel 1:13–14). In the Testament of Simeon, Simeon says that his murderous jealousy against Joseph prompted God to paralyze his right hand (T. Sim. 2:12). "I knew ... that this had happened to me because of Joseph," he confesses, "so I repented and wept" (T. Sim. 2:13). Simeon prayed that his hand "might be restored" and that he "might refrain from every defilement and grudge and from all folly" and then he "chastened [his] soul by fasting for two years" (T. Sim. 2:13; 3:4 [Kee, *OTP* 1:785–86]).

During his own much shorter period of fasting and prayer, Paul must have thought through the implications of seeing Jesus alive, surrounded with the glory of heaven, and sending him both to his own people and to the gentiles (Acts 26:17). The very Jesus whom the high priest had sentenced to death, and whose fledgling movement both Paul and the high priest had tried to stamp out, was the "Son of Man" that Stephen had seen in the last moments of his life "standing at the right hand of God" (Acts 7:55–56). He was the suffering "Son of Man" of Daniel 7 whom God had vindicated, the messianic king who shared God's authority in Psalm 110, and he was alive, indicating that the last days and the time of the resurrection had now begun.

A NEW UNDERSTANDING OF THE RELATIONSHIP
BETWEEN THE LAW AND SIN

It is possible that the seeds of Paul's theology of the Mosaic law were planted during this early period of repentance. While Paul was "advancing in Judaism beyond" his peers, expressing his zeal for Jewish tradition (Gal 1:14), and rigorously keeping the Mosaic law (Phil 3:6b), he was also violently persecuting the Jesus movement and trying to destroy it (Gal 1:13; Phil 3:6a). Like the unbelieving Israelites he describes in Romans 10:2, he had a "zeal for God, but not according to knowledge."[5] His intense pursuit of the law had been misguided and led him to stumble over Christ rather than to embrace him in faith (cf. Rom 9:30–33). This "stone" that "the builders rejected" turned out to be "the cornerstone" of God's new temple, the church (Matt 21:42; Mark 12:10–11; Luke 20:17).[6]

It was perhaps the combination within himself of a sincere devotion to God's law with a murderous desire to snuff out the followers of God's Messiah that led Paul, after his conversion, to a deep appreciation of the insidious nature of sin. His love for the law had led him to hate the Messiah and his people. The human tendency to rebel against God, then, ran so deep that it could even use God's holy, righteous, and good law (Rom 7:12) to oppose God and the faithful remnant of his people (Rom 7:10–11; cf. Phil 3:6).[7] The law itself was not the problem. Rather, the problem lay with sin's ability to take what was good and use it for evil (Rom 5:20; 7:5; 1 Cor 15:56).

The self-deception involved was so profound that only God himself could break through it, and that breakthrough was like release from slavery (Rom 7:6). It was like having the veil removed from one's eyes (2 Cor 3:14–16) or being raised from the dead (Rom 6:1–14; Col 3:1; Eph 2:1–10). That is what God had done through the appearance of the risen Lord Jesus to Paul outside Damascus.

A New Understanding of God's Concern for All People Groups

This new approach to the Mosaic law meshes well with the universal nature of the commission that Jesus gave to Paul at the time of his vision. He told Paul that he would not only rescue him from his "own people" and "from the gentiles" but that he was sending him "to them to open their eyes and turn them from darkness to light, and from the power of Satan to God, so that they may receive forgiveness of sins and a place among those who are sanctified by faith in me" (Acts 26:17–18 NIV).[8] Both the people of Israel and the gentiles were equally in darkness, under Satan's power, in need of forgiveness for sin, and in need of taking their place in a new people, set apart from others by their faith in Christ. These words implied that all people, both Jews and gentiles, were so tainted by rebellion against God that apart from God's forgiving and sanctifying power they were beyond hope. Through faith in Christ, however, both forgiveness and membership in God's people were available to all.

Paul's accounts of his conversion in his letters also emphasize the universal reach of the gospel that Jesus revealed to him on that occasion. In Galatians, he speaks of his conversion primarily as a call to "preach" God's Son "among the gentiles" (Gal 1:16). In Philippians, he describes it as a loss of confidence in his own righteousness, based on the law, and his gain of the righteousness that comes from God through faith in Christ (Phil 3:4–9).[9] His conversion was, in other words, a dramatic interior transformation, an about-face that shifted the source of his righteousness from himself to God, from his own social location and accomplishments to "faith in Christ," that is, to "the righteousness from God that depends on faith" (Phil 3:9). Paul does not refer directly to forgiveness here, but later, in his letter to the Romans, he explains that God accounts righteousness to the ungodly apart from works and then illustrates this principle with a reference to forgiveness in Psalm 32: "David ... speaks of the blessing of the one to whom God counts righteousness apart from works: 'Blessed are those whose lawless deeds are forgiven, and whose sins are covered; blessed is the man against whom the Lord will not count his sin'" (Rom 4:6–8; cf. Ps 32:1–2a).

It seems reasonable, then, to think of Paul's conversion experience as a moment in which he understood that God had freely forgiven him for his pursuit of the law and Jewish tradition in ways that blinded him to what God was doing in Jesus and his followers. It was also a moment in which he began to understand the universal need for the gospel. Both gentiles and Jews—even Jews zealously committed to the Mosaic law and to Jewish tradition—needed the forgiveness that God was now offering through Jesus.

The Catechesis of Paul in Damascus and His Proclamation of the Gospel There

Luke tells his readers that after Paul's baptism and recovery from the physical effects of his vision he spent "some days ... with the disciples in Damascus" (Acts 9:19b). Like Ananias, the "disciple" whom the Lord sent to Paul after his conversion, these disciples were probably still part of the Jewish community in Damascus and, at least at this time, had a good reputation within that community (22:12). It was within this community that Paul first began to obey his commission to "open the eyes" of his own people and of the gentiles (26:17–18).

Damascus was a large and ancient city with both a huge Jewish population and a non-Jewish population devoted to its gods, particularly to the worship of Zeus. A massive temple to this Greek god was under construction during Paul's stay there.[10] The synagogues of the city, moreover, had attracted the devotion of a significant number of non-Jewish women (*B.J.* 2.559–561). It is not surprising, then, that Luke speaks of "synagogues" (in the plural), in Damascus (Acts 9:2, 20), and it is also not surprising that Paul would head to those synagogues to fulfill his commission to take the gospel to both Jews and gentiles.[11]

Luke tells his readers that once Paul had recovered his sight and spent some time among the Jesus followers of Damascus, he "immediately" began preaching in the synagogues that Jesus was the Son of God (Acts 9:20). This message recalls Luke's earlier narrative of Jesus's trial before the Sanhedrin where the elders, the chief priests, and the scribes condemn Jesus precisely for claiming about himself that he is the Son of God and interpreting that title through the lenses of Psalm 110:1 and Daniel 7:13. Apparently speaking of himself, Jesus had said that "the Son of Man shall be seated at the right hand of the power of God" (Luke 22:67–71), and they had taken this to mean that he was claiming to be "Christ, a king" (Luke 23:2). The theological implications of Jesus's claim that he would sit at God's right hand and the political implications of his claim to be the Messiah provided enough evidence to bring to Pilate and negotiate for his death. With Paul's connections to the high priest (Acts 9:1), he would have known that the case against Jesus took this shape.

Now, his message in the synagogues of Damascus was that this case against Jesus was all wrong. Jesus was not a blasphemer but precisely the "Son of God" and the "Christ" that he had claimed to be (Acts 9:20, 22). He was God's Son and Israel's king, raised from the dead, ascended to heaven, and seated at God's right hand (Mark 12:36; Acts 2:33–36; 5:30–31; cf. 7:55–56).

Luke's focus on Paul's early preaching of Jesus as God's Son and Messiah meshes well with what Paul says in his letters about the theological change that came over him at his conversion. In Galatians 1:16 he describes his conversion as God revealing "his Son to me." In Romans 1:1–5 he says that when God called him to be an apostle, the message he sent him to proclaim was about God's "Son, who was descended from David according to the flesh" and "declared to be the Son of God in power according to the Spirit of holiness by his resurrection from the dead" (Rom 1:3).

Following Christ in Damascus and Arabia

Paul's preaching must have also included the good news of "the forgiveness of sins [ἄφεσιν ἁμαρτιῶν]," as Jesus puts it to Paul (Acts 26:18). Up to this point, Luke has used this phrase four times in Acts to describe the preaching of the earliest Christians and of Paul himself (Acts 2:38; 5:31; 10:43; 13:38). Paul also indicates that he preached this element of the gospel as critically important and that, when he did so, he was only handing on an understanding of Christ's death that earlier Christians had handed down to him. He tells the Corinthians, "I delivered to you as of first importance what I also received: that Christ died for our sins in accordance with the Scriptures" (1 Cor 15:3).[12] Paul would have understood immediately from Jesus's words to him at the time of his conversion that the very Lord Jesus whose teaching and followers he had so vigorously opposed was forgiving even him for what he had done.

It was probably through the theological nurture of the Christian community in Damascus that he first learned of the role Jesus's death played in the forgiveness of sins. That early community must have known what Jesus had taught his followers about his death. "The Son of Man came not to be served but to serve," Jesus had said, "and to give his life as a ransom for many" (Mark 10:45). At his final Passover meal with his disciples, he had taught that his body would be broken, like the bread at the supper, and "given for" them, and that his blood would be "poured out," like the wine, "for" them (Luke 22:19–20; cf. 1 Cor 11:24–25).[13] The benefit that Jesus's followers received from his death, then, was the forgiveness of sins.

Paul's Proclamation of the Gospel in Arabia

Paul tells the Galatian Christians that sometime within a three-year period after his call to proclaim the good news about God's Son among the nations, he left for Arabia.[14] On the heels of his dramatic call to proclaim good news to the nations, it is likely that his foray into Arabia was in obedience to this new vocation (Gal 1:15–18). There was no Roman province of Arabia at this point. The term was an ethnic expression that referred to the lands in which "the ancients encountered Arabs," and this, according to G. W. Bowersock, stretched "from the northern reaches of Mesopotamia to the southern shores of the great peninsula that lies between the Red Sea and the Persian Gulf."[15] In Paul's time, much of this region was under the control of Aretas IV, who was king of the Nabateans from the winter of 9–8 BC until AD 40.[16]

Some have speculated that Paul already had in mind his strategy of taking the gospel where Christ had not yet been preached (Rom 15:20–21). Knowing that the Christian message had already reached the coastal cities to the west (e.g., Sidon, Tyre, Ptolemais), Paul set out for a region where he knew the gospel had made no or little progress.[17] Perhaps he took an incremental approach to his mission to the gentiles, attempting to reach the Arabs first since they too were descendants of Abraham and practiced circumcision.[18]

It is possible that there were some Christians in this vast region, since "Arabians" appear in the list of Jews and proselytes present at Peter's Pentecost sermon (Acts 2:11). Some of them may have been among the three thousand people who believed Peter's message and received baptism that day (Acts 2:41). Even so, Arabia would have been fertile territory for taking the gospel to all ethnic groups, both Jewish and otherwise. The ancient geographer Strabo, writing in the early first century AD, says that one of his friends had visited Petra, the leading city of the Nabatean Kingdom, and "found many Romans and many other foreigners spending time there" (*Geogr.* 16.4.21). The Nabateans themselves were a formerly nomadic people who had, by Paul's time, blended their way of life with Hellenistic and Roman customs, developed sophisticated methods of irrigating crops in their largely desert region, and founded well-run cities connecting a network of trade routes.

They were close neighbors to the Jews in Judea, and the literary and inscriptional evidence from the time points to a relationship between the two groups that was usually peaceful. Herod the Great's mother was Nabatean, Herod himself had lived in Petra briefly during his childhood, and Herod's son Antipas married the daughter of Aretas IV. More ordinary Jews, moreover, also lived in Nabatea. A tomb inscription from Hegra, the kingdom's second-largest city, and dated July-August, AD 42, reads in part, "This is the tomb which Shubaytu son of 'Ali'u, the Jew, made for himself and for his children and for 'Amirat, his wife."[19] Clearly, Shubaytu had settled down and made a life for himself and his family in Nabatea.

The Nabateans themselves worshiped a god they called Dushara, but whom they identified variously with Dionysius, Zeus, and possibly Osiris,

Following Christ in Damascus and Arabia

Isis, and the sun.[20] They also worshiped their former king Obodas, whom they had deified after his death in the early first century BC, and identified with Zeus.[21] "Arabia," then, was fertile ground for Paul's proclamation to both Jews and gentiles of God's power over spiritual darkness and God's willingness both to forgive the sins of all who had faith in Jesus and to give them a place among his newly configured people (Acts 26:18).

At some point during this work in Arabia, Paul seems to have fallen afoul of the authorities. He does not say why or where this happened, but his two references to Damascus imply that when he returned to the city from Arabia (Gal 1:17), "the governor [ὁ ἐθνάρχης] under King Aretas was guarding the city... in order to seize" him, but he "was let down in a basket through a window in the wall and escaped his hands" (2 Cor 11:32–33). This statement is the only historical evidence that King Aretas's rule ever extended as far as Damascus. The city had come under Roman control in 65 BC through the eastern conquests of the general Pompey (Josephus, *A.J.* 14.29) and was still under Roman control during the time of the emperor Tiberius, as Roman coins minted in Damascus show. Even though there are no known examples of Roman imperial coins minted in Damascus during the years that Paul would have been in the city, no one would think to question that the Romans controlled this important Hellenistic city on their eastern frontier continuously through the first century apart from Paul's statement in 2 Corinthians 11:32–33.[22]

Many scholars believe it likely, therefore, that Paul's term for "governor" (ἐθνάρχης) refers not to a ruler of the city who was subordinate to King Aretas but to the leader of a particular ethnic group within a city. The Jews of Alexandria had such an "ethnarch" (Josephus, *A.J.* 14.117), and it would make sense for the Nabateans who lived in Damascus and who were often involved in commerce to have their own consul that represented the interests of King Aretas to the Romans.[23]

The "governor" Paul describes, however, was more powerful than a consul.[24] If he had the power to guard the city gates from the inside, forcing Paul to sneak through an opening in the city's walls so that he could flee to the outside, then he must have had military powers. This means that King Aretas, whom he served, must have been in military control of the city.[25] Several scholars have made a persuasive case that Paul's escape from Damascus coincides with a period of political turbulence in precisely the region where Paul was located, and this turbulence probably gave Aretas IV the opportunity to control Damascus for a short time roughly from the fall of AD 36 through the spring of AD 37.[26]

Luke's narrative is highly compressed at this point, never mentioning Paul's time in Arabia and covering his three years there with the phrase "When many days had passed" (Acts 9:23). He then tells the story of Paul's escape from Damascus in language that converges closely with Paul's firsthand account, but with one major difference. In Luke's account it is not the "governor" of King Aretas who was guarding the city to take Paul into custody but "the Jews" who "were watching the gates day and night in order to kill him" (9:23–24). Some interpreters believe Luke used a later, inaccurate tradition that portrayed the Jews as Paul's "customary" enemies, or that Luke made this up, being "only too ready to blame any bad feeling towards the Christians on the Jews" (cf. 20:3, 19).[27]

A merger of the two accounts, however, produces a historically plausible result. Paul himself says that the same Jewish leadership who plotted Jesus's death opposed his own attempts to proclaim the gospel to the gentiles (1 Thess 2:14–15; cf. 2 Cor 11:24).[28] The Jewish leadership in some of the Damascus synagogues may well have aligned themselves with the Jerusalem leadership and, like them, considered this dramatically changed Paul an enemy. Originally, he had come to help them by arresting troublemakers in their midst, and now he had himself become a troublemaker. Jews had lived in relative peace among the Nabateans for decades, and now, in these troubled times, Paul was proclaiming as Son of God a Messianic pretender, condemned to death by their own high priest and Sanhedrin.

Moreover, as a Jew, perhaps they thought, he was publicly implying that Nabatean devotion to their own gods was idolatry and needed forgiveness. Extant legal inscriptions and documents from two Nabatean cities, Hegra and Mahoza, show that Jews living in the Nabatean Kingdom in the first and early second centuries felt comfortable depositing their legal documents in Nabatean temples and could nod in the direction of Nabatean deities for purposes of ratifying contracts.[29] Most Jews had probably adopted a live-and-let-live approach to Nabatean religion.

It is not farfetched, then, to think of the Jewish leadership in Damascus helping the Nabatean governor of the city arrest and silence Paul's preaching of the gospel in synagogues both in Damascus and in the politically sensitive areas south of the city. Both Jewish and Nabatean authorities may have seen Paul's preaching as too socially disruptive to tolerate.

The wider context of Paul's own record of his escape from Damascus tells us something about how he himself understood it, at least from a distance of almost two decades. Paul mentions his escape as the last, climactic item in a list of humiliating disasters that he had encountered in his work proclaiming the gospel. These disasters were his ironic "boast" in contrast to his opponents in Corinth who bragged on having the standard badges of honor in the culture of the time, such as sophisticated oratory and impressive letters of recommendation. The final item in Paul's ironic list of counter-boasts is his descent from the Damascus city wall in the sort of basket used for carrying raisins, figs, or cuts of fish (2 Cor 11:32–33).[30]

When he made his escape, Paul must have been aware of the profound contrast between his former self and what he had now become. What he calls the "necessity . . . laid on" him to preach the gospel (1 Cor 9:16) had reduced this highly educated and well-connected young man to fleeing the Jewish leaders of an important Hellenistic city, and its gentile governor, by disguising himself as a basket of dried fruit. This was only one early instance of a long line of hardships he would face both from his own people and from the gentiles as he sought faithfully to carry out his commission to proclaim to everyone the good news of reconciliation to God through Jesus, the Messiah. Such events must have contributed from the early days of his work to his conviction that God's "power is made perfect in weakness" (2 Cor 12:9).

4

Return to Jerusalem

Both Paul and Luke say that after Paul left Damascus he traveled to Jerusalem (Gal 1:18; Acts 9:26). He clearly fled Damascus to escape arrest, but he decided that Jerusalem would be his destination because he wanted to get to know Peter (Gal 1:18). He also saw "James the Lord's brother" there (Gal 1:19).[1] It is perhaps significant that in 1 Corinthians 15:3–11, where Paul quotes a Christian tradition "of first importance," the names of both "Cephas" (the Aramaic form of "Peter") and James appear. This old and important tradition covers the significance of Jesus's death, how his death fulfilled the Scriptures, and the historicity of his bodily resurrection (1 Cor 15:3–5). Paul must have received instruction in such basics before he set out for Jerusalem, but perhaps he chose to flee there precisely to meet these two prominent apostles and tap into the valuable access that they both, and especially Peter, had to the memory of Jesus.

"James the brother of the Lord" (Gal 1:19) had not been his brother's follower during his lifetime (Mark 3:21, 31–35; John 7:3–5) and had only later, probably through seeing the risen Jesus, become both a disciple and an apostle (1 Cor 15:7; cf. Gal 2:9). Peter, however, was one of Jesus's first disciples (Mark 1:16) and could provide especially helpful information on Jesus's teaching, actions, death, and resurrection. When Paul went to Jerusalem, he focused his attention on Peter, and "remained with him fifteen days" (Gal 1:18).

PAUL'S KNOWLEDGE OF JESUS'S LIFE AND TEACHING

Paul must have known enough about Jesus's teaching before his conversion and call to form a basis for the persecution of Jesus's followers, and he probably learned much more from the disciples in Damascus before his journey to Arabia. It seems likely that he also learned much from his fifteen days with Peter in Jerusalem. His knowledge of Jesus's life and teaching is clear from his letters.[2]

Paul knew that Jesus was born into the Davidic line (Rom 1:3; cf. Gal 4:4), that he lived in poor circumstances (Phil 2:7), that he lived a sinless life (2 Cor 5:21), and that at Passover time he was betrayed (1 Cor 5:7; 11:23), but that, before his betrayal, he reinterpreted the Passover meal in terms of his own death (1 Cor 11:24–25). Paul knew that the governing authorities (1 Cor 2:8), including the Jewish authorities (1 Thess 2:14–15), condemned Jesus to crucifixion, and that Jesus both died by crucifixion and was buried (1 Cor 15:3–4). He knew that Jesus came back to life on the third day after his death and appeared to the apostles and to many others (1 Cor 15:4–7).

Paul's letters also contain echoes of Jesus's teaching. His comment that sexual union leads to a union of flesh (1 Cor 6:16; cf. Eph 5:31) mirrors Jesus's teaching on marriage, and, like Jesus's teaching, recalls Genesis 2:24 (Matt 19:5–6; Mark 10:7–9). His further comment that "the wife should not separate from her husband" recalls Jesus's teaching that what "God has joined together" human beings must not "separate" (Matt 19:6; Mark 10:9). Not only is there verbal agreement between Paul and the gospel tradition here, but Paul specifically cites "the Lord" as the source of his teaching (1 Cor 7:10).[3] He follows the same pattern on the issue of whether "those who proclaim the gospel should get their living by the gospel" (1 Cor 9:14; cf. 1 Tim 5:18). The Lord's saying "the laborer deserves his food," he argues, shows the truth of this principle (Matt 10:10; Luke 10:7).[4]

He probably knew the eschatological teaching of Jesus about the Son of Man coming on the clouds, sending out his angels "with a loud trumpet call," and gathering the elect (Matt 24:30–31; cf. Mark 13:26–27; Luke 21:27; 1 Thess 4:16–17). He seems to have known that Jesus taught all this would happen suddenly, "like a thief in the night" (1 Thess 5:2–4; cf. Matt 24:43–44; Luke 12:39). He also knew about Jesus's teaching that just before the unfolding of these events, a period of extreme rebellion would break out against God, including the rise of one particularly godless leader who would proclaim his own divinity (2 Thess 2:3–4; cf. Mark 13:9–20; Matt 24:9–22).[5]

CHAPTER 4

It is not clear how much of this information came from his fifteen days with Peter, and exactly what Peter himself knew and believed is not entirely clear. Mark's Gospel and 1 Peter, however, are reasonably understood to reflect Peter's teaching, and those texts also have close connections to Paul's theology, especially to Paul's understanding of Christ's death.

PETER AND THE MEMORY OF JESUS IN MARK'S GOSPEL

Around the turn of the second century, Papias, the bishop of Hierapolis in the Roman province of Asia, spoke of a tradition in Christian circles, already ancient, that linked Mark's Gospel with the apostle Peter. Papias described this link in a few sentences from his five-volume work titled *Exposition of the Logia of the Lord*.[6] Only fragments of that work remain, preserved in quotations from it in the fourth-century church historian Eusebius, but, from a historical perspective, these fragments are valuable.

Hierapolis, Papias's home, was an important city near the intersection of major roads connecting the eastern Roman Empire with regions to the west, and Papias was apparently a native of the region.[7] He seems to have taken advantage of his strategic location to learn all he could from those who belonged to the second and first generations of Christians. He knew personally, for example, the daughters of Philip the Evangelist, one of "the seven men of good repute" chosen to oversee the daily distribution of food to the early Jerusalem church (Acts 6:5; 21:8–9; Eusebius, *Hist. eccl.* 3.31.9).[8]

Papias also heard reports of what at least two disciples of Jesus were teaching who lived into Papias's own lifetime.[9] In the prologue to his *Exposition*, Papias explains how he treated his sources:

> I will not hesitate to set down for you, along with my interpretations, everything I carefully learned then from the elders and carefully remembered, guaranteeing their truth. For unlike most people I did not enjoy those who have a great deal to say, but those who teach the truth. Nor did I enjoy those who recall someone else's commandments, but those who remember the commandments given by the Lord to the faith and proceeding from the truth itself. And if by chance someone who had been a follower of the elders should come my way, I inquired about the words of the elders—what Andrew or Peter said, or Philip or Thomas

or James or John or Matthew or any other of the Lord's disciples, and whatever Aristion and the elder John, the Lord's disciples, were saying [λέγουσιν].[10] For I did not think that information from books would profit me as much as information from a living and abiding voice.[11]

Papias, then, was in close touch with those who had learned from the disciples of Jesus and makes special mention of those who were closest to him chronologically and probably geographically, namely Aristion and "the elder John." These living voices, who formed a tight chain of eyewitness testimony back to Jesus himself, were more valuable to him than what he could learn from books.

As Richard Bauckham has shown, in saying this, Papias was following a well-worn convention of ancient historiography. Ancient historians, such as the third-century BC historian Polybius, sometimes advocated the notion that personal experience was a better way to learn anything than bookish research. For the historian, this meant that one achieved accuracy in reporting what really happened by witnessing events oneself, or, failing that, interviewing eyewitnesses and those who had themselves learned of events from those eyewitnesses (Polybius, *Hist.* 12.27–28).[12]

Papias assures his readers that he has followed this procedure, having "carefully learned and carefully remembered" what "the elders" taught him. This included testimony from "the elder John," himself a disciple of the Lord, about a link between the apostle Peter and Mark's Gospel. According to Papias, "the elder used to say [ἔλεγε] this":

> Mark, having become Peter's interpreter, wrote down accurately everything he remembered, though not in order, of the things either said or done by Christ. For he neither heard the Lord nor followed him, but afterward as I said, followed Peter, who adapted his teaching as needed but had no intention of giving an ordered account of the Lord's sayings. Consequently Mark did nothing wrong in writing down some things as he remembered them, for he made it his one concern not to omit anything that he heard or to make any false statement in them.[13]

Although scholars have often called into question the reliability of Papias on this point, there are good reasons for accepting the idea that Peter was one of Mark's primary sources. First, Papias is not the only second-century writer who connects Mark's Gospel with Peter. Justin Martyr, writing after Papias in the mid-second century, makes the same connection, but does so in a way that makes it unlikely he was dependent on Papias. In a section of his *Dialogue with Trypho*, devoted mainly to showing how Psalm 22 predicted numerous events surrounding Jesus's death and resurrection, Justin refers repeatedly to what he calls "the memoirs of his apostles" (*Dial.* 100.4; 101.3; 102.5; 104.1; 106.4) or simply "the memoirs" (*Dial.* 103.6, 8; 105.1, 5, 6; 107.1). Once he calls these writings "the memoirs that I say were composed by his apostles and their followers" (*Dial.* 103.8), and once he refers to a passage that only Mark's Gospel contains (Mark 3:16–17) as written in "his memoirs."[14] The antecedent of "his" is not entirely clear, but the most likely candidate is "Peter," to whom Justin has just referred.[15]

It is possible that Justin learned about the connection between Peter and Mark's Gospel from Papias, but the only notable verbal similarity between the two passages is their use of "remember" (ἀπομνημονεύω) to describe the connection.[16] Irenaeus (*Haer.* 3.10.5) and Tertullian (*Marc.* 4.2.5) confirm the same connection, and although they may be dependent on Papias, this is not certain. It is possible that they bear witness to the widespread currency in the second century of a tradition earlier than Papias himself.[17]

Second, Peter is the most prominent disciple of Jesus in Mark's Gospel.[18] He is the first disciple Mark names (1:16), and he and his brother Andrew are the first disciples who follow Jesus (1:17). His name always comes first in the trio of disciples ("Peter, James, and John") whom Jesus sometimes selects out of the twelve for special experiences or instruction (5:37; 9:2; 14:33; cf. 13:3). He is the disciple who climactically names Jesus as "the Christ" in the middle of the narrative (8:29). He also is the last disciple named in the narrative, and that last occurrence of Peter's name both sets him apart from the other disciples ("But go, tell his disciples and Peter that he is going before you to Galilee," 16:7) and effectively restores Peter to the circle of the twelve after his threefold denial of Jesus (14:66–72). It is reasonable to think of the story of Peter's failure and restoration as coming from Peter himself: the story involves a level of personal regret and reflection that plausibly reflects Peter's own perspective.[19]

Third, there are other links between Peter and Mark in the New Testament. Peter retreated to Mark's house after he was released from prison

(Acts 12:12), and, in 1 Peter 5:13, Peter, who is in Rome, sends greetings to his readers from Mark, whom he calls "my son." The reference to Mark as his "son" implies a close personal relationship consistent with the idea that Mark was Peter's understudy.[20]

It is likely, then, that when Paul went to Jerusalem "to visit" Peter (Gal 1:18), he was going to one of the primary keepers of the tradition of Jesus's words and deeds. Mark's Gospel probably provides a good sample of what Paul either had confirmed about his own knowledge of Jesus or learned for the first time during his fifteen days with Peter.

Peter and Paul on the Significance of Christ's Death

The theological significance of Jesus's crucifixion is central within both Mark's narrative and Paul's letters. For both, Jesus's shameful and undeserved death on the cross is the means God uses to atone for the failures of God's people to live in the way he has called them to live. Mark makes clear the undeserved nature of Jesus's death and its significance as an atonement for sin. A group of closed-minded and power-hungry community leaders engineered Jesus's death. They believed that Jesus had blasphemed God when he pronounced the sins of a sick man forgiven (Mark 2:5–7), when he allowed his disciples to gather grain to eat on the Sabbath (Mark 2:24), and when he healed a disabled man on the Sabbath (Mark 3:2). After this last incident, "The Pharisees went out and immediately held council with the Herodians against him, how to destroy him" (Mark 3:6). Yet, Mark makes clear, Jesus had authority, given to him by God, to do all this. He was the "Son of Man" of Daniel 7:13–14 to whom God, according to Daniel, would give "dominion and glory and a kingdom, that all peoples, nations, and languages should serve him" (cf. Mark 2:10, 28).

Still, in the end, the religious and political power brokers seemed to get their way. In a sham trial that recalled for Mark the silent suffering servant of Isaiah 53:7 (Mark 14:60–61), Jesus was finally convicted and sentenced to death on the charge of blasphemy because of his claim to be the Son of Man of Daniel 7:13–14 (Mark 14:62–64). His crucifixion was filled with public shaming: the Roman soldiers charged with crucifying him first mocked his claims to kingly authority (Mark 15:16–20), "and those who passed by derided him," saying, among other things, "save yourself, and come down from the cross!" (Mark 15:29–30). Referring to his healing ministry, "the chief priests with the scribes mocked him to one another, saying, 'He saved others; he cannot save himself. Let the Christ, the King of Israel, come down now from the cross that we may see and believe'" (Mark 15:31–32).

For Mark, however, this was not merely a tragic miscarriage of justice but the means God had chosen to atone for the sins of all who were in rebellion against him and were willing to turn from that rebellion. Jesus came "not to be served but to serve, and to give his life as a ransom for many" (Mark 10:45). His shed blood sealed a covenant between God and his people because it was "poured out for many" (Mark 14:24). These texts are again intentionally reminiscent of Isaiah's innocent, suffering servant, who "had done no violence, and there was no deceit in his mouth" (Isa 53:9), but who "poured out his soul to death and was numbered with the transgressors; . . . he bore the sins of many" (Isa 53:12).

In Mark's Gospel, Peter is perhaps the clearest example of Jesus's atoning death at work. He and his brother Andrew were Jesus's first followers (Mark 1:16–17), and yet they, along with the rest of the twelve, abandoned Jesus at his arrest (14:50). Mark describes Peter's abandonment in detail—his protest of loyalty to Jesus (14:29), his sleepiness during Jesus's agonized prayer in the garden where he was arrested (14:37), his threefold denial that he was Jesus's follower during the time of Jesus's trial before the high priest (14:68, 70, 71), and his weeping at the thought of what he had done (14:72). Despite all this, the words of the angel to the two Marys who discovered Jesus's tomb empty show that Jesus was willing to be reconciled to Peter: "But go, tell his disciples and Peter that he is going before you to Galilee. There you will see him, just as he told you" (16:7; cf. 14:27–28). Peter was among the many whom Jesus had ransomed at the cost of his life, and for whose sins Jesus's shameful death had atoned.

As Bauckham and others have argued, it is reasonable to connect this detailed account of Peter's failure, sense of regret, and restoration with the claim of John the Elder, according to Papias, that Peter was a primary source for Mark's Gospel. It seems equally reasonable to think of Peter telling this story to Paul during their fifteen days together only a few years after the death and resurrection of Jesus. Their stories, as it turned out, were similar. Paul too had been zealous for God but then failed miserably as the blindness of his zeal led him to target God's people with violence (Gal 1:13–14; 1 Cor 15:9; Phil 3:6; 1 Tim 1:13). Despite this, the Christ who "died for our sins in accordance with the Scriptures" had also died for his sins, and "the grace of God" had powerfully transformed Paul, the persecutor of the church, into an apostle of the very message he had tried to silence (1 Cor 15:3, 9–10a; cf. Gal 1:23). The transformation was so complete that he became the hardest working of all the apostles, "though," he says, "it was not I, but the grace of God that is with me" (1 Cor 15:10b).

For Paul, Christ's death was the instrument of transformation, and this was probably true for Peter. Paul puts it this way in Galatians: "I have been crucified with Christ. It is no longer I who live, but Christ who lives in me. And the life I now live in the flesh I live by faith in the Son of God, who loved me and gave himself for me" (Gal 2:19b–20). Paul's old way of life died with Christ on the cross, and faith in the resurrected Son of God now fueled his new way of life.[21] From Paul's perspective, Christ loved him and, out of this love, made the transformation of Paul's life possible by his death. The way Paul words this ("who ... gave [παραδόντος] himself for me") is reminiscent of Isaiah 53:12 (LXX), where Isaiah says that the servant "was given over [παρεδόθη] for their sins," referring to the sins of God's people (my trans.).

Paul goes into more detail about the sense in which Christ gave himself for him a few paragraphs later: "Christ redeemed us from the curse of the law by becoming a curse for us—for it is written, 'Cursed is everyone who is hanged on a tree [ξύλου]'" (Gal 3:13). The "curse of the law" here is the curse of destruction and death that the law pronounces on all who disobey it, and, for Paul, this includes all humanity (Gal 3:10; cf. Deut 27:26). Christ, however, absorbed this curse by being hung "on a tree" (Deut 21:23). Paul is quoting from a part of the Mosaic law that governs how Israel should carry out the common ancient Near Eastern custom of exposing the corpse of an executed criminal (cf., e.g., Gen 40:19; Esth 5:14). In Israel, this custom should illustrate the theological truth that, when the condemned person was alive, his criminal behavior placed him under the curse of God (Deut 21:22–23).[22]

Since Christ was sinless, however, his crucifixion functioned in a substitutionary way: he received the penalty of destruction, death, and God's curse that rests on all who disobey the law and, in this way, rescued all Christians from this plight. As Paul put it elsewhere, "For our sake [God] made him to be sin who knew no sin, so that in him we might become the righteousness of God" (2 Cor 5:21). Paul believed that those who trusted God to deal mercifully with the sin of his creatures in this way became united with Christ, both in his death and in his resurrected, ascended existence. They were united with Christ's death in the sense that they had turned away from their previous acts of unfaithfulness to God, and they were united with Christ's present existence in the sense that they lived in the way he outlined in his teachings (Rom 6:1–14, 17).

There is much less evidence for Peter's theology of conversion, but what does exist shows a similar pattern. First Peter displays the same pattern of allusions to the substitutionary, atoning death of Isaiah's suffering servant that appears in Mark's description of Jesus's passion. During an argument that Christian household slaves should continue to be respectful to their masters, even when treated unjustly, Peter recalls the example of Christ: "He committed no sin, neither was deceit found in his mouth. When he was reviled, he did not revile in return; when he suffered, he did not threaten, but continued entrusting himself to him who judges justly. He himself bore our sins in his body on the tree [ξύλον], that we might die to sin and live to righteousness. By his wounds [μώλωπι, "welt"] you have been healed. For you were straying like sheep, but have now returned to the Shepherd and Overseer of your souls" (1 Pet 2:22–25).

Peter's description of Jesus here is deeply indebted to the description of the suffering servant in Isaiah 53:4–12, and in ways that closely parallel Mark's indebtedness to the same text. Just as the servant had "done no violence, and there was no deceit in his mouth" (Isa 53:9), and just as he "bore the sin of many" (Isa 53:12), so Jesus "committed no sin, neither was deceit found in his mouth" (1 Pet 2:22). Just as the servant was silent in the face of oppression (Isa 53:7), so Jesus did not revile those who reviled him (cf. Mark 14:60–61). Just as the undeserved "welt" (μώλωπι) on the servant's back substituted for the divine chastisement that God's people deserved and, in this sense, healed them (Isa 53:5 LXX), so Jesus's "welt" (μώλωπι) has healed those who follow him.[23] And just as the servant took on himself all the iniquity of the people of God, who, like sheep, had gone astray (Isa 53:6), so Jesus now serves as the shepherd of those who once strayed, like sheep, away from God (cf. Mark 10:45; 14:24).

It is significant that in the middle of this Isaianic description of Jesus's atoning death, Peter makes a statement that is also reminiscent of Paul's understanding of Jesus's death. Just as Paul thought of Jesus's death as both atonement for sin and the beginning of a transformative union with Christ, so Peter seems to couple these two ideas in one brief sentence: "He himself bore our sins [τὰς ἁμαρτίας ἡμῶν αὐτὸς ἀνήνεγκεν] in his body on the tree, so that, having died to sins, we might live for righteousness" (1 Pet 2:24 CSB). The reference to Christ himself bearing our sins is strongly reminiscent of the ancient Greek translation of Isaiah 53:12 where Isaiah, describing the servant, says that "he himself bore the sins of many" (my trans.). This is in turn reminiscent of Mark's record of Jesus's statements that he would give his life as a ransom and pour out his blood "for many" (Mark 10:45; 14:24). The substitutionary and atoning nature of Jesus's death in both 1 Peter and Mark, then, is structurally like Paul's articulations of Christ's death "for me" and "for us" (Gal 2:20; 3:13).

Peter's reference to Jesus's bearing "our sins in his body on the tree" makes the connection to Paul's understanding of the substitutionary and atoning nature of Christ's death even more plausible. Underlying Peter's use of "the tree" (τὸ ξύλον) as a name for the cross (ὁ σταυρός) is probably the same understanding of Deuteronomy 21:23 that appears in Galatians 3:13.[24] In both texts, the exposure of Christ's body on the upright wooden frame of the cross (the "tree") is a sign that he suffered the curse that those who had rebelled against God deserved, and he did so in their place. Peter's connection with this understanding of Deuteronomy 21:23 also appears in Acts, where he twice describes Jesus's crucifixion as "hanging him on a tree" (Acts 5:30; 10:39). The only other reference to the cross as a tree in Acts appears in Paul's speech in the synagogue at Pisidian Antioch (Acts 13:29).

Someone might argue that 1 Peter is pseudonymous and that, like Acts, was written after Paul, so it simply borrows the reference to the cross as a tree from commonly accepted Christian tradition. It is just as historically plausible, however, to think that both Acts and 1 Peter preserve Peter's own theology of the atonement and that Paul picked up this theology, with its reference to Deuteronomy 21:23, sometime during the early years of his ministry. His fifteen days with Peter in Jerusalem would have provided an opportunity during which this could have happened. He would have understood the atoning nature of Christ's death from the time of his conversion when Jesus had commissioned him to preach the gospel to both Jews and gentiles who, on believing it, would "receive forgiveness of sins" (Acts 26:18). Still, his fifteen days with Cephas could easily have provided an opportunity for a deepened understanding of the atonement in the direction of his description of it in Galatians 3:13. This may have been the time Paul was referring to in 1 Corinthians 15:3 where he says that he had "delivered to" the Corinthians the critically important truth that he had "*also received*: that Christ died for our sins in accordance with the Scriptures" (my emphasis).

This is not all, however. After describing the substitutionary and atoning nature of Christ's death, Peter moves seamlessly into a description of union with Christ that recalls Galatians 2:19b–20 and especially Romans 6. Christ "bore our sins," says Peter, "so that, having died to sins, we might live for righteousness" (1 Pet 2:24 CSB). The term Peter uses here for "having died" (ἀπογενόμενοι) never shows up in Paul's writings (or anywhere else in the New Testament), and where it does appear in Greek literature, it often carries the sense of keeping away from something or not participating in it.[25] Peter might simply be saying, then, that Christ died so that we might depart from sinning and live in the right way. His thought might be, in the words of Edward Gordon Selwyn, "ethical and psychological" rather than "mystical" in the sense of union with Christ's death.[26]

The term could also refer, however, to departing this life, or dying, and since it is coupled with the notion of living with respect to righteousness, that is probably what it means here.[27] It is not exactly the way Paul speaks in his letters, but it is close, for example, to Romans 6:2b, "How can we who died [ἀπεθάνομεν] to sin still live in it?" or 6:11, "So you also must consider yourselves dead [νεκροὺς] to sin and alive to God in Christ Jesus." Paul makes these comments, moreover, within a context that goes on to thank God that the Roman Christians "have become obedient from the heart to the standard of teaching to which you were committed, and, having been set free from sin, have become slaves of righteousness" (Rom 6:17–18). Here Paul's supposedly "mystical" idea of union with Christ takes a decidedly ethical turn, and Peter's ethical use of the term "righteousness" seems to match Paul's use of the term "righteousness" in this context as obedience to a set body of teaching.[28] It is true that Paul characteristically uses the term "righteousness" to refer to God's saving power, his gift of a right standing with himself, and his impartiality, but here he uses it, like 1 Peter, to mean simply "doing what is right."[29]

Again, it is common to say that such similarities between 1 Peter and the Pauline literature, especially Romans, arose from 1 Peter's use of a common

Return to Jerusalem

Christian tradition already informed by the language of those letters.[30] It seems no less historically reasonable, however, to think of 1 Peter expressing ideas that sound Pauline, but in somewhat different terms and with different emphases because it preserves evidence of the sort of actual, personal contact between Peter and Paul to which Galatians 1:18 testifies.[31] Paul's own testimony to his relationship with Peter reveals that even when Paul did not think Peter was acting in a way that was consistent with the gospel, he and Peter agreed on the essence of the gospel. In Antioch, after Peter had withdrawn from table fellowship with gentile Christians, Paul was able to correct Peter's hypocrisy by describing the essence of the gospel, on which the two apostles agreed: "We know that a person is not justified by works of the law, but through faith in Christ, so we also have believed in Christ Jesus, in order to be justified by faith in Christ and not by works of the law" (Gal 2:15–16).[32] That agreement probably began with Paul's fifteen-day stay with Peter in Jerusalem.

THE THREAT OF VIOLENCE AND PAUL'S FLIGHT FROM JERUSALEM

Paul says nothing about his first post-conversion visit to Jerusalem apart from his brief statements that he stayed with Peter for fifteen days, and, among the other apostles, saw only James (Gal 1:18–19). Luke goes into more detail. He says that when Paul came to Jerusalem, he was slow to win acceptance among the disciples of Jesus there because they did not trust his claim to have become one of them. A man named Barnabas, however, introduced Paul "to the apostles" and explained the story of his conversion and of his proclamation of the gospel in Damascus (Acts 9:26–27).

"Barnabas" was a nickname for a man whose given name was Joseph. His nickname originated with the apostles who seem to have known him well (Acts 4:36). Although he was originally from Cyprus, his aunt Mary and cousin John Mark lived in Jerusalem, and their house was the first place Peter went after he was miraculously released from Herod Agrippa's prison (Acts 4:36; 12:12; Col 4:10). John Mark is the same Mark that Peter considered a "son" (1 Pet 5:13), who acted as his interpreter, and who used Peter's information about Jesus as a source for his gospel (Eusebius, *Hist. eccl.* 3.39.15). This John Mark later became an assistant to Barnabas and Paul during their gospel-preaching mission to Cyprus (Acts 12:25; 13:5),

CHAPTER 4

and after Barnabas and Paul parted company, he became an associate of Barnabas in helping the churches on Barnabas's native island of Cyprus (Acts 15:37, 39).

All of this demonstrates how small and tightly knit the top leadership of the early Jewish-Christian community in Jerusalem was, and how, from an early date, Paul was an important part of that tightly knit community. It quickly became clear, however, that, unlike the other members of this leadership circle, Paul could not stay in Jerusalem.

There were two reasons for this. First, Paul had received a clarifying and empowering vision when he was praying in the Jerusalem temple in which the Lord told him that the people of Jerusalem would not accept his testimony about Jesus. He was therefore to go "far away to the gentiles" (Acts 22:17–21). This may, at first, seem confusing, since elsewhere in Acts Paul's commission to take the gospel to the gentiles had come to Paul at the time of his conversion near Damascus (Acts 26:17–18; cf. Gal 1:16).[33] In addition, according to Paul's own testimony, he had already spent three years in Damascus and Arabia preaching Jesus Christ among the gentiles as God had intended (Gal 1:16–17).

The problem is resolved, however, if the temple vision to which Paul refers in Acts 22:17–21 was not a commissioning vision, but a clarification of that original commission. Paul had spent three years proclaiming the gospel to gentiles in Damascus and Arabia before returning to Jerusalem where he probably continued to focus his gospel message on the inclusion of gentiles within the people of God. These were all regions close to, or within, Judea. Now, in his trance in the Jerusalem temple, Paul saw and heard the Lord urging him to change the geographical location of his ministry: he must go "far away" (μακράν) to the gentiles (22:21).[34]

Second, as the Lord had indicated in this vision, his witness would not be accepted within Jerusalem (Acts 22:18). This meshes with the description of what happened to Paul in Acts 9:29. During his stay in Jerusalem, Paul engaged in the same kind of debates with Greek-speaking Jews that Stephen had conducted with diaspora Jews (including some from Paul's native province of Cilicia) and that had led to Stephen's death (cf. 6:8–10; 7:54–60). Paul had been part of that group, but now opposed the group, or one like it. Paul's approach was probably even more radical than Stephen's approach to the issue of including non-Jewish peoples within the people of God. The result was predictable: this group of Greek-speaking Jews in Jerusalem began trying to kill Paul.

When Paul wrote 1 Thessalonians 2:14–16, he was probably referring to this period of opposition in Jerusalem. If we read this passage according to the most likely understanding of the Greek and omit the comma that appears in most modern translations at the end of verse 14, then the beginning of verse 15 is a restrictive relative clause and does not refer to the Jewish people as a whole.[35] The NIV is among the very few translations that get this right:

> [14] For you, brothers and sisters, became imitators of God's churches in Judea, which are in Christ Jesus: You suffered from your own people the same things those churches suffered from *the Jews* [15] *who killed the Lord Jesus and the prophets and also drove us out*. They displease God and are hostile to everyone [16] in their effort to keep us from speaking to the Gentiles so that they may be saved. In this way they always heap up their sins to the limit. The wrath of God has come upon them at last. (1 Thess 2:14–16 NIV, emphasis added)

Paul was sympathizing with the Thessalonian Christians who had suffered a kind of marginalization in their own city that was like what many Christians across the eastern Mediterranean had experienced. The churches in Judea were also suffering, Paul says, not at the hands of the Jews generally (virtually all Christians in Judea in this period were Jews), but at the hands of the very Jews "who had killed the Lord Jesus and the prophets and also drove us out" (1 Thess 2:15 NIV). Paul is speaking here of the chief priests, scribes, and elders of the people who had engineered Jesus's crucifixion and continued to oppress his followers in Jerusalem and Judea.[36] These were the leaders (and they included the pre-Christian Paul) who had colluded with "those who belonged to the synagogue of the Freedmen . . . , and of the Cyrenians, and of the Alexandrians, and of those from Cilicia and Asia" to put Stephen through a mock trial similar to Jesus's trial and condemn him to death (Acts 6:8–7:1, 54–60).

In 1 Thessalonians 2:14–16, Paul is probably looking back not only on events like the deaths of Jesus and Stephen but also on his own experience in Jerusalem during his first post-conversion visit there. His own preaching

CHAPTER 4

of the inclusion of gentiles as gentiles within the people of God had probably led to the efforts of the Greek-speaking Jews (perhaps with the blessing of the chief priests, scribes, and elders of the people) to kill him. They are, Paul says, "hostile to everyone in their effort to keep us from speaking to the Gentiles so that they may be saved" (1 Thess 2:15–16 NIV). A powerful group of leaders had sent Jesus to his death, and an alignment of these same leaders with a zealous crowd of diaspora Jews had also sent Stephen to his death. Now they had turned their attention to him.[37]

Paul says that they "drove us out" of Judea (1 Thess 2:15), and in a passage in Galatians that probably touches on the same period of his life, he says that after leaving Jerusalem he "went into the regions of Syria and Cilicia" (Gal 1:21).[38] Luke fills in some detail on Paul's exit from Jerusalem. When Paul's fellow believers in Jerusalem discovered that the Greek-speaking Jews were trying to kill him, "they brought him down to Caesarea," a roughly seventy-mile journey to the closest major port city.[39] They then "sent him off to Tarsus" (Acts 9:30).

There are no details on the route Paul took from Caesarea to Tarsus, but a logical way to get there would be to take a coastal vessel working its way north to the Syrian port city of Seleucia.[40] It was then a relatively short distance by ship from Seleucia to the lake on the coast of eastern Cilicia that served as the seaport for Tarsus.[41] A traveler from Seleucia to Tarsus could also take an overland route that ran east through Antioch. According to Strabo, "One sails up from the sea to Antiocheia on the same day" (Strabo, *Geogr.* 16.2.7). If that is what Paul did, he might then have traveled north to a town called Pagrai on the southeastern side of the Amanus mountain range, through a pass in the mountains, up the coast into Cilicia and on to Tarsus. It was a journey of about a hundred and forty miles.[42] Either way, just as he says in Galatians, Paul would have stopped at Syrian ports, or Syrian towns farther inland, on his way into Cilicia.

5

Ministry in Syria and Cilicia

It is not clear how long Paul spent in Tarsus before Barnabas found him there and brought him to Antioch "for a whole year" (Acts 11:25–26) to help with the new, ethnically diverse church in that city. Paul's next time marker in Galatians simply indicates that fourteen years after his conversion he went to the meeting in Jerusalem that probably corresponds with the Jerusalem Council in Acts 15 (Gal 2:1–10). If Paul's conversion took place around AD 33, and his work in Arabia lasted until about AD 36, then that meeting took place around AD 47. Luke recounts Paul's travels and work on Cyprus, in Pamphylia, and in southern Galatia (Acts 13:4–14:23). He also describes his eventual return to Antioch sometime during this eleven-year period (Acts 14:24–28). Neither Paul nor Luke, however, says anything about what Paul did before Barnabas brought him to Antioch, and little about the "whole year" he spent there.

After telling his readers that Paul and Barnabas spent a year in Antioch, Luke's attention shifts to Jerusalem and his time indicators become vague: "now in these days" (Acts 11:27); "about that time" (Acts 12:1); "then he went down . . . and spent time there" (Acts 12:19). He implies, however, that Paul's year in Antioch was chronologically close to the time of Herod Agrippa I's death, which Luke also describes, and which, according to Josephus, took place in the third year of Claudius's rule, or AD 44 (Acts 11:27–30; 12:20–25; Josephus, *A.J.* 19.351). This means that Paul's work in "the regions of Syria and Cilicia" probably lasted about seven years, from roughly AD 37 until 44. This was a period stretching through the whole reign of the emperor Gaius (AD 37–41) and into the early years of Claudius ("Caligula," AD 41–44). It overlapped closely with the rise to power of the

CHAPTER 5

Hasmonean Jewish king Herod Agrippa I who ruled first over Trachonitis and Gaulanitis, then over Galilee and Perea, and eventually over Judea, Samaria, and Caesarea (AD 37–44).[1]

A TIME OF POLITICAL TURMOIL

This was a time of immense turmoil for many Jews, whether in Judea or in the Jewish diaspora of the eastern Mediterranean. In AD 38, Herod Agrippa I set out from Rome to secure his rule in the territories Gaius had given him in the east, and along the way he stopped in Alexandria, the capital of Egypt. The city was experiencing a nasty political dispute between its Greek population, which enjoyed special privileges, and the Jews. The Jews, for well over a century, had formed a discrete civic body within the city with the legal right to live in their own city sector and to govern their own affairs.[2] The Greeks, however, were the most privileged class within Alexandria, and all who were members of the city's special center for Greek education and culture (the "gymnasium") enjoyed the privileges of full citizenship, including exemption from a burdensome tax the Romans had imposed on the working male population nearly a century earlier.[3] During the early thirties AD, at least some people within the Jewish population began to lobby for admission to this full form of Alexandrian citizenship, and Greek leaders resisted this encroachment on their social and cultural space.[4]

Greek resentment against the Jewish population was at the boiling point right at the time Herod Agrippa I stopped in Alexandria on his way to Syria (Philo, *Flacc.* 26; *Legat.* 179). Herod was a Jewish king with the enormous social advantage of friendship with the new Roman emperor Gaius. After initially wanting to keep his visit to Alexandria short and secretive, he decided to stay long enough to send a petition to Gaius supporting the Jewish cause, and, during his stay, made an open display of his military guard and his wealth.[5] This only enflamed Greek resentments against the Jews. Greek leaders successfully blackmailed Flaccus, the Roman procurator of Egypt, into turning a blind eye to the organization of a "parade" mocking King Agrippa and his displays of wealth and royalty (Philo, *Flacc.* 36–40).

That parade was the catalyst for a violent popular uprising of Greeks against the Jews, which the politically weakened Flaccus did nothing to stop. The primary evidence for these events comes from the Alexandrian Jewish philosopher Philo, who lived through them.[6] His account of the beatings, torture, murder, theft, poverty, famine, and loss of long-standing political protection for Alexandria's Jewish community is stomach-turning. Two statements in the account stand out as particularly important, however, for understanding how this riot must have affected Jewish people who knew about it. First, Philo comments that when the rioters could not succeed in tearing or burning down synagogues because the numbers of Jews protecting them were too great, they resorted to desecrating the synagogues with images of Gaius (Philo, *Legat.* 134; cf. *Flacc.* 41–43). The message seems to have been that the Jews, as people who did not worship Gaius, were enemies of the emperor. Second, at one point in his account of the horrors that the Alexandrian Jews experienced at the hands of rioters, Philo says that a group of Jewish women were seized, taken to the theater and presented with swine's flesh, which they were told to eat. Those who refused were handed over for torture (Philo, *Flacc.* 95–96).

The desecration of places of worship with a ruler's image and forced consumption of swine's flesh would have suggested to most Jews that what was happening in Alexandria was similar to what had happened in Judea almost two centuries earlier when the Jews were at the mercy of the philhellenic Syrian king Antiochus IV Epiphanes.[7] At that time, too, the king built "altars and sacred precincts and shrines for idols" in Judea and Jerusalem (1 Macc 1:54). He renamed the temple in Jerusalem "the temple of Olympian Zeus" (2 Macc 6:2), and he set up statues of both Zeus and himself in the temple.[8] Jews were expected to abandon their religious traditions and participate in the worship of Greek gods. Those who refused these orders died horrific deaths, and the king's subordinates used eating swine's flesh as a litmus test of Jewish willingness to cave in to the king's program of Hellenization (1 Macc 1:41–50; 2 Macc 6:1–7:42).

Philo seems to have thought that the events in Alexandria set the feelings of the Jewish people on edge wherever they were located. "It was perfectly clear," he says, "that the rumour of the overthrowing of the synagogues beginning at Alexandria would spread at once to the nomes of Egypt and speed from Egypt to the East and the nations of the East and from the Hypotaenia and Marea, which are the outskirts of Libya, to the West and the nations of the West" (*Flacc.* 45 [Colson, LCL]). He then makes the point that Jews live "in very many of the most prosperous countries" and would hear of the troubles in Alexandria (*Flacc.* 46 [Colson, LCL]). Throughout the world, Jewish people would fear "that people everywhere might take their cue from Alexandria, and outrage their Jewish fellow-citizens by rioting against their synagogues and ancestral customs" (*Flacc.* 47 [Colson, LCL]). There is some slight evidence that these fears were realized. The sixth-century chronographer John Malalas, who lived in Syrian Antioch, preserves an otherwise unknown account of an uprising in the city in AD 40 in which "the Hellenes of Antioch fought with the Jews there in a faction brawl, killed many Jews and burnt their synagogues."[9]

Just as Paul's seven years of ministry in Syria and Cilicia were getting started, then, many Jews in the diaspora may well have been afraid that they were entering a period when the non-Jewish majorities and Roman rulers in the places where they lived would try to force them to adopt Greek, or other non-Jewish customs in the way Antiochus IV had done, and, as it seemed, the Greek majority in Alexandria was doing. Despite the arrival of authorities from Rome to arrest Flaccus and restore calm a few months later, political trouble for the Jews of the eastern Mediterranean was not over. Only two years later, Jewish fears of attacks on their way of life must have increased exponentially when Gaius glibly decided to transform the Jewish temple in Jerusalem "into a temple of his own to bear the name of Gaius, 'the new Zeus manifest,'" as Philo puts it (Philo, *Legat.* 346). The image was actually a likeness of Jupiter (whom the Romans identified with Zeus) rather than a likeness of Gaius himself, but subtleties such as these probably mattered as little to Jews generally as they did to Philo (Philo, *Legat.* 188, 265).[10] The whole project must have sounded in Jewish ears like a repetition of the draconian Hellenizing policies of Antiochus IV Epiphanes, and, even accounting for some exaggeration in the reports, the reactions to it were extreme.

The differing accounts that Philo and Josephus give of what prompted Gaius's odd move are instructive for understanding the mood of the times. When the incident occurred, Philo was in Rome with a delegation of four other Alexandrian Jews seeking an audience with Gaius in the hope that he would be willing to help the city's Jewish population. He claims that Gaius's order was an angry response to a report that Jewish people in the Judean coastal town of Jamnia had torn down an altar for sacrifice to the emperor. An anti-Jewish element had hastily erected the altar simply to goad the Jews into destroying it and then to get them into trouble (Philo, *Legat.* 200–202). Josephus claims that Apion, one of the Alexandrians who was in Rome to speak against the Jewish cause, told Gaius that the Jews alone among all of Rome's subject peoples "scorned to honor him with statues and to swear by his name" (Josephus, *A.J.* 18.257–258; cf. *Ag. Ap.* 2.73). In other words, they failed to treat him as a god alongside other gods. Apion was a well-known scholar and orator "who drew crowds to his lectures all over Greece in the days of Gaius Caesar" (Seneca, *Ep.* 88.40 [Gummere, LCL]).

Gaius's plan never materialized thanks to an anguished petition from his friend Herod Agrippa I, the delaying tactics of Gaius's Syrian legate Petronius, and, finally, Gaius's death in AD 41 (Philo, *Legat.* 275–333; Josephus, *A.J.* 18.273–309). The same kinds of provocations that created problems in Alexandria and Jamnia, and that fed the anti-Jewish rhetoric of Apion, however, seem to have continued under the emperor Claudius. He issued an edict shortly after succeeding Gaius concerning the tensions in Alexandria instructing "both sides to take the utmost care to ensure that there are no disturbances after this edict of mine has been published" (Josephus, *A.J.* 19.285).[11] A second edict went "to the rest of the world" and included the statement that "the Jews throughout the whole world under our sway should also observe the customs of their fathers without let or hindrance. I enjoin upon them also by these presents to avail themselves of this kindness in a more reasonable spirit, and not to set at nought the beliefs about the gods held by other peoples but to keep their own laws" (Josephus, *A.J.* 19.290 [Feldman, LCL]).

That Claudius felt the need to issue such edicts not only to Alexandria but to the whole empire shows that feelings were running high in many places. Not long after his edicts, trouble broke out in Dora, a coastal town just eight miles north of Caesarea. The story sounds familiar: some non-Jewish troublemakers in the city "brought an image of Caesar into the synagogue of the Jews and set it up" (Josephus, *A.J.* 19.300 [Feldman, LCL]). Violence was only avoided when Herod Agrippa I made a swift visit to Petronius, who was still serving as legate of Syria, and Petronius took equally swift action to quell any further trouble (Josephus, *A.J.* 19.299–311). Petronius issued an edict of his own to the people of Dora, and he was not too happy about having to do it: "It is ridiculous for me to refer to my own decree after making mention of the edict of the emperor which permits Jews to follow their own customs, yet also, be it noted, bids them live as fellow citizens with the Greeks" (Josephus, *A.J.* 19.306 [Feldman, LCL]). Clearly, relations remained strained on both sides in parts of Syria, despite Claudius's edicts.[12]

There is little evidence for the state of the Jewish community in Cilicia during this period, but the evidence that does exist indicates that it was large, and that some within that community had a tendency toward violence in defense of Judaism.[13] Within the group that claimed Stephen had spoken "blasphemous words against Moses and God," and that instigated Stephen's arrest, were "those from Cilicia" (Acts 6:9, 11–12).

Much later, and less reliable, is a story from the third-century orator Philostratus about the first-century philosopher Apollonius, who was a native of Tyana, seventy or so miles north of Tarsus, in Cilicia. Apollonius was supposedly present when the emperor Titus visited Tarsus and agreed to take a petition of some of the citizens of the city to his father, the emperor Vespasian. Philostratus claims that Apollonius "came forward and said, 'Suppose I show that some of these people are hostile to you and your father, that they have negotiated with Jerusalem about revolt, and have been secret allies of your most declared enemy'" (Philostratus, *Vit. Apoll.* 6.34.2 [Jones, LCL]).[14] This possibly indicates a group of Jewish people in Tarsus in the first century who were sympathetic with the Jewish revolt against Rome in AD 66–70. It is true that Philostratus's portrait of Apollonius is highly fictionalized, and that he composed it almost two hundred years after this period of Paul's career, but *The Life of Apollonius* may nevertheless provide a window onto the social realities of its first-century setting.[15]

Civil Unrest as the Setting of Paul's Syrian and Cilician Ministry

It seems reasonably clear from this evidence that both Syria and Cilicia in AD 37–44 were places where tension could easily flare up between the Jewish and the non-Jewish population. Yet these were also the places where Paul was preaching "among the Gentiles . . . the faith he once tried to destroy" (Gal 1:16, 23). This was the period, moreover, in which other Jewish

Ministry in Syria and Cilicia

Christians began "preaching the Lord Jesus" to the non-Jewish, Greek-speaking population of Syrian Antioch (Gal 1:21; Acts 9:20).

What response would Paul have received when he preached the gospel to gentiles in Syria and Cilicia? Much would have depended on exactly what he preached. He tells the Galatians that God revealed his Son to him at the time of his conversion so that he "might preach him among the Gentiles" (Gal 1:16). Right at the center of his preaching, then, would have been the significance of Jesus himself. A little later in the same letter, Paul reminds the Galatians that when they first heard the gospel "Jesus Christ was publicly portrayed as crucified" (Gal 3:1), so the crucifixion of Jesus seems to have figured prominently into Paul's preaching to the gentiles. He tells the Corinthians, similarly, that when he proclaimed "the testimony of God to them" he focused on "Jesus Christ and him crucified" (1 Cor 2:2; cf. 1:23).

Luke says that when Jesus appeared to Paul at the time of his conversion, he sent him to open the eyes of both Jews and gentiles "so that they may turn from darkness to light and from the power of Satan to God, that they may receive forgiveness of sins and a place among those who are sanctified by faith in me" (Acts 26:17–18). Paul discloses in passing in a letter written only a few years after his period of preaching in Syria and Cilicia that when the Thessalonian Christians believed the gospel he had preached to them, they "turned to God from idols to serve the living and true God, and to wait for his Son from heaven, whom he raised from the dead, Jesus who delivers us from the wrath to come" (1 Thess 1:9–10).

From the earliest days of his mission to the gentiles, then, Paul seems to have proclaimed both the Jewishness of Jesus and his worldwide significance. He was the "Christ," the Son of God and the anointed King of God that Jewish people expected on the basis of their Scriptures. He was also the human face of Israel's God who would one day hold all the nations accountable for failing to worship the God of Israel exclusively, for Israel's God was the Creator of the universe and the only true God (1 Cor 8:5–6). It was true that he had died the shameful death of crucifixion at the hands of ignorant governmental powers, both Jewish and Roman (1 Cor 2:8; cf. 1 Thess 2:14–15), but God had raised him from the dead and given him an immortal body (1 Cor 15:3–11, 42–44; Phil 3:20–21). Moreover, God, in his mercy, had transformed Jesus's death on the cross into a sacrifice through which he would forgive the sins of all people groups, including those of his own people, the Jews. All who accepted this forgiveness through the death of Jesus, whether Jews or gentiles, would escape God's wrath at Jesus's return and experience the same transformation from mortality to immortality that Jesus himself had experienced (1 Thess 4:13–18).

In an environment marked by tension between Greeks and Jews, it would not be surprising if a message like this ran into strong resistance. From a Jewish perspective, Paul's preaching must have seemed like an implicit attack on the Jewish authorities who ran the Jerusalem temple and had targeted Jesus for elimination and his early followers for marginalization. Paul's message about the great messianic king, Jesus, could also have been understood as an attack on Herod Agrippa's authority. Herod was the king of the Jews, and he had been a defender of Jewish rights. He had courageously opposed Gaius's ill-conceived plan to install an idol in the temple.[16] He had responded swiftly and angrily to the trampling of Jewish religious rights in Dora.[17] Perhaps some Jewish people in Syria and Cilicia even knew that Agrippa himself had opposed the Christian movement in Jerusalem because "he saw that it pleased the Jews" (Acts 12:3).[18] A message calling on people who appreciated Herod Agrippa and the temple leadership to repent of their sin and acknowledge a crucified Galilean rabbi as the Messiah may have seemed like a betrayal of the Jewish cause in divisive and difficult times.

From a Greek perspective, Paul's message may have seemed like an attack on traditional religious commitments and on the imperial cult. Such open criticism of the imperial cult from a Jew was exactly what Claudius, Petronius, and Agrippa wanted to avoid. It could only enflame tensions and make matters worse. Claudius's edict to the Alexandrians emphasizes the importance of allowing the various ethnic groups in the eastern empire to observe their own religious customs without interference from others. A live-and-let-live approach would reduce tensions and keep the peace. He points out that Augustus desired "that the several subject nations should abide by their own customs and not be compelled to violate the religion of their fathers." In Alexandria, the Jews were to be allowed to "abide by their own customs," and both parties, he says, were to "take the greatest precaution to prevent any disturbance arising after the posting of my edict" (Josephus, *A.J.* 19.283–285 [Feldman, LCL]).

Similarly, Petronius's decree about the Greek desecration of a synagogue in Dora with an image of Caesar emphasizes the need for the various religions to leave each other alone (Josephus, *A.J.* 19.303–311 [Feldman, LCL]). Caesar's image, he says, belongs in his own shrine, not in a Jewish synagogue. Jews, for their part, need "to follow their own customs" and "live as fellow citizens with the Greeks" (Josephus, *A.J.* 19.306 [Feldman, LCL]). He concludes by stressing his main point to the Dorians, whatever their cultural and religious identity: "I charge you to seek no pretext for sedition or disturbance, but to practice severally each his own religion" (Josephus, *A.J.* 19.311 [Feldman, LCL]).

Community leaders in the towns of Syria and Cilicia where Paul preached could easily have understood his gospel as a politically charged message. Here was a Jewish person telling non-Jews that they would fall under the wrath of a coming king if they did not turn away from their traditional religious practices, including devotion to the emperor, and follow the teachings of a Jewish messianic claimant that the Roman procurator of Judea had executed by crucifixion.

Writing to the Corinthians roughly twelve years after this period of his ministry had ended, Paul recounts his apostolic credentials as a list of hardships he had endured as part of his call to proclaim the gospel to both Jews and gentiles:

> Are they servants of Christ? I am a better one—I am talking like a madman—with far greater labors, far more imprisonments, with countless beatings, and often near death. Five times I received at the hands of the Jews the forty lashes less one. Three times I was beaten with rods. Once I was stoned. Three times I was shipwrecked; a night and a day I was adrift at sea; on frequent journeys, in danger from rivers, danger from robbers, danger from my own people, danger from Gentiles, danger in the city, danger in the wilderness, danger at sea, danger from false brothers; in toil and hardship, through many a sleepless night, in hunger and thirst, often without food, in cold and exposure. (2 Cor 11:23–27; cf. 12:10)

Luke describes an incident in Lystra prior to the composition of 2 Corinthians in which Paul was stoned and left for dead (Acts 14:19), and another incident in Philippi when the local magistrates had him beaten with rods (Acts 16:22, 37). The general descriptions of danger and difficulty, and even the three shipwrecks, could similarly fit within Luke's narration of Paul's travels in Acts 13–19. Luke says nothing, however, about lashings in Jewish synagogues and two further encounters with the Roman magistrate's rod. Perhaps these incidents fell within the seven years on which Luke is silent but during which Paul proclaimed the gospel in Syria and Cilicia.[19] "The marks of Jesus" that Paul bore on his body (Gal 6:17) might have come at least in part from severe treatment during this period, although the stoning in Lystra and the beating in Philippi would have certainly left their scars.

On the positive side, this was probably also the period during which the churches of "Syria and Cilicia" emerged, which Paul later revisited with his coworkers (Acts 15:23, 41). Paul's preaching and church-planting efforts during the politically volatile seven years between AD 37 and AD 44 are the most likely explanation for the existence of these churches.[20] Two centuries later, the church in Tarsus seems to have been flourishing, and the Christian communities in some Cilician towns were large enough to send their bishops to the Council of Nicaea in AD 325. Perhaps some of these churches came to life under the preaching of the apostle Paul.[21]

PAUL'S VISION OF PARADISE AND HIS THORN IN THE FLESH

Sometime during this period, Paul experienced a vision of paradise that he briefly describes in 2 Corinthians 12:1–4. Paul relates his vision at an awkward moment in the letter. His opponents in Corinth have tried to undermine his authority and capture the loyalty of the Corinthians by bragging about such things as their missionary accomplishments, rhetorical skill, authoritarian demeanor, connection to early Jewish Christianity, and endurance of hardship (2 Cor 10:12–13; 11:6, 20, 22–23). Judging by the uncomfortable way Paul introduces his own boasting in "visions and revelations of the Lord" (2 Cor 12:1), they were probably also bragging about their visionary experiences.[22] In an effort to win the Corinthians back, Paul answers "a fool according to his folly" (Prov 26:5), and, very uneasily, engages in his own boasting (2 Cor 10:15–18).[23] Paul was writing around AD 56, and he describes his vision as occurring fourteen years earlier, which would put it toward the end of his work in Syria and Cilicia, perhaps sometime in AD 42–43.

Since he was uncomfortable with boasting about such things, he does not go into a lot of detail. He was, he says, "caught up to the third heaven," "to paradise," and in the third heaven "heard things that cannot be told, which man may not utter" (2 Cor 12:2–4). Twice he says that he does not know whether this experience happened "in the body or out of the body" (12:2–3). The plural reference to "revelations" a little later in the passage (12:7) probably does not mean that experiences like this happened to Paul more than once but refers to the "things" he heard during this experience and that he could not describe.[24] Paul's specific dating of the event to "fourteen years ago" implies that whatever happened to him was a unique experience.

Jewish prophetic and apocalyptic writings from a time prior to Paul sometimes describe experiences that resemble this. Isaiah had a vision of the throne room of God (Isa 6:1–7). Ezekiel saw the throne-chariot of God (Ezek 1:4–28). Daniel had a vision of the Ancient of Days seated to render judgment (Dan 7:9–10, 13–14). Sometimes, as with Paul, these visions emphasized either the ineffable nature of the experience or its connection with secrecy and mystery. In one of his visions, Daniel was told to "seal" it "up" because it referred not to Daniel's time but to a later time (Dan 8:26). In another vision, Daniel heard things that "he did not understand" and was informed that "the words" were "shut up and sealed until the time of the end" (Dan 12:7, 9).

Closer to the time of Paul, someone taking the identity of the biblical Enoch (Gen 5:24) claimed that, after meditating on a petition for mercy from the fallen angels of Genesis 6:2, he fell asleep and experienced an ascent to heaven (1 En. 13:6–7). He flew on the wind through the clouds and the stars to parts of heaven so glorious that he found it impossible to recount them (1 En. 14:8, 16). Eventually he beheld God himself, sitting on his throne (1 En. 14:19–20). Similarly, someone identifying himself with Levi (Gen 34:25) claims to have fallen asleep while meditating on human depravity and to have found himself on a high mountain. From there he traveled through two heavens to the presence of God in the third heaven, and God commissioned him to "tell forth his mysteries to men" (T. Levi 2:3–10 [Kee, *OTP* 1:788]).

All these experiences probably occurred during a time of crisis for the individuals who had them and the communities they represented. Isaiah's vision happened after the death of a highly effective king, Uzziah, and under an ever-growing political threat from Assyria.[25] The visions of Ezekiel and Daniel emerged out of social upheaval created by exile in Babylon.[26] The historical settings of 1 Enoch 12–16 and the Testaments of the Twelve Patriarchs are less clear, but it seems likely that they too emerged from communities that felt only too heavily the weight of the rebellion against God that, in "Enoch's" account, the fallen angels and their human progeny had introduced into the world.[27] As "Levi" puts it, "Sin was erecting walls and injustice was ensconced in towers" (T. Levi 2:3 [Kee, *OTP* 1:788]).

A tantalizing passage in Philo provides a possible backdrop for Paul's own heavenly ascent. Philo tells his readers that he could remember a time when he "had leisure for philosophy and for the contemplation of the universe and its contents" (Philo, *Spec.* 3.1–6 [Colson, LCL]).[28] He "seemed always to be borne aloft into the heights with a soul possessed by some God-sent inspiration, a fellow traveler with the sun and moon and the whole heaven and universe" (Philo, *Spec.* 3.1). Then, however, he was tracked down by "envy" and pulled down "with violence" from heaven and "plunged . . . in the ocean of civil cares, in which I am swept away, unable even to raise my head above the water" (Philo, *Spec.* 3.3). Nevertheless, says Philo, sometimes he has a brief respite from these "civic turmoils" and can "take wings and ride the waves and almost tread the lower air, wafted by the breezes of knowledge which often urges me to come to spend my days with her" (Philo, *Spec.* 3.5).

Philo is probably referring in this passage to the outbreak of violence against Alexandria's Jewish population in AD 38, just a few years before Paul's heavenly ascent in AD 42.[29] In a way that is similar to some of Daniel's visions, and to parts of the visions of "Enoch" and "Levi," Philo's ascent led to knowledge that was not generally "known to the multitude."[30] Perhaps, like Philo, "Levi," and "Enoch," Paul experienced a heavenly ascent as a retreat from the societal turmoil around him.

The one piece of information Paul does divulge about the content of his vision was that he saw the "third heaven," which he calls "paradise." The third heaven is probably a reference to the region above the clouds (the first heaven) and the astronomical bodies (the second heaven) where God dwells in all his glory.[31] Paul's use of the term "paradise" (παράδεισος) to refer to this region recalls the Greek text of the creation narrative, which uses the term throughout Genesis 2–3 to refer to the fruitful and peaceful garden that God planted in Eden, and where God walked with Eve and Adam (Gen 3:8). Perhaps God gave to Paul an encouraging vision of the new creation where there would be no injustice, oppression, or war, and where God would walk again with his people in a place of abundance and safety (cf. Lev 26:11–12; Ezek 37:25–28; 2 Cor 5:17; Gal 6:15; Rev 2:7; 21:3–4; 22:2).

It was also at this time, and in connection with his ascent to paradise, that Paul experienced something he calls "a thorn . . . given me in the flesh, a messenger of Satan to harass me" (2 Cor 12:7b). Its purpose was to prevent Paul from "becoming conceited because of the surpassing greatness of the revelations" he had experienced (12:7a). He urged the Lord three times to take this suffering away, but instead the Lord told him that his grace was sufficient for Paul and that weakness was the context in which power was perfected (12:8–9). Paul's description of this weakness as "in the flesh" must mean that it was a physical malady, and Paul's three prayers for healing probably imply that it was a recurring illness. If this is right, then an especially severe bout of this same illness may account for Paul's near-death experience in Asia, which occurred much later, probably in Troas and probably in AD 56.[32]

Paul, however, was not interested in describing the details of his illness. He was much more interested in the principle that the Lord taught him through this illness, that power must be tempered in the fires of suffering. "I am content with weaknesses, insults, hardships, persecutions, and calamities," he says, "For when I am weak, then I am strong" (2 Cor 12:10). Paul did not believe that his illness was a good thing. It was the work of one of Satan's minions (ἄγγελος), sent to give him a sound beating (ἵνα με κολαφίζῃ). Nevertheless, God brought good from it. He used it to keep Paul from becoming proud because of the prestige that others might attach to his amazing visionary experience. The Lord, then, had used Paul's suffering to keep him from misusing the power the Lord had given him.

In years to come, Paul would continue to discover that God was often at work in his ministry precisely when opposition and difficulty were prevalent. Paul tells the Corinthian Christians that he will stay where he is in Ephesus until Pentecost, "for a wide door for effective work has opened to me, and there are many adversaries" (1 Cor 16:9). He tells the Roman Christians that they can boast in afflictions because from affliction God can bring the good qualities of endurance, character, and hope (Rom 5:3–4). Later, he tells the same audience that "for those who love God all things work together for good" (Rom 8:28). Although the distress of his work made him feel like a sheep led to the slaughter, he was nevertheless a victor because he saw God's love for him so clearly in the death and resurrection of Jesus (Rom 8:31–39). He told the Christians in Philippi, similarly, that he had watched as God found ways to advance the gospel through his imprisonment (Phil 1:12–14).

Paul's years preaching the gospel in Syria and Cilicia, then, may have been an extraordinarily difficult time for him. His politically provocative message probably met with violent opposition, and he was probably plagued with a painful illness. He was nevertheless continuing to learn that the gracious God who had called him to proclaim the gospel to the nations also empowered him to accomplish this task in the midst of weakness. "For the sake of Christ, then," he told the Corinthians, "I am content with weaknesses, insults, hardships, persecutions, and calamities. For when I am weak, then I am strong" (2 Cor 12:10).

6

Forming and Expanding the Multiethnic Church of God

Near the end of a description of how the Corinthian Christians can work for unity among themselves and bear a winsome witness to unbelievers, Paul urges them to "give no offense to Jews or to Greeks or to the church of God" (1 Cor 10:31–32). Paul implies here that he considers "the church of God" to be a new people, distinct from such groups as "Jews" and "Greeks." Although those who believed the gospel retained their social identity (see, e.g., Rom 9:3; Gal 2:3, 15), the identity of Christians as "the church of God" encompassed and took priority over that identity. Luke identifies the church in the Syrian city of Antioch as the location where this social shift first began to happen on a large scale, and he places Paul at the center of this shift.

THE ORIGINS OF THE CHURCH IN SYRIAN ANTIOCH

Writing only a few decades after Paul's time, Josephus tells his readers that "the Jewish race, densely interspersed among the native populations of every portion of the world, is particularly numerous in Syria" (*B.J.* 7.43 [Thackeray, LCL]). They were especially present in Antioch, he explains, where they had enjoyed civic privileges since the time of the city's founding in the third century BC, apart from the obvious exception of the rule of Antiochus IV (*B.J.* 7.43–44; cf. *Ag. Ap.* 2.39). "Moreover," he continues, "they were constantly attracting to their religious ceremonies multitudes of Greeks, and these they had in some measure incorporated with themselves"

(*B.J.* 7.45 [Thackeray, LCL]). When the gospel came to Antioch, therefore, it entered a social environment in which Jewish people had long been used to associating with the local non-Jewish population, and in which some of that population had found the Scriptures, the synagogue, and the Jewish way of life appealing.

It is not surprising, then, to learn from Luke that in the early Jerusalem church "Nicolaus, a proselyte of Antioch" was among those chosen to oversee the fair distribution of food aid to Greek-speaking disciples who needed it (Acts 6:5). As a proselyte to Judaism from Antioch, Nicolaus would have spoken Greek as his native tongue. It is also not surprising to learn that after an extensive persecution of Jesus's disciples broke out in Jerusalem (8:3), some of the disciples who were from Cyprus and Cyrene (and therefore spoke Greek) also went to Syrian Antioch and proclaimed the gospel in Greek to non-Jewish Greek-speaking people there. As a result, Luke implies, "a great number who believed turned to the Lord" (11:19–21).

This was such an unusual development that, according to Luke, when the Jerusalem church heard what was happening, they sent one of their leaders to Antioch, presumably to inspect the changes there and to be sure they met with the approval of the Jerusalem leadership (Acts 11:22; cf. 8:14). This multiethnic group of Jesus's disciples, meeting together, also required a new name. Those who comprised it were not simply Jews or Greeks but a third social group altogether. So, Luke tells his readers that "in Antioch the disciples were first called Christians" (11:26b).

The leader that the Jerusalem church sent to Antioch was Barnabas, and he was an obvious choice for overseeing the developments there. Not only was he "a good man, full of the Holy Spirit and of faith" (Acts 11:24), but he was from Cyprus and probably fluent in Greek (4:36). When he saw what was happening in Antioch, he not only approved of and encouraged it (11:23), but he thought of another Greek-speaking disciple of Jesus who could help teach the new, multiethnic church: Paul.

Barnabas had been kind to Paul during Paul's first trip back to Jerusalem after his conversion and had served as an intermediary, introducing him to Peter and James and explaining to them that Paul's conversion was real (Acts 9:27; Gal 1:18–19). Now, once again, Barnabas reached out to Paul, making the trip to Cilicia to search for him. After finding him in Tarsus,

Barnabas brought Paul to Antioch where they served together as prophets and teachers in the new church (Acts 11:25–26a; 13:1). Luke says that they continued to do this "for a whole year" (Acts 11:26b) before an urgent need in Judea interrupted their work.

Famine Relief in Judea

At some point during this year, a prophet named Agabus arrived from Jerusalem and predicted "a great famine over all the world," and, Luke continues, "this took place in the days of Claudius" (Acts 11:28; cf. 21:10). It is not clear how long before the famine Agabus made his prophecy, but it is likely to be the same famine Josephus describes as so severe in Jerusalem that "many were perishing from want of money to purchase what they needed" (Josephus, *A.J.* 20.51). That famine happened when Tiberius Alexander (the nephew of Philo) was procurator of Judea and therefore sometime during the period AD 46 to 48 (Josephus, *A.J.* 20.100–101).[1]

These dates receive confirmation from a constellation of evidence in Pliny the Elder, surviving official records on conditions in Egypt, and another report of Josephus. Pliny comments that during the reign of Claudius the Nile River in Egypt, which flooded regularly, crested at eighteen cubits. To his knowledge that was the highest the river had ever been. Sixteen cubits was ideal, and anything over that amount led to delayed planting and a poor yield at harvest time (Pliny, *Nat.* 5.10). Official records from Tebtunis in Egypt for the year AD 45 show a spike in the price of grain for August, September, and November, indicating a poor harvest, and so AD 45 makes sense as the year of Pliny's flood.[2] Several years later, when the famine was so severe in Jerusalem that "many were perishing," the royal family in Adiabene provided relief aid for the needy there, but, when they tried to buy grain in Egypt for this errand of mercy, they had to pay "large sums" for it (Josephus, *A.J.* 20.51).[3]

In the Jerusalem and Antioch of AD 44, all this lay in the future, but the church at Antioch took Agabus at his word and sent relief to their fellow Christians in Judea. The normal procedure for collecting such funds was the one that the royal family of Adiabene followed. A wealthy and powerful benefactor would supply the needed money.[4] Although the church in Antioch had such a well-connected person in its midst ("Manaen a member of the court of Herod the tetrarch," Acts 13:1), they followed a different procedure. Luke says that "The disciples decided they would send support [διακονία] to the brothers and sisters in Judea, with everyone contributing to this ministry according to each person's abundance" (11:29 CEB).[5]

Perhaps Barnabas and Paul encouraged this approach. Later, when Paul was collecting money among the Corinthians for the poor among the saints in Jerusalem, he also urged each person in the church to give according to his or her income (1 Cor 16:2; 2 Cor 8:1–5, 11–15). It was important for each person to give for theological reasons, however small their gift might be. Sacrificial giving demonstrated the genuineness of God's gracious work in the lives of believers (2 Cor 8:8–9; 9:7), and, in this instance, was the payment of a material debt that gentile Christians owed to needy Jewish Christians for the spiritual benefit they had received from their participation in the blessings God had given Israel (Rom 15:27). Perhaps the famine conditions in Judea in the midforties AD provided Paul an opportunity to think all this through with the other leaders of the church in Antioch. In any case, the church chose Barnabas and Paul to take the relief to Judea (Acts 11:30; 12:25).

Since Luke says this happened about the same time as the death of Herod (Acts 12:1, 20–25), it seems likely that Barnabas and Paul traveled to Jerusalem around AD 44, the year that Herod Agrippa I died. A journey to Judea with monetary support for the Judean church before the famine reached its peak in AD 46–48 would not only make good sense from a practical perspective but would also demonstrate earlier rather than later the desire of the Antiochene church, despite its ethnic diversity, to be united with the Jewish Christians of Judea.

Many students of Paul's career believe that this "famine relief" visit to Judea corresponds with the second Jerusalem visit Paul mentions in the narrative of his contacts with Jerusalem in Galatians 1:18–2:10. The argument for this position is strong, and almost persuasive. In Galatians, Paul says that he visited Jerusalem "because of a revelation" (Gal 2:2), and in Acts, a prophecy prompts the famine relief visit (Acts 11:28–29).[6] Paul says his visit occurred fourteen years after his conversion (Gal 2:1), and that would place it right in the thick of the famine, at roughly the same time that the royal family of Adiabene came to the aid of famine victims in Jerusalem.[7] In Galatians 2:10, moreover, Paul says that James, Peter, and

John asked him and Barnabas to remember the poor, and, Paul says, this was "the very thing I was eager to do." That eagerness coincides neatly with the purpose of the Acts 11–12 visit to meet the needs of people suffering from food insecurity.[8] Perhaps most important, on this view the number of Paul's visits to Jerusalem in this period of his life matches the number of visits that the Acts narrative describes: Paul visited once about three years after his conversion (Gal 1:18; Acts 9:26), and once about fourteen years after his conversion (Gal 2:1; Acts 11:27–30; 12:25).[9]

It seems slightly more likely, however, that the second visit Paul describes in Galatians does not correspond to the famine relief visit in Acts 11–12. It refers instead to a later visit that Paul and Barnabas made to Jerusalem, according to Acts 15. That visit was primarily for the purpose of deciding whether gentiles who had embraced the gospel in faith must also convert to Judaism (Gal 2:2–5; Acts 15:1–2, 5). The idea of remembering the poor comes into the picture at the end of Paul's account of the visit (Gal 2:10), as if it is a subsidiary concern, rather than the main purpose of Paul's visit to Jerusalem. This would make sense if Paul was looking back to a previous visit whose main purpose had been support for a future famine, a famine that by the time of the Jerusalem conference was fully under way. A conference in AD 47 during the famine might well end with an expression of concern that the Antiochenes "continue to remember the poor" (Gal 2:10 NIV), just as they had remembered the poor when they brought aid a few years earlier. This would mean, however, that Paul left any explicit reference to Luke's famine relief visit out of the account of his visits in Galatians.

Why would Paul do this? Paul's purpose in that account was not to describe his every visit to Jerusalem but, rather, to describe his contact with the Jerusalem apostles, James, Peter, and John (Gal 1:18–19; 2:9).[10] The aid described in Acts 11:30, however, went to the "elders" in the churches throughout Judea. Although Barnabas and Paul certainly went to Jerusalem as part of this trip (Acts 12:25), Luke says nothing about a meeting with "the apostles" there.[11] Since he typically distinguishes "apostles" from "elders" in the Jerusalem church and makes it clear when both groups are present (Acts 15:2, 4, 6, 22–23; 16:4), it is likely that Barnabas and Paul did not meet with the Jerusalem apostles but met with the elders of the various assemblies of Christians throughout Judea.

CHAPTER 6

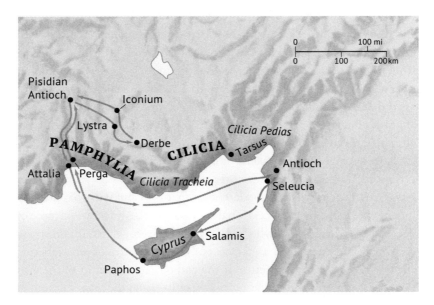

Map 2: From Syrian Antioch to Cyprus to Southern Galatia and Back to Syrian Antioch

Before returning to Antioch, they stopped in Jerusalem, and undoubtedly delivered aid there also (Acts 12:25), but, for whatever reason, they must have handed off their aid to the elders of the various Jerusalem assemblies rather than to the apostles James, Peter, and John. The apostles, or at least Peter, may have been in hiding at this point, trying to escape Herod Agrippa I, who had killed James (the disciple of Jesus) and had tried to imprison Peter, undoubtedly for the same purpose (Acts 12:1–11). They did meet John Mark, however, the associate of Peter (Acts 12:12; 1 Pet 5:13) and probable author of Mark's Gospel. John Mark then accompanied them back to Antioch (Acts 12:25).

The Multiethnic Church Expands to Cyprus

After Barnabas and Paul returned to Antioch, the church sent them out again at the direction of the Holy Spirit, probably through the church's prophets, saying, "Set apart for me Barnabas and Saul for the work to which I have called them" (Acts 13:1–2; cf. 11:27–28).[12] John Mark went with them as their "assistant" (ὑπηρέτης), a term that implies his subordinate role (13:5).

It made sense for Barnabas, Paul, and John Mark to set sail for Cyprus first, since that was Barnabas's native land (Acts 4:36), and he probably had both family and friends within the large and flourishing Jewish community there.[13] They first traveled to the port of Seleucia, an easy boat ride down the Orontes River from Antioch, or a sixteen-mile walk west along the road that joined the two cities. Either way, that part of the journey would have taken most of one day.[14] It was about a hundred and twenty nautical miles as the crow flies from Seleucia to Salamis on Cyprus, but one had to tack against prevailing winds from the north, making it a journey of over two days.[15]

They were not the first believers to take the gospel to Cyprus. Greek-speaking Jewish Christians from Jerusalem had already traveled there, and some Jewish Christians from Cyprus had been among the first people to preach the gospel in Antioch (Acts 11:19–20; cf. 8:1). Luke says that these pioneers spoke "the word to no one except Jews," and it seems likely that the Jewish Christians on the island remained connected with their local synagogues at this point.

Barnabas and Paul landed first at Salamis on the eastern side of the island, a large city and second only in importance to the capital, Paphos, on the western side.[16] Salamis had a Jewish community sizable enough to support more than one synagogue, and Barnabas and Paul went to the synagogues first (Acts 13:5). They may have been following the example of the earlier Jewish-Christian missionaries (Acts 11:19), or they may have been putting into practice a theological conviction of Paul that the gospel was for "the Jew *first* and also . . . the Greek" (Rom 1:16, emphasis added).[17] In either case, the work of Paul and Barnabas on the island followed a pattern that becomes familiar by the end of Acts. Paul typically takes the gospel first into the synagogue in a given region (Acts 13:14; 14:1; 17:1, 10, 17; 18:2–4, 19; 19:8; cf. 28:17).[18] Here, however, Luke omits a description of the response that the three Christians received from the synagogues and quickly moves the narrative along to Paphos, in the middle of the island's western coast.

Cyprus was a senatorial province, and Paphos was both the residence of the Roman proconsul and the location of the military headquarters of the Roman army on the island.[19] It must have been a busy seaport town. Aphrodite's best-known temple lay a few miles to the east in "Old Paphos" and celebrated a popular festival every year that, according to Strabo, attracted pilgrims to the site from "other cities" (*Geogr.* 14.6.3). The city was also an important stop for shipping traffic on its way to Alexandria, which lay about 250 nautical miles to the southwest.[20]

Somehow, the Roman proconsul heard that Barnabas and Paul were in Paphos and summoned them so that he could evaluate the message they were proclaiming (Acts 13:7). Luke identifies him only as "Sergius Paulus," leaving off the first of his three Roman names (the praenomen), and that, combined with the incomplete nature of the historical record on proconsuls of Cyprus, makes it hard to identify him precisely. Probably, however, he is the same person as L. Sergius Paullus, whose name shows up on a boundary stone listing the five custodians of the Tiber, and that dates to sometime between AD 41 and 47.[21] The Tiber River in Rome was prone to disastrous flooding, and so the emperor sensibly appointed government officials whose job was to mitigate the damage. "Custodian" of the Tiber and its banks was a responsible position and might well have served as a steppingstone to the higher office of proconsul around the time that Paul, Barnabas, and John Mark made their journey to Cyprus.[22]

Sergius Paulus seems to have been interested in matters of religion. Luke says that when Barnabas and Saul appeared before him, a Jewish magician, whom Luke calls a "false prophet," was also present (Acts 13:6–7). Roman officials sometimes consulted religious figures from various schools of thought for advice. Tiberius included an astrologer named Thrasyllus in his household (Suetonius, *Tib.* 14.4), for example, and Nero consulted an astrologer named Balbillus (Suetonius, *Nero* 36.1). Josephus, the Jewish historian, fancied himself able to foresee the future and, because of this ability, seems to have functioned as an adviser to the Roman general Vespasian (Josephus, *B.J.* 3.399–408).[23]

Elymas probably played something like these roles for Sergius Paulus. When Barnabas and Paul arrived, he sought to protect his position by turning the proconsul away from their message. In response, Paul told him that he would "be blind and unable to see the sun for a time," and, when this actually happened, "the proconsul believed" the gospel (Acts 13:8–12).

In addition to Cypriot Jewish Christians (11:19), therefore, there was now at least one gentile believer on the island, and it seems likely that Luke presents him as only the most unusual and politically powerful example of many other gentiles on Cyprus who also believed.

Problems in Pamphylian Galatia

There is convincing inscriptional evidence that the family of Lucius Sergius Paullus owned land around Pisidian Antioch, and this suggests that the proconsul had strong ties to that area.[24] On the basis of this evidence, several scholars have plausibly suggested that Paul, Barnabas, and John Mark set out from Paphos for Pisidian Antioch because the newly sympathetic proconsul suggested they go there and facilitated their introduction into the city.[25]

First, however, they traveled to Perga in the region of Pamphylia that lay along the coast of south-central Asia Minor, and in this period, was part of the massive province of Galatia (Acts 13:13).[26] Perga was a bustling, gleaming metropolis.[27] It was about ten miles inland from the major port of Attalia (cf. Acts 14:25), and either Attalia or Side, thirty-five miles east of Perga, would have been the obvious destination for a ship carrying passengers bound for Perga.[28] All three cities were major metropolitan areas, but Luke says nothing about Paul and his companions preaching the gospel in any of them. Why did the group make a beeline for Perga and then from Perga to Pisidian Antioch? If they were carrying letters of introduction from Sergius Paulus to influential members of his family in Pisidian Antioch, the answer may lie in their haste to get to that destination and take advantage of this unusual open door.

One of the Roman Empire's most important roads, the Via Sebaste, ran from Perga north to Pisidian Antioch and then southeast to Iconium and Lystra.[29] It ranged from twenty to twenty-six feet wide and could "carry wheeled traffic along its entire length."[30] It seems likely that Paul, Barnabas, and John Mark sailed to one of the coastal towns of Pamphylia and then made the journey to Perga in order to take the fastest route to Pisidian Antioch. There they could take advantage of connections with the family of Sergius Paulus and then move easily along the Via Sebaste southeastward to other important towns in southern Galatia.

CHAPTER 6

Even with this focused goal, however, it seems odd, as some scholars have noticed, that Paul did not pause to preach the gospel in the large, bustling city of Perga. Luke's account reveals another oddity about their time in Perga that has puzzled students of Paul for centuries: "John left them," says Luke, "and returned to Jerusalem" (Acts 13:13). When Paul proposed about three years later that he and Barnabas revisit the churches they had established on Cyprus and in southern Galatia, and Barnabas recommended that they bring John Mark along with them again, Paul refused so resolutely that he and Barnabas had to part ways. The reason, Paul said, was that John Mark "had withdrawn from them in Pamphylia and had not gone with them to the work," presumably the work in southern Galatia (15:38). Although three years old, the wound from John Mark's departure in Perga was still fresh.[31] It is natural to wonder whether these two oddities—the omission of preaching in Perga and John Mark's departure—were connected.

The great nineteenth-century classicist and archaeologist William Ramsay was convinced that Paul had suffered an attack of malaria that prevented work in Perga, and that he sought the healing higher altitudes of Pisidian Antioch to convalesce. John Mark's departure was a result of his disappointment that Paul failed to evangelize Pamphylia before moving on to Galatia.[32] If this is right, argued Ramsay, then it would explain why Paul reminded the Galatian churches in his letter to them that "it was because of a bodily ailment that I preached the gospel to you at first" (Gal 4:13). It might also explain why he referred to his "thorn in the flesh" as a "thorn" or a "stake" (2 Cor 12:7), since this was an apt description of the severe headaches that malaria could cause.[33]

Ramsay has filled too many gaps with speculation about malarial headaches and personal disappointments, and he could not have known in the late nineteenth century that Paul was already in Galatia when he was in Perga. Nevertheless, he does make some reasonable connections. At least according to Luke, Paul certainly viewed John Mark's departure as profoundly disturbing, and according to Paul himself he went to southern Galatia, which at this time included Perga, because of an illness. Using Acts and Galatians to illumine each other reveals that these two events happened at about the same time. Paul's statement that he appealed to the

Lord three times to remove his thorn in the flesh (2 Cor 12:8), moreover, does make the "thorn" sound like a recurring illness of some type.[34]

Perhaps Paul grew ill on Cyprus and Sergius Paulus arranged for his convalescence in Galatia. To get there, Paul had to pass through Perga, but he may have been too ill to preach in this important city. At this point, John Mark turned back for reasons related to this unanticipated development: Paul was ill and unable to preach, and they were headed into the interior of Asia Minor with no certainty of being able to continue the work they had set out to do.

Murray Harris, therefore, may well have been basically correct when he reasoned that Paul could not preach the gospel in Perga because he was suffering from one of three attacks of a recurring sickness corresponding to the "three times" that Paul prayed for the Lord to remove the thorn from him (2 Cor 12:8).[35] Harris argued that the first attack happened sometime during Paul's years in Syria and Cilicia around AD 43, shortly after Paul's rapture to paradise and fourteen years before 2 Corinthians (2 Cor 12:2–3).[36] The second and third attacks happened in Perga and Troas in AD 47 and 56. It seems just as plausible, however, to think of Paul's "three times" as an approximate expression referring to the frequency and intensity of his prayers for deliverance, and to imagine Paul suffering more than three attacks of his illness.[37] A third attack may have corresponded with the roadblock that Satan used more than once while Paul was in Athens to prevent his return to Thessalonica (1 Thess 2:18). Paul's near-death experience in Troas would then be at least the fourth such attack (2 Cor 1:8–9; cf. 2 Cor 2:12–13; 7:5).

Harris observes that although the attack in Perga and the attack in Troas at first prevented extensive efforts to proclaim the word in those places (2 Cor 2:12–13; 7:5), Paul later made up for these omissions by returning to both cities and preaching in them (Acts 14:25; 20:6–12).[38] One could add to this that after Satan hindered Paul from returning to Thessalonica, he also made up for his absence not only by sending Timothy (1 Thess 3:1–3) but by eventually traveling back to Macedonia, and probably to Thessalonica, himself (Acts 20:1–2; 2 Cor 2:13; 7:5).

In Galatians, whose audience would have included assemblies of Christians in Pisidian Antioch, Paul says that when he preached the gospel to them during his first visit he did so "because of a bodily ailment." They received him "as an angel of God, as Christ Jesus," and they did this, he says, despite the temptation this sickness presented to them to "scorn or despise" him (Gal 4:13–14). The word translated "scorn" here normally means "spit" (ἐξεπτύσατε), and spitting when seeing someone with a physical infirmity was a common way of keeping evil powers at bay in Paul's world. "We spit on epileptics in a fit," says Pliny the Elder; "that is, we throw back infection. In a similar way, we ward off witchcraft and the bad luck that follows meeting a person lame in the right leg" (*Nat.* 28.7.36 [Jones, LCL]).[39] Paul may have been obviously ill when he arrived in Pisidian Antioch and was appreciative that the people there not only did not treat him as involved somehow in witchcraft but, quite the contrary, received him as God's messenger, or as Christ Jesus himself (Gal 4:14).

7

Advancement and Opposition in Southern Galatia

Pisidian Antioch was in the Phrygian part of Galatia, but it was so close to Pisidia that it was called Antioch "near Pisidia" (Ἀντιόχεια ἡ πρὸς Πισιδίᾳ καλουμένη) according to Strabo (*Geogr.* 12.8.14).[1] The city was a large and gleaming Roman colony that at this time was part of the Roman province of Galatia. Paul and Barnabas would have seen its massive temple of Augustus rising above the city walls long before they actually reached the city itself.[2] As they climbed the road up to its main gate, they would have looked uphill at a series of artificial waterfalls created by a system of basins in the center of the road.[3] Once inside, they may have strolled along the *Tiberia Platea*, a broad street lined on either side with a sort of colonnaded food court of restaurants and gathering places.[4]

Perhaps they stared up at the triumphal arch constructed to celebrate Augustus's military victories, with its written proclamation of Augustus's greatness (*Res Gestae*).[5] According to James R. Harrison, "This bilingual inscription would have been a major tourist attraction that visitors to the city could hardly have missed."[6] Perhaps they walked by the new, massive statue of the emperor Claudius that was erected in the late forties AD by a member of one of the city's leading families, C. Caristanius Fronto Caisianus Iullus, to celebrate Claudius's military success in Britain.[7] Everything would have announced the grandeur and power of Rome, and the supposed fertility and peace that Augustus and his successors had brought to places as far away from Rome as Britain, Phrygia, and Pisidia.[8]

CHAPTER 7

A Synagogue Sermon in Pisidian Antioch

Just as they had done on Cyprus, Paul and Barnabas seem to have made straight for the synagogue in Antioch to focus their first efforts in the city on proclaiming the gospel to the local Jewish community. When the Sabbath day arrived, Luke says, they went to the city's synagogue and simply sat down (Acts 13:14). The gathering must have been small enough and the members of the synagogue well enough known to each other that Paul and Barnabas stood out. Or perhaps word had already circulated that Paul and Barnabas were friendly with the famous Sergii family. In any case, after the Scripture reading, the synagogue rulers invited Paul and Barnabas to speak (13:15), and Paul took full advantage of the opportunity (13:16–41).

It is reasonable to think that Luke's narrative gives the essence of what Paul said on this occasion.[9] Where he can be checked, Luke turns out to be a careful historian by Greco-Roman standards, and it is reasonable to think that he worked with a method similar to that of Thucydides when it came to speeches. Both historians wrote of events that occurred relatively recently and of which, at least some of the time, they had firsthand memory.[10] Thucydides says that when he could not remember a particular speech well, or did not have sources for it, he constructed a probable speech, but stuck as much as possible to "the general sense of what was actually said" (*P.W.* 1.22.1 [Smith, LCL]).

Polybius, similarly, implies that historians should either record speeches "verbatim" or provide an "accurate paraphrase," but in any case "give an account of what was actually said" (*Hist.* 12.25a [Waterfield]).[11] Inventing speeches for the purpose of showing off one's rhetorical ability, although sometimes practiced among historians, was not acceptable to Polybius (*Hist.* 12.25a–b). The speeches in Acts are neither rhetorically sophisticated nor do they try to mimic the length of actual speeches, which could run for hours (Acts 24:4; Pliny the Younger, *Ep.* 4.16).[12] It seems likely, then, that they represent a summary of what Luke thought the apostle said based on his sources or his own memory.

Luke has given Paul's speech in Pisidian Antioch its shape, and it certainly contains some of his own characteristic theological concerns, but it also echoes the theological thinking found in Paul's letters. Jesus as the promised descendant of David plays an important part in the synagogue sermon (Acts 13:22–23), just as he does at the beginning and near the end of Romans (1:2–3; 15:11–12; cf. Isa 11:1). The language Paul uses for this point in the speech is particularly close to Romans 1:2–3.[13] Those who plotted Jesus's crucifixion did so in ignorance according to both Paul in the synagogue (Acts 13:27) and Paul in 1 Corinthians (2:8). Although innocent, Jesus died on a "tree" according to the synagogue sermon (Acts 13:28–29). Similarly, Paul explains in Galatians that Christ died under the curse that both Jews and gentiles deserved since he died on a cross, and the public exposure of his body fulfilled the penalty of Deuteronomy 21:23, "Cursed is everyone who is hanged on a tree" (Gal 3:13; cf. 2 Cor 5:21).

Perhaps in the longer version of the sermon that Paul actually gave in Pisidian Antioch he went into the kind of detail on this point that would allow him to say later that he had portrayed Jesus as crucified before the very eyes of the Galatian Christians (Gal 3:1). Both Christ's death and his resurrection from the dead fulfilled the Scriptures according to the Paul of the sermon (Acts 13:29–37) and according to Paul's summary of his own preaching in 1 Corinthians (15:3–4). Should anyone doubt Jesus's resurrection, both the Paul of the sermon and the Paul of 1 Corinthians claim that the resurrected Jesus verifiably appeared to his followers, who began proclaiming the gospel (Acts 13:31; 1 Cor 15:5–8). Similarly, for both Pauls, the effect of Christ's death and resurrection is justification by faith, which is equivalent to the forgiveness of sins (Acts 13:38–39; Rom 4:1–8, 25).

It seems likely, then, that Luke has provided his readers with a summary of the kind of preaching that Paul often did in the diaspora synagogues that he entered during his travels. He traced the history of Israel down to the time of John the Baptist and Jesus, placed Jesus within this story, described how Jesus's unjust condemnation and death led to his resurrection and recognition as God's Son, showed how all of this both fulfilled the Scripture and provided forgiveness from transgression against the Mosaic law, and, like a prophet of old, called upon his audience to acknowledge the work that God was doing in their own time (Acts 13:16b–41).

The Aftermath of Paul's Sermon

Luke reports that the immediate response to Paul's sermon was promising. Not only ethnic Jews but also former gentiles who had now converted to Ju-

CHAPTER 7

daism found Paul's sermon persuasive (Acts 13:42–43). Perhaps they were the ones who spread the word to others during the following week and produced a huge crowd "to hear the word of the Lord" on the next Sabbath (13:44).

This larger crowd was much less sympathetic, however, and some who were there began contradicting and misrepresenting Paul, stymieing his efforts (Acts 13:45). As a result, Paul and Barnabas made a decisive shift in their strategy in Pisidian Antioch. They would leave the synagogue and pour their energy into spreading the gospel among the non-Jewish inhabitants, not only of the city itself but of the more rural area of Phrygia in which it was located (13:48–49).

According to Luke, with this shift in strategy they saw themselves fulfilling the role of the servant in Isaiah 49:6. The broader passage in Isaiah (49:1–6) describes someone variously identified as "Israel" and as an individual whom the Lord has formed in the womb for the purpose of gathering his people together and bringing them back to him (49:1–5). The servant's role will go beyond even this amazing feat, however, for the Lord will make him, according to the part of the passage that Luke quotes, "as a light for the nations" so that the Lord's "salvation may reach the ends of the earth" (49:6).

Paul's letters reveal that Isaiah 49 was important to his thinking. He alludes to or quotes from it at least four times (Gal 1:15, 24; 2 Cor 6:2; Rom 14:11), and he describes his conversion as God setting him apart from his mother's womb, using the language of Isaiah 49:1 and 5. Luke's reference to Paul's use of this passage at this point, then, meshes well with Paul's own appropriation of Isaiah 49.

Barnabas and Paul did not intend to turn permanently away from Jewish people, however, any more than the Lord turns away from Israel in Isaiah 49. Theirs was a strategic decision to turn to the gentiles in the full knowledge that God's purposes for Israel were not yet finished. Probably, at this point, Paul was beginning to formulate the strategy that he would describe ten years later in his letter to the Roman Christians. He would make much of his ministry to the gentiles as part of a plan that would eventually prompt the Jews to emulate the gentiles' obedience to the gospel and bring an end to their hardened hearts (Rom 11:13–16, 25–27; 15:8–9).

This turn to the gentiles, however, provoked a negative response to the message of Paul and Barnabas among some of the Jewish community's leaders in the region. Some of them with connections to prominent gentile women in the city and with the city's "leading men" joined forces to expel Paul and Barnabas not only from the city itself but from the surrounding region that the city controlled (Acts 13:50).

One of these "leading men" may have been C. Caristanius Fronto Caisianus Iullus. Caristanius's massive statue of Claudius featured an inscription announcing that he had served three times as one of the two most powerful people in the city (a *duumvir*). He was also a priest and a retired Roman army officer.[14] In his role as both priest in a local cult and either former or present *duumvir*, he could easily have seen the disruption that Paul and Barnabas were causing to long-standing religious and social customs in the city as a threat to its peace and prosperity.[15] Despite their expulsion, however, Paul and Barnabas left behind them in Pisidian Antioch a number of sympathizers and disciples of Jesus, both Jewish and gentile (Acts 13:43, 48, 52; 14:21–22).

Preaching and Suffering Southeast of Pisidian Antioch

The next Roman colony heading southeast on the Via Sebaste was Iconium, a little over ninety miles from Pisidian Antioch, and Paul and Barnabas set out for it.[16] Iconium was a multiethnic city with Jewish, Roman, Greek, and Phrygian influences mingling together. The strategy of Barnabas and Paul was the same as it had been on Cyprus and in Pisidian Antioch. They went first to the local synagogue with their message and met with great success among Jews and Greeks (Acts 14:1). Just as with Elymas on Cyprus, "the Lord . . . bore witness to the word of his grace, granting signs and wonders to be done" through Paul and Barnabas (Acts 14:3). Later, when Paul wrote his letter to the churches in southern Galatia, he would remind them that when they first believed the gospel, God had worked miracles among them by the power of his Spirit (Gal 3:5).

Despite this, just as in Pisidian Antioch, strong opposition also developed from Jews and a multiethnic group of non-Jews (Acts 14:2). When Paul and Barnabas sensed that the opposition was about to turn violent, they once again fled along the Via Sebaste to another Roman colony, Lystra, and the region surrounding it (14:5–6).

Luke has no record of Paul preaching in a synagogue at Lystra, and it is not clear what this means. Were Paul and Barnabas making good on their announcement in Pisidian Antioch that they were now turning to the gentiles (Acts 13:46)? Or did Luke decide simply to focus on one eventful day in a longer period of work in that place? Jewish people definitely lived in the city because Paul met his future coworker Timothy in Lystra, and Timothy's mother was Jewish (Acts 16:1; 2 Tim 1:5; 3:15). If both Timothy and his mother became Christians in Lystra, moreover, then it seems likely that Paul and Barnabas had not given up entirely on work among Jewish people in southern Galatia. Perhaps, then, Luke wanted to tell the story of one memorable day in a longer period of ministry in that city and the region around it. It was a moment that allowed him to balance his sample of Paul's synagogue preaching from Paul's ministry in Pisidian Antioch with the kind of preaching Paul did among gentiles who had no understanding of Jewish Scripture or theology.

Luke does not give a full account of Paul's preaching but focuses on what he said after he had healed a lame man in the audience (Acts 14:8–10, 15–17). The healing was so startling that many in the crowd concluded the gods Zeus and Hermes had visited them in the form of Barnabas and Paul. A popular story in the region claimed that the god Zeus and his son and messenger Hermes had once visited the nearby Phrygian countryside in the guise of mortal human beings. After they asked for hospitality from some residents and were turned away, one poor, elderly couple welcomed them into their home and entertained them lavishly despite their poverty. Later, the gods flooded the whole countryside, sparing only the old couple and their house, which they turned into a temple where the couple would serve as priests for many years and finally be transformed into two entwined trees that Ovid, writing in the early first century, claims to have seen himself (Ovid, *Metam.* 8.618–724).[17] The crowd around Paul and Barnabas identified Barnabas with Zeus and identified Paul, since he was the preacher, with Zeus's messenger, Hermes. The priest of the local temple of Zeus brought out bulls and garlands to sacrifice to them.

Luke makes a point of saying that these crowds were not speaking Greek (Acts 14:11). They were speaking their local language, Lycaonian, and for Luke this probably was another indicator that the gospel was for every human being, not simply Jews and Greeks. This was a point with which Paul fully agreed. He tells the Roman Christians that he is under obligation to proclaim the gospel "to Greeks and to barbarians, both to the wise and to the foolish" (Rom 1:14).[18]

Advancement and Opposition in Southern Galatia

Luke's summary of Paul's response also meshes well with the hints in Paul's letters of what he preached to gentiles who were utterly unfamiliar with Judaism.[19] In Luke's account, Paul's preaching of the gospel focuses on his hearers' need "to turn [ἐπιστρέφειν] from these vain things to a living God" (Acts 14:15). Similarly, Paul reminded the Thessalonian Christians a few years after preaching in Lystra that when he first brought the gospel to them (1 Thess 1:5) they "turned [ἐπεστρέψατε] to God from idols to serve the living and true God" (1 Thess 1:9).

Paul also tells his audience in Lystra that God had borne witness to himself even before Paul reached them through the good he had done for them in the natural world (Acts 14:17). This is not unlike Paul's description of God's self-witness in his summary of the gospel to the Roman Christians, where Paul says that God made known his "eternal power and divine nature" to people "in the things that have been made" (Rom 1:19–20).

Paul's statement in Lystra that "in past generations [God] allowed all nations to walk in their own ways" sounds like the precursor to a claim that those times had now reached an end with the coming of the gospel. This sounds a similar note to Paul's warning in Romans against those who "presume on the riches of [God's] kindness and forbearance and patience, not knowing that God's kindness is meant to lead you to repentance" (Rom 2:4; cf. 3:25).

Once again, however, violent opposition cut Paul's preaching short. Paul's Jewish opponents from Antioch and Iconium arrived in Lystra and persuaded the crowds to reject the apostle's message. Just as in Iconium, rejection turned to violence, but this time Paul had no time to flee. Some in the crowd began throwing stones at him, and some of those stones hit their mark, knocking Paul unconscious. The rabble then dragged what they thought was Paul's dead body outside the city and left him there (Acts 14:19). Some of those who had believed Paul's message, however, made a circle around him and, after helping him up, led him back into the city, perhaps maintaining their circle so that no one would see him (14:20a).

It was an experience Paul did not forget. About ten years later when recounting instances of hardship he had encountered in his itinerant preaching ministry, he told the Corinthian Christians, "Once I was stoned" (2 Cor 11:25). Similarly, Paul was probably thinking of this incident when, near the end of his life, he urged Timothy to remain faithful in the midst of

CHAPTER 7

hardship just as Paul had done: "You, however, have followed my teaching, my conduct, my aim in life, my faith, my patience, my love, my steadfastness, my persecutions and sufferings that happened to me at Antioch, at Iconium, and at Lystra—which persecutions I endured; yet from them all the Lord rescued me" (2 Tim 3:10–11).

FLIGHT FARTHER TO THE SOUTHEAST AND RETURN TO BELEAGUERED COMMUNITIES

The following day Paul and Barnabas fled Lystra, traveling southeast, and they eventually stopped in Derbe (Acts 14:20b). The journey would not have been easy. Paul would have been suffering from his wounds, and possibly a concussion, and their likely route meant a trek of roughly eighty miles.[20] The route and destination, however, were sensible choices for people trying to escape pursuers. Derbe lay just outside the boundaries of the Roman province of Galatia in the small client kingdom of Commagene. Commagene was currently under the direct rule of Antiochus, a friend of the emperor Claudius and son-in-law of Herod Agrippa I.[21] It lay, moreover, in the direction of the land route back through Cilicia to Tarsus and Syrian Antioch.[22]

The ministry of Paul and Barnabas in Derbe appears to have been successful. Luke mentions no opposition and comments that Paul and Barnabas "made many disciples" there (Acts 14:21). He gives no indication of how long they stayed, but it must have been long enough for this successful effort, and long enough that Paul and Barnabas believed the opposition to them in Lystra, Iconium, and Pisidian Antioch had cooled. Christians in those towns needed encouragement from Barnabas and Paul to continue in the faith, and they needed some kind of organizational structure so that believers could continue to encourage one another and instruct new followers of Jesus as their numbers grew. So, probably for this reason, Paul and Barnabas decided not to return to Syrian Antioch overland, but instead they retraced their steps to make sure that the multiethnic communities of Jesus followers in the towns where they had encountered such trouble would survive and thrive.[23]

They steeled the believers in Lystra, Iconium, and Pisidian Antioch against the kind of persecution they had already seen Paul endure, and they organized believers in each city into assemblies, or churches, like the churches in Jerusalem and Antioch (Gal 1:2). They then provided each church with leaders that Luke calls "elders" (Acts 14:21–23). Later, in his letter to the Galatian Christians, Paul would probably refer both to the persecution of the Galatian churches at the hands of unbelieving Jews (Gal 3:4; 4:29) and to the need to care for the churches' leaders by "sharing all good things with the one who teaches" (Gal 6:6).[24]

It is possible that the need to regularize their social status as assemblies of Jews (who were also Christians) and so to reduce persecution led some of the assemblies of mainly gentile Christians in southern Galatia to fall "so quickly" for the false teaching that later arrived in their midst (Gal 1:6).[25] It is also possible that a lack of attention to providing for the needs of their leaders contributed to their inability to answer the persuasive case that these false teachers presented to them and that Paul himself had to answer in his letter (in, e.g., Gal 3:15–4:7 and 4:21–31). All that, however, lay in the future.

For now, Paul and Barnabas set out from Pisidian Antioch, following the Via Sebaste again, this time in the opposite direction, to Perga where their journey into the interior of Asia Minor had started and where, perhaps, Paul had become ill. Luke recorded no proclamation of the gospel in Perga on that earlier visit (Acts 13:13–14a). Now, however, Paul and Barnabas made the most of their stop in this important city and "proclaimed the word" there (14:25 CEB).[26]

Luke says nothing about the response to Paul's preaching, and when Paul and his new partner Silas returned to Derbe and Lystra later (Acts 16:1), they were focused on going north toward Bithynia rather than moving south to Perga (16:6–7). This probably means that there was no Christian community to strengthen there.[27] If that is correct, then it seems likely that those who heard Paul's preaching in Perga did not find it persuasive, and few if any people there believed the gospel.

8

Resistance to the Multiethnic Church

After proclaiming the gospel in Perga, Paul and Barnabas went directly back to Syrian Antioch by ship from the nearby port of Attalia (Acts 14:25–26; cf. 13:13). When they reached Antioch, they called for a special gathering of the church there to report on what had happened as they did "the work" that the Holy Spirit, through the church, had sent them to do (14: 27a; cf. 13:2). The theme of their report was how God "had opened a door of faith to the Gentiles" (14:27b). News of their successful outreach to the gentiles on the Cyprus leg of their trip had probably already reached Jerusalem through John Mark after he parted company with them in Perga (13:13). He was a native of Jerusalem (12:12, 25), and it seems likely that he returned there after his departure.

THE SIGNIFICANCE OF CIRCUMCISION

The focus of the church in Antioch on including the nations within God's people apart from their observance of the Mosaic law, however, alarmed some Judean Christians who believed that a critical element was missing from the Antiochean form of the gospel. In Luke's words, they thought that "unless you are circumcised according to the custom of Moses, you cannot be saved" (Acts 15:1). Luke later identifies them as Jewish Christians who were also Pharisees, and they must have remained unconvinced of Peter's conclusions after he had seen the Roman centurion Cornelius and his family experience the power of the Holy Spirit (10:34–35, 45–47; 11:2–3, 18).

Circumcision had been the boundary marker of the Jewish people for centuries. It was the physical symbol of God's promise to Abraham, the father of the Jewish people, that he would be Abraham's God, and the God of his offspring, for generations to come. It was an outward sign that God would keep his promise to make Abraham the father of many nations and would give him the land of Canaan as his own (Gen 17:4–8, 10–11). This covenant, symbolized by male circumcision, was "an everlasting covenant," and any male who refused this physical marker was to be considered a covenant breaker and cut off from God's people (17:13–14).

As part of his strategy to Hellenize Judea in the mid-second century BC, Antiochus IV Epiphanes had forbidden circumcision (1 Macc 1:48, 60–61), and many Jews, seeing the political and economic advantages of compromising their faith, had succumbed to the pressure to abandon the rite. The author of 1 Maccabees puts it this way: "In those days lawless men came forth from Israel and misled many, saying, 'Let us go and make a covenant with the Gentiles round about us, for since we separated from them many evils have come upon us'" (1:11; cf. 1:43).

Other Jews courageously resisted Antiochus's commands and paid for their resistance with their lives (1 Macc 1:62–63; 2:29–41). Some both resisted and took up arms not only against Antiochus's forces but also against Jewish people who had compromised with him for their own advantage or had caved in to his bullying and given up observance of the Mosaic law: "They forcibly circumcised all the uncircumcised boys that they found within the borders of Israel. They hunted down [ἐδίωξαν] the arrogant men" (2:46–47). The "arrogant men" that the Jewish resistance fighters hunted down were probably the same group of "lawless men" that had initially "misled many" by urging them to "go and make a covenant with the Gentiles round about us" (1 Macc 1:11). Some of those whom Antiochus and his forces had persecuted, then, became persecutors themselves.

Was the Work of Paul and Barnabas with Gentiles Too Accommodating?

Although these events had happened 180 years before the journey of Paul and Barnabas to Cyprus and central Anatolia, it is reasonable to imagine that, after all the trouble between Jews and their non-Jewish neighbors in Alexandria, Dora, and perhaps in Cilicia in the late thirties and early forties AD, and after the terrifying threat of Gaius to erect a statue of Zeus in

CHAPTER 8

the temple, many Jews were concerned about anything that looked like an accommodation of Judaism to gentile ways.[1] The persecution that Barnabas and Paul experienced from some within the Jewish community in Pisidian Antioch and Iconium may have come, in a similar way, from people who feared that they were calling for a compromise of the Jewish way of life with gentile customs. Their response, at least, was like that of the Maccabeans. In Pisidian Antioch, they stirred up "persecution" (διωγμόν) against Paul and Barnabas (Acts 13:50). This might be the kind of activity Paul refers to in Galatians 4:29 when he distinguishes between two Jerusalems, one that is free from the law and heavenly, and one that is still enslaved to the law and even "now" was persecuting (ἐδίωκεν) its free, heavenly counterpart.

The procurator of Judea during this time (AD 46–48) was Tiberius Julius Alexander, and he may have provided an example to many Jews in Judea of what compromise with gentiles for political advantage could look like. Both his father, Alexander, and his uncle, Philo, were devout Jews of high social standing, and Alexander was a close friend of Herod Agrippa I, the recently deceased Jewish king of Judea. It seems likely that Agrippa had recommended Tiberius Julius Alexander to Claudius for service to Rome, and he had risen rapidly through the ranks. It also seems likely, however, that his rapid rise was related to his abandonment of Judaism. In the words of Josephus, he "did not stand by the practices of his people" (*A.J.* 20.100).[2]

Close to the time that Paul and Barnabas would have returned to Antioch, Tiberius Julius Alexander ordered the crucifixion of two sons of a Jewish revolutionary named Judas the Galilean (Josephus, *A.J.* 20.102). Judas had been an advocate for Judea's independence from Rome in the early first century after Augustus's census of AD 6. He insisted that Roman domination over Judea was a form of slavery and that the Jewish people should serve no master but God (Josephus, *A.J.* 20.4–10, 23–25; *B.J.* 2.118).[3] Josephus connects him with a group of assassins called "the Sicarii" who targeted Jewish people willing to sacrifice "the hard-won liberty of the Jews" (*B.J.* 7.255). This is a reference to the independence that freedom fighters had achieved from Antiochus IV Epiphanes and his successors many years before. Josephus gives the impression that Judas's "philosophy" continued unbroken through the time of open war against Rome that began in AD 66 (*B.J.* 7.253–258). It seems likely, therefore, that the apostate Roman procurator Tiberius Julius Alexander crucified two of Judas's sons because they posed a threat to Roman order in the province. He must have suspected them of carrying on the religious zeal of their father.[4] They, for their part, must have thought of Tiberius Julius Alexander as precisely the kind of compromising traitor that their forefathers two centuries earlier had fought to expel from the country.

In such an environment, it makes sense that some Jewish Christians would worry about the law-free inclusion of gentiles into God's people that was happening in Antioch. It probably seemed to some that the gospel Paul was proclaiming in the diaspora stretched the boundaries of God's people too far.[5] Paul, they probably thought, was truncating the requirements for following Jesus and preaching a people-pleasing form of the gospel, perhaps for his own advancement (cf. Gal 1:10). The story of Paul's newfound friendship with the well-placed Roman proconsul Sergius Paulus, which John Mark may have brought back to Jerusalem, would probably have done nothing to calm their fears.

The circumcision group may also have been fearful of particularly zealous Jews who would take the message and activities of the famous turncoat Paul as an example of what the entire movement believed. As if all this were not enough, the misunderstanding of Paul's intentions that James later repeats to him may have already been circulating: "You see, brother, how many thousands there are among the Jews of those who have believed. They are all zealous for the law, and they have been told about you that you teach all the Jews who are among the Gentiles to forsake Moses, telling them not to circumcise their children or walk according to our customs" (Acts 21:20–21).

The Jewish Christians of Acts 15:1 were not against incorporating gentiles into the movement. They believed, however, that full conversion to Judaism was a necessary part of following the Jewish Messiah, and that the church at Antioch, with Paul and Barnabas at the helm, was not communicating the entire truth of the gospel to the gentiles either in their own community or abroad.

They seem, therefore, to have undertaken a mission to correct Paul's teaching. They traveled from Jerusalem to Antioch, and they probably also went to other parts of Syria and to Cilicia (Acts 15:23), where Paul had preached the gospel for seven years. Eventually they would make their way farther to the northwest to the churches Paul and Barnabas had founded in south Galatia. There they would make such a convincing case that some gentile believers would begin to "desire to be under the law" (Gal 4:21) and to turn to the circumcision party's "different gospel" (Gal 1:6).

In his letter of response, Paul would insist that those who taught this distortion of the gospel and were trying to force the Galatians to be circumcised were doing this "in order that they might not be persecuted for the cross of Christ" (Gal 6:12b). Their efforts to turn Paul's gentile converts into Jewish proselytes would regularize the status of Christians in these places as people who were part of a movement within Judaism.[6] Moreover, just as Paul and Barnabas were able to recount the story of their mission to these churches in places like Antioch, Phoenicia, Samaria and Jerusalem (Acts 14:27; 15:3–4), so these countermissionaries could tell their own stories of bringing Paul's half-converts fully into the fold. Perhaps this is what Paul means when he says that his opponents in Galatia were trying to force the Galatian Christians to be circumcised not only to avoid persecution but also "to make a good showing in the flesh" (Gal 6:12a) and "that they may boast in" the Galatians' "flesh" (Gal 6:13).[7]

A Clash of Views in Jerusalem

Paul's first encounter with this group was in Antioch where, Luke says, they came to teach the view that "unless you are circumcised according to the custom of Moses, you cannot be saved" (Acts 15:1). In other words, in the final day of judgment, when God pours out his wrath on human rebellion against him, gentiles could only emerge unscathed if they not only had faith in Jesus but had become part of the Jewish people by keeping the Mosaic law. The ethnic component was critical.

Paul and Barnabas disagreed vigorously with this perspective, and, since these teachers had come from Jerusalem (Acts 15:24), the church at Antioch commissioned Paul and Barnabas "and some of the others" to travel there for a discussion of the issue with the Jerusalem church leaders (Acts 15:2). It is likely that this is the same journey to Jerusalem Paul describes in Galatians 2:1–10. In both places the meeting's purpose was to consider whether someone who was not Jewish should be forced to accept circumcision (Gal 2:3; cf. Acts 15:1, 5) and to determine whether the gospel as Christians in Antioch taught and believed it was the same as the gospel that the church leaders in Jerusalem taught (Gal 2:2, 6–9; cf. Acts 15:2, 6).

The result of the meeting is also identical in both places. Paul and Barnabas on one side and the Jerusalem leaders on the other side agreed that circumcision was not necessary for gentiles who wanted to be part of the Christian movement (Gal 2:6–9; Acts 15:19–21). The people who "troubled" (ἐτάραξαν) gentile Christians with this idea made much of their Jerusalem origins, but they did not, in fact, have the authorization of the Jerusalem church to teach their misleading form of the gospel (Gal 1:7; 5:10; Acts 15:24).

Paul's account of the meeting says that in addition to Barnabas, Titus accompanied him on the journey to Jerusalem, and this meshes well with the statement in Acts that not only Paul and Barnabas but also "some of the others" (Acts 15:2) comprised the group that went to Jerusalem.[8] Titus was an uncircumcised Greek (Gal 2:3), and Paul's later description of him as his "true child in a common faith" (Titus 1:4) is consistent with the idea that he became a Christian through Paul's ministry.[9] He was, therefore, a living illustration of the point Paul and Barnabas wanted to make in Jerusalem.

Paul's goal upon arriving in Jerusalem was to meet privately with the leadership of the Christian community there, particularly with James, Peter, and John (Acts 15:2; Gal 2:2), and that meeting eventually materialized (Acts 15:6; Gal 2:6–10), but only after a meeting with the entire church that had an unfortunately painful conclusion. The church and its leaders gave them a warm welcome when they arrived, and in a general meeting of the whole assembly, the group from Antioch described the astonishing events of the journey Paul and Barnabas had made through Cyprus and central Anatolia (Acts 15:4)—the silencing of Elymas the magician, the conversion of Sergius Paulus, the positive response to the gospel of many Jews and large numbers of gentiles in Pisidian Antioch and Iconium, the healing of the lame man in Lystra, the founding of groups of disciples, many of them gentiles, in Lystra and Derbe, and the great suffering that Paul, Barnabas, and many of these new believers had experienced for their faith.

What happened next, however, must have been difficult, especially because Titus was present (cf. Gal 2:3–4). Some believing Pharisees rose to their feet and insisted, just like those who had come to Antioch earlier, that it was necessary to circumcise gentile believers and instruct them to keep the Mosaic law (Acts 15:5).

Once again, the contingent from Antioch faced the outspoken view that gentile believers stood outside the boundaries of the people of God

CHAPTER 8

and could only come within those boundaries by becoming Jewish proselytes. Paul makes it clear in his later letter to the Galatian Christians that he viewed this conviction as itself outside the boundaries of legitimate Christian belief. Those who took it, and stood by it to the end, were "false brothers secretly brought in—who slipped in to spy out our freedom that we have in Christ Jesus, so that they might bring us into slavery" (Gal 2:4).[10]

The clash between these two ways of drawing the boundaries of Christian fellowship led to the private meeting that Paul had originally sought with the leadership of the Jerusalem church (Acts 15:6; cf. Gal 2:2). The extensive "debate" that Luke mentions within this meeting (Acts 15:7) probably reflects the same event Paul refers to in Galatians when he says that "we did not yield in submission even for a moment" to pressure to circumcise Titus (Gal 2:5). Some of the Jerusalem leadership may have argued at first for a more conciliatory approach to the Pharisees, but Paul drew a line in the sand at requiring circumcision of gentiles.

Luke does not describe how Paul argued his case theologically and exegetically, or even that he did so. Although Luke says that Paul and Barnabas retold the stories of God's marvelous deeds among the gentiles (Acts 15:12), Luke was mainly interested in summarizing what Peter and James had to say. Buried in Luke's "much debate" (15:7), however, may well be Paul's articulation of many of the arguments that would later surface in his letter to the Galatians.

There Paul contrasts the slavery of life under the Mosaic law with the freedom that believers have in Christ Jesus (Gal 2:4). Paul is not talking here about a life of freedom from the will of God as it is expressed in Scripture but a life of freedom from the curse that the law justly pronounces upon all those who disobey it. In Deuteronomy 27:26, the law pronounces a curse on everyone who fails to abide by all the things written in it, and this means that no one can expect to be released from God's just punishment (or "justified") on the basis of keeping the law (Gal 3:11a). No one can keep its every precept (Gal 3:11b–12). This is the predicament from which Christ "redeemed" (ἐξηγόρασεν) those who have faith in him, and he did this by dying on the cross in their place, absorbing in their stead the curse they deserved (Gal 3:13).

The term "redeemed" (ἐξηγόρασεν) is a natural expression for buying someone out of slavery. Although it is not a common word, the historian Diodorus Siculus used it twice in exactly this way in the first century BC.

In one passage he tells the story of how the philosopher Plato's friends "purchased his freedom" (ἐξηγόρασαν) after the tyrant Dionysius had sold him into slavery. In another passage he describes how a wealthy Roman knight fell in love with an enslaved woman and "purchased her freedom" (ἐξηγόρασεν) (*Bib. hist.* 15.7.1, 36.2, 2a [Oldfather, LCL]). Since Paul has already used the metaphor of freedom from slavery explicitly and clearly in Galatians 2:4, that idea is almost certainly present in his use of the word rendered "redeemed" in Galatians 3:13. If so, then, the "freedom" that Paul refers to in Galatians 3:13 is not freedom from the law's instruction and guidance—which no Jewish person would call "slavery"—but freedom from the penalty of death that the law justly pronounces on those who disobey it.[11]

Paul makes a further point in Galatians that he probably also made in the "debate" with the church leadership in Jerusalem. When God chose Abraham as the forefather of the Jewish people, he promised that Abraham would not only father a great nation, but that through him all the families of the earth would experience blessing (Gen 12:2–3) and that Abraham would be the father of many nations (Gen 17:4–6). Paul makes the case in Galatians that through the death of Christ and the giving of the Spirit, this promise is being fulfilled as gentiles believe the gospel (Gal 3:14). Everyone, whatever their ethnicity, social status, or gender, becomes part of Abraham's promised offspring through the Spirit's work and faith in Christ (Gal 3:26–29). They are now no longer slaves (Gal 4:1–3) laboring under the law's curse because God "sent forth his Son, born of a woman, born under the law, to redeem [ἐξαγοράσῃ] those who were under the law, so that we might receive adoption as sons" (Gal 4:4–5).

All this, both the redemption that comes through the substitutionary death of Christ, and the redemption that comes through adoption as God's sons, Paul maintains, is a matter of the grace of God. To attempt to avoid God's punishing wrath by submitting to the law's requirements is to reject that grace (Gal 2:21; cf. 1:6; 5:4). In the same way, limiting the inheritance of Christ and his benefits to those who submit to the law is to reject God's means of fulfilling the promise he graciously gave to Abraham (3:18).[12]

Although Luke tells us little about what Paul said to the Jerusalem leaders, he does summarize Peter's speech to the gathering after the extensive debate, and it is possible that Peter learned something from Paul during this time of free exchange. Luke's summary, in any case, sounds a theological note that is reminiscent of the way Paul uses the theme of slavery and freedom in Galatians. After referring to his own experience with Cornelius, Peter asks the advocates of circumcision for gentiles a rhetorical question: "Why are you putting God to the test by placing a yoke on the neck of the disciples that neither our fathers nor we have been able to bear?" (Acts 15:10). The metaphor of a "yoke" could be used positively (Matt 11:29), but it could also carry negative connotations, as it does here, and people sometimes used it to describe the burden of slavery (Sophocles, *Aj.* 944; *Fragments of Unknown Plays* 591; cf. Ezek 34:27). "For freedom Christ has set us free," Paul tells the Galatian Christians; "stand firm therefore, and do not submit again to a yoke of slavery" (Gal 5:1).

Most Jews did not consider the law to be an unobservable maze of burdensome commandments. Luke certainly knew this since at the beginning of his gospel he portrays Elizabeth and Zechariah, the parents of John the Baptist, as "righteous before God, walking blamelessly in all the commandments and statutes of the Lord" (Luke 1:6). Joseph and Mary, similarly, conscientiously kept the various laws surrounding the birth and circumcision of a male child, and they went to Jerusalem for Passover every year with no hint that these were anything but joyful observances (Luke 2:22–24, 27, 39, 41). Here in Acts 15:10, then, it is unlikely that Luke describes Peter as portraying the law itself negatively.[13]

It is more likely that, like Paul, Peter refers to the law's curse on the disobedient as an unbearable burden for the Jews. People only had to remember that an apostate Jew, Tiberius Julius Alexander, was currently ruling over them in the name of Rome to realize that the curse of foreign domination for disobedience to the law was not over. The Mosaic law itself had predicted that Israel would disobey its precepts and experience the curse of foreign domination as "a yoke of iron" (Deut 28:48). They only had to understand what Peter was saying through the lens of Psalm 130: "If you, O Lord, should mark iniquities, O Lord, who could stand?" (130:3). If the Mosaic law is viewed as a set of practices required for entry into God's people and for salvation from God's wrath on the final day, then it poses an unbearable burden because no one can keep it completely. Only God could "redeem Israel from all his iniquities" (Ps 130:8), and, Peter was saying, God had started to do this through "the grace of the Lord Jesus" (Acts 15:11). This undeserved gift of salvation was available then not through the

Mosaic law but simply by accepting the gift in faith. This was an avenue, Peter asserts, that God had opened to both Jews and gentiles.[14]

An Ambiguous Compromise

Peter's position carried the day, and after Barnabas and Paul had again told the story of God's miraculous work among the gentiles through them (Acts 15:12), James proposed a compromise decision. No one should cause unnecessary difficulty for gentiles who turn to God, but they should receive instructions "to avoid the pollution associated with idols, sexual immorality, eating meat from strangled animals, and consuming blood" (15:19–20 CEB). There was evidently some ambiguity about the intentions of the decree. In its later versions in Acts, the phrase "pollution associated with idols" becomes more specifically "food offered to idols" (15:29; 21:25 CEB). Do the decree's prohibitions, then, concern mainly food, making it easier for law-observant Jewish Christians to have table fellowship with otherwise unobservant gentile Christians?[15] Or do the prohibitions have more of a bedrock moral quality to them, implying that avoiding idolatry, sexual immorality, and blood consumption are God's nonnegotiable expectations for all nations?[16]

The most likely understanding of the decree finds its source in both concerns. The decree was probably designed to keep new gentile believers untainted by idolatry. This taint could easily happen through participation in rituals surrounding the consumption of meat and wine (1 Cor 10:7, 14–22; Rev 2:14, 20). It was probably also intended to keep gentile believers free from sexual immorality, a basic moral principle based on God's original creation of man and woman as companions for each other (1 Cor 6:16; cf. Gen 2:24). The prohibitions of what is "strangled" and of "blood" were probably efforts to facilitate table fellowship between Jewish and gentile Christians by urging gentile Christians to observe a basic Jewish dietary restriction against eating animals slaughtered in a way that retains blood in the meat, and against saving and eating the blood itself (Gen 9:4; Lev 17:10–14).[17]

Luke does not record Paul's response to this compromise, although he clearly implies that Paul did not object to it (Acts 15:30; 16:4). Paul also says that the meeting ended amicably on a note of agreement and mutual appreciation (Gal 2:7–9), but he never mentions the Jerusalem decree in his letters. Some interpreters have said that this absence is evidence Paul never had anything to do with the decree and that Luke's setting for it at the Jerusalem Council is a fiction.[18] It is more likely, however, that Paul felt his teaching already covered the decree's central concerns. His preaching to gentiles underscored the importance of abandoning devotion to idols (1 Thess 1:9–10) and of taking care not to cross the line into idolatry in ambiguous settings where meals were served (1 Cor 10:1–22). Avoiding sexual immorality was also a common theme in his teaching (1 Thess 4:2–8; 1 Cor 5:1–13; 6:12–20; Rom 13:13; Col 3:5; Eph 4:17–24; 5:3–14).[19]

He did not think that dietary restrictions were necessary for believers, whether Jewish or gentile (1 Cor 8:4–6, 8; 10:25–27; Rom 14:14), but he taught the importance of not giving offense to others by flaunting dietary freedoms in observant Jewish-Christian settings (Rom 14:15). Even meat that had been previously offered to an idol and then purchased in the marketplace posed no problem for Paul, as long as it was consumed in a private home rather than a temple, and as long as no one present was offended (1 Cor 10:25–30). His convictions about food, therefore, were not tied to the food itself (1 Cor 8:4–6; 10:25) but to the setting in which the food was consumed (1 Cor 10:19–21), to the potential for offending one's company (Rom 14:13–23; cf. 1 Cor 8:10), and to the prospect of advancing the gospel in a given setting (1 Cor 9:19–23; 10:31–33; Rom 14:19; 15:1–2).

This is probably different from what James had in mind, but it was also close enough to the spirit of the decree that Paul did not have a problem communicating it to the Christian assemblies in Syria (including Antioch) and Cilicia to whom the Jerusalem leaders had addressed it (Acts 15:23, 30).[20] The false teachers had visited those places, and the letter with the decree would make clear that their position varied from that of the Jerusalem leaders. They had gone out without authorization from the Jerusalem leaders (15:24), and the Jerusalem leaders did not require circumcision of gentile Christians, which was the false teachers' main concern (15:1).

Later, when he revisited the churches he and Barnabas had planted in south Galatia, he would also communicate the terms of the decree to them, although the false teachers had not yet arrived there (Acts 16:4). He may have thought that the decree would guard against a future visit the false teachers would likely make to these churches.[21] Conversely, Paul may have omitted any reference to the decree in his later letter to the Galatians because the result of its promulgation had been so disappointing. It failed to prevent the sort of deception and division the false teachers had created in southern Galatia, problems that required a vigorous response from Paul.[22]

Further Conflict in Antioch

Paul may have also been disappointed in the decree's inability to prevent another troubling incident in Antioch after the Jerusalem Council. Following the Council, Barnabas and Paul returned to Antioch with two emissaries from the Jerusalem church, Judas and Silas. These two emissaries seem to have accompanied them to bear witness that Jerusalem had, in fact, sided with Paul and Barnabas over the issue of circumcision (Acts 15:24). Eventually, Judas and Silas returned to Jerusalem (Acts 15:32–33), but Barnabas and Paul remained in Antioch "for some days" (Acts 15:35–36). It is probably at this point that Paul's narrative in Galatians picks up the historical thread of his relationship with Peter and other Christians in Jerusalem.[23] Right after his account of the Jerusalem Council (Gal 2:1–10), and probably in chronological sequence, Paul tells the story of an incident that occurred in Antioch whose ultimate source may have been the ambiguities in the Jerusalem Council's decree.

During the "some days" that Barnabas and Paul remained in Antioch after the Council, Peter came to Antioch, probably as part of his own calling as a traveling apostle. James, the brother of the Lord, was now clearly the leader of the Jerusalem community (Acts 15:13; 21:18), and, during this period, Peter traveled not only to Antioch (Gal 2:11–14) but eventually to Corinth (1 Cor 1:12; 3:22; 9:5) and Rome (1 Pet 5:13; 1 Clem. 5.4; 6.1). In Antioch, Peter joined Paul, Barnabas, and other Jewish Christians in eating with gentile Christians at the Christian community's common meals. Paul gives no specific information about the food served at these meals, but it evidently did not meet the standards of the Jewish-Christian community in Jerusalem, and this led to a conflict that Paul describes this way:

> [11] But when Cephas came to Antioch, I opposed him to his face, because he stood self-condemned; [12] for until certain people came from James, he used to eat with the Gentiles. But after they came, he drew back and kept himself separate for fear of the circumcision faction. [13] And the other Jews joined him in this hypocrisy, so that even Barnabas was led

astray by their hypocrisy. ¹⁴ But when I saw that they were not acting consistently with the truth of the gospel, I said to Cephas before them all, "If you, though a Jew, live like a Gentile and not like a Jew, how can you compel the Gentiles to live like Jews?" (Gal 2:11–15 NRSV)

This paragraph raises several questions. Who were the people who came from James? Did they bring some sort of ultimatum to Antioch, and, if so, did they really represent James's views? Who were "the circumcision faction," and why did Peter "fear" them? Most translations and commentators have filled the gaps in the Greek text of Galatians 2:12 in ways that communicate considerable tension between the conservative Jews in Jerusalem and the new, boundary-breaking church in Antioch. The "people from James" become "messengers" (REB) from the leaders of the Jerusalem church, and their message urges the church in Antioch to stop having common table fellowship between Jews and gentiles and to conform to the standards of "the circumcision faction" (NRSV). Peter withdraws from fellowship with gentiles because he is "afraid" (NIV) of this group.

In an important article on this passage, however, Mark A. Seifrid has argued persuasively that this common scenario reads too much into what Paul says.²⁴ The "people from James" (NRSV) simply came to Antioch from the Jerusalem church, and therefore "from James." Paul calls them "those from the circumcision" (τοὺς ἐκ περιτομῆς, Gal 2:12), but that phrase usually refers to Jewish Christians in Paul's letters (Rom 4:12; Col 4:11; cf. Acts 10:45), not to a pro-circumcision "faction" (NRSV), "party" (ESV), or "group" (NIV).²⁵ Paul does not say that they brought any message from James or from anyone else. They could easily have come more as observers, in the same way that the Jerusalem church "sent Barnabas to Antioch" as an observer at an earlier time (Acts 11:22).²⁶ Paul's expression that Peter "began to separate from" (ἀφώριζεν) gentile Christians "fearing those from the circumcision," moreover, need only mean that Peter was embarrassed and concerned about his own loss of honor and recognition in Jerusalem.²⁷ There is, therefore, no need to complicate the situation by suggesting that the people from James "came invested with some powers from James which they abused."²⁸

All that Paul says clearly in Galatians 2:12 is that before people from James arrived in Antioch, Peter was living like a gentile and, presumably, not asking questions about the origin and content of the food he was served. After their arrival, however, he began to be embarrassed by this practice and stopped "living like a gentile" when it came to food. Presumably, the delegation from James continued to maintain the Jewish dietary practices that all Christians observed in Jerusalem, and Peter was ashamed to reveal that he had not been doing this. Following his lead, the rest of the Jewish Christians in Antioch also withdrew from table fellowship with Christian gentiles, and, Paul says with pain in his voice, "even Barnabas was led astray by their hypocrisy" (Gal 2:13).

The problem may have centered on the ambiguity of the Jerusalem decree. The delegation from James probably did not think that the decree permitted Jewish Christians to share gentile food willy-nilly. Certainly, the Cornelius episode had made clear that God permitted a Jewish person, like Peter, to eat with a "devout" gentile "who feared God with all his household, gave alms generously to the people, and prayed continually to God" (Acts 10:2). They might have assumed that Cornelius and his family were avoiding food offered to idols, meat with blood in it, and blood itself. An observant Jewish person would go much further than this, and so these minimal requirements probably seemed appropriate to the Jerusalem leadership and consistent with their decision to accept Cornelius.

The food offered at meals in Antioch, however, probably did not rise to the standards that the Jerusalem leadership expected of people like Cornelius and his family, and that the Jerusalem leadership thought they had spelled out in the Jerusalem decree. Perhaps Christians in Antioch avoided extremely offensive items such as pork and blood, but they may well have understood the prohibition on "the pollution associated with idols" (Acts 15:20 CEB) merely as a warning against idolatry, not as a ban on common meat that may have incidentally been offered to an idol before hitting the market (cf. 15:29; 21:25).

Why did Paul get so angry about this that he "opposed" Peter "to his face" and considered him a self-condemned hypocrite who was "not acting consistently with the truth of the gospel"? Elsewhere Paul considers it inappropriate for gentile Christians to look down on Jewish Christians who want to maintain their Jewish identity through observing the food laws (Rom 14:3a). What, then, was so offensive about Peter's conduct here?

In Paul's view, Peter's powerful example had led to a large-scale breach of fellowship with gentile Christians in Antioch, all the more offensive because it came after a season of eating with them.²⁹ After Peter's withdrawal, Paul stood alone as the only Jewish Christian in the community willing to continue table fellowship with gentile Christians. This nearly unanimous action must have communicated to the gentile Christians that the Jewish Christians had become uncertain about the gentiles' status in the people of God. It was true that gentiles should not look down on Jewish people who wanted to observe the law, but it was equally important to Paul that observant Jewish Christians should not sit in judgment on gentile Christians who did not observe the dietary laws (Rom 14:3b, 10, 13). It was critical for leaders such as Paul, Barnabas, Peter, and James to find ways to "give no offense to Jews or to Greeks or to the church of God" (1 Cor 10:32) and to live in respectful harmony with each other on the matter of diet (Rom 15:5–7).

In Paul's view when observant Jewish Christians failed to do this, they implied that gentile Christians must "live like Jews" (Gal 2:14) or fall into the category of "gentile sinners" to be avoided (Gal 2:14–15). This is where the situation in Antioch began to parallel the problems the traveling false teachers created when they claimed that circumcision was necessary for salvation (Gal 2:4; Acts 15:1, 5). It is not that Paul believed Peter, Barnabas, the rest of the Jews, or probably even the people from James, really held this view. That is why Paul levels the accusation of hypocrisy. What they knew to be true about the gospel was not governing their behavior, and the result was both unloving treatment of their gentile neighbors (cf. Gal 5:14; 6:2) and division in the church (cf. Gal 5:15). All Jewish Christians, Paul argues, know that people are "justified by faith in Christ and not by works of the law," because, as Psalm 143:2 implies, "by works of the law no one will be justified." That leaves faith as the only possible avenue to justification (Gal 2:16). If Jews and gentiles are justified before God in the same way, then no Jewish person should break fellowship with gentile Christians because they do not "live like Jews" (Gal 2:14).

The Gospel of God's Grace Prevails

Paul's argument was probably persuasive with most of those present, including the "people from James," at least eventually.³⁰ When Paul mentions Peter later in 1 Corinthians, there is no hint of theological tension between them (1 Cor 1:12; 9:5; 15:5), and he still considers Peter a primary witness to the resurrection of Jesus and member of the important group of "twelve" disciples (1 Cor 15:5). Paul also continued to count James among the apostles (1 Cor 15:7), thought of gentile Christians as indebted theologically to the Jerusalem church (Rom 15:27), and later met with James and "all the elders" in Jerusalem on good terms (Acts 21:17–19).

Looking to the more immediate future, Paul would not have invited Barnabas to accompany him on another visit to the new Christian assemblies on Cyprus and in Asia Minor unless Barnabas had realized the truth of his point in Antioch (Acts 15:36). It is also doubtful that Paul would have eventually chosen Silas to accompany him on this trip if Paul had experienced a serious break in fellowship with Jerusalem after his stand in Antioch (Acts 15:40). Silas was a Jewish-Christian prophet (Acts 15:32), and one of two emissaries from Jerusalem that had accompanied Paul and Barnabas back to Antioch from the Jerusalem Council (Acts 15:22, 27). His role was to bear witness, from the Jerusalem perspective, that the leaders there agreed with Paul and Barnabas on the terms of the decree, and he had since returned to Jerusalem (Acts 15:33). He became Paul's trusted traveling companion and coworker, featuring prominently both in Luke's narrative of Paul's work in Macedonia and Achaia (Acts 16:16–39; 17:4, 10; 18:5; cf. 2 Cor 1:19) and as a co-sender of Paul's letters to the Thessalonian Christians (1 Thess 1:1; 2 Thess 1:1).

Paul and Barnabas did have a "sharp disagreement," however, over whether to take John Mark with them on their return trip to the mainly gentile churches they had planted on their recent journey west (Acts 15:36–39a; cf. 13:13b). John Mark was Barnabas's cousin, and they shared strong family ties to the Jerusalem church.[31] From a human perspective, it makes sense that Barnabas was not as ready as Paul to leave John Mark behind. Paul, however, was insistent. An argument ensued, and they decided to go their separate ways. Barnabas and Mark would cross the sea to Barnabas's native island of Cyprus. Paul and Silas would revisit churches on the mainland (15:39–40).

9

Advancing Westward with the Gospel

Before his argument with Barnabas, Paul had probably already planned to take a different route to visit the churches he and Barnabas had planted on Cyprus and in central Asia Minor. If false teachers were traveling around and spreading the idea that circumcision was necessary for salvation (Acts 15:1), and if there was misunderstanding over how Jewish Christians should interpret the Jerusalem Council's decrees (Gal 2:11–14), then it was important to exercise some helpful oversight of the churches in Syria and Cilicia that Paul had founded during his roughly seven years of work in those regions (Gal 1:21; cf. Acts 9:30; 11:25–26).[1]

Paul had probably intended to take a northern route mainly by land that would lead first to the churches he had planted in Syria and Cilicia and then westward toward Derbe, Lystra, Iconium, and Pisidian Antioch.[2] He and Barnabas could then travel south to Perga, sail to Cyprus from Attalia, and then return to Syrian Antioch. After their disagreement over John Mark, however, they decided to divide the route between them. Barnabas and John Mark would cover the work on Cyprus. Paul and Silas would travel north and mainly overland to Christian communities in Syria, Cilicia, and the southern part of the province of Galatia.

A Long Hike into the Anatolian Interior

No one knows how Paul and Silas traveled, but they probably made their way along the road that led north from Antioch, past Pagrai, through the pass in the Amanus Mountains, and along the coast to Tarsus, encouraging and instructing churches along the way.[3] From Tarsus they could have

Advancing Westward with the Gospel

Map 3: From Syrian Antioch to Southern Galatia to the Aegean Region to Jerusalem and Back to Syrian Antioch

headed north on the Via Tauri, following the Cydnus River up into the Taurus Mountains and through the mountain pass known as the Cilician Gates. Perhaps they then traveled along roads that connected Podandus, Tynna, Cybistra, Derbe, Lystra, and Iconium and then traveled the Via Sebaste from Iconium to Pisidian Antioch.

Another possibility is that after arriving in Tarsus they traveled southwest along the coast, perhaps by coastal vessel, to Corycus, a journey of about forty-five nautical miles. They would then have had a fourteen-mile walk to Seleucia (in "Rough" Cilicia) and perhaps struck out to the northwest along a road that may have followed the Calycadnus River. They would have had a steep walk up and then down the southwest part of the

Taurus Mountains but eventually would have arrived, after about eighty-five miles, at Laranda in Lycaonia and finally, fifteen miles farther, at Derbe and the other Christian communities in this region of Galatia.[4]

There was probably no direct route from Derbe northwest to Lystra. Paul and Silas may well have traveled along roads that led south through Laranda and then northwest, and, if so, the journey would have been around eighty-four miles and taken about four days.[5] The journey from Lystra to Iconium, however, was much simpler. An extension of the paved Via Sebaste joined the two towns, and they were only twenty miles from each other.[6]

If Paul and Silas traveled from Antioch mainly on foot and were able to walk in the neighborhood of eighteen miles a day, then whatever route they followed, it was both time-consuming and physically demanding. It was also risky: accidents at sea, swollen rivers, bandits, hunger, dehydration, and inadequate clothing were all possibilities (2 Cor 11:25–27). Why go to all this trouble? Paul may give us a glimpse into what drove him forward when he tells the Corinthians, "Even if I preach the gospel, I can claim no credit for it; I cannot help myself; it would be agony for me not to preach. If I did it of my own choice, I should be earning my pay; but since I have no choice, I am simply discharging a trust" (1 Cor 9:16–17 REB). At his call and conversion, God had entrusted Paul with the task of proclaiming the gospel to both Jews and gentiles, and that responsibility propelled him forward.

A New Co-worker

In Lystra, Paul and Silas met a young man named Timothy, who had a good reputation among Christians both there and in the neighboring town of Iconium. Timothy had probably become a follower of Jesus through the influence of his mother, Eunice, and grandmother, Lois, who themselves seem to have responded to Paul's gospel message during his first visit to Iconium and Lystra (Acts 16:1; 2 Tim 1:5). Perhaps it was on his first visit to Lystra, then, that Paul laid hands on Timothy and became the means through which God gave him the Spirit, the Spirit who would in turn give Timothy strength, love, and good judgment for the challenges that lay ahead (2 Tim 1:6–7; cf. Acts 8:14–17; 19:6).[7]

Timothy's mother, Eunice, was Jewish, but his father was Greek, and perhaps because his father had forbidden it, Timothy had never been circumcised. Judging from the way Luke describes the reputation of Timothy's father, however, he seems to have died by the time that Paul and Silas returned to Lystra. "The Jews who were in those parts," Luke says, "all knew that his father *had been* a Greek" (Acts 16:3).[8]

Paul invited Timothy to join him and Silas and to travel along with them as "God's coworker in the gospel of Christ" (1 Thess 3:2). At some point Paul called the leaders together that he and Barnabas had appointed in the church in Lystra (Acts 14:23) and they too laid their hands on Timothy, prophesying over him and confirming for the whole community that God had called and empowered Timothy to work with Paul (1 Tim 4:14).

This began a partnership that would extend through the rest of Paul's life. From early in their association, Timothy seems to have functioned almost as an extension of Paul himself. Timothy could serve as his emissary in Thessalonica, Corinth, Philippi, and Ephesus (1 Thess 3:2, 6; 1 Cor 4:17; 16:10; Phil 2:19; 1 Tim 1:3) and often joins Paul in the greetings that open his letters as if Timothy is their co-sender (2 Cor 1:1; Phil 1:1; Col 1:1; 1 Thess 1:1; 2 Thess 1:1; Phlm 1). When Paul was in prison, he wanted Timothy by his side (Phil 2:20, 22–23; 2 Tim 4:9, 21). "I have no one else like him," he tells the Philippians, "who will be genuinely concerned for your welfare. . . . You know Timothy's proven worth, how as a son with a father he has served with me in the gospel" (Phil 2:20, 22).

Timothy's Circumcision

In preparation for working with him, Paul circumcised Timothy. Luke explains that he did this because Jewish people in the area around Lystra and Iconium knew about Timothy's ethnically complex family background (Acts 16:3). Some interpreters of Acts have wondered whether this account could be true. Paul would later tell the Galatians that if they accepted circumcision Christ would be of no advantage to them (Gal 5:2). He would urge the Corinthians to remain in the social state in which they were called, whether circumcised or not (1 Cor 7:18). He has already decisively refused to circumcise Titus, who was a Greek, despite pressure to do so at the Jerusalem Council (Gal 2:3–5). Is it likely, the argument goes, that the same Paul would now circumcise Timothy?[9] Is it not more likely that Luke was the victim of the misinformation that stands behind the false charge Paul mentions in Galatians 5:11: "If I . . . still preach circumcision, why am I still being persecuted?" This rumor worked well for Luke according to this theory since he wanted to portray Paul as a law-observant Jewish Christian.[10]

The circumcision of Timothy, however, makes sense both from what is known about how Jewish people determined Jewish identity during this period and from the perspective of the ministry strategy that Paul articulates in his letters. Already in Ezra 9–10, the status of a child's mother seems to be the most important criterion in determining whether that child belongs to the nation of Israel. When Ezra discovers that "the people of Israel and the priests and the Levites have not separated themselves from the peoples of the lands with their abominations" and "have taken some of their daughters to be wives for themselves and for their sons so that the holy race has mixed itself with the peoples of the lands," the solution lies in sending the wives away with their children (9:1–2; 10:3, 44).[11] There is no corresponding mention here of any problem with Jewish wives taking gentile husbands.[12] Ezra, therefore, may reflect a tradition within Judaism that was beginning to stress the importance of the mother in Jewish identity.[13]

By the time the book of Jubilees appeared in the second century BC, moreover, intermarriage between Jews and gentiles was, at least in the eyes of those who produced and valued this book, a just cause for violence: "And if there is any man who wishes in Israel to give his daughter or his sister to any man who is of the seed of the Gentiles let him surely die, and let him be stoned because he has caused shame in Israel. And also the woman will be burned with fire because she has defiled the name of her father's house and so she will be uprooted from Israel" (Jub. 30:7 [Wintermute, *OTP* 2:112–13]). The author says this while retelling the story from Genesis 34 of how Jacob's sons Simeon and Levi took vengeance on the gentiles Hamor and Shechem for Shechem's rape of their sister Dinah. In the biblical text, Jacob scolds his sons for bringing trouble on him by their violence (Gen 34:30). The author of the book of Jubilees, however, views their zeal as commendable. It "was a righteousness for them and it was written down for them for righteousness" (Jub. 30:17). God chose the descendants of Levi for the priesthood, the author says, "because he was zealous to do righteousness and judgment and vengeance against all who rose up against Israel" (Jub. 30:17–18). In the mid-first century AD, feelings about intermarriage still ran high enough that even gentile men of high social standing who wanted to marry Jewish women sometimes had to accept circumcision as a requirement (Josephus, *A.J.* 20.139).

Luke implies that the marriage of Timothy's mother, Eunice, to an uncircumcised gentile was well known not only in their hometown of Lystra but in the neighboring town of Iconium (Acts 16:2–3) and that it had given offense to Jewish people in the area. With Timothy's father now deceased, and the family now entirely both Jewish and Christian, it made sense for Paul to avoid unnecessary trouble and regularize Timothy's status as a Jewish man by circumcising him. Tensions had already reached the breaking point with some of the unbelieving Jews in Pisidian Antioch and Iconium during Paul's original visit to the area with Barnabas (Acts 13:45, 50; 14:2, 5). In Lystra itself some unbelieving Jews from both Antioch and Iconium had traveled along the Via Sebaste and gathered a crowd that stoned Paul and left him for dead (Acts 14:19; cf. 2 Tim 3:11).[14] If Paul had already started to look westward to the province of Asia at this point (cf. Acts 16:6), he may have anticipated traveling along the Via Sebaste from Iconium not merely to Pisidian Antioch but also to the important commercial and political city of Apamea, just across the border of Asia, with its large Jewish community.[15] Circumcising Timothy would show that despite Paul's focus on bringing gentiles into the people of God, he did not intend to undermine the Jewish identity of Jewish Christians. In addition, it might prevent a repetition of the violent zeal that broke out against him in cities along the Via Sebaste during his first visit to the region.

The action was also consistent with Paul's policy, stated later in 1 Corinthians 9:20, and the problems he had to think through at this time may have helped him formulate that policy: "To the Jews I became as a Jew, in order to win Jews. To those under the law I became as one under the law (though not being myself under the law) that I might win those under the law."

Circumcising Timothy, however, was also not inconsistent with his earlier refusal to have Titus circumcised at the time of the Jerusalem Council (Gal 2:3). Circumcision was inappropriate for Titus precisely because "he was a Greek" (Ἕλλην ὤν).[16] As J. B. Lightfoot argued, Paul may have had Timothy's circumcision in mind when he wrote these words and may have been anticipating or answering the objection that he was inconsistent on the issue of circumcision (cf. 5:11).[17] From Paul's perspective, Titus could not be circumcised because to do so would communicate that someone who was Greek had to become Jewish in order to belong to God's people, and that would be a "different gospel" (1:6).

Since Timothy was Jewish, however, his circumcision could serve, as it did with Abraham, "as a seal of the righteousness that he had by faith while he was still uncircumcised" (Rom 4:11). Paul deeply valued the Jewish roots of the new multiethnic people of God and never opposed the idea that Jewish Christians should keep their Jewish identity intact through observing elements of the Mosaic law. He made a good faith effort to let the churches in the southern part of Galatia know the decrees of the Jerusalem Council (Acts 16:4). He admonished gentile believers in Rome not to look down on or sit in judgment on Jewish Christians who continued to follow their traditional customs of diet and festival observance (Rom 14:3, 5–6, 10, 13, 20–21). He seems to have made his first efforts at collecting funds for needy Jewish believers in Jerusalem among "the churches of Galatia" (1 Cor 16:1; cf. Gal 2:10). This collection he viewed as something gentile Christians owed to Jewish Christians, "for if the Gentiles have come to share in their spiritual blessings," he says, "they ought also to be of service to them in material blessings" (Rom 15:27).[18]

THE SPIRIT DIRECTS THE GROUP TO TROAS

After Timothy's circumcision, probably in Lystra, he would have accompanied Paul and Silas along the extension of the Via Sebaste joining Lystra with Iconium, and then along the main road westward to Pisidian Antioch. If they had continued along the Via Sebaste, they would have traveled southward along the border of the Roman province of Asia and eventually arrived at Perga where Paul and Barnabas had preached the gospel on the return leg of their first journey to the area (Acts 14:25). Luke says nothing about believers in Perga, however, and, if there was no church there to strengthen, Paul perhaps felt free to move westward toward Asia. If so, they perhaps followed the Via Sebaste southwest as far as Apollonia, still well within ethnic Phrygia, but also inside the boundaries of the Roman province of Galatia. Luke calls this corner of Galatia aptly "the Phrygian and Galatian region" (16:6 REB).[19] It was only a few miles from Apollonia to Apamea, just across the border of Asia.[20]

At this point, however, the three travelers hit a spiritual roadblock. Luke says that the Holy Spirit hindered them from speaking the word in Asia (Acts 16:6). Depending on how one understands the Greek participle here (κωλυθέντες), this hindrance could have occurred before, during, or after the trio went through "the Phrygian and Galatian region," although "after" is perhaps the least likely option from the standpoint of the grammar. Luke probably means that they traveled throughout Phrygian Galatia "*because* the Holy Spirit kept them from speaking the word in the province of Asia" (16:6 CEB, emphasis added).[21] It is not clear how or why the Holy Spirit communicated this hindrance to the group, although the role of Paul and Silas as prophets (13:1; 15:32) may mean that they had some special insight into the Spirit's guidance. In any case, the three perhaps stayed longer and traveled to more towns in Phrygian Galatia precisely "because" of the Spirit's prohibition "from speaking the word" in neighboring Asia.

The Spirit's prohibition was from speaking the word in Asia, however, not from traveling through it, and a journey northwest through Asia would have been necessary in order to reach the part of Bithynia near Mysia, which became the group's next destination (Acts 16:7).[22] It makes sense, then, to think of Paul, Silas, and Timothy setting out for Bithynia by leaving Apollonia in Phrygian Galatia, arriving in Apamea just on the other side of the Galatian border with Asia, traveling north to Cotiaeum, and eventually arriving at Dorylaeum near the border between Asia and Bithynia. Here, they would probably also have been near the territory of Mysia, although its boundaries were not clear by Paul's time (Strabo, *Geogr.* 12.4.4–6; 12.8.1–2).[23]

Once again, however, they received a spiritual prohibition. This time the prohibition was stricter than it had been with the province of Asia: they were not even to enter the province of Bithynia (Acts 16:7).[24] They must have then turned back down the same road that brought them to Dorylaeum, but, when they arrived at Cotiaeum, they probably continued south, traveling past Aezani and Cadi and making a sharp turn to the northwest to arrive at Ancyra. From Ancyra, they would have taken a road that probably led to the town later called "Hadrianuthera," and from there they would have turned west to Adramyttium and then north along the coast to Troas.[25]

The entire route from Phrygian Galatia to Troas, therefore, was within the Roman province of Asia, and the team of three probably traveled as quickly as they could, obeying the Sprit's direction not to "speak the word" in any of the towns they visited (Acts 16:6). Luke seems to emphasize this point in his comment on their approach to Mysia. Mysia was an ancient region mostly in northwestern Asia, and it included the coastal city of Alexandria Troas. Luke comments that the group, "disregarding Mysia, went down to Troas" (Acts 16:8, my trans.). The term translated "disregarding" (παρελθόντες) does not mean that they failed to travel through Mysia—Troas was *in* Mysia! Rather, it means that they passed through Mysia without stopping or interacting with the population (cf. 1 Macc 5:48).[26]

It seems that Luke wanted his readers to understand that God, through his Spirit, had directed the group to go as quickly as possible to the northwest coast of Asia. He did not want them to stop and preach the gospel or plant churches but simply to continue their journey until they could go no farther. Even in Troas, their purpose was not to preach the gospel, and Luke records no preaching efforts in this major port city.[27] That would change in years to come (2 Cor 2:12; Acts 20:6–12). For now, however, the prohibition against work in Asia was still in effect and meant that "speaking the word" in Troas was off limits.

Luke Joins the Group in Troas and God Guides Them to Macedonia

Everything changed quickly once Paul, Silas, and Timothy arrived in Troas. Another divine prompting, this time in the form of a nighttime vision to Paul, directed the group to cross the sea and help the Macedonians: "A man of Macedonia was standing there urging him and saying, 'Come over to Macedonia and help us'" (Acts 16:9). As soon as Paul had seen the vision, Luke says, "we sought to go on into Macedonia, concluding that God had called us to preach the gospel to them" (16:10). The Greek term translated "concluding" (συμβιβάζοντες) can refer to drawing the threads of evidence together to produce a coherent argument for a particular position (9:22). Here, the term may hint that when the group thought through their past experiences of the Spirit's guidance and added to them this most recent experience of a vision, they could not escape the impression that God had directed them to this point so that they would cross the Aegean Sea and proclaim the gospel in Macedonia.

This point in Luke's narrative not only marks a great geographical shift in the group's mission but also a shift in the perspective of the narration. For the first time in Acts, Luke throws the narrative into the first-person plural, something that will continue sporadically until Paul reaches Rome near the book's end. Scholars debate the significance of this. Has Luke suddenly started to incorporate a travel account from Timothy, Silas, or perhaps even Paul himself into his story? Has Luke simply started speaking in the first person to lend verisimilitude to his narrative? Does Luke both incorporate an eyewitness source and show himself, as the author of the narrative, to be a member of the group of early Christians who follow Paul? Did ancient authors simply like to tell stories of sea journeys in the first person?[28]

Certainly, the most natural way to take the shift into the first-person plural is to understand that the author of Luke-Acts was himself a participant in the events he describes. He began his two-volume work by saying that he intended "to compile a narrative of the things that have been accomplished among *us*" (Luke 1:1, emphasis added), and he has shown himself to be a competent and careful editor of Mark's Gospel. It is unlikely, then, that he would confuse his readers by sloppily leaving first-person plural narration in his account unless that narration included himself. He is, moreover, writing in the mode of ancient historiography, not fiction, and there is no sound evidence that ancient historiographers included themselves in a fictional way in the events they described.[29] No one knows whether Luke joined the three others in Troas, or at some earlier point, or had been with them since they left Syrian Antioch, but, at least for this part of the narrative, the group grows to four, with Luke playing mainly the role of observer in many of the events he will narrate.

The four Christian travelers "immediately" started looking for a ship to take them across the Aegean Sea to Macedonia (Acts 16:10). The sea journey from Alexandria Troas to Neapolis in Macedonia was one of the busiest routes across the northern Aegean, and Luke gives the impression that when the winds turned favorable, they had no trouble finding passage.[30] They made the journey to Neapolis in good time—only two days, with an overnight stop on the island of Samothrace (16:11). Now, finally, the Spirit's prohibition was lifted. They were in Macedonia.

10

Church Planting and Suffering in Macedonia

When Paul, Silas, Timothy, and Luke landed in the Macedonian port of Neapolis, they would have taken the Via Egnatia northwest for about ten miles to Philippi.[1] This road was one of the most important transportation routes in the Roman Empire. It stretched along the Aegean coast from Byzantium in eastern Thrace to Neapolis, Philippi, and Amphipolis. It then turned inland to take in Apollonia, met the sea again at Thessalonica, and continued westward across Macedonia finally to terminate at both Apollonia and Dyrrachium, just across the Adriatic Sea from Brundisium in Italy. Brundisium was at the southern end of the Via Appia, and the Via Appia led northwest to Rome, entering the city at the Porta Capena and terminating in a busy intersection just south of the Circus Maximus. Apart from a short sea journey across the Adriatic, therefore, the Via Egnatia was effectively a highway that connected the city of Rome with Byzantium, uniting Rome with the eastern empire.

The Romans had constructed the Via Egnatia for military purposes, but by Paul's time it functioned mainly as a travel route for trade and tourism, bringing Roman and Italian immigrants east, and along with them Roman goods and culture.[2] It also brought eastern peoples, along with their goods and cultures, westward to Rome. As the four Christians entered Philippi, the road became what was probably the city's main east–west street, paved and lined with columns.[3]

THE GOSPEL ADVANCES AND CREATES CONFLICT AT PHILIPPI

Philippi itself was a leading city in Macedonia (Acts 16:12), although Thessalonica was the capital of the province, and Amphipolis was the capital of the district within Macedonia that it shared with Philippi.⁴ Unlike those cities, however, Philippi was also one of only three Roman colonies along the Via Egnatia.⁵ People spoke Latin freely there and could be proud and protective of their own identity as Romans, as Luke's account of Paul's arrest shows. They could also feel threatened by people like Paul and Silas, who were Judeans from the east (16:20–21).

When the group arrived in Philippi, they followed the same strategy Paul had employed when he, Barnabas, and John Mark first arrived on Cyprus: they tried to find the places where Jewish people worshiped (Acts 16:13; cf. 13:5, 14; 14:1). There is some evidence that Jewish people who lived outside Judea tried, if possible, to locate their synagogues near bodies of water so that they could wash before engaging in sacred tasks such as prayer (Josephus, *A.J.* 12.106; 14.258; cf. Jdt 12:7).⁶ That probably explains why Luke says he, Paul, Silas, and Timothy "supposed" they would find "a place of prayer" by the river. The river would be the obvious place to look for a synagogue or some less formal gathering of Jewish people on the Sabbath. The Gangites River passed about a mile and a half from the city, along the Via Egnatia and outside an archway that probably marked the city's sacred boundary or *pomerium*.⁷

It was probably there that the four Christians found a gathering of women who were either Jewish or sympathetic with Judaism (Acts 16:13). At least one of them, Lydia, listened attentively to Paul and accepted baptism (Acts 16:14–15). Lydia was a woman of wealth, at least compared to most people of the time. Although she was an immigrant from Thyatira in the Roman province of Asia, she was a merchant who specialized in selling either expensive purple dye or the luxury items (perhaps cloth) that had been dyed with it.⁸ She was also the head of a household large enough to accommodate the four Christians on the spur of the moment. Luke remembered both her invitation of hospitality and her insistence that the four travelers accept her offer (Acts 16:15). Perhaps in the coming months she would be a significant contributor to the monetary gifts that would eventually help Paul devote more time to the proclamation of the gospel in Thessalonica and Corinth without violating his policy of refusing to become a financial burden to the churches where he ministered (Phil 4:15–16; 2 Cor 11:8–9; Acts 18:5).⁹

Luke gives the impression that Paul remained in Philippi for a number of days rather than months (Acts 16:12–13, 18), and he focuses on the beginning and the end of Paul's visit there, supplying no details about the number of other people from the Jewish prayer gathering who became Christians, or what and how Paul taught them.[10] Luke recounts no resistance to the group from unbelieving Jewish people in Philippi, and it seems possible that the entire group, or a majority of it, eventually became believers.[11] When Paul wrote to the Philippian Christians from Rome over a decade later, although there is no mention of Lydia, women still played an important role both in the community of believers and in supporting Paul's work in advancing the gospel generally (Phil 4:2–3). Perhaps the women in Paul's letter, whom Paul names as Euodia and Syntyche, emerged, like Lydia, from that original place of prayer.

At the end of Paul's stay, Luke records an incident that also made a deep impression on Paul because of the suffering and shame it involved. He told the Christians in Thessalonica about it when he arrived there not long after the incident, and he reminded them of it when he wrote to them (1 Thess 2:2). He also clearly remembered it over a decade later when he wrote from imprisonment to the persecuted Christian community in Philippi that they were "engaged in the same conflict that you saw I had and now hear that I still have" (Phil 1:30).

Paul and Silas were both Roman citizens, and, in the uneven justice of the Roman legal system, should have been exempt from judicial beating and shackling without a trial or sentence. They also had the right to have their case heard and, if necessary, to an appeal (Acts 16:37; cf. 22:25–26, 29).[12] The magistrates of Philippi, however, failed to follow this process when Paul and Silas fell afoul of some local slave owners. Paul had commanded the fortune-telling spirit of an enslaved girl to leave her, depriving her masters of the income that her "spirit of divination" brought them (Acts 16:16, 18–19). Her masters then "seized Paul and Silas and dragged them into the marketplace" where they charged them before the city officials with being Jews, disturbing the city, and advocating an un-Roman way of life (16:19–21). The magistrates assumed that Paul and Silas were foreigners of a low social class and therefore not entitled to due process, so they summarily stripped them, beat them with rods, and shackled them painfully in prison (16:22–24).[13] That night an earthquake struck the area, shaking the prison's foundations, jarring the doors so badly that they opened, and freeing the prisoners from their restraints (16:25–27). The frightened jailer believed the gospel as a result of the incident (16:30–34), and the next morning, the city magistrates sent their rod-wielding peacekeepers to the jailer with the message that he could free Paul and Silas (16:35).

It was only then that Paul was able to inform them that he and Silas were Roman citizens and that the magistrates had dealt with them illegally. Paul insisted that the magistrates themselves—the highest officials in the city government—come to them personally and lead them out of the prison (Acts 16:37).[14] Their accusers had called them un-Roman (16:21). Paul now showed that he understood Roman culture very well by entering a small contest of honor with the magistrates. They had deprived him and Silas of their honor through degrading treatment, so now he insisted the magistrates come to the prison themselves, at the expense of their own honor, and openly admit the injustice.[15]

This was not the only time Paul was beaten with the rods of local peacekeepers. "Three times," he tells the Corinthians, "I was beaten with rods" (2 Cor 11:25). Each time it happened Paul must have felt deeply not only the physical pain but also the profound sense of shame that was normal in the Greco-Roman world for someone facing such a demeaning experience.[16] We were "shamefully treated at Philippi," he says, using a word (ὑβρισθέντες) that refers to treating someone with "insolence" (ὕβρις). "Insolence," says Aristotle, "means to do and say things that bring shame to the victim" (Aristotle, *Rhet.* 2.2).[17]

Despite this painful experience, however, Paul refused to turn back. It would have been a greater agony not to preach the gospel with which God had entrusted him (1 Cor 9:16–17). "Though we had already suffered and been shamefully treated at Philippi," he tells the Thessalonians, "we had boldness in our God to declare to you the gospel of God in the midst of much conflict" (1 Thess 2:2).

Paul, Silas, and Timothy Travel to Thessalonica

Paul set out once again, then, along the Via Egnatia toward Thessalonica (Acts 17:1). Silas and Timothy were with him, but the first-person plurals drop out of Luke's narrative at this point, only to reappear again at Acts 20:5–6 where Luke says, "We sailed away from Philippi" for Troas.[18] This probably means that the group left Luke behind in Philippi, perhaps to continue teaching and nurturing the young group of believers there. The journey to Thessalonica passed through the important city of Amphipolis thirty-three miles away, although the territory of the city was so large that its boundaries stretched all the way to the western edge of Philippi.[19] Amphipolis was surrounded on two sides by the Strymon River, which the Via Egnatia crossed, and which emptied into the Aegean Sea only three miles to the south.[20]

After twenty-seven more miles, the group went through Apollonia, and, finally, thirty-five miles more brought them to Thessalonica. It is tempting to think of their journey as moving along in three stages with overnight stays in Amphipolis and Apollonia. Each leg of such a journey, however, would have been longer than three people could cover in a single day of travel on foot, especially if two of them were recuperating from a severe beating. Craig Keener has suggested that Lydia gave them a monetary gift that allowed them some faster form of transport, such as rented mules or horses (cf. Phil 4:15).[21]

After the Romans had fully subdued Macedonia in the mid-second century BC and plundered its capital Pella unmercifully, they made Thessalonica the seat of the new province's proconsul. It was a large and busy port city on the Via Egnatia and "became the junction between East and West, the meeting point of two worlds."[22] After the battle of Philippi in 42 BC, Octavian, Mark Antony, and Lepidus rewarded Thessalonica for its support against Brutus and Cassius with the status of a "free city," meaning that its inhabitants were exempt from paying tax to Rome. The imperial cult was prominent in the city, and many Roman merchants lived there in the first century.[23] Still, it was not as Romanized as Philippi. Its inhabitants spoke mainly Greek, came from a variety of cultures, and worshiped a wide range of gods.[24]

Paul's Multiethnic Outreach in Thessalonica

Not surprisingly, there was also a Jewish synagogue in Thessalonica, and Paul "as was his custom" (Acts 17:2) went there each Sabbath for three weeks and gave instruction. Luke says that his synagogue teaching focused on proving from the Scriptures that Jesus was the Messiah and that the Messiah was destined to suffer and then rise from the dead (Acts 17:3). It is true that these are standard themes of early Christian preaching as Luke describes it in Acts (cf. 3:18; 8:30–35; 26:23), but they are also the themes that Paul himself affirms as the most important subjects of his preaching in the Aegean area at this time (1 Cor 15:3–4). If Paul were filling out Luke's summary with more detail, he might add that he said the Messiah was destined not only to suffer but to suffer "for our sins" (1 Cor 15:3) and that because of this atoning death he would "deliver us from the wrath to come" (1 Thess 1:10).

Judging from the letters he later wrote to the Thessalonian Christians, he also spent a lot of time talking about the final day of judgment or, as he calls it, "the day of the Lord" (1 Thess 5:2; 2 Thess 2:2; cf. 2 Thess 1:10; 2:3). He could summarize their conversion in terms of their desire to be delivered from the destruction that would come on that day to those who had not acknowledged the one true God (1 Thess 1:10; 5:2), and he says that he repeatedly taught on the topic when he "was still with" them (2 Thess 2:5).[25] He seems to have known and conveyed Jesus's own teaching on the final day, using, for example, the metaphor of a thief coming in the night to describe the importance of being ready for his coming (Matt 24:36–44; cf. 1 Thess 5:2–10). He also seems to have taught extensively on Daniel 10–12, a passage important to Jesus (Matt 24:15; Mark 13:14; cf. Dan 9:27; 11:31; 12:11).[26] A "man of lawlessness," similar to the "contemptible person" of Daniel 11:21, would signal by his coming the immediate appearance of Jesus and the advent of the day of the Lord (2 Thess 2:3–12; cf. Matt 24:15, 24, 29–31).

Paul's audience at these synagogue teaching sessions was diverse. It included not only Jewish people but some of the city's leading women and Greeks who were sympathetic with Judaism. Luke says that a variety of people from all three groups found Paul's message persuasive, although he gives the impression that Paul had more success among non-Jewish people than among Jewish people (Acts 17:4). This matches Paul's own statement in his first letter to the Thessalonian Christians that they "had turned to God from idols" when they believed the gospel (1 Thess 1:9). It may seem surprising that gentiles within the synagogue would need to "turn from idols," but prior to embracing the gospel, they may have simply added elements of Jewish ritual to the range of religious activities in which they participated.[27]

We should also not imagine that Luke has told us everything Paul, Silas, and Timothy did in Thessalonica. He has probably condensed his description of their work just as he did with his description of their ministry in

CHAPTER 10

Philippi. For example, just as he offers no explanation of the "we" material at Philippi (Acts 16:10–17), so in his report on Thessalonica, he never identifies "Jason" (17:6). It seems probable, then, that Paul, Silas, and Timothy spent more than three weeks in Thessalonica, and that during this time Paul preached the gospel in non-Jewish settings, just as he would do later in Athens (17:16–21).[28]

Paul's Means of Support in Thessalonica

One such setting might well have been his workplace. Paul reminds the Thessalonians that he, Silas, and Timothy engaged in "labor and toil" while they were with them, working "night and day" so that they would not burden anyone in Thessalonica while they proclaimed the gospel to them (1 Thess 2:9; 2 Thess 3:7–8). When Paul says in a later letter that he has served Christ "in toil and hardship, through many a sleepless night" (2 Cor 11:27) he may be referring to the same experience of often working hard, long hours to provide for his own needs in the communities where he preached the gospel (cf. 1 Cor 4:12; 9:6, 18; 2 Cor 12:14). It is possible that the "Jason" who pops into Luke's narrative with no explanation and seems to have been the person who accommodated Paul and his coworkers in Thessalonica was, at the beginning, only their employer and through his contact with them became a believer (Acts 17:5–9).[29]

Paul believed that he and other preachers of the gospel were entitled to hospitality from the people among whom they worked (2 Thess 3:9; 1 Cor 9:4–5; Gal 6:6; 1 Tim 5:18). Their proclamation of the gospel and discipling of new believers was hard labor, and Jesus had "commanded that those who proclaim the gospel should get their living by the gospel" (1 Cor 9:14; cf. Matt 10:10–11; Mark 6:10; Luke 9:4; 10:7). By the time he reached Thessalonica, however, he had decided not to take advantage of this right (2 Thess 3:9; 1 Cor 9:15). He found that he could spread the gospel more effectively by working as a common laborer and earning his keep, although he had no objection to receiving support from Christians in other cities or from coworkers who came alongside him (Phil 4:16; 2 Cor 11:8–9; Acts 18:5).

Paul probably had at least three reasons for this approach. First, it put distance between himself and the professional orators and philosophers who were a common sight in the large cities of the mid-first-century Mediterranean world.³⁰ Not all "sophists" and "Cynic" philosophers had bad reputations, but they sometimes received criticism for being more interested in fame and fortune than in the well-being of the citizenry. Dio Chrysostom, speaking of Alexandria in the first century, for example, commented on Cynic philosophers there who had given philosophy a bad name:

> Cynics, posting themselves at street-corners, in alleyways, and at temple-gates, pass round the hat and play upon the credulity of lads and sailors and crowds of that sort, stringing together rough jokes and much tittle-tattle [σπερμολογίαν] and that low badinage that smacks of the market-place. Accordingly they achieve no good at all, but rather the worst possible harm, for they accustom thoughtless people to deride philosophers in general, just as one might accustom lads to scorn their teachers, and, when they ought to knock the insolence out of their hearers, these Cynics merely increase it. (*Or.* 32.9 [Cohoon and Crosby, LCL]).

These would-be philosophers, Dio continued, were more concerned with "their own profit and reputation [δόξης]" than with the improvement of their hearers. They rarely spoke with frankness (παρρησίαν), and, when they did, they made "a hurried exit" to avoid an embarrassing rejection from their audience (*Or.* 32.10–11). It was hard to find an honest orator or philosopher:

> But to find a man who in plain terms and without guile [ἀδόλως] speaks his mind with frankness [παρρησιαζόμενον], and neither for the sake of reputation [δόξης] nor for gain makes false pretensions, but out of good will and concern for his fellow-men stands ready, if need be, to submit to ridicule and to the disorder and the uproar of the mob—to find such a man as that is not easy, but rather the good fortune of a very lucky city, so great is the dearth of noble, independent souls and such the abundance of toadies, mountebanks, and sophists. (*Or.* 32.11)³¹

Paul, for his part, wanted to be just such a person of integrity to his audiences of often skeptical hearers and enthusiastic but inexperienced believers: "We have renounced disgraceful, underhanded ways. We refuse to practice cunning or to tamper with God's word, but by the open statement of the truth we would commend ourselves to everyone's conscience in the sight of God" (2 Cor 4:2). He refused, then, to become a deadweight on the generosity of his hearers, like a parasite that numbs the limb of its host (11:9; 12:13–14).³² Instead, he wanted new believers to see him as a parent providing for his children, spending and being spent for their souls (12:14–15).

A second reason for this approach seems to have been Paul's desire to teach what he considered an important principle for new believers to learn and follow. It was so important that he had boiled it down to a pithy one-liner: "If anyone is not willing to work, let him not eat" (2 Thess 3:10). In 2 Thessalonians, Paul reminds his readers of this aphorism and says that when he was with them, he taught it to them more than once both in word and in example (3:6–9). He had no rebuke for those who were sick, disabled, or could not find employment, but only for those who claimed to be believers and were not "willing" to work.³³

What broader theological concern did this saying represent? For Paul it may have represented the idea that working for one's food was a good activity God had woven into the order of creation. Genesis 2:15–16 said that after God created the first man, he "put him in the garden of Eden to work it and keep it" and told him, "You may surely eat of every tree of the garden." In the book of Jubilees, a second-century BC interpretation of Genesis and the first part of Exodus, the author reflects on Genesis 2:15–16 this way: "And during the first week of the first jubilee Adam and his wife had been in the garden of Eden for seven years tilling and guarding it. And we gave him work and we were teaching him to do everything which was appropriate for tilling. And he was tilling" (Jub. 3:15 [Wintermute, *OTP* 1:59]).³⁴ Paul's younger contemporary Josephus similarly interpreted Genesis 2:15–16 to mean that God brought both Adam and Eve into the "garden and bade them to tend the plants" (*A.J.* 1.38 [Thackeray, LCL]).³⁵

It was possible to avoid work in the Greco-Roman world in various ways—by attaching oneself to a wealthy patron, by posing as a philosopher, by relying on the Roman grain dole.³⁶ Paul believed, however, that productive work was part of God's good creation and that Christians should therefore engage in it (cf. 2 Thess 3:13; Acts 20:33–35; Eph 4:28). He was also concerned that Christians not share the bad reputation that loafers and meddlers often had in the Greco-Roman world (1 Thess 4:12).[37]

A third reason Paul insisted on working with his hands in the communities where he ministered was probably also to provide himself with a venue for explaining the gospel and its implications to others. Since Paul had the hand skills necessary to produce tents and awnings (Acts 18:3), he could have talked about the gospel while working with his hands.[38] The mid-first-century Roman philosopher Musonius Rufus addressed the question of "what means of livelihood is appropriate for a philosopher" and argued that working at farming was eminently suitable:

> What, perhaps someone may say, is it not preposterous for an educated man who is able to influence the young to the study of philosophy to work the land and to do manual labor just like a peasant? Yes, that would be really too bad if working the land prevented him from the pursuit of philosophy or helping others to its attainment. But since that is not so, pupils would seem to me rather benefited by not meeting their teacher in the city nor listening to his formal lectures and discussions, but by seeing him at work in the fields, demonstrating by his own labor the lessons which philosophy inculcates—that one should endure hardships, and suffer the pains of labor with his own body, rather than depend upon another for sustenance.[39]

In a similar way, it seems likely that Paul used his long hours making and mending tents, awnings, and sails to teach the gospel and its implications to those around him in the workshop. Many of those people would have been gentiles with little or no understanding of Judaism, its Scriptures, and its traditions.[40]

Accusations of Socially Disruptive Ideas in Thessalonica and a Hasty Departure

It is not clear how long Paul, Silas, and Timothy were in Thessalonica, but it was long enough for the Thessalonian believers to "become very dear" to them (1 Thess 2:8, 11, 17; 3:1, 5, 8–9, 12) and for Paul to instruct the new believers in the rudiments of the gospel (1 Thess 1:9–10; 4:2; 5:1–2). It was also long enough to establish a leadership structure for the group (1 Thess 5:12–13), just as he had done in the churches in southern Galatia (Acts 14:23; cf. Gal 6:6), and for him to receive a much-appreciated monetary gift to support his work in Thessalonica from the new believers in Philippi (Phil 4:15–16).[41] Paul hints, however, that he was forced to leave Thessalonica too soon for his liking. He says that he was "orphaned by being separated" from the Christians there, using a strong term (ἀπορφανισθέντες) that implies he was compelled to leave (1 Thess 2:17 NIV), and he also expresses an urgent desire to see them again so that he could "supply what [was] lacking" in their understanding of the faith (1 Thess 3:10 NIV).

Just as Luke had done in his description of Paul's work in Philippi, he describes in detail the scene that led to the exit of Paul and Silas from Thessalonica. Some of the Jewish people in Thessalonica opposed Paul's message out of concern that Paul was exercising influence over the non-Jewish people who attended the synagogue (Acts 17:5; cf. 13:45). This opposition group stirred up wider community resistance to the new movement, and this led a mob to attack Jason's house where Paul, Silas, and Timothy had been staying and perhaps working. They were not present when the mob arrived, so the crowd forced Jason and some other believers who happened to be present to appear before the city's "politarchs" (17:6). These were city administrators well-known from Macedonian inscriptions, and they seem to have normally come from the city's elite social classes.[42]

The charges against the Thessalonian Christians were serious and plausible. Paul had been teaching that there was "another king" (Acts 17:7) because he had taught that Jesus was the Christ, the anointed king of Jewish expectation (Acts 17:3). He had also taught that Jesus had risen from the dead and would arrive from heaven with a mighty army both as the agent of God's salvation for his people and as an agent of God's wrath on everyone who had not turned away from the worship of their traditional gods (1 Thess 1:9–10; cf. 4:6, 16). This coming king would arrive at a time when people were complacent, saying to each other, "There is peace and security" (1 Thess 5:2–3).

It is easy to see how the misunderstanding or mischaracterization of even a small part of this interconnected series of teachings could lead to a charge of subversion (Acts 17:6). Since the time of Caesar Augustus, Roman rulers had promoted throughout the empire the notion that both Augustus and his successors had brought order, peace, and a golden age of prosperity everywhere their rule had expanded.⁴³ The Roman Senate deified Augustus and his successors at various points, requiring as evidence for the deification that a witness should come forward who had seen the emperor's soul ascend to heaven.⁴⁴ James R. Harrison has argued persuasively that in the mid-first century, Romans and the societies under their rule frequently conceived of Augustus as reigning over the Roman Empire from the heavenly realm to which he had supposedly ascended after his death. From that position he was able to continue to guide the empire to peace and prosperity.⁴⁵

D. Clint Burnett, moreover, has provided clear evidence that the Thessalonians worshiped Augustus and other Julio-Claudian emperors, integrating their devotion to them with their devotion to their own traditional gods and to the deified personification of the city of Thessalonica itself.⁴⁶ Burnett argues persuasively that the Thessalonians engaged in this kind of worship as a means of showing gratitude to Rome for its benefaction and encouraging Rome to continue their favorable treatment of the city. There was a real sense in which the worship of the Julio-Claudian imperial family helped to maintain the city's well-being, or its "peace and security" as Paul might have put it (1 Thess 5:3).⁴⁷ Burnett makes the case that when Paul urged those who listened to his message in Thessalonica to turn "to God from idols to serve the living and true God" (1:9), many Thessalonians would have heard the exclusiveness of his message as a threat to the complex relationship between their worship of their traditional gods, their worship of the Julio-Claudians, and the prosperity of their city.⁴⁸

Against the backdrop of the religious culture of Thessalonica, then, Paul's gospel must have sounded many political alarm bells to those who heard but did not sympathize with it. His gospel implied not only that the religious myth of the reign of Augustus and his family over the world was untrue but, as Harrison argues, that Jesus had basically taken his place as the true heavenly power who, unlike Augustus, would return to earth. In addition, as Burnett has argued, Paul's message would have offended those who viewed Thessalonica's prosperity as dependent on the merger of Thessalonica's traditional religious cults with religious devotion to the Julio-Claudian emperors.

Such concerns could have motivated at least some in the mob from the marketplace that went looking for Paul and Silas and dragged "Jason and some of the brothers" before the city politarchs (Acts 17:5–6). This setting offers a reasonable explanation for the charges the mob brought against them. The "security" that the politarchs required of Jason may have been a way of ensuring that Jason would oversee the departure of Paul and Silas from the city.[49] This would absolve the politarchs of responsibility for dealing with them, but also make certain that Paul and Silas would not continue to make trouble.[50]

PAUL AND SILAS FLEE TO BEREA AND FIND A WARMER WELCOME

After this incident, Paul and Silas left Thessalonica for Berea at the prompting of the Thessalonian Christians (Acts 17:10), and perhaps because their exit was a condition of the bail that Jason had posted.[51] There is no reference to Timothy leaving with them, but his name resurfaces at the end of Luke's account of Paul's stay in Berea (Acts 17:14) revealing that he had been with Paul and Silas all along. Paul's comparison of their departure from the Thessalonians to children being wrenched from their parents captures not only its abrupt and involuntary nature but just how emotionally difficult it was for Paul himself (1 Thess 2:17).[52] Still, they had to go or bring further legal trouble to Jason and the new Christian community in Thessalonica.

Geographically, at least, Berea was a good choice for a flight from Thessalonica.[53] It was about fifty miles away, and roughly twenty miles of the route that Paul and Silas probably took went through a marshy lowland.[54] Berea was also a long way from the coast and from the well-traveled Via Egnatia.[55] Since the Thessalonian Christians "sent" Paul and Silas (and presumably Timothy) there (Acts 17:10), moreover, they may have known people in the city with whom the three companions could stay. The route they would have taken is not clear, but a logical journey would have continued westward along the Via Egnatia twenty miles or so to Allante, just across the Axios River. They might have spent whatever was left of the night there and then traveled the additional twenty-five miles southwest to Berea the following day.[56]

The three went directly to the synagogue after their arrival, following Paul's usual strategy (Acts 13:5, 14; 14:1; 16:13; 17:1) and found there both Jewish and Greek people who were more receptive to their message than people in the synagogue in Thessalonica had been (17:11).[57] Luke makes a point of mentioning that "not a few" socially well-positioned Greek women were among the Bereans who believed (17:12). Somehow, though, Paul's unbelieving Jewish opponents in Thessalonica got wind of Paul's success in the Berean synagogue and came there too, "agitating and stirring up the crowds" (17:13). The pattern was identical to what had happened to Paul much earlier in Lystra, when Jewish opponents came from Pisidian Antioch and Iconium and "persuaded the crowds" to stone him (14:19).

This time, however, the believers in the Berean synagogue sent Paul away before any harm could come to him. Paul had probably told them what had happened in Thessalonica, and they followed the same strategy the Thessalonian Christians had adopted. The Berean believers seem to have acted sooner, however, and before any judicial action against Paul and Silas could take place. They also took the step of sending Paul completely out of the province of Macedonia all the way to Athens in Achaia and providing him with an "escort" of Berean believers for this long journey, involving both land and sea (Acts 17:14–15 REB). The journey would have been quite expensive, and perhaps Paul used some of the monetary aid from believers in Philippi to pay for food and transportation for himself and his Berean companions.[58]

Just as Paul had already left Luke behind, perhaps in Philippi, so now he left Silas and Timothy behind in Berea, probably with the thought that they would nurture both the Berean and Thessalonian churches. All three Macedonian churches had come into existence through the labor pains of social upheaval, and Paul had left the believers in these cities to deal with a choppy wake of social and legal problems. He must have felt that it was only prudent also to leave his coworkers behind to help the believers in these cities mature in their newfound faith.

It must have been difficult, however, to part company especially with Silas, who had traveled with him all the way from Syrian Antioch and shared his suffering and humiliation in Philippi. Timothy too had probably already become by this time the unique, like-minded "son" of Philippians 2:20. It is understandable, then, that he gave his Berean guides instructions to send Silas and Timothy to him "as soon as possible" (Acts 17:15).

11

A Cool Reception in Athens and Laying a Foundation in Corinth

In the fifth century BC, Athens had supplied the world with the histories of Herodotus and Thucydides and the famous tragedies of Euripides, Sophocles, and Aeschylus. Its glory was so great that Aeschylus was content for people to forget his literary accomplishments if they remembered he had been a citizen of this city and a brave soldier in its defense (Pausanias, *Descr.* 1.14.5).[1] Socrates had once argued in its public spaces, Plato once flourished there, and there Aristotle had become his student.[2] By Paul's time Athens was still a popular tourist destination, thick with reminders of its famous past, and a center for philosophical study, but its days of independence and strategic importance were centuries in the past.[3] It was a good place for Paul to escape his pursuers and to wait for Silas and Timothy to arrive from Macedonia (Acts 17:16).

Paul and his Berean companions probably arrived at the port of Piraeus about five miles southwest of Athens and walked to the city itself. Once inside, they found symbols of religious devotion everywhere. "I perceive that in every way you are very religious," Paul would say in his speech to the city's governing council (Acts 17:22), and about a century later, the tourist guidebook writer Pausanias agreed: "The Athenians," he says, "are far more devoted to religion than other men" (*Descr.* 1.24.3 [Jones, LCL]). The city was especially famous for its distinctive displays of the head of the god Hermes atop square stone pillars. According to Thucydides, these stood "in great numbers both in the doorways of private houses and in sacred places"

(*P. W.* 6.27 [Smith, LCL]). Many were still standing in Paul's day. In Luke's apt phrase, "the city was full of idols" (Acts 17:16).[4]

Perhaps Paul and the Bereans climbed to the Acropolis using the staircase that the emperor Claudius had erected a few years earlier, and, once at the top, gazed up at the massive statue of Athena in front of them.[5] Walking a bit farther, they would have seen the Parthenon on their right, and, just twenty-five yards east of it, exactly on the Parthenon's east–west axis, they would have seen the temple of Roma and Augustus.[6] An inscription on the stone block between the columns and the roof announced that the governing body of Athens had dedicated the temple to "the goddess Roma and Augustus Caesar" when Pammenes was "Priest of the goddess Roma and Augustus Savior."[7] Down in the lower city Paul might have read not only an altar inscription "to the unknown god" (Acts 17:23) but inscriptions on altars dedicated to the worship of Augustus and his successors.[8] It is not clear exactly where in the city these altars were originally located, but many have been found around the Roman forum.[9]

Marketplace Evangelism, Anxiety for the Thessalonians, and (Possibly) Illness

Paul took all this in while he waited for Silas and Timothy to join him from Macedonia, and what he saw prompted him to action (Acts 17:16).[10] He not only went to the synagogue but, in a manner appropriate to the culture of Athens, Luke says that he went to "the marketplace," an area that included the Roman forum. There, like Socrates, he began discussions with those who happened to pass by hoping to lead them to an understanding of the gospel (Acts 17:17–18; cf. Xenophon, *Mem.* 1.10). According to Luke, he did this every day.

This effort to advance the gospel in Athens was not his only concern during this period. In 1 Thessalonians, which he wrote a few months later, he says that around the time he was in Athens he was in inner turmoil about how the Thessalonian believers were faring since his hasty, nighttime departure. One day, he told them, when they all stood before the Lord Jesus after Jesus's descent from heaven, he hoped that the Thessalonians, with their faith intact, would be his "crown," like the crown of a victorious athlete (1 Thess 2:19; cf. 4:16). Would this hope be realized, or would their commitment to the gospel fail to survive the suffering they were enduring because of it (1:6; 2:14–17; 3:1, 4–5)? "More than once," he tells them, his concern became so great that he tried to return to Thessalonica, "but Satan thwarted us" (2:18 REB).

This sort of "daily pressure . . . of . . . anxiety for all the churches" would later occupy a climactic place in Paul's list of difficulties he had to endure in his faithful apostolic service to Christ. "Who is weak, and I am not weak?" he tells the Corinthians. "Who is made to fall, and I am not indignant?" (2 Cor 11:28–29).

As if this were not enough, at some point during his work in Athens, Paul may have experienced another bout of the recurring illness that had (perhaps) plagued him in Perga before he traveled north to Phrygia (cf. Acts 13:13–14; Gal 4:13). His claim that "Satan thwarted" his repeated attempts to return to Thessalonica is reminiscent of his description of his "thorn . . . in the flesh" as a "messenger from Satan" given to "harass" him (2 Cor 12:7). If that "thorn" was an illness, then it makes sense to think of Satan hindering Paul's return to Thessalonica with a recurrence of it.[11]

Eventually Timothy arrived in Athens, and Paul must have been glad for the company, especially if he was both anxious and ill.[12] It is reasonable to infer from what Paul says in 1 Thessalonians, however, that Timothy was unable to say anything when he came to Athens that allayed Paul's fears about believers there. He comments neither on Timothy's arrival nor on any news he may have had of the Thessalonians but only says that when he could endure his anxiety no longer, he sent Timothy to them, probably meaning that he sent Timothy *back* to them (1 Thess 3:1–2, 5).[13] Perhaps he was still unable to travel himself because of his illness. If that illness was the hindrance that kept him from traveling, it is a measure of how anxious he was to receive news from Thessalonica that he was "willing to be left behind at Athens alone" (3:1) with no one to help him. That news would not come, however, until after he had recovered enough to continue his marketplace discussions and eventually leave Athens for Corinth.

Paul before the City Council of Athens

Luke often ends his description of Paul's tenure in a particular city by describing at length an incident of opposition to Paul. That is probably the function of his description of Paul's encounter with the governing council of Athens. At some point, probably after Timothy's departure and his recovery from illness, one of Paul's marketplace dialogues led to a hostile encounter that seems to have landed Paul in official trouble.[14]

Within his marketplace audience that day were Epicurean and Stoic philosophers who may have at first been interested in his ideas about the relationship between the human and the divine and how life is best lived (Acts 17:18). Their interest did not last long, however, and Luke says that some of them concluded Paul was a mere marketplace idler. They called him a *spermalogos*, a guttersnipe who picked up scraps of knowledge without understanding the coherence of the systems from which they came.[15] Demosthenes, Athens' greatest orator, could deploy the term in tandem with "marketplace loafer" and "poor devil of a clerk" against an enemy he wanted to paint as a pseudo-intellectual (Demosthenes, *Cor.* 127 [Vince and Vince, LCL]).[16] Much closer to Paul's own time, Dio Chrysostom could criticize Cynic philosophers who preached in public for "stringing together rough jokes and much tittle-tattle [σπερμολογίαν] and that low badinage that smacks of the market-place" (*Or.* 32.9 [Cohoon and Crosby, LCL]).

Others thought Paul was proclaiming "foreign divinities," an ominous allegation for any of Luke's readers who knew the charges against Socrates.[17] According to Socrates's contemporary and associate Xenophon, the Athenian judicial council executed him for "not worshipping the gods worshipped by the state and . . . bringing in other novel divinities" (Xenophon, *Mem.* 1.1.1 [Marchant, Todd, and Henderson, LCL]).[18] It would not have helped that Paul was probably teaching the foolishness of idolatry in a context filled with attempts to merge traditional Greek religion with the worship of various Roman emperors. The unhappy part of the crowd "took" Paul "and brought him to the Areopagus" to hear him further (Acts 17:19). Since Luke most often uses the word translated "took" here (ἐπιλαβόμενος) in a hostile sense (cf., e.g., 16:19; 18:17), it seems likely that this was something like an arrest.[19]

The Romans allowed the traditional Athenian governing council (the Areopagus) to adjudicate matters of possible civil unrest, and in Paul's time it sometimes met in the area called the Royal Porch near the marketplace where Paul had been talking with passersby. That was probably the setting for the court hearing that Luke describes, and for Paul's speech in Acts 17:22–31.[20]

²² Men of Athens, I perceive that in every way you are very religious. ²³ For as I passed along and observed the objects of your worship, I found also an altar with this inscription: "To the unknown god." What therefore you worship as unknown, this I proclaim to you. ²⁴ The God who made the world and everything in it, being Lord of heaven and earth, does not live in temples made by man, ²⁵ nor is he served by human hands, as though he needed anything, since he himself gives to all mankind life and breath and everything. ²⁶ And he made from one man every nation of mankind to live on all the face of the earth, having determined allotted periods and the boundaries of their dwelling place, ²⁷ that they should seek God, and perhaps feel their way toward him and find him. Yet he is actually not far from each one of us, ²⁸ for

"In him we live and move and have our being";

as even some of your own poets have said,

"For we are indeed his offspring."

²⁹ Being then God's offspring, we ought not to think that the divine being is like gold or silver or stone, an image formed by the art and imagination of man. ³⁰ The times of ignorance God overlooked, but now he commands all people everywhere to repent, ³¹ because he has fixed a day on which he will judge the world in righteousness by a man whom he has appointed; and of this he has given assurance to all by raising him from the dead.

Is Luke's Version of Paul's Speech a Fiction?

Many scholarly interpreters of Acts have denied that the authentic Paul of the letters could have given a speech like this in Athens.[21] In Romans, Paul says that God is in the process of revealing his wrath against sinful gentiles for failing to worship him as he is revealed in the natural world (1:18–32), and that he will judge gentiles for failing to do the law written on their hearts (2:14–16). Would this Paul really say to gentiles in Athens about their idolatry that up until now God had simply "overlooked" their ignorance (Acts 17:30)?[22] Would the Paul who set the wisdom of the cross in contrast to the wisdom of the Greeks (1 Cor 1:18–2:5) really preach an evangelistic sermon in Athens in which the cross was missing?[23]

A Cool Reception in Athens and Laying a Foundation in Corinth

Those who defend the idea that Paul spoke to the Areopagus in Athens, and that Luke provides a concise review of what he said, however, have the better argument. That Paul was in Athens and that he was in Athens alone is not in doubt, since Paul himself says this in 1 Thessalonians 3:1.[24] If he was there by himself, it is consistent with what we know of this phase of Paul's work that he would have proclaimed the gospel openly if his physical health permitted it. It is also clear from Paul's own letters that when he preached the gospel at this point in his work, he both preached against idolatry and described the return of the resurrected Jesus from heaven to bring God's wrath against the unrighteous (1 Thess 1:9–10; 4:6; cf. Acts 17:29–31).[25]

It is indeed odd that the Paul of the speech does not mention the cross since, according to Paul's letters, the cross occupied a central place in his evangelistic preaching to gentiles in places like Corinth (1 Cor 2:1–2) and Galatia (Gal 3:1).[26] His mention of God's forbearance in overlooking sin, however, is consistent with Paul's own theology (Rom 3:25), and Luke's summary must have left out much of what Paul said.[27]

The classicist Victor Davis Hanson suggests that one question to ask in determining whether a particular speech in Thucydides is historical is this: "Does an oration logically follow a course of events and in turn have an immediate effect on the conduct of subsequent actions in the narrative?"[28] Paul's arrest and defense of himself before an Athenian court logically follows from his public discussion of a religiously and politically provocative message. The meager response to his speech (Acts 17:32–34) also makes sense considering its concluding focus on Jesus's bodily resurrection, a notion that Greeks with their understanding of the dissolution of the body at death would have found odd. The speech, then, probably reflects what Luke remembered of Paul's own description of his ministry in Athens.

Common Ground—to a Point

The speech begins on a positive note, trying to find common ground with Paul's Athenian audience. They were very religious people, Paul begins, and Paul wants to make their religious devotion more accurate and truthful (Acts 17:23). About a century after Paul was in Athens, Pausanias the travel writer went there and commented that at the harbor of Phalerum, near Athens, there were "altars of the gods named Unknown" (*Descr.* 1.1.4 [Jones, LCL]). Paul had seen an altar like this and read the inscription. This provided him with a platform for explaining his understanding of the one true God, a God that his audience did not know (Acts 17:24).

When Paul began describing him, his audience at first may have thought that this God resembled Zeus. At least among some Stoic philosophers, Zeus was the source of human life just as with Paul's God, and Paul quotes a well-known Stoic poet, Aratus, to make this point (Aratus, *Phaen.* 5; cf. Acts 17:24–26, 28). Zeus governed the movements of the stars and the change of the seasons just as Paul claimed his God had "determined allotted periods" (Aratus, *Phaen.* 5–13; cf. Acts 17:26). In Stoic thought, Zeus was everywhere: "Full of Zeus are all the streets and all the market-places of men; full is the sea and the havens thereof" (Aratus, *Phaen.* 2–4 [Mair and Mair, LCL]). For Paul, too, God was "not far from each one of us, for 'In him we live and move and have our being'" (Acts 17:27–28), a statement that may be a paraphrase of Aratus.[29] Clearly Paul believed that his God was "the Lord of heaven and earth" (Acts 17:24), and some within his audience might have thought this also made him compatible with Zeus, whom some considered "mighty for ever, king for evermore" (Callimachus, *Hymn.* 1.2 [Mair and Mair, LCL]).

Even Paul's ideas of righteous judgment through a man whom God appointed may not have been entirely unfamiliar to his audience.[30] Vergil could describe Minos, supposedly the ancient king of Crete and Zeus's son, as presiding in the underworld over a "conclave of the silent" where he learned the "lives and misdeeds" of people (Vergil, *Aen.* 6.432–433).[31] Minos's brother Rhadamanthys, similarly, "chastises, and hears the tale of guilt" in the underworld, "exacting confession of crimes, whenever in the world above any man, rejoicing in vain deceit, has put off atonement for sin until death's late hour" (6.566–569 [Fairclough and Goold, LCL]).

At this point, however, Paul's speech and Greco-Roman views of judgment after death sharply differed.[32] In Paul's speech the nature of judgment and of the judge whom God had appointed clearly set his God apart from the theological thinking of his audience. Paul's God would judge the entire inhabited world (Acts 17:31), not simply those who were especially wicked, and he would judge them for things as seemingly innocent to a Greek audience as using gold, silver, and stone to represent divine beings in human form (17:29–30).

God had also confirmed the man whom he had appointed as judge in his position by raising him bodily from the dead (Acts 17:31). The judgment of which Paul spoke, then, must have sounded like a restoration of the physical universe in which both the judge and those whom he judged were returned to life within physical bodies. How else would God's human judge, who was now re-occupying a physical body, be able to provide righteous judgment to the world? That the crowd came to this conclusion seems to be the implication of Luke's summary statement of its response. "Now when they heard of the resurrection of the dead, some mocked" (17:32). "The dead" in this statement is plural (νεκρῶν), so the crowd understood Paul to be talking not simply about the resurrection of Jesus from among the dead but the return of a vast company of dead people to their physical bodies.

This idea, however, seemed ridiculous and repulsive to most of them. The Athenian playwright Aeschylus could have Apollo, the son of Zeus, say that "once a man has died, and the dust has sucked up his blood, there is no rising again" (*Eum.* 644–651 [Sommerstein, LCL]).[33] Not even Zeus, however mighty, could bring a dead person back to life. Pliny the Elder, writing only thirty or so years after Paul's visit to Athens, considered it a great good that, unlike God, human beings died and that even the deity could not take this away from them by making them immortal or recalling them from the dead (*Nat.* 2.5.27). Much later, in mockery of the Christian idea of the bodily resurrection of the dead, Celsus could ask, "For what sort of human soul would have any further desire for a body that has rotted?" (Origen, *Cels.* 5.14).[34] Celsus misunderstood the doctrine (cf. 1 Cor 15:42–44), but it is unlikely that most of Paul's audience in Athens understood it any better.

The result of Paul's speech was largely mockery (Acts 17:32). A few in his audience were more open to his ideas, and some of those few believed the gospel (Acts 17:34). The yield was so small, however, that Paul did not count it as the founding of a church. Instead, the members of Stephanus's household in Corinth a few months later were, in his view, "the first crop of the harvest to come from the mission to Achaia" (1 Cor 16:15 CEB).[35]

CHAPTER 11

Laying Foundations in Corinth

Shortly after his experience with the Areopagus council, and probably sometime early in AD 50, Paul left for Corinth (Acts 18:1).[36] If it was winter, when shipping on the Mediterranean slowed down and the expense of passage went up, Paul may well have chosen not to travel by sea but to walk west from Athens to the coast and then around the Eleusinian Gulf and past the city of Eleusis, home of an annual religious festival that attracted pilgrims from all over the world.[37] His route would have taken him along the southern coast of the region called Megara, where "the road is exceedingly near to the rocks, so that it often is on the edge of the precipice because the mountain lying above it is impassable and high" (Strabo, *Geogr.* 9.1.4).

Until a railroad was built through this area in the nineteenth century, the route included a six-mile stretch that, in the words of the famous anthropologist James George Frazer, was "a narrow crumbling ledge halfway up the face of an almost sheer cliff, at a height of six to seven hundred feet above the sea. On the right rose the rock like a wall; on the left yawned the dizzy abyss, where, far below the waves broke at the foot of the precipices in a broad sheet of white curdling foam."[38] Strabo, moving in the opposite direction along the same path, describes winds that "come violently down from the heights on the left" (*Geogr.* 9.1.4). It was also a spooky road, notorious for brigands. Mythical stories circulated, at least among the Athenians, of how the mighty Minotaur-killer, Theseus, had eliminated two ruthless thieves that terrorized travelers along this route.

If Paul took this path, his journey probably lasted two stressful days, walking twenty-five to twenty-six miles each day.[39] Perhaps he stopped overnight in the city of Megara, as Dio Chrysostom would do several decades later when traveling from Corinth to Athens (*Tyr.* [*Or.* 6] 6). A rugged journey like this may have been in Paul's mind when he told the Corinthians later that his service to Christ had involved him in "danger from robbers . . . danger in the wilderness" (2 Cor 11:26).

When he finally arrived in Corinth, he found himself within a large and busy commercial thoroughfare. "Corinth is called 'wealthy' because of its commerce," said Strabo, who had visited the city in 29 BC (*Geogr.* 8.6.20; cf. 8.6.23).[40] It was strategically located near the southern side of the nar-

A Cool Reception in Athens and Laying a Foundation in Corinth

row, natural land bridge that connected the Peloponnesian Peninsula to the Greek mainland, and two major harbors serviced it. One (Lechaeum) was on the Gulf of Corinth only two and a half miles to the north and at the end of one of the city's main thoroughfares. The second harbor (Cenchreae) was just eight miles to the east on the Saronic Gulf.[41] Aelius Aristides (AD 117–180) claimed that this geography was the key to the city's wealth. The isthmus is so narrow, he said, that a single breeze both blows ships in on one side and out on the other side. As a result, "everything from everywhere comes here both by land and sea, and this is the reason why the land even from the earliest times was praised as 'wealthy' by the poets" (*Orat.* 46.22).[42]

Strabo succinctly states why this location gave Corinth an economic advantage: "It is . . . master of two harbors, one to Asia, the other near to Italia, making the interchange of cargo easy between places so far apart" (*Geogr.* 8.6.20). Ships from Italy with cargo for ports in the eastern Mediterranean could avoid the dangerous voyage around the jagged Peloponnesian peninsula by sailing into the Gulf of Corinth, transporting their cargo the short distance across the isthmus, and reloading it into ships on the other side in the Saronic Gulf.[43] From the east, the process was simply reversed. If the ships were small enough, they could be "carried across the isthmus on trolleys" (Pliny, *Nat.* 4.10).[44]

Corinth, then, was a wealthy, cosmopolitan city, "the crossroads of Greece," as Dio Chrysostom called it a few decades after Paul (*Virt.* [*Or.* 8.5]).[45] In the mid-first century, it was the sort of place where Junia Theodora lived—a wealthy citizen of Corinth, but a native of Lycia, many miles to the east on the southwestern coast of the Anatolian peninsula. The coastal towns of Lycia honored her with a series of inscriptions that they sent to Corinth at different times and that were eventually collected after her death as a memorial to her. According to these inscriptions, when Lycian citizens traveled to Corinth, Junia Theodora showed them hospitality, welcoming them into her house, supplying them with whatever they needed, and serving as their patron.[46] At some point in his Corinthian ministry, Paul would meet Phoebe, who would become a deaconess of the church at Cenchreae and perform a similar function for Paul and for many others (Rom 16:1–2).

According to Dio, Corinth was the kind of place that a philosopher like Diogenes, or an orator like himself, might show up and attract a crowd, not of Corinthians, who were inured to the pulse of the city, but of strangers: "One could hear crowds of wretched sophists around Poseidon's temple shouting and reviling one another, and their disciples, as they were called, fighting with one another, many writers reading aloud their stupid works, many poets reciting their poems while others applauded them, many jugglers showing their tricks, many fortunetellers interpreting fortunes, lawyers innumerable perverting judgment, and peddlers not a few peddling whatever they happened to have."[47]

It was the sort of city where a young student might show up in the school of a philosophy teacher expecting to be trained as a professional orator. Then, through clever rhetorical skills, a fashionable appearance, and the right social connections, he might make it into a position of power and influence within the city's most influential structures. So, for example, just such "a young student of rhetoric" from Corinth once wanted to learn from the early second-century philosopher Epictetus.[48] This student's "hair was somewhat too elaborately dressed," and his "attire in general was highly embellished" (Arrian, *Epict. diss.* 3.1.1 [Oldfather, LCL]). He had also put on jewelry and plucked out unwanted body hair to make himself look more attractive (3.1.14–15, 42).[49] With its excellent lines of communication to other parts of the Roman world, its transient population, and its willingness to hear traveling orators, Paul must have thought of Corinth as an ideal location to preach the gospel.

By the time he arrived in the city after his exhausting journey, he had probably also exhausted his financial resources. The help that the Philippian church had given him several months earlier (Phil 4:15–16), and any funds he had been able to save from his hard manual labor in Thessalonica must have been depleted by this time (1 Thess 2:9; 2 Thess 3:8). So, he began his apostolic work in Corinth by looking for manual labor among the city's tent and awning makers. He found it with a couple whose background was like his own (Acts 18:2).

PRISCA AND AQUILA

Like Paul, Prisca and Aquila were tentmakers, and Aquila, at least, was a Jewish person of the diaspora.[50] All three of them had also recently arrived in Corinth.

A Cool Reception in Athens and Laying a Foundation in Corinth

Prisca and Aquila had come from Rome, where the emperor Claudius just a few months earlier (in AD 49) had issued a command expelling "all the Jews" from the city (Acts 18:2). Tiberius had issued a similar decree in AD 19, and Claudius had restricted Jewish meetings in Rome when he first came to power in AD 41. Both emperors seem to have been concerned to show how devoted they were to traditional Roman religion and customs by expelling religious groups of eastern origin.[51] So, when unrest sprang up among Jewish people in Rome over someone whom the Roman historian Suetonius called "Chrestus," Claudius once again issued an anti-Jewish edict in which "he expelled them from Rome" (*Claud.* 25.4 [Rolfe, LCL]).[52] Although it is unlikely that all Jews actually left, enough had to go for Claudius to make his public relations point, and Prisca and Aquila were among them (Acts 18:2).[53]

Prisca and Aquila were almost certainly already Christians when they set out for Corinth, especially if, as Suetonius hints, the order of expulsion originated in the connection between Judaism and Christianity. Not only do they seem to have supported Paul's mission to the synagogue in Corinth (Acts 18:3–4), but Luke says nothing of their conversion, and when he next mentions them in the narrative, they are Paul's traveling companions and coworkers, able to instruct ill-informed Christians in "the way of God more accurately" (Acts 18:18–19, 26). Similarly, when Paul lists the people whom he baptized in Corinth, he says nothing about Prisca and Aquila (1 Cor 1:14–16).

Twice in his letters Paul mentions that an assembly of Christians meets in the couple's house. Writing from Corinth to Christians in Rome, he sends greetings not only to Prisca and Aquila, who have by this time returned there, but to "the church in their house" (Rom 16:3–5).[54] Similarly, writing from Ephesus to Corinth, he sends greetings from Aquila and Prisca "together with the church in their house" (1 Cor 16:19). This means that in both Rome and Ephesus, Prisca and Aquila could afford accommodations large enough for an assembly of Christians to meet there. It seems likely that in Corinth too they accommodated Paul and eventually an assembly of Christians in their new home.

This does not mean that Prisca and Aquila were affluent. They may well have rented space that doubled both as a workshop and a residence. If their house was like some other commercial and domestic spaces from the area just east of the city's theater, it might have had a door or window open to the street, with living and sleeping space either at the back of the shop or in an upstairs area.⁵⁵ Customers probably entered the workshop through a door where they could see its employees, such as Paul, producing awnings, canopies, and tents and could perhaps survey some of the finished products.⁵⁶

Hard Work Yields New Growth

From Paul's perspective the work was hard and the hours long. We can probably imagine Paul and his companions working six days a week cutting and sewing linen and leather, selling their products to customers, taking orders, and keeping the books. At the end of a list of the hardships he has had to endure as an apostle, Paul tells the Corinthians, "We labor, working with our own hands," right after the hunger, thirst, shabby clothing, beatings, and homelessness he has had to endure (1 Cor 4:10–12; cf. 2 Cor 6:5; 11:23).⁵⁷ In another list, after mentioning the "toil and hardship" that marked his service as an apostle, he continues with "many a sleepless night" (2 Cor 11:27). This statement is reminiscent of his comment to the Thessalonians that when he was with them, he "worked night and day, that we might not be a burden to any of you" (1 Thess 2:9; cf. 2 Thess 3:8).

They must have all been grateful when the Sabbath arrived, and they could enjoy both rest from their hard labor and the opportunity that synagogue meetings offered for discussions of the gospel. Luke says that some of the people in the synagogue found Paul persuasive, and among them were not only Jews but also Greeks (Acts 18:4). Just as with Paul's ministry in Thessalonica, there is no need to think of the "Greeks" in the synagogue as having already abandoned their worship of traditional Greek and Roman gods. Apart from their full conversion to Judaism, they were welcome in the synagogue as inquirers, just as unbelieving inquirers were later welcome in Christian assemblies in Corinth (1 Cor 14:23–25). This may explain why Paul's letter addresses a church that is mainly non-Jewish but that, according to Luke, originated in the synagogue. At this early point in Paul's ministry, these new Corinthian Christians, both Jewish and Greek, seem to have remained within the synagogue. Perhaps, in addition, they met separately with each other in the workshop of Prisca and Aquila "on the first day of every week" (1 Cor 16:2).

A Cool Reception in Athens and Laying a Foundation in Corinth

Later, when Paul reflected on these early days of his ministry in Corinth, he commented on the distinctly unimpressive nature of his oratorical abilities, at least compared to the usual fare available in the busy, cosmopolitan city of Corinth: "And I, when I came to you, brothers, did not come proclaiming to you the testimony of God with lofty speech or wisdom. For I decided to know nothing among you except Jesus Christ and him crucified. And I was with you in weakness and in fear and much trembling, and my speech and my message were not in plausible words of wisdom, but in demonstration of the Spirit and of power, so that your faith might not rest in the wisdom of men but in the power of God" (1 Cor 2:1–5). Perhaps as Paul wrote these words, he remembered his arrival in Corinth in a state of physical exhaustion after a lonely, difficult, and marginally productive ministry in Athens. Perhaps he remembered how difficult it was to carry on intelligent discussions in the synagogue after working hard all week in the workshop, or to preach the gospel in the workshop early the following morning before it opened for business. He may also have had in mind the professional orators that entertained crowds and gathered awestruck students around them in Corinth and how modest his own oratorical abilities were by comparison.[58]

He definitely remembered that the people who were interested in the gospel were not impressive intellectually, socially, or spiritually: "Consider your calling, brothers: not many of you were wise according to worldly standards, not many were powerful, not many were of noble birth. But God chose what is foolish in the world to shame the wise; God chose what is weak in the world to shame the strong; God chose what is low and despised in the world, even things that are not, to bring to nothing things that are, so that no human being might boast in the presence of God" (1 Cor 1:26–29). When he first preached the gospel in Corinth, he had to begin at the most elementary level. "I fed you with milk," he tells them, "not solid food, for you were not ready for it" (1 Cor 3:2).

Despite these many inadequacies, both in himself and in his audience, God had established an assembly in Corinth of those who believed the good news. The God of Israel had made a new covenant with his people (1 Cor 11:25), a covenant that cut across ethnic lines to include both Jews and gentiles (10:32) and across social lines to include both the few who were powerful and nobly born and the many who, as far as the world outside the church was concerned, were low and despised.

CHAPTER 11

The beginning of an assembly of God's newly created people in such unpromising circumstances was a sign to Paul that this church could only have come into being by God's power and grace. Perhaps it was the hard labor involved that first suggested to Paul metaphors drawn from the worlds of farming and building to describe the Corinthian church. He had "planted" the church and "laid" its "foundation" (1 Cor 3:6, 10), but Paul followed these metaphors with important qualifiers pointing to God's power. God both gave the church its growth and gave to Paul the ability to lay its foundation skillfully (1 Cor 3:7, 9).

By this time, the Corinthian church was only one of many churches that God had used Paul and his coworkers to "plant" and "found." Multiethnic churches now also existed in Syria, Cilicia, Cyprus, southern Galatia, and Macedonia. Silas, Timothy, Luke, Prisca, and Aquila were all helpful coworkers who aided Paul in nurturing these new communities of Jesus followers. When Paul received a disturbing report of developments among the churches scattered across southern Galatia, however, it probably became clear that he needed to add literary resources to his human helpers as a means of encouraging these churches to remain faithful to the gospel.

12

An Urgent Letter from Corinth to Christians in Galatia

Paul stayed in Corinth at least a year and a half (Acts 18:11, 18), the longest period he had spent in any one place since he and Barnabas had first ventured forth from Antioch to take the gospel westward. It was during this time that the apostle may have first found it necessary to use some means other than his coworkers to nurture the new communities of Christians he had left behind. Like other people of his time, he used letters for a task like this.

LETTER WRITING IN THE ROMAN EAST AND PAUL'S LETTER TO THE GALATIANS

People wrote letters for many different reasons in Paul's time. They wrote with news of themselves, or to ask for news from friends and family. They wrote letters of recommendation. They wrote to give instructions and ask questions about instructions given, or because they needed something. They wrote to send love and greetings, to extend sympathy, or to instill courage in difficult times.[1] One, more specific, reason for letter writing was to provide authority and direction in an emergency that the writer could not tend to personally because of his or her distance from the letter's recipient.

At some point in the second century AD, for example, an Egyptian man named Diogenes received a letter from a "dear friend" named Apollogenes with questions about how to manage Diogenes's land. Diogenes wrote back, annoyed: "A thousand times I've written to you to cut down the vines at Phai [?], as Demetrius the gymnasiarch and Adrastus and Sotas decided. But today again I get a letter from you asking what I want done. To which I reply: cut them down, cut them down, cut them down, cut them down, cut them down: there you are, I say it again and again."[2]

A few lines later, Diogenes expresses astonishment that Apollogenes needed three yoked animals for irrigating another vineyard whose yield was too small for that much attention: "I am astonished [Θαυμάζω]," he says, "if there is a need for three yokes for the irrigation of the vineyard in Chalothis!"[3] At the end of the letter, he took the pen from the scribe to whom he was dictating it and added in his own unsteady hand some comments about receiving a container of olive oil and about some "other things" that he wanted Apollogenes to keep safe until he arrived.[4] He concluded on a friendly note: "Farewell, my dear friend Apollogenes."[5]

Like so many other letter writers from antiquity, when Paul wrote Galatians, he wanted to be there in person, but he was too far away. "I wish I could be present with you and change my tone," he tells them, "for I am perplexed about you" (Gal 4:20). Like Diogenes, he had received some upsetting news: "I am astonished [Θαυμάζω] that you are so quickly deserting him who called you in the grace of Christ and are turning to a different gospel" (Gal 1:6).[6] He could not understand the obtuseness of his readers: "O foolish Galatians! Who has bewitched you?" (Gal 3:1). Like Diogenes, he found it necessary to repeat himself (Gal 1:8–9; 5:2–3). Yet, just as Diogenes considered Apollogenes a "dear friend," Paul had deep affection for the Galatian Christians, whom he considered his "little children" (Gal 4:19). He closed his letter to them, just as Diogenes did, with a sentence in his own ungainly writing: "See with what large letters I am writing to you with my own hand" (Gal 6:11).[7] This provided a personal touch just as it did in Diogenes's letter. For Paul, however, it also authenticated the letter, assuring its audience that this missive described the gospel as Paul the apostle understood it.[8]

The stakes were quite different for Paul than they were for Diogenes. Paul had no interest in making his own financial affairs more efficient and profitable. He hoped to rescue the relationship of his readers to the one true God who had created the universe and was now beginning to re-create it through the Lord Jesus Christ (Gal 1:4; 6:15). With its world-encompassing concerns, then, Paul's letter is much longer and more rhetorically sophisticated than most private letters from antiquity.

Was Galatians Paul's First Letter?

The great scholar Theodor Zahn made a persuasive case in the late nineteenth century that 1 Thessalonians provides a hint about when Paul wrote Galatians. Zahn believed that Paul wrote Galatians from Corinth after the visit of a group of people from Galatia but before Timothy and Silas arrived in Corinth from Macedonia (Acts 18:5).[9] He argued that Paul almost certainly wrote 1 Thessalonians from Corinth, not long after leaving Athens (1 Thess 3:1) and shortly after Timothy's arrival in Corinth with news of how the Thessalonians were doing (Acts 18:5; cf. 1 Thess 3:6).[10] Near that letter's beginning, Paul commends the Thessalonians for their perseverance in the faith despite the difficulties they have experienced. They have served as an example to believers not only in their own region, Paul says, but even farther afield: "The word of the Lord has sounded forth from you not only in Macedonia and Achaia, but *in every place* your faith in God has become known, so that we have no need to speak about it. For the people of those regions report about us what kind of welcome we had among you, and how you turned to God from idols, to serve a living and true God" (1 Thess 1:8–9 NRSV, emphasis added).

Zahn argued that Paul speaks here of a group of believers outside Macedonia and Achaia ("in every place"), and that this group is most reasonably identified at this point in Paul's work with the churches of Pisidian Antioch, Derbe, Iconium, and Timothy's home town of Lystra, all located in the southern part of the Roman province of Galatia.[11] If this identification is correct, then Paul likely heard not only good news about the Thessalonians from the Galatian Christians, but distressing news about the Galatians themselves. It is unlikely that this information came from Timothy because Paul never mentions Timothy in his letter to the Galatians, and that would be odd if he was with Paul at the time he wrote. Not only was Timothy from Lystra in southern Galatia, and well known to Christians in the region (Acts 16:1–2), but Paul mentions him (and Silas) at the beginning of both letters to Thessalonica.[12] So, Zahn reasoned, Paul probably wrote Galatians before the arrival of Timothy and Silas in Corinth (Acts 18:5), and the Thessalonian letters after their arrival.[13]

Another piece of evidence from the Thessalonian correspondence tends to confirm Zahn's approach. At the end of 2 Thessalonians, Paul authenticated his letter with a few words in his own handwriting, just as he did in Galatians (6:11) and 1 Thessalonians (5:27):[14] "I, Paul, write this greeting with my own hand. This is the sign of genuineness in every letter [ἐν πάσῃ ἐπιστολῇ] of mine; it is the way I write" (2 Thess 3:17). The reference to "every letter" would be more natural if Paul had not only written 1 Thessalonians before 2 Thessalonians but written a second previous letter with an authenticating signature. If he wrote Galatians, 1 Thessalonians, and 2 Thessalonians from Corinth during this initial stay in the city, then his other letter would have to be Galatians.

The Circumstances That Prompted Paul to Write

Paul, then, probably decided to write the letter during the first part of his first stay in Corinth, while he was working hard with Prisca and Aquila and after hearing from a group of Christians from southern Galatia about a distressing development in the churches there. During the recent journey of Paul and Silas through southern Galatia, they had communicated the decision of the Jerusalem Council to the various assemblies of Christians in the region (Acts 16:4). They probably thought that if the same people who had insisted on circumcision for gentile Christians in Syria and Cilicia (Acts 15:1; Gal 2:3–5), or people under their influence, made their way west to the Christian assemblies in southern Galatia, the decrees of the Jerusalem Council would guard against their arguments.[15] The Jerusalem leaders had already decided against the necessity of circumcision for gentiles and had issued instructions that would make the fellowship of Jewish and gentile Christians more palatable to Jewish Christians (Acts 15:29; cf. 15:20; 21:25).

Paul now learned, however, that, just as in his disagreement with Peter and Barnabas at Antioch after the Jerusalem Council (Gal 2:11–14), the Council's decision and its decrees were not successful in guarding against misunderstanding and in keeping the peace and unity of the church. People teaching a distorted form of the gospel were now "intimidating" these churches (1:7; cf. 5:10, 12, my trans.) telling them that they must live by the Jewish law to be in a right relationship with God (2:15–16).[16] This included adopting the Jewish calendar (4:10), observing circumcision (5:2), and, probably, keeping the law's dietary requirements (2:12). Basically, their argument was that these gentile Christians must become Jewish to belong to God's people.

The troublemakers' intimidation tactics probably involved shutting gentile Christians in the Galatian churches out of table fellowship with themselves (Gal 4:17), just as the Jewish Christians in Antioch had once withdrawn from table fellowship with gentile Christians in that city (Gal 2:12–13). They probably used this tactic to apply social pressure to the Galatian gentiles to adopt their position (Gal 4:17; cf. Acts 15:24). Paul claims that the troublemakers' motivation for all this was to avoid persecution (Gal 6:12), but from Paul's perspective, their tactics were *inflicting* persecution on genuine Christians (Gal 4:29).

Part of the troublemakers' appeal to the Galatian Christians may have been that, by becoming Jewish, these gentiles would regularize their social status and prevent the sort of hardship they had experienced when Paul and Barnabas had preached to them the gospel without circumcision (cf. Acts 13:50; 14:5, 19, 22). If they became Jewish Christians, the false teachers must have said, then, like other Jews, they would be exempt from any expectation to participate in the imperial cult.

The imperial cult was firmly established in this area.[17] Temples dedicated to Augustus and his family dotted the landscape of southern Galatia in the mid-first century. This included the massive temple in Pisidian Antioch with its recent addition of a triple-arched gateway dedicated to the emperor Claudius in AD 50.[18] Worship of the emperors was an important form of political diplomacy by which both the Romans and the native populations whom they controlled recognized the legitimacy and inevitability of Roman rule. The eminent historian of Anatolia, Stephen Mitchell, in describing the effect of Claudius's triple-arched gateway, puts it this way: "This massive and symmetrical design provides one of the most notable examples of the transformation of civic space, whereby imperial buildings literally took over and dominated the urban landscape, thus symbolizing unequivocally the central position that emperor worship occupied in city life, and the overwhelming manner in which the emperor dominated the world view of his subjects."[19]

Gentile Christians in the region who had little or no connection to the synagogue might easily find themselves in trouble with family and neighbors if they suddenly began refusing to observe the "days and months and seasons and years" that marked the calendar of the imperial cult (Gal 4:10).[20] By adopting Jewish customs alongside their newfound faith in Christ, however, they would have a place to fit in religiously, and at least some of the offense would fall away.[21]

The troublemakers seem to have incorporated into their arguments an attack on Paul's qualifications and integrity. Much of the first major section of Paul's letter is a defense of himself (Gal 1:10–2:14), and isolated statements toward the letter's end seem to arise from accusations against him (5:11; 6:17). He describes in detail his relationship with the apostles in Jerusalem. He insists that the gospel he preached, and his authority to preach it, came from God rather than from them (1:1, 11–24; 2:6). At the same time, he makes clear that they and he preached the same gospel and agreed with each other at the Jerusalem Council on its essential tenets (2:7–10, 14). The letter also denies that he was willing to compromise the truth to please people (1:10; cf. 6:17), and it denies he once preached the same circumcision-oriented gospel as the false teachers (5:11).

Where did these troublemakers come from? They were probably the same Jewish Christians who had originally traveled from Judea to Syria and Cilicia pressuring Christians in those regions to adopt circumcision (Acts 15:1, 23). Although Paul had not yielded to this idea for a moment (Gal 2:5; Acts 15:12), and the apostles in Jerusalem had also rejected it (Gal 2:9; Acts 15:28–29), the circumcision movement did not disappear.[22] Members of the movement probably followed the path of Paul and Silas westward to Derbe, Lystra, Iconium, and Pisidian Antioch. By the time that a group of believers from these towns decided to make their way to Paul and ask for his help, many Galatian Christians were on the verge of capitulating to the false teachers (Gal 4:9–11, 21; 5:4), and nasty divisions had arisen (Gal 5:26).

Paul was puzzled about why so many Christians in southern Galatia found these false teachers persuasive. Why had he become their enemy? Why was he having to go through the anguish of giving birth to these Christian communities once again (Gal 4:16–19)? He wished he could be there with them in person to deal with the problems that the false teachers had created (4:20), but, as with so many problems in the mid-first-century Roman Empire, a letter of instruction would have to suffice.

An Urgent Letter from Corinth to Christians in Galatia

Paul's Response

Paul's letter is a spirited defense both of his own integrity and of the gospel that he and Barnabas had originally preached in southern Galatia.[23] His point throughout is that from the time of his conversion to the present time, his life had been intertwined with the one true gospel (Gal 1:11–2:14). This was the same form of the gospel that God had revealed to him at his conversion (1:11–17) and that Christians in Judea and the leaders of the Jerusalem church, who knew Jesus personally, also proclaimed (1:18–19, 23; 2:6–10). At the center of this gospel was the principle that God, as an act of his free grace, had dealt with the rebellion of his creatures against him and put them right with himself through the death of his Son, the Messiah, Jesus. The only requirement on their part was trust that God had, in fact, done this (2:15–21). Close to the center of this same gospel, and as an inevitable consequence of it (2:14), lay the principle that a right standing with God was available not only to the Jewish people but to anyone, including gentiles, willing to turn away from worshiping any other gods (4:8–9) and to turn toward the one true God in the belief that God would make them right with himself through the atoning death of Jesus, the Messiah (1:16; 2:2–3; 3:6–9, 22, 27–29).

All this was not only consistent with the Jewish Scriptures, Paul argued, but a necessary fulfillment of them. Abraham, the forefather of the Jewish people, received a right standing with God through faith (Gal 3:6; cf. Gen 15:6). Abraham's faith, moreover, was in God's ability and willingness to fulfill his promise to bless "all the nations" through him (Gal 3:8; cf. Gen 18:18). God was in the process of fulfilling that very promise by including gentiles within his people through faith just as Abraham had received a right standing with God by faith (Gal 3:6, 9).

The "different gospel" that had invaded southern Galatia, however, was inconsistent with the Jewish Scriptures at precisely the two critical points of the true gospel: inclusion within God's people by trusting in God's grace through Christ on one hand and the inclusion of the gentiles, as gentiles, within God's people on the other hand. All Jewish people should know from their own Scriptures, Paul argued, that keeping the Jewish law could play no role in a right standing before God: "We are Jews by nature and not sinners from among the Gentiles; nevertheless knowing that a man is not

CHAPTER 12

justified by the works of the Law but through faith in Christ Jesus, even we have believed in Christ Jesus, so that we may be justified by faith in Christ and not by the works of the Law; since by the works of the Law no flesh will be justified [δικαιωθήσεται]" (Gal 2:15–16 NASB). The last clause in this statement alludes to Psalm 143:2 (142:2 LXX), "No one living will be counted righteous [δικαιωθήσεται] before you", and this allusion hints that all Jewish people should know from their Psalter that doing what the Mosaic law requires does not put anyone in a right relationship with God.

Later in the letter, Paul explains from the Jewish Scriptures why this is true (Gal 3:10–13). The law gives life to those who do it and pronounces a curse on those who do not live by everything in it (Lev 18:5; Deut 27:26). The law, for example, pronounces a curse on the executed criminal whose body, after execution, is hung on a tree (Deut 21:23). Paul might also have pointed to the lengthy narration in the Mosaic law of the ways God would punish his people if they disobeyed the law (Lev 26:14–39; Deut 28:15–68).[24] Perhaps he intended his audience, familiar as they were with the Jewish Scriptures, to recall such prominent passages in the law. In any case, he argues that the prophet Habakkuk had said that those who are righteous by faith will live (Hab 2:4). These Scriptures imply that although no one can keep the law fully and avoid its curse (cf. Ps 143:2), God, in his mercy, puts people in a right standing with himself by their faith in him. What becomes of the law's curse? Christ absorbed it when he was "hung" on the "tree" of the cross. The death of Christ brought the curse of the Mosaic law to an end, and in this sense at least brought the law itself to an end.

The death of Christ also brought the law to an end in the sense that it formed a barrier between God's people, Israel, and the other nations of the earth (Gal 3:14). The Mosaic law was in effect for a time to make crystal clear that all people, even Israel, were in rebellion against God (3:19, 22), but it was only in effect "until Christ came," so that a right standing with God might come by faith (3:24–25) and be available to everyone, not just to Israelites whose social boundaries were marked out by the Mosaic law. In this way, God had started to fulfill his promise to Abraham in the preaching of the gospel to the gentiles (3:26–29). The era of a new creation had begun (6:15) with its promise of return to the harmony between God's creatures that reflected their peaceful coexistence with God and each other in the garden after their creation (Gen 2:8, 15–23; 3:8a).

If gentile believers in southern Galatia now came back under the law as if conversion to Judaism were a requirement for a right standing with God, they rejected the sufficiency of Christ's death to accomplish this task (Gal 5:2–4; cf. 2:21). This not only meant rejecting the grace of God revealed in Christ's death but also coming back under the law's just curse on those who were in rebellion against God. Under these circumstances, the Galatians were no better off than when they had worshiped idols (4:9; cf. 2:18). The results of this backpedaling for their relationships with each other were hardly consistent with the peace and harmony of the new creation: "But if you bite and devour one another, watch out," Paul says, "that you are not consumed by one another" (5:15; cf. 5:19–21, 26).[25]

GALATIANS AS A SUMMARY OF PAUL'S LONG-STANDING THEOLOGICAL CONVICTIONS

Beginning in the early twentieth century, some interpreters of Paul's letters have thought that Paul's description of his understanding of the gospel in this letter is buried beneath layers of specifically Jewish argument that have obscured his real convictions. In the thinking of William Wrede, for example, Paul's real gospel did not center on a biblically based understanding of transgression, atoning sacrifice, and justification but began with the idea that all humanity lay under the cosmic dominion of sin, and the dominion of sin led to death for everyone. The divine Christ redeemed humanity from this cosmic power and its consequences by his own assumption of human flesh, his death, and his resurrection. Paul's gospel was simply that people should believe these truths and be baptized into the new community of people who believed them.[26]

Since in Galatians and Romans Paul was debating with people under the influence of Judaism, the theory goes, he tried to win them back over to his side by framing his argument in terms they would find familiar. His heavy engagement with Scripture, his talk of justification through faith and not by works of the law, and his focus on the substitutionary nature of Christ's death were not at the heart of his gospel but were instead rhetorical efforts to win an argument by using Jewish terms and concepts.[27] Other interpreters have described the nature of Paul's argument about justification by faith apart from works of the law in Galatians in ways that are structurally similar to Wrede's analysis, despite deviating from Wrede in some of the details.[28]

This understanding of Paul's description of the gospel in Galatians, however, is not persuasive from a historical perspective. Paul's explanation of the gospel in Galatians 2:15–16 as justification through faith in Jesus Christ and not by works of the law defines the phrase "the gospel" as he has used it up to this point in the letter. This is the gospel that Jesus Christ revealed to him at his conversion (Gal 1:11–12), that he preached for fourteen years before the Jerusalem Council (2:1–2), and to which the leaders of the Jerusalem church added nothing (2:6). If many Jewish Christians, including Cephas and Barnabas, retreated from its social implications in Antioch, they did so not because they had renounced its truth but because they acted in ways that were inconsistent with what both Paul and they knew to be the gospel (2:13–14). The gospel summarized in the principle "a person is not justified by works of the law but through faith in Jesus Christ" is something that all Jewish Christians should embrace (2:15).

There is a hint, moreover, in Paul's citation and explanation of Deuteronomy 21:23 ("Cursed is everyone who is hanged on a tree") in Galatians 3:13 that his convictions about the substitutionary and atoning nature of Christ's death were central to his presentation of the gospel from the first. The understanding of Jesus's death that lies beneath Paul's use of this text probably goes back to the earliest Jewish-Christian community and is part of what Paul claims he received from that community (1 Cor 15:3) and considered foundational common ground (Gal 2:6–9).

Deuteronomy 21:22–23 regulates a gruesome ancient Near Eastern custom of impaling the dead bodies of executed criminals and allowing them to hang in the open to be devoured by wild animals (e.g., Gen 40:19). The public nature of this act would shame the family or tribe of the person executed and was probably thought to deter crime (Josh 8:29; 10:26; Esth 5:14 [LXX]; 6:4).[29] In its full form, the text Paul cites reads this way: "And if a man has committed a crime punishable by death and he is put to death, and you hang him on a tree, his body shall not remain all night on the tree, but you shall bury him the same day, for a hanged man is cursed by God. You shall not defile your land that the LORD your God is giving you for an inheritance" (Deut 21:22–23).

Jewish interpreters of Scripture had applied this text to crucifixion well before Paul's time (11Q19 LXIV, 6–13; 4Q169 3–4 I, 7–8 [cf. Josephus, *A.J.* 13.380]).[30] Moreover, the Jewish leaders who plotted Jesus's death were concerned to bury him before nightfall on the day of his crucifixion (John 19:31), which was unusual for victims of crucifixion. This shows that they interpreted Jesus's crucifixion through the lens of Deuteronomy 21:23 ("His body shall not remain all night on the tree").[31] It is reasonable to conclude that they thought of Jesus as a false prophet who tried to lead Israel astray (Luke 23:2, 14), and they thought of this as a capital crime that deserved God's curse (Deut 13:5).[32]

Luke's description of Peter's preaching in the earliest days of the church pictures him as also using this text, but now as part of a message that the Jewish leadership had *unjustly* killed Jesus by "hanging him on a tree" (Acts 5:30; 10:39). God had shown through Jesus's resurrection and exaltation that Jesus was who he claimed to be (Acts 5:31; 10:40).[33] Close on the heels of these two references to Jesus's undeserved death by hanging and subsequent exaltation, Peter mentions the availability now of "forgiveness of sins" (Acts 5:31; 10:43).[34]

The idea that the curse of God fell on Jesus in the place of sinners is not explicit in these passages, but it is a short step from the collection of these elements in Peter's preaching to Paul's claim in Galatians 3:10–13 that Jesus suffered under the curse that violators of the law deserved. Deuteronomy 27:26, which Paul quotes in Galatians 3:10, appropriately summarizes the theme of Deuteronomy 27:9–28:68 that God's curse rests on those who violate the Mosaic law, and that the history of Israel shows the nation has violated this law.[35] If Jesus died unjustly under God's curse, Paul concluded, then he died in place of those who deserved God's curse, taking the punishment they deserved for them.

Although Paul would have preached this biblical form of the gospel in a different way to a non-Jewish audience than to a Jewish audience, he must have preached its basic principles in the same way. He understood the Bible to teach that everyone (not merely the Jewish person) who violated the Mosaic law was under God's curse and needed Christ's redemption from that curse.[36] Deuteronomy 27:26 says, "Cursed be *everyone* [πᾶς] who does not abide by all things written in the Book of the Law, and do them" (emphasis mine).

This was the gospel that Paul preached, therefore, when he and Silas came to southern Galatia. According to Luke, Paul alluded to Deuteronomy 21:22–23 when he preached the gospel in the synagogue in Pisidian Antioch.[37] People living in Jerusalem and their rulers, Paul says, asked Pilate to execute Jesus. Then, he was taken "down from the tree [ξύλου]" and placed in a tomb (Acts 13:29). Roman writers occasionally referred to a cross as a "tree" (Seneca, *Ep.* 101.14; Cicero, *Rab. Perd.* 4.13), but there is no doubt that Luke's other two references to Jesus's death on a "tree" reflect Deuteronomy 21:22 (Acts 5:30; 10:39), and this third and final reference is likely an echo of those two prior references.[38]

Paul proceeds in language that echoes Peter's message after alluding to this text, referring to God raising Jesus from the dead after he was removed from "the tree" (Acts 13:30; cf. 5:31a). Paul gives this announcement near the end of his sermon: "Let it be known to you therefore, brothers, that through this man forgiveness of sins is proclaimed to you, and by him everyone who believes is freed from everything from which you could not be freed by the law of Moses" (Acts 13:38–40; cf. 5:31b). This sounds very much like Luke's version of Paul's understanding of Jesus's redemptive work in Galatians 3:10–13. The death of Jesus on the "tree," followed by his resurrection, has led to the offer of the forgiveness of sins and freedom from problems that the Mosaic law could not solve.

Paul had originally preached this gospel of Christ crucified in unmistakable terms when he and Silas came to Galatia after the Jerusalem Council (Gal 3:1). His letter was now an urgent effort to preach that same gospel again, but in a form specifically designed to refute Jewish-Christian teachers who had refused to accept the conciliatory terms of the Jerusalem Council.

13

Urgent Letters to Thessalonica and Overcoming Opposition in Corinth

Writing to the Corinthians several years after leaving Corinth, Paul says that at some point during this first stay in the city, he fell into need (2 Cor 11:9). Perhaps business declined at the tent and awning shop where he worked with Aquila and Prisca (Acts 18:2–3) or his teaching in the local synagogue began to consume more of the productive hours of the week and ate into his income (Acts 18:4).

Whatever the reason, his convictions about staying in the labor force of the communities where he worked kept him from asking the new Christian assembly in Corinth for monetary help. He would continue to present "the gospel free of charge" and set an example of the importance of productive work for the Corinthians (1 Cor 9:18; 2 Cor 11:7; 2 Thess 3:9), although this meant "toil and hardship, through many a sleepless night" and, when business was slow, going without food and proper clothing (cf. 2 Cor 11:27).

In addition, during this period of his ministry he experienced "the daily pressure ... of ... anxiety for all the churches" (2 Cor 11:28). "Who is weak," he says, "and I am not weak? Who is made to fall, and I am not indignant?" (11:29). Certainly, he became indignant when the Galatian Christians were "made to fall." But what about Christians in Macedonia, particularly the Thessalonians? Paul was also worried about them.

On one hand, believers from elsewhere in Macedonia and Achaia and even further afield had given him encouraging reports about the Thessalonians' steadfastness. They were continuing not only to trust the gospel they had heard from Paul but to spread it to other regions (1 Thess 1:7–10).[1]

They were standing steadfastly by their commitment to worship the one God through his coming Son, Jesus (1 Thess 1:9b–10). They did this, moreover, within a social context where their neighbors could interpret their refusal to participate in rituals of religious devotion to the traditional Greek gods and to the Julio-Claudian family as a threat to the security and prosperity of the city (Acts 17:6–7; 1 Thess 5:3).[2]

On the other hand, Paul had been unable to cover some secondary but important aspects of the Christian faith during his short stay with these young believers. He had sent Timothy back to them from Athens to help with this problem (1 Thess 3:2), but he still had a strong desire to see them himself and make sure that their understanding of the faith was not "lacking" (3:10).

A Letter of Self-Defense and Instruction to the Thessalonians

For more than one reason, then, he must have been relieved when Silas and Timothy arrived in Corinth from Macedonia (Acts 18:5). He had probably not seen Silas since leaving him in Berea (Acts 17:14). He had not seen Timothy since sending him from Athens back to Thessalonica "to establish and exhort" the Thessalonian Christians in their faith (1 Thess 3:1–5). Now that they were all together again, his two coworkers could join him in the work of teaching the new Christians in Corinth about Jesus (2 Cor 1:19). Silas and Timothy also brought monetary gifts from the Christian assemblies in Macedonia, and these gifts took the place of Paul's lost wages (2 Cor 11:8–9). Perhaps most important to the worried Paul was Timothy's "good news," that the Thessalonian Christians' "faith and love" were intact, as well as their kind feelings toward him (1 Thess 3:6). Perhaps it was the ability of Silas and Timothy to do some of the teaching in Corinth, and the easier work schedule that the funds from Macedonia probably provided, that gave Paul time to write to the Thessalonians and address some of their deficits in understanding their new faith (1 Thess 3:10).[3]

Just as his letter to the Galatians addressed his unfairly tarnished reputation before moving to detailed argument against the false teachers, so in 1 Thessalonians, Paul wanted first to clear up any possible misunderstanding about his integrity before instructing the Thessalonians on several important theological points. In his opening prayer of thanksgiving to God for the

Thessalonian Christians, he briefly reminded them "what kind of persons we proved to be among you for your sake" (1 Thess 1:5 NRSV), and he then devoted the first major part of his letter to a defense of his character (2:1–12).

He insisted that he spoke candidly when he declared the gospel to them (1 Thess 2:2), that his appeal to them arose from neither error nor impurity nor deceit (2:3), and that his speech was designed not to please people but God (2:4). He "never came with words of flattery ... nor with a pretext for greed" (2:5).[4] He sought glory from no one (2:6), worked hard night and day in order not to be a financial burden on them (2:9), and lived among them in a holy, righteous, and blameless way (2:10). He treated them the way loving parents treat their children (2:7–8, 11), and not, he seems to imply, the way fake philosophers, only interested in their own fame and the money of their audience, treat those who listen to them.

He left them involuntarily, like a child torn from his mother or father, and left them only physically, not emotionally (1 Thess 2:17). That is why he sent Timothy to them from Athens (3:1–5) and was so relieved when Timothy appeared with his good news about the state of their faith and love (3:6).

He also had some concerns, however, and so, like a good friend, he devoted a large section of the letter to these anxieties.[5] First, he wanted the Thessalonian Christians, who were mainly gentiles, to know that they were, in a sense, no longer gentiles. They were now part of the people of God and needed to live in ways that demonstrated their separation from the rest of the world around them (1 Thess 4:4–5, 7), just as God had required ancient Israel to separate itself from the surrounding nations in their sexual ethics (Lev 18:1–30). God had now given to the Thessalonian Christians, whatever their ethnicity, the Spirit that Ezekiel had prophesied God would give "into" his people at the time of their restoration, providing them with an interior transformation that would enable them to keep his commands (1 Thess 4:8; cf. Ezek 36:27; 37:6, 14 LXX).[6]

Second, he wanted to correct misunderstanding about the status of believers who had already died (1 Thess 4:13–18). Apart from Jews, people in the Greco-Roman world did not believe in an embodied afterlife. Some thought that death led to a shadowy, unpleasant existence, and others that life after death could be pleasant precisely because it was divorced from the pain and suffering of an embodied existence. Many people simply thought that death led to extinction and left memorial stones engraved with an abbreviation for the ditty, "I wasn't, I was, I am not, I don't care."[7] Outside Jewish thought, the resurrection of the dead into an embodied, immortal existence was unknown.[8]

Some among the Thessalonian Christians, therefore, seem to have believed that unless they were living at the time of Jesus's coming, they would miss out completely on the salvation Jesus would bring. If some Thessalonian Christians had already died, perhaps those who remained began to wonder if God had punished the deceased with death and whether the living too would fall under his wrath when the day of the Lord came like a thief in the night (1 Thess 5:1–3).[9]

Paul's response must have seemed as strange to most Thessalonian Christians as the notion of the resurrection had seemed a few months earlier to his audience of philosophers at the Athenian Areopagus (Acts 17:32). The dead would not miss out on the future saving work of the Lord Jesus Christ. Rather, they were still "in Christ" and would rise to a new, immortal life at Christ's coming. The remainder of God's people who had not yet died would then join these resurrected believers. Together they would process out to meet Christ and accompany him as he entered the world (1 Thess 4:15–17).[10]

Behind this description of the future existence of believers lay Paul's belief that, in some sense, their future existence had already started. God had already called the Thessalonian Christians "into his own kingdom and glory," and they were supposed to be living already in a way that was consistent with life in this new age (1 Thess 2:12).[11] When Christ came to establish his kingdom in all its fullness, therefore, he was coming into a world in rebellion against its Creator to reclaim it, and the Thessalonian Christians would be part of this transformation.[12] There was no need for them to fear the coming day of the Lord. They were "not of the darkness" but were "children of light" (5:5) and belonged "to the day" (5:8). God had not destined them for wrath, Paul assured them, "but to obtain salvation through our Lord Jesus Christ" (5:9; cf. 1:10).[13]

THE POLITICAL IMPLICATIONS OF PAUL'S TEACHING

To Paul, there was nothing unreal or shadowy about any of this. Instead, the language he uses is so this-worldly that it must have made clearer than ever the conflict between anything like the Roman political system and the future reign of the Lord Jesus Christ. The word Paul uses for the "coming" (παρουσία) of the Lord appears frequently in literature, inscriptions, and papyri to refer to the arrival of a ruler in a particular place.[14]

It sometimes referred to the advent of a rival to Roman rule in a locale where he wanted to assert his authority. Polybius, for example, tells the story of how in the early second century BC the Roman consul Gnaeus Cornelius went to King Philip V of Macedonia to urge him to make peace with Rome and to warn him against any alliance with Antiochus III of Syria: "Encountering him near Tempe," says Polybius, "he conveyed his other instructions to him and advised him to send an embassy to Rome to ask for an alliance, that they might not think he was watching for his opportunity and looking forward to the arrival [παρουσία] of Antiochus" (Polybius, *Hist.* 18.48.4 [Paton, Walbank, and Habicht, LCL]). Later, Mithridates VI, the great king of Pontus, could refer in an inscription to his invasion of Asia and war against the Romans there in 88 BC as "my coming [παρουσία]."[15]

Closer to the time of Paul, in AD 19, something similar happened with the proconsul Germanicus, the adopted son of the emperor Tiberius. Germanicus broke the custom that no high-ranking Roman should visit the province of Egypt since this might be seen as an attempt to control the grain supply and thus as a power grab (Tacitus, *Ann.* 2.59). After going to Egypt, Germanicus issued proclamations that referred both to his "visit" (παρουσία) and to how upset he was that the Egyptians had welcomed him with acclamations that were normally addressed to the gods. Those acclamations, said Germanicus, "are appropriate only to him who is actually the saviour and benefactor of the whole human race, my father, and to his mother, my grandmother."[16]

Similarly, Paul's term for the "meeting" (ἀπάντησις) of believers with the Lord could have political connotations of meeting a politically powerful dignitary before he entered a city or territory. Cicero, writing in Latin, could use the term in its Greek form to refer to "the town deputations [ἀπαντήσεις]" that would greet Julius Caesar as he arrived (*Att.* 8.16.2 [Schackleton Bailey, LCL]).[17] The Greek word, then, was well-known in the mid-first century BC as a technical term for such a meeting.[18]

It seems likely that Paul was aware of the political connotations of the terms he was using. Rather than emphatically denying the original politically charged accusation that in Thessalonica he preached "another king, Jesus" (Acts 17:7), Paul filled in the details of that claim. People in Thessalonica could have paid their rent with coins that featured Julius Caesar's crowned head on one side with the letters θΕΟΣ ("god") forming a column right in front of his nose.[19] They worshiped Augustus, "son of god," together in the same temple with the Greek god Hercules and the personification of their city, and they believed that this merger of traditional devotion with Roman devotion would encourage Roman benefaction and keep their own city safe and prosperous.[20]

Paul insisted, however, that there was only one God and one Savior. God would arrive in the person of his anointed king ("Christ") Jesus, commanding an army of angels "with a cry of command" and "the sound of a trumpet" (1 Thess 4:16). Their mission would be "salvation" (5:8–9), the reclamation of the world for God and his people. No one knew when this would happen, but it would come at a time when self-satisfied people assumed, as Roman propaganda also proclaimed, that the powerful would always have the "peace and security" their political and military institutions provided (5:2–3).[21]

Troubling Developments

There is no way to know who carried Paul's first letter to the Thessalonian Christians to its destination, or how another report on conditions in Thessalonica reached Paul, but it is likely that only a few months passed before Paul received bad news from the Christians there. This scenario assumes, however, that 2 Thessalonians is an authentic letter from Paul, and not everyone would agree with this assumption. Some interpreters of the letter have observed that its structure, expressions, and themes are like 1 Thessalonians, but then, these interpreters claim, its approach to the day of the Lord differs significantly from the approach in 1 Thessalonians.[22] Whereas 1 Thessalonians emphasizes the suddenness of the Lord's appearance on that day (5:1–11), 2 Thessalonians concentrates on the events that must precede the Lord's coming (2:1–12). Paul is unlikely to have penned them both, especially within a few months of each other.[23]

These interpreters theorize, therefore, that after Paul's death someone patterned a new letter on the old letter to correct the view that the day of the Lord had already come (2 Thess 2:2), a view that had arisen from 1 Thessalonians.[24] This person failed, however, to duplicate the "personal warmth" or intellectual energy of 1 Thessalonians.[25] The references in 2 Thessalonians to "a letter seeming to be from us" (2:2), to the necessity for work (3:6–15), and to Paul's personal signature as a sign of authenticity "in every letter of mine" (3:17), moreover, betray a time much later than Paul when pseudonymous letters (including this one) circulated in Paul's name, a time when the church needed to adapt to life in a world that had failed to end, and when Paul's letters were circulating around various churches.[26]

On scrutiny, however, this position loses much of its persuasive power. The idea that the letter lacks "warmth" and intellectual creativity is a subjective judgment with which not everyone will agree. Even assuming it is true, however, it is unclear why Paul had to write warmly and engagingly in every letter.[27] It does not seem unlikely, moreover, that Paul would write in a similar form and express himself in a similar way in two letters written within a few months of each other.[28]

The claim that Paul's eschatologies in the two letters are "contradictory" is particularly puzzling.[29] The day of the Lord will come like a thief in the night for unbelievers—those who "are saying, 'There is peace and security'" although they stand in danger of God's judgment (1 Thess 5:3). Paul is clear in 1 Thessalonians, however, that the Thessalonian Christians do not fall into this category: "But you, brothers and sisters, are not in darkness so that this day should surprise you like a thief" (5:4 NIV).[30] In 2 Thessalonians, then, he reminds them of the events that must precede the day of the Lord and for which they will be watching because they are believers (2:1–12).

The reference to Paul's authenticating signature at the end of the letter, moreover, is difficult to explain on the theory that someone wrote it in the decades after Paul's death. The statement assumes that every letter Paul has written up to the time of 2 Thessalonians also has an authenticating signature. This claim would be verifiably false, however, in the final decade of the first century when most or all of Paul's thirteen-letter corpus was well-known.[31] Most of his thirteen letters have no such authenticating signature. The statement does make sense if Paul wrote 2 Thessalonians after Galatians, which has such a signature (Gal 6:11), and after 1 Thessalonians, where the first-person reference in the letter's next to last sentence makes it likely that Paul picked up the pen to close out the letter (1 Thess 5:27). By the time Paul wrote his authenticating statement in 2 Thessalonians, he had penned three letters, and in all of them he had written part of the conclusion in his own, unprofessional but distinctive "large letters" (Gal 6:11).

Second Thessalonians, then, is very likely an authentic Pauline letter, and it provides a reasonably clear picture of what happened to the Thessalonian Christians between the two letters. The suffering of these new Christians for their commitment to the gospel had continued unabated (2 Thess 1:4). In addition, a deeply disturbing misinterpretation of Paul's teaching had arisen, perhaps based on a supposedly Spirit-led utterance about what Paul had *really* meant either through the spoken word or through his first letter: the day of the Lord had already come (2 Thess 2:2; cf. 1 Thess 5:19–21)![32] The community did not receive this as good news but as a profoundly upsetting idea. If the day of the Lord had already happened, then salvation had passed them by.[33]

Paul was unsure where this weird idea came from, but he seems to have thought that it was a misinterpretation of something he had said, whether in his original teaching in Thessalonica or in his first letter (2 Thess 2:2).[34] He had taught often in Thessalonica about the coming of "the day of the Lord" (2 Thess 2:2–3, 5).[35] This teaching, however, was extraordinarily difficult. It was based on a complex section of Scripture, Daniel 10–12, and on some teaching of Jesus that itself had a complex relationship with that passage (Mark 13:14–27; Matt 24:15–31).[36] It is easy to see how the mainly gentile Thessalonian Christians might have become confused, especially if, as with Paul's teaching on the resurrection of the dead (cf. Dan 12:2–3), he had not been able to say everything he intended to say about Daniel 10–12 before his unexpected departure from the city (1 Thess 2:17; 3:10; 4:13; cf. Acts 17:10).

The Thessalonians may well have known, for example, about Gaius Caligula's attempt about a decade earlier to set up a statue of Jupiter (or Zeus) in the Jerusalem temple.[37] Was Gaius (or Zeus) "the abomination of desolation" (Dan 9:27; 11:31; 12:11; cf. 2 Macc 6:2; Matt 24:15; Mark 13:14)? Was their own suffering for the faith the time of unprecedented suffering that Jesus had said would shortly precede the gathering of his elect "with a loud trumpet call" from the four corners of the earth (Mark 13:19, 27; Matt 24:21, 31; cf. 1 Thess 4:16)? Had he already gathered his elect and left the Thessalonian believers behind because they were not chosen?

As if this were not enough, some manual laborers in the community were taking advantage of various cultural means of avoiding work, and they were using the time and energy this freed up to make themselves a nuisance to others.[38] Paul had addressed this problem when he first came to Thessalonica (1 Thess 4:11; 2 Thess 3:6, 10), and he was still concerned about it when he wrote to them (1 Thess 4:11–12; 5:14), but the problem had persisted (2 Thess 3:6–15).

Another Letter

Paul responded to these problems with another letter designed both to comfort and to challenge the Thessalonian community. He began with comfort. He continued to thank God that their faith was growing, their love for each other increasing, and that they remained steadfast despite their heavy load of persecution and suffering (2 Thess 1:3–4). He also assured them that the day of the Lord would reveal God to be just and the Thessalonians to be beneficiaries, not victims, of his justice (1:5–12).[39] God had chosen them "as the firstfruits to be saved, through sanctification by the Spirit and belief in the truth" (2:13).

The day of the Lord, moreover, had not come as some in Thessalonica claimed. Before that day arrived, a man even more unrestrained in his lawlessness than the "contemptible person" of Daniel 11:21 must first appear. Wicked rulers such as Antiochus, Pompey, and Pontius Pilate had certainly desecrated Jerusalem and the temple before. Gaius had come close to doing it again.[40] No one, however, had yet taken his seat in God's temple, proclaimed himself to be the loftiest of all gods, and tried to prove his claim with "false signs and wonders" (2 Thess 2:4, 9).

That meant that no one had yet completely fulfilled Jesus's interpretation of Daniel's "abomination of desolation" as a person (not a pagan altar) "standing where *he* ought not to be" (Mark 13:14, emphasis added).[41] There was plenty of "lawlessness" presently at work (2 Thess 2:7), but God's restraining hand, perhaps in the form of his angel Michael, would continue to keep the worst manifestations of lawlessness in check until "the lawless one" appeared (2 Thess 2:6–7; cf. Dan 10:13; 12:1).[42] Even when that happened, however, the Lord Jesus would match the lawless one's appearance (παρουσία) with an appearance (παρουσία) of his own, and he would terminate him with a mere breath (2 Thess 2:8).

After this word of encouragement, Paul ended his letter with instructions to the Thessalonians about the necessity of work. Exactly why some Thessalonian believers were "not willing to work" (2 Thess 3:10) is unclear. It is tempting to search for a connection between this unwillingness and their misinterpretation of Paul's teaching on the day of the Lord.[43] Paul never makes that connection, however, and he says that he addressed the problem when he first preached the gospel in Thessalonica, long before misunderstandings about the day of the Lord had time to develop in his absence (2 Thess 3:7–10; 1 Thess 4:11–12).[44]

It is more likely, then, that Paul was concerned about some Thessalonian believers taking advantage of various cultural customs, such as the Roman system of patronage, to "live off someone else's crumbs," as Juvenal describes it (*Sat.* 5.1–2 [Braund, LCL]).[45] As Juvenal's satire reveals, this was a custom that would not place Christians in an attractive light with respect to the rest of society (cf. 1 Thess 4:12). Productive work for those who were able to do it, moreover, was an important expression of a theological principle that God designed human beings to engage in useful activity (Gen 2:15–16; cf. Jub. 3:15; Josephus, *A.J.* 1.38).

This was now the third time Paul had admonished the Thessalonians on this issue, and he could only regard those who refused to comply with his instructions as intentionally disorderly and rebellious. The Thessalonian Christians, he says, should stay away from those in their midst who refused to work (2 Thess 3:6, 14). This act of disassociation would result in their shame (3:14), and since the Greek and Roman cultures that dominated Thessalonica considered loss of honor disastrous, this would be a powerful incentive for the disorderly within the community to conform to Paul's teaching on work.[46] The purpose was not to make enemies of those who refused to work but to teach them just as one would teach a family member (3:15).

Opposition to Paul and a Significant, Favorable Legal Decision

Near the end of 2 Thessalonians, Paul refers briefly to the difficulty he was facing from opponents to the gospel in Corinth: "Finally, brothers, pray for us, that the word of the Lord may speed ahead and be honored, as happened among you, and that we may be delivered from wicked and evil men" (3:1–2a). This may be a reference to opposition that arose in the synagogue in Corinth during Paul's efforts to convince those in attendance that "the Christ was Jesus" (Acts 18:5–6).[47]

The idea that Jesus was the Messiah was a "stumbling block" to many Jewish people because Jesus had suffered crucifixion for his controversial approach to the Mosaic law and the temple (1 Cor 1:23; 2:2; cf., e.g., Mark 3:6; 14:58; John 5:18; Matt 27:39–40; Gos. Thom. 71), and so, in his case, crucifixion seemed to represent the punishing curse from God that he deserved (Deut 13:5; 21:22–23; Luke 23:2, 14). The view that Paul had just articulated a few months earlier in Galatians was quite different. Jesus had suffered God's curse not for his own sins but for the sins of everyone who violated the Mosaic law, Jews as well as gentiles. Trust in the necessity of his death to reconcile any human being with God was the one crucial step for entering the people of God. In Paul's view, everyone who wanted to belong to God's people, whether Jewish or gentile, had to take this step (Gal 3:10–13).

The vigor of the opposition to such ideas among some Jewish leaders in Corinth led Paul to break with the synagogue (Acts 18:6–7), and as Paul's comment in 2 Thessalonians shows, he was concerned that this opposition might hinder the gospel's spread in the city. Writing to Corinth later, he recalls how when he preached the message of "Jesus Christ and him crucified" in the city, he did so "in weakness and in fear and much trembling" (1 Cor 2:2–3).[48]

Instead of encountering a roadblock, however, the word of the Lord sped forward, perhaps in answer to the Thessalonian Christians' prayers. A gentile sympathizer with Judaism named Titius Justus provided his house next door to the synagogue as a substitute venue for Paul's teaching (Acts 18:7). Titius Justus's name probably indicates that he was a Roman citizen, and both his citizenship and his home may have helped facilitate the spread of the gospel.[49] Similarly, a synagogue leader named Crispus and his whole family believed the gospel (Acts 18:8; 1 Cor 1:14). Paul himself received an encouraging nighttime vision from the Lord assuring him that he would come to no harm as he preached the gospel and that the Lord had already set apart many Corinthians to belong to the Christian community in the city (Acts 18:9–10).

In practical terms, however, perhaps the most important development came with the ruling of the newly arrived proconsul of Achaia, L. Iunius Gallio Annaeanus, older brother of Seneca the Younger and, like Seneca himself, an important Roman statesman under both Claudius and Nero.[50] A letter of Claudius, inscribed in the temple of Apollo in the important Achaian religious center of Delphi, pinpoints Gallio's service in Achaia with a fair degree of certainty to AD 51. It was not long after Gallio arrived that the unbelieving Jews in Corinth brought to him a complaint against Paul for "persuading people to worship God contrary to the law" (Acts 18:12–13).[51]

Gallio seems to have assumed that their reference to "the law" meant their "own law" (Acts 18:15), and his decision that the Roman legal system was uninterested in the fine points of Jewish law seems to have cleared the way for Paul to continue teaching in Corinth without legal interference and for Christians to meet there uninhibited by the legal authorities.[52] Since Gallio was himself such a high-ranking official, his decision probably had even wider implications for the treatment of Christians for several years. Roughly eight years later, and many miles away in Caesarea Maritima, the Judean procurator Festus took an approach to Paul and his movement in AD 59 that echoed Gallio's legal judgment (25:19). When Festus inherited from his predecessor a complaint against Paul from the leaders of Jerusalem's ruling council (cf. 24:1, 5–6), he expressed surprise at the nature of the complaint in terms reminiscent of Gallio's ruling: it involved no serious wrongdoing (25:18; cf. 18:14). Like Gallio, he then summarized it as an inner-Jewish "dispute" (25:19; cf. 18:15).[53]

Probably a short time after Gallio's verdict, he developed a respiratory illness. Rather than finish his yearlong term as proconsul, he decided to tend to his health and escape to the sea (Seneca, *Ep.* 104.1), a common remedy for his condition, and one that he would employ more than once (Pliny, *Nat.* 31.33).[54] Paul, too, left Corinth, perhaps sensing that after Gallio's ruling the seeds of faith that he and his coworkers had planted in the city were safe to leave in the hands of local leaders.

Together with his faithful friends Prisca and Aquila, then, he said farewell and left for the harbor of Cenchreae on the Saronic Gulf, an eight-mile walk to the east (Acts 18:18). Cenchreae was probably already home to the Christian community where Phoebe, a friend and benefactor of Paul's work, played an important role (Rom 16:1–2). It was the obvious place from which to catch a ship for points east.

14

A Visit to Jerusalem, a Collection for Its Needy Christians, and a New Beginning in Ephesus

When Paul and Silas set out to strengthen churches in Syria, Cilicia, and southern Galatia and to share with them the decision of the Jerusalem Council (Acts 15:40–16:5), they may not have known how long their mission would take. Paul's work had extended far beyond the regions where he and Barnabas had planted churches prior to the Council, and Paul had settled in Corinth for a year and a half. The important ruling of Gallio, moreover, could have been a turning point for Paul: it set a legal precedent that might keep him and any potential believers in other cities out of legal trouble if opponents to his message complained to the Roman authorities again.[1] This was a good time, then, to move to another major Aegean city with the gospel. Before taking this major new step, however, Paul first wanted to offer himself and his ministry anew to God and to reconnect in person with the believers in Jerusalem and Syrian Antioch.

Paul Undertakes a Vow

The idea that Paul offered himself and his ministry anew to God is an inference from Luke's puzzling statement that when Paul was in Cenchreae "he had cut his hair, for he was under a vow" (Acts 18:18). Luke says nothing about why Paul took this vow, nor does Luke describe it as a Nazirite vow, but the only vow ritual in the Scriptures that involves cutting one's hair is the Nazirite vow (Num 6:1–21), and most interpreters agree that this is what Luke intended to describe.[2] The purpose of a Nazirite vow was "to separate" oneself "to the Lord" (Num 6:2), and it entailed three personal requirements for the duration of the vow. First, one had to abstain from wine and any product made from grapes (6:3–4). Second, one's hair had to remain uncut (6:5). Third, one could not touch a dead body (6:6–12). During the period for the vow, the one undertaking it brought a series of offerings to the priest at "the tent of meeting" (6:13–17). Then, at the end of the vow period, he or she offered the hair of their shaved head on the sacrificial fire (6:18).

Eliezer Diamond has produced a well-reasoned argument that while one was under a Nazirite vow, he or she served as both priest and sacrifice, offering oneself to God.[3] He shows that in many cultures from ancient to modern times offering one's hair was symbolic of offering the essence of oneself to the deity.[4] Abstention from wine and corpse impurity, moreover, echo requirements for ritually pure sacrifices and active-duty priests (Lev 7:19–21; 10:9; Ezek 44:21). "The essence of the Nazirite vow," Diamond concludes, "is that by means of consecrating one's hair for a certain period and then offering it on the altar one symbolically offers oneself to God, and in doing so one is both offering and officiant."[5] Paul's contemporary Philo, at least, understood the ritual this way. He described people who took the Nazirite vow as those who not only sacrifice material things but "dedicate and consecrate themselves, thus showing an amazing sanctification and a surpassing devotion to God" (*Spec.* 1.248 [Colson, LCL]).[6]

Paul, then, may have been dedicating himself anew to the taxing work that God had given him to do. His year and a half in Corinth had been filled with hard work (1 Thess 2:9; 2 Thess 3:8; 2 Cor 11:27), with anxiety for the churches he had left behind in Galatia and Macedonia (1 Thess 3:1, 7; 2 Cor 11:28), and with opposition from unbelievers (1 Thess 2:2; Acts 16:16–24; 18:6, 12). God had brought him safely to this turning point in his ministry, and Paul responded by turning to this traditional biblical ritual as an expression of his continued, total commitment to the task that lay ahead. It is true that Paul cut his hair long before he could have made an offering of it in the temple (Num 6:18; 1 Macc 3:49–53; *B.J.* 2.309–313), but he may have varied the standard procedure by shaving his head at the beginning of his vow, intending to offer the hair that grew in the meantime in Jerusalem when he arrived there.[7]

A Visit to Jerusalem and a New Beginning in Ephesus

THE FULFILLMENT OF PAUL'S VOW AND THE PLIGHT OF THE JERUSALEM POOR

After he had undertaken his vow, he set sail for Syrian Antioch with two important intermediate stops in Ephesus and Jerusalem along the way (Acts 18:19, 22). He probably already had in mind at this point his eventual return to Ephesus for a longer Corinthian-style mission there. Perhaps this was why he took Prisca and Aquila with him and left them there after giving some initial instruction in the synagogue in Ephesus (Acts 18:19–21). Their job would have been to engage in the beginning stages of this new work. Perhaps they rented the "house" that would double as their new tent-making workshop and as a meeting place for at least one of the Christian assemblies in the city (1 Cor 16:8, 19). In addition, they could continue the discussions Paul had started in the synagogue and stay in touch with the churches in Corinth and Cenchreae while Paul continued his journey east (cf. Acts 18:26–27).

Instead of traveling directly to Antioch, which was his destination, Paul disembarked at the large Judean port city of Caesarea and then traveled inland "up" to Jerusalem. Luke only says that "when he landed at Caesarea, he went up and greeted the church, and then went down to Antioch," omitting any mention of Jerusalem (Acts 18:22). The only reason for Paul to travel to Antioch by way of Caesarea, however, would be to visit Jerusalem. The normal sea route from Ephesus to Antioch ran along the southern coast of Asia Minor, many miles to the north.[8] The traveler, moreover, did not go "down" from Caesarea to Antioch but certainly would go "down" from Jerusalem to Antioch.[9] The implication of Luke's report, then, is that after a short time in Ephesus, Paul made his way to Jerusalem where he spent a relatively short time with the Jewish Christians in the city. If Paul took one of the large, fast ships that plied the eastern Mediterranean between major cities, his journey from Ephesus to Caesarea might have taken something like six days.[10] The sixty-five-mile walk to Jerusalem would have taken him three or four days more.[11]

This journey made sense for two reasons. First, it would allow Paul to make the necessary offerings in the temple, including the offering of his hair, in fulfillment of his vow. Second, as James D. G. Dunn suggested, a visit to Jerusalem also made sense after the debacle among the Galatian churches. Paul probably went there in part to meet with James, and any other Jerusalem church leaders still in town, to make sure that he and they both still agreed on the legitimacy and necessity of each other's work (cf. Gal 2:6–10).[12] If he followed standard procedure for a Nazirite vow, he would have stayed in Jerusalem for at least thirty days before offering his hair (Josephus, *B.J.* 2.313). This provided plenty of time for him to confer with the Jerusalem church leadership.

It also provided an opportunity for Paul to observe the difficult political and economic situation that the Jerusalem church found itself in at this time.[13] In late AD 51 and early AD 52, Judea was a powder keg waiting to explode.[14] These were the last years of the procuratorship of Ventidius Cumanus, a period marked by increased tensions between the Jews and the Romans who occupied their land. At one of the pilgrimage festivals, and probably within months of the time Paul arrived in Jerusalem, people in Samaria massacred a group of Galilean Jewish pilgrims who were traveling south to Jerusalem for the festival. The leaders of the pilgrims appealed to Cumanus to bring the murderers to justice, but Cumanus refused to do this, and the Jews took matters into their own hands. The resulting conflict eventually led Cumanus to restore order with a sizable military action against the Jews. At least some of the Jewish combatants believed that Cumanus's unfair treatment of them proved that the Jews were merely slaves to the Romans. They thought of themselves as freedom fighters against Roman oppression (Josephus, *A.J.* 20.120).

The conflict only died down when Jewish leaders in Jerusalem traveled to Samaria and were able to convince enough of the Jews that further fighting would "bring down the wrath of the Romans on Jerusalem" (Josephus, *B.J.* 2.237; cf. *A.J.* 20.123 [Thackeray, LCL]). In the end, both sides appealed to Ummidius Quadratus, the legate of Syria who outranked Cumanus, and, after an investigation, Quadratus sent Cumanus to Rome to explain himself to the emperor. Claudius sent him into exile.

Josephus, at least, believed that this conflict had lit a fuse. "Many," he says, "... had recourse to robbery, and raids and insurrections, fostered by the more reckless, broke out all over the country" (*B.J.* 2.238 [Thackeray, LCL]).[15]

Josephus was a member of the tiny group of wealthy elites and had little interest in what actually motivated peasants in the Judean countryside to

A Visit to Jerusalem and a New Beginning in Ephesus

turn to "robbery," but Martin Goodman has made a persuasive case that poverty was a leading cause.[16] The wealthy ruling class in Jerusalem, he argues, had gained their riches over the course of the first century in part by loaning rural landowners money when harvests were bad and then taking their land and forcing the farmers to become tenants on it when they could not repay their loans.[17] The tax burden on these tenants was also great.[18] As a result, argues Goodman, some people turned to stealing from the wealthy in order to survive, and they received support from their villages when they did this.[19]

Eleazar, son of Deinaeus, the military leader of the Jewish action against the Samaritans and Romans, was just such a person. He had become a Robin Hood–style hero to many, and, as Goodman puts it, "tales of his exploits, suitably romanticized, survived into the rabbinic literature of the second century AD (cf. *m. Sot.* 9.9)."[20] Others of the desperate poor during this period flooded Jerusalem, which was one of the few cities in the ancient world where most people valued charitable giving as an act of piety.[21] These social and economic movements were in full swing in the late forties and early fifties after the famine conditions that dominated the forties.[22]

It seems likely, then, that when Paul arrived in Jerusalem, perhaps in the closing months of AD 51, he encountered crowds of desperately poor people. This may have been the period during which he developed a plan to help "the poor among the saints at Jerusalem" (Rom 15:26; cf. 2 Cor 9:12).[23] He would collect funds from the churches that he and his coworkers had planted and nurtured in central Anatolia and along the western Aegean coast, and that they hoped to nurture in the province of Asia. Representatives from these churches could then take this relief to Jerusalem, and Paul might go with them, if it seemed prudent (1 Cor 16:3–4; 2 Cor 8:19–21; Acts 20:4).

Paul probably saw several advantages to this plan. First, it would meet a real human need, and the Scriptures taught that meeting the needs of the poor was an important characteristic of God's people (Deut 10:17–19; 24:10–22; Ps 146:5–9; Isa 10:1–4; Jer 7:5–7; cf. Gal 2:10).[24] Second, Paul believed the churches he had planted, despite their mainly gentile composition, constituted the restored people of God. Just as during the time of Israel's wilderness wanderings, God wanted his people to distribute fairly the gifts of food he had given them. If one part of God's people suffered poverty, those who were not as poor should come to their aid (2 Cor 8:13–15; cf. Exod 16:18; 1 Cor 12:26).

Third, the churches that would make this contribution were mainly gentile. The offering, then, would be a way for gentiles to reciprocate materially for the spiritual blessings that Jewish Christians had shared with them from Israel's heritage (Rom 15:27), blessings such as adoption into God's family, a glorious future as God's people, the fulfillment of God's covenant promises to his people, God's law, the worship of the one true God, the heritage of the patriarchs, and living under the rule of Israel's Messiah (Rom 9:4–5; cf. Eph 2:11–13).[25]

With his vow fulfilled, his meeting with the Jerusalem leaders completed, and his plan to help the Jerusalem church in place, Paul set out for Antioch. He probably made the seventy-mile trek back to Caesarea and then arranged for passage on a coastal vessel sailing north and calling at ports such as Tyre, Sidon, Beirut, and Tripolis along the way. It was perhaps a journey of seven days.[26]

Luke says nothing about what Paul did in Antioch or how long he stayed, only that he spent "some time there" (Acts 18:23). It seems likely that he reported on his work with Silas in the churches of Syria, Cilicia, Lycaonia, Phrygia, Macedonia, and Achaia. Again, Dunn is probably right that a meeting with the Antioch church after the incursions of false teachers into Galatia and Paul's strong letter would make strategic sense.[27] It would also help ensure the expanding church's unity across the ethnic divide between Jews and gentiles, and this was something that Paul valued deeply (Rom 15:8–12; Eph 2:11–22).

Dunn believed that these meetings of reconnection in Jerusalem and Antioch did not go well. Otherwise, why would Luke describe them so briefly and vaguely?[28] There is a small hint in Paul's letters, however, that these meetings were more harmonious than Dunn thought. Both Barnabas and Mark were on good terms with Paul in later years, after the tensions described in Galatians 2:13 and Acts 15:36–40. These meetings in both Jerusalem and Antioch, within a short time of each other and only a few years after those tensions, may have provided the opportunity for forgiveness and reconciliation, laying the foundation beneath the teamwork visible in Paul's positive references to Barnabas and Mark in later letters (1 Cor 9:6; Phlm 24; Col 4:10; 2 Tim 4:11).

A Visit to Jerusalem and a New Beginning in Ephesus

STRENGTHENING THE GALATIAN CHRISTIANS AND EXPLAINING THE OFFERING

If the winter of AD 51–52 was at the door, Paul would probably have spent the season in Antioch. The weather on the Mediterranean and in the mountain passes of Cilicia would make traveling those routes difficult until the spring.[29] When spring came a few months later, however, Paul made his way, either by land or by a combination of land and sea, to the interior of Asia Minor, or, as Luke puts it, to "the territory of the province of Galatia and its Phrygian region" (Acts 18:23; cf. 16:6).[30] Here he would have visited the churches that he and Barnabas had established in Pisidian Antioch, Iconium, Lystra, and Derbe (13:14–14:28) and that he and Silas

Map 4: From Jerusalem to Syrian Antioch to Southern Galatia to Ephesus to Macedonia, Illyricum, Achaia, and Back to Jerusalem

had revisited on the phase of their work they had just ended in Corinth (15:41–16:1). Their valued coworker Timothy was from this area (16:1–3), and roughly two years earlier Paul had written his letter "to the churches of Galatia" to Christians here. If part of the reason for Paul's departure from Ephesus had been to make sure that he and his coworkers were still theologically unified with Christians in Jerusalem and Antioch, then it made sense to visit the Christian communities to whom he had written his fiery letter to let them know about his recent visit and to check on their condition.

Luke says that Paul traveled through Galatia and its Phrygian region in an orderly way (Acts 18:23), probably indicating that he visited each of the churches in these areas as he moved from east to west.[31] One reason for such an orderly approach, making sure not to miss a single Christian community, was the need to explain carefully to each community the reason for the project of collecting relief aid for poor believers in Jerusalem and Paul's proposed method of doing it (1 Cor 16:1).

Paul's method emphasized the collection's financial integrity. Within a culture where fake philosophers sometimes collected money from people for their teaching and then quit philosophy to live in luxury, and professional orators charged exorbitant fees for their performances, Paul wanted the honorable nature of his motivations to be clear "not only in the Lord's sight but also in the sight of man" (2 Cor 8:21).[32] So, he wanted to avoid giving the wrong impression by arriving in a particular area and immediately beginning to collect money. Rather, he asked that each person within the church set aside an amount every Sunday that was commensurate with his or her income. When Paul visited each area, the churches in that area would choose representatives who would travel with Paul and the collected funds to Jerusalem. Paul would make the trip with the money, however, only if the participating churches deemed it appropriate (1 Cor 16:2–4).

Paul also wanted the method of the collection to emphasize its noncoercive, freewill character. Those who contributed to the collection should be motivated by the transforming work that God's abundant grace had accomplished in their lives.[33] The Greek term Paul uses for "the collection" (λογεία) highlighted its religious nature, and Paul may have chosen the term specifically because he did not want the collection to appear to be a "tax."[34] He wanted it to be "an act of grace" (2 Cor 8:19) and "a voluntary gift," not "an extortion" (9:5 NRSV). "Each one," he says, "must give as he has decided in his heart, not reluctantly or under compulsion, for God loves a cheerful giver" (9:7). Paul's ultimate hope for the collection was that through it the needy Christians in Jerusalem might glorify God when they understood how fully gentile believers had submitted to the gospel, and how completely God's abundant grace had transformed them (9:13–14).

Return to Ephesus

From the Phrygian corner of Galatia, Paul set out west, almost certainly traveling along the wide and well-paved Via Sebaste toward Apollonia.[35] At Apollonia, which was still within Phrygian Galatia, the road forked, and Paul probably went west to Apamea just across the Galatian border in Asia, and an important crossroads.[36] On his earlier journey through this area with Silas and Timothy, Paul had probably gone north at Apamea and along roads that led to Cotiaeum and Dorylaeum (Acts 16:6–8).[37] Now, however, he most likely took the ancient and well-traveled road that went southwest from Apamea and then, after about thirty miles, west from Lake Sanaos, past Colossae, and through Laodicea, Antioch-on-the-Maeander, Tralles, and Magnesia.[38] Perhaps Paul stopped long enough in Colossae to meet and explain the gospel to Epaphras and Philemon, residents of that city who eventually became instrumental in the spread of the gospel in Colossae, Laodicea, and Hierapolis (Col 1:6–8; 4:9, 12; Phlm 1, 7, 10, 17, 19, 23). Finally, Luke says, Paul emerged from "the inland country and came to Ephesus" (Acts 19:1).[39] It was probably the late summer or early fall of AD 52.[40]

If Paul's strategy in spreading the gospel was first to establish churches in major cities, such as Corinth, from which the gospel could then easily spread outward to other areas, he could not have chosen a better base of operations on the east coast of the Aegean Sea than Ephesus. It was, in the words of numerous inscriptions from the period, "the first and greatest metropolis of Asia" and one of the largest cities in the Roman Empire.[41] Although its harbor tended to silt up because of deposits from the Cayster River, it was well maintained, and a deeper harbor that could accommodate larger vessels lay only a few miles to the north.[42] Two major road systems connected at Ephesus, one of them running north and south basically along the coast of Asia Minor, and the other—the one Paul traveled into Ephesus—running east all the way to Susa in what is today western Iran.[43]

CHAPTER 14

Immigrants and tourists filled the city, just the people to take the gospel to a wide range of other places once they had heard and believed it themselves. Probably the city's main attraction was its fame as the birthplace of the goddess Artemis and the worldwide hub for her worship. An Ephesian inscription from about a century after Paul puts it this way: "Since the goddess Artemis, leader of our city, is honoured not only in her own homeland, which she has made the most illustrious of all cities through her own divine nature, but also among Greeks and also barbarians, the result is that everywhere her shrines and sanctuaries have been established, and temples have been founded for her and altars dedicated to her because of the visible manifestations effected by her" (IEph 24B 8–14).[44]

Pausanias the travel writer agreed. "All cities worship Artemis of Ephesus," he claimed, "and individuals hold her in honour above all the gods" (*Descr.* 4.31.8).[45] She had temples as far west as Iberia (modern Spain) and Massilia (Marseilles, France), but Ephesus was her "temple keeper" (νεωκόρος, Acts 19:35), a title attested on coins and in inscriptions from the time of Nero.[46] No city was as closely merged with the reputation and worship of Artemis as Ephesus.

The temple of Paul's time had been there for four and a half centuries, but it was the last of five temples stretching back many centuries earlier.[47] According to one second-century BC writer, it was the greatest sight in all the world.[48] Pliny the Elder says that the temple took 120 years to build, and he describes a massive structure roughly 460 feet long and 238 feet wide with 127 columns that towered upward 65 feet (*Nat.* 36.21.95–96).[49] It was adorned throughout with the work of famous sculptors and painters.[50]

In addition to its convenient location for travelers and its attraction as the city of Artemis, Ephesus was also a governmental and banking center. It was the capital of the province of Asia and therefore home to the proconsul, whose impressive palace may have been the building that overlooked the theater and whose ruins are still visible.[51] The temple of Artemis, moreover, was the depository for massive amounts of money from all over the Roman world. Fear of the goddess's wrath kept the money safe from theft or embezzlement.[52]

With its excellent location for travel both west across the Aegean and east through Asia Minor, Ephesus also allowed Paul to stay in close touch

A Visit to Jerusalem and a New Beginning in Ephesus

with his other churches in those areas. As Jerome Murphy-O'Connor put it, "Not only was it roughly equidistant from his churches in Achaia, Macedonia, and Galatia, but as a capital city at the head of an excellent road system and with an important port it offered him superb communications."[53] Here was a place where Paul and his coworkers could settle down and spend many fruitful months of ministry.

15

Ministry in Ephesus and a Letter to Christians in Corinth

Paul spent three busy years in Ephesus, and his strategy there seems to have followed roughly the pattern of his work in Corinth. He began in the synagogue and workshop, but when opposition to his teaching made continued association with the synagogue impossible, he retreated to a separate venue. Just as in Corinth, moreover, he expanded his ability to oversee the churches he had planted elsewhere through sending them co-workers and writing them letters. In Ephesus, however, his ministry lasted longer and had a wider reach than his work in Corinth. Two factors may have made a long stay in Ephesus appealing: the city's central location for travel to points west and east, and a period of relative calm for the Christian movement that Gallio's favorable verdict possibly introduced.

Beginnings in the Workshop, Synagogue, and Lecture Hall

By the time Paul arrived back in Ephesus, there was already a cohesive community of believers there, well versed in the faith, and active in their efforts to encourage other believers elsewhere.[1] The origins of this community are not clear. Perhaps it originated with Paul's brief involvement in the synagogue before he left for Jerusalem and Antioch (Acts 18:19–20). Perhaps it emerged from the work of Prisca and Aquila in the synagogue before Paul returned (18:19, 26).

There are indications from Luke's narrative, however, that there were disciples of Christ in Ephesus before Paul, Prisca, and Aquila arrived in the city. The way Luke tells the story hints that when Prisca and Aquila attached themselves to a synagogue after Paul's departure, they discovered Apollos, a learned Alexandrian Jew, was already there teaching "accurately the things concerning Jesus, though he knew only the baptism of John" (Acts 18:25). After Prisca and Aquila instructed him on this point, they became allies. Eventually, Apollos wanted to travel to Achaia, probably after hearing about the churches in Corinth and Cenchreae from Prisca and Aquila, and Luke says that "the brothers" supplied Apollos with a letter of recommendation to the Christians there (Acts 18:27). These "brothers" appear to be a group of Jesus followers who were associated with Apollos and the synagogue before Paul and his coworkers arrived in the city. We may even know one of their names: Epaenetus. Immediately after greeting Prisca (or "Priscilla," as Luke calls her) and Aquila in his letter to the Romans, Paul sent Epaenetus greetings and referred to him as "the first convert to Christ in Asia" (Rom 16:3–5).[2]

Paul's contribution to the advancement of the gospel in Ephesus seems to have started as soon as he arrived back in the city (Acts 19:1; cf. 18:21). Luke's passing reference to the face cloths and the aprons Paul used (19:12) implies that he was hard at work in the tentmaking shop, and it seems likely that this was a shop Prisca and Aquila set up during his absence (cf. 18:3). Later in Luke's narrative, Paul himself will reflect on his nearly three years in Ephesus and comment that he worked hard with his hands to meet his own needs and the needs of others, especially "the weak" (20:33–36). Writing from Ephesus, he comments to the Corinthian Christians, "To the present hour we hunger and thirst, we are poorly dressed and buffeted and homeless, and we labor, working with our own hands" (1 Cor 4:11). Simply having a job, friends, and coworkers did not mean life was easy. Even on the Sabbath, when paid work ceased, he would have gone to the synagogue where Luke says he "spoke boldly, reasoning and persuading" those in attendance "about the kingdom of God" (Acts 19:8).

At some point in these endeavors, Paul discovered a group of people who, like Apollos, had an attachment to John the Baptist (Acts 19:1–7). Luke calls them "disciples" and reports that Paul asked them about receiving the Holy Spirit "when [they] believed" (19:1–2). The language of discipleship and faith makes them sound like Christians, but Luke does not describe them as having faith specifically in Jesus, and he says clearly that they had never heard of the Holy Spirit.[3] It seems likely, then, that they were simply followers of John the Baptist who were either unfamiliar with Jesus or did not understand the significance that John placed on Jesus. Josephus's brief description of John the Baptist in his Jewish history shows that such interpretations of John's teaching were possible. Josephus says nothing that links John to Jesus or to teaching on God's Spirit but portrays him as merely a good man and eloquent preacher who urged people to accept baptism as a sign of their willingness to live the righteous life God desired (*A.J.* 18.116–119).

In any case, when Paul informed the group that John had instructed people to believe in Jesus, they accepted baptism in Jesus's name (Acts 19:4–5). Paul laid his hands on them as part of their initiation, and the Holy Spirit confirmed their entry to the church by giving them the ability to speak languages they had not learned ("tongues") and to prophesy (Acts 19:6).[4] It is clear from Paul's letters that these two signs of the Holy Spirit's powerful presence in the believing community had accompanied Paul's work in Thessalonica and Corinth (1 Thess 5:19–20; 1 Cor 12:8–10; 14:4–6, 22, 39). As soon as the newly baptized disciples in Ephesus began manifesting these two gifts of the Spirit, therefore, Paul must have known that their belief in Jesus, the one who came after John, was authentic.[5] They probably joined Paul, Prisca, Aquila, and other Ephesian believers in the home of Prisca and Aquila for Christian instruction and worship (1 Cor 16:19).

The Gospel Spreads

This arrangement of dialogue in the synagogue on the Sabbath, a separate home-based meeting for Christians, and hard work in the tentmaking workshop continued for three months, perhaps the fall months of AD 52 (Acts 19:8). When some tension broke out in the synagogue over Paul's teaching, however, Paul and the Jesus followers separated entirely from the synagogue (19:9). They probably continued to meet for worship and instruction both in the home of Prisca and Aquila and in the other homes Luke had in mind when he later said that Paul taught in Ephesus "in public and from house to house" (20:20).

The "public" space was "the lecture hall of Tyrannus" (Acts 19:9 NRSV), probably a local teacher's classroom that Paul rented during the time of day when Tyrannus's classes were not in session.⁶ As James D. G. Dunn commented, this would have opened Paul's message to a broader audience unrelated to Judaism.⁷ With a good port for connections to the west and well-traveled roads providing access to the other three points of the compass, over the next two years the gospel spread throughout the province of Asia (19:10).

Luke makes clear, however, that the wide impact of the gospel on both Ephesus and the whole province was not merely a matter of Paul's persuasive powers or the strategic location of his teaching. The word about the apostle and the gospel spread because "God was doing extraordinary miracles by the hands of Paul" (Acts 19:11). The face cloths he used to wipe sweat from his face in the workshop and lecture hall, and the aprons he used at his work bench carried healing power to the sick (19:12). In addition, the demonic powers that were so prevalent in the magic-soaked culture of Ephesus recognized Paul and fled from him just as they had recognized and fled from Jesus (19:11–20; cf. Luke 4:41).⁸

Paul must have been extraordinarily busy during this phase of his career, probably from the winter of AD 53 to the spring of AD 56 (cf. Acts 20:31).⁹ Between the workshop, the lecture hall, and teaching from house to house, there would have hardly been enough hours in a normal weekday for sleep. Paul's own excitement about the growth of the church in Asia during his work in Ephesus shines through 1 Corinthians. Although there were pressing needs in Corinth (1 Cor 4:18–19), Paul explained why he could not leave Ephesus at that time to visit the Christians there: "A wide door for effective work has opened to me" (1 Cor 16:9).

Paul Sends a Letter to Corinth and Coworkers to Macedonia and Achaia

Still, Paul did not leave the Corinthian church unattended. Sometime during his two to three years in Ephesus, Apollos recrossed the Aegean Sea from Corinth and got to know Paul (1 Cor 16:12). Perhaps it was Apollos, then, who brought him the news that some Corinthian Christians needed instruction on how God expected his people to behave sexually.¹⁰ It seems likely that these were the Christians of high social standing Paul had in view when he wrote 1 Corinthians 5–6.¹¹ Pornography and prostitution were common in Roman cities of the time and were not relegated to certain districts, and the banquets of upper-class Romans often featured prostitutes.[12] "If there is anyone who thinks that youth should be forbidden affairs even with courtesans," said Cicero, "he is doubtless eminently austere, but his view is contrary not only to the licence of this age, but also to the custom and concessions of our ancestors" (Cicero, *Cael.* 20.48).[13]

Paul would certainly have taught on this subject while he was in Corinth. His first letter to the Thessalonian Christians, written from Corinth, covers lucidly God's expectations for abstention from sexual activity outside of marriage (1 Thess 4:2–8). Since Paul's departure from Corinth, however, some Corinthians had started to revert to the norms of the culture around them, and, in response, Paul wrote to them "not to associate with sexually immoral people" (1 Cor 5:9).[14] He gives no further information about the content of this letter, and the letter itself has disappeared, but it is clear from references to it in 1 Corinthians that the problems Paul meant for it to address continued unabated (1 Cor 5:1–13; 6:12–21; 2 Cor 12:21).

At about the same time Paul sent this letter, he probably sent Timothy and other "brothers," including a brother named Erastus, to Macedonia and Achaia (Acts 19:22; 1 Cor 4:17; 16:10–11).[15] One of the nameless "brothers" may well have been Titus, and at some point in their travels the group seems to have split up.[16] In 2 Corinthians, Paul implies that Titus and another "brother" had initiated the collection in Corinth (and throughout Achaia) during the previous year (2 Cor 8:6, 10; 9:2; 12:18).[17] He does not mention Timothy here, however, and this would be strange if Timothy, who joins Paul in writing 2 Corinthians (1:1), had been this other "brother." Timothy and Erastus seem to have traveled only as far as Macedonia, and Luke reflected this in his much later narrative. That narrative condenses the various complications into the statement that Paul "sent into *Macedonia* two of his helpers, Timothy and Erastus" (Acts 19:22, emphasis added).[18] Paul may have asked Apollos to join the group also, but "it was not at all his will" to go along (1 Cor 16:12). Was Apollos already aware from his time in Corinth that fractures were beginning to appear in the church's foundation based on partisan loyalties either to him or to Paul (cf. 1:12; 3:4)?[19]

Luke says nothing about the trip's purpose, but, according to Paul, one reason for the journey was to remind the Corinthians of Paul's "ways in

Christ Jesus" as he taught "them everywhere in every church" (1 Cor 4:17). Perhaps another reason was to explain to all Christians along the western side of the Aegean Sea, including Christians in Macedonia, the reason and method for collecting relief aid for believers in Jerusalem. The verb Luke uses in Acts 19:22 to say that Paul sent his "helpers" (τῶν διακονούντων) Timothy and Erastus to Macedonia is the same term that Paul uses, in both its verb and noun forms, to describe the collection (2 Cor 8:4, 19–20; 9:1, 12–13; Rom 15:25).[20]

More News from Corinth

There is no way to know exactly when during Paul's Ephesian ministry he received further disturbing information about the state of the Corinthian church, but two detailed reports came to him, and their basic concerns are clear. First, a group of Ephesian Christians working for a woman named Chloe had traveled from Ephesus to Corinth and met some people in the church there.[21] When they returned to Ephesus, they approached Paul with several concerns about Christianity in Corinth. The church there was splitting into mutually hostile factions based on the Christian leader they prized the most, whether Paul, Apollos, or Cephas (Peter) (1 Cor 1:10–12).[22] Similar divisions showed up when the church gathered for worship, although now the division was along socioeconomic lines (11:18–19).[23] At the Lord's Supper the few who were rich greedily feasted on as much food and drink as they wanted while the poor went hungry and felt humiliated (11:21–22, 33–34).[24]

Chloe's people also "reported" to Paul that sexual immorality had infected the church: a man was living with his stepmother (1 Cor 5:1), and some people in the church were having sexual relations with prostitutes (6:15–16). They were engaged in this behavior, moreover, despite Paul's letter of instruction on these matters (5:9) and were even attempting to justify it by arrogantly claiming, "I have the right to do anything" (6:12 NIV; cf. 5:2). In addition, some people in the church had taken other people before the local courts over everyday problems that the accusers claimed amounted to fraud (6:1, 3, 7–8).

Second, a delegation of three Corinthian believers, Stephanas, Fortunatus, and Achaicus, arrived in Ephesus (1 Cor 16:17) and probably brought with them a letter from Corinth that Paul refers to in 1 Corinthians 7:1

CHAPTER 15

("Now concerning the matters about which you wrote . . ."). Since Paul often changes topics in 1 Corinthians by repeating the phrase "now concerning" (περὶ δέ; 7:25; 8:1; 12:1; 16:1, 12), or simply using the word "now" (δέ; 11:2, 17; 15:1), he may have been signaling to the Corinthians that he was moving through topics raised in their letter to him. If so, their letter seems to have convinced Paul that they needed further teaching on the advisability of marriage (7:1–40), the wisdom of eating food that had been involved in non-Jewish sacrificial rituals (8:1–11:1), women wearing head coverings in Christian assemblies (11:2–16), the relative importance of spiritual gifts (12:1–14:40), the nature of the bodily resurrection of believers from the dead (15:1–58), the collection for poor Christians in Jerusalem (16:1–4), and the travel plans of Apollos (16:12).

As if all this were not enough, something in either or both reports revealed that some Corinthian Christians had become disillusioned with Paul. They were sitting in judgment on him and finding him deficient in the qualities they valued in a leader and teacher (1 Cor 4:3–5). Unlike Apollos and the professional orators so common in their city, Paul's rhetorical skills were unimpressive (1 Cor 1:17, 20; 2:1, 3–4; 2 Cor 10:10; cf. Acts 18:24, 28). Unlike Cephas and Jesus's brothers, who required the communities in which they worked to support them financially and who had experienced the immense privilege of knowing Jesus personally, Paul had to work hard at manual labor in the communities where he taught, and everyone knew that his call to be an apostle had come after the call of all the others.[25]

As this disillusioned group would say about Paul later, "His bodily presence is weak, and his speech of no account" (2 Cor 10:10). The exciting professional orators who visited and lived in Corinth made plenty of money on their oratorical and educational skills.[26] Could the sweaty, disheveled Paul, often ill and constantly stooped over his workbench, really be an apostle? How could someone with such uninspiring oratorical skills and so few important social connections carry the authority that Paul claimed for himself (1 Cor 9:2; 15:9–11)?

Perhaps some of the wealthier Corinthians treated the church like one of the clubs that were so common among people of a similar religion, merchandizing enterprise, or trade. These clubs encouraged their members to compete against others for honor by serving as benefactors.[27] A person like Paul with his emphasis on building up every member of the community,

Corinthian Pride and Its Antidote

Paul's answer to all this comes in the form of his own letter back to Corinth, probably written in the spring of AD 55.[28] The group from Corinth that Stephanas headed, and whom Paul commends at the end of the letter (1 Cor 16:15–16), probably carried it for him.[29] The letter diagnoses the Corinthians' spiritual disease as fundamentally a problem of pride. They had been infected with the desire for glory, a craving that was endemic to Roman society generally. "There is no one so humble that he cannot be touched by the charm of glory," said the first-century Roman moralist Valerius Maximus (8.14.5 [Walker]).[30] Although in the Corinthian church there were "not many . . . wise according to worldly standards, not many . . . powerful, not many . . . of noble birth" (1 Cor 1:26), many nevertheless wanted glory for themselves, often at the expense of others. And for the few who possessed worldly power and social status, the drive to attain glory in Roman Corinth, spurred on by what James Harrison calls the "endless 'chatter'" of honorific inscriptions, would have simply been second nature.[31]

The competition between the groups who followed various celebrity Christian teachers, although natural in a setting used to catapulting dazzling orators to fame, was a symptom of arrogance—of being "puffed up" (φυσιοῦσθε) as Paul memorably puts it (1 Cor 4:6, 18, 19). The Greek term was well known in Paul's world as an image for arrogance. Cicero, writing in Latin about a century earlier, could use it in Greek to refer to himself after bragging on his own integrity.[32] "Recte πεφυσίωμαι," he says of himself: "I have a right to a swollen head" (*Att.* 5.20.6 [letter 113] [Shackleton Bailey, LCL]). The image possibly recalled for Paul's readers an inflated animal bladder—an ancient flotation device—with its large, impressive exterior hiding a complete lack of substance.[33]

"The power of eloquence," said Valerius Maximus in the preface to a whole section devoted to the subject, "is supreme" (8.9 [Walker]). The preface to his next section describes "how much importance lies in proper enunciation and appropriate physical gestures." He continues, "When eloquence is supplied with these, it affects people in three ways: eloquence itself captures their minds, it hands over their ears to be charmed by enunciation, and it hands over their eyes to be charmed by gesture" (8.10).

Paul, however, had been anything but eloquent when he preached the gospel and discipled believers in Corinth, as he emphatically points out. From a Corinthian cultural perspective, the message he preached, centered as it was on a crucified Jewish king, was "folly" (1 Cor 1:18, 23), and Paul delivered it "in weakness and in fear and much trembling" (2:3), without speaking "in plausible words of wisdom" (2:4). Moreover, the Corinthian church itself consisted mainly of the foolish, weak, lowly, and despised elements of Corinthian society (1:26–28). God had nevertheless used Paul's unpromising speaking abilities and demeanor to demonstrate his Spirit's presence and power in Corinth. It was from the ragtag band of those who heard Paul preach that God assembled the people who would begin to fulfill God's long-awaited prophetic promises for the restoration of his people (1 Cor 2:9; cf. Isa 52:15; 64:3–4; 65:16; Jer 3:16). Neither their status nor any human leader had given them what they really needed in life. Rather, God had provided for them "righteousness and sanctification and redemption" (1 Cor 1:30).

Why had God worked this way? Precisely so that "no human being might boast" in his presence (1 Cor 1:29; cf. 1:31). "What do you have that you did not receive?" Paul asks the Corinthians; "If then you received it, why do you boast as if you did not receive it?" (1 Cor 4:7; cf. 3:21).

By shifting their focus off this truth and placing it instead on attaining glory in Corinthian terms, some of the Corinthians had become so "puffed up" that they failed to see how dysfunctional their moral compass had become (5:1–2). In their pride some of them had begun to assert, "All things are lawful for me" (6:12; 10:23). This idea had led some into sexual immorality (6:12–20; cf. 5:1–2) and participation in the sacred meals of locally worshiped "gods," even if the example of their participation threatened to influence other less sophisticated believers back into the actual worship of those gods (8:10). This drive for recognition had blinded the wealthy who hosted the community's gatherings to the needs of the Christian poor in their midst as they gobbled down their own rich fare, oblivious of the effect this had on the poor who went hungry and left humiliated (11:20–22).[34]

Ministry in Ephesus and a Letter to Christians in Corinth

Some whom the Spirit had given the ability to speak in languages they had not learned looked down on those who did not have this gift (1 Cor 12:10, 28, 30; 13:1, 8; 14:1–40), and again the result was shame. Using an illustration common in ancient Greek and Roman political discussions, Paul imagines the Corinthian Christian community as a body where some parts, probably those who had the dramatic gift of speaking in unlearned languages, told others with less impressive gifts, "I have no need of you" (12:21) and these despised others felt they were not even part of the body (12:14–16).[35]

If the theological antidote to all this was to refocus on God's gracious initiative in the salvation of them all, then the practical antidote was to focus on showing love to each other by building one another up and therefore building up the whole community. God had given Paul the ability to lay the community's foundation "like a skilled master builder," and now the Corinthians needed to be careful how they were building on that foundation (1 Cor 3:10). That foundation was none other than Jesus Christ himself (3:11), and the Corinthians were the temple of God, the dwelling place of his Spirit's presence (3:9, 16–17).

So, the Corinthian Christians who claimed the "right" (1 Cor 8:9) to eat "in an idol's temple" needed to give more thought to how their actions would "build up" another believer who might be tempted to worship the idol in that temple. If the exercise of this right would only "build up" this other believer toward destruction (8:10, my translation), then it was necessary to give up that right, even if one "knows" that this right exists. "'Knowledge' puffs up," says Paul, "but love builds up" (8:1). In the same way, even if one has worked out theologically that "all things are permitted to me" (6:12), one's conduct should not be governed by this principle but by consideration of what builds the community up and is therefore beneficial to all (10:23).

The same principle of edification ought to govern the Christian community's approach to using their gifts in community gatherings. Paul recommended that when the church assembled, they should emphasize the use of prophecy, which everyone could understand, and de-emphasize the use of tongues-speaking since it was more confusing and therefore less edifying to all (1 Cor 14:1–25). Again, love for others should guide one's conduct (13:1–14:1).

CHAPTER 15

The Corinthians' Identity as the People of God

Apart from the epidemic of pride that plagued the Corinthian church, Paul also detected a serious lack of appreciation for what it meant to be the people of God. The Corinthians' problems with sexuality, legal disputes, and idolatry all reflected a misunderstanding of who they were as "those who have been made holy to God in Christ Jesus, who are called to be God's people" (1 Cor 1:2 CEB). Just as God had said to his ancient people Israel that he wanted them to "be holy to me, for I the LORD am holy and have separated you from the peoples" (Lev 20:26), so the Corinthians were now also God's people and were to be separate from the culture around them, living in the way God created all human beings to live.[36]

As a result, Paul was obviously upset when he learned that someone within the Corinthian Christian community was living in a sexual relationship with his stepmother. It was "a type of immorality that isn't even heard of among the Gentiles" (1 Cor. 5:1 CEB). Paul assumed here that, from a theological perspective, the Corinthian Christians were not gentiles, even though from an ethnic perspective that is clearly what most of them were (1 Cor 12:2). Despite being non-Jews, they were God's people, and like God's people as they are described in the Scriptures, Paul wanted them to live according to a distinct pattern of conduct that set them apart from the godless cultures around them. Their own sexuality, therefore, needed to be expressed in ways that were compatible with the pattern laid down in the Mosaic law. God had insisted that Israel not imitate the often bizarre and abusive sexual practices of the nations surrounding them (Lev 18:1–30), and so having sexual relations with a stepmother was not an option (Lev 18:8).

Because Christians were God's people, moreover, their sexuality needed to be expressed within the boundaries of marriage as Scripture defined it in its account of God's creation of the first married couple (Gen 2:18–25). Sexual intimacy created a relational bond that should only be experienced in marriage (1 Cor 6:13–17; Gen 2:24), and God had designed marriage as the appropriate place for sexual expression (1 Cor 7:1–40). Scripture also revealed that marriage was a place where the equal worth and mutual respect God intended for men and women should be on display (1 Cor 11:7–12; cf. Gen 1:26–27; 2:21–22). For married women to remove the head coverings that in Roman Corinth showed their married status, therefore, was inappropriate within Christian assemblies for worship (1 Cor 11:5, 13).[37]

Paul takes a similar approach to the willingness of some Corinthians to dabble in idolatry by participating in dinners inside the sanctuaries of locally worshiped gods (1 Cor 8:10). In the first part of his argument on this topic, he takes the position that participation in such dinners is unloving and unedifying for those whose consciences are weak (8:7–13). In the final part of that argument, he argues that involvement in these dinners is also wrong because it is, in fact, idolatry (10:20–22).[38] The "knowledge" that "'an idol has no real existence' and that 'there is no God but one'" was certainly correct according to Scripture (8:4; cf. Deut 6:4), but the Corinthians had drawn from this knowledge the wrong conclusion that they could participate in dinners honoring one or more of the "gods" without bringing upon themselves the Lord's judgment.

They should learn, Paul says, from the experience of "our fathers" (1 Cor 10:1), meaning the ancient Israelites with whom the mainly gentile Corinthians now stood in continuity. The ancient Israelites experienced God's redemption and gifts in their exodus from slavery in Egypt and in their wilderness wanderings (Exod 13:21–22; 14:19–31; 17:6), but when they were tempted by sexual sin to participate in idolatry, God poured out his wrath on them (1 Cor 10:1–13; cf. Num 14:21–45). If the Corinthians were God's special people "on whom the end of the ages" had "come," then they should be careful not to repeat the mistakes of ancient Israel (10:12).

It was fine, therefore, to accept dinner invitations to private homes and eat the meat served without asking any questions about whether it had been previously involved in a sacrificial ritual (1 Cor 10:23–11:1). Believers invited to eat dinner in the temple of one of the many gods worshiped in Corinth, however, should run the other way (8:10; 10:14).

The Scriptures had promised that the future restoration of God's people would also begin his restoration of all creation to the form he intended when he created it, prior to Adam's rebellion against him. As part of that restoration, God would remove the curse of death that Adam, by his disobedience, had brought on the whole world (1 Cor 15:21–22, 25–49; cf. Gen 3:17–19).[39] Scripture taught that God would do this by raising his people from the dead, and just as Adam's original existence had been an embodied existence, so the new existence of his people would be embodied.

Since Paul had already encountered opposition to and misunderstanding of this teaching in both Athens and Thessalonica (Acts 17:32; 1 Thess 4:13–18), he was probably not surprised to discover from the Corinthian Christians' letter that some of them had problems with it also.

The Corinthian Christians who rejected the bodily resurrection of believers were not quite as pessimistic about resurrection as the prevailing culture. Paul's contemporary Pliny the Elder had said that God could not "bestow eternity on mortals or recall the deceased" (*Nat.* 2.5.27 [Rackham, LCL]), but the Corinthians believed that at least Jesus had experienced resurrection. They simply denied his resurrection implied anything about a general resurrection of the dead (1 Cor 15:12–13). Perhaps they thought of Jesus's resurrection as merely a one-time marvelous deed that demonstrated his great power. They also seem to have accepted the notion of an afterlife, just not an embodied afterlife. This seems to be the implication of Paul's insistence that they could not have one without the other (15:18), and of their insistence on the odd practice of baptism on behalf of those who had already died (15:29).[40] These Corinthian believers had difficulty imagining "what kind of body" people who had died could possibly occupy that would make them immortal. By their definition, bodies were subject to weakness, decay, and death (15:35).[41]

Paul responded to this error with a recap of the Christian case for the reality of Christ's bodily resurrection (1 Cor 15:1–11), a summary with which he assumes the Corinthians will agree (15:12). He then explained the inseverable connection between the bodily resurrection of Jesus and the hope contained in "the gospel" that he had "preached" to the Corinthians. This connection could only be explained in biblical terms.[42] Adam had brought death to all humanity through his rebellion against God, and all human beings had repeated his rebellion and experienced its consequences themselves (15:21–22; cf. 15:3, 17, 56; cf. Gen 3:19). If God's people had been left in this condition, death would have been victorious over them (15:54–55). Instead, however, God provided another "Adam," the anointed king Jesus (15:23–28; cf. 15:45, 47), who overcame sin and death through his resurrection and made it possible for God's people, through identification with him, to experience the same embodied, spiritual, immortal existence that he had in his resurrected state (15:45–49).[43] He was, therefore, the first of the general resurrection of the dead to come (15:20), and without both his resurrection in the past and the general resurrection in the future, there was no hope for eternal life (15:16–19, 30–32). Sin would remain unforgiven, death would remain victorious over the body, and all humanity would perish (cf. 15:54–57).

Paul also explained, however, that the Corinthians who rejected a general bodily resurrection seemed to have misunderstood what it entailed. He agreed with them that "flesh and blood cannot inherit the kingdom of God" (1 Cor 15:50), but this did not mean that existence in God's future kingdom would be disembodied. Rather, God would change the bodies of believers so that they would be incorruptible and immortal (15:51–53). Just as Isaiah prophesied, "Death" would be "swallowed up in victory" (15:54; cf. Isa 25:8).[44]

For Paul, this teaching was not an abstract fine point tacked onto the end of his letter.[45] Rather, the incorrect belief of some Corinthians on this point had led to much of the concrete misbehavior within the community. Paul believed that the lawsuits among believers in the Corinthian church reflected a failure to appreciate the significance of the future existence of believers in the kingdom of God (1 Cor 6:3, 10). Much of the sexual immorality in the church arose from a misunderstanding of the importance and immortality of embodied existence (6:13–14). Paul probably also thought that the readiness of affluent participants in the Corinthian Christian community to treat the Lord's Supper as a typical upper-class banquet (11:17–34) arose from a failure to appreciate the reality of the coming bodily resurrection of the dead (15:32–34).

Paul's Plans to Revisit Corinth

As Paul drew his letter to a close, he gave the Corinthians the same set of instructions about the collection for needy Judean Christians that he had given the Galatians on his journey westward toward Ephesus some months earlier (1 Cor 16:1–4). Paul probably hoped that Timothy, Erastus, and Titus would be able to reinforce these same instructions whenever they arrived in Achaia, but it made sense to include the procedure for the collection in this letter also. The uncertainty in Paul's statement that Timothy should have nothing to fear from the Corinthians "if" (ἐάν) he comes to them (16:10 NRSV, REB, NIV) shows that Paul did not know whether Timothy, Erastus, and Titus would even get to Corinth.[46]

Paul also wanted the Corinthians to know his own travel plans. Some of them had been claiming he was unlikely ever to return to Corinth (1 Cor 4:18), but at this point he planned to return soon (4:19; cf. 11:34).[47] He would wait until later in the spring ("Pentecost"), which would allow him to continue to address the opportunities and challenges that faced him in Ephesus (16:8–9). Then, he would make his way first to the churches in Macedonia, then to Corinth (16:5; Acts 19:21). Since he planned to spend the winter months in Corinth, he probably intended to spend the late spring, summer, and fall of AD 55 in Macedonia strengthening the churches in Philippi, Thessalonica, and Berea and coordinating the collection among Christians in those places.[48]

Paul phrases the narrative of his travel plans diplomatically. "Perhaps I will stay with you or even spend the winter," he tells them, as if to say that he does not mean to distribute his attention to the various churches on his itinerary unequally (1 Cor. 16:6). When easier travel resumed again in the spring of AD 56, he would either go to Jerusalem with the contribution for the needy Christians there ("if it seems advisable," 1 Cor 16:4) or go somewhere else (1 Cor 16:6).[49] He was already thinking of the extension of his work westward toward Rome (Acts 19:21; Rom 1:9–15; 15:23–24).[50] Although these plans eventually materialized, they only materialized after a significant delay, the result of an unexpected and difficult series of circumstances in both Ephesus and Corinth.

16

Trouble in Corinth and Strange Teaching in Ephesus

Some months after sending 1 Corinthians, and during his hectic life in Ephesus, Paul received more distressing news about the Corinthian Christians. How the news came to him is not clear, but at the end of 1 Corinthians, Paul had mentioned that he was expecting Timothy and "the brothers" to return to Ephesus before he left the city (1 Cor 16:11). If this group consisted of Timothy, Erastus, Titus, and another nameless "brother" (Acts 19:22; 2 Cor 12:18), and if Timothy and Erastus stayed in Macedonia while Titus and "the brother" pressed on to Achaia to start the collection (2 Cor 8:6, 10; 9:2; 12:18), then Titus may well have been the messenger who brought these bad tidings to Paul in Ephesus.[1]

It is difficult to know how closely the situation in Corinth at this point resembled the mess it became in the months before Paul wrote 2 Corinthians. Since Paul responded to this report with the drastic step of interrupting his work in Ephesus, where "a wide door for effective work" had "opened" to him and he was facing significant opposition (1 Cor 15:32; 16:9), the situation must have been grave.

Titus's Distressing News and Paul's Painful Visit to Corinth

Titus perhaps told Paul that his long letter to the Corinthians had done little to quell the "quarreling, jealousy, anger, hostility, slander, gossip, conceit, and disorder" that had prompted it (2 Cor 12:20). "Impurity, sexual immorality, and sensuality" were still problems (2 Cor 12:21; 13:2). Some within the Corinthian community, moreover, continued to oppose Paul because of his unimpressive "outward appearance" (2 Cor 5:12; cf.

1 Cor 4:3–5, 18, 20), and the whole community's affection for him had become "restricted" (2 Cor 6:12). It is difficult to imagine the community had taken his advice to discipline the man living in a sexual relationship with his stepmother (1 Cor 5:1–5).[2]

Paul had hoped that when Timothy arrived in Corinth, the Christians there would "put him at ease" (1 Cor 16:10). Now he learned that Timothy had never made it to Corinth but was still in Macedonia and that Titus, who had made it to Corinth, was decidedly not "at ease" about developments in the city. Clearly, this Christian community needed a personal visit from Paul himself. Some months earlier, when Paul had written 1 Corinthians, he had planned to "come . . . soon" to Corinth (4:19), and he was uncertain whether this visit would need to be a disciplinary visit or something milder: "Shall I come to you with a rod," he had asked them, "or with love in a spirit of gentleness?" (4:21). Now was the time to make this visit, and it was going to involve a metaphorical "rod."

The situation was too urgent to follow the plan laid out in 1 Corinthians of traveling to Corinth only after the long journey north to Troas, across the northern Aegean Sea, and through Macedonia (1 Cor 16:5). He would take the shorter route, sailing directly across the Aegean to Corinth, and thus visit Corinth "first" (2 Cor 1:15).[3] He apparently then intended to travel on to Macedonia where he would finish gathering the Macedonian funds for the collection and assemble the Macedonian delegates. Together they would travel back to Corinth, where more delegates would join the entourage, and the whole group would then sail with the funds to Judea (2 Cor 1:15–16; 8:19; cf. 1 Cor 16:3). A plan like this would make sense if Paul was optimistic when he set out for Corinth that he could straighten out the situation there and put the final touches on the collection efforts of his team in both Achaia and Macedonia.

Luke mentions none of this, and Paul gives few details. Paul says that he came to Corinth "in sorrow" (2 Cor 2:1 NASB), using a term (λύπη) that means "pain of mind or spirit, *grief, sorrow, affliction.*"[4] The expression probably reflects the distress he felt at hearing the report that prompted the visit. He also indicates that once he arrived in Corinth, he issued a warning to the Christians there that he hoped would lead them to turn away from their sin, especially the sexual immorality that 1 Corinthians identified as such a serious problem (2 Cor 12:21; 13:2). He spared them the most painful elements of Christian discipline, however, in the hope that, given time, they might change (2 Cor 1:23; 13:2).[5]

Many interpreters of 2 Corinthians have thought this visit was extraordinarily unpleasant for Paul. In the view of one distinguished scholar, an unnamed person in the community had vigorously opposed Paul on his arrival (2 Cor 2:5–11), and the visit ended in "disaster" with Paul hurrying "back to Ephesus hurt, angered, and perplexed."[6] This scenario is not consistent, however, with Paul's comment that he had boasted to Titus about the Corinthians, a boast that must have happened shortly after Paul's return to Ephesus from his painful visit to Corinth (7:14).[7] It also fails to mesh with Paul's description of his demeanor during his second visit to Corinth: "I warned those who sinned before and all the others, and I warn them now while absent, as I did when present on my second visit, that if I come again I will not spare them" (13:2). These do not sound like the words of a person who on his "second visit" had fled from opposition feeling injured and confused.[8]

It is more likely that this visit to Corinth was sorrowful because Paul took no pleasure in having to make the visit at this point and for this reason. He left behind the "open door" for his work in Ephesus sooner than he intended (1 Cor 16:9) and had to change his plan of visiting Macedonia before visiting Corinth, expressed to the Corinthians in his recent long letter to them (1 Cor 16:5–6). That same letter also reveals that Paul was facing difficult challenges in Ephesus: he had fought "with wild beasts" in the city and had "many adversaries" there (1 Cor 15:32; 16:9). Although by this time, Timothy had probably returned to Ephesus (cf. 1 Cor 16:11) and Paul could leave the situation in his capable hands (cf. 1 Cor 4:17; Phil 2:19–22), it must have been less than ideal to leave Ephesus for Corinth and Macedonia before straightening out the problems in Ephesus. In addition, he would not have relished the task of warning the Corinthian Christians against the very sins he had already addressed in 1 Corinthians (2 Cor 12:20–21; 13:2). As Paul set out on his journey, he may well have been discouraged to think that most Corinthian Christians were still not ready for a diet of solid food and, still, like infants, had to be fed with milk (cf. 1 Cor 3:1–3).

Exactly what happened during this second visit to Corinth is not at all clear, but, if Paul boasted to Titus about the Corinthians not long after his return to Ephesus, he must have left Corinth more hopeful than when he had set out. It is true that in his later letter, written before his third visit, he says that he hopes God will not "humiliate me *again*" (2 Cor 12:21 REB, my emphasis).[9] This probably does not refer to the humiliation he had suffered at the hands of the Corinthians on his second visit, however, but to Paul's feelings of humiliation when he realized just how unresponsive they had been to the two letters that preceded his painful visit. Paul probably announced his changed travel plan to the Corinthians, optimistically thinking they would approve of it: although staying with them the whole winter would not now be possible (cf. 1 Cor 16:6), they would have the benefit of not one but two visits (2 Cor 1:15).[10]

There is no reason to think that after Paul left Corinth he deviated from his original plan of visiting Macedonia next and beginning to gather the Macedonian funds and delegates.[11] In a somewhat puzzling passing comment describing the end of Paul's three years in Ephesus, Luke seems to confirm this. Out of the blue, he says that the Macedonians Gaius and Aristarchus were with Paul in Ephesus and says further that they were "his companions in travel" (Acts 19:29). This would make sense if Paul had traveled from Corinth to Macedonia and Gaius and Aristarchus had joined him as Macedonian delegates intending to travel with him back to Corinth and on to Judea. Aristarchus, at least, appears in Luke's actual list of delegates later in the narrative (20:4).[12] When Paul's plans were interrupted, and he traveled from Macedonia on to Ephesus instead of back to Corinth and Judea, Gaius and Aristarchus apparently did not abandon Paul but continued with him to Ephesus.

An Administrative Letter to Timothy

It is possible that among the "many adversaries" (1 Cor 16:9; cf. 15:32) Paul faced in Ephesus before he left for Corinth and Macedonia were people within the Ephesian churches who were teaching a form of Christianity Paul considered false. In response, Paul may have composed an administrative document for Timothy, instructing him in Paul's reluctant absence to resist the false teachers and promote a form of Christianity that emphasized "a pure heart and a good conscience and a sincere faith" (1 Tim 1:3–5). Paul says in 1 Timothy that he had left Ephesus for Macedonia (1:3) but hoped to return to Ephesus soon (3:14; cf. 4:13), and so the letter would fit nicely within this stage of Paul's Ephesian ministry.

Many scholars who study Paul and his letters, however, believe that the apostle did not write 1 Timothy. The letter's vocabulary and style differ markedly from most of the other canonical letters attributed to Paul.[13] It uses expressions like "good conscience" (1 Tim 1:5, 19) and "sound doctrine" (1:10; cf. 6:3), for example, that appear to some interpreters more like the language of Hellenistic literature and philosophy than like the letters everyone agrees Paul wrote.[14]

The letter's instructions on women (1 Tim 2:9–15), moreover, seem to some interpreters to reflect a stage in the history of Christianity later than Paul when Gnostic Christians were beginning to advocate "that marriage and procreation are from Satan" (Irenaeus, *Adv. Haer.* 1.24.2; cf. 1 Tim 2:15).[15] Its assumption of Christian communities organized under the leadership of "overseers," "elders," and "deacons," some of whom at least have been ceremonially appointed (1 Tim 3:1–13; 4:14; 5:17–22), appears to some interpreters to emerge from a time later than Paul and closer to the subapostolic age when church organizational structure was more complex than in Paul's day.[16]

In addition, most scholars who think the letter is pseudonymous believe that attempts to fit it into the narrative of Paul's travels in Acts are implausible. They also think that the efforts of those who believe the letter is genuine to locate it in a period of Paul's life after the close of the book of Acts are unpersuasive.[17] When, in Acts, does Paul leave Timothy behind in Ephesus and travel without him to Macedonia (1 Tim 1:3)?[18] What evidence is there that Paul survived the Roman imprisonment that Luke describes, other than a few late and vague references in the church fathers?[19]

These arguments, while substantive, are not conclusive. First, arguments from vocabulary and syntax are not safe indicators of forgery. Just as Cicero could leave one letter recipient on the edge of his seat with a breathtaking description of mob violence in Rome, he could bore another letter recipient to tears with a pedestrian description of entertainments in Pompey's new theater.[20] This is a reminder that if, as with Cicero, hundreds of authentic Pauline letters had survived, 1 Timothy might look much more "Pauline" than it looks within the context of a mere thirteen-letter corpus.

A letter's style depends significantly on what sociolinguists call its "register," the language that an author used with a particular audience, for a particular purpose, or in a particular time of life.²¹ First Timothy, and its stylistic companions, Titus and 2 Timothy, were written to individuals, with second-person singulars everywhere but in each letter's closing words where Paul sends a grace benediction to a group of people affected by the instructions he gives to his coworkers (1 Tim 6:21; Titus 3:15; 2 Tim 4:22).²²

Paul wrote 1 Timothy, moreover, to a trusted subordinate in an administrative capacity. First Timothy is full of commands and instructions on how to handle a difficult situation that doctrinal and social problems had created. These characteristics bring the letter into the orbit of ancient Hellenistic and Roman administrative letters, which are often terse, are filled with commands, and give instructions to subordinates for handling tricky economic and political problems.²³ Under these circumstances, then, it is not surprising that Paul would write in a different register than in his undisputed letters.

Second, the problem of false teaching that 1 Timothy addresses probably explains why the letter's instructions are so focused on church offices and church order. "Overseers and deacons" receive brief mention in other contexts (Phil 1:1; cf. Acts 14:23; 20:17), but Paul probably discussed them more extensively in 1 Timothy because some of the occupants of these offices had fallen prey to a twisted form of the Christian faith. It is difficult, moreover, to see why the ceremonial appointment of group leaders through laying hands on them signals a later church development (cf. Gen 48:14; Acts 6:6; 9:17).

Third, the complex fabric of travel plans and actual journeys that Paul presupposes in 1 and 2 Corinthians makes clear that Luke has compressed many details of Paul's travels, and 1 Timothy fits reasonably easily into the more detailed picture that 2 Corinthians provides. When Paul describes his plans as they stood just before leaving Ephesus on the "painful visit," he implies that his turnaround point was to be Macedonia (2 Cor 1:16).²⁴ It is therefore reasonable to match these plans with his comment in 1 Timothy that he left Timothy in Ephesus when he "was starting for Macedonia" (1 Tim 1:3 REB).²⁵ It is true that his statement about returning to Ephesus soon (1 Tim 3:14) and his instructions about what Timothy should do in the meantime (1 Tim 4:13) find no parallel in Paul's description of his "painful visit" in 2 Corinthians. There he only indicates that he planned to travel to Corinth, Macedonia,

Trouble in Corinth and Strange Teaching in Ephesus

back to Corinth, and on to Judea (2 Cor 1:16). At this stage of his planning, however, he might easily have intended to spend a short time in Ephesus after visiting Corinth but before going on to Judea (cf. Acts 20:16–17).

As things turned out, Paul did return to Ephesus, probably sooner than he had intended when he set out for Corinth and Macedonia on the "painful visit" trip. When he describes what happened rather than what he planned to do, it becomes clear that he only visited Corinth once on this journey and then went back to Ephesus. He probably did not return to Ephesus, however, by simply sailing east across the Aegean Sea.[26] Rather, he went from Corinth to Macedonia, his original turnaround point. Then—and here is where his plans changed—he traveled on to Ephesus rather than back to Corinth. From Ephesus, he eventually visited Corinth for a third time, passing through Troas and Macedonia on his way (2 Cor 1:23; 2:1, 12–13; 7:5; 12:14; 13:1; Acts 20:1–2), and probably after a brief trip westward from Macedonia into Illyricum (Rom 15:19; Acts 20:2a).

If Paul wrote 1 Timothy during this period of his work, therefore, he probably wrote from Macedonia, not long after his "painful visit" to Corinth. The letter's purpose was to instruct Timothy about "how one ought to behave in the household of God, which is the church of the living God, a pillar and buttress of the truth" (1 Tim 3:15). This instruction was necessary because false teaching had infiltrated the Christian community in Ephesus, and this false teaching seems to have led some people within the church to behave in ways that were at odds with sound Christian teaching.

The intellectual structure of the false teaching is hard to discern because Paul did not consider it coherent enough to merit refutation. Its promoters thought of themselves as "teachers of the law" (1 Tim 1:7) and denigrated both marriage and the enjoyment of food (4:3), but beyond these tenets it is difficult to go. In Paul's view, the false teaching promoted "useless speculations" (1:4, cf. BDAG 303), "vain discussion" (1:6), "irreverent, silly myths" (4:7), "an unhealthy craving for controversy and for quarrels about words" (6:4), and "the irreverent babble and contradictions of what is falsely called knowledge" (6:20). The false teachers lacked "understanding either [of] what they [were] saying or the things about which they [made] confident assertions" (1:7). They were "depraved in mind and deprived of the truth" (6:5).

CHAPTER 16

In Paul's view, the false teachers did not sincerely believe what they taught. Rather, their consciences were "seared" (1 Tim 4:2), and they imagined religion to be a path to riches (6:5). "The love of money" prompted them to "wander away from the faith" (6:10).

Interpreters of 1 Timothy sometimes chalk this kind of language up to the common invective that philosophers and religious intellectuals used against their opponents in antiquity.[27] Jewish magicians and Greek prophets in Roman times, however, frequently charged for their services. Juvenal describes a particular type of Jewish woman who claims to be "an expounder of the laws of Jerusalem" and whom he calls a "high priestess" and "reliable intermediary of highest heaven." This woman, he says, "will sell you whatever dreams you like for the tiniest copper coin" (6.542–547 [Braund, LCL]).[28] Lucian says that the Paphlagonian prophet Alexander of Abonoteichus began his career by associating as a boy with "one of those who advertise enchantments, miraculous incantations, charms for your love affairs, 'sendings' for your enemies, disclosures of buried treasure, and successions to estates" (*Alex.* 5 [Harmon, LCL]). Later, Alexander posed as a priest of Asclepius and issued oracles to inquirers, some of which prescribed medical cures (*Alex.* 22). He charged one drachma and two obols per oracle (*Alex.* 23).

Juvenal and Lucian were writing of events in the second century, but Jewish magicians seem to have operated in a similar way at almost exactly the time of Paul (Philo, *Spec.* 3.100–101; 4.48–50; Pliny, *Nat.* 30.2.11; Josephus, *A.J.* 20.142; cf. Acts 13:6–12).[29] Luke identifies a "Jewish high priest" named Sceva whose "seven sons" practiced exorcism in Ephesus and the surrounding area at the time of Paul's work in the city.[30] They apparently used names whose utterance they considered spiritually effective for driving away "evil spirits," and they attempted to use Jesus's name in the same way (Acts 19:13–14).

Luke says nothing about the sons of Sceva charging for their services, but it seems likely that they did this. If so, then the false teaching Paul opposes in 1 Timothy may have arisen within, or may have been influenced by, the same sort of Jewish folk religion that the sons of Sceva and other "freelance experts" in religion practiced.[31] In his second letter to Timothy, written several years later, Paul compares the false teachers against whom he warns Timothy to the Egyptian magicians that opposed Moses and about whom stories circulated widely in the first century (e.g., CD 5,

17b–19; and Pliny, *Nat.* 30.2.11).[32] Paul may have referred to these well-known magicians because the false teachers, located somewhere in Asia, used magical practices (2 Tim 3:8, 13).[33]

Clearly the false teachers brought more to the game than magical incantations. They emphasized esoteric knowledge (1 Tim 1:4; 4:7), a concern with the Jewish law (1:7), a negative view of marriage, and certain dietary prescriptions (4:3), and they communicated all this to their devotees for a price (6:5). Perhaps just as in Juvenal's Rome, some of the false teachers were women who "expounded the laws of Jerusalem." Were they the younger widows who went "from house to house . . . saying what they should not" (5:13)?

Paul responds with instructions to Timothy on how to restore "healthy teaching" (1 Tim 1:10; cf. 6:3, my trans.) and "proper conduct" (3:15 REB) to the Christian assemblies in Ephesus. His primary concern is that the Ephesians see their assemblies as a single "household of God" testifying by its way of life to the truth about Christ that the church confesses (3:15). Speaking of the person who oversees each assembly, Paul observes, "He must manage his own household well, with all dignity keeping his children submissive, for if someone does not know how to manage his own household, how will he care for God's church?" (3:4).

It seems likely that the false teaching had affected the order of Christian households with its message that people should avoid marriage and certain foods. At a practical level, therefore, many of Paul's instructions focus on domestic matters. He is concerned with the way men on one hand and women on the other hand have been behaving when Christians in Ephesus assemble (1 Tim 2:8–15). Men should pray rather than quarrel; women should avoid displays of wealth, should "learn quietly," and should not teach. The assembled Christian community should reflect the roles of Adam and Eve at creation, with "Eve" avoiding the role of teacher, which led to transgression, and instead focusing on childbearing, faith, love, holiness, and self-control.

Paul then describes the qualities that should characterize "overseers" and "deacons" (1 Tim 3:1–13), and most of these qualities are domestic in nature: the overseer should be faithful to one woman, sober, well-behaved, hospitable, not a drunkard, not pugnacious, not obsessed with money. He should lead his household well and have obedient children.[34] Similarly, deacons should be dignified, straightforward in their speech, not addicted to "much wine," innocent of dishonest financial affairs, loyal to one woman, and leading their children and houses well. Women deacons should be dignified, not guilty of slander, sober, and trustworthy.

The church should take care of widows "who are truly widows" (1 Tim 5:3), but instead of picking up the slack for irresponsible children and grandchildren, it should teach them "to show godliness to their own household and to make some return to their parents" (5:4). Failing to take care of the "members of" one's "household" is a denial of the faith and equivalent to not being a believer at all (5:8).

Younger widows receive special instructions because they seem to be among the primary purveyors of the false teaching. Rather than making the rounds of houses "saying what they should not" (1 Tim 5:13) and straying "after Satan," they should marry, bear children, manage their households," and care for relatives who are widows (5:16). These are probably precisely the domestic activities that the false teaching resisted with its prohibitions of marriage and abstinence from various foods (4:3).

Paul's letter gives the impression that the false teaching, with its negative view of marriage and the enjoyment of food, appealed especially to young, widowed women in the Christian assemblies in Ephesus. These women seem to have then spread the false teaching from house to house and, in the process, disrupted those households.

At a theoretical level, Paul emphasizes the necessity of holding the Christian faith with sincerity rather than as a body of outward rules and regulations. Luke Timothy Johnson has shown that Paul opens the letter with a lengthy expression of this idea, and that it runs like an undercurrent through the rest of the document.[35] "The aim of our charge," says Paul, "is love that issues from a pure heart and a good conscience and a sincere faith" (1 Tim 1:5). The false teachers, however, focus on their unhealthy outward practices. They fancy themselves teachers of the law with its rules and regulations (1:7). The "law (νόμος) is good" Paul counters (1:8), but only when one uses it "appropriately" (νομίμως) to distinguish between the just person and the lawless person (1:9–11).[36] In the hands of those whose heart and conscience have not experienced the transforming effects of the gospel, Paul's argument implies, it can become a vehicle for the very vices it forbids, as Paul knows from firsthand experience (1:13). Timothy should charge these teachers, then, to stop spreading their "different doctrine," and Timothy himself should hold on to "the faith and a good conscience" (1:19) as he fulfills Paul's instructions.

Similarly, in the middle and at the end of the letter, Paul mentions the false teachers' rules on marriage and diet as evidence that they are insincere "liars whose consciences are seared" (1 Tim 4:2). Their focus on outward practices, he says, masks inward corruption and depraved minds that imagine "godliness" to be "a means of gain" (6:5).[37] Again, Timothy, for his part, is to provide for the Ephesian Christians an example of how to live in his "speech, in conduct, in love, in faith, in purity" (4:12). He is to "pursue righteousness, godliness, faith, love, steadfastness, gentleness" (6:11).

Paul also seems concerned in 1 Timothy with the reputation of Christians before Ephesian society, perhaps because of the impact that the false teaching has had on the conduct of Christians in Ephesus.[38] It is necessary, he says, to "lead a peaceful and quiet life, godly and dignified in every way" (1 Tim 2:2). The reason for this seems to be, at least in part, that God "desires all people to be saved and to come to the knowledge of the truth" (2:4). If Christians were behaving in ways that the wider society found offensive, and these behaviors arose from a warped theology, then the church was failing in its role as "a pillar and buttress of the truth" within that society (3:15). It was important, then, that the "overseer" of a Christian assembly "be well thought of by outsiders" (3:7; cf. 3:2) and that "deacons . . . prove themselves blameless" (3:10).[39]

Pauline churches in Ephesus came into existence under a cloud, when some opponents of Paul in the synagogue where he taught "publicly maligned the way" (Acts 19:9 NIV). In such an environment, Paul's concern for the public image of Christians in the city makes sense. The last thing the Ephesian church needed was a reputational crisis brought on not by the offense of the truth it proclaimed about God but by the "silly myths," harmful rules, "envy, dissension, slander, evil suspicions, and constant friction" that the false teaching had produced (1 Tim 1:4; 4:3; 6:4–5).

When Paul wrote 1 Timothy he intended to return to Ephesus "soon" (3:14), but clearly not so soon that a letter was unnecessary. After sending it, he probably intended to spend ample time working among the Christian assemblies in Philippi, Thessalonica, and Berea to gather their funds and delegates for the collection and then to travel to Corinth and on to

Judea via Ephesus. That plan only materialized later, however, and in a modified form.

More Bad News from Corinth, a Change of Plan, and a Third Letter

It was probably sometime during this busy period in Macedonia that Paul again received distressing news from Corinth, news that once again involved a disruption to his plans. An opponent of Paul within the Corinthian community had started expressing his views in a way that clearly and severely wronged both Paul and many within the community itself. Most people within the community seem not to have agreed with the opinions of this anti-Paulinist, but they also seem not to have risen to Paul's defense (2 Cor 7:9, 12).

Paul responded in two ways. First, he canceled his return trip to Corinth. With such opposition stirring against him, it was not the time for the gathering of delegates from a wide geographical area in Corinth to finish the collection project. The busy port of Corinth was the ideal staging area for the final phase of the collection, but if the Christians of Corinth were themselves unenthusiastic about Paul, then trying to launch the journey to Judea from there might only bring humiliation both to Paul and the Corinthian Christians (cf. 2 Cor 9:4). In any case, a return visit to Corinth under the present circumstances was bound to be as painful as the visit he had just made (1:23; 2:1). He would simply return to Ephesus rather than travel back to Corinth and on to Judea.

Second, he decided that once he was back in Ephesus, he would send Titus to Corinth again, this time with a letter of warning that he hoped would correct the problem by urging the Corinthian Christians to discipline the erring brother in formal proceedings and to repent of their own unwillingness to do this without prompting from Paul (2 Cor 2:9; 7:12).[40] It must have been with a heavy heart that Paul set out for Ephesus, probably with the Macedonians Gaius and Aristarchus (Acts 19:29).

It was probably sometime after their arrival in Ephesus that Paul composed his next letter to Corinth "in much affliction and anguish of heart and with many tears" (2 Cor 2:4). The Corinthian Christians could easily understand his failure to return to Corinth as a sign that he did not take his relationship with them seriously (2 Cor 1:17; cf. 1 Cor 4:18–19). He must have hoped, however, that they would see his decision not to return and his present letter—with its stern advice about church discipline—as evidence of his love for them (2 Cor 2:4). In addition, he hoped they would understand this letter as an expression of his desire for them to love him in return (2 Cor 2:9; 7:12).

After assuring Titus of his conviction that most Corinthian Christians probably did not support the opposition to him (2 Cor 7:14), Paul sent this letter with his trusted coworker (2 Cor 8:23) and asked him to restart the collection if enthusiasm for it had waned during all the trouble (2 Cor 8:6). Paul already had plans in place by this time to travel north from Ephesus to Alexandria Troas, Macedonia, and Corinth and from there first to Jerusalem and then to Rome (Acts 19:21; 2 Cor 2:12). He seems to have asked Titus to meet him in Troas after Titus's work in Corinth was complete, or, if Titus could not make it as far as Troas, to wait for him in Macedonia, probably in either Thessalonica or Philippi (2 Cor 2:13–14).

17

"Fighting Without and Fear Within"

It was a particularly dangerous encounter with Ephesian civic pride, centered on the goddess Artemis, that seems to have precipitated Paul's departure from the city and the end to his roughly three years of ministry there. The bond between Artemis and Ephesus was so long-standing and so tight that depictions of the goddess on coins could serve symbolically as depictions of the city itself, and her cult statue in her magnificent temple sported a crown symbolizing the city's walls.[1] A second-century AD inscription describes Ephesus as the goddess's "nurturer."[2] She was worshiped in public processions from her temple that went around and through the city, and the city celebrated three major annual festivals in her honor.[3] Friends, neighbors, and family members of the Ephesian Christians would have viewed their failure to attend these festivals as a societal transgression.[4]

It is easy to see how as Paul's work in the city progressed, pressure might build on Christians to tone down their commitment to the principle that "gods made with hands are not gods" (Acts 19:26). The lavishly dressed cult statue of Artemis, whether in her temple or on parade through the city, was clearly "made with hands." As the goddess of the hunt, moreover, Artemis's arrows could offer either protection or destruction to the city and individuals within it, depending on how well they honored her in return.[5]

These were the considerations that may have prompted a silversmith named Demetrius to gather a large group of his fellow craftsmen and lead them in a public demonstration against Paul and his followers. On a normal workday, Demetrius oversaw smiths who made "silver shrines of Artemis" (Acts 19:24), perhaps copies of the sanctuary in which her cult statue normally stood.⁶ On this day, however, he explained to the craftsmen he had called together about his concern that Paul's monotheistic convictions, duly taught to others, had brought their trade and "the great goddess Artemis" into disrepute (19:26–27).

The typical place for a civic assembly in Ephesus was the massive theater, and such an assembly would have to be coordinated through the chief administrative officer of the city—"the town clerk" (γραμματεύς, Acts 19:35)—whose office was probably near the theater. The enraged crowd of artisans, then, entered the theater, dragging with them Paul's Macedonian friends Gaius and Aristarchus and chanting, "Great is Artemis of the Ephesians!" Paul wanted to go into the fray, but his "disciples," and some wealthy city officials known as Asiarchs, urged him to stay away (19:30–31).⁷

As the chanting and chaos worsened, the town clerk addressed the crowd, telling them they were being too disorderly and should bring their complaint before the next regularly scheduled assembly (Acts 19:39). There was at least one such assembly per month, and up to three if needed, so the town clerk's point seems to have been that with a little patience the artisans would be able to have a fair and orderly hearing of their complaints. This would avoid the present risk that government officials would view their disorderly conduct as rioting (19:40), a development that could have had profound implications for the independent governance of the city under the Romans.⁸ After his speech, the city clerk dismissed the assembly (19:41), and everyone seems to have gone home without further trouble for the Christians, at least for the moment.

Paul's Difficult Journey to Macedonia

Paul may have thought it advisable to take his Macedonian "companions in travel" (Acts 19:29) and his coworker Timothy and leave the city before the next "regular assembly" rolled around. In addition to his political troubles in Ephesus, he had arranged to meet Titus in the important port city of Alexandria Troas, just across the Aegean Sea from the Macedonian cities of Thessalonica and Philippi, and a place where he intended to preach the gospel (2 Cor 2:12–13).

Probably most important of all, however, was the anxiety he felt about the effect of his most recent letter to Corinth. Had his boast to Titus as he sent him off with the letter (2 Cor 7:14) been too optimistic? Perhaps when the Corinthians received the letter, they would be unwilling to discipline the person who had opposed Paul so strongly. Perhaps they would by now be firmly opposed to Paul themselves and unwilling to contribute to the collection. Toward the end of his time in Ephesus, Paul had started to dread what he might hear from Titus (7:5) and even to regret sending his anguished letter (7:8). It must have been with a heavy heart that he set out for points north.

A typical ship bound for Alexandria Troas would have traveled along the coast of Asia, weaving a route between the islands of Chios and Lesbos (cf. Acts 20:14–15). The journey would have been unpredictable because of the prevailing winds from the northwest, but barring a storm or some other difficulty, might have taken between three and four days.[9]

Paul had been to Troas at least once before when he, Silas, and Luke had passed through the city on their way to Macedonia six years earlier (Acts 16:8–11). For unknown reasons, God's Spirit had at that time prohibited Paul from preaching the gospel in Asia (Acts 16:6), and since Troas was in Asia, it would have fallen under this ban. Now, however, the ban on Paul's preaching in Asia had long been lifted, and when Paul arrived in Troas the Lord opened a door of opportunity for the gospel's advancement (2 Cor 2:12).[10] Although neither Paul nor Luke says anything about a church in Troas at this point, soon there would be a flourishing community of believers meeting on Sunday evening, gathering "to break bread" (probably a reference to the Lord's Supper), and listening to Paul's teaching (Acts 20:7).[11] It seems likely that this community was the fruit of Paul's labors as he waited for Titus's arrival.

Titus, however, never arrived, and Paul's troubles only increased. In addition to his anxiety over the impact of his most recent letter, he may have also suffered another bout of the debilitating illness that occasionally attacked him. In references to his afflictions in this period that parallel each other closely, Murray Harris has observed that he first says his "spirit was not at rest" (2 Cor 2:13) and then that "our bodies had no rest" (7:5). He experienced "fighting without and fears within" (7:5).[12] This description is consistent with the idea that Paul was not only worried about the Corinthian believers' response to his letter but also plagued with some bodily ailment (cf. Gal 4:13).

"Fighting Without and Fear Within"

Paul's illness may well have been a recurrence of the "thorn in the flesh" that had occasionally afflicted him since AD 43 (2 Cor 12:2, 7–9), and was probably also "the deadly peril" he "experienced in Asia" (1:8, 10). The desperate language he uses to describe the experience fits a serious recurring illness: "We were so utterly burdened beyond our strength," he says, "that we despaired of life itself," and "we felt that we had received the sentence of death" (1:8–9). This last statement uses a perfect-tense verb (ἐσχήκαμεν) appropriate to an occurrence whose effects continued to linger even after the episode itself had passed. Paul thought he would need deliverance from this affliction again (1:10), and he was confident that if the Corinthians prayed for him God would deliver him from future recurrences.[13] When that happens, he says, "many will give thanks on our behalf for the blessing granted us through the prayers of many" (1:11).

Discouraged by his failure to find Titus, and perhaps weakened by the "deadly peril" of his illness, he abandoned the open door the Lord had provided in Troas, said goodbye to the infant church there, "and went on to Macedonia" (2 Cor 2:12–13). Neither Paul nor Luke tells us how Paul traveled to Macedonia or where he went when he got to the province. Alexandria Troas was a busy and important port, and it would make sense for Paul to sail from there to either of the similarly busy Macedonian ports of Neapolis or Thessalonica. If Paul's Macedonian friends Gaius and Aristarchus were with him on this journey, they may have sailed directly to Thessalonica, Aristarchus's hometown (Acts 19:29; 20:4). If so, perhaps they stopped on the island of Lemnos on their way, as the physician Galen did when he sailed from Troas to Thessalonica a century or so later (*Simpl. Med.* 9 [Kühn 12.171]).[14]

If they went to Neapolis, then they probably retraced the route Paul had taken six years earlier with Silas, Timothy, and Luke, stopping at Samothrace on the first day and landing at Neapolis on the second day. If this was their plan, then perhaps they waited to make the roughly ten-mile trek to Philippi until the third day (Acts 16:11–12).[15] Philippi would have had several advantages over Thessalonica as a backup meeting point with Titus.[16] The Christians at Philippi had been uniquely supportive of Paul and his team during his first foray into Macedonia and had continued to provide support when they moved outside the province to Athens and Corinth (Phil 4:15–16; cf. 2 Cor 11:8–9). After Paul's public shaming in Philippi and his insistence on an apology for this mistreatment (Acts 16:37–39), moreover, his legal situation in Philippi would have been clear. In other places in Macedonia, such as Thessalonica and Berea, he might have had more legal trouble (Acts 17:8–9, 13).

While Paul waited for Titus to arrive, he busied himself with arrangements for the collection among the Macedonians. Although they were quite poor themselves (2 Cor 8:2), he believed it was important for them to support this effort for the beleaguered Jewish Christians in Jerusalem, and Paul used the eagerness of the Corinthians to contribute during the previous year as an example to them (9:2). To Paul's surprise, the Macedonians accepted the challenge enthusiastically and gave generously (8:3–5; 9:2). Their eagerness to give "themselves first to the Lord and then by the will of God to" Paul (8:5) must have comforted the apostle amid his illness and anxiety as he hoped for good news from Titus.

Finally, Some Qualified Good News

It was probably during his efforts on behalf of the collection in Macedonia that Paul finally met Titus and heard the latest news from Corinth. The news was mainly good. Titus reported that at least most of the Corinthian Christians had been mortified to learn from Paul's letter that he thought they had been unsupportive when one of their number had opposed Paul (2 Cor 7:7, 11). They had responded by disciplining this person, perhaps too harshly (2:6–7; 7:11). Despite the difficult discipline, Paul's former opponent had reacted positively and asked for forgiveness (2:7). Most of the Corinthians, moreover, responded well to Titus, receiving "him with fear and trembling" (7:15) and refreshing "his spirit" (7:13). Paul's boast to Titus when he sent him off to Corinth with the last letter had proved correct, much to Paul's relief (7:14). He had reason to be "filled with comfort" and "joy" at Titus's report (7:4).

Nevertheless, all was not well. First, and most important, there was still a faction within the Corinthian church that was opposed to Paul and had failed to take on board the corrections Paul had urged upon the church in 1 Corinthians. They were not convinced Paul really cared for them. He had mentioned spending the winter with them at the end of the letter

(1 Cor 16:6) but then had failed to do so, making a hasty visit instead to enforce that letter's principles. He had then set out for Macedonia soon after arriving, claiming that he would return shortly but, again, failed to follow through (2 Cor 1:15–17). Instead of a second visit from Paul, they received a harsh letter (2 Cor 1:23; 2:3–4; cf. 10:10). Paul seemed to be taking the Corinthians for granted ("Did I lightly change my mind?" 2 Cor 1:17 REB) rather than showing them love (2 Cor 2:4; cf. 1 Cor 4:21). His brief second visit, moreover, was a reminder of all the off-putting characteristics he had exhibited during his original eighteen months with them: unskilled in public speaking (1 Cor 1:17, 20; 2:1, 3–4; 2 Cor 10:10), insistence on the significance of Christ's death (1 Cor 1:18; 2:2; 2 Cor 4:10; 5:14–15), and a refusal to follow the conventions of patronage and accept support from the wealthy members of the church (1 Cor 9:11–12, 15, 18; 2 Cor 11:7–11).[17]

Second, a rival group claiming both to be apostles and to have strong links to Judea and the early apostles had arrived in Corinth and aligned themselves with the opposition to Paul already present there. They had come with letters of recommendation in hand, probably from churches in Judea (2 Cor 3:1; 11:22) and boasted in their style of ministry and social connections (2 Cor 10:18; 11:12, 18, 20–22).

They applauded the Corinthian emphasis on Paul's flaws and added some observations of their own. Paul had arrived in Corinth with no letters of recommendation from anyone in Judea, the epicenter of the Jesus movement (2 Cor 3:1; 4:2; 5:12; 6:4; 10:12, 18; 12:11). Nothing about Paul, moreover, commended him as an apostle on a par with the twelve Judean apostles (2 Cor 11:5; 12:11).[18] Could Paul match the stunning healings and expert speaking ability that authenticated the apostleship of Peter and John (2 Cor 12:11b–12; cf. Acts 3:1–10; 4:13)? As the Corinthians had already noticed (1 Cor 9:1–2), unlike the original apostles, Paul had not known Jesus himself. At Antioch, perhaps they said, none of the important people from Jerusalem stood with Paul on the issue of dietary observance (Gal 2:11–13). They conceded that Paul's letters had a certain *gravitas* (2 Cor 1:13; 10:10), but was even this merely an attempt to frighten people (2 Cor 10:9)? In any case, the Corinthians were surely right that his speaking ability left much to be desired, and, in person, he exuded weakness (2 Cor 10:1, 9–10; cf. 11:6). If people of substance and his own abilities failed to commend

CHAPTER 17

him, could the Corinthian Christians trust him? He claimed to work in order not to burden them with his support, but did he intend to siphon off financial support from his collection for the Jerusalem poor (2 Cor 11:7–10; 12:13–18; cf. 8:20–21)?[19]

The theological foundation from which these opponents taught is not clear. Many interpreters have thought that since they highlighted their Jewishness (2 Cor 11:22), and since Paul argues at length in 2 Corinthians for the superiority of his "new covenant" ministry to the Mosaic ministry of the law's condemnation (3:4–18), his opponents emphasized that the Mosaic covenant was still in force. They were, in other words, Judaizers. They were like Paul's opponents in Galatia who insisted that gentiles conform to the Jewish law in order to enter the people of God, but without a requirement for circumcision.[20] Paul does not formulate his comparison of his ministry of righteousness with the Mosaic ministry of condemnation, however, as an answer to his opponents' theology. It is, rather, an argument for the dignity of his role in "the ministry of righteousness" against his opponents' claims that he is not fit to be an apostle.[21]

It is likely, then, that Paul objected, in equal measure, both to the behavior of his opponents and to the truncated, superficial theology from which it arose. They were content to win positions of influence among the Corinthians by slandering Paul (2 Cor 1:12, 17; 3:1; 5:13; 7:2; 12:16), focusing on what was transient (4:18), boasting about outward appearance (5:12), and adulterating the word of God (2:17; 4:2), probably by downplaying the significance of Christ's suffering (4:10; 5:14–15).

This was all enough for Paul to consider their teaching beyond the pale. They taught "another Jesus . . . a different spirit . . . a different gospel" from the Jesus, Spirit, and gospel that Paul had taught the Corinthians (2 Cor 11:4). Although they had come to Corinth from the outside (11:4), and they had probably come from Judea (11:22), they do not seem to have been concerned to impose the Mosaic law on non-Jewish Christians. They were much more interested in the patronage of the Corinthian Christians, in, as Lucian would satirically describe these sorts of arrangements, "having the noblest of the Romans for their friends, eating expensive dinners without paying any scot, living in a handsome establishment, and travelling in all comfort and luxury, behind a span of white horses, perhaps with their noses in the air" (*Merc. cond.* 3 [Harmon, LCL]).[22]

"Fighting Without and Fear Within"

Why a Letter Instead of a Visit?

All this called for a response, but once again, Paul felt he could not give that response in person. Perhaps he believed that even with most of the Corinthians back on his side, there was still too much acrimony and disobedience in Corinth to make a personal visit productive. The Corinthians were still "restricted in" their "own affections" for him (2 Cor 6:12; 7:2), and he was afraid that "perhaps when I come I may find you not as I wish, and that you may find me not as you wish—that perhaps there may be quarreling, jealousy, anger, hostility, slander, gossip, conceit, and disorder" (12:20). In other words, he was afraid that too many of them had learned nothing from 1 Corinthians, his painful second visit, and his most recent, severe letter.

By writing a letter of response to the criticisms of his opponents and of appeal to the Corinthians and sending it with Titus and two other "brothers" (2 Cor 8:18, 22; 9:3), Paul could prepare the Corinthians for his third visit (12:14; 13:1). Titus and the two brothers would be going to Corinth anyway to prepare the final stages of the collection (8:16–24; 9:5), and Titus seemed to get along well with the Corinthians (7:13, 15; 8:16–17). If he sent a letter with this trio, perhaps he could prevent his third visit from taking the disciplinary tone that his second visit had required (10:2; 13:2–3). "For this reason," he says at the letter's end, "I write these things while I am away from you, that when I come I may not have to be severe in my use of the authority that the Lord has given me for building up and not for tearing down" (13:10). If the letter had its intended effect, then Paul could fulfill his earlier suggestion that he spend the winter with the Corinthians, and he could do so in peace. He would then be able to conclude the Achaian part of his collection and oversee the assembly of delegates from the churches who would convey it to Jerusalem.

There may have also been a logistical reason why Paul needed to write to the Corinthians rather than visit them immediately. Luke says that when Paul reached Macedonia he went "through those regions" and gave "them much encouragement" (Acts 20:2). This implies that Paul did not stay in one place but traveled around, and he may have even ventured outside Macedonia. A few months later, when writing to the Roman Christians during the winter that he eventually spent in Corinth (Acts 20:2–3; Rom 16:1), Paul says that he had fulfilled his commission to proclaim the gospel of Christ "from Jerusalem and all the way around to Illyricum" (Rom 15:19). Since Paul had preached the gospel *within* the city of Jerusalem (Acts 9:28), this statement must mean that by the time he penned these words he had also preached the gospel *within* Illyricum, not merely up to its border.[23] Traveling to Illyricum and proclaiming the gospel there, however, would take time, and this provided another reason not to visit Corinth yet but to write the church there a substantial letter.

Paul the Mediator

Paul's letter is a deeply personal reflection on the character of his vocation as an intermediary who runs from place to place with the good news that God, who created the world, has taken the initiative in reconciling the world to himself in Christ (2 Cor 5:18). Second Corinthians has by far the highest concentration of words in the Greek Bible related to this task of mediating God's revelation to humankind (διακονία, διάκονος, διακονέω). These words, usually translated into English with the terms "ministry" and "minister," could refer to running around, assisting someone in need (e.g., Mark 1:31; Luke 10:40; 17:8; 22:27), but John N. Collins has ably demonstrated that both Jewish and non-Jewish peoples in Greek-speaking antiquity used these terms to describe those who carried messages from divine to human beings.[24] Hermes, for example, could function as the messenger (διάκονον) of Zeus (Aeschylus, *Prom.* 942; cf. Lucian, *Char.* 1).[25] Similarly, the Jewish general Josephus, writing, like Paul, in the first century, used the word to describe how he became convinced that God had given him the responsibility of prophesying the future fate of the Jews to the Romans.

Josephus was so close to Paul in culture, language, and time that his use of the word is particularly instructive. He surrendered to the Romans with this prayer to God: "Since it pleases thee who didst create the Jewish nation, to break thy work, since fortune has wholly passed to the Romans, and since thou hast made choice of my spirit to announce the things that are to come, I willingly surrender to the Romans and consent to live; but I take thee to witness that I go, not as a traitor, but as thy minister [διάκονος]" (*B.J.* 3.354 [Thackeray]).

Josephus would serve as a "go-between" who would interpret the word of God to the conquerors of God's people.[26] It was a role that, at least in Josephus's telling, the emperor Vespasian fully understood and acknowledged, calling Josephus "a minister [διάκονον] of the voice of God" (*B.J.* 3.626 [Thackeray]).²⁷

Paul was also a "go-between" or "mediator" of God's voice to the non-Jewish world. Since the role itself was widely recognized in Paul's world, 2 Corinthians is Paul's attempt to define it in a way specific to the Christian gospel, over against his opponents in Corinth who had their own ideas of what an authentic mediator of Christ should look like (2 Cor 11:23).

The letter makes it clear from the beginning that Paul did not take his role as God's mediator lightly, particularly with respect to his relationship with the Corinthians. The changes in his travel plans, and his decision to write to the Corinthians rather than visit them a third time on his way back to Ephesus, were not signs that he did not care for the Corinthians or went about his task of proclaiming the gospel in an opportunistic way (2 Cor 1:17).²⁸ His conduct with respect to the Corinthians always arose from his love for them and his desire for their joy to increase (1:24; 2:3–4).

Paul's task as a go-between, carrying the gospel of God's reconciliation to humanity, could never measure up in its outward appearance to the world's standards for influential teachers. His ministry in Troas served as an example of this: it was a disaster. Paul's unease about the Corinthians and his physical impairment led him to abandon a door that the Lord had opened for him there. God nevertheless used this seeming defeat to spread the aroma of Christ elsewhere (2 Cor 2:12–16).²⁹

Paul's failure to present the Corinthians with letters of recommendation is another example of the outwardly disastrous, but inwardly triumphant, nature of his ministry. Paul had no real "letters of recommendation," but in one sense the Corinthians themselves functioned in the same way. They were like a letter written on Paul's heart, and God himself had written a letter of recommendation for Paul on their hearts when God had transformed their lives by means of the Spirit (2 Cor 3:1–6). The gospel's transforming work happened inside a person, changing them so that they no longer stood under the condemnation of the Mosaic law. Instead of experiencing God's condemnation, they began to reflect more faithfully than before their conversion the divine image that God intended them to bear when he created human beings in the first place (3:7–18).

Paul had himself experienced this transformation at his own conversion and calling to proclaim the gospel, and it was God's dramatic work of re-creation in his own life that kept him from discouragement amid all the hardship he experienced as a mediator of the gospel (2 Cor 4:1). It was also God's transformative work in his own life that led him to repudiate "disgraceful, underhanded ways" and to "refuse to practice cunning or to tamper with God's word" (4:2). Perhaps Paul alludes here on one hand to the tactics of his opponents in Corinth (cf. 2:17; 5:12) and on the other hand to his own character prior to his conversion as he moved within the same politically powerful circles as the high priestly family that put Jesus to death and persecuted his first followers (cf. Acts 9:1–2).

The inwardly transformative, and therefore hidden, nature of Paul's success as a mediator of the gospel derived its character from the gospel itself. The gospel proclaims that the present is the time to embrace God's offer of salvation (2 Cor 6:2) because Jesus died in the past, and, by dying, brought life to those who accepted his death as a reconciling gift from God (4:10–11; 5:14, 19). Furthermore, the "salvation" that this reconciliation with God gives has future implications. God will one day judge the earth with equity and restore and renew creation from the ravages of human sin. On that day, those who have received God's gift of reconciliation and lived in a way consistent with this transforming gift will experience salvation and life in the new creation (4:14; 5:1, 4, 10, 17).

So, Paul's present service as a mediator of the gospel often involved suffering and perplexity, but God used these difficult circumstances to bring spiritual life to others (2 Cor 4:7–12). As Paul experienced the suffering that faithfulness to his role entailed, moreover, he avoided discouragement (5:6) by looking to the future when "what is mortal" would "be swallowed up by life" (5:4) and when everyone would "appear before the judgment seat of Christ" to "receive what is due for what he has done in the body, whether good or evil" (5:10). God had called him to persuade others of the gospel, and he constantly had in mind the day on which he would give an account to God for how well he had executed this responsibility. The sobering reality of this coming day (5:11), and his love for the Corinthians (2:4; 8:7; 11:11; 12:15), motivated the apostle's prayers for their restoration and all his efforts through correspondence, coworkers, and personal visits, to build them up (13:9–11; cf. 10:8; 12:19). The suffering he endured, the quality of his character, and his perseverance through false accusations, personal peril, punishment, sorrow, and poverty all should commend him to the Corinthians as a genuine mediator of God and should belie any accusation that he was an impostor (6:3–10).

Paul hoped that by reminding the Corinthian believers of the hidden nature of the gospel—its inner work and future focus—he was giving them a reason to reject "those who boast about outward appearance and not about what is in the heart" (2 Cor 5:12). Paul wanted the Corinthians to live in ways that prioritized their commitment to Christ rather than themselves (5:15). It seems likely that he thought of his opponents, with their focus on outward appearance, eloquence, and money (10:10; 11:6; 11:7–12; 12:13; cf. 2:17), as pushing the Corinthian believers in the opposite direction.

Paul's role as a mediator of God during this period also entailed the organization of relief aid for the needy in Jerusalem. To Paul, this was itself an act of mediation (2 Cor 8:4, 19, 20; 9:1, 12, 13) involving the conveyance of these gifts from his predominantly gentile churches on the Anatolian peninsula and around the Aegean Sea to the Jewish Christians in Jerusalem. Interest in the collection had waned in Corinth, probably while opposition to Paul was on the rise. Now that Paul's severe letter had effected a change in the attitude of most of the Corinthian church toward Paul (2:6; 7:6–13a), and with the encouraging report from Titus that many Corinthians had received Paul's coworker with respect and obedience (7:13b–15), Paul could appeal with confidence to them to renew their earlier support of this project (7:16–9:15). If the Corinthians were willing to lend their support, then Corinth could serve as the staging area for the conveyance of the collection to Jerusalem. Emissaries from the various participating churches could meet there and then take advantage of the busy port of Cenchreae to set sail with the collection for Judea.

With false accusations flying around about his handling of money (2 Cor 11:7; 12:16; cf. 2:17; 6:8), Paul was particularly eager in this part of the letter to spell out a transparent procedure for bringing the collection to a conclusion in Corinth (8:20–21). He would send Titus back to Corinth with two widely respected colleagues whom other participating churches had approved as trustworthy companions for Paul and the collection (8:18–19, 22–23). Paul had boasted to Titus and to these two "brothers" of the Corinthians' generosity, and Paul expresses his hope that when they arrive in Corinth his "boasting about [them] may not prove empty in this matter, so that [they] may be ready, as [he] said [they] would be" (9:3).

CHAPTER 17

Paul concluded the letter with a strongly worded appeal to the Corinthians not to succumb to the wiles of his opponents, whom Paul now explicitly describes as "false apostles, deceitful workmen, disguising themselves as apostles of Christ" (2 Cor 11:13). So far from being "mediators [διάκονοι] of Christ" (11:23, my trans.), they were "mediators [διάκονοι] of Satan" (11:14–15, my trans.). As part of their disguise, they boasted to the Corinthians that they were true, flesh-and-blood descendants of Abraham and mediators of Christ to the world (11:22–23) and that their loyalty lay not with Paul but with the much more impressive "super-apostles" in Jerusalem, Peter, James, and John (11:5; 12:11; cf. Gal 2:9). They had also adopted the Roman cultural trappings of clients under the patronage of the wealthier and more influential members of the Corinthian church (11:20).[30]

Now, writing in more direct response to them and to the Corinthian Christians under their influence, Paul decided to meet them on their own turf and to boast, like them, in himself. Paul's discomfort with this approach is palpable as he apologizes and makes several false starts (2 Cor 11:1, 16–18, 21), but he was so desperate to stem the tide of his opponents' influence and to win back the minority of Corinthians who remained skeptical of him, that he was willing to "answer a fool according to his folly" (Prov 26:5).[31] Even as he dives into this tactic, he shouts in midair, "I am speaking as a fool" (2 Cor 11:21).

Paul's boast, however, is chiefly and paradoxically a description of his many experiences of suffering and humiliation as he carried out his mediatorial work on behalf of God. He begins with a long list of dangers and deprivations that he has suffered in his effort to be faithful to his vocation, ending climactically with the incident in Damascus many years earlier when he was humiliatingly bundled into a large basket, lowered through a window in the city wall, and forced to flee for his life from the city governor's guards (2 Cor 11:21b–33). "If I must boast," he insists, "I will boast of the things that show my weakness" (11:30).

He then suddenly changes course and recounts something that even his opponents in Corinth would consider boastworthy: fourteen years earlier he had been the recipient of a vision of paradise in which he had received a revelation from God himself (2 Cor 12:1–6; cf. 12:11–12). Even here, however, the boast turns into disappointment as Paul admits that he was forbidden from revealing the content of these visions and revelations

"Fighting Without and Fear Within"

(12:4).³² The disappointment is complete when Paul ends his boast with a description of the suffering that God allowed Satan to inflict on him precisely because of these magnificent visions and revelations: "To keep me from becoming conceited because of the surpassing greatness of the revelations, a thorn was given me in the flesh" (12:7). Paul completes this roller-coaster ride by stating its point with clarity: "For the sake of Christ, then, I am content with weaknesses, insults, hardships, persecutions, and calamities. For when I am weak, then I am strong" (12:10).

The Corinthians who were still under the influence of the false apostles should reject them and their ill-conceived idea that what matters is outward appearance, eloquence, and money. God works through weakness, not through the trappings of prestige and power that Roman culture prized so highly.

When Paul had finished his letter, he gave it to Titus and the two brothers (2 Cor 8:16–24; 9:3) and sent them to Corinth with instructions to ready the collection there in anticipation of his arrival in the city with representatives from the Macedonian churches (2 Cor 9:3–5). Meanwhile, Paul probably spent several months continuing to collect funds from the Macedonians and then traveling westward along the Via Egnatia. Eventually he crossed over into Illyricum (Rom 15:19) and preached the gospel farther west than ever before. It was probably the summer of AD 56.

18

A Turning Point

Why did Paul delay his arrival in Corinth with a journey into Illyricum? His travels during this period, and his reasons for them, are unclear, but hints from his letters put his motive into slightly sharper focus. Paul was at a turning point in his career.

As he dictated the closing paragraphs of 2 Corinthians, he reflected on how he had first carried out the assignment he had received from God to preach the gospel to the nations. He had been "the first to come all the way to" Corinth with the gospel (2 Cor 10:13–14). He had been a pioneer, proclaiming the gospel to people groups that had never heard it, preferring to work where no one else had established churches before him, and unwilling to "boast beyond limit in the labors of others" (10:15). He does not say so, but he may have reflected on how for most of the previous four years he had worked in Corinth, Ephesus, and, to a smaller extent, Macedonia, trying to improve and repair the gospel foundations he had laid in those cities.[1] Now it was time once again to engage in pioneering work, and he hoped that the Corinthian Christians would repudiate his opponents in Corinth, continue their growth in faith, and support him and his coworkers "so that we might preach the gospel in lands beyond" Corinth (10:16).

A few months later, when writing to the Romans from Corinth, he explained that he had "fulfilled the ministry of the gospel of Christ" in the area between Jerusalem and Illyricum—roughly the area around the eastern half of the Mediterranean Sea—and that his ambition was to preach the gospel "not where Christ has already been named, lest I build on someone else's foundation" (Rom 15:19–20). He then supported his ambition with a quotation from the prophet Isaiah. "As it is written," he says, "'Those

A Turning Point

who have never been told of him will see, and those who have never heard will understand'" (Rom 15:21; cf. Isa 52:15 LXX).

The source and original context of this quotation are significant. The quotation comes from the beginning of a passage that describes the suffering of the Lord's servant for the sins of God's people (Isa 53:4–6). Since Paul understood the pronoun "him" in the passage to be Christ, and since in its original context "him" referred to the Lord's servant, Paul probably believed that Isaiah 52:13–53:12 expressed the essence of the gospel he had just explained at length in his letter to Rome.[2] Its description of the vicarious suffering of the Lord's innocent servant for the transgressions of his people paralleled the way God had reconciled people to himself through the death of Christ Jesus (cf. Rom 3:21–26; 5:6–8).[3]

Here, then, Paul makes clear that God had called him to take the gospel he had set down in the letter to people who had never heard it before, and to places where no gospel messenger had ever traveled. This idea taps into Isaiah's concern that not merely Israel but "the end of the earth" and "the coastlands" (Isa 42:10) would one day sing God's praise and that the Lord's servant would be the salvation of "the end of the earth" (Isa 49:6).[4] There would be no better way to fulfill this commission than to take the gospel to Spain, the Roman province lying at the western edge of the known world. Perhaps Paul was even thinking of Gadeira, a flourishing island city in western Spain that Strabo had described as sitting "at the extremity of the earth" (*Geogr.* 3.1.8).[5] It was a city that Paul likely knew.[6] Spending some time in Illyricum, where the gospel had never traveled, would not only be consistent with Paul's plan to turn again toward unevangelized peoples but would provide cultural preparation for ministry in the western part of the empire.[7]

Taking the Gospel to Illyricum

Augustus had laid the groundwork for dividing Illyricum into two smaller, more manageable provinces after a united Illyricum had rebelled against Roman rule in a war that had lasted from AD 6 to 9.[8] Tiberius was on his way to the province when he learned of Augustus's death in AD 14, and he was probably headed there to oversee the new administrative arrangements of a divided Illyricum, split in two by a border that ran somewhere south of the Sava River and north of the Dinaric Alps (roughly the modern political boundary between northern Bosnia-Herzegovina and Croatia). The northern part would be the new province of "Pannonia," and the southern part would be the new province of "Dalmatia."[9] In an offhand comment in what was probably his last letter, Paul will tell his coworker Timothy that Titus had gone "to Dalmatia" (2 Tim 4:10). This probably means that Titus had gone to work within churches established there. It is somewhat speculative to say so, but it would make sense if those churches came into existence during the time that Paul proclaimed the gospel in what he called "Illyricum" in his letter to the Romans.[10]

Paul could have reached Dalmatia by traveling west from Thessalonica along the Via Egnatia to the port city of Dyrrhachium, a journey of about 239 miles or about thirteen days.[11] Sixteen days more of walking along the northern extension of the Via Egnatia would have brought him to Salona, the administrative center of Dalmatia.[12] Since Salona was a busy port city farther up the Adriatic coast from Dyrrhachium, however, he probably went by ship if he went there at all. A coastal vessel could have made the journey in about four days, although Paul may have wanted to stop and preach the gospel in the ports of Lissus, Epidaurum, and Narona, natural stops along the way.[13] Recently built roads stretching from Salona to the northwest and southeast along the coast and into the interior connected the city with other major ports along the Dalmatian coast and with Pannonia to the northeast. It would have been an ideal location for moving the gospel into the surrounding area.[14]

The coastal cities of Dalmatia had large populations of Roman settlers, and the area was heavily Latinized. Roman religion had made inroads to the region and merged with the worship of indigenous gods. Work here not only would have provided Paul with a foundation for understanding the cultural challenges of ministry among the Romanized peoples of Spain but would have brought him culturally and linguistically closer to the city of Rome, whose Christians Paul hoped would support his new work in the west (Rom 15:24; cf. 2 Cor 10:15–16).[15]

There is no way to know how long Paul stayed in Illyricum, but it was probably only for a short period. Paul's main goal at this point in his work seems to have been to finish organizing the collection project in Corinth and then to set sail for Judea with the group of delegates who would accompany this gift. From Salona, it would have taken a little over six days to sail to Corinth; from Dyrrhachium, a little over four days.[16]

Luke says that Paul spent three months in Greece (Acts 20:2–3), the ethnic name that covered the Roman province of Achaia and the location of churches in Athens, Corinth, and Cenchreae.[17] It must have been an extraordinarily busy time. Not only did Paul need to attend personally to the Corinthian church in the wake of his recent turbulent relationship with them (2 Cor 12:14–15, 21; 13:1–4), but he needed to finish organizing the collection (2 Cor 9:3–5), and to prepare for the next phase of his work of proclaiming the gospel to the nations (2 Cor 10:15–16).

Thankfully, Paul had help. His coworker Timothy had been with him since he left Ephesus (2 Cor 1:1) and was with him still (Rom 16:21). Jason, who had hosted him and Silas in Thessalonica during their first visit to Macedonia (Acts 17:5–7), may have also accompanied Paul on his journey to Illyricum and Corinth (Rom 16:21).[18] Aristarchus too seems to have been with Paul since he left Ephesus (Acts 19:29; 20:4).

In addition to these traveling companions, Paul had friends in Corinth. This was his third visit to the city (2 Cor 12:14; 13:1), and Gaius, whom he had baptized during his first, eighteen-month stay (1 Cor 1:14), hosted him (and probably Timothy and Jason) in his house (Rom 16:23). Phoebe, a well-to-do deacon of the nearby church in Cenchreae, supported him financially (Rom 16:1–2). Titus and the two unnamed Christian "brothers" who had taken 2 Corinthians to Corinth (2 Cor 8:16–18, 22–24) were probably still there. Titus, at least, would have been there since he had "been appointed by the churches to travel with" Paul when he took the collection to Jerusalem (2 Cor 8:19).

As Paul turned his thoughts eastward toward the conclusion of the collection project in Jerusalem and then westward to his plan to proclaim the gospel in Spain, he prepared to write a substantial letter to the Christians in Rome, some of whom he knew personally (Rom 16:3–16). A letter as long and thoughtful as Romans would have taken planning, time, and the skills of a careful scribe.[19] In the case of Romans, this scribe's name is known. He was Tertius, a fellow Christian who viewed his considerable labor of taking down Romans at Paul's dictation as service to the Lord Jesus (16:22).[20]

CHAPTER 18

WHY ROMANS?

Romans is an unusual Pauline letter. Not only is it the apostle's longest letter, but he wrote it to a Christian community that neither he nor any of his coworkers had planted.[21] Although he had close relationships with people who had eventually moved to Rome (Rom 16:3–4, 5, 8, 9–10a, 11a, 12–13), Paul himself had never visited the city (1:13; 15:22–23), and by the time of his letter, the Christian community there was well established. "Your faith," Paul tells them, "is proclaimed in all the world" (1:8), and he considered them "full of goodness, filled with knowledge and able to instruct one another" (15:14). Moreover, Paul clearly articulates in the letter what some scholars have called his "principle of noninterference": "I make it my ambition to preach the gospel, not where Christ has already been named, lest I build on someone else's foundation" (15:20).[22]

So, why write an unusually long letter to such a famous, well-established Christian community? Was he mainly looking ahead to his mission in Spain and writing to the Romans to prepare for that mission in some way?[23] Was he thinking of his collection from gentile believers for the relief of Jewish believers in Jerusalem and reflecting on the relationship between his mission to the gentiles and the Jewish zeal he had left behind at his conversion?[24]

Spain and Jerusalem were both in Paul's mind as he composed this letter (Rom 15:22–32), but it seems likely that he wrote Romans primarily with the Roman church in mind. He wanted, as he says in Romans 1:11–12, both to give a "spiritual gift" to them in his role as apostle to the gentiles and to receive "encouragement" from them considering the tasks that lay ahead of him in both Jerusalem and Spain (cf. 15:15–16, 24, 28, 30–32).

Is this purpose for the letter consistent, however, with the "noninterference principle" of Romans 15:20? If Paul is writing the letter and planning a visit to Rome with the intention of encouraging humility and unity among Christians, isn't he building "on someone else's foundation"?

In answer to this question, it is important to pay close attention to Paul's wording in Romans 15:20. Paul says that he "makes it" his "ambition" to proclaim the gospel and plant churches where no one has done this before him, but he speaks here of an aspiration, not of an ironclad rule.[25] His aspiration led him to plan for work in Spain, but he needed to temper

A Turning Point

that aspiration in the case of the Roman Christians, just as he had done many times in the past. He had worked with a preexisting group of Jesus followers shortly after his conversion in Damascus (Acts 9:19–22). Several years later he had worked with an established group of Christians in Syrian Antioch (Acts 11:26). Christians were probably already present in Ephesus by the time he, Prisca, and Aquila arrived there (Acts 18:24–27).[26] Now the Romans needed pastoral oversight, and Paul delicately suggests that he is the person for the job (Rom 1:11, 13; 15:15–16).

Although famous (Rom 1:8), the church in Rome had no founding apostle, and it seems to have had a distinctive history as a primarily Jewish community at first that became increasingly gentile with the passage of time. What better authority to address their pastoral needs than Paul, who was both steeped in the traditions of Israel and called to be "a minister of Christ Jesus to the Gentiles" (15:16; cf. 1:5)?

A Spiritual Gift to the Roman Church

The "spiritual gift" (Rom 1:11) Paul wanted to give the Roman church was instruction about how they should live in unity with each other. Toward the end of the letter, he looks back on all that he has just composed and says that he has written to them "very boldly by way of reminder" in his capacity as "a minister of Christ Jesus to the Gentiles" (15:15–16). Paul describes his calling here as "the grace given me by God" (15:15).

This phrase provides the key to unlocking the mystery of what Paul means when he says that he has written "very boldly" to the Roman Christians. It recalls a similar phrase Paul had used in Romans 12:3, near the opening of the letter's lengthy section of ethical admonitions (12:1–15:7): "For *by the grace given to me* I say to everyone among you not to think of himself more highly than he ought to think, but to think with sober judgment, each according to the measure of faith that God has assigned" (12:3, emphasis mine).[27] Paul wanted to exercise among the Roman Christians his graciously given apostolic vocation of preaching the gospel to the gentiles because the Christians in Rome needed to hear that there was no place in the Christian community for haughtiness. Part of the purpose of the letter, therefore, was to encourage the Roman Christians to treat each other with humility and deference.[28]

CHAPTER 18

Paul applies this principle to the Roman community at length in Romans 14:1–15:13. There he reveals that various understandings of the place of Jewish law in the life of the Christian had generated the hostility that made Paul's bold admonitions about humility and deference necessary. On one hand, some of those who believed it was unnecessary to observe the commands in the Mosaic law on diet and days regarded with contempt those who thought these observances important. On the other hand, some of those who observed these commands sat in judgment on those who neglected them (14:3). Paul wanted each group to welcome the other, just as Christ had welcomed them (15:7). Paul had explained at length how Christ had welcomed them in the immediately preceding exposition of the gospel.

The Roman Church's Encouragement of Paul

The encouragement Paul wanted to receive from the Roman Christians (Rom 1:12) was closely related to the turning point he now faced in his career. Paul was on the cusp of engaging in two enormous projects that would take him nearly the entire length of the Mediterranean Sea, and at both ends of this long journey he faced great challenges.[29] He was heading immediately to Jerusalem with his collection of relief aid for Jewish believers (15:26–27), and he was concerned about the success of this venture into which he had poured such energy. Would unbelievers in Judea try to kill him, as they had done in the past (15:31a; cf. Acts 9:29)? Would the collection from his mainly gentile churches prove unacceptable to the Jewish Christians in Jerusalem because of misinformation they had received about Paul's attitude toward the Jewish law (15:31b; cf. Acts 21:20–22)? Paul hoped that the Roman Christians would join him in fervent prayer that neither of these fears would materialize (15:30).

The Spanish mission was also on Paul's mind as he wrote, and he had a specific request of the Roman Christians concerning this venture. "I hope," he says, "to see you in passing as I go to Spain, and to be helped on my journey there by you, once I have enjoyed your company for a while" (Rom 15:24). The verb "to be helped" (προπεμφθῆναι) had a range of meanings, from a cheerful farewell to supplying a traveler "with food, money . . . companions, means of travel, etc."[30] When Paul used the word elsewhere

(1 Cor 16:6; 2 Cor 1:16; Titus 3:13), it seems to have had this last, more substantial, meaning in mind. If that is correct, then Paul is asking the Roman Christians for significant support for the difficult challenges of preaching the gospel in Spain. Robert Jewett has usefully described what this help might have looked like: language instruction, introductions to immigrants, and contacts with Roman bureaucrats who worked in one or more of the major cities.[31]

The Jewish Character of Roman Christianity and a Misunderstanding of Paul's Gospel

Paul knew, however, that these requests for support, both for the work he was about to undertake in Judea and that he would later undertake in Spain, might face resistance in some parts of the Roman church. It is reasonably clear that Christianity first came to Italy and to Rome as a form of Judaism. It was already present in Puteoli in the mid-first century (Acts 28:13–14), and Puteoli was both Italy's busiest port and home to a large Jewish community (Josephus, *B.J.* 2.104; *A.J.* 17.328). Goods and ideas from the east flowed over the well-traveled trade route from Puteoli to Rome, and it is easy to imagine with Peter Lampe that Christianity first arrived in the synagogues of Puteoli and then made its way to the synagogues of Rome along this trade route.[32] At least by AD 49 it had created such a stir in the synagogues of Rome that Claudius could use the unrest as an excuse to expel Jewish people from the city (Suetonius, *Claud.* 25.4; cf. Acts 18:2).[33]

All this means that even if Roman Christianity at the time Paul wrote his letter was mainly gentile (Rom 1:13; 11:13), it nevertheless contained some Jewish Christians (16:3, 6, 7, 11). It also contained some Christians, whether Jewish or gentile, who continued to observe the Mosaic law (14:2–3, 5–6). It would be important, therefore, for Paul to explain the gospel in his letter in a way that put to rest any misinformation circulating in Rome about his attitudes toward the Mosaic law and Judaism.[34]

The letter contains hints at various points of what that misinformation might have looked like. It seems to have focused on two ideas. First, some people in Rome seem to have been worried that Paul's teaching on the availability of God's grace in Christ to all ethnic and social groups threatened the special place of Israel in God's affections (Rom 3:1). Second, people were concerned that Paul so marginalized the importance of the Mosaic law for the people of God that he opened the door to moral chaos (3:8, 31; 6:1, 15). Paul's approaches to Israel's election and to the Mosaic law were complex, and this complexity made it an easy target for opponents, so Paul took pains in his letter to explain the interface between the gospel and these issues. The rumors about Paul were unfounded, and once people understood what Paul really thought, this would become clear.

In summary, Paul wrote Romans both to encourage unity within a group of believers experiencing division over whether to observe the dietary and calendrical parts of the Mosaic law and to ask for encouragement from the Roman church for the success of his future efforts in Jerusalem and Spain. To accomplish these goals, he gave a full exposition of his understanding of the gospel in his letter to Rome and shaped his exposition to show that the gospel both encouraged the unity of believers and fulfilled rather than contradicted the Jewish Scriptures.

The Gospel as the Revelation of the Righteousness of God

Paul pursued these aims by explaining the gospel as the revelation of "the righteousness of God." This phrase, or something like it, appears seven times in Romans (1:17; 3:5, 21, 22, 25, 26; 10:3), and its importance to Paul's understanding of the gospel becomes clear when he begins to "preach the gospel" (1:15) to the Roman Christians using the same phrase. "For I am not ashamed of the gospel. It is the saving power of God for everyone who has faith—the Jew first, but the Greek also—because in it the righteousness of God is seen at work, beginning in faith and ending in faith; as scripture says, 'Whoever is justified through faith shall gain life'" (Rom 1:16–17 REB). "The righteousness of God," Paul says, is what makes the gospel God's saving power for everyone who believes, whatever their ethnicity.[35] Immediately, Paul begins to stress the socially unifying aspect of the gospel.

The way Paul frames his definition of the gospel here, moreover, also makes the point that the gospel is consistent with Israel's Scriptures. The two phrases "the saving power of God" and "the righteousness of God" stand parallel to one another and are mutually defining. This parallelism, and the claim that God's righteousness contains non-Jewish peoples within its scope, is a feature of the concept of God's righteousness in the Jewish Scriptures. "The LORD has made known his salvation," says the psalmist; "he has revealed his righteousness in the sight of the nations" (Ps 98:2–3). Isaiah, similarly, describes the Lord comforting his people with the words, "My righteousness draws near, my salvation has gone out, and my arms will judge the peoples; the coastlands hope for me, and for my arm they wait" (Isa 51:5).[36]

Writing from the heavily Romanized city of Corinth, Paul may have also anticipated that his audience in Rome would understand the term "righteousness" in the everyday sense of "equity" or "fairness." Nero minted coins in Alexandria in AD 56–57, at almost exactly the time Paul was writing Romans, with Nero's profile on one side and, on the other side, an image of the goddess ΔΙΚΑΙΟΣΥΝΗ ("Righteousness"). In the goddess's right hand is an evenly balanced scale communicating the propaganda that Nero was "fair"—probably meaning that he was fair in handling the grain supply that shipped mainly from Alexandria.[37]

Origen, the earliest extant commentator on Romans, seems to have taken Paul's reference to "the righteousness of God" here this way: "The righteousness of God is revealed in the gospel through the fact that with respect to salvation no one is excluded whether he should come as a Jew, Greek, or barbarian. For the Savior says equally to all, 'come to me, all you that labor and are burdened.'"[38]

The gospel, then, reveals God's righteousness as his saving power first to Israel and then to the nations. The revelation of his righteousness in this biblical sense to everyone, whether Jewish or non-Jewish, reveals his righteous character. He is equitable in the distribution of his saving power to all kinds of human beings regardless of their ethnicity, "for," as Paul will put it a few paragraphs later, "God does not show favoritism" (Rom 2:11 NIV).

Paul wraps up his thesis statement with a quotation from the prophet Habakkuk: "Whoever is justified [or 'righteous'] through faith shall gain life" (Hab 2:4). This quotation advances his argument in two ways. First, it demonstrates explicitly to his audience that the gospel he has just summarized and that he is about to explain in detail is consistent with the Jewish Scriptures. Paul had already hinted at this with his biblically informed definition of "God's righteousness" as his saving power, but now he drives this point home with an explicit quotation from one of Israel's prophets (cf. Rom 3:21).

Second, this quotation shifts the quality of righteousness from God to the person who believes. Now the believer is the one who is righteous, and this righteousness comes to the believer by faith.[39] Paul will explain what he means by this in the paragraphs that follow.

No one, he will say, can claim to be righteous based on anything within themselves, whether their ability to judge others (Rom 2:1, 3), their possession of the Mosaic law (2:12, 17, 20), their hearing of the Mosaic law in the synagogue each Sabbath (2:13, 18), their ability to teach the Mosaic law to others (2:20–22), or their circumcision (2:25–29). As Paul will summarize it, "No one will be declared righteous in God's sight by the works of the law; rather, through the law we become conscious of our sin" (3:20). Paul's quotation of Habakkuk 2:4 in Romans 1:17 implies, therefore, that the only way anyone can be righteous and escape the just penalty of death for rebellion against God on the day of judgment is to have a righteousness that comes from outside themselves. That righteousness must come to them as a gift from God, and God gives it to all who receive it by faith. In the words of a letter Paul later wrote to the Christians in Philippi, it is "the righteousness that comes from God on the basis of faith" (Phil 3:9).[40]

This raises an important question. How can God be righteous in the sense that he is fair and just and, at the same time, give righteousness to people who are unrighteous, thus saving them from his justified, punishing wrath? Paul answers this question in Romans 3:21–26. There Paul describes Jesus as the "place" where God freely and graciously acquits those who trust him from their rebellion against him and secures their ransom from the bondage in which this rebellion has placed them (3:24).[41] The crucified Messiah Jesus, Paul says, is "the place of atonement" between God and his estranged creatures, and this has allowed him to be both just and the justifier of the one who has faith in him (3:25–26). In the death of Christ, God both justly punishes the sin of those who are united with Christ by faith and releases them from any future punishment (3:26).[42]

Paul's use of the rare term "place of atonement" (ἱλαστήριον) recalls the way that the Greek Bible of Paul's time described the top of the ark of the covenant. This was the place where once a year, on the Day of Atonement, the high priest sprinkled the blood of a bull and a goat to make "atonement for himself and for his house and for all the assembly of Israel" (Lev 16:17).[43] Someone carefully reading Leviticus 16 today might assume that

A Turning Point

these rites only served to cleanse the temple, priest, and people of their ritual impurity, but Stephen Hultgren has shown that by the second century BC some Jewish people may have understood these rites as sacrifices for the forgiveness of moral guilt (11Q19 XXVI, 9–10; Jub 34:12, 18–19; cf. Lev 16:29–30).[44]

That is, in any case, Paul's understanding of Christ Jesus's role as the "place of atonement" (Rom 3:9–20, 23). He is, in the words of Stephen Hultgren, "'the place' where divine justice and mercy meet."[45] God in his mercy provided the substitutionary death of animals in the temple as a way in which the sinful worshiper could both die, by identification with the animal, and receive his or her life back from God. In the Jewish Scriptures, this happened quintessentially in the death of the bull and the goat in the Day of Atonement ritual.[46] For Paul, Christ's death was in a similar way God's gracious provision for the forgiveness of the believer's sin and the means of their reconciliation.[47] Because of their union with Christ Jesus by faith, his death substituted for their death, and rather than receiving the death that their own sin required, they received life by union with his resurrection (Rom 4:25). In the crucified Christ, therefore, God justly punishes sin with death and, at the same time, becomes the gracious "justifier of the one who has faith in Jesus" (3:26).

The rest of the letter puzzles out the implications of this critically important event. Paul argues that God's justification of the ungodly by faith is consistent with his relationship with Abraham, the great patriarch of Israel (Rom 4:1–8). It opens the door of God's people to the nations, and so it provides for the fulfillment of God's promise that Abraham would be "a father of many nations" (Rom 4:17; cf. Gen 17:5). It was an act of such power that it began reversing the effects of Adam's disobedience (Rom 5:12, 18) and establishing a new realm in which sin and death no longer hold sway over believers' lives (Rom 5:17, 21; 6:12, 14; 8:1–6, 12–13).[48]

Paul argues that although presently non-Jewish believers outnumber Jewish believers, God's promises to be faithful to Israel have not failed (Rom 9:6). Some Jewish people have believed (Rom 11:1, 5), and one day "all Israel will be saved" as God establishes a new covenant with his people and takes away their sins (Rom 11:26–27; cf. Jer 31:33; Isa 27:9).

Paul concludes the letter's argument by describing some of the gospel's ethical implications for the Roman Christian community. The gospel's

CHAPTER 18

humbling message that all are in need of God's saving mercy (Rom 12:1) implies that Christians should live in ways that foster humility (12:3, 16), the reconciliation of enemies (12:14, 17–21), love for others (13:8–10), and a welcoming attitude toward all, especially toward the weak (14:1; 15:1, 7).

As Paul and Tertius finished their work on the letter, the delegates from churches that had contributed to the collection were arriving in Corinth. At the letter's end, Paul says that Macedonia and Achaia had contributed to the collection, and he sends greetings to Rome from both Timothy and Sosipater (Rom 16:21).[49] When Luke lists the delegates who eventually gathered in Corinth and accompanied Paul with the collection to Jerusalem, he includes both Timothy and Sopater (the short form of Sosipater) in that list (Acts 20:4). Delegates from Galatia, other than Timothy, and from Asia seem not to have yet arrived (Rom 15:26).

Eventually, however, representatives from the four Roman provinces where Paul had spent most of the last decade assembled in Corinth with the funds from the churches in their areas. Paul and his coworkers may have already started looking for a ship that would take them all from the port city of Cenchreae to Syria. Tyre, in Syria, was a popular stop for ships from the west to unload their cargoes (Acts 20:3; cf. 21:3), and a city from which they could easily reach Judea and Jerusalem.[50]

19

Back to Jerusalem with the Collection Delegation

As Paul finished his letter to Christians in Rome, he was thinking about unbelieving Jewish opposition to him and to his gospel. "I urge you, brothers and sisters," he tells the Roman Christians, "by our Lord Jesus Christ and by the love of the Spirit to join me in my struggle by praying to God for me. Pray that I may be kept safe from the unbelievers in Judea" (Rom 15:30–31a NIV). When he had faced opposition from unbelieving Jewish people in Corinth six years earlier, at the end of his eighteen-month stay there, the accusation against him before Gallio had been that he was "persuading people to worship God contrary to the law" (Acts 18:12–13). Paul's letter to Rome shows that these misunderstandings of his position on the Jewish law were still circulating widely, and he may have already suspected that he could face trouble in Corinth before he and his entourage of delegates set sail for Syria.[1]

Luke says that just before their journey began, Paul learned that a group of Judeans had "hatched a plot against" him (Acts 20:3a CEB). Because the Judeans' plot seems to have developed immediately before Paul and his companions set sail, some interpreters have wondered whether Paul intended to sail on a pilgrim ship, packed with people headed to Jerusalem to celebrate Passover.[2] A shipboard murder would be easy to execute and hard to detect if it simply involved shoving someone overboard.[3] About a century later, the charlatan Alexander of Abonoteichus tried to murder his skeptical enemy, Lucian of Samosata, by pretending reconciliation with him and offering to furnish him with a coastal sailing vessel and a crew for a trip along the southern coast of the Black Sea.[4] In mid-voyage, Lucian discovered that Alexander had instructed the sailors to throw him and his traveling companion overboard. He survived to tell the story only because the conscience-stricken captain refused to follow through with the deed, confessed everything, and dropped them off at a nearby seaport (*Alex.* 56–57).

Whatever the details of the plot against Paul, it prompted him to change the delegation's travel route to something safer (Acts 20:3b), and this change created another problem. Paul now had to worry about missing a deadline he had imposed on the group. "He was hastening," Luke says, "to be at Jerusalem, if possible, on the day of Pentecost" (20:16).

Paul's Changed Itinerary and the Symbolism of His Arrival Time

Paul decided that rather than sailing directly from Cenchreae to Syria the group should return to the province of Asia by traveling north to Macedonia and then onward from there to Jerusalem (Acts 20:3b–6).[5] Many interpreters assert that Paul made this trip overland.[6] According to the Stanford Geospatial Network Model of the Roman World, however, a land journey from Corinth to Philippi would have taken the group through rugged terrain and lasted over three weeks. Traveling mainly by sea, however, they could have made the journey in just over eight days, stopping at various ports in Macedonia (e.g., Thessalonica and Amphipolis) along the way.[7] This is within hours of the same amount of time that it would have taken Paul and the group to sail from Cenchreae to Tyre in Syria. Luke says that Paul arrived in the Macedonian city of Philippi in time to celebrate the Feast of Unleavened Bread (Acts 20:6), the seven-day Jewish festival that began immediately after Passover. This makes it likely that Paul had originally hoped to arrive in Jerusalem by Passover, the greatest pilgrimage festival of the Jews.[8]

If that was Paul's original plan, and he had been able to see it through, he would have arrived in Jerusalem on the anniversary of Jesus's final meal with his disciples, a meal that all Christians by Paul's time observed in memory of Jesus's death. Paul interpreted Christ's death to the Corinthian Christians, and probably other Christians also, through the lens of the Passover sacrifice. Since "Christ, our Passover lamb, has been sacrificed" for believers, he said, Christians should cleanse the "leaven of malice and evil" from their lives and replace it "with the unleavened bread of sincerity and truth" (1 Cor 5:7–8; cf. 11:20, 23–26). They should live with each other in harmony—caring for each other—as "one body," just as the bread from which they ate was one loaf (1 Cor 10:17; cf. 12:25).

The collection was a practical expression of how the gospel had transformed the lives of gentile believers in these ways. It demonstrated that gentile Christians appreciated their indebtedness to the rich theological heritage of Judaism (Rom 15:26–27). It also showed their concern to alleviate the suffering of other members of the body of Christ, despite the differences between them in location and ethnicity.

Another theological motivation might also have connected the collection to the Jewish calendar in Paul's thinking. The Feast of Weeks, or Pentecost, arrived fifty days after the Feast of Unleavened Bread (Josephus, *A.J.* 3.249, 252) and was the normal time for people to come to Jerusalem to present their "first fruits" to the priest in the temple (cf. Lev 23:16; Num 28:26; Deut 16:10).[9] "First fruits" were the first part of a harvest, or the firstborn of any female, whether animal or human, or the first products made from produce such as bread, olive oil, and wine. They belonged to the Lord and were paid to the priests who used them to support themselves (cf. Num 18:12–16). Money could substitute for these offerings, providing a means by which someone, for example, could "redeem" a firstborn son, and the priests depended on these offerings for their livelihood.

This posed a problem, however, for Jewish people who were not affluent enough to attend more than one pilgrimage festival. Most of them would have wanted to attend Passover, the most important festival, and they would have found it difficult to come back to Jerusalem fifty days later for the Feast of Weeks. There is some evidence that, in answer to this problem, it was possible for people to bring their "first fruits" during the Feast of Unleavened Bread, which had by this time become part of Passover.

Perhaps Paul, who often spoke of gentile believers as "the first fruits" (Rom 11:16; 16:5; 1 Cor 16:15; 2 Thess 2:13), thought of the group of delegates with their relief aid as an offering to God of the "first fruits" of his work among the gentiles.[10] Or, perhaps he thought of the group of delegates as representative of all gentile Christians, the "first fruits" of a multinational "offering to the Lord" that, according to Isaiah, would one day converge on Jerusalem, bringing their own offering "to the house of the Lord" (Isa 66:20; cf. Rom 11:16).[11] Paul may have thought it appropriate to bring these "first fruits" to Jerusalem at this important turning point in his career when he had "fulfilled the ministry of the gospel of Christ" in the eastern Mediterranean and now looked forward to carrying his work westward to Rome and to Spain (Rom 15:18–21, 24; cf. 15:16).

Paul may not have been entirely disappointed, therefore, when he had to change his travel plans in response to the plot against his life and lead the group to Philippi. He could now arrive in Jerusalem for the Feast of Weeks ("Pentecost") itself, and he could present the collection and the delegation of mainly gentile believers to Jewish Christians there at this significant time in the Jewish calendar for offering one's first fruits to God. In the meantime, he could celebrate the Feast of Unleavened Bread with its new, Christian significance with any believers in Philippi who wanted to participate (cf. Rom 14:5–9).[12] Since the church in Philippi had come into existence among women gathered on the Sabbath for prayer (Acts 16:13), chances are good that Paul found others in the city interested in observing the feast as a celebration of the new exodus that God had accomplished for his people in Christ's death.[13]

Instructing the Young Church in Troas

Sometime before this feast, either the whole group of delegates, or, more likely, the last two members of the group in Luke's list, set out for Troas. Luke's list ends with "the Asians, Tychicus and Trophimus" (Acts 20:4), and his next statement begins, "These went on ahead and were waiting for us at Troas" (Acts 20:5). "These" probably refers not to the whole list of delegates but, as some commentators have suggested, only to Tychicus and Trophimus.[14] Since they were from the Roman province of Asia, perhaps they had the most detailed knowledge of how to make sailing arrangements for the next stage of the journey in the important Asian port city of Alexandria Troas, or perhaps they simply made advance arrangements for accommodation of the rest of the group with the people in Troas who had believed the gospel the year before (2 Cor 2:12–13).[15] In any case, Paul and the rest of the delegates spent the seven days of the Feast of Unleavened Bread in Philippi and after it was over made the nine-mile journey along the Via Egnatia to the port city of Neapolis and from there set sail for Troas (Acts 20:6).

Back to Jerusalem with the Collection Delegation

This is the point in the narrative where Luke begins again to include himself with Paul in his account of the apostle's travels. He has not been a participant in the story since Paul, Silas, Timothy, and Luke first crossed the Aegean Sea to Macedonia (Acts 16:10). In chronological terms that was about eight years earlier, and Luke had probably been in and around Philippi the whole time overseeing the development of the church there. Now he joined Paul and the other delegates on their journey to Troas, the city where Luke seems to have first teamed up with Paul, Silas, and Timothy (16:10). At that time, they sailed in the opposite direction, from Troas to Neapolis and then made their way to Philippi (16:11–12), and they were able to make the crossing in two days with an overnight stop on the island of Samothrace. Now, however, the ship that took Paul and his entourage to Troas took five days to make the crossing (20:6).

Biographers of Paul and commentators on Acts often comment that the trip took longer this time because the ship was sailing against the wind.[16] The prevailing winds in this region, however, are from the north and northeast, so sailing in either direction could have been somewhat difficult.[17] It seems more likely that on this trip, Paul and the group of delegates simply took a vessel that stopped more often along the way to Troas, perhaps hopping from island to island (e.g., Thasos, Samothrace, Imbros, Lemnos) or calling on ports along the coast of the Thracian Sea (e.g., Abdera, Maroneia, Zone, Sale, Ainos, Sigeion).[18] The ship would probably have unloaded and loaded cargo and passengers at each stop.[19]

When they arrived in Troas, they reconnected with Tychicus, Trophimus, and the Christians in the city. Paul, Luke, and the delegates spent seven days there and met with the city's Christians on Sunday night "to break bread" and for Paul to provide them with instruction (Acts 20:7). It seems likely that this was a regular Christian gathering for worship on the day of the week that Christ rose from the dead (cf. Matt 28:1; Mark 16:2; Luke 24:1; 1 Cor 16:2), and that behind the reference to breaking bread stands a full meal that included the celebration of the Lord's Supper (cf. 1 Cor 11:17–34; Jude 12).[20] The meeting took place in the evening, presumably because people had to work during the day.

Everyone must have known that with Paul and his entourage of delegates in town this regular meeting would be unusual. They probably did not anticipate just how unusual it would be. Paul's teaching took place first, before the meal (Acts 20:11), and because Paul knew he would be leaving the next day, he spoke at great length (Acts 20:7, 9). This was a young church—less than a year old—and he had left it behind earlier than he had intended after its original founding (2 Cor 2:12–13). If Titus had not appeared in Troas with news of the Corinthian church, perhaps Paul would have stayed there longer and put the group on a firmer theological foundation. Paul had left the city in a state of anxiety, however, hoping to meet Titus in Macedonia and profoundly worried that the foundations of the Corinthian church were ready to crumble (2 Cor 2:13; 7:5–7). On this return visit to Troas, then, Paul may have spoken at such length to pack as much information about the Christian faith as possible into the time available before he had to leave. He was under pressure to arrive in Jerusalem by Pentecost (Acts 20:16). Having just finished dictating Romans, perhaps, as N. T. Wright has suggested, the theologically rich themes of that letter informed his teaching and account for the length of his discourse.[21]

Luke says that there were "a good many lamps" in the third-story apartment where the church was meeting.[22] These would have been vessels with wicks and spaces for olive oil (Matt 25:1, 3–4, 7–8), and it is easy to see how, even with a window open, they could raise the temperature and lower the oxygen level of a small, already warm, upper-story room.[23] A complex theological discourse at the end of a long workday in a stuffy room was a recipe for what happened next: a young man named Eutychus, who was perched on the sill of an open window, dozed off and plummeted two and a half stories to his death.

The language Luke uses to describe Paul's reaction implies that he was horrified. He went down—probably rushing through several flights of narrow, dark stairs—and "fell upon" Eutychus, wrapping his arms around him. It is true that Paul's action resembles the actions of Elijah and Elisha when they each raise young men from the dead (1 Kgs 17:21–22; 2 Kgs 4:32–35), but the resemblance is probably accidental.[24] The terms Luke uses to describe what Paul did reflect the impulsive action typical of emotionally powerful scenes (Tob 11:9, 13; Xenophon, *Anab.* 7.4.10).[25] Paul was profoundly disturbed and probably desperately hoping that somehow the young man had not been injured. Luke makes it clear that by the time Paul got down the stairs the crowd assembled below had already pronounced him dead. Paul's embrace, however, seems to have led him to a different conclusion:

there was no need for alarm—Eutychus was alive! Although he was dazed by the fall and had to be led away at the meeting's end (ἤγαγον ... τὸν παῖδα ζῶντα, Acts 20:12), he was well enough immediately after the incident for the meeting to continue.[26] Paul picked up his discourse and, after he finished, the group had their meal together as the sun was coming up.

A Walk to Assos

The next phase of the group's journey to Jerusalem could now begin, but for some reason Paul, once again, decided to split up the group. He would travel on foot to the port of Assos (or Apollonia, as it was sometimes called in the first century), and the rest of the group would sail there (Acts 20:13).[27] Those traveling in the ship would have a journey of about thirty-three nautical miles, eighteen nautical miles to the cape called "Lekton" and, after rounding the cape, fifteen nautical miles farther to Assos.[28] If a coasting vessel could travel four to six knots, and that seems to be the scholarly consensus, then, under normal sailing conditions, the travel time for the delegation in the ship would have been somewhere between five and nine hours.[29] They would have arrived, therefore, in the evening of the same day as their departure.

Meanwhile, Paul's land journey took about twice as long. It totaled thirty-one miles, sixteen miles along the road that followed the coast south, across a still-visible pedestrian bridge that spanned the Satnioeis River, and then slightly inland to the temple of Apollo Smintheus (Apollo the Mouse God).[30] Another fifteen miles along a road, traces of which also remain visible, would have taken Paul from the temple to Assos.[31] Glen L. Thompson and Mark Wilson speculate reasonably that Paul would have spent the night somewhere around the temple.[32] It attracted many pilgrims and had at least two Roman baths that were in use during the first century. Paul could have easily found facilities there for rest and recovery midway through his long walk. He probably arrived at the port of Assos in the late afternoon or evening of the second day, a full day after his companions' arrival. If something like this is what happened, then Luke's description of the situation makes perfect sense. Luke, who was among the delegates who arrived by ship the day before Paul, says that Paul "met up with us at Assos" (Acts 20:14), implying that the delegation was already in Assos when Paul arrived and found them.[33]

Interpreters of Acts have offered a colorful array of theories about why Paul separated from the group and walked alone to Assos. Perhaps Paul wanted to train the group to get along without him, to make special travel arrangements, or to avoid sea sickness, or perhaps he wanted to reflect quietly on the suffering that lay ahead of him (cf. Acts 20:23; Rom 15:31).[34] Luke offers no hint of Paul's reasoning but makes clear that, whatever his reasons, Paul "had arranged" the walk, which implies that it was not an impulsive decision but carefully planned (Acts 20:13). At least as far as the planned itinerary was concerned, Paul's arrangements seem to have worked well. He met the rest of the group in Assos and, probably the next day, boarded their ship on schedule. Perhaps the suggestion most consistent with a planned travel itinerary across the peninsula is that Paul wanted to visit believers along his route, especially during his overnight stop.[35] Paul was already laboring under the divinely given impression that he might face suffering, imprisonment, and death in Jerusalem, and this knowledge may have renewed his urgency to maximize his instruction of believers during this period (Acts 20:23).

Sailing from Assos to Miletus

From Assos, the ship's first stop was Mitylene on the island of Lesbos, about twenty-four nautical miles to the south-southeast, a journey of about four to six hours in open water with following winds (Acts 20:14).[36] According to the geographer Strabo, writing in the early first century, Mitylene was "the largest city" on the island (*Geogr.* 13.2.2), and Duane W. Roller, in his commentary on Strabo, says that "from its foundation at an early date into the Roman period it was the most important city in the northeastern Aegean."[37] It had two harbors, a northern harbor that serviced commercial vessels and a southern harbor for military purposes.[38] The city's northern harbor was an obvious place for the ship's captain to unload and load cargo and passengers, and for him to reprovision the ship for the next day.

The following day, the ship set out in the direction of the island of Chios (Acts 20:15). Strabo implies that the journey from the city of Chios north to Mitylene was about four hundred stadia if the ship traveled with the south wind (*Geogr.* 14.1.35).[39] That would mean a journey of somewhere between thirty-eight and forty-three nautical miles, or between ten and fourteen hours.⁴⁰ Paul was traveling in the opposite direction, and perhaps against the wind, so although Paul and his team made the trip in one day, it may well have been a particularly long day of sailing.⁴¹ Luke says that the ship "came ... opposite [ἄντικρυς] Chios," implying that it did not actually anchor in its harbor but was "off" or "near" the island city, perhaps in the mainland port of Erythrae, which had close ties to neighboring Chios.⁴²

Whether Paul and the delegation spent the night in Chios or Erythrae, it would take less than a day to sail to Ephesus, and at least Paul, Timothy, Aristarchus, and Trophimus, all of whom had spent time with the Christian community there, must have debated at some point whether to include Ephesus in their travel itinerary. Paul's decision, says Luke, was "to sail past Ephesus, so that he might not have to spend time in Asia, for he was hastening to be at Jerusalem, if possible, on the day of Pentecost" (Acts 20:16).

With all the social connections between Paul, the delegation, and the Ephesian Christian community, Paul probably anticipated that if he arrived in the city, he and those with him would become entangled in social obligations that would keep them from reaching Jerusalem with the collection by Pentecost with its important symbolism for the Jewish people, and especially for the Jewish-Christian community.⁴³ It is not clear when Paul made this decision. Since Luke indicates later in the narrative that Paul and the group changed ships at Patara to get to Phoenicia (Acts 21:1–2), it seems likely that Paul made the decision to skip Ephesus during the week in Troas, and that the delegation intentionally booked passage on a ship that would take them from Troas to Patara but bypass Ephesus.⁴⁴

In any case, it is easy to imagine the ship's crew working all afternoon taking on a load of "the best of the Hellenic wines" that Strabo says were produced in the rugged northwest section of Chios (*Geogr.* 14.1.35). The ship set sail, probably in the morning, for the island of Samos, with its port city by the same name. It bypassed Ephesus on its way and probably arrived at Samos city late in the evening of the same day (Acts 20:15).⁴⁵ According to Strabo, Samos had wine that was puzzlingly inferior to the wine in other large ports in the area (*Geogr.* 14.1.15), so perhaps Paul's ship unloaded some of its better wine from Chios for sale there and then weighed anchor for the large, busy port of Miletus something like twenty-eight nautical miles, or five to seven hours, away.

CHAPTER 19

An Important Meeting in Miletus

Miletus might easily have been a major destination for "the ship." In the mid-first century, the city had four harbors and the largest known marketplace in the ancient Greek and Roman world.[46] Paul and the delegation would have probably sailed into the main harbor, passing through a recently constructed sixteen-columned gateway and beside a temple to Apollo Delphinios (Apollo the Dolphin God).[47] Miletus was an important commercial hub, with ships dropping off passengers and products such as wine, and then taking on loads of grain, olives, olive oil, wool, woven products, dyes, and other goods before leaving port for their next destination.[48] Although Luke does not say how long Paul and the delegation stayed there, the ship's crew may have spent a number of days loading and unloading passengers and cargo and transacting business before it was ready to leave again.[49]

It was perhaps his realization that the ship's layover in Miletus would take ample time that prompted Paul to contact the Christians in Ephesus and summon (μετεκαλέσατο) the church elders to meet with him in Miletus (Acts 20:17). In Luke's summary of Paul's comments at this meeting, he describes Paul as saying that he does not know what will befall him in Jerusalem, "except that in city after city the Holy Spirit assures me that imprisonment and hardships await me" (Acts 20:23 REB). The present tense here ("assures me" [διαμαρτύρεταί μοι]) seems to refer most naturally to prophetic revelations Paul was experiencing in the current phase of his travels and thus in the cities whose churches he had visited most recently: Corinth, Philippi, and Troas.[50] This receives confirmation from the letter he had just written to Rome where he asks the Roman Christians to pray fervently for him that he would "be delivered from the unbelievers in Judea" (Rom 15:31).[51] Paul may well have thought it important to give instruction to the church leadership in Ephesus because he might never see them again (Acts 20:25).

If the idea is correct that Paul wrote 1 Timothy from Macedonia sometime during the previous year, then the meeting may have been urgent for another reason. Harmful notions had infiltrated the church recently, seemingly through its teachers (1 Tim 1:3–4, 6–7; 6:3–5, 20), and, in that letter, Paul had urged Timothy to make sure the overseers and deacons in the church were doctrinally and morally qualified to serve in those capacities (3:1–13; 5:22). Although Paul had been back to Ephesus since these troubles, a final meeting with these elders for warning and instruction would make sense.

Perhaps it was the Asian contingent in the delegation—Tychicus and Trophimus—who separated from the group and made their way to Ephesus to summon the church leaders there to Miletus for a meeting with Paul.[52] The messengers would have had a boat ride of about two and a half nautical miles across the Latmikos Gulf, a six-mile walk to Priene, a roughly twenty-six-mile walk around the eastern end of Mount Mycale, and then northward along the coast to Ephesus.[53] It was a journey of two days. Allowing the messengers two more days in Ephesus to recuperate from the journey and gather the church leaders who could make the trip back to Miletus, nearly a week must have passed before the elders gathered in Miletus for their meeting with Paul.

If Luke followed the method of the Greek historians Thucydides and Polybius, then the speech he attributed to Paul as the next step in his narrative (Acts 20:18b–35) gives "the sentiments most befitting the occasion, though at the same time" adhering "as closely as possible to the general sense of what was actually said" (*P.W.* 1.22.1 [Smith, LCL]; cf. Polybius, *Hist.* 12.25a.5). Since Luke was present with Paul, it seems reasonable to take the speech he records as "the general sense" of a session that, like the evening meeting in Troas, probably lasted many hours.

Paul's instruction was both a retrospective defense of his manner of life during the time he worked in Ephesus (Acts 20:18b–21, 27, 33–35) and a prospective description of what would happen both to him (20:22–23, 25) and to the Ephesian church (20:29–30). Paul primarily wanted to warn the Ephesian church against people from within the Christian movement, and within the Ephesian church itself, who would attack the church (20:28–30) and, considering the apologetic tone of the speech (20:18–21, 33–35), would attack Paul himself. Paul anticipates, moreover, that these attacks would come at a time when he would no longer be able to defend himself or a correct understanding of the gospel in person (20:25, 29, 38).

The element of self-defense in the speech may have arisen from his experience with opponents in southern Galatia and Corinth who attacked his character as a way of separating the Christians in these places from the apostle's teaching (Gal 1:10; 4:16; 5:11; 6:17; 2 Cor 10:10, 14; 11:5–12; 12:17–18). In response, Paul emphasized the sincerity and consistency of his long relationship with the Ephesian elders (Acts 20:18b–21). He had suffered persecution from the Jewish community for what he taught (20:19), and he did not vary or curtail his teaching to suit his audience. He taught repentance toward God and faith in the Lord Jesus Christ both in public and in private (20:20), and he taught these truths to all people, whether Jewish or Greek (20:21). His goal was, and always would be, to testify to the gospel of God's grace regardless of the suffering this would entail (20:24). Paul may have thought of these as helpful reminders if in the future people began to slander him in his absence.

Paul was also convinced that after he had suffered in Jerusalem (Acts 20:22–23, 29), false teachers would try to create havoc in the Ephesian church, and so he warned the Ephesian elders to be on guard against them (Acts 20:28, 31).[54] He emphasized his example of hard work and generosity during his three years in Ephesus (Acts 20:31, 34–35) and how during that time he had given no thought to gaining gold, silver, or apparel (Acts 20:33), classic signs of wealth and status. Not only would this provide a defense against anyone who accused him of taking financial advantage of the churches where he worked (cf. 2 Cor 12:17–18), but it provided a reminder to the Ephesian elders of the importance of resisting the kind of greed that had fueled their recent bout with false teaching (1 Tim 6:5, 10).

On to Patara, Syria, and Jerusalem

After a sorrowful parting (Acts 20:36–38), Paul and the delegation set sail from Miletus and "made a straight run . . . to Cos" (21:1 REB). They made the journey of about forty-five nautical miles in one day, so they probably had a following wind and sailed along at four to six knots, the average speed for favorable conditions in open water.[55] The trip to Rhodes was longer, although how long depends on how closely the ship's pilot hugged the coasts of Cos, the Datça peninsula, and the island of Syme. Ancient ship pilots tended to navigate by means of visible landmarks, so this could have been a journey of more than sixty nautical miles and, even with favorable winds, a long voyage of ten to fifteen hours.[56]

Rhodes was probably still a magnificent place when Paul and the delegation landed there. Strabo says that "in harbors, roads, walls, and other constructions it is so much better than other places that I cannot speak of any other that is equal or even superior to this city" (*Geogr.* 14.2.5). Luke gives the impression, however, that "the ship" did not remain there long but pressed on the next day to Patara about fifty-four nautical miles away over open water.

With favorable winds, the journey would have taken between nine and fourteen hours and placed Paul and the delegation in the capital city of the relatively new Roman province of Lycia, organized in AD 43. Patara was one of two good harbors in this mountainous region and connected to a network of roads recently constructed, or at least measured, during the two years after Rome's creation of the province.[57] Patara would have been a busy port city with good connections to the province's interior and opportunities for larger ships to load up on cargo. The city would have offered ample opportunity, then, for finding a ship willing to take the delegation on the long, open-water journey to Phoenicia (Acts 21:2), the coastal strip of the Roman province of Syria and the gateway to Jerusalem.[58]

The way Luke describes the ship's journey from Patara to Tyre in Phoenicia implies that it sailed the roughly 340 nautical miles without stopping, but only sighting Cyprus and then "leaving it on the left" (21:3).[59] The prevailing winds in this part of the Mediterranean blow from west to east, and Luke gives the impression that the ship's captain made use of these winds to sail directly to Tyre.[60] At the top speed of six knots, the journey would have taken a little over two days and involved navigating by the stars over two nights.[61]

When "the ship" arrived in Tyre, it began unloading its cargo. Since the delegation boarded "the [same] ship" seven days later to travel to Ptolemais (Acts 21:6), its unloading schedule must account for the seven days Paul spent in Tyre.[62] Paul and the delegation made good use of the time by finding fellow "disciples" in the city and meeting with them. What they heard from the Tyrian Christians confirmed what the Holy Spirit had been revealing to Paul since his journey to Jerusalem began. "Through the Spirit they were telling Paul not to go on to Jerusalem," probably out of fear for his safety (21:4; cf. 20:23). "The ship" made a brief stop in Ptolemais, a few hours sailing to the south, and the delegation "greeted the brothers and sisters and stayed with them for a day" (21:7 NIV). Their next stop was the massive port of Caesarea (21:8), a coastal sail about twenty-seven nautical miles to the south, and a journey, with favorable winds, of about seven hours.[63]

Paul and the church of Caesarea were probably well known to each other by this time. It seems likely that Philip had proclaimed the gospel to people there when he came to the city two decades earlier (Acts 8:40), and Paul had perhaps met some of these believers when, shortly after his conversion, he escaped to Caesarea from attempts on his life in Jerusalem (9:29–30). He had visited the Caesarean church again on his way to Jerusalem after his residency in Corinth in the early fifties AD (18:22). Observing the difficult conditions for believers during that visit may have prompted Paul to plan the collection of relief aid that he was now bringing through Caesarea to Jerusalem.

Considering the extent of Paul's probable acquaintance with Christians in Caesarea, a lengthy visit made sense, and Luke says that the delegation stayed in Philip's house "for many days" (Acts 21:10a). During this stay, the Jewish-Christian prophet Agabus traveled from somewhere in Judea, probably Jerusalem (cf. Acts 11:27–28), and gave another dark prophecy about Paul's fate in the city: unbelieving Jews would bind Paul and turn him over to the gentiles (Acts 21:10b–11). Paul and those with him probably did not miss the echo here of Jesus's fate in Jerusalem (cf. Luke 18:32). Everyone responded to this with an attempt to persuade Paul to give up his plan to travel to Jerusalem, but Paul refused, insisting that he was ready to suffer imprisonment and death "for the name of the Lord Jesus" (Acts 21:13).

The roads from Caesarea to Jerusalem covered about sixty-five miles and would have taken about three and a half days to travel on foot. It was a long journey, much of it uphill, and the group took some time to prepare (Acts 21:15). Some of the Caesarean Christians went with the group, perhaps as a show of solidarity and to provide an introduction of this mainly gentile company to the conservative Jewish Christians of Jerusalem. Once there, they would stay with a fellow believer named Mnason who was known to the contingent from Caesarea. Luke points out that he was both a Cypriot and "an early disciple" (21:16). As a Cypriot he would have known Greek, and as an early disciple he would have credibility with the Jerusalem church. He was well positioned, therefore, to serve as a host to the mainly gentile delegation that came with Paul and to serve as a mediator between them and the traditionally Jewish Jerusalem church.

20

Violence and Arrest in the Jerusalem Temple

In the six years since Paul last visited Jerusalem (Acts 18:22), political problems in Judea had increased. The emperor Claudius recalled Cumanus and appointed Felix procurator in AD 52, shortly after Paul's departure. Two years later, Nero ascended to power in Rome and confirmed Felix as governor of Judea where, according to Josephus, "matters were constantly going from bad to worse" (*A.J.* 20.160 [Feldman, LCL]). Josephus pins the blame for the trouble on two causes: "brigands and impostors."

BRIGANDS AND IMPOSTORS

The people Josephus calls "brigands" were not common criminals but members of a religiously motivated group that had been active in Judea for decades and whose goal was freedom for the people of Israel from Roman domination (*A.J.* 18.4–7).[1] According to Josephus, they had "a passion for liberty that is almost unconquerable, since they are convinced that God alone is their leader and master" (*A.J.* 18.23 [Feldman, LCL]). Apart from this special interest, Josephus says, they agreed with the beliefs of the Pharisees (*A.J.* 18.23). The Pharisees had a reputation for strict observance of the Mosaic law according to their interpretation and expansion of it (Acts 22:3; 26:5; Phil 3:5–6; Josephus, *Vita* 191), and many of those laws dealt with the purity of the temple.[2] Judging from the coins these "brigands" produced when they briefly gained control of Jerusalem, they were especially interested in "Zion's freedom," probably referring to the liberation of the temple (located on Mount Zion) from foreign control and pollution.[3]

From among these "brigands" a group of assassins emerged, the so-called *sicarii* who seem to have become especially active after Nero's confirmation of Felix. This group specialized in assassinating—with concealed weapons—Jewish people whom they suspected of collaboration with the Romans, and they did this specifically in the crowded conditions of the pilgrimage festivals at Jerusalem (*B.J.* 2.254–255).[4]

Apart from the brigands, says Josephus, another group arose who also "ruined the peace of the city" (*B.J.* 2.258 [Feldman, LCL]). Josephus calls them "deceivers and impostors" who "under the pretense of divine inspiration" encouraged "revolutionary changes" (*B.J.* 2.259 [Feldman, LCL]; cf. *A.J.* 20.167–168). The most famous of the group was a man from Egypt who claimed to be a prophet and led a large group of people around the desert and to the Mount of Olives. There the group overlooked the walls of Jerusalem which, the prophet said, would fall on his command. He believed that his followers would overtake the Romans in Jerusalem and then appoint him king.

This description evokes the time of Israel's exodus from Egypt, with its desert trek and its echo of Joshua's conquest of Jericho.[5] Perhaps the Egyptian thought of himself as the prophet like Moses whose coming Moses had predicted (Deut 18:18), and whom some still expected in the first century (John 6:14; 7:40). Here too the ultimate motive was probably the liberation of the Holy City of Jerusalem from the domination of the Romans. Josephus comments that "deceivers and impostors" like this led their followers "out into the desert under the belief that God would there give them tokens of deliverance" (*B.J.* 2.259 [Thackeray, LCL]).[6] The phrase Thackeray translates "tokens of deliverance" could also be rendered "signs of freedom" (σημεῖα ἐλευθερίας) and is redolent of the "signs" that God used to display his power when he liberated Israel from slavery in Egypt (Exod 4–11).

Paul and the Delegates Meet with the Jerusalem Church Leadership

This was the atmosphere in Jerusalem when Paul and the delegation of mainly gentile Christians with him arrived at Mnason's house. Perhaps Paul's sister, or at least his nephew, joined them (cf. Acts 23:16), and the next day they met with James and the elders of the Jerusalem church (21:17–18). This was probably the point at which Paul and the delegates with him handed the collection over to the Jerusalem leadership.[7]

Luke says nothing substantive about the collection and only hints once in his narrative that the collection even existed (Acts 24:17). Some scholars have suggested that this omission arose from Luke's embarrassment that the Jerusalem leaders had rejected the offering, belying Luke's notion of a unified early church.[8] The Jerusalem leaders themselves, however, had impressed on Paul at the Jerusalem Council that he should make sure to incorporate into his mission to the gentiles a concern for the poor (Gal 2:10). It would be odd, considering this emphasis, if they now rejected alms from those very gentiles.[9]

It seems reasonable, then, to trust Luke, who claims to have been present at the meeting (Acts 21:17–18), when he says that the Jerusalem leaders "glorified God" after hearing Paul's report of what God had done through his ministry among the Gentiles" (Acts 21:19–20). This was basically the response Paul had hoped the collection would receive. As he told the Corinthians, "By their approval of this service [the collection] they [the Jerusalem church] will glorify God because of your submission that comes from your confession of the gospel of Christ, and the generosity of your contribution for them and for all others, while they long for you and pray for you, because of the surpassing grace of God upon you" (2 Cor 9:13). Luke's language is less effusive than Paul's expressed hopes, and the mystery of Luke's omission of the collection remains, but it seems historically sensible to include within the Jerusalem leaders' positive response to Paul their acceptance of the gentiles' generous offering.

Along with all the good news and cheer, however, came a more ominous report. Paul had developed a bad reputation in Jerusalem among the thousands of Jewish Christians in the city, all of whom, the Jerusalem leaders said, were "zealous for the law" (Acts 21:20b). These believers had heard that Paul taught diaspora Jews in the regions where he worked to abandon Moses, the rite of circumcision, and the practice of Jewish customs (Acts 21:20b–21). The concerns Paul had expressed a few months earlier in his letter to the Romans about slanders against him, and about the possibility of violence against him from unbelievers in Judea, were not unfounded (Rom 3:8; cf. 6:1, 15; 2 Cor 6:8).[10]

CHAPTER 20

The Jerusalem Church Leadership Has a Plan

The leadership of the Jerusalem church felt that Paul's reputation in Jerusalem, and the likelihood that his arrival in the city would become known, required some remedial action (Acts 21:22). Their plan may well have been an effort to refute the slander of a good man.[11] It would also have the benefit of making sure that his presence did not implicate them in the same rumors that were making the rounds about Paul. The ruling class in Jerusalem already considered them to be the leaders of a dangerous sect (24:5; cf. 24:14), and only a few years later the high priest and the ruling council would find James "and certain others" guilty of transgressing the law and execute them by stoning (Josephus, *A.J.* 20.200 [Feldman]).

The Jerusalem church leaders proposed, then, that Paul undertake two acts of Jewish piety that would show his continuing commitment to the Mosaic law. He would go through a purification rite necessary for entry to the temple and pay the expenses of four Christians who had placed themselves under a Nazirite vow and were nearly ready to bring their vow to an end (Acts 21:23–24).[12] Perhaps they thought Paul would welcome this solution since the purpose of his last visit to Jerusalem was to complete his own Nazirite vow (18:18, 22).

Ending a Nazirite vow involved not merely the shaving and sacrifice of one's hair (Num 6:5, 18) but three animal sacrifices (a lamb of each gender and a ram) plus fine unleavened bread, meal, and wine. It was an expensive process, especially when multiplied by four. Paul's own ritual of purification, which he would need to perform to enter the temple with the Nazirites, was itself not inexpensive. If it was a purification ritual to rid himself of corpse impurity, which seems likely, then, in addition to the water ritual prescribed in the Mosaic law (Num 19:11–13) he probably had to offer the two lambs that Josephus says were required for people who had been in a state of corpse impurity for more than a week (Josephus, *A.J.* 3.262).[13] The intersection of the request that Paul undertake and underwrite these expensive rituals in Luke's narrative with the concern for the collection in Paul's letters is probably not coincidental. It seems reasonable to conclude that the Jerusalem leadership believed the expenditure of at least part of the collection money in this way would be an appropriate use of it.

If the Jerusalem leaders did make this suggestion, Paul must have wondered about its propriety. Was it appropriate to use the funds this way, even if the delegates gave their permission? Would complying with such a plan compromise his teaching that observance of the law was not necessary for inclusion within God's people, even for Jewish people?

Paul's Response to the Plan

How would Paul have thought about these issues? On the financial question, he was probably torn between wanting to respect the request of the Jerusalem church leaders and wanting to bend over backward to avoid any impression of the funds' misuse. Paul was meticulously careful when organizing the collection to avoid the idea that he would personally benefit from it. He wanted the initiative in taking up the collection to belong to the churches themselves (1 Cor 16:2; cf. 2 Cor 12:17–18). He insisted that a team of delegates from the churches who had contributed to the collection travel with it (1 Cor 16:3; 2 Cor 8:19–21). He was willing to stay behind himself unless the churches approved his own involvement in taking the funds to Jerusalem (1 Cor 16:4). His aim was to do "what is honorable not only in the Lord's sight but also in the sight of man" (2 Cor 8:21). If he had imagined that using the collection to pay the expenses of the Nazirites (and possibly his own expenses) could compromise this overarching principle, he would not have done it.

Regardless of where the money for these rituals came from, though, would Paul have felt that the plan compromised his theological convictions about the Mosaic law? In the letter he had just written to the Roman Christians, he had made clear that he felt no need to follow the Mosaic laws of purity himself. "I know and am persuaded in the Lord Jesus that nothing is unclean in itself," he had said (Rom 14:14), and, in 1 Corinthians, he had commented that "food will not commend us to God. We are no worse off if we do not eat, and no better off if we do" (1 Cor 8:8; cf. Gal 2:11–14). He clearly did not believe it necessary for Christians, even Jewish Christians, to maintain the laws of purity when it came to their diet. Circumcision, too, was unnecessary (Gal 6:15; 1 Cor 7:18–19).

At the same time, he believed that Christians might continue to observe the Mosaic law as an act of devotion to God, if their conscience led them to do so. Just as Abraham had "received the sign of circumcision as a seal of the righteousness that he had by faith" (Rom 4:11), so, presumably, Christians could continue to circumcise their male children as a demonstration of their faith. In the same way, observing the food laws and the Jewish calendar could be ways of honoring the Lord Jesus (Rom 14:5–6).

The important principle in all this was that "each one should be fully convinced in his own mind" (Rom 14:5). No one should feel compelled, nor should one compel anyone else, to act in ways that were inconsistent with their inner convictions. The goal was for Christians of various ethnicities and persuasions "to live in such harmony with one another, in accord with Christ Jesus, that together" they might "with one voice glorify the God and Father of our Lord Jesus Christ" (Rom 15:5–6; cf. 1 Cor 10:31–11:1). This was a principle that Paul tried to live by in his own ministry:

> To the Jews I became as a Jew, in order to win Jews. To those under the law I became as one under the law (though not being myself under the law) that I might win those under the law. To those outside the law I became as one outside the law (not being outside the law of God but under the law of Christ) that I might win those outside the law. To the weak I became weak, that I might win the weak. I have become all things to all people that by all means I might save some. I do all for the sake of the gospel, that I may share with them in its blessings. (1 Cor 9:20–23)

In the end, Paul decided that he should comply with the wishes of James and the Jerusalem church elders. He went to the temple with the four Christian Nazirites, initiated the rite of purification for himself, and arranged for their own "vow of purification" to be completed (Acts 21:26). If the Jerusalem church wished it, and the delegation agreed, it does not seem impossible that Paul used part of the collection funds to pay for these rituals.[14]

Mobbed and Arrested in the Temple

At some point close to the end of his seven-day waiting period, and when he was himself in a state of ritual purity (Acts 24:18), Paul went to the temple (21:27). Luke does not say why he went there, nor does he mention the four Nazirites, but it seems reasonable to think of Paul making a trip to the

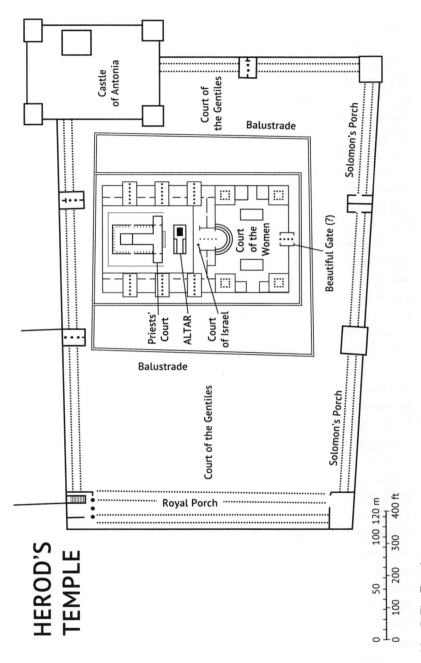

Map 5: The Temple

temple for some purpose connected with the end of his own purification or the sacrifices that the Nazirites needed to make.

The temple's architecture plotted out five areas of increasing holiness.[15] The outermost court was open to everyone whether Jewish or gentile, except for women during menstruation.[16] The next court was open to all Jewish people, although Jewish women had to be in a state of ritual purity. A flight of stairs and a wall separated the court of gentiles from this next court, and on the wall notices in Greek and Latin read, "No foreigner is to enter within the forecourt and the balustrade around the sanctuary. Whoever is caught will have himself to blame for his subsequent death."[17] The Romans allowed the Jewish people "to put to death any who passed it, even were he a Roman" (Josephus, *B.J.* 6.126).

A level terrace lay beyond this balustrade, and ritually pure Israelite men and women could cross it, climb a flight of stairs, and separate. Women would walk to entry gates on the east and west side of the wall that enclosed a court reserved for them. This court probably included a gallery from which they could see the work of the priests in the next court.[18] Men would enter a gate in the southern side of the same wall, probably walk along a corridor that passed through the women's court, and enter through another gate in a wall that enclosed an area reserved for ritually pure Israelite men.[19] Another wall separated this court from an area reserved for the priests alone. The final area of holiness was the inner sanctuary, reserved for the high priest clad in his special vestments, and entered once a year on the Day of Atonement.

When Paul entered the temple area, he probably walked up the stairs to the main entrance in the southern wall, through the tunnel that connected this entrance with the court that everyone could enter, passed the barrier with its warning signs, and entered the precincts of the inner temple reserved for ritually pure Israelites alone.[20] He was probably somewhere in the area reserved for Jewish men when some men from the Roman province of Asia spotted him (Acts 21:27). They must have been from Ephesus, and, like Paul, they had probably made the pilgrimage to Jerusalem for the Feast of Weeks. They knew what Paul looked like from encounters with him in Ephesus, and they probably knew that he was a controversial figure among Jewish people not only in Ephesus but throughout the province of Asia (19:9–10, 26; 20:19).[21] They had already seen him in Jerusalem with

Trophimus, an Ephesian Christian they recognized and knew to be a gentile (21:29).

For some reason, they suspected that Paul had led Trophimus, and perhaps other non-Jewish members of his group, beyond the fatal barrier and into the inner temple area. Perhaps they had heard Paul describe his own ministry the way he had characterized it in his letter to the Roman Christians a few months earlier. He was, Paul had told the Romans, "a minister of Christ Jesus to the Gentiles in the priestly service of the gospel of God, so that the offering of the Gentiles may be acceptable, sanctified by the Holy Spirit" (15:16).

The Asians, then, seem to have believed that Paul had facilitated the desecration of the temple, and as the warning notice on the barrier implied, should face death immediately, without a trial.[22] The Mishnah would later say that "if a priest served in the Temple while impure, his fellow priests do not bring him to court. Rather, young priests take him out of the Court and split his skull with clubs" (m. Sanhedrin 9:6).[23]

Something like this seems to have been the intention of the Asians when they seized Paul and called for reinforcements from the crowd (Acts 21:27–28, 30). The resulting mob dragged him out the two gates, down the stairs, across the terrace, through the warning barrier, and down the stairs to the court of gentiles where they began beating him with the intention of killing him (21:31–32, 36; 22:22). They may have believed that the temple would remain defiled until Paul was dead.[24]

Meanwhile, "the gates were shut" (Acts 21:30), probably to keep any bloodshed outside the inner temple area.[25] These were probably the two gates at either end of the corridor running through the court of women and connecting the men's court to the terrace and the temple's outer court. Each gate had two doors, and each door was forty-five feet high by twenty-two feet wide, about the same square footage, says E. P. Sanders, "as a small house today."[26] Closing such doors would have been an enormous undertaking and gives an impression of the size and raucous nature of the disturbance.[27]

Someone, perhaps Luke or one of the four Nazirites, reported the trouble to the Roman tribune stationed with the one thousand soldiers under his command in the massive Antonia Fortress at the northwest corner of the temple (Acts 21:31).[28] The fortress towered above the porches on the western and northern sides of the outer temple enclosure and had "stairs leading down to both of them, by which the guards descended; for a Roman cohort was permanently quartered there, and at the festivals took up positions in arms around the porticoes to watch the people and repress any insurrectionary movement" (Josephus, *B.J.* 5.243–244 [Thackeray, LCL]).

The Roman military officer in charge of the Antonia Fortress, a tribune named Claudius Lysias (Acts 23:26), responded to the chaos below with an overwhelming military force, and, when the mob saw soldiers coming, they stopped beating Paul (Acts 21:31–32). A lynching for defiling the temple was not illegal from Rome's perspective (Josephus, *B.J.* 6.126), and the mob may well have expected that a few words of explanation to the tribune would permit them to continue their gruesome task.

Claudius Lysias, however, suspected the bloodied man before him of a much more serious crime. The size of the mob and the obvious fame of the man at the center of all the trouble may have indicated to the tribune that Paul was the Egyptian who had tried to lead an assault on the Roman soldiers occupying the temple mount some time earlier (Acts 21:38). That troublemaker had fled Jerusalem with a few of his followers when the Roman procurator Felix had met his devotees with an armed force (Josephus, *B.J.* 2.263). If this man was the Egyptian, the tribune must have thought, he was a political prisoner that Felix, presently in Caesarea, would want to deal with personally, and perhaps even send to Rome.[29] The two chains with which the tribune commanded that Paul should be bound would prevent another escape (Acts 21:33).

As the soldiers carried Paul up the stairs, the tribune was surprised to hear him ask in elegant Greek for permission to speak.[30] Claudius Lysias would have known that Greek was widely spoken across the Roman world, including Egypt, but Paul had formulated his question in a way that the tribune believed was inconsistent with the fugitive Egyptian's level of education and culture.[31] "Are you not the Egyptian, then, who recently stirred up a revolt and led the four thousand men of the Assassins [σικαρίων] out into the wilderness?" (Acts 21:37–38). Paul let him know that, to the contrary, he was a Jewish man from the important city of Tarsus in Cilicia and held citizenship there. He wanted to address the restive crowd that had followed the soldiers to the fortress staircase calling for his lynching (21:36, 39–40).

The tribune permitted this, perhaps hoping that Paul would calm the crowd. Luke, who may have overheard the speech, took it as Paul's "defense" of his conduct (Acts 22:1).[32] They had accused him of contempt for the Jewish people, its customs, and its sacred place of worship (21:28), but he was only trying to obey the command of the God of Israel to bring the nations to God. Like his accusers, he had been so zealous for Israel's traditions that he had violently persecuted followers of Christ (22:3–5). God had shown him through a vision of Jesus of Nazareth, however, that this was a grave error (22:6–11). The law-observant Jewish Christian Ananias had explained to Paul the significance of what had happened to him (22:12–14), and Ananias had told him that he would be God's witness "to all people" (22:15 NIV). Jesus himself, moreover, had appeared to him in the temple and confirmed that he should take his message about the God of Israel and his Righteous One Jesus far away to the nations (22:21).

The mention of non-Jewish people groups seemed to confirm for the mob what they had suspected—that Paul had brought Greeks into the inner temple and defiled it. So, once again, they clamored for his death (Acts 22:22; cf. 21:36). Claudius Lysias, who probably did not understand Paul's Aramaic speech, no longer suspected him of being the seditious Egyptian but was still not clear about why the crowd was so angry with him. He felt it his duty to find out what it was about Paul that had created such a disruption in such a sensitive place at such a volatile time.

Assuming Paul was his distant social inferior, he ordered his subordinates to question him under the lash (Acts 22:24), an interrogation technique reserved for foreigners and others of low social standing.[33] Paul, however, was a Roman citizen, and subjecting him to the lash without formal legal proceedings ran contrary to Roman custom (cf. 16:37–39).[34] Some interpreters of Acts and biographers of Paul have thought that at this point the apostle asserted his legal rights because he wanted to avoid the harshness of the lash, often depicted as "a flail with knotted cords, or possibly ... with pieces of metal or bone inserted into the leather straps."[35]

Two considerations make this unlikely. First, Luke's picture of Paul reveals no concern about the physical suffering he is on the verge of facing. Instead, Paul coolly asks about a point of law: "Is it lawful for you to flog a man who is a Roman citizen and uncondemned?" This calm approach to his own suffering and death is consistent with the portrait Luke draws of Paul throughout his journey to Jerusalem. He is ready to suffer and die in the city, if necessary, to testify truthfully there to "the facts about" Jesus (Acts 23:11; cf. 20:23; 21:13).[36]

Second, the common description, sometimes accompanied by illustrations, of the Roman scourge as an instrument embedded with metal and bone and so forth needs to be dropped.[37] In a careful study, the historian Andrea Nicolotti has shown that such descriptions rest on eighteenth-century misinterpretations of artwork and artifacts from Roman antiquity.[38] Like anyone else, Paul would have wanted to avoid the physical pain and social shame involved in a lashing, but Luke pictures him, even in this extreme situation, as focused on his status as a Roman citizen to facilitate his faithful witness to the facts about Jesus in Jerusalem, and eventually, in Rome (Acts 23:11; cf. 19:21).

The tribune took Paul's claim to citizenship at face value, probably recognizing that he would not risk death by faking it (cf. Suetonius, *Claud.* 25.3) and not wanting to make things worse for himself. After all, he had publicly chained and nearly flogged a Roman citizen, and that was no small breech of Roman custom.[39] Less than a century earlier, Cicero had imagined the horror of a situation in which a Roman citizen found himself in a foreign land but among Roman officials there who neglected their duty to follow the law:

> Take away this confidence, take away this defence from Roman citizens; lay it down that to cry "I am a Roman citizen" shall help no man at all; make it possible for governors and other persons to inflict upon a man who declares himself a Roman citizen any cruel penalty they choose, on the plea that they do not know who the man is; do this, accept that plea, and forthwith you exclude Roman citizens from all our provinces, from all foreign kingdoms and republics, from every region of that great world to which Romans, above all other men, have always had free access until now. (Cicero, *Verr.* 2.5.65 [Greenwood, LCL])

The tribune's vulnerable legal position with Paul probably explains why he released Paul from any restraints and detained him in comfortable circumstances within the Antonia Fortress.[40] He still needed to find out why Paul had created such a dramatic disturbance in the temple, but he probably wanted to be careful not to alienate Paul further to avoid legal trouble for himself.[41]

A Hearing, a Plot, and Paul's Transfer to Caesarea

Claudius Lysias had a problem. From his perspective, Paul had caused a massive disturbance in the inner part of the Jewish temple during a crowded Jewish festival. On one hand, as a Roman citizen, Paul was entitled to due process. On the other hand, if he had desecrated the temple, then even Roman citizenship would not protect him against the death penalty (Josephus, *B.J.* 6.126). If he were guilty and not handed over, the crowds in town for the festival could create massive disturbances, and a failure to control those disturbances might look like incompetence to the procurator Felix, who was sixty-five miles away in Caesarea. Only a few years before, the governor of Syria had sent the lower-ranking Judean procurator Cumanus and his tribune Celer to Rome after their mismanagement of a series of violent events. Those events had started, according to Josephus, with a disturbance in the temple over an act of desecration at the jam-packed Passover festival. Cumanus suffered exile, and Celer was executed (Josephus, *A.J.* 20.105–136; *B.J.* 2.223–246).[42]

It is understandable, then, why Claudius Lysias would want greater clarity on Paul's case from the Jewish nobility who normally ran the affairs of Jerusalem and the temple and who must have heard about the disturbance (Acts 21:30). This wealthy and influential group ("the council" or "Sanhedrin") functioned as an advisory body to the high priest and as a court for local criminal matters.[43] According to Luke, Claudius Lysias "commanded" (ἐκέλευσεν) them to meet.

Despite the objections of some commentators on Acts, it was entirely possible for a high-ranking Roman official to give orders to this body of Jerusalem nobles, including orders to meet with him.[44] So, for example, only nine years after Paul's appearance before the Sanhedrin, the Roman procurator Florus "ordered" (ἐκέλευσεν) "the chief priests, the nobles, and the most eminent citizens" of Jerusalem to hand over people who had insulted him (Josephus, *B.J.* 2.302 [Thackeray, LCL]), and he could send for (μεταπέμπεται) "the chief priests and the leading citizens" to instruct them on how they could get back into his favor (*B.J.* 2.318).[45] As the highest-ranking Roman official in Jerusalem, then, Claudius Lysias would certainly have had the authority to "order" the local nobility to meet and help him decide what to do in this case.[46]

The meeting did not go well. Paul was able to win some sympathy from his fellow Pharisees by emphasizing their common belief in the resurrection of the dead (Acts 23:6–9), but the high priest Ananias, himself corrupt (Josephus, *A.J.* 20.206–207), completely rejected Paul's claim to have a clear conscience before God (Acts 23:1–2). The resurrection issue, moreover, generated such controversy that things turned violent, and Claudius Lysias commanded his soldiers to bring Paul back into the fortress (Acts 23:7, 9–10).

The tribune had not learned much. What he did learn was that the charge against Paul seemed to hinge not on temple defilement (a charge he would have understood) but on a fine point of Jewish belief that he neither comprehended nor cared about. The tribune felt that Paul had done nothing to deserve punishment (Acts 23:29), but probably since the rich and powerful Ananias had expressed such a strong objection to Paul, he felt that he had to send the case to the procurator Felix at his headquarters in Caesarea. In the Roman provinces, only the governor could try a case, and for Lysias, that meant sending Paul and his accusers to Felix with a letter of explanation (23:26–30).[47]

Paul, then, remained in the fortress. The following day he received a visit from his young nephew, who had sobering news (Acts 23:12–22). The young man had overheard people plotting against Paul's life and had picked up enough of the conversation to know how the plot would unfold. A group of over forty men had sworn they would observe a strict fast until they had killed Paul, and they had urged some of the city council to cooperate with the plot. The group could only kill Paul, however, if they got him out of the Antonia Fortress, and they wanted to do this by asking the council to request another meeting with Paul from the tribune. The request for a follow-up meeting would make sense, since the first meeting had not even touched on the main issue of temple defilement.

Luke says nothing about the motivation for this plot, but intrigue and murder were part of the atmosphere at festival times in Jerusalem, and especially around the temple during Felix's procuratorship.[48] Felix had tried to suppress the murderous activity of the *sicarii* against Jewish collaborators with Rome, but he had also not been above making secondhand arrangements for the *sicarii* to focus their violence on his own political enemies (Josephus, *A.J.* 20.161, 163–164). According to Josephus, this conduct had resulted in a rash of similar murders both for political ends and for monetary gain (*A.J.* 20.165). Perhaps, then, the forty men who wanted to kill Paul were *sicarii* and were attempting to purify the temple by executing one who had defiled it.[49] To this end they may have made common cause with the city council whose leading priests and elders stood in a decades-long tradition of opposing the Christian movement and certainly had no interest in sparing a Christian accused of temple defilement (e.g., Mark 14:55; Acts 4:5, 16–18; 5:17–18, 27–28, 33; 9:1, 14, 21).

Claudius Lysias responded to the threat by sending Paul to Felix immediately, before he received the disingenuous request of the city nobility, and before he had to alienate the high priest by denying it. The threat against Paul made a large military escort necessary for the now-treacherous journey to Caesarea, the worst part of which would have been the thirty-six-mile stretch from Jerusalem to Antipatris.

The easiest way to travel through the steep hills and valleys northwest of Jerusalem was the route that ran through the Beth Horon pass, the two-mile descent from upper Beth Horon to lower Beth Horon.[50] In antiquity, the road between these two settlements was narrow, curved sharply, and often looked up to steep hills and down into precipitous ravines.[51] In the words of a learned professor of Jewish history at the University of Tel Aviv, "A small detachment occupying the hills can easily prevent the advance of a much superior force and push it down into the ravines."[52] This pass had been the waterloo of armies opposing Jewish freedom fighters in the past (1 Macc 3:13–26) and would be the place of disgraceful retreat again in the near future (Josephus, *B.J.* 2.546–550).[53] Only a few years earlier, under the procurator Cumanus, "brigands" had robbed one of the emperor Claudius's slaves at this spot, and Cumanus's response had led to a major political uprising (Josephus, *B.J.* 2.228–231 [Thackeray, LCL]).[54]

Claudius Lysias may have guessed that the "more than forty" conspirators against Paul had anticipated his next move and stationed part of their group, or sympathizers with them, on the hills overlooking the descent from upper to lower Beth Horon. A large military escort would reduce the risk of a simple prisoner transfer spiraling out of control and into a career-ending disaster.[55]

CHAPTER 20

The escort departed with their prisoner, and with a letter from Claudius Lysias to Felix informing him of the basic facts of Paul's case. Paul's accusers, the letter said, would follow Paul to Caesarea where they would make their case against him (Acts 23:25–30, 35).[56] After reaching Antipatris safely, a large part of Paul's military escort returned to Jerusalem, and the rest traveled thirty miles northwest to Caesarea. There Paul made an initial appearance before Felix, who read the letter from Claudius Lysias and informed Paul that he would hear his case when the plaintiffs arrived (23:35).

21

A Taste of Roman Justice in Caesarea-by-the-Sea

Caesarea-by-the-Sea was the Roman military and administrative headquarters for the province of Judea, and the main residence of the province's procurators.[1] It was a critically important port city along the eastern Mediterranean coast, providing a safe harbor for the gigantic clippers loaded with grain that sailed from the empire's breadbasket in Egypt to Rome. Winds on the Mediterranean tend to blow from the northwest, so ships could sail from Rome to Egypt swiftly, but the journey from Egypt to Rome was long and difficult, requiring navigation first to points north and then westward. Some of these ships traveled due north to places like Myra along the southern coast of Asia Minor (Acts 27:5–6). Other ships found that Caesarea on the coast of Judea was an ideal stopping point with its carefully engineered harbor and all the advantages of a large Roman city.[2]

There was also a multiethnic church in Caesarea. It had been helpful to Paul and the collection delegation when they had passed through the city only a couple weeks earlier (Acts 10:24, 44, 47–48; 21:8, 16). Now Paul was back, but this time as a prisoner of the Roman governor Felix.

In the Custody of Felix

Felix kept Paul in the enormous palace that Herod the Great had built around seventy years earlier (Acts 23:35).[3] This does not mean, however, that his detention was comfortable, at least during the first phase of his ordeal. The palace occupied a small peninsula jutting out into the ocean and consisted of two terraced sections: a lower terrace, which was private, and an upper terrace, which was public. The public area contained an audience hall that functioned as a courtroom (Acts 25:23) and, among other facilities, a prison.[4] Herod the Great had kept and eventually executed his son Antipater somewhere within the palace compound (Josephus, *A.J.* 17.185; *B.J.* 1.663), and, unless Herod had more than one palace in the city, Paul was likely kept in the same prison.[5]

Brian Rapske has observed that according to Luke, Felix relaxed the severity of Paul's confinement after his initial hearing and allowed his circle of friends to attend to his needs. This implies that prior to this time he was in grim circumstances with no provision for his needs from outside the prison (Acts 24:23).[6]

Perhaps it was something of a relief, then, when Ananias the high priest and a group of city leaders from Jerusalem arrived to make their case against Paul. At least now there was the possibility for some change in Paul's circumstances, and Paul had reason to believe that, in terms of the gospel's progress, the change would be for the better. Only a few days earlier, the Lord Jesus had appeared to him in a vision and assured him that he would make it to Rome and testify to the facts about Jesus (Acts 23:11).

From a practical, human perspective, however, Paul's legal situation must have looked bleak to an outside observer. He had two significant strikes against him. His first disadvantage was that, unlike Ananias and the dignitaries from Jerusalem, he had no advocate (ῥήτωρ) to speak on his behalf. The litigants in a trial before a Roman magistrate commonly entrusted the presentation of their case to a professional orator who knew something about the law, but whose primary skills lay in oral persuasion. Court records from a case in Egypt in AD 49 show how the system worked.[7] In it the plaintiff never speaks, but his "advocate" (ῥήτωρ), whose words seem to have been recorded almost exactly as spoken, makes a brief, orderly case for his client, dating relevant events with polite exactness to "the seventh year of our sovereign Tiberius Claudius Caesar" and submitting documentary evidence to prove his client's claims. The defendant, however, speaks for herself, stating her case in an unadorned way and providing no evidence.[8] In the same way, Paul's opponents have an advocate, but he is forced to speak for himself.

Paul's second disadvantage lay in the social status of his accusers. Ananias, as the high priest, was not only the most politically powerful Jewish figure in Judea, and enormously wealthy, but may have had a hand in Felix's appointment to his post as procurator.⁹ Six years earlier Ananias had been a member of a group within the high priestly circle that the Syrian legate Quadratus sent to Rome to account to the emperor Claudius for the violent resistance to Roman rule that was gaining momentum in AD 51–52 (Josephus, *B.J.* 2.243; *A.J.* 20.131). The Jewish leaders, including Ananias, had a powerful ally in the Judean prince Herod Agrippa II, who was living in Rome at that time. Agrippa's father had been a close friend of the emperor Claudius.¹⁰ Through his intercession with the emperor, the Jewish leaders not only prevailed in their hearing before Claudius but one of their group, the former high priest Jonathan, was able to convince the emperor to replace the Judean procurator Cumanus with his favorite pick—Felix (Josephus, *B.J.* 2.245; *A.J.* 20.135–136, 162).¹¹ Josephus does not mention Ananias's involvement, but since he was part of the small high priestly circle that Quadratus sent to Rome, it is possible that he joined in the effort to have Felix appointed to this post.¹²

None of this would have been lost on Felix as Ananias and his advocate Tertullus stood before him. Felix had little affection for Jonathan, and presumably his circle, but these were powerful people with strong ties to Rome, and it would be important not to alienate them unnecessarily in these uncertain political times.¹³

Tertullus the advocate began with a compliment to Felix for his effective work at remedying precisely the kind of riotous conduct that he then claimed Paul had promoted (Acts 24:2–5).¹⁴ Felix had brought peace and reform to the province (probably a reference to all the "banditry" and religious fanaticism Felix had brutally suppressed), but Paul's conduct, he implied, showed the need for constant vigilance. Paul was "a plague," Tertullus said, "one who stirs up riots among all the Jews throughout the world" (24:5). This sort of language was circulating in the legal atmosphere of the time.¹⁵ In a public letter from sixteen years earlier, the emperor Claudius had warned the Jews of Alexandria "not to bring in or admit Jews sailing from Syria or Egypt, which will inevitably increase our suspicions. Otherwise I shall proceed against them in every way as spreading what amounts to a world-wide epidemic."¹⁶ Tertullus mentioned what he called Paul's attempt to profane the temple (24:6), but that charge now simply became a supporting prop to the more serious idea that Paul was the ringleader of a weird sect that promoted sedition. The portrait of Paul that Tertullus was painting had

CHAPTER 21

an uncanny resemblance to "the Egyptian" who had escaped Felix's troops. Did Tertullus intentionally paint his portrait in that style?[17]

If Ananias thought Paul would be at a disadvantage because he had no advocate, he was mistaken. Luke, who might have been present for this speech, or might have consulted nearly verbatim court records, gives the impression that Paul mounted an effective legal defense.[18] Paul began with an emphasis on Felix's strong qualifications for judging his case. The procurator had worked as a judge in the region "for many years," and, therefore, Paul implies, was able to understand the religious and political complexities of life in the region (Acts 24:10).[19] Paul does not mention it, but this was all the truer since Felix's wife was the young Jewish princess Drusilla (Acts 24:24; Josephus, *A.J.* 20.141–144), daughter of Herod Agrippa I (Josephus, *B.J.* 2.220).

Tertullus's claim that Paul was the head of a troublesome local sect did not square with the fact that he had arrived in Judea only twelve days before his initial hearing with Felix (Acts 24:11).[20] The "sect" to which he belonged was only a particular way of worshiping the same God that his accusers worshiped, believing the same Scriptures they believed, and looking forward to the same hope of the resurrection that many of his accusers held (24:14–16).

He had only come to Jerusalem to worship and bring alms (Acts 24:17). He had come, in other words, for the same reasons that hordes of other pilgrims also came regularly to Jerusalem. He did not violate the temple's sanctity, and those who initially charged him with this crime had not even taken the trouble to show up for the hearing (24:19). Ananias and the elders, who were present, could only charge him with the "crime" of believing in the resurrection of the dead, something that Paul's appearance before their council had shown not to be a crime at all (24:21; cf. 23:6–9, 29).

Luke says that Felix had "a rather accurate knowledge" of Christianity (Acts 24:22), implying that he knew that what Paul had said about the relationship between Christianity and Judaism was true. Christianity was a different "way" of worshiping the God of the Jews and following their law, but there was nothing criminal about it.

Josephus, Tacitus, and Luke agree, however, that Felix was not an honorable person. He married Drusilla after looking at her, finding her attractive, and persuading her through a fake magician to leave her husband (Josephus, *A.J.* 20.141–143). He had used the very terrorists he was supposed to arrest to assassinate the high priest Jonathan because Jonathan pushed him too hard to make reforms to his way of governing the province (Josephus, *A.J.* 20.162–164). He "practiced every kind of cruelty and lust" (Tacitus, *Hist.* 5.9 [Moore, LCL]; cf. *Ann.* 12.54).

It is not surprising, then, to find him leaving Paul in prison, despite his innocence, in the hope of receiving a bribe from him (Acts 24:26). It is also unsurprising to discover him trying to please Paul's powerful enemies among the Jerusalem nobility (24:27). Felix did improve the conditions of Paul's custody so that he could have some freedom and his circle of acquaintances in Caesarea could attend to his needs (24:23). Thankfully, Paul had friends such as Luke and Aristarchus (20:4–6; 27:2) who stayed with him through the whole ordeal, and the church in Caesarea probably also offered him help (21:8–16).[21]

A New Procurator Arrives

Outside Paul's palace prison, the city of Caesarea was in a state of turmoil generated by the competing civic claims of its Syrian and Jewish inhabitants. The Syrians in the city claimed that their civil rights should trump those of the Jewish people because they had inhabited the city first, before Herod the Great's building program. Even Herod, they argued, recognized the city's Syrian character, since many of his projects involved statues and temples unfitting for the monotheistic Jews. The dispute devolved into daily violence, and Felix, unable to quell the violence, sent the leaders of the two parties to Rome to argue their cases before Nero (Josephus, *B.J.* 2.266–270; *A.J.* 20.173–178). About this time, Nero recalled Felix to Rome and replaced him with a new procurator, Festus. The reason for this is unclear, but it may have had something to do with his failure to quell the violence in Caesarea and with an accusation against him from the leaders of the Caesarean Jewish community (*A.J.* 20.182). It was probably the late summer or early fall of AD 59, and Paul had been in prison for the better part of two years (Acts 24:27).

Within a few days of his arrival in Caesarea, Festus made the journey to Jerusalem to meet with the city's leaders (Acts 25:1–2), an important first step for ensuring a successful term as procurator. The high priest, former high priests, and Jewish nobility were not only the local power brokers, but since the time of Claudius they had often been successful in requests they had made of the Roman emperor on issues related to the observance of their religious customs in their own land.[22] Fourteen years earlier (in AD 45), when the procurator Fadus wanted to control possession of the high priest's special garments, the Jewish leadership traveled to Rome and got Claudius's permission to control the garments themselves. "I have consented to this measure," said Claudius in a letter on the subject, "first because of my own piety and my intention that each should worship according to his ancestral practices" (Josephus, *A.J.* 20.13 [McKechnie]).[23] A new procurator, then, would do well to pay a visit to the Jerusalem authorities as soon as possible after arriving in the province.

The first item on the authorities' agenda was Paul and the need to dispose of his case, preferably by disposing of Paul himself (Acts 25:2–3, 15, 24). To this end, the Jerusalem elites who met with Festus requested that he do them a "favor" (χάρις) and transfer Paul's case to Jerusalem (25:2–3). Their true intent, according to Luke, was to make another attempt at ambushing and killing Paul, this time on a journey in the reverse direction, from Caesarea to Jerusalem (cf. 23:12–15, 19–21, 30).

Some scholars believe that this second attempt at an ambush was Luke's creative effort to intensify the involvement of the Sanhedrin in injustice and lay the foundation for Paul's appeal to Caesar.[24] There is nothing historically implausible about the scene, however. The hierarchy in Jerusalem during this period was actively involved in trying to snuff out the Christian movement by attacking its leaders (1 Thess 2:14–16; Acts 12:1–19; Josephus, *A.J.* 20.200).[25]

Festus seems to have suspected that something was amiss in their request, and as a new procurator, he must have been unsure exactly how much trouble he might create for himself with a favor for the Jewish leadership at the expense of Paul. He told the Jerusalem authorities that they would need to face Paul in Caesarea where they could accuse him at a formal hearing (Acts 25:5, 16). By the time Festus got back to Caesarea a little over a week later, he seems to have settled on a compromise: once Paul had faced his accusers in Caesarea, perhaps Paul would agree to a trial in Jerusalem, but a trial before him rather than the Sanhedrin. This would provide the needed "favor" (χάρις) for the Jerusalem authorities and still give Paul the Roman justice he deserved (25:9).

Paul, however, smelled a rat. After his hearing, when Festus presented his idea to Paul, Paul responded that if he had done anything worthy of death, he was ready to die for it. "But if there is nothing to their charges against me, no one can give me up [χαρίσασθαι] to them [as a favor]" (Acts 25:11, modified).[26] Paul knew that the Jerusalem authorities' case against him was weak, and that so far various Roman officials viewed it as an in-house Jewish affair swirling around arcane religious issues undeserving of punishment (Acts 23:29; 25:18–19, 25; cf. 18:14–16). Paul, therefore, had no intention of sacrificing himself so that Festus could grant a diplomatic "favor" to the Jerusalem elites. Although there had been some personnel changes, these elites were basically the same group that for years had oppressed Jewish Christians in Judea and tried to drive Paul out of the province (1 Thess 2:15).[27]

PAUL APPEALS TO CAESAR

Paul needed a strategy for escaping Judea entirely. So, although he had not yet received a judgment against himself, he exercised his right as a Roman citizen to appeal his case to Caesar (Acts 25:11–12). To appeal a case before receiving a verdict might at first seem strange, but the laws governing appeals in this period are not entirely clear. Heike Omerzu makes a persuasive case that it was only after the first century, with a dramatic increase in the number of Roman citizens, that the Romans developed strict rules about the timing and circumstances of appeals to the emperor.[28] In the early empire, someone who was in legal trouble and a Roman citizen seems to have been able to appeal their case to the emperor at any point.[29] Although she believes that Festus actually condemned Paul to death and that Paul appealed to Caesar after this verdict, she argues that there is nothing historically implausible about Luke's account from the perspective of known Roman law in the mid-first century.[30]

Omerzu believes that Luke's apologetic interests motivated him to portray Paul as innocent and the Romans as just in recognizing Paul's innocence.[31] Luke has already revealed, however, that Festus was inclined to pervert justice by giving political favors to the Jerusalem elites (Acts 25:9; cf. 25:3, 11). It seems equally likely, therefore, that Luke faithfully relates what happened, and that Paul's request for a trial before Caesar was an attempt to find a more just courtroom for his case (25:11–12).

CHAPTER 21

Before sending Paul to Rome, Festus would need to put into writing the charges against him, but those charges were so bound up with Jewish religious ideas that Festus did not know how to formulate them (Acts 25:26; cf. 25:7–8).[32] Festus was probably grateful, therefore, that Herod Agrippa II and his sister, Bernice, had planned a visit to Caesarea to welcome him to his office. Before Nero had become emperor, the emperor Claudius had made Agrippa the king of a large region northeast of the Sea of Galilee (Batanaea, Trachonitis, and Abila, Josephus, *A.J.* 2.138).[33] He was a thoroughgoing loyalist to Rome, and he must have seen it as a politically prudent step to welcome Festus to the region with great fanfare (Acts 25:23).[34]

It makes sense, then, that he would comply with Festus's request to hear from Paul and interpret for Festus any particularly Jewish matters that the new procurator failed to understand (Acts 25:22; cf. 26:3). According to Luke's report of Paul's speech (and Luke may have witnessed it, 27:1), Paul defended himself as a pious adherent to Judaism who only believed that the vision for the future found in "the prophets and Moses" had "come to pass." This fulfillment had happened in the resurrection of Jesus and the proclamation to the nations that they needed to repent of their sins (26:20, 22–23). Luke's impression was that Festus remained uncomprehending (26:24) but that Agrippa found Paul persuasive (26:28) and assured Festus that apart from Paul's insistence on a hearing before the emperor, he could be released (26:32).

It was really to Festus's advantage, however, that Paul had made his appeal. As A. N. Sherwin-White put it, "Festus was naturally only too glad, politically, to rid himself of the prisoner. To have acquitted him despite the appeal would have been to offend both the emperor and the province."[35] The emperor might be offended that Festus had denied to him the authority of passing judgment on the case, and the indigenous leaders of the province would clearly take offense that Festus had denied them what they wanted. Paul was bound for Rome, but under far different circumstances than he imagined when he wrote his letter to the Romans from Corinth as a free man roughly three years earlier.

22

A Turbulent Journey West and Respite on Malta

Festus arranged for Paul to travel to Rome with a group of other prisoners and placed them all under the care of a centurion named Julius from a local cohort, the "cohort of Augustus" (Acts 27:1).[1] They set sail in a ship from Adramyttium, a port on the coast of Mysia just to the northeast of the island of Lesbos. It seems to have been headed from Caesarea back to Adramyttium with the intention of stopping first in Sidon, some sixty-nine nautical miles to the north, and then at ports on the southern coast of Asia Minor (27:2–3).[2]

Paul's Entourage

At least two other people were with Paul, Luke (who begins including himself in the narrative at this point) and "Aristarchus, a Macedonian from Thessalonica" (Acts 27:2). Aristarchus seems to have been with Paul since Paul's journey to Macedonia following his painful visit to Corinth (Acts 19:29). He had accompanied him when he left Ephesus for the last time and traveled with him back through Macedonia to Corinth. He then traveled on to Jerusalem with the collection and the other delegates (Acts 20:4) and stayed with Paul all the way through his long confinement in Caesarea, qualifying him, in Paul's view, as a "fellow prisoner" (Col 4:10; cf. Phlm 24).

Luke had also been with Paul for a long time at this point. He had joined the collection delegation in Philippi (Acts 20:5) and, seemingly, had been with Paul ever since.

Is it likely that anyone else was with Paul? The movements of Tychicus in Acts and Paul's letters hint that he was with the group. He was one of two

CHAPTER 22

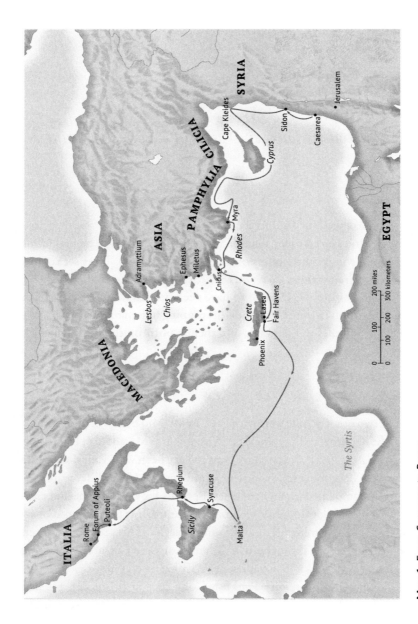

Map 6: From Caesarea to Rome

Christians from the province of Asia that traveled with the collection to Jerusalem (Acts 20:4), and he was later with Paul in Rome where he served as Paul's courier for letters back to Asia (Col 4:7; Eph 6:21; cf. 2 Tim 4:12). Trophimus the Ephesian may have still been with Paul (Acts 20:4; 21:29) since the ship's stop at Cnidus could have been the point at which Paul sent him to nearby Miletus (Acts 27:7; 2 Tim 4:20). If Paul left Titus on Crete when the ship stopped at the small harbor of Fair Havens (Acts 27:8; Titus 1:5), then he must be added to the group, and if Paul wrote his letter to Titus during his three-month stay on Malta, then the otherwise unknown "Artemas," whom Paul considers sending to Crete to relieve Titus, may have been with him also (Titus 3:12). Timothy may have been with him as well. He was present in the group that left Corinth for Jerusalem (Rom 16:21; Acts 20:4) and later joined Paul in writing letters from Rome (Phil 1:1; 2:19; Col 1:1; Phlm 1). This would be a group of eight (Paul, Aristarchus, Luke, Tychicus, Trophimus, Titus, Artemas, and Timothy), and the size of the group naturally prompts the question whether Paul could have embarked in a coasting vessel with such an entourage.

There is no way to know the precise size of the ship that Paul and his friends occupied when they left Caesarea, although it was large enough to sail safely across the open ocean at one point in its voyage (Acts 27:5). Ancient Roman ships averaged "75–80 tons," and "a maximum capacity of about 70 tons might necessitate a basic length around 20 m" or roughly sixty-six feet—in today's terms, a reasonably sized yacht.[3] If this was the size of Paul's ship, there was probably plenty of room for its crew members, Paul's seven companions, the centurion Julius, and the other prisoners of which Julius had charge.[4]

A Difficult Voyage to Myra

The group, however large, arrived the next day in Sidon, with its good natural harbor (Strabo, *Geogr.* 16.2.22), and the ship probably lingered there loading and unloading cargo.[5] Luke points out that the centurion Julius was friendly toward Paul and allowed him enough freedom to receive care from his friends in town (Acts 27:3). When the ship was ready for departure, they must have sailed north to some point east of Cyprus, hugging the coast as they went. They probably then tried to sail west toward Cape Kleides on the northeast tip of Cyprus with the intention of eventually traveling the roughly fifty nautical miles north from Cape Kleides to the coast of Cilicia.[6]

Contrary winds, however, forced a change of plans: they would have to sail "under" (ὑποπλέω) Cyprus, or on the side of Cyprus sheltered from the wind (Acts 27:4). Luke was probably referring to winds prevailing from the northwest. If so, then it is most likely that the ship traveled along the eastern side of Cyprus, turned west to sail along its southern side, and then crossed the open ocean between western Cyprus and Cilicia Tracheia (27:4–5).[7] From there, it made its way along the coast of Cilicia Tracheia and Pamphylia to Andriake, the busy port of Myra in Lycia (27:5). Most of the journey along this coast would have been hard going against contrary winds from the west-southwest.[8]

Myra was roughly three hundred nautical miles north of Alexandria, and a port of call for ships laden with Egyptian grain trying to make it to Rome. With winds blowing mainly from the west, a direct journey to Rome was virtually impossible, so ships from Alexandria often headed north for the southern coast of Asia Minor with the wind blowing over their port side and then worked their way west, now with the wind blowing over their starboard side. In this ponderous way they could eventually reach the west coast of Italy.[9] Julius the centurion found just such a ship for the next stage of their journey (Acts 27:6). It was a large Alexandrian grain ship, capable of taking on two hundred and seventy-six crew and passengers (27:37).

A Slow Journey South and Shelter on Crete

With the westerly wind trying to blow them back toward Cyprus, they made their way "slowly" along the Lycian Sea between the island of Rhodes and the mainland and eventually arrived "off Cnidus" at the tip of the Datça Peninsula (Acts 27:7).[10] Cnidus provided deep harbors on either side of its rocky perch, one that faced northwest and one that faced southeast, providing safety and rest for ships in a variety of wind and weather conditions. The southeastern-facing harbor could have provided welcome shelter from the westerly winds that had made progress so slow for Paul's ship.

Luke does not describe an extended stop at this point, but the ship may have waited long enough to allow Paul to perform a deed of mercy for one of his group who was sick. In his last extant letter, written while awaiting the resolution of his case in Rome, he says that he "left Trophimus, who was ill, at Miletus" (2 Tim 4:20). This is probably a reference to "Trophimus the Ephesian" (Acts 21:29), who two years earlier had accompanied Paul to Jerusalem and whom the Jewish pilgrims from Asia assumed Paul had brought into the parts of the temple reserved only for Jews. He had evidently stayed with Paul through the ordeal of his arrest and detention in Caesarea and may well have been in Paul's group aboard the ship to Rome. At this point in its journey, the ship was only seventy-seven miles from the large port city of Miletus, not far from Trophimus's native Ephesus. Sailing there in the fall would take just over twenty-four hours.[11] Although it is a bit speculative to say so, Paul may have sent Trophimus back to Miletus at this point.

In any case, the ship's pilot realized that he had no chance of sailing directly into the prevailing westerly winds and turned southwest toward Crete. There they found shelter from the wind on the eastern side of the island.[12] As the ship turned west to travel along Crete's southern coast, the northwesterly winds that dominate this part of the island's coastline in October once again made progress difficult (Acts 27:8a).[13] Eventually, however, they arrived at a harbor called "Fair Havens," about two miles west of the city of Lasea (27:8).[14] Luke's use of "the city" Lasea as a geographical marker for the location of "Fair Havens" implies that Fair Havens itself was little more than a natural harbor, and there is no evidence to indicate that Lasea was a town of any significant size.[15] It must have been an uninviting stopping point for a large ship with hundreds of passengers and crew and a load of valuable wheat. In addition, in the often-repeated words of James Smith, "it was a bay open to nearly one-half of the compass," perhaps leaving the ship vulnerable to foul weather.[16]

The problem was that "the Fast was already over," meaning that the Day of Atonement had already passed, and it fell on October 5 in AD 59.[17] This was late in the year for safe travel on the open ocean (Acts 27:9–10), and even the ship's owner seems not to have thought that the financial incentive for getting to Rome with his load of wheat in the winter was worth the risk.[18]

The ship, then, needed to find a suitable place to spend the winter. Paul with his entourage, his Roman citizenship, and his possible future appearance before Nero was probably perceived as a person of high social status, and so he was allowed a voice in the discussions between Julius the centurion, the ship's pilot, and the ship's owner.[19] Luke says that he counseled caution: going on would endanger both the ship and its company (Acts 27:10, 21). The others prevailed, however, and "the majority decided to put out to sea from there," not to try to reach Rome, but simply to sail farther to the west along Crete's southern coast to the more suitable harbor of Phoenix where they hoped to spend the winter (27:11–12).

Did Paul Leave Titus on Crete?

How long did this stop at Fair Havens take? Interpreters of Acts usually assume that it was brief, but Luke says nothing one way or the other about the length of time the ship and its crew stayed at Fair Havens. Since Luke often compresses time in his narrative (e.g., Acts 9:23; 20:2), it is not unreasonable to imagine this stay lasted long enough for Paul to have contacted Christians in the area with the permission of Julius, the friendly centurion (cf. Acts 27:3; 28:14–16). Jewish pilgrims from Crete had been present at Pentecost (Acts 2:11), and Paul might easily have heard of Christians on the island during his eighteen months in Corinth or his nearly three years in Ephesus (Acts 18:11; 19:10; 20:31).[20] Apollos, Paul's friend and fellow laborer in the spread of the gospel in the Aegean region, may have already been on the island at this point (Titus 3:13).

If so, it seems natural to think of Paul sending one of his group, such as Titus, out to villages near Fair Havens to inquire about the state of Christian associations in the region and the location of Apollos. Such a procedure would not have been unlike his efforts to contact Christians in Sidon, or later, in Puteoli (Acts 27:3; 28:13–14). There is no need, then, to imagine Christianity emerging on Crete recently, and certainly no need to think that Julius allowed Paul to evangelize the island.[21]

If it is possible to take the letter to Titus as evidence of what Paul found out about Christianity on Crete at this point, then what he discovered was troubling. At least in the villages that Paul heard about, the church was under the influence of Jewish teachers who emphasized the need to observe purity regulations and to learn from Jewish mythology (Titus 1:10, 14–15). Judging from Paul's use of the term "myths" and his implied claim that the teaching on purity arose from "the commands of people" (1:14–15), it is likely that both aspects of the false teaching were untethered from Scripture and had an esoteric and ascetic character. Like the false teachers that had created such trouble in Corinth and Ephesus, moreover, the teachers on Crete insisted on payment for their services (1:11; cf. 2 Cor 11:7–15; 1 Tim 6:10).[22]

The result was quarreling and division, especially over the interpretation of the Jewish law (Titus 3:9). Households were in disarray (1:11), and the basics of morality and civility were in danger of neglect (1:12, 16; 3:8, 11, 14).

If this was what Paul learned, then it would make sense for Paul to leave Titus on Crete to aid these troubled churches (Titus 1:5). Perhaps Paul intended for Titus to join forces with others, such as "Zenas the lawyer and Apollos" (3:13), who may have been on the island and sympathetic with Paul's concerns.[23]

Shipwreck!

Whether any of this is on target, it is at least clear from Luke's narrative of his voyage with Paul that the ship's owner, ship's pilot, and Julius the centurion all disagreed with Paul's advice not to sail away from Fair Havens. Instead, they would sail to Phoenix (Acts 27:12). They probably considered this town a safe place to spend the winter and thought the area might offer more amenities than Fair Havens. It was about forty nautical miles to the west, without hugging the coast tightly.[24] Judging from an inscription found near Phoenix dating to a few decades after Paul's journey, it was also a common place for the pilots of Alexandrian ships to spend long periods of time, probably as they sheltered from winter weather (IC 2.20.7).[25] The ship's pilot and owner had likely been there before.

So, when a mild wind from the south began to blow, it must have seemed the perfect opportunity to sail west, hugging the coast for a few miles, and then, at Cape Matala, where the coast turns north, to make a straight run slightly north of west for Phoenix. Unfortunately, the wind quickly and dramatically changed and began blowing the ship in the opposite direction. This wind, apparently well known to the sailors, and now well known to Luke, was called the *Eurakylōn*, a term that mixed Greek and Latin and was probably sailing lingo for the violent northeast wind that could blow at this time of year in this part of the Mediterranean.[26]

CHAPTER 22

With its square-rigged sails, an ancient ship was helpless before such a wind, and Paul's ship simply gave way to it.[27] Thankfully, the *Eurakylōn* blew the ship near the small island of Cauda, which provided enough shelter for the sailors to take two important steps to keep it from taking on water or breaking apart. First, they hauled the troublesome ship's boat on board. They had been dragging it along behind them and it was probably filled with water, adding to the ship's instability (Acts 27:16).[28] Second, they ran their emergency cables, kept on board for moments like this, underneath the ship to hold its planking together more tightly (27:17a).[29]

With these problems solved they began to fear that the *Eurakylōn*, blowing hard from the northeast, would drive them south into the dreaded shallow gulf off the coast of Libya ("the Syrtis," Acts 27:17b). This area was not only a navigational nightmare, with "shoals, crosscurrents, and long sand-bars extending a great distance out," but stories circulated of uncanny, man-eating animals that lurked around the shoreline and sometimes feasted on shipwrecked mariners (Dio Chrysostom, *Or.* 5.5–11 [Cohoon, LCL]). To slow their progress in this direction, they lowered all the ship's sails and any removable equipment the wind might use to blow them along.[30]

As one stormy day led to another, they began to jettison first some of the ship's cargo and then the ship's equipment (Acts 27:18–19), probably because the ship was taking on more and more water. There were no compasses for navigation in this period, and so when the guiding light of the stars, sun, and moon remained obscured for the next eleven days, Luke says that most everyone on board gave up hope of surviving (27:20): having avoided the shallows off the Libyan coast, the ship would nevertheless sink at sea.[31]

Paul, however, had not given up hope. During the night, he had experienced one of the visions that so often came to him when his work seemed to be at a turning point or in crisis (Acts 27:23; cf. 16:9; 18:9–10; 22:17–21; 23:11). A messenger of God had stood beside him and told him not to be afraid because it was necessary for him to stand before Caesar, and he would therefore survive this trial. Moreover, God, in his generosity, had decided that everyone on board the ship would survive along with him (27:24). Luke remembered that Paul had conveyed this message to others on the ship as a way of encouraging them (27:21–26).

After thirteen days in the storm, the sailors' suspicion that they were nearing land received confirmation from a series of decreasing depth measurements: 121 feet of ocean depth became, a little later, 92 feet (Acts 27:28). This development was both a blessing and a curse. It certainly increased their chances of survival, but it introduced its own new danger. If their large ship broke apart on rocky shallows farther than swimming distance from the shore, they could perish as easily as if the waves had swamped the ship on the high seas.

Their only hope for survival was a controlled crash into the shore. In an effort in this direction, the ship's crew lowered four anchors from the rear of the ship. They would have either dropped them over the ship's side or sent the cables holding them through the portals on either side of the ship that accommodated its two rudders. Perhaps they did both.[32] They probably also pulled up their rudders, secured them to keep them from banging around in the storm, and felled their main mast.[33] They must have also readied their foresail for hoisting. At the first light of day, they would cut away their anchors and, powered by surf and foresail, attempt to use the rudders to guide the ship into the most favorable landing spot they could see (Acts 27:40).[34]

The sailors, however, did not like their own chances of outliving such a maneuver.[35] On the pretext of helpfully stabilizing the ship further by also lowering anchors from its front, they attempted to launch the ship's boat and escape in it, thus avoiding a plunge into the deep as the larger vessel broke apart (Acts 27:29–30). Paul observed what they were doing, told the soldiers on board that they needed the sailors' expertise to survive, and the soldiers stopped the sailors' plan by cutting the ropes holding the boat to the ship and setting it adrift (27:31–32).

As morning light approached on the fourteenth day of their ordeal, Paul again took the initiative with advice and encouragement. He urged people on the ship to eat something in preparation for their rough landing and reminded them that he believed no one would perish (Acts 27:33–35). Luke reports that people took Paul's advice and then pitched in to help lighten the ship by throwing its wheat cargo overboard (27:36–38).

When morning came, the sailors were able to make out a bay with a beach they believed might work for driving the ship aground, and they enacted their plan. They simultaneously cut the anchor ropes, untied the rudders, and hoisted the foresail (Acts 27:40).[36] The ship must have lurched forward toward the beach and safety. Before it could reach the beach, however, it ran aground in a shallow area and began breaking apart (27:41). With the ocean depths behind them and shallower water ahead, they could only swim to safety or float there on pieces of debris from the ship.[37] In one way or the other, however, everyone made it safely to shore (27:43–44).

A Winter of Hospitality on Malta

Soon after this harrowing experience, they discovered the island was Malta and met some of the locals. The islanders were not native Greek speakers (Acts 28:2, 4), but they spoke eloquently the language of human kindness. They knew that traumatized and water-soaked wreck victims needed a warm fire, particularly in the cold and rain that had descended on the group (28:1–2). Once the fire was lit, Paul, true to the initiative he had taken throughout the voyage, immediately became helpful and started gathering wood to keep the fire going.

Luke says that Paul's efforts led to a snake bite and to alarm among the Maltese, who had probably learned that some of the shipwreck survivors were Roman prisoners and thought that justice had caught up with Paul. Paul, however, suffered no more harm from the snake than he had suffered from the shipwreck, just as the heavenly messenger had promised him a few days earlier (Acts 28:3–5). God would preserve him because Paul's destiny was to stand before the emperor (27:23–24). When the islanders who had heard about the snake bite realized that Paul was unharmed, they withdrew their negative opinion of him and decided that he was a god in human form (28:6).

Malta, with its friendly people, turned out to be a comfortable place to spend the worst of the winter months and wait for safe passage to Sicily and eventually to Rome (Acts 28:11). It was a place rich in Punic, Roman, and Greek culture and had been under Roman domination since the Second Punic War in the late third century BC. Although the Romans governed it as part of Sicily at first, they seem to have given Malta its own procurator by the first century AD.[38]

Paul was probably there from late October AD 59 through early February AD 60 and seems to have quickly made friends with Publius, "the chief magistrate of the island" (Acts 28:7 REB).[39] Publius's father was suffering from fever and dysentery, and, when Paul prayed for his healing, he recovered. When word of this spread, other islanders afflicted with ailments also came to Paul for healing (28:8–9). Luke implies that because of these healings, Paul and the whole group received "many honors" from the islanders. This deep respect for Paul, and the hospitality that went with it, seems to have continued throughout their stay (28:10).

Such circumstances would have made it possible for Paul to write his letter to Titus sometime during these three months. These relatively pleasant conditions would also explain why Paul never mentions his imprisonment in that letter.[40] There is no indication that Paul was actually treated as a prisoner during this time. He was free to enjoy the friendship, hospitality, and honor of both Publius and other islanders, and Luke never mentions Julius the centurion or the other soldiers charged with guarding Paul while the group was on Malta.

Since Festus thought Paul was innocent of the accusations against him (Acts 26:32), it is also easy to imagine Paul making optimistic plans for a return to the east sometime in the next year. Rather than traveling west to Spain as he had planned to do before his arrest (Rom 15:24, 28), he would spend the winter of AD 60–61 in Nicopolis (Titus 3:12) in Epirus.[41] Titus could meet him there once Artemas or Tychicus arrived to take Titus's place on Crete (Titus 3:12). Paul was not sure at the moment when he closed the letter which of these two coworkers he would ask to carry it, but since Tychicus would later be with him in Rome and Paul would send him to Asia with letters for Christians in Ephesus and Colossae (Col 4:7–9; Eph 6:21–22; cf. Acts 20:4), he may have eventually decided to send the letter eastward to Crete with Artemas. His plans for "Zenas the lawyer and Apollos," who were with Titus on Crete, were more definite. He wanted Titus to make sure that they were well equipped for their journey to their next assignment (Titus 3:13), although he does not mention what that assignment is.

Is Titus a Genuine Letter of Paul?

Many scholars who write about the letter to Titus believe, however, that someone other than Paul produced it in Paul's name in the late first or early second century, long after Paul's death. Most of those who read the letter this way believe that the same author produced 1 and 2 Timothy at about the same time. This would account for the stylistic differences between Titus and Paul's authentic letters on one hand and the stylistic similarities of Titus to 1 and 2 Timothy on the other hand.[42]

A date in the late first or early second century would also explain, according to this view, why the letter to Titus is so concerned with church structure. The fervent expectation of Christ's second coming had faded, heretical sectarianism was on the rise, and in this changed situation there was a need to perpetuate and protect the church through a more organized system of offices than was necessary during Paul's lifetime.[43] A date after Paul's death, when the expectation of Christ's second coming had faded, would also account for the letter's concern to accommodate the church's ethics to the values of the wider society, especially in matters of the home (Titus 1:11; 2:1–10; 3:1–2).[44] In the view of one scholar, a second-century date for the letter would help explain its supposed attempt to elevate the social standing of Christians by disparaging both Cretans and Jews in ways that Romans would find appealing (1:10–14).[45]

The arguments from the vocabulary and style of Titus, however, are no more conclusive with this letter than they are with 1 Timothy. Paul may have simply written Titus in a different "register" than his other letters since, like 1 Timothy, he sent it to a trusted individual to provide him with administrative instructions. Just as with 1 Timothy, Paul uses the second-person singular throughout the letter until he gets to the final sentence, "Grace be with you all" (Titus 3:15). Here he probably uses the plural to signal that the letter's final words have in view the large group of people whom his instructions to Titus will affect.[46]

Similarly, the references to church structure in Titus are simple and compatible with the references to church structure in the letters that all would agree Paul wrote (1 Thess 5:12–13; Gal 6:6–7; Phil 1:1).[47] The most plausible way of reading the references to "elders" and to an "overseer" (Titus 1:5, 7), for example, is to see them as describing the same role, and if this is correct, then the letter speaks not only of a leadership position without a fixed title but of a single leadership position without the complications of "deacons" or "widows" (cf. 1 Tim 3:8–13; 5:9, 11).[48] The letter's concern with order in the home, moreover, might just as easily have arisen from the disruption that the false teachers had caused in Christian households (Titus 1:11) as from an effort to accommodate the church to the values of Roman culture.

Administrative Instructions for Cretan Churches

The letter recaps for Titus why he is on Crete and briefly describes the primary theological themes he should emphasize in his teaching on the island. It also reviews Paul's plans both for himself and his coworkers, including Titus, during the next year. Like 1 Timothy, Titus resembles an ancient Ptolemaic or Roman "administrative letter."[49] These letters often begin not merely with the sender's and the recipient's names but with the titles of one or the other or both, stressing their authority to deal with the problem that is the letter's subject. They then move quickly past the formal greeting right to the subject at hand and issue instructions either to a peer or to a subordinate. The instructions to peers often include deferential language, but in letters to subordinates, these niceties are missing.[50] The main thing in these letters is to get the job done.[51]

That job in common Ptolemaic or Roman administrative letters had to do with practical, everyday tasks such as enforcing the law and collecting revenue. The substance of these letters, therefore, is much less concerned with the moral philosophy that undergirds these duties than is the letter to Titus. This difference is understandable, however, in a letter written to deal with the administration of what, in ancient terms, would be a philosophical club or scholastic community.[52]

Paul's description of his own apostolic credentials at the beginning of the letter emphasizes its main theme: the marriage of theological truth and piety. Paul is an apostle who communicates the "knowledge of the truth" to others (Titus 1:1), and the God "who never lies" commissioned him to do this (1:2–3). The appointment of elders (or overseers) in various Cretan Christian communities is necessary precisely because (1:10) there are false teachers who illustrate the truth of a Cretan prophet's negative assessment of Cretan culture: "Cretans are always liars, evil beasts, lazy gluttons" (1:12).

This rhythmic line expressed what many people apparently thought about Cretan culture. Cretans "lied" about the god Zeus, who they said had died on their island and whose tomb was there.[53] Commenting on Titus 1:12, Theodore of Mopsuestia observes that "The poet said this about the Cretans because he wanted to slander them on the grounds that they were claiming they could show the tomb of Jupiter in their land, since the

CHAPTER 22

poet believed that Jupiter was not a man but a god."[54] Cretans also had a widespread reputation for avarice.[55]

Paul probably picked up this line somewhere and understood it as expressing a link between telling lies about divine things and vicious behavior, a link that was precisely the problem with the false teachers.[56] Their mythology and strange exegesis of Scripture led to chaos in households (Titus 1:11, 14; 3:9), controversy, dissension, quarreling, and division (3:9–10).

In contrast to the false teaching, Titus should tell the Cretans about behavior that is in harmony with healthy teaching.[57] Older men should exhibit qualities that would be highly valued of older people in any society. They needed to be levelheaded, serious, and thoughtful. As "healthy" Christians, however, they should, in addition, embrace the three especially Christian virtues of faith, love, and patience (Titus 2:2; cf. 1 Thess 1:3).[58] Older women should have a similar demeanor and should also have a special role in teaching younger women how to conduct their lives with wisdom (Titus 2:3–5). Titus should himself provide an example of the marriage between healthy teaching and good deeds (Titus 2:6–8).

Paul focuses on the basics of morality in this section (Titus 2:2–8), especially in the home (2:4–5, 9–10). Young women, for example, need to learn how to love their husbands and their children (2:4), young men should learn self-control (2:6), and slaves should work for their masters in "all good faith" (2:10).

His primary concern was the appearance of the church to the outside, unbelieving world. Young women needed to learn the moral basics of home life "that the word of God may not be reviled" (Titus 2:5). Titus's example of good works, integrity, dignity, and healthy speech was especially important "so that an opponent may be put to shame, having nothing evil to say about us" (2:8). Slaves should submit to their masters "so that in everything they may adorn the doctrine of God our Savior" (2:10). It seems likely that this concern arose from the disruption that the false teaching had created in the homes of Cretan Christians (1:11).

The witness of the church to the unbelieving world is so important, says Paul, because the appearance of God's grace in the redeeming work "of our great God and Savior Jesus Christ" was designed to train people how "to live self-controlled, upright, and godly lives in the present age" and "to purify for himself a people for his own possession who are zealous for good works" (Titus 2:11–12, 14). Paul does not say so explicitly, but he implies that if Christian mothers are failing to love their own children (for example), then the church cannot claim with any plausibility that its message of God's redeeming work through Jesus Christ is effective and therefore true.

Paul means for none of this to imply that the Cretans generally or the false teachers and their followers are in some special category of bad belief and behavior. If the Cretan Christians need to learn the basics of civil behavior and moral conduct (Titus 3:1–2), Paul makes clear that no one else, including himself and Titus, was any different (3:3). God's kindness, generosity, and goodness, not their own upright behavior, came to their rescue and set them on a path away from God's wrath and toward eternal life (3:4–7).

If Paul wrote his letter to Titus from Malta, then he may have eventually put it in Artemas's hands and sent him to Crete to carry on the work of instruction and renewal in the Cretan churches that Titus had started. Paul and the others in his entourage would resume their journey.

23

House Arrest in Rome

Paul's contemporary Pliny the Elder says that "spring opens the seas to voyagers" (*Nat.* 2.47.122 [Gummere, LCL]) and claims this happens on February 8, a surprisingly early date. That date, however, meshes neatly with Luke's account of what happened next to Paul and his company. If Paul's ship crashed into the Maltese shore in late October (Acts 27:41), then Luke's statement that the group set sail from Malta "after three months" (Acts 28:11) would place their departure sometime in late January or early February.[1] If this is right, then Julius found a ship willing to make the journey from Malta to the Italian mainland early in the sailing season.[2]

Luke does not say that it was another grain ship, but his description of it as from Alexandria and headed for Puteoli (Acts 28:11, 13) fits a grain ship precisely. Puteoli's position in the northwest corner of "the Crater" (today's Bay of Naples), and its high-tech anchorages, fashioned from the area's famous waterproof cement, helped to make it the most important marketplace in southern Italy (Strabo, *Geogr.* 5.4.6).[3] Grain ships from Egypt could discharge their grain there for the overland journey to Capua, a short distance to the north, and then to Rome using the famous Via Appia. These same ships then probably filled their holds with food and wares from the fertile Campanian countryside for profitable resale when they arrived back in Alexandria.[4] In Paul's time, the arrival of the grain fleet from Alexandria in Puteoli's port generated considerable excitement with "everybody . . . bustling about and hurrying to the water-front" (Seneca, *Ep.* 77.3 [Gummere, LCL]).[5]

It would make sense for a grain ship's pilot who had spent three long months in Malta to sail as soon as possible for Puteoli and get paid for his grain. The journey would not have exposed the ship to much open ocean. Portus Pachyni on the southeastern tip of Sicily was only seventy-eight miles away, and a ship could sail within sight of land from that point onward.[6]

Luke remembered that the ship Julius chose sailed under the sign of the twin gods Castor and Pollux, probably meaning that their images were carved on either side of its bow.[7] The "Dioscuri," as Luke calls them (Acts 28:11), were famous for rescuing sailors in winter storms.[8] Was the ship's pilot perhaps emboldened to set sail in early February by the thought of their protection?

The journey from Malta to the ship's first stop in Syracuse was about 110 nautical miles and would have taken all of one day and part of the next.[9] Luke says the ship "stayed there for three days" (Acts 28:12). Perhaps the pilot was just waiting for a favorable wind, but Syracuse was a large and important city with two good harbors, and he may have thought that the time it took to load and unload passengers and cargo there was worth the delay.[10] In any case, the ship soon headed north for Rhegium, an important access point from Sicily to the Italian mainland and, from Syracuse, a day-long journey.[11] The ship waited there for a day, and then a strong wind from the south "sprang up"—so strong that it shaved a half day off the typical two-and-a-half-day trip up the coast to Puteoli (Acts 28:13).[12] Paul's ship would have sailed past the island of Capri and then into "the Crater" and within sight of Mount Vesuvius rising above the bay to well over its current four thousand feet. Perhaps as the ship sailed into port, Paul could see the lavish mansions of the Roman elite on the mountain tops above the nearby resort city of Baiae (Seneca, *Ep.* 51.11 [Gummere, LCL]).[13]

As the entry point into Italy of ships and products from the east, it is not surprising that Puteoli had a Jewish community during this period (Josephus, *B.J.* 2.104; *A.J.* 17.328), and perhaps it was through this community that Christianity first came to the city.[14] When Paul arrived, his traveling companions found believers there, and Julius seems to have allowed Paul to receive their hospitality, just as he had allowed his friends in Sidon to care for him several months earlier (Acts 27:3). Luke says that they stayed with these believers for seven days and then set out for Rome (Acts 28:14).[15] Perhaps sometime during these seven days, someone was able to send a message to Christians in Rome that Paul and his coworkers were on the way.[16]

CHAPTER 23

A WARM WELCOME FROM A GROUP OF ROMAN CHRISTIANS

Some students of Acts believe that when Paul and his party left Puteoli they traveled first to the major city of Capua, twenty miles to the northeast, and then joined the Via Appia for the final leg of their trek to Rome.[17] It is also possible, however, that the group took a more direct route. If so, they traveled four miles northwest to Cumae and then followed the road that hugged the coast. The emperor Domitian would rebuild this road on a grand scale thirty-five years later, but the poet Statius could remember what it was like before it became the Via Domitiana: "Sticky ruts slowed the hampered journey, while the fainting beasts crawled beneath their high yoke, grumbling at too heavy a load." It was, he says, a "route that used to wear out a solid day" (Statius, *Silv.* 4.3.32–37 [Shackleton Bailey and Parrott, LCL]). Even with these annoyances, this route would probably have eaten up less time than taking the more circuitous route that ran through Capua.

Either way, Julius and his prisoners would have eventually passed through the coastal town of Sinuessa with its well-known healing springs, crossed the wooden bridge that spanned the Liris River (now the Garigliano) and arrived at Minturnae.[18] A little over nine miles farther would bring them to the port of Formiae.[19] About twenty-two miles farther still, they would have come to Tarracina, located just below a magnificent temple of Jupiter perched on a mountain 650 feet above the sea. Next, they would have traveled down the slope leading away from Tarracina and, after about three miles, passed a sanctuary devoted to Feronia, the goddess of agriculture and freed slaves.[20]

From that sanctuary, the famous Via Appia made an almost entirely straight line for fifty-three miles to Rome, where it entered the city at the Porta Capena and melted into a busy intersection just across from the southern end of the Circus Maximus.[21] For the first fourteen miles or so of this stretch, the road ran through a marshy region that, at least in the late first century BC, accommodated a canal running parallel to the Via Appia.[22] People and goods could travel this section of the road using canal boats hitched to mules, and some, like the Roman official and satirist Horace, made the journey (going the opposite direction) in a boat and overnight so that they could sleep along the way (Horace, *Sat.* 1.5.3–24).[23] The canal terminated at a town called "the Forum of Appia," which in

Horace's time was a bustling village filled with boatmen, enslaved people, and commercial traffic. It was about forty miles from Rome and, together with the village of Three Taverns, roughly ten miles farther on, was an obvious stopping point and meeting place.[24]

As Paul labored along the muddy road from Cumae to Formiae to Terracina and the fourteen buggy miles from Terracina to the Forum of Appia, a party of Christians from Rome who had heard he was coming were traveling along the Via Appia in the opposite direction to meet him. They must have left Rome from the Porta Capena, an area where, according to Juvenal writing roughly half a century later, one could easily meet with Jewish beggars (*Sat.* 3.10–16) and where a lengthy tirade against the flood of immigrants from the east could plausibly be set (3.58–125).[25] It would have been a short walk from the Porta Capena up the Aventine hill to the neighborhoods where the ancient churches of Saint Prisca and Saint Sabina now stand.[26] It is perhaps reasonable to wonder whether the Christians who set out to meet Paul were Jewish Christians from a neighborhood somewhere around the southern end of the Circus Maximus. That was the end of the Circus where a devastating fire broke out in market stalls a little over four years later, a fire that Nero blamed on Christians (Tacitus, *Ann.* 15.38, 44).

In any case, Luke says they "came as far as the Forum of Appius and Three Taverns to meet us" or, to translate more woodenly, "for a meeting with us" (Acts 28:15). The word Luke uses for "meeting" here (ἀπάντησις) could sometimes refer to a meeting with an important official (Polybius, *Hist.* 5.26.8) or person of high standing (Polybius, *Hist.* 5.43.3). Josephus could use a closely related word (ὑπάντησις) to describe how the people of Antioch rushed four miles outside the city walls to meet the Roman general Titus after his victory over the Jews (*B.J.* 7.100).[27] Luke may have been trying to communicate, therefore, that this group of Roman Christians conveyed to Paul, and perhaps more importantly, to the Roman soldiers who had charge of him, that he was a person of high standing deserving respect and good treatment.[28]

If that was their intention, they seem to have succeeded. Not only did Paul take courage (Acts 28:15) but, when he arrived in Rome, he "was allowed" by whatever Roman official decided on the terms of his custody "to lodge privately, with a soldier in charge of him" (28:16 REB).[29]

CHAPTER 23

Paul's Lodging in Rome

An ancient Latin tradition claims that Paul lived under these arrangements "outside the barracks" (ἔξω τῆς παρεμβολῆς).[30] There is little chance that this tradition reflects more than an educated guess, but if it is correct, Paul would have lived somewhere in the vicinity of the *Castra Praetoria*, the barracks of the emperor's elite personal guard that Tiberius had built about forty years earlier (AD 20–23).[31] The barracks were located northeast of the city, beyond its walls, and a short walk from the Viminal Gate, which is still visible just outside the northeastern corner of the Termini train station.[32] In the modern geography of Rome, the praetorian barracks occupied a rectangle roughly defined by the area just east of the Castro Pretorio metro station and the right angles of the Viale del Policlinico.[33]

Literary and archaeological evidence implies that the area around the barracks was largely uninhabited. Tiberius wanted a location away from the city to encourage discipline among the troops (Tacitus, *Ann.* 4.2), and the location he chose was one of the highest points in the area, looking both south and southwest over the city and north and northeast toward the roads leading into it.[34] Archaeologists have found nearby a field for military training exercises with no remains of ancient housing.[35] When Nero, at the end of his life, searched for a "retired place" to flee from his pursuers, he went north of Rome to a friend's suburban villa and, as he got near the house, had to bushwhack his way through an undeveloped area.[36] On the way "he heard the shouts of the soldiers from the camp hard by, as they prophesied destruction for him and success for Galba" (Suetonius, *Nero* 48.2–3 [Rolfe, LCL]). It is perhaps worth wondering whether the Acts of Paul, a second-century fantasy, preserves a memory of this location when it says that Paul (who is not yet imprisoned) "rented a barn outside of Rome in which he taught" (14.1 [Pervo]).[37]

If Paul lived in this region during his two years in Rome, then he probably lived in a less congested area, perhaps with more room for less money than would be the case closer to the city center.[38] Luke describes Paul's "lodging" (Acts 28:23) with a term (ξενία) that appears three times in an edict of Tiberius from AD 19 to refer to private property seized for military lodging.[39] It seems just possible that Luke has used a technical term for lodging that Paul rented (Acts 28:30), but that was also his official place of judicial confinement (28:16).

A soldier guarded him there (Acts 28:16), and this soldier may or may not have been a member of the praetorian guard, the emperor's massive military contingent, numbering something like twelve thousand soldiers in Nero's time.[40] It is true, as some scholars argue, that Paul's relatively low social status would make any involvement of the praetorian guard in his case surprising.[41] It is also true, however, that Paul's accusers, the Jerusalem nobility, were very high status people who might have made Paul's case and confinement of more than usual interest to the authorities in Rome. Either way, if Paul lived near the praetorian barracks northeast of the city walls, it is easy to see how praetorians within those barracks might hear that he was in prison for Christ (Phil 1:13).

In addition to his military guard, Paul's imprisonment entailed wearing restraints that he referred to sometimes as "bonds" and sometimes simply as "a chain" (Phil 1:7, 13–17; Eph 6:20; Col 4:18; Phlm 10, 13; 2 Tim 1:16; 2:9; Acts 28:20).[42] These bonds would not only have been uncomfortable but would have entailed a loss of personal dignity, an issue that seems to have become a problem for Paul toward the end of his imprisonment (2 Tim 1:8, 12, 16; 2:9).[43]

Paul Continues His Work

Despite these restrictive conditions, Paul was far from idle. According to Luke, only three days after his arrival, he invited the city's Jewish leaders to meet with him (Acts 28:17). He wanted to make clear to them that the Jewish leadership in Jerusalem had wrongly accused him of flouting Jewish customs and opposing the Jewish people and that, quite the contrary, he was a prisoner "because of the hope of Israel" (Acts 28:17–20). A further meeting, with larger numbers present, apparently gave Paul the opportunity to explain the gospel in greater detail, and, as usual, "some were convinced by what he said, but others disbelieved" (Acts 28:24). Luke insists, moreover, that this level of activity continued for the whole two years of his confinement (Acts 28:30–31), and Paul confirms this with the comment in his last remaining letter that although he was "bound with chains as a criminal . . . the word of God is not bound!" (2 Tim 2:9).

CHAPTER 23

How was Paul able to keep this up under house arrest? Both the coworkers around him and his physical living conditions may have facilitated such activity. At the beginning of his two years in Rome, he had Timothy's invaluable help (Phil 1:1; 2:19–24; Phlm 1; Col 1:1). Luke and Aristarchus were also still with him, and he seems to have reconnected with John Mark in Rome (Phlm 24; Col 4:10). Eight other coworkers (Epaphroditus, Onesimus, Demas, Epaphras, Tychicus, Onesiphorus, Crescens, and Titus) also seem to have been with Paul at some point during this period (Phil 2:25–30; Phlm 10, 23–24; Eph 6:21; Col 1:7; 4:7, 12; 2 Tim 1:16; 4:9–12).[44]

The hints that Paul's imprisonment letters provide about the movements of these and other coworkers point to a situation in which Paul had ample help spreading the gospel in Rome and nurturing Christian faith in the cities where he had worked in previous years. Timothy appears with Paul at the beginning of the period but shows up in Asia Minor toward its end (Phil 1:1; Col 1:1; Phlm 1; 2 Tim 4:11; cf. Col 4:10). Epaphroditus travels from Philippi with assistance for Paul, and Paul sends him back with an instructional thank you note (Phil 2:25–30). Epaphras and Onesimus find Paul in Rome (Col 1:7–8), and Epaphras stays with Paul (Col 4:12; Phlm 23), but Onesimus travels with Tychicus and a packet of letters back through Ephesus to his home in the Lycus River Valley (Col 4:9; 2 Tim 4:12). Tychicus himself is much more than a courier: he will report on Paul's circumstances to Christians in Ephesus and Colossae, and, at the same time, encourage them in their Christian commitment (Eph 6:21–22; Col 4:7–8).

The language Paul uses about Epaphroditus and Onesimus is particularly revealing. His description of Epaphroditus in his letter to the Philippians shows that the Philippians intended their messenger to stay with Paul to help him and that it was only Epaphroditus's brush with death through a serious illness that prompted Paul to send him home (Phil 2:25–30). Similarly, Paul's letter to Philemon about Onesimus shows that only the pressure of a strained relationship between Christian brothers led Paul to send Onesimus back to his master. Had circumstances been different, Paul "would have been glad to keep him with me, in order that he might serve me on your behalf during my imprisonment for the gospel" (Phlm 13). Paul, therefore, maintained a busy network of coworkers that allowed him to continue the work God had called him to do despite his confinement.

House Arrest in Rome

The configuration of much of the rental property in Rome during this period, moreover, may have facilitated this beehive of activity. In a careful study of housing in ancient Rome, Andrew Wallace-Hadrill has argued cautiously but persuasively that people of various social classes lived in neighborhoods, and that these neighborhoods often featured buildings and networks of buildings that mixed large well-appointed space for the upper classes with much smaller rental space for the less well-off.[45] The whole complex might be surrounded by baths, toilets, meeting halls, and eating shops, all of which served the neighborhood.[46] This is consistent, moreover, with the commonsense observation that in a large city with no fast means of transportation, such shops, meeting halls, baths, and public latrines would have to be within walking distance of the places where people lived.[47]

As a result, in large cities like Rome and Ephesus such concentrations of multiuse buildings and multistory apartments could "function," in the words of Bradly S. Billings, "as the locus of community" and "provide a physical place for highly bonded groups such as families and communities gathered around a common interest of cultic practice to establish a presence in the city."[48] From both ancient literature and ancient inscriptions, it is clear that people with a common bond banded together for mutual support. Bakers, fishmongers, wine merchants, people who wanted a guarantee of a decent burial, and ethnic groups who wanted to worship their own gods, for example, came together in associations and sometimes invested in property together.[49] In Rome, Jewish people certainly banded together in large numbers in the region on the right side of the Tiber River (Philo, *Leg.* 23.155), but also in other areas: the Subura, the Campus Martius, and around the Porta Capena.[50] Two inscriptions from Puteoli, the first dating from AD 79, testify to a group of merchants from the Syrian city of Tyre who rented property together. They dedicated their building to their own Tyrian god and worked together importing products from the Syrian coast.[51]

Something like this arrangement could account for Paul's ability to carry on his apostolic mission of supporting multiethnic Christian communities while he was under house arrest in his own rented space. Luke, Aristarchus, and Timothy, for example, might have found rental space close to Paul's own rented apartment, and Paul's coworkers who came and went over the next two years could have shared the space of coworkers who were more permanent residents of the city, or they might have found their own short-term rentals in the same neighborhood.⁵²

The public bath may have been particularly important as a meeting place for Paul's network of coworkers. The Romans considered these baths an absolute necessity of urban planning, and the larger ones were like miniature cities with "public halls, latrines, fountains, archways, and exedras, and sometimes peristyles as well, all set at different intervals along ritual armatures."⁵³ In them, people sat in a circle to encourage social interaction, and the art and architecture of the building encouraged social cohesion.⁵⁴ It is easy to imagine Paul's coworkers in Rome taking advantage of all this to meet among themselves, with other Christians, and with interested inquirers into the faith. There is a hint from about a century after Paul's residency in Rome that this may have been the case. In a text that seems to be a reliable account of Justin Martyr's examination by the Roman urban prefect Q. Iunius Rusticus, the prefect asks Justin where Christians in Rome meet. The exact text of Justin's reply is not clear, but the two earliest versions refer to a public bath, and Justin's dwelling above it. That is the one Christian meeting place in Rome that Justin knows.⁵⁵

Opposition from Some Christians and an Unpromising Legal Environment

Paul had much to be thankful for: he was not confined in the darkness, squalor, and terror that characterized the existence of most Roman prisoners, and he could continue to advance the gospel through his letters and coworkers.⁵⁶ There was also cause for concern. For one thing, some groups of Christians within Rome were opposed to Paul and willing to make his circumstances worse.

Paul's own letter to Rome, his letters from Rome, and the witness of later Christian literature all hint that Christians in the imperial capital were not entirely unified, and that Paul himself was a controversial figure among them. His letter to Rome reveals his awareness that some Christians within the city had heard slanderous rumors about his teaching, especially his teaching on the Mosaic law. Some people, he says, "slanderously charge us with saying" that people should "do evil that good may come" (Rom 3:8). After concluding one of his complex passages explaining the role of the law in making sin worse and God's grace correspondingly abundant, he introduces the next section with "What shall we say then? Are we to continue in sin that grace may abound? By no means!" (6:1; cf. 6:15).

Later in the letter, it becomes clear that Paul was also aware of divisions among Roman Christians over whether to observe some of the distinctively Jewish elements of the Mosaic law: "One person believes he may eat anything, while another person eats only vegetables. Let not the one who eats despise the one who abstains, and let not the one who abstains pass judgment on the one who eats, for God has welcomed him.... One person esteems one day as better than another, while another esteems all days alike" (Rom 14:2–3, 5a).

Paul himself was convinced that "nothing is unclean in itself" (Rom 14:14) and "everything is indeed clean" (14:20), but he advises patience with those who do not think this and urges both groups to "welcome one another as Christ has welcomed you, for the glory of God" (15:7).

Closer to the letter's conclusion, he urges the Roman Christians to steer clear of people "who cause divisions and create obstacles contrary to the doctrine that you have been taught" (Rom 16:17). This group uses "fine speech and blessing" to persuade naive Christians of its erroneous positions (16:18).[57] It is possible that Paul was warning the Roman Christians of the type of false teachers he had encountered elsewhere in his work, but a warning against unsound Christian teaching in Rome itself would be consistent with the other hints about such teaching in the letter.

If Paul wrote Philippians from Rome, moreover, it reveals that Christianity in the city was still divided and that Paul remained a controversial figure among those who knew about him. When he turns in the letter to the subject of his own circumstances, he tells the Philippians that most of his fellow Christians in Rome have become bolder in their efforts to communicate the gospel to others because they have heard about his imprisonment (Phil 1:14). Another group, however, proclaims Christ "from envy and rivalry" (φθόνον καὶ ἔριν, Phil 1:15) and "out of selfish ambition" with the motive of increasing Paul's suffering while he is in prison (Phil 1:17). This lack of support for Paul among some Christians in Rome would also make sense of Paul's claim, in what was probably his last letter, that at his first legal hearing in Rome ("my first defense") no one stood by him, "but all deserted me" (2 Tim 4:16).

CHAPTER 23

A letter from Christians in late first-century Rome to Christians in Corinth confirms this picture and hints ominously that it had fatal consequences for Paul. The author of the letter, traditionally called "Clement," seems to have lived in the second generation of Christians (1 Clem. 44.1–3), and by his time Nero's horrific persecution of Christians in AD 64 seems to have been part of the collective memory of the Roman Christian community (6.1–2; cf. Tacitus, *Ann.* 15.44).[58]

Clement and his fellow Christians in Rome were concerned about how "jealousy" (ζῆλος), "envy" (φθόνος), and "strife" (ἔρις) had led Christians in Corinth to rebel against their community's elders. Near the beginning of his letter, Clement runs through a long list of examples from Scripture, nearly all of them concerned with the havoc that "jealousy and envy" could wreak within families or within the people of Israel (1 Clem. 4.1–13 [Holmes]).[59] He then turns to the same problem among "those champions who lived nearest to our time" (1 Clem. 5.1) beginning with "the good apostles" Peter and Paul. After a brief reference to Peter, he says this about Paul:

> Because of jealousy [ζῆλον] and strife [ἔριν] Paul showed the way to the prize for patient endurance. After he had been seven times in chains, had been driven into exile, had been stoned, and had preached in the east and in the west, he won the genuine glory for his faith, having taught righteousness to the whole world and having reached the farthest limits of the west. Finally, when he had given his testimony before the rulers, he thus departed from the world and went to the holy place, having become an outstanding example of patient endurance. To these men [Peter and Paul] who lived holy lives there was joined a vast multitude of the elect who, having suffered many torments and tortures because of jealousy [ζῆλος], set an illustrious example among us. (1 Clem. 5.5–6.1 [Holmes])

Clement uses basically the same language that Paul used in Philippians to describe the evil that led to the apostle's death, and he rolls directly from Paul's death into a reference to the persecution under Nero that happened "among us," that is, in Rome.[60] He does this in a letter to a Christian community plagued by these same vices, and at the end of a list of the destructive results of these vices among members of the same families and people groups. It seems reasonable to conclude that Clement believed Paul had perished in part because members of his own metaphorical family in Rome—other Christians—had opposed him.[61]

It seems clear, therefore, that Paul's residency in Rome was not a period in which the large Christian community in the city rallied behind him with one voice. Three years earlier, when he wrote his letter to the Romans, he greeted five discrete groups of Christians, and perhaps we can imagine these groups as house churches that were sympathetic to Paul.[62] One or more of these groups probably sent the welcome party that met Paul and his fellow travelers shortly after they had arrived in Italy (Acts 28:15). Other house churches in Rome, however, must have opposed Paul. It is easy to imagine that some Roman Christians found his approach to the Mosaic law in his letter to them offensive, perhaps taking exception to his claim that "the law came in to increase the trespass" (Rom 5:20) or that believers are "released from the law, having died to that which held us captive" (Rom 7:6). If rumors could spread among the Christians of Jerusalem that Paul taught Jewish people to "forsake Moses" and "not ... circumcise their children or walk according to" Jewish "customs" (Acts 21:21), similar rumors may have spread among those Christians in Rome who were equally committed to the Mosaic law.[63]

In addition to opposition from some Roman Christians, the legal atmosphere in Nero's court at the time of Paul's imprisonment might have caused him concern. For many years, cases that came before the emperor involving the Jewish priestly class tended to favor them.[64] Sixteen years earlier, in AD 44, Claudius had ruled against his own procurator Cuspius Fadus and in favor of the Jerusalem priests in a dispute over whether the high priest's vestments should be stored in the Antonia Fortress or the priests themselves should keep them (Josephus, *A.J.* 20.6–14).[65] Similarly, in AD 52, Claudius decided in favor of the Jewish high priest and against the Roman procurator Cumanus and the Syrian legate Quadratus in a hearing over who was responsible for political disturbances in Samaria (Josephus, *B.J.* 2.232–246; *A.J.* 20.118–136).[66]

A third case is especially interesting because it involved the two officials that had up to this point ruled in Paul's favor, the Roman procurator Felix and the Jewish king Herod Agrippa II. Nero would have heard this case about the time that Paul's two years in Rome ended (AD 62). The temple authorities had built a wall that blocked the view from Agrippa's Jerusalem residence and from the Antonia Fortress into the inner temple. When Festus commanded the temple authorities to tear the wall down, they asked permission to take the case to Nero, which he granted.

Had Festus understood better the tendency of the imperial court to find in favor of the Jerusalem priests, and the atmosphere in Nero's court at the time of this request, he probably would not have granted it: "Nero, after a full hearing, not only condoned what they had done, but also consented to leave the building as it was. In this he showed favour to his wife Poppaea, who was a worshipper of God and who pleaded on behalf of the Jews" (*A.J.* 20.195 [Feldman, LCL]).

Josephus knew Poppaea personally (Josephus, *Vita* 16), so it makes sense to trust him when he attributes the verdict to her influence. It was also a verdict, however, that was consistent with the long-standing tendency of Roman emperors to favor the upper priestly class of Jerusalem in cases that involved them. As Paul McKechnie puts it in an essay that lays out all this evidence, "In order to rule in favor of the Jerusalem priests in the middle decades of the first century, the emperors ruled against three procurators of Judaea, a legate of Syria, and Claudius' personal friend Agrippa II."[67]

McKechnie makes the further point that this legal atmosphere would not have been favorable to Paul. He too would appear before Nero in a case that pitted him against the priestly nobility in Jerusalem.

24

Visitors from Philippi and the Lycus River Valley

Amid the turmoil that his Christian enemies and his difficult legal position created for him, Paul must have been refreshed when, at various unknown points during his two years in Rome, visitors from churches to the east arrived on his doorstep. Epaphroditus arrived from Philippi, a church that had often been generous to Paul, with yet another act of generosity. In addition, Epaphras and Onesimus arrived from Colossae in the Lycus River Valley, a church that Epaphras seems to have founded and nurtured under Paul's influence. Although Paul does not say so explicitly, it is possible that they too arrived to help him. All three visitors, however, seem also to have come to Paul with pastoral problems, and Paul responded with a series of letters.

A Thank-You Note to Christians in Philippi

Epaphroditus arrived from the Christians in Philippi with a charge to stay and help Paul during his imprisonment, and with gifts that probably provided the monetary means for this support. Paul had a deep appreciation for Epaphroditus, for the risk he had taken in making the journey from Philippi, and for the gift that he brought from the Philippians (Phil 2:25–30; 4:18). If Paul's commendation of him as a "brother and fellow worker and fellow soldier" (Phil 2:25) springs from the time he spent with Paul in Rome and not from prior acquaintance, then Paul seems to have been especially appreciative of Epaphroditus's hard work advancing the gospel alongside him in Rome. Paul uses the term "fellow worker" in his letters to describe people especially committed to helping him in his work, people such as

Prisca, Aquila, Timothy, and Apollos (Rom 16:3, 21; 1 Cor 3:9). The term "fellow soldier" probably indicates that Epaphroditus, like Paul, had braved significant conflict in his efforts to further the cause of the gospel.[1]

At some point in these efforts (and this may be the conflict Paul was imagining), Epaphroditus became seriously ill and nearly died (Phil 2:26–27, 30).[2] His illness, and the thought of losing him, was a serious blow to Paul, who speaks of being wracked with grief ("sorrow upon sorrow") until, mercifully, Epaphroditus recovered (2:27). Somehow, though, Epaphroditus learned that his fellow Christians in Philippi knew about his illness and had started worrying about him. This in turn made Epaphroditus eager to return home (2:26).[3]

Epaphroditus seems to have brought to Paul's attention some problems in the Philippian church. First, the church was struggling with division (Phil 2:14). The source of the disagreement is unclear, but it may have involved a difference of viewpoint between two prominent women in the Philippian Christian community, Euodia and Syntyche. The language Paul uses in his letter when he urges these women to "be of the same mind" (4:2 NIV) recalls language he has used elsewhere in the letter when he urges the wider community to "be of one mind" or "have the same mindset as Christ Jesus" (2:2, 5 NIV). Perhaps these hardworking women, with important roles in the community, had differing views on some point of doctrine or practice, and their disagreement had affected the entire church.

Second, the Philippian church was continuing to suffer persecution from the wider society in which it existed. The church was born amid suffering (Acts 16:16–40; 1 Thess 2:2), and it continued to face opposition (Phil 1:28–30) from the "crooked and twisted generation" in which it lived (Phil 2:15). Paul seems concerned in his letter that this intimidation from their opponents might lead the Philippian Christians to deviate from a way of life that was faithful to "the gospel of Christ" (Phil 1:27–28).

When Epaphroditus had recovered from his illness and started to express a strong desire to return to Philippi, Paul used the opportunity to write a relatively short letter to the Christian community there, and especially to its leaders, the "overseers and deacons" as Paul calls them (Phil 1:1). He wanted to thank them for their gift (and perhaps explain why Epaphroditus was returning earlier than they had expected), but he also wanted to use the opportunity of Epaphroditus's return to address both the problems

Epaphroditus had described and the problems that Paul thought might arise in the context of a Roman colony like Philippi.

The main purpose of his letter was to help the Philippian Christians "decide what really matters" (Phil 1:10 CEB) amid the present threats of disunity and persecution and the potential threat of perverse teaching about how Christians should live. His strategy seems to have been threefold.

First, he would provide the Philippians with examples of people they knew (himself, Christ Jesus, Timothy, and Epaphroditus) who had centered their lives on the gospel in the face of hardship and lived in loving, sacrificial unity with others.

Second, he would warn them of the kinds of theological error that, looking back over the last decade of his work, had sometimes damaged the Christian communities in the cities where he had planted churches.

Third, he would save his thanks for their gift until the end, perhaps to leave it ringing in their ears, and he would thank them in a way that demonstrated both his dependence on God and his concern for them. Even here the goal would be to model for them how they might focus on "what really matters."

After his greeting, Paul moves, as usual, into a prayer section that anticipates the letter's main concerns. Looking back over his proclamation of the gospel in Macedonia and Greece, he tells the Philippians that when he remembers them in prayer, he is joyful. They have been partners with him "in the gospel from the first day until now" (Phil 1:5), whatever the circumstances (1:7). Thus, he anticipates his longer thank-you note at the end of the letter (4:10–20) and encloses his admonitions in the letter's center within an atmosphere of gratitude.

Paul next begins to model for the Philippians what it means to prioritize the advancement of the gospel ("what really matters") over one's own difficult circumstances (cf. Phil 3:17; 4:9).[4] He opens the main body of the letter with a conventional phrase ("I want you to know . . .") that would have led his readers to expect information about the details of his imprisonment. Instead, however, he provides a statement of how his imprisonment has contributed to "the greater progress of the gospel" and his confidence that its outcome will serve "the progress and joy" of the Philippians in their "faith" (1:12, 25 NASB). Although he was in prison, and although his imprisonment provided the occasion for some of his Christian enemies to make greater trouble for him, the gospel was making inroads among the praetorian guard in the massive barracks near where he lived. His imprisonment was even providing his enemies a platform for preaching Christ (1:12–18a).

Paul expresses his attitude toward the opposition of his enemies with a claim that, ultimately, it failed the test of what is really important: "But what does it matter? The important thing is that in every way, whether from false motives or true, Christ is preached. And because of this I rejoice. Yes, and I will continue to rejoice" (Phil 1:18 NIV). Paul certainly cared whether people preached Christ "from false motives or true" (2 Cor 2:17; 4:1–2; 11:13–15), but relative to the actual progress of the gospel, such considerations did not matter to him.[5]

Paul next turns to the Philippians and implicitly urges them to live in the same way: they should live in a way that is commensurate with the worth of the gospel. This means standing united with each other and standing firm against the intimidation of their unbelieving opponents in Philippi (Phil 1:27–30). Paul has already provided himself as an example of how to do this by focusing not on his opponents but on the gospel's progress (1:12–18). Now he provides three other examples of focusing on "what really matters" (1:10 CEB): Christ Jesus himself, Timothy, and Epaphroditus (2:1–30).

As the Philippians seek to make Paul's joy complete by "being of the same mind," doing "nothing from rivalry or conceit," and counting "others more significant" than themselves (Phil 2:2–3), they should think the way Jesus thought (2:5). Precisely because he was in the form of God, who is gracious and merciful toward others, he did not think of his divinity as something to be exploited for his own selfish gain (2:6).[6] Instead, he emptied himself of divine privilege (2:7) and became like human beings, dying not merely as a man but as a slave might die, on a cross (2:8). God responded to this expression of selflessness by exalting Jesus (2:9–11).

The Philippians should follow the same pattern in their relationships with each other, working out the implications of their own salvation by abandoning their grumbling and holding tight to the gospel (Phil 2:12–16). The willingness of both Timothy and Epaphroditus to prioritize the welfare of others and the progress of the gospel (2:19–30) offers a down-to-earth example, from people whom the Philippians knew well, of how they too should exhibit "the same mindset as Christ Jesus" (2:5).[7]

Visitors from Philippi and the Lycus River Valley

Paul next turns to two concerns he had covered before with the Philippians but that he felt needed reiteration (Phil 3:1). First, he warns the Philippians against Christians who thought that adherence to the Mosaic law, especially the law of circumcision, was necessary for a right standing with God (3:2–16). If Paul wrote Philippians from Rome and the Christians who opposed him "from envy and rivalry" (1:15) rejected the view of the Mosaic law he had expressed in Romans, then it is easy to see why he might have this error in mind as he wrote. He had faced opponents in Corinth a few years earlier who seemed to have boasted in their pedigree as "Hebrews," "Israelites," and "offspring of Abraham" while they claimed to be "servants of Christ" (2 Cor 11:22–23), and he may well have thought that something like this error could make its way north to Philippi.

Against this idea, Paul writes a very short autobiography. He had once considered both his thoroughly Jewish upbringing and his unimpeachable zeal for the Mosaic law as the basis of his right standing with God (Phil 3:4–6). He then realized, however, that such confidence was merely trust in things of "the flesh" (3:3) or, to put it differently, in his "own righteousness" (3:9 KJV). When he understood who Christ really was, however, he considered such fleshly credentials to be "loss" rather than "profit," and through union with and faith in Christ he gained a righteousness not of his own but a righteousness that came to him from God (3:7–9). Paul's implication for the Philippians is clear: anyone who arrives in Philippi claiming that adherence to the Mosaic law together with faith in Christ is necessary for a right standing with God has shifted their confidence to the flesh and away from the work of God's Spirit and God's Messiah, Jesus (3:3).

Paul also warns the Philippians against allowing Roman culture to lead them astray. Philippi was a proud Roman colony (Acts 16:21), and Paul knew from his work with the Corinthian Christians how easy it was for Roman values to distort the principles that should characterize Jesus's followers. Through the distortions of Roman culture, the crucifixion of Jesus appears not as evidence that God's power works through weakness but as an embarrassment (Phil 3:18; cf. 1 Cor 1:22–25).[8] It also becomes easy to allow Roman dining customs, with the drunkenness and mistreatment of social inferiors that often accompanied them, to invade Christian observance of the Lord's Supper (Phil 3:18–19; cf. 1 Cor 11:17–34).[9] Instead of conforming to Roman society, the Christians of Philippi should focus on their status as citizens of the new society that Christ will establish when he comes out of the heavens and transforms his people so that their immortal bodies are like the immortal body he currently has (Phil 3:20–21).

After outlining some practical steps for encouraging Euodia and Syntyche to overcome their differences (Phil 4:2–3) and giving some pithy ethical admonitions (4:4–9), Paul concludes the letter by circling back to the theme of his gratitude to the Philippians for sending Epaphroditus and the things he brought with him (4:10–20). He composes his thank-you note carefully to be sure that the Philippians knew he considered their gift valuable, but not because of what it would do for him. He wanted them to understand that he did not imagine God would leave him unable to cope with having "little," going "hungry," and being "in need." Instead, he valued their gift because it showed that the Philippians had the right priorities: worshiping God through the practical support of the gospel's advancement (4:11–13, 17–18; cf. 2 Cor 8:1–5; 9:11–14 NRSV).

Epaphras and Onesimus Arrive from the Lycus River Valley

Paul's letter to Christians in Colossae is one of the six letters in the New Testament that fly under Paul's name but whose authorship is disputed. If Paul wrote it, why does the letter's vocabulary and style deviate from the undisputed letters?[10] Why does it assert that the church is a body of which Christ is the head (Col 1:18; 2:19) rather than simply comparing the church to a body that is also Christ (Rom 12:5; 1 Cor 12:12)? Why does the tension between the believer's present death with Christ in baptism and future union with Christ's resurrection (Rom 6:3, 5) seem to collapse into the notion of the believer's present union with Christ's resurrection and existence with him in regions above the earth (Col 2:12–13; 3:1–3)?[11] Why does a "household code" appear in the letter, presumably aiding its readers to adopt a less radical posture toward marriage and family life than Paul's preference for celibacy seems to allow?[12] Some careful interpreters of the letter have decided that the only likely answer to these questions is that someone penned the letter after Paul's death in his name.

Many others, however, think that the best explanation for the letter is that Paul wrote it. Nothing in the letter, including its long sentences, redundant phraseology, and slightly unusual vocabulary, deviates so far from Paul's "undisputed" letters that Paul's authorship becomes unlikely.[13] This is especially true for those who are not willing to concede that only the undisputed seven letters are likely to be Paul's. If Paul wrote Ephesians, for example, there is nothing unusual about long sentences, redundancy, union with the risen Christ, and Christ as the head of the church (e.g., Eph 1:3–23; 2:5–6; 4:12, 15–16).

Paul could easily have produced both Colossians and Ephesians in a different "register" from his undisputed letters for a variety of reasons.[14] He may not have had the time or desire to shorten his sentences before dictating them, or to deploy his more usual argumentative style. He may also have wanted to use a vocabulary and sentence structure more suited to prayer, or to his audience's context (e.g., Col 1:3–14; 2:8–23). The corpus of Paul's letters is not large enough for a letter's vocabulary and style to play a role in the determination of its authorship.[15]

If the letter is not genuinely Paul's, moreover, the personal details at the end of the letter are hard to explain.[16] They fit hand-in-glove with the personal details in Philemon, especially if Paul sent the two letters together to Colossae with Tychicus and Onesimus. The five people who send greetings to the church that meets specifically in Philemon's house (Phlm 2, 23–24) also appear at the end of Colossians and greet all the believers in the city (Col 1:2; 4:10–14). This would easily fit with a scenario in which these coworkers of Paul had special ties to Philemon, who was also Paul's coworker (Phlm 1). Paul's omission of any reference to Tychicus in Philemon makes sense if Onesimus rather than Tychicus took that letter to his master Philemon, and Paul's commendation of Tychicus in Colossians makes sense if he was responsible for overseeing the reading and dissemination of that letter in the Lycus River Valley.[17] A forger might make all this up and include the artificially intense statement—e.g., "Say to Archippus, 'See that you fulfill the ministry that you have received in the Lord'" (Col 4:17; cf. Phlm 2). If that is what happened, however, it is difficult to understand why the forger, having used Philemon as a source for the names in his letter, failed to include the letter's most significant figure, Philemon himself.[18]

At some point in his Roman imprisonment, then, two visitors from Colossae near the Lycus River in Asia appeared at Paul's door, Onesimus and Epaphras. Whether they came together or separately is not clear. Colossae's

CHAPTER 24

Christian community would not have been large, and it is perhaps more realistic to think of them traveling from that community together than to think of them as arriving separately and unknown to each other.[19] Paul had not been to the Lycus River Valley since Christian communities had appeared there (Col 2:1), but he may have passed through it as he traveled along the major east–west road he likely took on his journey from Jerusalem to Antioch to Ephesus roughly eight years earlier.[20] At that point, however, he was probably traveling quickly to rejoin Prisca and Aquila, to get the collection for the poor Christians in Jerusalem started, and to make sure that the churches he and his coworkers had founded in the Aegean region remained sound. A long stop in Colossae to plant churches probably did not make sense.

Perhaps Paul stayed long enough, however, to meet and explain the gospel to two residents of the city, Epaphras and Philemon.[21] It was through Epaphras that the first churches in Colossae came into existence (Col 1:7), including the church that met in Philemon's house (Phlm 1–2). Soon Christian communities sprang up in the nearby cities of Laodicea and Hierapolis and, as the years passed, Epaphras seems to have become a leader of the Christian communities in all three cities (Col 4:13). According to Ulrich Huttner, "a strong walker could visit all three cities in the course of a one-day circular hike."[22] We can reasonably imagine Epaphras calling on Christians in the three cities regularly. Paul considered him a "much loved fellow slave" and "faithful minister of the Messiah" on behalf of the Colossians (1:7 CSB), implying that he knew him well and that they had worked together to advance the gospel. Perhaps during Paul's three years in Ephesus, Epaphras sometimes made the six-day trek west to visit and learn from Paul.

Paul also considered Philemon a beloved coworker (Phlm 1) and partner (v. 17) who had provided him with joy and encouragement and shown generosity to many other Christians (v. 7). He must have been a person of relatively high social standing. He either owned or rented a dwelling large enough to accommodate an assembly of Christians and comfortable enough to provide Paul with a guest room (Phlm 2, 22). His household included, moreover, at least one enslaved man, Onesimus.[23] Perhaps it is appropriate to think of Philemon as a prosperous businessperson who had profited in some way from the rich agricultural products that the Lycus River Valley produced or from the wool, leather, metalworking, or milling industries that probably flourished there.[24]

Two Letters to Colossae and a Letter to Laodicea

Why Onesimus came to Paul is a mystery, and interpreters of Paul's letter to Philemon, which appeals to Philemon on behalf of Onesimus, have put the evidence from the letter together in different ways.[25] The traditional view is that Onesimus ran away from Philemon, somehow encountered Paul, and then, having become a Christian, returned to Philemon with Tychicus and Paul's letter (cf. Col 4:7–9).[26] As it stands, however, this simple explanation leaves unexplained how Onesimus managed to connect with Paul, who not only knew his master but had some authority over Philemon (Phlm 8–9).[27]

Perhaps, then, Onesimus had wronged Philemon and fled to Paul for the purpose of asking him to intercede for him with his master.[28] The *Digest* of Roman law, assembled and edited under the sixth-century Roman emperor Justinian, contains legislation that may go back to the first century and that shows this sort of flight to a master's friend was legal and not unusual, at least in some Latin-speaking places.[29] Another option is that the church in Colossae sent Onesimus to Paul to help him in prison. The letter never describes Onesimus as a runaway, and the mission of Epaphroditus to Paul for the Philippian church would provide an analogy to this scenario.[30]

Despite the ability of these alternative views to explain how Paul and Onesimus encountered each other, they also come with problems. The legislation concerning slaves who flee to friends of their masters for refuge is in Latin and is of uncertain date. Exactly what customs and laws would have prevailed among Greek-speaking inhabitants of the Lycus River Valley is uncertain.[31] It also seems unlikely that Christians would have always felt compelled to follow whatever laws and customs prevailed in their own regions.[32] Paul, at least, counseled following the law as far as possible, but also believed that the most important law to follow was the principle of loving others (Rom 13:1–10).

The notion that the Colossian church sent Onesimus to Paul, moreover, seems unlikely since the letter reveals that the relationship between Philemon and Onesimus was strained.[33] When Paul says to Philemon, "This perhaps is why he was parted from you for a while, that you might have him back forever" (Phlm 15), he seems to be gently pushing Philemon to understand that an otherwise unhappy parting has nevertheless resulted in something good.[34] Paul's plea to "receive him as you would receive me" (v. 17), moreover, implies that Onesimus might not get a cheerful reception from Philemon. The reason for this probably lies behind Paul's promise to cover any damages that Onesimus owed Philemon (v. 18). Philemon had done something that cost his master money.

As Jeffrey Weima points out, the traditional view of Onesimus as a runaway slave has the advantage of fitting neatly into the large body of evidence that enslaved people frequently ran away from their masters.[35] The only real problem with this view is that it becomes hard to know how Onesimus would have encountered Paul and become a Christian while he was with him.

Perhaps, then, the situation was complicated. Onesimus may have run away from Philemon's household but done so in the company of Epaphras who was sympathetic to his plight and already heading for Rome to visit Paul about problems in the churches of the Lycus River Valley. Epaphras, at least, would likely have known something about Paul's attitude toward slavery—that, for example, he urged masters to "give up using threats" and to be fair and kind to enslaved people in their households (Col 4:1; Eph 6:9 REB)—and it is easy to imagine Epaphras convincing Onesimus to seek Paul's help with the problems he was experiencing in Philemon's household. Whatever the backstory of Paul's letter to Philemon, it probably did not fit neatly into any legal category, and it is not clear that Epaphras, Paul, Onesimus, or even Philemon would have cared much about which of the prevailing laws and customs applied to the situation. Philemon would have wanted his slave back, and Epaphras and Paul would have wanted to respond to the whole messy situation by prioritizing love and the gospel's advancement.

In any case, after Onesimus met Paul they became friends, and at some point, through their friendship, Onesimus became a Christian (Phlm 10, 12). Paul would probably have been happy to intercede on Onesimus's behalf whether he had become a believer or not. He had a robust view of the equality of all human beings before God (1 Cor 1:26–29; Rom 2:6–11; 3:29–30; 10:12) and believed that Christians should "do good to everyone" (Gal 6:10a). He also believed, however, that Christians should "especially" do good to those who belonged to "the household of faith" (Gal 6:10b).

Visitors from Philippi and the Lycus River Valley

Onesimus's membership in this new kind of household gave Paul the opportunity to argue in his letter to Philemon, and to the church that met in his house, that Onesimus's conversion entailed a radical reorientation of Philemon's relationship with his master. Onesimus was now Paul's child: Paul had "fathered" him during his imprisonment (Phlm 10 CSB), and Philemon should treat him "no longer as a slave, but better than a slave, as a dear brother" (Phlm 16 NIV).

Indeed, when Onesimus returned, Philemon should treat him as he would treat Paul himself. If Onesimus was indebted to Philemon, Paul should be held responsible. But, of course, Philemon would not hold Paul responsible for some debt—theirs was hardly a transactional relationship. So it should be with Philemon (Phlm 17–18).

Paul was interested in more than encouraging Philemon to rethink his relationship with his slave. He had another request: that Philemon send Onesimus back to him so that he might engage in Christian ministry in Rome while Paul was confined to his apartment (Phlm 13).[36] One way that Philemon could serve Paul as his "beloved fellow worker," then, would be to allow Onesimus's return to Paul for gospel service among the network of Paul's coworkers in Rome.

This loving elevation of Onesimus to the status of a family member equal in standing to his master was a practical outworking of the theology that Paul articulated elsewhere in his extant letters. Paul's settled conviction was that within the people of God the accepted hierarchies of the Roman world had to come crashing down. Jews, Greeks, barbarians, Scythians, circumcised, uncircumcised, slaves, free, male, female were all categories that had to give way before the new status of all believers as children of God and brothers and sisters of one another (1 Cor 12:13; Gal 3:26–28; Col 3:9–11). Because Christians lived in a world ordered by the standard categories, they had to work within them, but the categories themselves had to submit to the overarching truth of God's impartiality and the overarching requirement of love (Rom 12:9; 13:8–10; Eph 5:2; 6:9; Col 3:14; Phlm 9).

So, Paul could say things that from the perspective of the standard hierarchies seemed nonsensical. Philemon should treat Onesimus in the same way that Philemon would treat Paul (Phlm 17), and slave masters should treat those they had enslaved in the same way they expected the enslaved members of their household to treat them. This included abandoning the threat of violence (Eph 6:9). When Paul urged Christian slave masters to treat their slaves like their social superiors, told them to stop threatening their slaves with violence, and reminded them that they themselves had an impartial master in heaven, he cut the thread that held the institution of slavery together.[37] Philemon probably got the message, and that is probably why this small letter survived.

In addition to his concern for Onesimus, Epaphras brought Paul another pastoral problem. Someone identifying himself as a Christian had been influencing churches in the Lycus River Valley with "plausible arguments" (Col 2:4) that shifted the focus of these believers from Christ's victory over the invisible "rulers and authorities" in the universe (2:15) onto a series of mechanisms for controlling those powers themselves. This false teacher emphasized observance of a Jewish religious calendar (2:16), "religious ritual" (θρησκεία) involving angels (2:18), concern with "the elemental spirits [στοιχεῖα] of the world" (2:8, 20), visions he had seen, and ascetic practices (2:18, 21, 23).[38]

Identifying this religious movement with precision is impossible, but Clinton E. Arnold has made a convincing case that it involved an amalgam of Judaism and magic.[39] From a time well before Paul, King Solomon was thought to have possessed a vast body of esoteric wisdom, including "the structure of the world and the activity of the elements [στοιχείων] . . . the powers of the spirits and the reasonings of human beings, the varieties of plants and the virtues of roots" (Wis 7:17, 20; cf. 1 Kgs 4:29–34). In a part of the pseudonymous Testament of Solomon that probably predates Colossians, thirty-six "elemental spirits" (στοιχεῖα) identifying themselves as the "world rulers of the darkness of this age" appear before "Solomon" (T. Sol. 18:1–2 [Duling, *OTP* 1:977]).[40] These elemental spirits then acknowledge with one voice that God has given Solomon authority "over all the spirits of the air, the earth, and [the regions] beneath the earth" and, since they too are "spirits," they take their place submissively before him (T. Sol. 18:3 [Duling, *OTP* 1:977]).

Each spirit then divulges to Solomon what harm it causes and what angel, when called upon, or what ritual, when enacted, will cure the harm (T. Sol. 18:4–42). Ruax, the elemental spirit of headaches, will stop causing pain when it hears, "Michael, imprison Ruax" (T. Sol. 18:5 [Duling, *OTP* 1:978]). Oropel, the elemental spirit that causes sore throats and congestion, will "retreat immediately" when it hears "Raphael, imprison Oropel" (T. Sol. 18:8 [Duling, *OTP* 1:978]). An elemental spirit causing domestic discord yields to the utterance of "Angel, Eae, Ieo, Sabaoth" when combined with a ritual involving laurel leaves and sprinkling with water (T. Sol. 18:15 [Duling, *OTP* 1:979]). This was roughly the sort of magic that Sceva and his seven sons were practicing in Ephesus in the first century (Acts 19:13–20), and it seems reasonable to think of these practices as also present a hundred miles to the east in the Lycus River Valley.

If this is on the right track, then the Colossian philosophy mixed Judaism, Jewish magical practices, ascetic routines, and Christianity in a way that probably appealed to Christians in the region as a means of addressing everyday problems. By observing the right calendar, performing the right rituals, and calling on the right heavenly beings, including Jesus, they could gain control over everything from ear wax and indigestion to jealousy and divorce.[41] They could do this through controlling the transcendent powers trying to harm them. Just as the sons of Sceva were happy to use Jesus's name in their methods of exorcism, then, the Colossian philosophy probably viewed the name of Jesus as just one device in a large box of spiritual tools.

Exactly how the visions the false teacher claimed to experience and the asceticism that he promoted figured into his "philosophy" is not clear. Perhaps there was some connection to the oracle at Claros, which was still functioning in the first century just north of Ephesus and Colophon (Tacitus, *Ann.* 2.54; Pliny, *Nat.* 2.232). Evidence from a later time shows that delegations from the Lycus Valley sometimes visited the prophets there, and the prophets themselves fasted before they "entered" (ἐνεβάτευσαν; cf. Col 2:18) a grotto to receive oracles from Apollo.[42]

Another possibility is that the teacher in Colossae inherited the connection between visions and asceticism from Jewish apocalyptic literature where the seer sometimes fasts or eats and drinks a special diet before receiving a vision.[43] In 4 Ezra, for example, Ezra fasts for a week before each of three visions and, before one vision, eats a special diet of flowers and field plants (4 Ezra 5:20; 6:31, 35; 9:23–26). Later, he gathers five men around him and is mysteriously offered a full cup of fire-colored liquid. This liquid sharpens his mind, spirit, and memory and prompts him to dictate to the five men a long series of writings which they produce in a script they do not know (14:37–48). The "five men" themselves had to fast during the day when they were busy writing and could only eat "their bread at night" (14:42 [Metzger, *OTP* 1:555]).

Whatever the exact ingredients in the melting pot that made up the Colossian philosophy, Paul responded with a letter that urged the city's Christians to remain faithful to the true gospel as Epaphras originally taught it to them (Col 1:5–7). Paul told them that he prayed fervently for them to understand fully God's will so that their lives might produce "every good work," might reflect growth in understanding God, might be empowered to remain steadfast, and, especially, might give thanks to God for all he had done for them through his beloved Son, particularly his provision for dealing with their sin (1:9–14).

Paul's emphasis fell on this last item in his list—what God had done for them through his Son. Taking off from this point, Paul first described who God's Son was, then what God did through him, and finally what God did through him specifically for the Colossian Christians.

God's Son was the visible image of the invisible God, the Creator of everything, whatever its location, mode of existence, or place in the hierarchy of powerful beings. He did not merely create all things, but he created them to serve his purposes, and they all held together because of him. He was preeminent over them all. It was through this powerful person (the first to rise from the dead) and by his sacrificial crucifixion, that God reconciled everything to himself "whether on earth or in heaven" (Col 1:15–20). In particular, he reconciled the Colossian Christians to God through his death (1:21–22). That reconciliation would only turn out to be effective if the Colossians remained steadfast in the gospel that they heard and for which Paul himself was a humble courier (1:23).[44]

This opening description of God's Son as the image of God and involved in creation echoes the portrayal of wisdom in Scripture and in Hellenistic Jewish literature as the means through whom God created all things (e.g., Ps 104:24; Prov 3:19; 8:22–31; Wis 7:26; 9:1–2).[45] By describing God's Son this way, Paul was probably preparing the ground for his more direct admonition later to reject the "philosophy" (φιλοσοφία) which only appeared to be "wisdom" (σοφία) (Col 2:8, 23). Paul may have been planting the thought early in the letter that although the "philosophy" claimed to have special "wisdom" about how to call on angelic beings to ward off evil spirits, God had already rescued the Colossian Christians from such beings through the one who created everything and has authority over everything, including the invisible powers.

When the Colossian Christians were baptized, they were buried and raised with Christ, participating in both his death and his new life. In this participation, Christ wiped out the debt against God that their sin had accrued by nailing the record of that debt to the cross. At the same time, Christ stripped himself of the "rulers and authorities" clinging to him to do him harm and triumphed fully over them through the cross (Col 2:12–15).[46] This is why, Paul says, the Colossian Christians should reject the philosophy's attempt to convince them to participate in various religious rituals and to share its teacher's fascination with visions (2:16–23). Considering Christ's accomplishment, and their union with Christ, the philosophy's religious gymnastics were totally unnecessary.

They were also unhelpful in resisting "indulgence of the flesh" (Col 2:23).[47] Fixing one's mind on Christ's present position of victory at God's right hand, the place where he ascended after his death and resurrection, was far more valuable than "self-made religion and asceticism and severity to the body" in living the way God created human beings to live (3:1–4:6).

At about the same time that Paul wrote his letters to Christians in Colossae, he also wrote a letter to Christians in Laodicea that has not survived. Paul told the Colossian Christians at the end of their letter that after reading it they should "have it also read in the church of the Laodiceans; and see that you also read the letter from Laodicea" (Col 4:16). Although the reason for and content of Paul's letter to Laodicea remain wholly unknown, Paul's encouragement to the Colossians to exchange letters with the Laodiceans implies that he thought his letters would be useful beyond the local assemblies of Christians to whom he addressed them.[48] Perhaps his imprisonment had prompted him to think of his letters as a body of instruction he could leave behind if the unpredictable system of Roman justice failed to go his way.[49]

25

Fighting from Prison against Discouragement in Ephesus

There is some evidence in the letters from this phase of Paul's life of a growing realization that he might not make it out of prison alive. If he wrote to Titus from Malta or shortly after his arrival in Italy, then his plan to meet his coworker in Nicopolis the following winter (Titus 3:12) shows that he hoped for a relatively speedy and favorable resolution to his case. Festus and Agrippa had thought him innocent (Acts 25:25; 26:31). Why would the emperor, or some other magistrate in Rome, ignore their opinion? His letter to the Philippians is more guarded about his prospects, but on balance, he was still optimistic. "Christ will be honored in my body," he tells them, "whether by life or by death" (Phil 1:20), but then, a few sentences later, "I know that I will remain and continue with you all, for your progress and joy in the faith, so that in me you may have ample cause to glory in Christ Jesus, because of my coming to you again" (Phil 1:25–26; cf. 2:23–24). Similarly, in his letter to Philemon, Paul seems optimistic about a positive outcome and again plans to travel east before too long. "Prepare a guest room for me," he tells Philemon, who was in Colossae, "for I am hoping that through your prayers I will be graciously given to you" (Phlm 22).[1]

Paul's next missive was probably his letter to the Ephesian Christians. Timothy was present with Paul when he wrote Philippians, Colossians, and Philemon (Phil 1:1; Col 1:1; Phlm 1) but is missing from Ephesians. This is somewhat surprising since Paul wrote Colossians and Ephesians at roughly the same time, as the close similarity of Colossians to Ephesians and especially the identical commendation of their courier Tychicus indicate (Col 4:9; Eph 6:21). Timothy's absence from Ephesians makes sense, however, if he had left Rome for Asia (2 Tim 1:15; 4:13) between the time that Paul finished writing Colossians and started writing Ephesians.[2] That scenario would also explain why Paul needed to tell Timothy that he had sent Tychicus to Ephesus (2 Tim 4:12): he sent him (and Onesimus) there with a letter for the Ephesians and instructions to give them encouragement (Eph 6:21–22; cf. Col 4:9).[3]

If this order of the letters is correct, then the optimistic tone in Philippians, Colossians, and Philemon gives way in Ephesians to a slightly grimmer tone of concern about the legal hearing that Paul awaits. Near the end of the letter, he asks the Ephesians to pray for him "that words may be given to me in opening my mouth boldly to proclaim the mystery of the gospel" (Eph 6:19). He knows that, as an "ambassador" of the kingdom of Christ and of God (6:20; cf. 5:5), he should proclaim "the mystery of the gospel" with boldness, but he is an ambassador "in chains" and so needs the prayers of the Ephesians to strengthen him for this task. He has already connected the word "mystery" at the beginning of the letter with God's plan to unite all things in heaven and earth in the Messiah (1:9–10), a plan that involves the assertion of the Messiah's hegemony over "all rule and authority and power and dominion" (1:21). Paul needs courage not to flinch from describing this politically volatile message when discharging his ambassadorial duties before the authorities.[4]

By the time Paul wrote 2 Timothy his legal situation seems to have worsened. His "first defense" was behind him, and the phrase "first defense" implies that another hearing lies ahead. People Paul had expected to come to his aid had deserted him (2 Tim 4:16), and he speaks as if death is near: "For I am already being poured out as a drink offering, and the time of my departure has come. I have fought the good fight, I have finished the race, I have kept the faith. Henceforth there is laid up for me the crown of righteousness, which the Lord, the righteous judge, will award to me on that Day" (4:6–8a).

Ephesians and 2 Timothy, therefore, may be the apostle's last extant letters. In them Paul summarizes the gospel (Ephesians) and urges his closest colleague to remain faithful to the gospel in the face of persecution from the outside and defections from within (2 Timothy).

CHAPTER 25

THE SETTING AND GENUINENESS OF PAUL'S LETTER TO THE EPHESIANS

It is not clear how Paul heard that Christians in Ephesus were discouraged (Eph 3:13). As Epaphras and Onesimus traveled west from the Lycus River Valley to visit Paul, they would probably have passed through Ephesus and taken a ship from there to Italy. Perhaps Epaphras met with Christians in the city and heard from them that Paul's suffering had disheartened them. The challenges they had experienced from false teaching several years earlier still seem to have posed a problem (Eph 4:14, 20–21; 5:6; cf. 1 Tim 1:3–4; 4:1–3; 5:13; 6:3–10; Acts 20:29–30).[5] It is unlikely, moreover, that tension between Christians in Ephesus and other religious groups, whether Jewish or pagan, had abated since Paul's residency there (Acts 19:9, 23–38).

In any case, Paul decided to send the Ephesian Christians a letter of encouragement and basic instruction and to include it in the packet of letters that Tychicus and Onesimus would take with them on their journey eastward to Colossae. It is the most general of Paul's extant letters: Paul, Tychicus, and Jesus are the only personal names in the letter, and other than brief, general warnings against false teaching (Eph 4:14; 5:6) and a passing reference to his readers' discouragement (Eph 3:13), the letter does not seem to address a specific pastoral situation. Paul refers to having heard of his readers' faith and love (Eph 1:15), but he does not seem to know his readers well and he is unsure whether they know him (Eph 3:2; 4:21). This has seemed odd to many interpreters since Paul spent between two and three years in Ephesus and must have known many Christians in the city (Acts 19:10; 20:31).

Some scholars explain this inconsistency with the theory that Paul did not actually write the letter but that someone wrote it in Paul's name a generation after the apostle. Its purpose was to bolster his authority and to lend weight to the author's own interpretation of Paul.[6] This would explain both the general nature of the letter and its often-verbatim similarity to Colossians, which the author had in hand and imitated. The lack of a place name in the letter's greeting in its earliest manuscripts could lend weight to the theory, moreover, since without a place, it appears to be a letter simply "to the saints who are also faithful in Christ Jesus" (Eph 1:1 RSV).[7]

It also makes sense, though, to read Ephesians as a letter that Paul composed and sent to Christians in Ephesus. The letter is certainly like Colossians, but if Paul wrote these letters at about the same time and intended to send them off together, the similarities are understandable.[8] Ephesians, moreover, expresses a strong commitment to telling the truth. "Speaking the truth in love" is necessary for the unity of the church, and the unity of the church is one of the most important themes of the letter: "Having put away falsehood, let each one of you speak the truth with his neighbor, for we are members one of another" (Eph 4:15, 25). The letter's moving conclusion, instructing its audience to put on the armor of God, tells them first to fasten "on the belt of truth" (6:14). In the complex world of Christian pseudepigraphy, such inconsistencies certainly occurred.[9] The simple, unaffected, and sweeping admonitions to be truthful in Ephesians, however, would be odd in a letter that not only uses Paul's name but speaks with pathos of "Paul" suffering in prison (3:1, 13: 4:1) and in need of prayer for courage (6:18b–20).[10]

The general nature of the letter, then, probably reflects the long period of time that had passed since Paul was last in Ephesus.[11] It had been six or seven years since his work in the city concluded, and he could not assume that his audience fully understood the basics of either his apostolic authority to help them or the way of life that the message of Jesus implied. Did they know that God had given him a special commission to preach the gospel to the nations (Eph 3:2)? Did they appreciate the insight God had given him into the role that the church played in God's plan to bring all nations into his people on an equal footing (3:3–7)? Had they heard and been taught the truth about Jesus (4:21)? The general nature of the letter, then, reflects the general nature of the problem: a relatively large group of Christians in one of the Roman Empire's largest cities needed encouragement to persevere in the face of suffering and false teaching.

Praise to God and Intercession for the Ephesians

Paul decided to begin this word of encouragement in an unusual way. At least in the letters from him that are still extant, Paul normally followed his opening greeting with a report on how he prayed for the letter's recipients. Second Corinthians breaks this pattern with a single long sentence of praise to God for the way he has used Paul's suffering, paradoxically, to supply comfort to both Paul and others (2 Cor 1:3–5).[12] Similarly, in

Ephesians, Paul follows the greeting with a prayer of praise to God, but here the prayer—still one sentence—is much longer, with clause tumbling over clause for 202 words (Eph 1:3–14).

The intention of this unusual prayer seems to be to offer encouragement to the Ephesian Christians by reminding them of the benefits God had conferred on his people through the Messiah, Jesus.[13] He chose them, adopted them into his family, and graciously forgave their trespasses against him through Jesus's death (Eph 1:3–7). He gave them "wisdom and insight" so that they might understand his plan to put everything in the universe, whether visible or invisible, in its proper place under Jesus's authority (1:8–10). He predetermined that all believers—both the believers of Paul's own generation and more recent believers in Ephesus—would live "for the praise of his glory" both now and in the future (1:11–12).

Paul then shifts to his more usual prayer report format, briefly mentioning that he thanks God for the Ephesian Christians' faith in Jesus and love for one another (Eph 1:15–16) but then quickly moving into how he intercedes with God for the Ephesian Christians (1:17–23). In this description of his intercessory prayer for them, Paul reveals the main burden of the letter.[14] He prays (and his letter seeks to be part of the answer to this prayer) that God will enlighten "the eyes" of the Ephesians' "heart" so that they might understand the immense magnitude of the power God has placed at their disposal through their union with the risen and victorious Messiah (1:18–23).

Paul describes the Messiah's place of victory in language reminiscent of Psalm 110, where the God of Israel says to Israel's king, "Sit at my right hand until I make your enemies your footstool" (Ps 110:1; Eph 1:20–21), and Psalm 8 where the psalmist praises the God of Israel for giving human beings a lofty position in creation, putting "everything under their feet" (Ps 8:6 NIV; Eph 1:22). Probably for many in Paul's audience, this imagery would have also recalled the common depiction of conquering Roman emperors with defeated subject peoples under their feet.[15] Paul reminds the beleaguered Ephesian Christians that because of their union with Christ by faith (Eph 1:13–14), God had given them power over all the visible and invisible forces ranged against them, whether local Roman magistrates, who represented the emperor's power, or the many spiritual beings that their neighbors sought to control through magic.

Three Examples of God's Gracious Power

Next, Paul describes three examples of how God has used his great power in gracious ways on behalf of believers, including the Ephesian Christians (Eph 2:1–3:13). First, he describes how God used his power to transfer believers out of their lives of rebellion against God and helpless fealty to the prince of the demonic powers (2:1–3) into the sphere of Christ's victory over those powers (2:4–6). They were once spiritually dead, walking in transgression and sin, but now they are God's handiwork, newly created to walk in the good works God intended for his human creatures from the beginning (2:10).

Second, he describes how God used his great power to transfer all believers out of a world of social discord into a society of peace (Eph 2:11–22). The world was once divided into competing social groups. On one side stood God's people, Israel, with their access to God's Messiah and God's promises, and on the other side stood the nations outside Israel, alienated from God's people and from God himself (2:11–12). Now, however, God had brought this dividing wall, with the enmity it spawned on both sides, crashing down through the Messiah's death on the cross (2:13–18).

Both Jewish and non-Jewish peoples had now come together to form a new society built on the foundation of the apostles and prophets, with the Messiah Jesus himself as the building's most important stone. This building, it turns out, is a temple where God dwells by his Spirit. Obviously, this project of peace and unity among the nations was not complete—it had only started to take shape in the church. In the church, however, God was in the process of creating a "holy temple," a dwelling place for his Spirit where both Jewish and non-Jewish peoples would live in peace with himself and with each other (Eph 2:19–22).[16]

Third, Paul says that God's power enabled him to become a messenger of this good news to everyone, and especially to the gentiles (Eph 3:1–13). Although he was "the very least of all the saints," God nevertheless transformed him into someone with insight into the surprising nature of God's work through the gospel (Eph 3:8). Paul was probably thinking here of how God had transformed him from a persecutor of the church into an apostle to the nations (1 Cor 15:9–10).[17] Remarkably, God had revealed to him, of all people, "the mystery" that the Creator of all things was using the socially unified church to show "the rulers and authorities in the heavenly places" the multifaceted nature of his wisdom in the creation of both the world and the church (Eph 3:9–10). Paul's proclamation of the gospel, in other words, led the church to fulfill its own role in making God's wisdom known. The church would reveal to the inimical spiritual forces of the universe that their scheme to hatch chaos within God's world would not succeed. Ultimately, they would be unable to usurp God's authority and divide God's creatures from God and each other.[18]

Paul ends this first major section of the letter with a prayer that God might give the Ephesian Christians inner strength to grasp the implications of all that he has just told them. The dimensions of God's love are so vast, he says, that they surpass knowledge, and yet Paul prays that God might enable the Ephesian Christians to know this love and to receive encouragement from it (Eph 3:14–21).

A Way of Life Consistent with the Church's Mission and God's Great Love

Most of the rest of the letter focuses on the practicalities of living in peace and unity with one another despite the social forces that work against these goals. If the church's mission is to proclaim by its unity the manifold wisdom of God in bringing humanity back to the peaceful state God intended for it at creation, then it is necessary to be humble, gentle, and patient with one another, even when patience means putting up with annoyances (Eph 4:1–2). For the church to complete its mission, it needs to be "eager to maintain the unity of the Spirit in the bond of peace" (4:3; cf. 2:22).

Paul explains to the Ephesian Christians that God has not left the church without resources for accomplishing this goal (Eph 4:7–16). The risen and victorious Messiah, seated at God's right hand in the heavenly places, has given apostles, prophets, evangelists, shepherds, and teachers to the church to aid it in its mission (4:7–11). Their assignment is to equip the rest of God's people to grow in maturity until each believer individually, and the body of believers together, begin to take on the character of the Messiah himself (4:12–16).

As God's people leave behind their former ways of life, mired in ignorance, sexual immorality, and greed, and adopt their new way of life, marked by truthfulness, gracious speech, kindness, forgiveness, and love, they are beginning to live as new creatures, re-created in the image of God and imitating both him and the Messiah, who "loved us and gave himself up for us" (Eph 4:17–5:2; cf. 2:10). As they live in this way, moreover, they will not only avoid the deception that sexual immorality and greed are harmless (5:5–6) but they will become powerful beacons of light for others. Their light will expose for others the harm that comes from "unfruitful works of darkness" (5:11–12). It will also become the means through which the risen Christ sheds his light on them, calling them out of spiritual death and transforming these newly illuminated people into beacons of light as well (5:14; cf. 2:1).[19]

Rather than participating in the drunken debauchery that sometimes characterized mealtime gatherings in Roman antiquity, the Ephesian Christians should gather for Spirit-guided times of instructional singing characterized by thanksgiving to God (Eph 5:15–20).[20] Probably since these times of gathered worship happened mainly in homes, Paul naturally moves next to a set of instructions on submitting to the needs of others in the home (5:21).[21] Wives should submit to their husbands, and husbands should love their wives just as Christ loved the church (5:22–33). Christ showed his love for the church by giving himself up for "her" (the term for "church" in Greek is in the feminine gender). This is how husbands should submit to and love their wives (5:25–33). Children should obey their parents, and fathers should not expect too much of their children (6:1–4).

Slaves should obey their masters with sincerity in the sight of God (Eph 6:5–8). In a move, however, that stands the institution of slavery on its head, Paul surprisingly says that slave masters should do for their slaves what he has just told slaves to do for their masters, and that masters must not threaten their slaves with violence (6:9).[22] It is unclear how the institution of slavery could survive in anything like its normal form under these conditions.

Paul concludes all this instruction with the phrase "there is no partiality" with God (Eph 6:9; cf. Rom 2:11; Gal 2:6; Col 3:25). This statement, and these instructions generally, are consistent with the theology Paul had developed in the first part of the letter on the equality before God of all his human creation. There he had said we all "once lived in the passions of our flesh" (Eph 2:3), and Christ offers peace to all, both the far and the near, both with God and with each other (Eph 2:14–17).

CHAPTER 25

Paul ends the letter with a rousing call to arms, urging his readers to stand and defend the world that God created and that he empowered Christ to recapture when he raised him from the dead and seated him at God's right hand (Eph 6:10–20; cf. 1:20–23; 2:5–6; 4:8–10). He recalls a passage from the prophet Isaiah in which the prophet expressed his great distress at the injustice prevailing among God's people in his own time: "Justice is turned back, and righteousness stands far away; for truth has stumbled in the public squares, and uprightness cannot enter. Truth is lacking, and he who departs from evil makes himself a prey" (Isa 59:14–15). In response, the Lord himself intervenes: "He put on righteousness as a breastplate, and a helmet of salvation on his head; he put on garments of vengeance for clothing, and wrapped himself in zeal as a cloak" (Isa 59:17). Similarly, Paul pictures God's people clothing themselves with truth, righteousness, peace, faith, salvation, the Spirit's work through the gospel, and prayer. With this armor, which God both wears and supplies, the Ephesian Christians should fight off both discouragement and compromise with the world's values (Eph 6:14–20). They should be the instruments through which God intervenes within an unjust, deceptive, and evil world to establish justice and proclaim God's gracious salvation.

This astonishingly countercultural vision of peace and unity, articulated within a world of dog-eat-dog betrayal and violence, provides a concise summary of Paul's theology and its practical application.[23] It picks up critical themes that Paul has articulated elsewhere in his letters: the source of the world's ubiquitous evil in rebellion against God the Creator, God's mercy in sending Christ to remedy this situation through his sacrificial death, the transforming nature of union with the risen Christ through faith, and the practical, socially unifying vision of a people—and eventually a world—living in harmony. F. F. Bruce's memorable description of Ephesians as "the quintessence of Paulinism" is not wrong.[24] Here, near the end of his life, Paul summed up for the church in Ephesus the message God had called him to proclaim and the transforming effect it could have on all who embraced it in faith.

26

Paul Finishes the Race

Sometime after Paul wrote Colossians and Philemon, but before he wrote Ephesians, Timothy left Rome and traveled eastward. It is not clear exactly where he went. The false teaching Paul mentions in 2 Timothy bears some resemblance to the false teaching Paul warned against in Ephesus when he wrote 1 Timothy several years earlier, and Paul mentions Ephesus and people with connections to that city several times in the letter (2 Tim 1:18; 2:17; 4:12, 19). When Paul tells Timothy, however, that he has "sent" Tychicus "to Ephesus" (4:12) he seems to assume that Timothy is *not* in that city and that Timothy needs to know Tychicus is there.

It seems slightly more likely, then, that Paul had sent Timothy not merely to Ephesus but to other locations in Asia also, perhaps especially to the Lycus River Valley where the amalgam of Christian teachings and magic had been creating confusion. If so, then this would make sense of Paul's comment, "You are aware that all who are in Asia turned away from me" (2 Tim 1:15). A location for Timothy somewhere in Asia would also make sense of Paul's instructions to "get Mark and bring him with you, for he is very useful to me for ministry" (2 Tim 4:11). From Philemon and Colossians, it seems that Mark had been with Paul in Rome (Phlm 24; Col 4:10a), but that Paul planned to send him eastward, possibly as far as Colossae: "If he comes to you," Paul tells the Colossians, "welcome him" (Col 4:10b).[1] If Timothy was supposed to "get Mark and bring him" to Paul, then it is reasonable to assume Timothy was within striking distance of Colossae where, Paul hoped, Mark was now located.

CHAPTER 26

Two Significant Events

After Timothy's departure, Paul experienced two significant events. First, a Christian from Ephesus named Onesiphorus, whose whole family Paul seems to have known during his work in that city, came to visit him (2 Tim 1:16–18; 4:19). Chained prisoners suffered a serious loss of honor in Roman society, and so Paul was grateful that Onesiphorus was not ashamed of his condition and worked hard to find him in Rome.[2] Paul was also thankful for the "breathing space" that Onesiphorus's visit gave him.[3]

It seems that when Paul wrote 2 Timothy, however, Onesiphorus was no longer with him. The lonely tone of the letter implies this. Everyone in Asia, he says, has turned away from him (2 Tim 1:15). Phygelus, Hermogenes, and Demas have defected from the faith (1:15; 4:10). "Luke alone" was with him (4:11). No one had taken his side at his first defense (4:16). He longed to see Timothy (1:4) and urged him to come to Rome quickly (4:9, 21).

Second, Paul had been summoned to his "first defense" (2 Tim 4:16). From the perspective of Roman law, perhaps this corresponded to the "first" of two or more presentations of evidence and argument in a Roman trial. Something like this, at least, was the procedure in 70 BC when Cicero prosecuted the corrupt governor of Sicily, Gaius Verres.[4] An early fourth-century AD account of the legal proceedings that ended in the death of the Christian martyr "Phileas, bishop of Thmuis and ruler of Alexandria" envisions the possibility of other hearings also. Using language close to 2 Timothy 4:16, but with no sign of dependence on it, this document says that "at the time of [Phileas's] first defense" (ἐν μὲν τῇ πρώτῃ ἀπολογίᾳ) the bishop was insulted, tortured, and then imprisoned.[5] The text briefly describes what happened at Phileas's "third and fourth appearances" and then, at much greater length, gives the details of his defense when he was "summoned for a fifth time."[6]

If the same procedure was in effect in the first century, then Paul's "first defense" was probably a formal hearing before a magistrate in which, for the first time, he attempted to defend himself against the charges of his accusers. As a Roman citizen, Paul would not have been tortured (cf. Acts 22:25). He would also have been entitled to a presumption of innocence (*Dig.* 22.3.2), and, under normal procedure, his accusers would have to be present for the trial to proceed (Acts 25:16).[7] Waiting for their arrival may have been one of the main reasons that nearly two years passed before Paul's formal legal proceedings got underway.

This "first defense," however, did not go well from a legal perspective. Roman courtrooms were spacious and open to the public.[8] Their proceedings were often raucous events with large, vocal audiences who weighed in freely with their opinions on the litigants, their guilt or innocence, and the punishment they should receive.[9] The first-century advocate Quintilian recalls an incident when a famous orator named Trachalus spoke so loudly and eloquently over the normal uproar in the judicial building that he could be heard, and was applauded, across the building's four sections where juries were being empaneled (Quintilian, *Inst.* 12.5–6). Quintilian's student Pliny the Younger complained a few years later about hired groups calling out their support for the orator who hired them during court proceedings. This kind of thing happened at a more subdued level in the days of his teacher Quintilian, continues Pliny. Back then, he recalls Quintilian saying, orators merely sent invitations to people to come and support them in court (*Ep.* 2.14).

In a setting like this, having the support of one's family, or at least one's friends, was critical to the success of one's case, and testimony from people of "dignity, faith, morals, and gravity" was important (*Dig.* 22.5.2).[10] Paul says, in contrast, "No one took my side at my first court hearing. Everyone deserted me" (2 Tim 4:16 CEB).

Concern about False Teaching

As if all this were not enough, Paul was deeply concerned about the emergence in Asia (and possibly Rome) of deviant forms of Christian belief and practice. When Paul had written to Timothy in Ephesus several years earlier, he had warned against a type of false teaching that engaged in esoteric speculation, expressed in what seemed to Paul to be senseless blather (1 Tim 1:4, 7; 4:1–2, 7; 6:4–5, 20–21). Its teachers also claimed the inspiration of spiritual forces, criticized marriage, and advocated a restrictive diet (1 Tim 1:4; 4:1–3). At that time Paul had already placed two of the leaders of this movement, Hymenaeus and Alexander, under church discipline (1 Tim 1:20), and in Ephesians he had urged Christians in Ephesus not to "be children, tossed to and fro by the waves and carried about by every wind of doctrine, by human cunning, by craftiness in deceitful schemes" (Eph 4:14) or to yield to the deception of "empty words" to the effect that God would not judge those who practiced sexual immorality and greed (Eph 5:5–6).

More recently, Epaphras had informed him of a similar movement in Colossae. It was also speculative, engaged with transcendent beings, and emphasized a special diet (Col 2:4, 8, 16–23). Both movements advocated a distorted morality. The false teachers in Ephesus were "liars whose consciences were seared" (1 Tim 4:2; cf. 1:19), and those in Colossae seemed to have been promoting their ascetic regimen as a way of "stopping the indulgence of the flesh" (Col 2:23).

When Paul wrote 2 Timothy, he was still concerned about movements like this in Asia. The "irreverent babble" and "foolish, ignorant controversies" were continuing apace (2 Tim 2:16, 23). Hymenaeus was still in the picture, despite his excommunication, although it is not clear whether he was teaching in Ephesus or somewhere else. He had, in any case, now joined with someone named Philetus, and both were claiming that "the resurrection [had] already happened" (2:17–18). Paul continues to express concern about a broken moral compass. The false teachers were "corrupted in mind" (3:8), although their corruption seems to have less to do with asceticism than with sexual immorality (3:6; cf. 2:19, 22; 4:3; cf. Eph 5:5–6).

In addition, Paul is now more explicitly concerned about a magical component to this religious movement. The people Paul has in mind in 2 Timothy remind him of the magicians Jannes and Jambres, names given in popular accounts of the first century to the magicians who opposed Moses in Pharaoh's court (2 Tim 3:8; cf. Exod 7:11, 22). Later he refers to them as "impostors who will go on from bad to worse, deceiving and being deceived" (2 Tim 3:13). The Greek word behind "impostors" could just as easily be rendered "sorcerers" or "wizards."[11]

The spirit world, magic, and a present resurrection also converge in a second-century description of the teacher Menander, who probably flourished in the late first century. According to Justin Martyr, who was writing in Rome less than a century after Paul, Menander came "from the village of Kapparetaia," in Justin's home region of Samaria and about twenty-eight miles south and slightly east of Caesarea.[12] Justin regarded him as demon-possessed ("worked on by demons") and says that after moving to

Antioch he "beguiled many through magic art." He also "persuaded his followers that they would never die," and some of those followers, Justin says, were still alive in his own time (*1 Apol.* 26.4; cf. 56.1 [Minns and Parvis]).[13] Perhaps the movement in Asia that so concerned Paul near the end of his life was something like Menander's movement in Antioch.[14]

It is perhaps not insignificant that Menander's teacher was another Samaritan named Simon. Justin claims that Simon was active "in the time of Claudius Caesar." He too, "through the art of the demons who moved him, performed magical deeds" in Rome (*1 Apol.* 26.2 [Minns and Parvis]). The idea that Simon was in Rome may derive from nothing more than Justin's misinterpretation of a statue inscription he had seen on Tiber Island.[15] It is possible, however, that it reflects a first-century movement in Rome that mingled magic, spirit possession, and elements of Christianity. Perhaps when Paul wrote 2 Timothy he was just as concerned about Timothy's encounter with something like this movement when he returned to Rome as he was with Timothy's exposure to it in Asia.

A FINAL LETTER, TO TIMOTHY

The prospect of impending death, a disappointing lack of support, and various defections from the faith seem to have prompted Paul to write what was probably his last letter. It is a letter, however, that like 2 Thessalonians, 1 Timothy, Titus, Colossians, and Ephesians, some interpreters believe to be a fiction.

The vocabulary and style of 2 Timothy closely resemble the vocabulary and style of 1 Timothy and Titus, and many scholars reject those letters as authentically Pauline in large part because of their unusual discourse, more reminiscent of Hellenistic tractates on philosophy than of Paul's undisputed letters. As in 1 Timothy and Titus, the author of 2 Timothy could speak of a "good conscience" (2 Tim 1:3; cf., e.g., 1 Tim 1:5; Titus 1:15) and of the need to follow "healthy" teaching (2 Tim 1:13; 4:3; cf. 1 Tim 1:10; Titus 1:9; my trans.), expressions that echo ethical discussions in ancient philosophical deliberation (e.g., Seneca, *Tranq.* 3.4; Epictetus, *Diatr.* 1.11.28) and later Christian literature (e.g., Ign. *Magn.* 4) but that never appear elsewhere in Paul's letters.[16]

In the view of these interpreters, then, 2 Timothy, like 1 Timothy and Titus, emerged long after Paul's death to shore up the organization of the church by providing it with instruction on church order. The function of 2 Timothy within the trio was to supply Paul himself as an example of faithful endurance to church leaders amid the challenges of persecution and false teaching.[17] The realistic-sounding personal notes throughout the letter are fictional (although possibly containing some accurate historical information) and participate in a general trend in the second century to produce legends about the apostle's life (as in, e.g., the Acts of Paul).[18]

It does not seem implausible, however, that Paul himself wrote this letter in a "register" like that of 1 Timothy and Titus. Once again, he was writing to an individual who was a trusted coworker, using the second-person singular until the letter's final sentence when he may have had in view other people with Timothy (2 Tim 4:22). The language of Hellenistic philosophy that appears in these letters, moreover, was in use in the first century, and Paul might easily have picked it up. Philosophers in Rome contemporaneous with Paul were discussing the importance of teaching others "the blessing of a good conscience" (Seneca, *Tranq.* 3.4 [Basore, LCL], and Paul's contemporary Philo could claim that Abraham kept the commandments of God not because he had them in written form but because he allowed inner stirrings to lead him that were "healthy and free from sickness" (*Abr.* 275).[19] None of this seems impossible within the context of Paul's thought as he expresses it in the undisputed letters (e.g., Rom 2:15). Paul, then, wrote this letter, shifting into the tone that he used with trusted subordinates and reflecting the conceptual world of his environment.

The letter seems to have had several quotidian purposes. Paul needed his coat as protection against winter's advancement (2 Tim 4:13). He needed company, and Timothy was his "beloved child" (2 Tim 1:2, 4; 4:9, 21; cf. Phil 2:20, 22). He also needed some important documents, perhaps related to his legal troubles (2 Tim 4:13).[20] Since his coat and documents were with a friend in Troas, and Timothy would need to go there to get them, Paul also wanted to warn Timothy against "Alexander the coppersmith," who had done some great unknown harm to Paul and was probably in Troas (2 Tim 4:13–14).[21] He might harm Timothy too (2 Tim 4:15). These mundane concerns were reason enough to get a message to Timothy.

The letter's primary purpose, however, was to urge Timothy to remain faithful to the gospel and to his and Paul's many years of work together for its advancement. Paul did this mainly by placing both positive and negative examples before Timothy.[22]

Near the beginning of the letter, he includes his usual thanksgiving prayer report, but he shapes it to express his purpose clearly. When Paul thinks of Timothy, he says, he thinks of the sincerity of his faith and of the firm heritage that Timothy received from both his grandmother and his mother (2 Tim 1:5). This is a solid foundation for Timothy to build on as he exercises the divine gift that Paul recognized when he participated in the gathering of elders that set Timothy apart for the work of gospel ministry (2 Tim 1:6; cf. 1 Tim 4:14).[23] Paul wants Timothy "to fan" this gift "fully into flame" (ἀναζωπυρεῖν) as he faces the difficulties of suffering for the gospel and correcting false teachers.[24]

Paul then moves to a series of positive and negative examples illustrating how Timothy can do this. Paul himself supplies a positive example to follow. He tells Timothy not to "be ashamed" either of "the testimony about our Lord" or "of me his prisoner" (2 Tim 1:8). Included in "the testimony about our Lord" would be the account of his crucifixion, one of the most shameful of all punishments in antiquity. Imprisonment, too, seriously damaged one's supply of honor. In a world where honor was highly valued and was like a substance that could be depleted or gained, people would have been tempted to avoid a message or way of life viewed as dishonorable.[25] Although his commitment to proclaim the gospel had landed Paul in prison and had, therefore, depleted his honor, he was "not ashamed" of the suffering he had to endure. He was confident that on the final day, when God put right what was wrong with the world, the gospel he proclaimed would find vindication (1:12; cf. 1:18; 2:12; 4:8, 18).[26]

Those in Asia who had defected from the faith, including two people he and Timothy knew (Phygelus and Hermogenes), provide counterexamples (2 Tim 1:15). There is no mention of shame here, but they nevertheless are illustrations of people who have failed to guard the good deposit of the gospel, a failure that Timothy should avoid (1:14).

Onesiphorus, however, provides a model of someone who "was not ashamed" of Paul's imprisonment. He was willing to risk his own honor to find and help him (2 Tim 1:17–18).

Such examples should impel Timothy to cooperate with the gifts of the Spirit and of salvation God has given him (2 Tim 2:1). These will enable him to live a life not of cowardice but of "power . . . love and . . . self-discipline" (1:6–7, 9 NRSV) and will equip him to hand on to other

CHAPTER 26

trustworthy people the gospel as he had learned it from Paul. These people will then be "qualified," like Timothy, to pass it along to others (2:2).[27] As Timothy engages in this task, he will need to remember the centrality to the gospel of Jesus's resurrection from the dead (2:8), and also remind the teachers he trains of the resurrection's importance (2:14).[28] A twisted understanding of "the resurrection" lay at the heart of much of the false teaching that Timothy would need to resist (2:18), and Paul considered "the hope of the resurrection of the dead" to be both critical to the gospel and the reason for his arrest and imprisonment (2:8–9; Acts 23:6).

Hymenaeus and Philetus are negative examples of faithlessness with respect to this central doctrine (2 Tim 2:16–18). Timothy should "avoid" and "have nothing to do" with their senseless false teaching, refusing to engage in the quarrels that it generates (2:16, 23; 3:5). He should instead gently correct those who have fallen prey to it in the hope that "God may perhaps grant them repentance leading to a knowledge of the truth" (2:25).

Rather than becoming involved with the immoral conduct of the false teachers and their victims, Timothy should remember the character and doctrinal emphases of those who taught him from his youth onward (2 Tim 3:10–15). From the time Paul met Timothy in southern Galatia to the present, he has shown Timothy what it means to "live a godly life in Christ Jesus" (3:12). People like his grandmother and mother who taught him the Scriptures in his youth are also models to follow (3:14–15).

The Scriptures themselves will provide a touchstone for Timothy's work as a courier of the good news that Paul has handed on to him. They will show him what to emphasize in his teaching, how to refute his opponents, how to correct those who have strayed from the right path, and how to instruct people to live righteous lives (2 Tim 3:16). They are a toolbox, providing the equipment Timothy needs to do a good job (3:17).

So, Paul concludes, Timothy should faithfully proclaim the message of the gospel and teach people what it means for their lives. He should do this both when it is convenient and when it is inconvenient (2 Tim 4:2). Encounters with false teachers and with suffering should be assumed, but in the face of it all, Timothy's calling is to "always be sober-minded, endure suffering, do the work of an evangelist, [and] fulfill [his] ministry" (4:3–5).

Paul draws the main portion of his letter to a close by again providing an example for Timothy to follow. The drink offering of his life, poured out in sacrifice so that others might embrace the gospel, is almost expended (2 Tim 4:6; cf. Phil 2:17). Nevertheless, Paul is far from discouraged. The hardship he has faced in the service of the gospel has been a "good fight" (2 Tim 4:7) and the victor's crown lies just in front of him (2 Tim 4:8a). As he writes this letter, then, Paul is conscious of stretching past the winning post, like a victorious athlete at the end of a race. He also wants to be clear, however, that this race has more than one winner. The crown goes to "all who have longed" to see the Lord at "his appearing" (2 Tim 4:8b), and that includes Timothy, if, like Paul, he remains faithful.

What Happened after Paul's Final Letter?

How Paul sent his letter to Timothy is completely unclear. Perhaps he included it with the growing package of letters that Tychicus would carry east to Ephesus and the Lycus River Valley. If so, then Paul's need to tell Timothy, "Tychicus I have sent to Ephesus" (2 Tim 4:12), implies that Tychicus would not be able to hand the letter to Timothy personally.

Whether Timothy and Mark ever made it back to Rome is also uncertain. When Paul asked Timothy to return to him in Rome, he may have envisioned Timothy and Mark passing through Ephesus, Troas, Philippi, and Corinth. He would greet Prisca, Aquila, and the household of Onesiphorus in Ephesus (2 Tim 4:19; cf. 1:16, 18). He would then sail north to Troas where he would pick up Paul's coat and critical documents and hopefully steer clear of Alexander the coppersmith (2 Tim 4:13–15). If he had not visited Philippi on his journey outward from Rome, he might easily sail westward from Troas to Neapolis and Philippi, fulfilling Paul's promise to the Philippian Christians that Timothy would come to them soon (Phil 2:19, 23). Whether from Troas or Neapolis, Timothy could sail back to Rome without too much trouble—assuming he made the journey "before winter" (2 Tim 4:21), as both Paul and Timothy knew all too well.

Did any of this actually happen? Early Christian tradition associates Mark with Rome (1 Pet 5:13; Eusebius, *Hist. eccl.* 2.14.6–15.2), and scholars have become increasingly interested in the question whether the gospel attributed to Mark displays signs of composition in Rome. It contains numerous Latinisms, mentions a "Rufus" that could be identical with the "Rufus" of Rom 16:13 (Mark 15:21), and shows significant theological overlap with Paul's letter to Christians in Rome.[29] It seems just possible, then, that Timothy did "get Mark" and "bring him" back to Rome (2 Tim 4:11), where he settled and wrote his gospel.

What Happened to Paul?

What happened to Paul, the resolution of his legal problems, and how he died are also unclear. Although Luke was with Paul when he wrote 2 Timothy and must have known what happened to him, his own narrative famously goes silent after recording that Paul welcomed all, proclaimed God's kingdom, and taught about the Lord Jesus Christ for two years from his rental unit in Rome (Acts 28:30–31; 2 Tim. 4:11). It is hard to escape the hints in Luke's narrative, however, that Paul is moving closer to death as the story proceeds.[30] The Ephesian church elders will not see his face again (Acts 20:25), a point that Luke emphasizes (Acts 20:38). In Tyre the disciples tell Paul ominously not to follow through with his plan to travel to Jerusalem (Acts 21:4). In Caesarea, Agabus dramatically prophesies Paul's arrest in Jerusalem, which leads everyone to plead with him not to go there (Acts 21:10–12). Paul responds, however, that he is ready not only for imprisonment but death "for the name of the Lord Jesus," a fate to which the crowd around Paul seems resigned (Acts 21:13–14). It is true that Luke emphasizes Paul's innocence of the charges against him and shows that both a Roman governor and a Jewish king recognized his innocence, but these elements parallel his story of Jesus, whose legal ordeal ended in an unjust condemnation and death.[31]

On balance, then, it seems best to take Luke's narrative as evidence of Paul's condemnation and death in Rome at the end of his two years there. Perhaps because his story of Paul was only part of his larger story of the gospel's progress "to the end of the earth" (Acts 1:8), he did not want to focus the conclusion of his narrative on Paul's death. This might be especially so if he knew from firsthand experience (2 Tim 4:11) that Christian "jealousy and strife" were partly responsible for it (1 Clem. 5.5 [Holmes]; cf. Phil 1:15; 2 Tim 4:16).[32] Luke probably considered it more consistent with his goals to end on the high note that, despite Paul's imprisonment, he taught about the Lord Jesus Christ for two full years with courage and without hindrance (Acts 28:31).

If this is correct, then Paul's "first defense" (2 Tim 4:16), was probably an initial hearing, perhaps after his accusers from Jerusalem finally arrived to pursue the case against him. It is reasonable to assume that these accusers were members of the priestly upper class in Jerusalem, just as they were several years earlier when "the high priest Ananias" had traveled from Jerusalem to Caesarea with a group of elders and a professional advocate named Tertullus to accuse Paul before the Judean procurator Felix (Acts 24:1). At that time, these powerful people leveled two accusations against Paul: he created social discord among Jewish people across the world, and he had tried to desecrate the temple (Acts 24:5–6).[33]

There was now a new high priest in Jerusalem, but there is no reason to think that the accusations of the Jerusalem nobility had changed, and, if these were still their charges against Paul, the authorities in Rome would have taken them seriously. The charge of setting riots in motion among a particular ethnic group would have been considered sedition—an effort to undermine the good order of the empire, personified in the emperor himself.[34]

The charge of attempted temple desecration would also have been serious.[35] The Romans had accepted the responsibility of preserving the temple's sanctity. According to Josephus, who himself carried the message, the emperor Titus scolded the Jews in control of the temple in AD 70, just before its destruction, for desecrating it: "Exchange the arena of conflict for another and not a Roman shall approach or insult your holy places; nay, I will preserve the temple for you, even against your will" (*B.J.* 6.128 [Thackeray, LCL]).[36] Josephus, at least, would have his readers believe that the Romans took the sanctity of the Jerusalem temple as seriously as (in this case, more seriously than) the Jews themselves.

Closer to the time of Paul's trial—indeed possibly in the same year—the high priest Ishmael son of Phabi arrived in Rome and pleaded with Nero to allow the Jerusalem priests to keep a wall they had recently added to the temple. The wall's construction had blocked the view of the inner temple from the west and thus both from the observation of Roman soldiers stationed atop the temple's western portico and from the view of Herod Agrippa II, whose palace overlooked the temple (Josephus, *A.J.* 20.192).[37] Festus had ordered them to take the wall down, but Ishmael had requested that Festus allow the priests to appeal their case to Nero. The governing nobility of Jerusalem, Ishmael told him, "could not endure to live any longer if any portion of the temple was demolished" (Josephus, *A.J.* 20.193 [Feldman, LCL]). E. Mary Smallwood took this to be a "sophistical argument."[38] There is no reason, however, not to see the petitioners as sincere: to destroy the wall was to defile part of this holy site.

Nero, at least, seems to have been sympathetic with Ishmael's reasoning. When the meeting finally happened, he commended the Jerusalem nobility for building the wall and, agreeing to their request, "consented to leave the building as it was" (Josephus, *A.J.* 20.195). If this same, or a similar, group appeared before Nero accusing Paul of attempting to defile the temple, it is unlikely that Nero would have looked favorably on Paul's defense. When Paul finally stood before Caesar (Acts 27:24), then, Caesar probably decided against him and ordered his execution.[39]

If the authorities allowed Paul a death consistent with his social standing, then the mid- to late second-century tradition that he was beheaded is probably correct (Acts Paul 14.3–5). According to an important study by David Eastman, ancient tradition identifies two sites south of Rome where this took place.[40] One tradition, stretching back to the fourth century, identifies the place of Paul's death as a marshy spot along the banks of the Tiber River and on the Via Ostiensis. Both the early fifth-century Christian poet Prudentius and a fourth-century sarcophagus that depicts the place of Paul's execution agree on this location.[41] Another tradition, traceable to a Greek text composed in the sixth century, places Paul's execution on the Via Laurentina at the site of an estate known as Aquae Salvias. Eastman argues persuasively that this Greek text relies on an earlier Latin source that originated in Rome. It is not at all clear, however, that either tradition accurately preserves the location of Paul's death.

Somewhat more reliable is the tradition that Paul's remains were buried in a cemetery just outside the city walls in a marshy area near the Tiber and on the road to Ostia. It is not improbable that after Paul's execution the Roman authorities allowed his friends to bury his remains: it was customary for Roman citizens who had been executed to receive a decent burial (*Dig.* 48.24.1, 3).[42] By the late second or early third century, moreover, Christians already seem to have been making pilgrimages to a memorial along the road to Ostia to visit the place where Paul's remains rested (Eusebius, *Hist. eccl.* 2.25.7).[43] A century later, the site of the apse of the present-day Basilica of Saint Paul Outside the Walls was so thoroughly identified with this spot that the emperor Constantine built a basilica there to commemorate Paul's martyrdom.[44] Excavations to the north and east of the apse have revealed a cemetery with some tombs that go back to the

Paul Finishes the Race

early first century AD and therefore add plausibility to the idea that this is, in fact, the place of Paul's burial.[45]

It is unlikely that Paul himself would have cared much about the disposition of his body once he had died physically. If a brick-and-mortar monument on the Via Ostiensis somehow pointed people to the reality of a future resurrection and a new creation, Paul would have been pleased.[46] From the apostle's perspective, however, the treatment of his physical remains was irrelevant. As he told the Corinthian Christians, after his death "what is mortal" would be "swallowed up by life" (2 Cor 5:4).

It is not that the physical body was unimportant to him. He had staked his whole life on the doctrine of the resurrection from the dead (1 Cor 15:29–32). This resurrection, however, was not the resuscitation of a corpse. Comparing what happens to a believer after death to what happens to a seed planted in the soil, Paul had said this to the Corinthians: "What is sown in decay is raised in decay's reversal. It is sown in humiliation; it is raised in splendor. It is sown in weakness; it is raised in power. It is sown an ordinary human body; it is raised a body constituted by the Spirit. If there is a body for the human realm, there is also a body for the realm of the Spirit" (1 Cor 15:42–44; cf. Phil 3:20–21).[47]

Real life, then, was much more than inhabiting a body in the process of breaking down. Jesus's resurrection from the dead was the first of the general resurrection of God's people from the dead (1 Cor 15:20). It was God's first step in establishing the re-created world that prophets like Isaiah had promised would eliminate death (1 Cor 15:54–55; 2 Cor 5:17; cf., e.g., Isa 25:6–8).

For this reason, Paul seems to have neither feared death nor to have been concerned about what happened to his body after he died. Since the time of his encounter with the crucified and risen Jesus on the way to Damascus, he had spent his whole turbulent life in Jesus's service, proclaiming the good news of reconciliation with God through faith in his Messiah. Speaking of this life, Paul had once reflected, "I do it all for the sake of the gospel" (1 Cor 9:23). He wanted to stay in the fray as long as God could use him there for the gospel's advancement, but once his work was finished, he would be glad. "For me to live is Christ," he said, "and to die is gain" (Phil 1:21; cf. 2 Cor 5:9).

APPENDIX I

The Evidence for Paul

What are the reliable sources for Paul's life and thought? The earliest texts that talk about Paul also turn out to be the most important texts for understanding the apostle. Paul's own letters are a critical, firsthand source of information. In addition, the Acts of the Apostles, which is chiefly about Paul, presents itself as a carefully researched narrative whose author was at times a participant in the events it narrates. Two questions, however, bedevil the scholarly discussion about using these sources in accounts of Paul's life and theology. Which letters that bear Paul's name did he write? Is the Acts of the Apostles a reliable account of Paul's movements and motivations?

WHICH PAULINE LETTERS DID PAUL ACTUALLY WRITE?

Paul's canonical letters are the earliest evidence of Christianity. Either 1 Thessalonians or Galatians is the earliest extant Christian document. Of the thirteen New Testament letters that bear Paul's name, however, only seven are universally regarded as authentic: Romans, 1 Corinthians, 2 Corinthians, Galatians, Philippians, 1 Thessalonians, and Philemon.

Even if, for the sake of avoiding controversy, a biographer of Paul took evidence for Paul's life only from these "undisputed" letters, they would contain a gold mine of information. We would know that he persecuted the church before God called him to preach the gospel through a vision of the risen Lord (Gal 1:12–16; 1 Cor 15:8–9). We would know the basic outline of his church-planting efforts from Jerusalem to Illyricum (Gal 1:16–2:10; Phil 4:15–16; 1 Thess 1:7–8; 2:2; 1 Cor 16:5–9; 2 Cor 2:12; 7:5; Rom 15:19).

APPENDIX I

We would know about the importance of his collection for the poor among the Christians in Jerusalem (1 Cor 16:1–4; 2 Cor 8:1–9:15; Rom 15:25–28) and understand the significance of that collection in demonstrating a critical Pauline theological principle: God had reconciled believers to himself and torn down the walls of division that separated ethnic groups in the process (2 Cor 8:9; Rom 15:27). We would know something about Paul's relationships with important coworkers such as Timothy, Titus, Prisca, and Aquila (Phil 2:19–23; 1 Cor 4:17; 16:19; 2 Cor 2:13; 7:6–7; 8:6, 16, 23; Rom 16:3–5, 21). We would know that Paul understood himself to be an apostle of Christ Jesus to the gentiles (Rom 1:5; 11:13; 15:15–16; 1 Cor 15:9–10; 2 Cor 12:12) and that, despite some tension, other apostles based in Jerusalem also recognized the legitimacy of his ministry (Gal 2:1–10;). We would also know that Paul often suffered violence from those who opposed his message, sometimes landing in prison (1 Cor 4:9–13; 16:8–9; 2 Cor 2:14; 4:8–12; 11:23–25, 32–33; Phil 1:13; Phlm 1, 23). In addition, we would know the great themes of his theology (Romans, Galatians, 1–2 Corinthians).

If the other six New Testament letters that bear his name are authentic, however, we could add much to this picture. From 2 Thessalonians, 1 and 2 Timothy, Titus, Ephesians, and Colossians we could gain a higher-resolution picture both of Paul's theology and of his relationship with Christians in Thessalonica, Asia, and Crete. In 2 Thessalonians we would see Paul nuancing the teaching in 1 Thessalonians on the imminent return of Christ and filling out the details of how he understood church discipline (2 Thess 2:1–12; 3:6–15). In the other five letters we would find details of the history of Pauline Christianity in Asia's largest city, Ephesus (Eph 3:13; 4:14, 17; 5:6; 1 Tim 1:3; 2 Tim 1:18; 4:12). We would also get a much clearer picture of Paul's relationship with coworkers such as Timothy and Titus (1 Tim 1:2, 18; 4:12; 2 Tim 1:3–7; 2:1, 22; 3:10–11, 15; Titus 1:5) and learn much about how Paul handled questions of order in the churches he founded and in the homes that, from these letters, seem so important to the smooth functioning of those churches (1 Tim 2:1–3:13; 4:1–5; 5:1–6:2; 2 Tim 3:6–7; Titus 1:5–9, 11; 2:1–10).[1] Who would guess that Paul was involved in the nurture of Christianity on the island of Crete apart from his letter to Titus (Titus 1:5)?

Many historians of early Christianity, however, believe that Paul did not actually write these six letters but that someone else wrote them in his name. This would not necessarily mean that the authors of any of these letters created them with malicious intent. Some pseudonymous documents, including letters, in antiquity appear to have been innocent fictions or attempts to present the teaching of important historical figures to a later generation.[2] Whatever motivated their production, however, if the "disputed" letters are not from Paul they hold little or no value for understanding the geographical movements and theological convictions of Paul himself.

Scholars who take this approach to the six disputed letters point to five types of evidence for their position. First, they argue that literary forgery was common in antiquity and was particularly common within early Christianity. Second, they argue that forgers used a set of techniques to disguise their deceit that also show up in at least some of the six disputed letters. Third, they observe that the literary style (including the vocabulary) of the disputed letters differs from the style of the authentic letters. Fourth, they point out that some of the disputed letters reveal literary dependence on other Pauline letters. Fifth, they argue that the disputed letters sometimes contradict what we know of the authentic Paul's theology or historical context.[3]

There can be little reasonable doubt that literary forgery, including the forging of epistles in the name of some respected person, was common in antiquity and that many examples exist of literary forgery in ancient Christianity. It is also beyond dispute that literary forgers used certain techniques to give their work an air of authenticity and that some of the disputed Pauline letters contain elements matching these techniques.

Since the early first century AD, for example, editions of Plato's writings have concluded with a collection of thirteen letters, all supposedly written from Plato to important people with whom he had connections in Sicily, southern Italy, Macedonia, the area around Troas, and possibly Thrace. Debate continues about the authenticity of these letters, but among the letters widely considered forgeries, numbers 9, 12, and 13 are particularly instructive for understanding the arguments against the disputed letters of Paul. The writing style of these three letters differs from that of the authentic Plato, and they are so banal that it is difficult to know why the important political figures to whom they are addressed would have saved them.[4] At least with letter 12, the forger's motivation is clear: "We have been wonderfully pleased at receiving the treatises which have come from you," writes the fake Plato, "and felt the utmost possible admiration of their author;

indeed we judged the man to be worthy of those ancient ancestors of his" (359c–d [Bury, LCL]). The letter's forger himself probably composed the treatises "Plato" was so thrilled to receive and intended the letter to lavish Plato's approval on his ideas to gain them a hearing. In addition, the author has "Plato" trace the ancestors of the treatises' author to a colony of noble immigrants from Troy to Italy, a detail for which no evidence exists in the historical record. It is probably sheer invention designed to inflate the dignity of the treatises' author and encourage acceptance of "his" ideas.[5]

Letters 9 and 13, similarly, contain intricate details from a clearly fictional day-in-the-life of Plato: "We are looking after Echecrates now and we shall do so in the future also" (358b); "Philaides ... was talking about you; and if it had not required a very long letter I would have told you in writing what he said; but as it is, ask Leptines to tell you" (363b–c [Bury, LCL]). These irrelevancies provide the letters with an air of everyday reality but also raise the question of why anyone would preserve a letter, such as 13, that contains almost nothing else but such details. The forger seems to have anticipated this objection in his final sentence, "Preserve ... this letter," he instructs Dionysius (363e).[6] Letter 13 contains other, similar techniques for guarding against suspicion: "Let this greeting not only commence my letter but serve at the same time as a token that it is from me" (360a); "Concerning the sign which indicates which of my letters are seriously written and which not ... bear it in mind and pay the utmost attention" (363b [Bury, LCL]).

The Platonic epistolary forgeries are only one particularly clear example of a common occurrence in antiquity. As Bruce Metzger says, in an often-quoted statement, "There is scarcely an illustrious personality in Greek literature or history from Themistocles down to Alexander, who was not credited with a more or less extensive correspondence."[7] Ancient Christians, moreover, seem to have sometimes produced documents in the names of the apostles, or a famous Christian, to lend support to their theological positions (e.g., the Epistle of the Apostles supporting Jesus's physicality) or to satisfy curiosity (e.g., the Epistle to the Laodiceans supplying the letter mentioned in Col 4:16), and some of these pseudonymous documents were letters.[8]

The question, then, is not whether pseudonymity was common and clever in the world of the early Christians, but whether, in any given case, a document is likely to be a fiction. It is true that the six disputed Pauline letters have features that duplicate the techniques of known forgeries from antiquity. For example, in 2 Thessalonians 2:2 the author asks his readers not to be "alarmed, either by a spirit or a spoken word, or a letter seeming to be from us, to the effect that the day of the Lord has come" and in 3:17 says, "I, Paul, write this greeting with my own hand. This is the sign of genuineness in every letter of mine; it is the way I write." Are these devices like those used in, for example, pseudo-Plato's letter 13 to guard against detection? In the same way, are the references to the travels of Demas, Crescens, Titus, and Tychicus, the note that "Luke alone is with me," and the instructions to bring Paul's coat and books from Troas in 2 Timothy 4:10–13 all attempts at verisimilitude, similar to details from mundane life that show up in the forged epistles of Plato? Is the instruction to Timothy to "use a little wine for the sake of your stomach" (1 Tim 5:23) roughly equivalent to pseudo-Plato's humdrum but realistic comment that he is sending to Dionysius "twelve jars of sweet wine for the children and two of honey" (*Ep.* 13 361 A)?

This is certainly possible, but it is worth asking how an author might write a letter that was genuinely concerned about false epistles circulating in his or her name or a letter that might incorporate newsy details of everyday life into a discussion of important philosophical, theological, or political matters. If the ancient world was awash with everything from forged inscriptions to forged apocalypses, it makes sense that a well-known and influential author might guard against fraud within a letter. The Hasmonean prince Aristobulus II, around 63 BC, required the governors of his fortified cities to obey instructions given to them in his "own hand," clearly, it is implied, to guard against forged letters that might instruct them to surrender (Josephus, *B.J.* 1.137 [Thackeray, LCL]). In the same way, the Roman military leader L. Munatius Plancus, writing in 43 BC, could be very nervous about whether the correspondence he received from other high-ranking officials was genuine, trusting only, as he says to Cicero, in the "autograph originals" (Cicero, *Fam.* 10.21).[9] The political and strategic issues at stake were far too weighty to fail to certify the genuineness of the letters on which their negotiation depended.[10]

For Paul, the issues at stake in his letters were certainly no less important than this, and so it is not surprising to find him finishing 1 Corinthians with, "I, Paul, write this greeting with my own hand" (16:21) and Galatians with, "See with what large letters I am writing to you with my own hand"

(6:11). The classical philologist Steve Reece, after examining a large number of ancient letters, concluded in his monograph on such signatures that Paul added his signature to Galatians for several reasons, but "primarily to assert his letter's authenticity."[11] Such "warnings against forged writings" and "literary prophylaxes" should be removed from the list of arguments against, for example, the Pauline authorship of 2 Thessalonians (2:2; 3:17; cf. Col 4:18).[12] Since these "tools of the forger's trade" were also standard tools in authentic letters for guarding against forgery, their use does not reliably signal forgery.[13]

Genuine letters also sometimes combined philosophical comments with the discussion of down-to-earth matters. A certain Chairas, for example, wrote a letter to his doctor in AD 58 that waxes philosophical in its opening section on the meaning of life and the nature of friendship but then gets down to the business of clarifying the ingredients for a medical prescription to treat ailing feet.[14] Similarly, the undisputed letters of Paul can end with tantalizingly brief references to people and controversies that are otherwise unknown, for example to Phoebe the deaconess from Cenchreae (Rom 16:1), the apostles Andronicus and Junia (Rom 16:7), Rufus's mother "who has been a mother to me as well" (Rom 16:13), and the feuding Euodia and Syntyche (Phil 4:2–3). The personal details and mundane comments in the Pastorals are more numerous, but they are not qualitatively different.

The first two of the four main reasons for considering the disputed six Pauline letters to be forgeries, then, are not conclusive. This leaves the other three criteria: differences in style, literary dependence, and contradictions of what is known either about Paul's theology or about his historical context.

Most of these other criteria are also not particularly useful in determining the authenticity of the disputed Pauline letters. Stylistic comparisons are difficult because it is hard to know based on the available evidence just how elastic Paul's stylistic abilities were.[15] Studies in sociolinguistics reveal that an author's style changes with "register," a term that refers to the context in which an author produced a document. A single author can vary the register in which he or she writes depending on the genre they have chosen, the audience they address, or the time of life in which they are writing.[16] Paul, for example, might write in a different register when addressing a letter to an individual, such as Timothy or Titus, than when addressing a letter to a church. His register might also vary from earlier to later letters and from letters written in freedom to those written from prison.[17]

These findings have received confirmation in Jermo van Nes's extraordinarily sophisticated study of the vocabulary and syntax of the New Testament letters attributed to Paul. Van Nes concluded that although there is a large amount of variation in the vocabulary and syntax of the Pauline letters, the only statistically significant variations among the five linguistic characteristics he studied appear in 1 and 2 Timothy and Ephesians.[18] The letters to Timothy have a high number of words that appear only once among the Pauline letters, and Ephesians has a low number of sentences that are grammatically incomplete. He made the case, further, that other factors besides author variation can account for these differences, for example, emotion, aging, and the difference between oral and written discourse.[19]

Literary dependence of one letter upon another (e.g., of 2 Thessalonians on 1 Thessalonians or Ephesians on Colossians), moreover, is not necessarily indicative of forgery since authors sometimes kept copies of letters.[20] "Don't distress yourself about the letter which you are so sorry you tore up," Cicero assures M. Fabius Gallus, "I have it safe at home" (*Fam.* 7.25 [Shackleton Bailey, LCL]). If Paul sometimes kept copies of his letters, or wrote them at basically the same time (as he might have done with Colossians and Ephesians), he could easily have used material from one letter in the composition of another letter.[21]

Supposed theological contradictions between the disputed and undisputed Pauline letters are, likewise, not a reliable guide to forgery since even carefully considered judgments of this type are inevitably subjective. What one interpreter sees as a contradiction another interpreter views as a plausible expression of Paul's thought in a changed environment.[22]

Historical inconsistencies between Paul's known context and a letter supposedly from him provide a more reliable guide to forgery. If, for example, 1 Timothy 6:20 warns its readers against the *Antitheses* of Marcion, who lived in the mid-second century, this would obviously betray a forgery.[23] "O Timothy," the verse reads, "guard the deposit entrusted to you. Avoid the irreverent babble and contradictions (ἀντιθέσεις) of what is falsely called knowledge." But, as Jerome D. Quinn and William C. Wacker point out, the Greek text at this point will not allow a reference to Marcion's *An-*

titheses.²⁴ Just as in English, so in Greek, the article "the" (τάς) goes with both "babble" and "contradictions," showing that the reference is not to some well-known book called the *Antitheses* but to "counter-propositions" that the false teachers whom the letter resists have laid against orthodox Christian teaching.²⁵

Decisions about anachronism in the disputed Pauline letters within the New Testament canon, however, are rarely this clear-cut. Is the structured church order described in 1 Timothy 3:1–13 too advanced for Christianity as it existed in Paul's lifetime? Does the series of events that will precede the coming of "the day of the Lord" in 2 Thessalonians 2:3–12 reflect a time after Paul's death when hope for the return of Jesus had faded? Do the references to the travels of Paul and his coworkers in 1 and 2 Timothy and Titus fit within a plausible, coherent historical background? Honest answers to these questions must inevitably be ambiguous: good arguments exist on both sides of the debate.

How, then, is it possible to tell whether a given Pauline letter is authentic or a very clever forgery? In the end, the judgment will be impressionistic and subjective, but it is reasonable to write the story of Paul's ministry on the basis of all thirteen canonical letters.

In the early fifth century, Augustine of Hippo recognized the difficulty of proving the genuineness of any document written in his era. Augustine knew that the Greek physician Hippocrates had both an authentic corpus of writings and some spurious writings attached to his name. He maintained that the only way to tell them apart was to trust the writings handed down from Hippocrates's own time as authentic and to distrust those that had appeared more recently. "How do people know," asks Augustine, "that the books of Plato, Aristotle, Varro, Cicero, and other such authors are their works except by the same unbroken testimony of the ages following one upon another?" How will anyone know that his own writings are authentic, Augustine asks, apart from the testimony of those who live in his own time, know his writings to be genuine and then pass this knowledge down to others? So it is with the Scriptures, he says. They have been handed down as genuine from one generation to another in the church from the time of their composition (*Faust*. 33.6).²⁶

This is not a bad argument. If no other arguments for or against a particular Pauline letter's genuineness are decisive, and if the ancient world was awash in forgeries, then it made, and makes, sense to consider the antiquity of the document itself and the antiquity and reliability of those who testify to its authorial claims. The disputed Pauline letters fare reasonably well under these considerations, and so it seems intellectually justifiable to use them as sources to construct the apostle's career and thought.

Is Acts a Reliable Source for Paul's Movements and Motivations?

Assessments of the historical value of Acts range from the view that it is an invaluable independent source for the apostle's life and thought composed by Luke, a companion of Paul, to the idea that it bears a strong resemblance to ancient historical novels.[27] It could be a historical monograph covering a relatively brief period of great importance to the history of a certain people, something like Sallust's *War with Catiline*. Or it could be a heavily fictionalized account featuring real people and places important to a particular people group, something like Judith, or even the love story by Chariton called *Chaereas and Callirhoe*. Perhaps, say some scholars, the Acts of the Apostles lies between these poles.[28]

If the beginning of an ancient book is important for alerting the reader to the kind of book it is, however, there can be little doubt that the Acts of the Apostles looks much more like the *War with Catiline* than a historical novel.[29] Judith begins with a historical "mistake" so glaring that it seems reasonably clear the author was trying to signal an intent to write fiction.[30] Any Jewish reader old enough to appreciate the story of Judith would know from the Bible itself that Nebuchadnezzar ruled not Assyria but Babylon (Jdt 1:1; 2 Kgs 24–25).[31] Chariton's second sentence is, "I am going to tell you the story of a love affair that took place in Syracuse."[32] As the story develops, it becomes clear that it really does not matter whether it actually "took place," for its point is to entertain the reader with an exciting tale of youthful love, wicked pirates, and intrepid travelers.

Sallust's *War with Catiline* is also an exciting account of greed, daring, and woe, but it is quite different from these heavily fictionalized stories. Sallust begins with a reflection on what he is doing by writing the composition that will follow. Doing great deeds, he admits, is more difficult, but "the writing of history" has difficulties of its own. The historian's "words must match the deeds recorded," and whenever one truthfully records the "great merit and renown of good men" some people inevitably think the author is writing something false, something "tantamount to fiction" (*Bell. Cat.* 3.2 [Rolfe and Ramsey, LCL]). So Sallust will write "a brief account" of the greedy Catiline and his conspiracy against the Republic and make his "narrative" as truthful as he can (*Bell. Cat.* 4.3–4).

Sallust, then, is writing a type of prose for which truth-telling mattered. He will fail to accomplish the service he wishes to provide to the Republic if he fails to tell the truth, and he sees no point in writing apart from providing that service.

If we can assume that the prologue to Luke's Gospel also reflects on what Luke will do in Acts (cf. Luke 1:3; Acts 1:1), then, like Sallust, Luke begins with a brief reflection on what he wants to accomplish in his gospel and its sequel. He speaks of writing a "narrative" that focuses on accomplishments among his people (Luke 1:1). His reference to eyewitnesses is reminiscent of Sallust's preliminary defense of his own truthfulness (Luke 1:2). Like Sallust, moreover, Luke was writing not long after the events he records and even seems to have participated in some of them (Acts 16:10–17; 20:5–15; 21:1–18; 27:1–28:16). As Colin J. Hemer has observed, he does not brag in his preface about his status as an eyewitness—something one might expect of an author only posing as an eyewitness. Rather, he distinguishes between those who witnessed the foundational events surrounding Jesus ("those who from the beginning were eyewitnesses," Luke 1:2) and his own participation, which came later ("it seemed good to me also, having followed all things closely for some time past," Luke 1:3).[33]

Interpreters of Acts who think that Luke's narrative provides a reliable source for reconstructing early Christian history have sometimes received criticism for thinking of "ancient historiography in terms of a fact-based enterprise."[34] Ancient historians, it is said, were more interested in the plausibility of their narrative than its factual accuracy.

Ancient readers, however, certainly knew the difference between fact and fiction and some, at least, seem not to have appreciated attempts to cover a lack of knowledge with a plausible narrative. Polybius, writing more than two centuries before Luke, distinguishes between the poet and the historian, arguing that they serve different purposes. Some historians, he complains, do not seem to understand the difference: "It is the job of a tragic poet to astound and entertain his audience for a moment by means of the most convincing words he can find, but it is the job of a historian to instruct and persuade his readers for all time by means of deeds that actually took place and words that were actually spoken" (*Hist.* 2.56.10 [Waterfield]).[35] The best historians do not simply do research while reclining on a couch in a library but travel and talk to people who can give insight into the events they want to describe (12.27.4–6; cf. 4.2.1–3). They question as many knowledgeable people as possible and use good judgment about whom to believe (12.4c.4–5). Lucian feigns surprise at the number of writers, among them historians, who "have concocted long, fantastic yarns" and supposed "that nobody would notice they were lying" (*Ver. hist.* 1.2, 4 [Harmon, LCL]).

It does not seem unlikely that Luke knew about historical standards like the ones that Polybius describes. He may have also been aware of the kind of criticism Lucian reflects. Like Polybius, he emphasizes an active form of research that valued eyewitness testimony and personal involvement. Occasionally in his narrative of Paul's career, Luke seems to signal with the first-person plural ("we") that he was himself a participant in the action (Acts 16:10–17; 20:5–15; 21:1–18; 27:1–28:16). Some scholars have been unwilling to concede that this surface reading of these sections can be correct. Objections to it take various forms. One scholar, for example, thinks that Luke's presentation of Paul's theology varies so widely from the theology Paul expresses in his letters that someone who knew Paul as well as the "we" sections imply is unlikely to have written Acts. He proposes, therefore, that Luke knew and learned from the companion of Paul who supplied the information in the "we" sections and that Luke used the first-person plural to mark the places in the narrative that reflected this source's experiences with Paul.[36] Another scholar believes that Luke took over the "we" from Paul himself who frequently uses it in his letters when describing his travels (as in 2 Cor 7:5).[37]

Still another scholar has argued at length that the "we" sections in Acts always show up in connection with sea voyages, and that they are part of a special sea voyage "genre" that regularly shifts into the first-person plural when the sea voyage begins.[38] Since this is simply the way sea voyages were often written up in antiquity, the "we" sections of Acts would not imply that the author of the text participated in the events.[39] Instead, the author has placed himself and his readers imaginatively into the text just as he could say in the preface to his work that the things about which he writes were not only delivered to "us" but that they happened "among us" (Luke 1:1–2).[40] To this scholar, Hemer's meticulous work showing the accuracy of the final "we" section (Acts 27:1–28:16) reflects his "distrust of imagination" and arises from "a 19th century view of faith grounded in historical rationalism."[41]

Hemer's case cannot, however, be easily dismissed. Descriptions of sea voyages in ancient literature certainly often shift into the first person when the voyage begins, but this happens in both real and unreal voyages (e.g., Josephus, *Vita* 3.15; Chion of Heraclea, *Ep.* 4.2). It is, as A. J. M. Wedderburn points out, a natural way of talking about the common experience of people on a ship, "exposed together to the hazards and uncertainties which went with such a form of travelling."[42] Hemer has shown, moreover, that Acts 27:1–28:16 looks much more like a real travel narrative than fiction. The account is verifiably accurate at the levels of geography, wind direction, maritime terminology, and understanding of the Roman grain shipments from Egypt, and it seems unstudied in its accuracy.[43] It is therefore reasonable to think that Luke wrote this section this way because he was present for the events he describes.

If that is true of the final "we" section, then this conclusion can also reasonably extend to the first-person parts of the narrative in chapters 16, 20, and 21, although they are shorter and less detailed. The "we" there is unlikely to be anyone other than the "we" in the sea voyage narrative, and those narratives, too, are likely to be the firsthand accounts of someone involved in the events they describe. This impression of the "we" sections, combined with Luke's explicit but understated truth claim in the gospel prologue (Luke 1:1–4), can provide confidence to the historian that Luke did not believe himself to be writing fiction and that he witnessed some of what he describes.

This impression only increases with a comparison of the details of Paul's work as they appear in his letters with Luke's description of Paul's career in Acts. It is perhaps not surprising that Acts and Paul agree on matters that loom large in the Acts narrative, such as Paul's conversion, his meeting with the apostles in Jerusalem, or the focus of his work on the eastern Mediterranean. Even a highly fictionalized account of the apostle might get those basic details right, especially if, as some scholars believe, the author of Acts wrote with a knowledge of Paul's letters.⁴⁴ A reasonable case exists, however, that although the correspondence between Acts and Paul's letters reaches to small details, it does this in a way that is consistent with independent accounts.

According to both Luke and Paul, for example, Paul's conversion happened near Damascus (Acts 9:3; Gal 1:17), and a long time lapsed before he visited Jerusalem after his conversion (Acts 9:23; Gal 1:18). When he did leave Damascus, he had to escape in a basket and through an opening in the wall because the authorities there wanted to arrest him and were watching the normal city exits (Acts 9:25; 2 Cor 11:32–33). It is possible that Luke retrieved all of this from Galatians and Second Corinthians. Some scholars have pointed especially to the story of Paul's escape from Damascus as an indicator that Luke both found the story in Paul's letters and then edited it according to his supposed tendency to blame the Jews for the persecution of the early Christians. So, the theory goes, Luke changed what he found in 2 Corinthians to picture Paul fleeing from the Jews (Acts 9:23) rather than from "the governor under King Aretas" (2 Cor 11:32).⁴⁵

There is nothing historically implausible, however, about Paul experiencing persecution from some people within the massive Jewish population of Damascus (Josephus, *B.J.* 2.561; 7.368; cf. 1 Thess 2:14–15).⁴⁶ In addition, as one interpreter has noticed, Luke's "basket" (σπυρίς) is smaller than Paul's "basket" (σαργάνη), diminishing the physical size of Paul himself in the narrative and working against Luke's "valorization of Paul elsewhere (e.g., 9:22)."⁴⁷ Did Luke edit the story he found in 2 Corinthians to turn Paul's persecutors into Jewish people but also edit it to contradict his tendency to make a hero of Paul? It seems at least as reasonable to think of Luke reflecting the details of a source other than Paul's letters.

Similarly, according to Acts, Paul's Hebrew name was "Saul," and this is information that only Acts conveys (7:58–13:9). It fits neatly, however, with Paul's own claim that he belonged to "the tribe of Benjamin" (Phil 3:5) whose most famous member was King Saul (1 Sam 9:1–2).⁴⁸ Again, it seems as reasonable to think of Luke preserving historically accurate information about Paul on this point as to think of him creating Paul's Hebrew name.

When Paul narrates a moment of theological tension with the apostle Peter and others at Antioch, he comments that "even Barnabas" failed to support his viewpoint (Gal 2:13). Paul's disappointment becomes comprehensible against Luke's portrait of Barnabas as an unselfish, encouraging person who had taken "Saul" under his wing and worked closely with him both in Antioch and on an extensive church-planting effort (Acts 4:36–37; 9:27; 11:24; 13:1–3). At the same time, although Acts never speaks of the dispute at Antioch, it does indicate that eventually Paul and Barnabas argued and parted ways (Acts 15:39).

After parting ways with Barnabas, Paul's new traveling companions according to Luke were Silas (the "Silvanus" of Paul's letters) and Timothy (Acts 15:40; 16:1–3). On a journey around the Aegean Sea, they established groups of believers in Philippi, Thessalonica, Athens, and Corinth among other places (Acts 15:39–18:18a). In Paul's letters to these communities, these same companions show up in ways that synchronize neatly with Acts. Timothy joins Paul in writing to the Philippians (Phil 1:1) and was well-known to them (Phil 2:22). Silvanus and Timothy both join Paul in writing to the Thessalonians (1 Thess 1:1; 2 Thess 1:1), and Paul mentions in passing in 1 Thessalonians that he had traveled to Athens after establishing the Thessalonian church (1 Thess 3:1). He also mentions in passing in 2 Corinthians that "Silvanus and Timothy and I" proclaimed Jesus Christ in Corinth (2 Cor 1:19).

The order in which they visited these places, moreover, is the same in both sources. Paul indicates in 1 Thessalonians that he, Silvanus, and Timothy (1:1) traveled from Philippi, where they were "shamefully treated," to Thessalonica where, again, they met with "much conflict" (2:2; cf. Phil 4:16). After being "torn away" from Thessalonica (1 Thess 2:17), Paul and Timothy, at least, traveled to Athens (1 Thess 3:1). Paul says in passing that he sent Timothy from Athens back to Thessalonica to check on the new and beleaguered believers there (1 Thess 3:1–3), and then, again in passing in 2 Corinthians, he indicates that he, Silvanus, and Timothy were together in Corinth where they preached the gospel (2 Cor 1:19). Luke's narrative parallels all of this remarkably closely—persecution in Philippi and Thessalonica (Acts 16:19–34; 17:5–9), separation from each other around the time of the journey to Athens (Acts 17:14–15), and then reunion in Corinth (Acts 18:5).

Luke's account and Paul's letters, moreover, can be mutually illuminating. For example, Luke says that "when Silas and Timothy arrived from Macedonia, Paul was occupied with the word" (Acts 18:5), implying that before this time he was not as fully occupied with proclaiming the gospel. In 2 Corinthians 11:9, as Murray Harris points out, we find out why.[49] "When I was with you and was in need," Paul tells the Corinthians, "I did not burden anyone, for the brothers who came from Macedonia supplied my need." When Silas and Timothy arrived from Macedonia, Paul was able to devote himself to preaching the word (Acts) because they brought gifts from the Macedonians (Paul's letters) that allowed him to work at manual labor less and at preaching the gospel more.

The only complication arises around the separation in Athens. Reading 1 Thessalonians 3:1–3 by itself leaves the impression that Paul, Timothy, and perhaps Silvanus were together in Athens, and that Paul sent Timothy from Athens to Thessalonica. This left Paul "behind at Athens alone," perhaps with Silvanus, if he is part of Paul's "we" (1 Thess 3:1). Reading Acts by itself, however, gives the impression that Silas and Timothy stayed behind in Macedonia while Paul pressed on to Athens (Acts 17:14–15) and that Paul did not see his companions again until their reunion in Corinth "when Silas and Timothy arrived from Macedonia" (Acts 18:5).[50] Luke hints that the situation was more complicated than his highly condensed narrative reveals, however, when he says that after Paul arrived in Athens he "was waiting" there—in Athens—for Silas and Timothy to join him (Acts 17:16). Evidently, Paul traveled to Athens alone, but Timothy, at least, traveled back and forth from Macedonia to Athens and then, eventually, together with Silas from Macedonia to Corinth (Acts 18:5; 2 Cor 1:19).[51]

The significance of this complication is not that it calls into question Luke's intention and ability to write an accurate historical narrative but that it teaches us how to read Luke. He wants to tell the story truthfully, but his space, knowledge, and purposes were limited, so he often compressed his narrative in ways that leave out information important to Paul.[52] Thus, Luke's "many days" separating Paul's conversion near Damascus and his first visit to Jerusalem (Acts 9:23) turns out from Galatians to have been three years, most of it spent in what Paul calls "Arabia" (Gal 1:17–18), or the Nabatean Kingdom whose northern border extended to an area just east of Damascus.[53] Similarly, Luke's comment that "when Paul had gone through" the regions of Macedonia "and had given them much encouragement, he came to Greece" (Acts 20:2) probably covers an enormous and complex journey from Ephesus to Troas (2 Cor 2:12) to Macedonia (2 Cor 2:13; 7:5) to Illyricum (Rom 15:19).

APPENDIX 1

It is possible that Luke creatively constructed all this from his reading of Paul's letters.⁵⁴ The correspondence between the cities on which Luke focuses in Acts 15:36–20:16 and the cities to which Paul wrote letters is indeed close.⁵⁵ It is not, however, exact. Paul never mentions Berea in his letters, but Luke tells the story of Paul's work in the city.⁵⁶ Perhaps it is possible to account for this exception by theorizing that Luke created his story of Paul's ministry in Berea out of a literary knowledge of the geography of the region (cf. Cicero, *Pis.* 36.89) and the mention of Berea in a list of the collection delegates to which he had access (Acts 20:4).⁵⁷ Is this explanation more plausible, however, than the theory that Luke's source was the historical Paul himself? Those who opt for a connection between Luke and Paul do not seem to be making an unreasonable choice. Paul's letters and the cities of Luke's narrative focus would then correspond fairly closely because these were the cities where Paul's gospel flourished and where people wanted to preserve the letters Paul had written to them.

On the theory that Luke knew and occasionally accompanied Paul, he would certainly have known that the apostle wrote letters. It is hard to imagine, for example, that he was with Paul in "Greece" just before his journey to Jerusalem but was unaware of the apostle's letter to the Romans (Acts 20:2–6).⁵⁸ It is not unreasonable, however, to take the combination of similarities and divergences between Acts and Paul's letters to indicate that Luke probably did not use the corpus of Paul's letters as a source.

In Conclusion

Luke, then, was a careful historian by ancient standards. He certainly had his own viewpoint and purposes, and he felt free to compress details, but when we can check him against Paul's letters, a plausible case can be made for his accuracy. It is reasonable to consider Acts an early and reliable source for Paul's career and thought, able to supplement the firsthand information that comes from Paul's thirteen canonical letters. Together these two sources are the earliest available for Paul and show evidence of authenticity and reliability.

APPENDIX 2

The Historical Setting of Paul's Imprisonment Letters

Five New Testament letters that bear Paul's name claim to have come from prison, and Colossians refers to yet another letter from prison (Col 4:16), no longer extant, bringing the total to six. How many of these letters are genuine? Where was Paul in prison when he wrote them? These questions are controversial in New Testament scholarship, with many scholars limiting the genuine letters to two (Philippians and Philemon), others accepting three (Philippians, Philemon, and Colossians), a few accepting four (Philippians, Philemon, Colossians, and 2 Timothy), and many still advocating the traditional view that Paul wrote all five letters (Philippians, Philemon, Colossians, Ephesians, and 2 Timothy).[1]

An interpreter's answer to these questions, moreover, tends to correlate with his or her confidence in the authenticity of these letters and level of confidence in the historical accuracy of Acts. Those who accept only Philippians and Philemon as genuine tend to have a low level of confidence in Acts. One such scholar, for example, believes that the Acts narrative distorts the real identity of Paul as a person of low social status whom magistrates often imprisoned as a religious troublemaker.[2] It is necessary, then, to think of possible locations for Paul's imprisonment when he wrote these letters that derive from Paul's own, authentic letters rather than from Acts. Caesarea and Rome are unattractive possibilities to these interpreters since apart from Acts, and a particular understanding of "praetorium" and "Caesar's household" in Philippians (Phil 1:13; 4:22), no one would guess that Paul had been imprisoned in either Caesarea or Rome. These scholars tend to opt for an imprisonment in the Aegean area, perhaps Ephesus or some unknown location in Asia.[3] Those who have higher levels of confidence in Acts gravitate toward one of three possibilities: Ephesus, Caesarea, or Rome.

APPENDIX 2

As appendix 1 explains, it makes historical sense to accept all five imprisonment letters as genuine and to understand Acts as a valuable historical source for Paul's life, at times providing the narrative of a participant in his travels. If that is right, it also makes sense to reconstruct the place of Paul's imprisonment when he wrote these letters using all five letters and Luke's account of Paul. Determining the order of the imprisonment letters is speculative, but deciding on Paul's location when he wrote them enables a plausible scenario to emerge.

Ephesus, Caesarea, or Rome?

Some scholars argue that part or all of the imprisonment letters come from Ephesus.[4] Although Acts never mentions an Ephesian imprisonment, the argument goes, Paul himself speaks of frequent imprisonments (2 Cor 6:5; 11:23), and since he says that he experienced great conflict and suffering that brought him to the brink of death around the time of his work in Ephesus (1 Cor 15:32; 2 Cor 1:8–10), he might well have been imprisoned there.[5] An Ephesian imprisonment might then be the moment when Prisca and Aquila "risked their necks for [Paul's] life" (Rom 16:3) or when Paul was in prison with Andronicus and Junius (Rom 16:7).[6]

If this is right, then Paul's letter to the Philippians fits neatly into an Ephesian imprisonment. When Paul wrote the letter, he was planning to travel to Philippi after his release (Phil 1:26–27; 2:24), just as during his Ephesian period in Acts he was planning to travel next to Macedonia, where Philippi was located (Acts 19:21).[7] When he wrote Philippians, moreover, he planned to send Timothy to Philippi in his place as soon as he had a good idea what his fate would be but before he could go to Philippi himself (Phil 2:23–24). According to Acts, this is exactly what happened while he was in Ephesus: "And having sent into Macedonia two of his helpers, Timothy and Erastus, he himself stayed in Asia for a while" (Acts 19:22).[8] If, however, Paul wrote Philippians from Rome, it becomes necessary to imagine that he changed the travel plan he expressed in Romans 15:24 and 28 to go to Rome and then to Spain.[9]

The multiple trips for himself and his coworkers that Paul presupposes between his current location and Philippi and Colossae (Phil 1:26; 2:19–30; Phlm 12, 22), moreover, are much easier to imagine if Paul was in Ephesus when he wrote Philippians, Colossians, and Philemon. Philippi and Colossae were relatively close to Ephesus but distant from both Rome and Caesarea.[10]

Opponents of an Ephesian location for Philippians used to point out that Paul says his imprisonment for Christ had become known "throughout the whole imperial guard" and to argue that the phrase most likely refers to the praetorians, Caesar's elite group of soldiers stationed mainly in Rome. A more literal translation of what Paul says, however, is that his imprisonment for Christ had become known "in the whole praetorium" (1:12 ESV margin). The word "praetorium" here could refer simply to a civic building of some kind, whether in Ephesus or elsewhere in the province of Asia.[11]

It is harder to account for Ephesians and 2 Timothy as genuine Pauline letters if they originated in an Ephesian imprisonment. Ephesians pictures Tychicus carrying the letter to its destination and reporting on Paul's circumstances to its readers (Eph 6:21–22) who could hardly, then, be in Ephesus. Second Timothy, moreover, clearly refers to Paul's place of imprisonment in Rome (2 Tim 1:17). One scholar who thinks that Ephesians is authentic but originated in Ephesus takes advantage of the textual uncertainty at the beginning of the letter and omits the phrase "in Ephesus" in its address (Eph 1:1). Perhaps, he argues, this letter was the "letter from Laodicea" that Paul refers to at the end of Colossians (Col 4:16).[12] If 2 Timothy is authentic, there is really no plausible way to argue that Paul penned the word of gratitude for Onesiphorus who found him in Rome from an Ephesian prison (2 Tim 1:17). One scholar believes that the other imprisonment letters (or at least the ones he considers authentic) came from Ephesus, but that Paul wrote 2 Timothy from prison in Rome.[13]

The plausibility of an Ephesian imprisonment rises and falls with one's willingness to assign other contexts to these two letters or to set Acts aside as historically problematic. No matter how one fits the puzzle together, though, the fact remains that there is no reliable evidence Paul was ever in prison in Ephesus.[14] The statements in Paul's letters about struggles in Ephesus and suffering in Asia do not mention imprisonment, and Paul's references to multiple imprisonments do not mention Ephesus. All of this is compatible with an Ephesian imprisonment, but the imprisonment itself remains speculative. Similarly, it is easy to think of reasons why Luke might omit an imprisonment in Ephesus from his narrative, but Luke's silence on an imprisonment despite his long account of Paul's work in the city (Acts 18:19–21; 19:1–20:1, 18–21, 26–27, 31, 33–35; 21:29) still counts against the theory.

As an alternative to either Rome or Ephesus, a small cadre of careful scholars over the last three centuries has maintained that some or all of Paul's prison epistles came from the long confinement that, at least according to Luke, Paul experienced in Caesarea (Acts 23:33–27:1). The case is surprisingly persuasive.

In his letter to the Philippians, the argument goes, Paul's reference to the gospel's advancement "in the whole praetorium" (1:13 ESV margin) most naturally refers to a building, and Luke says that Felix imprisoned Paul in Caesarea in "Herod's praetorium" (Acts 23:35).[15] Paul says in Philippians, moreover, that he will send Timothy to the Philippian Christians "soon" (Phil 2:19). In the meantime, perhaps he wrote Colossians and Philemon. Timothy joins Paul as a co-sender of those letters, and both letters mention Aristarchus and Luke, who, judging from the Acts narrative, were with Paul at this time (Acts 20:4–6; 27:2).[16] The picture of Aristarchus as Paul's "fellow prisoner" (Col 4:10) fits this situation neatly, moreover, since Aristarchus accompanied Paul from Caesarea to Rome (Acts 27:2).[17]

Tychicus was also with Paul at this point (cf. Acts 20:4), and before Tychicus took Colossians and Philemon to Colossae, Timothy probably left for Philippi as Paul had promised the Philippian Christians he would do (Phil 2:19).[18] Paul then wrote Ephesians, which does not mention Timothy as a co-sender, and sent Colossians, Philemon, and Ephesians with Tychicus to their respective destinations. As a co-sender of the letter to the Colossians, Timothy would have known that Tychicus would be taking Colossians and Philemon to Colossae since he and Paul mention this plan at the end of Colossians (Col 4:7–9). Timothy would not have known, however, that Paul had written a letter to the Ephesians and sent it with Tychicus who would now need to go to Ephesus as well as Colossae. This explains why Paul informs Timothy in 2 Timothy that he has sent Tychicus to Ephesus (2 Tim 4:12).[19]

If Timothy was in Philippi when he received 2 Timothy, then it would be no trouble for him to return to Paul via Troas and Colossae. He would stop in Troas to collect Paul's poncho from Carpus (2 Tim 4:13) and travel through Colossae to collect Mark (Col 4:10; 2 Tim 4:11). These would be natural stopping points on his way back east to Paul in Caesarea.[20]

Paul, for his part, would have still hoped in the early months of his imprisonment that he would soon be released and that from Caesarea he could put his plan to reach Rome and eventually Spain into effect. On his way west, he would stop in Colossae where, he hoped, Philemon would receive him as a guest (Phlm 22).[21] This expectation had faded, however, by the time he wrote 2 Timothy, and the loss of hope for release in Caesarea led him finally to appeal to Caesar in Rome (Acts 25:11–12; 26:32; 28:19).[22]

This is such a plausible scenario that at first it seems like the obvious way to put the puzzle pieces together. Unfortunately, for this form of the theory to work it is necessary to take two unsteady exegetical steps.

First, the theory must assign Philippians to a city other than Rome, yet Rome seems to be the most likely location for the letter. It is true that the word "praetorium" that Paul uses in Philippians (Phil 1:13) commonly designated a building and therefore could refer to the praetorium where Paul was imprisoned in Caesarea (Acts 23:35). The emperor Vespasian, however, could speak of soldiers serving "in my praetorium," meaning that they served in the special group of soldiers assigned to him in Rome (*ILS* 1993).[23] Paul also seems to use the phrase "in the whole praetorium" to refer to a group of people (the praetorian guard) because he immediately follows the phrase with "and to all the rest," referring to a parallel group of people.[24] Paul, then, could have used the word "praetorium" to refer to the emperor's personal soldiers in their large encampment a short walk northeast of Rome's Viminal Gate.

Michael Flexsenhar has argued passionately that a Roman imprisonment for Paul does not work in part because Paul's social status was far too low to merit the praetorian guard's involvement in his confinement.[25] Paul's statement, however, does not say that the praetorians were guarding him but only that "the whole praetorium" knew he was in prison for Christ. This could easily mean that Paul thought some of the soldiers quartered in the praetorian barracks had heard rumors about him.[26] Perhaps they remembered, or had heard of, the disturbances that "Chrestus" had caused in Rome about a decade earlier (Suetonius, *Claud.* 25.4) and took a special interest in this Christian prisoner who had appealed his case to Caesar.

If this reference to the "praetorium" stood alone, it would not imply a Roman location for Paul as he wrote the letter. It combines, however, with the greetings he sent at the end of the letter to the Philippians from "the saints . . . of Caesar's household" (Phil 4:22) to support the letter's Roman origin. Flexsenhar has shown that "Caesar's household" is a reference to a specific group of slaves "who worked in a particular part of the broader imperial bureaucracy" and therefore need not be located in Rome. The highest concentration of such slaves, however, as Flexsenhar concedes, would be in Rome.[27] Paul's reference to "saints . . . of Caesar's household" in the location from which he writes, combined with his mention of "the whole praetorium," makes Rome the most likely location for the letter.

Second, if 2 Timothy originated in Caesarea, then it becomes necessary to explain in extraordinarily improbable ways Paul's statement that when "Onesiphorus . . . arrived in Rome he searched for me and earnestly found me" (1:16–17).[28] Bo Reicke and John A. T. Robinson both suggested, for example, that this statement means Onesiphorus arrived in Rome expecting to find Paul there, failed to do so, and earnestly searched for him by traveling to Caesarea.[29] Without a clear indication otherwise from the text, however, Paul's statement that Onesiphorus searched for him in Rome and found him would be extremely odd if it meant that Onesiphorus found Paul anywhere but in Rome.

Once 2 Timothy finds its home in Rome, the overlap of the names mentioned in the letter and the names mentioned in Colossians and Philemon makes it likely that those letters come from the same city. Mark, Demas, and Luke all show up in Colossians and Philemon, just as they show up in 2 Timothy and nowhere else in Paul's letters (Col 4:10, 14; 2 Tim 4:10–11; Phlm 24). All of them, moreover, had been with Paul in the city from which he writes each letter. This makes it likely that all three letters originated in the same city, and, as 2 Timothy 1:17 makes clear, that city was Rome.

The Order of Paul's Letters from Prison

If it is difficult to know where Paul was in prison when he wrote some or all of his imprisonment letters, it is even more difficult to know the order in which he wrote them. It is possible, however, to make a reasonable guess. Perhaps the letters should come first that express optimism about Paul's release. In Philippians, Paul expresses some doubt about his fate (Phil 1:20) but, in the end, is "convinced" that he will survive (Phil 1:25) and expects to be able to visit the Philippian Christians "shortly" (Phil 2:24). In Philemon, too, Paul is hopeful that he would be released and able to take advantage of Philemon's guest room in Colossae (Phlm 22).[30] Since Philemon and Colossians send greetings from many of the same people (Epaphras, Mark,

The Historical Setting of Paul's Imprisonment Letters

Aristarchus, Demas, and Luke), and since Archippus is in the audience of both letters, it seems likely that Paul wrote them at basically the same time (Col 4:10, 12, 14, 17; Phlm 1, 23–24).

Paul wrote Philippians, Philemon, and Colossians, moreover, while Timothy was with him in Rome. Paul allies himself with Timothy in the opening greeting of all three letters. At first it seems puzzling, then, that Timothy does not appear in the opening greeting of Ephesians, nor anywhere else in that letter. Paul must have written Ephesians at roughly the same time as Colossians and Philemon since Paul commends Tychicus as the letter carrier to the readers of Colossians and Ephesians and does so in almost identical language near the end of each letter (Col 4:7–8; Eph 6:21–22). Furthermore, the subject of Philemon is the return of Onesimus to his master, a return that happened in the company of Tychicus (Col 4:9). If Philippians, Philemon, Colossians, and Ephesians were written near in time to each other, then why is Timothy missing from Ephesians? The answer to this puzzle may lie in Paul's comment in Philippians that he will send Timothy to the Christian community there "as soon as" he gets some clarity about his own situation in Rome (Phil 2:23–24).[31]

At some point shortly after Paul wrote Philemon and Colossians, Timothy may have left for points east (including Philippi), and Paul wrote Ephesians after his departure. He then sent Tychicus and Onesimus to Ephesus, Laodicea, and Colossae with all three letters, and with the mysterious letter to the Laodiceans (Col 4:16).

Paul probably wrote 2 Timothy last. Among the scholars who think that the letter is genuine, most ascribe it to a theoretical second imprisonment of Paul in Rome.[32] This rests on the ancient idea that Paul was released from his first imprisonment, traveled freely for a time, and then was rearrested in Rome where he wrote 2 Timothy and was executed late in Nero's reign. This would be a period of Paul's life, therefore, that falls outside the narrative of Acts (Eusebius, *Hist. eccl.* 2.22).[33]

Among those scholars who adopt this idea, a typical approach to the data locates Philippians, Philemon, Colossians, and Ephesians within Paul's first Roman imprisonment, but 1 and 2 Timothy and Titus, whose style and ethos are similar, in a period after the close of the Acts narrative and before his death in Rome.[34] The travel and personal details that appear sparsely in 1 Timothy and Titus, but more prolifically in 2 Timothy, can therefore find a home in the open space between Paul's two imprisonments.

On this reading of 2 Timothy, then, at some point Paul decided to travel east rather than to Spain after his release (Phil 1:18–19, 24–26; 2:24; Phlm 22). Once free, he traveled to Crete where he left Titus (Titus 1:5), then on to Ephesus where he left Timothy (1 Tim 1:3). He then traveled to Nicopolis (Titus 3:12) via Macedonia (1 Tim 1:3) but on his way back to Ephesus (1 Tim 3:14) was arrested in Troas where he left his coat and books with Carpus (2 Tim 4:13). Somewhere in these travels, he left Trophimus ill at Miletus and left Erastus in Corinth (2 Tim 4:20), both places that he might easily have stopped along this route.

A scenario like this avoids the seemingly intractable problem of trying to account for the travel plans and personal references of 2 Timothy within the single Roman imprisonment that Luke describes. Why would Paul tell Timothy to pick up clothing and books that he had left before his arrest years earlier at Troas (cf. Acts 20:6–12)? Why would he say that Erastus "remained" at Corinth or that he had left Trophimus ill at Miletus, places that Paul did not pass through on his way to Rome as a prisoner?[35] If Paul were speaking of events that occurred before his arrest several years earlier, what would be their relevance now? Since Timothy had been with Paul in Rome (Phil 1:1; Col 1:1; Phlm 1), surely he would know these details anyway.

The trouble with solving the problem of the travel details in 2 Timothy by means of a second imprisonment, however, is that Luke hints strongly throughout his narrative that Paul would not make it out of his legal tangle with the Jerusalem nobility alive. In the speech that Paul gave to the Ephesian elders in Miletus during his final journey to Jerusalem, Paul casts a shadow over his future: "I do not account my life of any value nor as precious to myself, if only I may finish my course and the ministry that I received from the Lord Jesus, to testify to the gospel of the grace of God. And now, behold, I know that none of you among whom I have gone about proclaiming the kingdom will see my face again" (Acts 20:24–25). Luke notes that as Paul left the elders after the speech, "there was much weeping on the part of all." They were sad "most of all," says Luke, "because of the word [Paul] had spoken, that they would not see his face again" (20:38). Paul had given a long speech, but this was the part of it Luke chose to highlight.[36]

Only a few sentences later, Luke describes Paul's visit with believers in Tyre and Caesarea, stopping places along Paul's route to Jerusalem. In Tyre, Luke says, the disciples "were telling Paul not to go to Jerusalem," an ominous note that Luke strengthens with the comment that the disciples said this to Paul "through the Spirit" (Acts 21:4). Several sentences later still, when Paul is in Caesarea, the prophet Agabus foretells Paul's arrest in Jerusalem (21:11), and Paul responds with, "I am ready not only to be imprisoned but even to die in Jerusalem for the name of the Lord Jesus" (21:13).

It is true, as interpreters often observe, that Luke also shows the case of Paul's accusers to be weak and emphasizes that the officials in charge of his case believed he was innocent (Acts 23:29; 25:18–19, 25; 26:31, 32).[37] Counterbalancing this, however, is the narrative parallel Luke must have intended between the passion of Jesus and the arrest and various legal hearings of Paul. Both appeared before the Sanhedrin (Luke 22:66–71; Acts 22:30–23:10), both appeared before the Roman governor of Judea (Luke 23:1–5; Acts 23:33–24:23), both appeared before a Herodian ruler of an area neighboring Judea (Luke 23:6–12; Acts 25:6–26:32), and both were innocent of the charges against them (Luke 23:4, 14–15, 22; Acts 23:9, 29; 25:18–19, 25; 26:31, 32). Without further indication to the contrary, it seems that Luke's story of Paul's arrest hints that Paul, like Jesus, faced an unjust execution at the end of his judicial ordeal. If 2 Timothy came from Paul's final imprisonment, therefore, and Luke describes the imprisonment experiences that led to Paul's death, then 2 Timothy came from the final imprisonment Luke describes.

What, then, of the difficult references to Paul's cloak and books in Troas, to Erastus remaining at Corinth, and to Paul leaving Trophimus sick at Miletus? Can these references find a plausible place within the span of Paul's ministry covered in Acts 20–28? Why would Paul refer to the location of possessions and coworkers from years earlier when he was a free man?[38] Any effort to answer these questions will be speculative, but it is not too difficult to imagine circumstances that answer them satisfactorily.[39]

Paul might have easily left his books and cloak in Troas when the collection delegation passed through the city on the way to Jerusalem (Acts 20:6). If "Erastus" is the same person whose greetings Paul sends from Corinth to the church in Rome (Rom 16:23), then it is not hard to think of why, at some point, he might have wanted to remain at Corinth. Moreover, if Trophimus was with the prisoner Paul on his journey to Rome (and this does not seem unlikely since he was involved in the incident that led to Paul's arrest), then Paul might have sent him nearer to his home in Ephesus (Acts 21:29) at some point in that journey when he got sick. Perhaps this happened when Paul's ship found shelter in one of the harbors of Cnidus, a simple one-day sailing journey south of Miletus (Acts 27:7).

APPENDIX 2

To understand why Paul might tell Timothy this information several years after it happened, it is necessary to understand one of the main purposes of 2 Timothy 4:9–21. This purpose was so important to Paul that he bookended the passage with clear statements of it: "Do your best to come to me soon," and "Do your best to come before winter" (4:9, 21). The passage calls Timothy to Paul's side and explains why it is so urgent that Timothy should come to him. Between the passages' calls to hasten to his side, Paul repeatedly mentions the distant locations of his coworkers (4:10, 12, 20). Paul might easily have done this not to inform Timothy of geographical details but to emphasize how unavailable most of his coworkers were to him.[40] "Luke alone is with me," he says at one point (4:11). With very few people around to help him, Timothy needed to come to Paul "soon," preferably "before winter," and preferably bringing Mark and Paul's belongings with him (4:9, 11, 13, 21).

Since communicating a sense of urgency was a main point of the passage, the passage itself probably mixed information that Timothy did not know (e.g., Demas had deserted Paul, 4:10) with information he knew (e.g., Trophimus had to be left in Miletus, 4:20). The timing and reason for these absences did not matter as much as the fact of the absences and the necessity, therefore, that Timothy should make haste (4:9, 21).

It does not seem improbable, therefore, that when Paul wrote the five extant imprisonment letters (and his missing letter to the Laodiceans) he was in prison in Rome. If this is right, it is reasonable to think of him writing Philippians first and sending it with Epaphroditus to Philippi. He then wrote a series of letters to the Lycus River Valley in Asia (Philemon, Colossians, and the letter to the Laodiceans) but waited for some reason to send them. When problems emerged in churches somewhere in Asia, Paul sent Timothy to help them, instructing him to visit the Christians in Philippi at some point in his travels. Paul then wrote Ephesians and, eventually, 2 Timothy. Tychicus and Onesimus would have carried Ephesians to Ephesus and Colossians and Philemon to Colossae. It is impossible to know who carried 2 Timothy, but perhaps Tychicus handed it off to someone who knew Timothy's location in the province of Asia.

APPENDIX 3

The Place, Manner, and Time of Paul's Death

The massive nineteenth-century sculpture of Saint Paul in the courtyard of the Basilica of St. Paul Outside the Walls in Rome stands near the spot where, according to ancient tradition, Paul's remains were located after his death. In Paul's right hand is a sword depicting the tradition, also ancient, that Paul died by beheading, like many other Roman citizens convicted of a capital crime. Is this what happened, and, if so, is there any indication of when it happened? Is the tradition dating at least as far back as the third century correct that Paul was released from his Roman imprisonment and traveled to Spain? Is the even more ancient tradition likely to be correct that he died around the same time as Peter in Rome and roughly about the time of Nero's horrific persecution of Christians? There are no definitive answers to these questions, but exploring them does yield some useful information about what happened to Paul.

WHERE AND HOW DID PAUL DIE?

The late first- or early second-century letter from the church of Rome to the church of Corinth (usually called "1 Clement") is the earliest witness outside the New Testament to Paul's death.[1] It couples Peter with Paul and briefly describes their demise but, other than saying that Paul testified before rulers, gives no details of his condemnation or execution. Just as Luke was more interested in showing the unhindered progress of the gospel's proclamation than in the details surrounding Paul's death, so Clement was more interested in moral instruction than in anything beyond the most general description of Peter's and Paul's persecution and fight "to the death" (1 Clem. 5.2).

The church at Corinth should avoid internal discord, he argues, because this same problem had led to Peter's "many trials" and to the need for Paul to show "the way to the prize for patient endurance" (1 Clem. 5.4–5). Paul "won the genuine glory for his faith" (5.6), and "when he had given his testimony before the rulers, he thus departed from the world and went to the holy place, having become an outstanding example of patient endurance" (5.7). Clement believed that Paul had appeared at some sort of court hearing and suffered execution as a punishment for his commitment to the Christian faith, but as Wolfgang Grünstäudl has put it, the details are "hidden in praise."[2]

The letter next says that to the suffering and witness of Peter and Paul "there was joined a vast multitude of the elect" who also suffered "torments and tortures because of jealousy" (1 Clem. 6.1). Here Clement becomes slightly more specific about what those "torments and tortures" involved. "Women," he says, "were persecuted as Danaids and Dircae" (6.2). This probably refers to the Roman imperial practice of using condemned criminals in re-enactments of violent stories and would be consistent with the theatrics to which Nero condemned Christians in AD 64 when he blamed the fire of Rome on them.[3] He had them "covered with wild beasts' skins and torn to death by dogs," says the Roman historian Tacitus, or "fastened on crosses, and . . . burned to serve as lamps by night." Nero intended these punishments to be a "spectacle" and presented them in "his Gardens" and as "an exhibition in his Circus" (*Ann.* 15.44 [Jackson, LCL]).[4]

Peter and Paul, according to 1 Clement, were "champions who lived nearest to our time" compared to the great heroes of biblical times, and both the deaths of Peter and Paul and the deaths of the "vast multitude" that suffered like them belong "to our own generation" (5.1). Clement, then, seems to have lived during a time when the persecutions under Nero were in the not-too-distant past.[5] Although he never says so explicitly, moreover, his idea that the Christians whom Nero rounded up and punished were "joined" (συνηθροίσθη) to Peter and Paul seems to imply that both apostles had died in Rome not long before the outbreak of the persecution.

It is important to emphasize, however, that there is no explicit information here.[6] Like Luke, Clement knew what happened to Peter and Paul, but he assumed that his audience in Corinth knew this too and did not deviate from his purpose of moral instruction to describe the details.

The Place, Manner, and Time of Paul's Death

The mid- to late second century saw a proliferation of "information" about the fate of Paul in Rome. Dionysius, bishop of Corinth sometime in the latter half of the second century, wrote a letter to the Roman Christians in which he spoke of Paul's martyrdom occurring "in Italy" at the same time as Peter's death (Eusebius, *Hist. eccl.* 2.25.8). Dionysius was familiar with 1 Clement, however, and his information may only be a conjecture based on that letter (Eusebius, *Hist. eccl.* 4.23.11).

Slightly more significant is the evidence that comes from a Roman Christian of roughly the same time named Gaius.[7] Gaius was an opponent of a Christian movement centered in Phrygia in Asia Minor called Montanism (Eusebius, *Hist. eccl.* 6.20.3). This movement valued the utterances of prophets within its community and claimed some connection to "Philip," the evangelist by that name mentioned in Acts (Acts 6:5; 8:4–8, 26–40; 21:8). Philip's four daughters were prophets (21:9), and the Montanists seem to have asserted that these women were early leaders of their movement.[8] Gaius was familiar with the writings of one of the second-century teachers within this movement named Proclus, and Proclus maintained that Philip and his four daughters had lived in Hierapolis in the Lycus River Valley. "Their tomb is there," said Proclus, "and that of their father."[9] Apparently in answer to this statement, Gaius, who was a resident of Rome, claims this: "I myself can point out the trophies of the apostles. For if it is your will to proceed to the Vatican, or to the Ostian Way, you will find the trophies of those who founded this church."[10] A "trophy" (τροπαῖον) was a "monument for having put the enemy to flight."[11] The enemy in this instance would have been Nero, and the monuments would have been physical memorials to the martyrdom of Paul and Peter. In the competition for an attachment to the earliest Christians, Gaius seems to have thought he had bested Proclus.

Gaius spoke as if these monuments were well-known, and if that is correct, then by the time he was writing in the late second or early third century, they had already been around for some time. Within the second century, therefore, probably no later than a century after the deaths of Peter and Paul and only slightly later than 1 Clement, Christians in Rome knew where monuments were located celebrating the triumph of Peter and Paul over their enemy Nero through their faithful death.

Around the same time that Gaius wrote his anti-Montanist essay, someone constructed an account of Paul's ministry and travels that deviates wildly from the canonical Acts.[12] Like the travels of Paul in Luke's account, however, the apostle's journeys in the Acts of Paul end in Rome, and, once he arrives there, the Acts tells a detailed story of his martyrdom (Acts Paul 14). This story begins not with Paul in confinement, as in the canonical Acts, but with the apostle preaching to jam-packed crowds in a barn he has rented outside the city. The overcrowding leads to disaster when a cupbearer in Nero's court falls Eutychus-like out of a high window. Although a prayerful appeal to the Lord Jesus Christ raises him from the dead, Nero becomes first frightened and then angry, especially when he learns that his cupbearer and others in his court have become soldiers in the army of another king—Christ. This leads to mass arrests and executions, including Paul's, who was, however, beheaded rather than burned like the rest. After his execution, Paul appears to Nero, convincing him to stop the carnage. He then appears to two sympathetic officials in Nero's court who have gathered at Paul's grave and spooks them into accepting baptism.

At first this tale seems to confirm independently the information in 1 Clement that Paul died in Rome in connection with Nero's persecution of Christians. It even seems to add to this the plausible information that Paul was beheaded. There are signs, however, that the author of the Acts of Paul had read 1 Clement. Prior to the story of Paul's martyrdom, when Paul is in Corinth, he reveals that his ultimate destination is Rome. On learning this, a Corinthian Christian prophet announces that when Paul arrives and begins teaching, he will become a victim of envy, which will lead to his death (Acts Paul 12.3). When Paul gets to Rome and starts teaching in the barn, the devil becomes envious of the love of Christians for each other and oversees the accident that eventually leads to Paul's demise (Acts Paul 14.1). The connection of envy with Paul's death makes it likely that the author was familiar with this same connection in 1 Clement (1 Clem. 5.5).[13]

The author might have easily derived the datum that Paul was beheaded, moreover, from combining a knowledge of Paul's Roman citizenship, learned from Acts, with a knowledge of the Roman legal custom of often beheading (rather than torturing to death) high status prisoners. "Caesar," he says, "... ordered ... Paul ... to be decapitated in accordance with Roman law" (Acts Paul 14.3).[14]

The author would not have received any information about Paul's "grave" (τάφον) from 1 Clement, however, and since he had Montanist

The Place, Manner, and Time of Paul's Death

sympathies, he is unlikely to have studied Gaius's anti-Montanist treatise with its reference to the apostles' "trophies."[15] His mention of a gravesite for Paul where Christians gathered, therefore, is probably independent confirmation that after Paul's death in Rome a monument was raised to him at the place of his burial.

This idea probably receives further confirmation from archaeological evidence found at the site of the Basilica of Saint Paul Outside the Walls in Rome, which burned in 1823. Art historian Nicola Camerlenghi has plausibly suggested that part of the trophy Gaius mentioned appears in the notebooks of an archaeologist who, in 1838, participated in the reconstruction of the church. These notebooks contain a drawing of part of a structure built in the distinctive crosshatch design of *opus reticulatum*. That design seldom occurred in structures built after the second century, and, in this case, a pavement of black-flecked volcanic stone seems to have surrounded the larger structure of which it was a part. When the emperor Constantine built the first basilica over the site in the early fourth century, he seems to have preserved this much older structure. Camerlenghi speculated that the emperor did this because this structure was the ancient "trophy" around which Christians had gathered for centuries to commemorate Paul's martyrdom.[16]

The evidence after the close of the second century does not seem to offer any further reliable information. Near the turn of the century, Tertullian assumes that Paul was beheaded in Rome but also speaks of Paul's reappearance after suffering the penalty reserved for Roman citizens, revealing that he was familiar with the story of Paul's death in the Acts of Paul (*Scorp.* 15). Origen of Caesarea mentioned Paul's death in Rome (*Hist. eccl.* 3.1.3), but he too was familiar with the Acts of Paul and probably knew its tale of Paul's beheading.[17] Eusebius himself connects the death of Paul with Nero's persecution of Christians in Rome (*Hist. eccl.* 2.22.8; 2.25.4–5; 3.31.1) and is clear that sources before him spoke of Paul's beheading there (*Hist. eccl.* 2.25.5), but, once again, he was familiar with the Acts of Paul (*Hist. eccl.* 3.3.5).[18]

It seems reasonably certain, then, that Paul died in Rome at the end of a judicial process which, according to Luke (Acts 27:24), entailed an appearance before Nero.[19] Since condemned Roman citizens were often permitted execution by beheading as a relatively painless death consistent with their social status, and since they also were often allowed burial, the tradition that Paul was beheaded in Rome outside the city along the Ostian Way and that his friends and coworkers were allowed to preserve his remains at a memorial there is certainly possible, perhaps even likely.[20]

When Did Paul Die?

If that is correct, then when did this happen? Was Paul arrested as part of the widespread persecution of Christians in Rome on the heels of the great fire of AD 64, or did he appear before Nero at some earlier time?

An old tradition, going all the way back to 1 Clement in the late first or early second century, claims that Paul died in Rome after he "had preached in the east and in the west" and after reaching "the furthest limits of the west" (1 Clem. 5.6–7). The author of 1 Clement may have simply been commenting in a general way on the sweep of Paul's ministry from east to west.[21] His claim that Paul reached "the furthest limits [τὸ τέρμα] of the west," however, sounds like he meant to refer to Spain, the western extent of the Roman Empire. This is especially true since the author was writing from Rome, and it is difficult to imagine someone in Rome referring to the city itself as the western boundary of the inhabited world.[22]

It is reasonable to think, therefore, that the author believed Paul had made it to Spain. This would fit nicely with Paul's own plans in his letter to the Romans (Rom 15:24, 28), a letter that the author most likely knew (1 Clem. 31.2; 50.6). The question is whether the author simply inferred from Paul's remarks in his letter to Rome that he had reached Spain, or whether he knew from reports about Paul that were circulating around Rome decades later that the apostle had reached "the furthest limits of the west." If Paul had reached Spain after being released from a first Roman imprisonment, then the close association in 1 Clement of the death of Paul with what looks like the persecution of Nero would make chronological sense.

It is only in the mid-third century, however, that an extant Christian text refers explicitly to a journey of Paul to Spain. This text, the so-called Muratorian Canon, probably came from the pen of Victorinus of Pettau around AD 258.[23] In it, Victorinus (or the unknown author) says that in the Acts of the Apostles, Luke's governing principle was to record "only what fell under his own notice" and that this is evident from "the omis-

The Place, Manner, and Time of Paul's Death

sion of the passion of Peter, and also of the journey of Paul, when he went from the city—Rome—to Spain" (§2 [Salmond, *ANF* 5:603]). Victorinus simply assumed as an agreed body of knowledge that Paul was released from confinement after his two years in Rome and traveled from Rome to Spain.[24] There is nothing here about a return to Rome or the fate of Paul, but Victorinus tends to confirm the suspicion that Clement's comment about Paul reaching the limit of the west referred to a journey to Spain.

Roughly half a century later, Eusebius confirms the currency of the theory that Luke ended Acts before Paul's release because he was not with the apostle at the time of his release (*Hist. eccl.* 2.22.6). In addition, he fills in this picture with a wealth of detail that he seems to derive from a close reading of 2 Timothy 4:6–18. He begins his treatment with a general statement of where his exegesis is going: "Tradition has it that after defending himself the Apostle was again sent on the ministry of preaching" (*Hist. eccl.* 2.22.2 [Lake, LCL]). The phrase "tradition has it" (λόγος ἔχει) is probably a reference to 2 Timothy, since Eusebius immediately dives into a picture of Paul's final years derived from that letter.[25] He begins with 2 Timothy 4:17: "The Lord stood by me and strengthened me, so that through me the message might be fully proclaimed and all the Gentiles might hear it. So I was rescued from the lion's mouth."

Eusebius says that he thinks the "lion" is Nero, an appropriate metaphor because of his "ferocity," and that Paul was delivered from his mouth so that he could fulfill the rest of his preaching ministry (*Hist. eccl.* 2.22.4 [Lake, LCL]). He also observes that at the time Paul was writing 2 Timothy he expected to die, since Paul says, "I am already being poured out as a drink offering, and the time of my departure has come" (2 Tim 4:6; *Hist. eccl.* 2.22.5). This means, argues Eusebius, that Paul describes two imprisonments, one that he was in as he wrote the letter and a previous imprisonment that ended in his release and further ministry.

Moreover, Eusebius continues, no one was with Paul at the time of his first defense, but Luke was with him as he wrote 2 Timothy. Eusebius is thinking of Paul's statements that at his "first defense no one came to stand by" him (2 Tim 4:16) and that "Luke alone" was with him when he wrote the letter (4:11). In Eusebius's mind, Luke did not stand with Paul at his first defense because Luke was absent from Rome at that time, and, just as in the Muratorian Canon, Luke's silence in Acts about the outcome of Paul's

369

APPENDIX 3

trial confirms this. Luke *was* with Paul later, however, when Paul wrote 2 Timothy, as Paul clearly states (*Hist. eccl.* 2.22.6). The implication is clear to Eusebius: Paul was in prison in Rome twice, one time that ended in Paul's release, a release that Luke was not there to see and record, and one time when Luke was present with Paul, which Paul refers to in 2 Timothy.

Eusebius's close reading of 2 Timothy 4 does not inspire confidence that he was aware of any evidence beyond what he could have read in 1 Clement (which he knew), or what he might have heard or read about why the Acts of the Apostles ended where it did. He never mentions a journey of Paul to Spain, and his elaborate theory about Paul's first and second imprisonments in Rome seems to arise only from his own reading of 2 Timothy.[26] He clearly believed that Paul had died at the same time as Peter during Nero's persecution of Christians in Rome, but it is unclear whether this belief rested on anything other than what many assumed to be true on the basis of 1 Clement and the presence in Rome of the "trophies" of Peter and Paul.

There is, therefore, no reliable evidence beyond the vague account in 1 Clement and the skimpy archaeological evidence in Rome about what happened to Paul and when it happened. It seems reasonable to conclude that Paul died in Rome, a conclusion that Luke's foreshadowing of his death in Rome confirms. The evidence in 1 Clement is also consistent with the idea that he and Peter both died prior to the outbreak of Nero's more widespread persecution of Christians after the great fire of Rome in AD 64. Those who died after the great fire were "joined" to Peter and Paul in their faithful deaths (1 Clem. 6.1). The idea that Paul reached Spain and that he traveled to Spain after his release from the Roman imprisonment Luke describes might easily reflect speculation on Romans 15:22–29 and Acts 28:30–31, and the further details in Eusebius seem to arise from his own exegesis of 2 Timothy 4.

Notes

CHAPTER 1

1. "When Rabban Gamaliel the Elder died, the glory of the Law ceased and purity and abstinence died" (m. Sotah 9:15, trans. Herbert Danby, *The Mishnah: Translated from the Hebrew with Introduction and Brief Explanatory Notes* [Oxford: Oxford University Press, 1933]). On Gamaliel, see Bruce Chilton (s.v. "Gamaliel," *ABD* 2:904–6), who doubts, however, that Paul was ever his student. For reasons why I accept the accuracy of Luke's portrait of Paul, see appendix 1.

2. See the discussions in Jerome Murphy-O'Connor, *Paul: A Critical Life* (Oxford: Clarendon, 1996), 1–4; and Craig S. Keener, *Acts: An Exegetical Commentary*, 4 vols. (Grand Rapids: Baker, 2012–2015), 2:1447–53.

3. Rainer Riesner, *Paul's Early Period: Chronology, Mission Strategy, Theology*, trans. Douglas W. Stott (Grand Rapids: Eerdmans, 1998), 63.

4. Translations of Strabo throughout come from Duane W. Roller, *The "Geography" of Strabo: An English Translation with Introduction and Notes* (Cambridge: Cambridge University Press, 2014).

5. W. M. Ramsay, *The Cities of St. Paul: Their Influence on His Life and Thought* (London: Hodder & Stoughton, 1907), 93, 109.

6. C. Bradford Welles, "Hellenistic Tarsus," *Mélanges de l'Université Saint Joseph* 38 (1962): 47, 52.

7. Cited in Welles, "Hellenistic Tarsus," 52.

8. Welles, "Hellenistic Tarsus," 54; C. P. Jones, *The Roman World of Dio Chrysostom* (Cambridge, MA: Harvard University Press, 1978), 72.

9. Welles, "Hellenistic Tarsus," 61–62. John Clayton Lentz Jr. doubts that many Jews were full citizens of Greek cities like Tarsus, but he admits that "the terms citizen (πολίτης) and citizenship (πολιτεία) are ambiguous" (*Luke's Portrait of Paul*, SNTSMS 77 [Cambridge: Cambridge University Press, 1993], 32–43). Even on his analysis, Jews could attain recognition and protection within a city and their community within the city could be described as a πολίτευμα.

10. Martin Hengel, *The Pre-Christian Paul*, trans. John Bowden (London: SCM, 1991), 2–3.

11. Lentz (*Luke's Portrait of Paul*, 56) is unwilling to accept at face value that there were Pharisees living in a diaspora city such as Tarsus but admits that "the evidence is far from conclusive."

12. Hengel, *Pre-Christian Paul*, 29–34.

13. Joachim Schaper, "The Pharisees," in *The Early Roman Period, Part 2*, ed. William Horbury, W. D. Davies, and John Sturdy, vol. 3 of *The Cambridge History of Judaism*, ed. W. D. Davies and Louis Finkelstein (Cambridge: Cambridge University Press, 1999), 402–4.

14. Cf. Schaper, "The Pharisees," 403–4.

15. H. G. M. Williamson, *Ezra, Nehemiah*, WBC 16 (Nashville: Thomas Nelson, 1985), 334.

16. Williamson, *Ezra, Nehemiah*, 335–36. The half-shekel tax connected with the census in Exod 30:11–17 was for the construction of the tabernacle and for a memorial of atonement. On this, see J. Liver, "The Half-Shekel Offering in Biblical and Post-Biblical Literature," *HTR* 56 (1963): 176–77.

17. Schaper, "Pharisees," 406–8.

18. Joel Marcus, *Mark 1–8*, AB 27 (New York: Doubleday, 2000), 440–41, 521.

19. Even Chilton, who is skeptical that Acts is historically accurate in its portrayal of Gamaliel, believes that "Gamaliel's relative tolerance of Jesus' followers is, in itself, plausible" ("Gamaliel," 905).

20. On the date and meaning of this mishnah, see David Instone-Brewer, *Prayer and Agriculture*, vol. 1 of *Traditions of the Rabbis from the Era of the New Testament*, 6 vols. (Grand Rapids: Eerdmans, 2004), 178–79.

21. For what follows in this paragraph, see Martin Hengel and Roland Deines, "E. P. Sanders' 'Common Judaism,' Jesus, and the Pharisees," *JTS* 46 (1995): 45–47; and Hannah K. Harrington, "Did the Pharisees Eat Ordinary Food in a State of Ritual Purity?," *JSJ* 26 (1995): 42–54.

22. Instone-Brewer, *Prayer and Agriculture*, 169–94.

23. Schaper, "Pharisees," 424.

24. Cf. Schaper, "Pharisees," 424–25.

25. Schaper, "Pharisees," 425.

26. E. P. Sanders, *Jesus and Judaism* (Philadelphia: Fortress, 1985), 177–88.

27. Marcus, *Mark 1–8*, 226, 230.

28. David Instone-Brewer, *Feasts and Sabbaths: Passover and Atonement*, vol. 2A of *Traditions of the Rabbis from the Era of the New Testament*, 6 vols. (Grand Rapids: Eerdmans, 2011), 43.

29. See BDAG 1011, s.v. τόπος 1b, although the editors acknowledge that the term is ambiguous.

30. Cf. 1 Clem. 40.5; BDAG 1011–12, s.v. τόπος 3.

31. Hengel, *Pre-Christian Paul*, 82.

32. Luke's term "delivered" (παρέδωκεν) is closely related to Paul's term "traditions" (παραδόσεων).

33. See Torrey Seland, "Saul of Tarsus and Early Zealotism: Reading Gal 1,13–14 in Light of Philo's Writings," *Biblica* 83 (2002): 449–71; and James D. G. Dunn, *Beginning from Jerusalem*, vol. 2 of *Christianity in the Making*, 3 vols. (Grand Rapids: Eerdmans, 2009), 344.

34. Seland, "Saul of Tarsus," 461.

35. Seland, "Saul of Tarsus," 461.

36. Cf. Seland, "Saul of Tarsus," 463–66.

37. BDAG 1022, s.v. ὑβριστής.

38. The term Luke uses here (ἐμμαινόμενος) refers to being "filled with such anger that one appears to be mad" (BDAG 322, s.v. ἐμμαίνομαι).

39. See BDAG 539–40, s.v. κέντρον 2. See, e.g., Euripides, *Bacch.* 794–795, where the phrase is used to portray Pentheus as nonsensically rebelling against a god, and Aeschylus, *Ag.* 1624, where Aegisthus points out how crazy it would be for the Chorus to continue to criticize him. Pindar seems to use the phrase to refer to the irrational lengths to which envy can drive a person (*Pyth.* 2.89–96).

40. In the case of James (Josephus, *A.J.* 20.200), Herod Agrippa II, who was sympathetic to the Romans, deposed the high priest Ananus for assembling a Sanhedrin without Roman permission (Josephus, *A.J.* 20.203). Nevertheless, both the high priest and the Sanhedrin were willing to flout Roman authority on religious matters when they thought they could get away with it.

41. The verdict on Luke's historicity at this point of Simon Légasse, "Paul's Pre-Christian Career according to Acts," in *The Book of Acts in Its Palestinian Setting*, ed. Richard Bauckham, vol. 4 of *The Book of Acts in Its First Century Setting*, ed. Bruce W. Winter (Grand Rapids: Eerdmans, 1995), 388.

42. I came to these figures both using the Stanford Geospatial Network Model of the Roman World and using a Scalex MapWheel with J. A. Talbert, ed., *Barrington Atlas of the Greek and Roman World* (Princeton, NJ: Princeton University Press, 2000), 69, 70, 71. The route Paul followed is not certain, and the ancient roads between Jerusalem and Damascus in the first century are not entirely clear, so the distances and times are approximate figures.

43. Josephus gives various figures for the Jewish population of Damascus during the Jewish war against Rome in AD 66–70: 10,500 in *B.J.* 2.561 and over 18,000 in *B.J.* 7.368.

44. That is, to the "governor [ἐθνάρχης]" of Damascus "under King Aretas." Aretas IV seems to have controlled the city briefly during AD 36. On this, see Douglas A. Campbell, "An Anchor for Pauline Chronology: Paul's Flight from 'The Ethnarch of King Aretas' (2 Corinthians 11:32–33)," *JBL* 121 (2002): 279–302.

CHAPTER 2

1. These translations are my own.
2. LSJ 897, s.v. καταλαμβάνω 2.2. On this, see Johannes Munck, *Paul and the Salvation of Mankind*, trans. Frank Clarke (Atlanta: John Knox, 1977), 23–24.
3. Munck, *Paul*, 22–23; Seyoon Kim, *The Origin of Paul's Gospel* (Grand Rapids: Eerdmans, 1982), 4–5.
4. E.g., Christoph Burchard, *Der dreizehnte Zeuge: Traditions- und kompositionsgeschichtliche Untersuchungen zu Lukas' Darstellung der Frühzeit des Paulus*, FRLANT 103 (Göttingen: Vandenhoeck & Ruprecht, 1970), 52–118; Richard I. Pervo, *Acts: A Commentary*, Hermeneia (Minneapolis: Fortress, 2009), 234–36.
5. On the date, see Randall D. Chesnutt, *From Death to Life: Conversion in Joseph and Aseneth*, JSPSup 16 (Sheffield: Sheffield Academic Press, 1995), 80–85; and Ross Shepard Kraemer, *When Aseneth Met Joseph: A Late Antique Tale of the Biblical Patriarch and His Egyptian Wife, Reconsidered* (New York: Oxford University Press, 1998), viii–ix, 225–44. For the possibility of Christian authorship, see Kraemer, *When Aseneth Met Joseph*, 253–72.
6. Craig S. Keener, *Acts: An Exegetical Commentary*, 4 vols. (Grand Rapids: Baker, 2012–2015), 2:1608n105.
7. On the historical figures behind this text, see Daniel R. Schwartz, *2 Maccabees*, CEJL (Berlin: de Gruyter, 2008), 185–92.
8. See the discussion of this possibility in Hans Windisch, "Die Christusepiphanie vor Damaskus und ihre religionsgeschichtlichen Parellelen," *ZNW* 31 (1932): 1–23.
9. See the CEB's translation of ἄφνω ... πεσόντα πρὸς τὴν γῆν καὶ πολλῷ σκότει περιχυθέντα as "he suddenly fell to the ground unconscious." On other differences between the narratives, see Windisch, "Die Christusepiphanie," 6–7.
10. See, e.g., Kim, *Origin of Paul's Gospel*, 5–11; Martin Hengel and Anna Maria Schwemer, *Paul between Damascus and Antioch: The Unknown Years*, trans. John Bowden (Louisville: Westminster John Knox, 1997), 42.
11. Translations of the Septuagint throughout come from the NETS, unless otherwise noted.
12. Karl Olav Sandnes, *Paul—One of the Prophets? A Contribution to the Apostle's Self-Understanding*, WUNT 2.43 (Tübingen: J. C. B. Mohr, 1991), 62–63.
13. Sandnes, *Paul—One of the Prophets?*, 65; Karl Olav Sandnes, "Prophet-Like Apostle: A Note on the 'Radical New Perspective' in Pauline Studies," *Biblica* 96 (2015): 551.
14. Sandnes, "Prophet-Like Apostle," 556–57, 560.
15. Cf. Sandnes, "Prophet-Like Apostle," 553–54.
16. Stanley E. Porter, *When Paul Met Jesus: How an Idea Got Lost in History* (Cambridge: Cambridge University Press, 2016), 105–19.
17. Dale C. Allison, "Acts 9:1–9, 22:6–11, 26:12–18: Paul and Ezekiel," *JBL* 135 (2016): 812–19.
18. The three Greek words in each text that refer to hearing a voice (of some-

one) speaking are virtually identical: ἤκουσεν φωνὴν λέγουσαν (Acts 9:4); ἤκουσα φωνῆς λεγούσης (22:7); ἤκουσα φωνὴν λέγουσαν (26:14); ἤκουσα φωνὴν λαλοῦντος (Ezek 1:28 LXX).

19. Cf. Allison, "Paul and Ezekiel," 824–26.

20. Allison, "Paul and Ezekiel," 824–25.

21. Dieter Böhler, "Saul, Saul, warum verfolgst du mich? Zum alttestamentlichen Hintergrund der Damaskusberichte (Apg 9; 22; 26)," *BZ* 61 (2017): 137–47.

22. E.g., Hengel and Schwemer, *Paul between Damascus and Antioch*, 49; Allison, "Paul and Ezekiel," 824–26.

23. Hengel and Schwemer, *Paul between Damascus and Antioch*, 48. Paul's vision in the Jerusalem temple after his conversion (Acts 22:21) contains a similar statement ("Go, for I will send you [ἐξαποστελῶ σε] far away to the Gentiles"). That statement, however, came to Paul later and for a somewhat different purpose.

24. Eph 3:1–10 also hints that Paul's conversion (to which Paul alludes in v. 9) was the point at which God gave him the "revelation" (v. 3) that he should proclaim the inclusion of the gentiles within the people of God through the gospel (v. 6).

CHAPTER 3

1. C. K. Barrett thinks this was a possibility (Barrett, *A Critical and Exegetical Commentary on the Acts of the Apostles*, ICC, 2 vols. [Edinburgh: T&T Clark, 1994–1998], 1:453).

2. Cf. Martin Hengel and Anna Maria Schwemer, *Paul between Damascus and Antioch: The Unknown Years*, trans. John Bowden (Louisville: Westminster John Knox, 1997), 81.

3. For the last two suggestions, see Kirsopp Lake and Henry J. Cadbury, *English Translation and Commentary*, vol. 4 of *The Beginnings of Christianity, Part I, The Acts of the Apostles*, ed. F. J. Foakes Jackson and Kirsopp Lake (London: Macmillan, 1933), 102. For the position taken here, see Hengel and Schwemer, *Paul between Damascus and Antioch*, 83–84.

4. On the reasons for fasting in Jewish and Greco-Roman antiquity, see Noah Hacham, "Fasting," *EDEJ*, 634–36; and Craig S. Keener, *Acts: An Exegetical Commentary*, 4 vols. (Grand Rapids: Baker, 2012–2015), 2:1642–44.

5. Cf. Robert Jewett, *Romans: A Commentary*, Hermeneia (Minneapolis: Fortress, 2007), 616–17.

6. Frank Thielman, "Paul's View of Israel's Misstep in Rom 9.32–3: Its Origin and Meaning," *NTS* 64 (2018): 367–71.

7. Cf. Jewett, *Romans*, 444–45, 452–53.

8. The inclusion of both Jews and gentiles in Acts 26:17 is clearer in the Greek than it is in many English translations. The relative pronoun often translated "whom" (οὕς) in the phrase "delivering you from your people and from the Gentiles—to whom I am sending you" (ESV; cf. RSV, NASB, NRSV) is masculine rather than

neuter. Since the noun for "gentiles" is neuter in Greek, this indicates that "people," which is masculine and refers to the Jewish people, is included within the relative pronoun's purview. On this, see Keener, *Acts*, 4:3519, and, in addition to the NIV, the CEB and CSB.

9. Seyoon Kim, *Paul and the New Perspective: Second Thoughts on the Origin of Paul's Gospel* (Grand Rapids: Eerdmans, 2002), 13.

10. Fergus Millar, *The Roman Near East 31 BC–AD 337* (Cambridge, MA: Harvard University Press, 1993), 312–14.

11. On the importance of Luke's plural, see Hengel and Schwemer, *Paul between Damascus and Antioch*, 54, 82.

12. Hengel and Schwemer, *Paul between Damascus and Antioch*, 99.

13. Hengel and Schwemer, *Paul between Damascus and Antioch*, 99.

14. In Gal 1:16–18 Paul is trying to describe the length of time between his call to preach the gospel to the gentiles and his first post-conversion visit to Jerusalem, so his "after three years" means that sometime in the third year after his conversion he visited Jerusalem. (Ancient writers often reckoned time inclusively, so "after three years" could mean one full year and parts of the two years on either side of that year.) Paul's time in Arabia occurred sometime during that period, but the length of time he spent there is not clear. See Douglas J. Moo, *Galatians*, BECNT (Grand Rapids: Baker, 2013), 108; and A. Andrew Das, *Galatians*, Concordia Commentary (Saint Louis: Concordia, 2014), 137–38.

15. G. W. Bowersock, *Roman Arabia* (Cambridge, MA: Harvard University Press, 1983), 1.

16. Bowersock, *Roman Arabia*, 51, 59, 68.

17. Martin Hengel, "Paul in Arabia," *BBR* 12 (2002): 61.

18. Hengel, "Paul in Arabia," 62.

19. Jane Taylor, *Petra and the Lost Kingdom of the Nabataeans* (Cambridge, MA: Harvard University Press, 2002), 163.

20. Taylor, *Petra*, 122–26.

21. Taylor, *Petra*, 47–48.

22. Coins from the time of Caligula and Claudius are missing from Damascus. It is only with Nero that Roman rule once again becomes clear. On this, see Emil Schürer, *The History of the Jewish People in the Age of Jesus Christ (175 B.C.–A.D. 135)*, rev. and ed. by Geza Vermes et al., 3 vols. (Edinburgh: T&T Clark, 1979), 2:129; Justin Taylor, "The Ethnarch of King Aretas at Damascus: A Note on 2 Cor 11:32–33," *RB* 99 (1992): 724, 725.

23. Rainer Riesner, *Paul's Early Period: Chronology, Mission Strategy, Theology*, trans. Douglas W. Stott (Grand Rapids: Eerdmans, 1998), 85; Hengel and Schwemer, *Paul between Damascus and Antioch*, 131.

24. It is true (Das, *Galatians*, 154) that when the Nabateans used Greek to describe their governors, they typically used a different word (στρατηγός) than the term Paul uses here (ἐθνάρχης), but inscriptional evidence reveals that the Nabateans

could sometimes use both terms to describe the same official. On this, see Taylor, "Ethnarch of King Aretas," 723; and Douglas A. Campbell, "An Anchor for Pauline Chronology: Paul's Flight from 'The Ethnarch of King Aretas' (2 Corinthians 11:32–33)," *JBL* 121 (2002): 285.

25. Bowersock, *Roman Arabia*, 68; Taylor, "Ethnarch of King Aretas," 720; Campbell, "Anchor for Pauline Chronology," 283.

26. Bowersock, *Roman Arabia*, 68–69; Fergus Millar, *The Roman Near East 31 BC–AD 337* (Cambridge, MA: Harvard University Press, 1993), 56–57; Campbell, "Anchor for Pauline Chronology," 287–98. For the date range, see Campbell, "Anchor for Pauline Chronology," 298–99.

27. See, respectively, Ernst Haenchen (*Acts of the Apostles: A Commentary* [Louisville: Westminster John Knox, 1971], 331) and Barrett (*Acts*, 1:466).

28. For this understanding of 2 Thess 2:14–15, see Thielman, "Paul's View of Israel's Misstep," 371–76.

29. Taylor, *Petra*, 163, 183. Hegra is now known as Mada'in Saleh in Saudi Arabia, and Mahoza is probably present-day Ghor as-Safi in Jordan.

30. For the meaning of the rare word for "basket" (σαργάνη) in 2 Cor 11:33, and for the technique of secretly smuggling contraband over a city a wall by using such a "basket," see Aeneas Tacticus, *Poliorcetica*, 29.6–8; Lucian, *Lexiphanes* 6.10; and the discussion in Isaac T. Soon, *A Disabled Apostle: Impairment and Disability in the Letters of Paul* (Oxford: Oxford University Press, 2023), 170–71. Soon argues on the basis of 2 Cor 11:33, Acts 9:25, and Acts Paul 3 that the basket was a small container and that Paul himself was physically very small.

CHAPTER 4

1. Peter and James, then, correspond to "the apostles" to whom, according to Luke, Barnabas introduced Paul (Acts 9:27). A reader of Acts might well assume that Luke meant all the apostles, since the last reference to them was in 8:1 where the whole Jerusalem church was scattered because of persecution "except for the apostles." Luke was not reaching for the level of precision that Paul required in his careful defense in Galatians. On this, see especially Craig S. Keener, *Galatians: A Commentary* (Grand Rapids: Baker, 2019), 101–2.

2. Jerome Murphy-O'Connor, *Paul: A Critical Life* (Oxford: Clarendon, 1996), 91–93.

3. David Wenham, *Paul: Follower of Jesus or Founder of Christianity?* (Grand Rapids: Eerdmans, 1995), 242–45.

4. Wenham, *Paul*, 382.

5. Wenham, *Paul*, 289–337, 382–83.

6. Richard Bauckham, *Jesus and the Eyewitnesses: The Gospels as Eyewitness Testimony* (Grand Rapids: Eerdmans, 2006), 12. See Eusebius, *Hist. eccl.* 3.39.1.

7. Bauckham, *Jesus and the Eyewitnesses*, 15; Michael W. Holmes, ed. and trans., *The Apostolic Fathers: Greek Texts and English Translations*, 3rd ed. (Grand Rapids: Baker, 2007), 722

8. Philip seems to have eventually immigrated with his daughters to Hierapolis (Eusebius, *Hist. eccl.* 3.31.3).

9. Bauckham, *Jesus and the Eyewitnesses*, 15–30.

10. As Bauckham points out (*Jesus and the Eyewitnesses*, 17), the present tense here indicates that Aristion and the elder John were teaching during Papias's lifetime.

11. Eusebius, *Hist. eccl.* 3.39.3–4 (trans. Holmes, *Apostolic Fathers*, 735).

12. Bauckham, *Jesus and the Eyewitnesses*, 21–30, especially 24–25 on Polybius.

13. Eusebius, *Hist. eccl.* 3.39.15 (trans. Holmes, *Apostolic Fathers*, 741).

14. These are my translations.

15. Markus Bockmuehl, *The Remembered Peter in Ancient Reception and Modern Debate*, WUNT 1.262 (Tübingen: Mohr Siebeck, 2010), 85. See also Graham N. Stanton, *Jesus and the Gospel* (Cambridge: Cambridge University Press, 2004), 101.

16. Bauckham, *Jesus and the Eyewitnesses*, 212–13.

17. Henry Barclay Swete, *The Gospel according to St. Mark* (London: Macmillan, 1898), xxvii–xxviii. Swete includes the "so-called Muratorian fragment" with Irenaeus and Tertullian as second-century witnesses to this tradition, but it now seems reasonably clear that the "Muratorian fragment" comes from Victorinus of Pettau around AD 258. On this, see Jonathan J. Armstrong, "Victorinus of Pettau as the Author of the Canon Muratori," *VigChr* 62 (2008): 1–34.

18. See especially Bauckham, *Jesus and the Eyewitnesses*, 155–82; and Martin Hengel, *Saint Peter: The Underestimated Apostle*, trans. Thomas H. Trapp (Grand Rapids: Eerdmans, 2006), 39–42.

19. Bauckham, *Jesus and the Eyewitnesses*, 177–79; Hengel, *Saint Peter*, 43–44. Cf. Robert H. Gundry, *Mark: A Commentary on His Apology for the Cross* (Grand Rapids: Eerdmans, 1993), 1040.

20. Swete, *St. Mark*, xvi.

21. For the connection between the title "Son of God" for Christ and Christ's resurrection, see Rom 1:4.

22. J. G. McConville, *Deuteronomy*, Apollos Old Testament Commentaries (Downers Grove, IL: InterVarsity, 2002), 332–33.

23. For the translation "welt" here, see BDAG 663, s.v. μώλωψ.

24. Martin Hengel, *The Atonement: The Origins of the Doctrine in the New Testament*, trans. John Bowden (Philadelphia: Fortress, 1981), 44.

25. MGS 244, s.v. ἀπογίνομαι.

26. Edward Gordon Selwyn, *The First Epistle of St. Peter*, 2nd ed. (London: Macmillan, 1947), 181.

27. BDAG 108, s.v. ἀπογίνομαι.

28. *Pace* John H. Elliott, *1 Peter*, AB 37B (New York: Doubleday, 2000), 536.

29. A qualification appropriately expressed by Reinhard Feldmeier, *Der erste Brief des Petrus*, THKNT 15/I (Leipzig: Evangelische Verlagsanstalt, 2005), 118n402.

30. See, e.g., Ernest Best, *1 Peter*, NCB (London: Marshall, Morgan & Scott, 1971), 34; Elliott, *1 Peter*, 38.

31. On this, see especially Dunn, *Beginning from Jerusalem*, vol. 2 of *Christianity in the Making*, 3 vols. (Grand Rapids: Eerdmans, 2009), 1151.

32. Oscar Cullmann, *Peter: Disciple, Apostle, Martyr*, trans. Floyd V. Filson (Philadelphia: Westminster, 1953), 65; Hengel, *Atonement*, 54–55; Martin Hengel and Anna Maria Schwemer, *Paul between Damascus and Antioch: The Unknown Years*, trans. John Bowden (Louisville: Westminster John Knox, 1997), 148.

33. Gerd Lüdemann views the geographical discrepancy as proof that "Paul's vision in the temple is certainly unhistorical." Lüdemann, *Early Christianity according to the Traditions in Acts* (Minneapolis: Fortress, 1989), 240.

34. There is perhaps an allusion here to Isa 57:19 LXX ("Peace upon peace to those that are far [μακράν] and to those that are near") and Acts 2:39, as some commentators maintain (e.g., Joseph A. Fitzmyer, *The Acts of the Apostles*, AB 31 [New Haven, CT: Yale University Press, 1998], 239; Craig S. Keener, *Acts: An Exegetical Commentary*, 4 vols. [Grand Rapids: Baker, 2012–2015], 3:3240), but these echoes are not the sole purpose of the adverb.

35. F. D. Gilliard, "The Problem of the Antisemitic Comma between 1 Thessalonians 2.14 and 15," *NTS* 35 (1989): 481–502.

36. Thielman, "Paul's View of Israel's Misstep," 371–76.

37. Thielman, "Paul's View of Israel's Misstep," 375.

38. Since Luke only mentions Paul's journey from Jerusalem to Caesarea to Tarsus and does not mention Syria, some scholars (e.g., Rainer Riesner, *Paul's Early Period: Chronology, Mission Strategy, Theology*, trans. Douglas W. Stott [Grand Rapids: Eerdmans, 1998], 266) have thought that when Paul spoke of Syria and Cilicia in Gal 1:21 he was using the official administrative name of the province, "Syria-Cilicia." This is unlikely from a grammatical perspective, however, since Paul repeats the article before each region (τῆς Συρίας καὶ τῆς Κιλικίας). On this, see A. Andrew Das, *Galatians*, Concordia Commentary (Saint Louis: Concordia, 2014), 143.

39. I calculated the distance using J. A. Talbert, ed., *Barrington Atlas of the Greek and Roman World* (Princeton, NJ: Princeton University Press, 2000), 69 and 70.

40. Cf. Mark Wilson, "Cilicia: The First Christian Churches in Anatolia," *TynBul* 54 (2003): 17.

41. On the sea route between Cilicia and Seleucia, see Strabo, *Geogr.* 14.5.20, and on the lake that formed the seaport for Tarsus, see Strabo, *Geogr.* 14.5.10.

42. On the route, see Strabo, *Geogr.* 16.2.8; and the maps in Talbert, ed., *Barrington Atlas*, 66, 67; and David H. French, *An Album of Maps*, fasc. 3.9 of *Milestones*, vol. 3 of *Roman Roads and Milestones of Asia Minor*, Electronic Monograph 9 (Ankara: British Institute at Ankara, 2016), 81. See also Mustafa H. Sayar, "Römische

Straßen und Meilensteine im Ebenen Kilikien," in *Roman Roads: New Evidence—New Perspectives*, ed. Anna Kolb (Berlin: de Gruyter, 2019), 159.

CHAPTER 5

1. On details of the regions and dates of the reign of Herod Agrippa I, see Josephus, *A.J.* 18.237, 252; 19.350–351. See also the helpful overview in S. Safrai and M. Stern, eds., *The Jewish People in the First Century: Historical Geography, Political History, Social, Cultural and Religious Life and Institutions* (Philadelphia: Fortress, 1974), 1:288–300.

2. E. Mary Smallwood, *The Jews under Roman Rule from Pompey to Diocletian: A Study in Political Relations* (Leiden: Brill, 1981), 225–26.

3. Smallwood, *Jews under Roman Rule*, 231–32.

4. Smallwood, *Jews under Roman Rule*, 234–35, 237.

5. Smallwood, *Jews under Roman Rule*, 238. See Philo, *Flacc.* 27–30, 103; *Legat.* 179.

6. See Pieter W. van der Horst, *Philo's "Flaccus": The First Pogrom*, Philo of Alexandria Commentary Series 2 (Leiden: Brill, 2003), 2–3.

7. Antiochus had grown up in Rome and Athens and understood little of Judaism. See Otto Mørkholm, "Antiochus IV," in *The Hellenistic Age*, ed. W. D. Davies and Louis Finkelstein, vol. 2 of *The Cambridge History of Judaism*, 8 vols. (Cambridge: Cambridge University Press, 1984–2021), 279–80.

8. Mørkholm, "Antiochus IV," 286.

9. Elizabeth Jeffreys, Michael Jeffreys, and Roger Scott, *The Chronicle of John Malalas: A Translation* (Melbourne: Australian Association for Byzantine Studies, 1986), 130 (10.20). See the analysis of Glanville Downey, *A History of Antioch in Syria from Seleucus to the Arab Conquest* (Princeton, NJ: Princeton University Press, 1961), 192–95.

10. See the comments of Erich S. Gruen, *The Construct of Jewish Identity in Hellenistic Judaism* (Berlin: de Gruyter, 2016), 404.

11. I am using the text as translated and discussed in Smallwood, *Jews under Roman Rule*, 246.

12. For a discussion of tensions in Antioch during this period, see Martin Hengel and Anna Maria Schwemer, *Paul between Damascus and Antioch: The Unknown Years*, trans. John Bowden (Louisville: Westminster John Knox, 1997), 183–91.

13. On the size of the community, see Philo, *Legat.* 281, and the discussion in W. M. Ramsay, *The Cities of St. Paul: Their Influence on His Life and Thought* (London: Hodder & Stoughton, 1907), 169–80.

14. For discussion of this passage, see Ramsay, *Cities of St. Paul*, 178–80.

15. On the historical worth of Philostratus's *Life of Apollonius of Tyana*, see Christopher P. Jones, *Philostratus: The Life of Apollonius of Tyana*, 2 vols. LCL 16–17 (Cambridge, MA: Harvard University Press, 2005), 1:7–13.

16. Hengel and Schwemer, *Paul between Damascus and Antioch*, 244. See Philo, *Legat.* 275–333; and Josephus, *A.J.* 18.297–298.

17. The incident "provoked Agrippa exceedingly, for it was tantamount to an overthrow of the laws of his fathers" (Josephus, *A.J.* 19.301 [Feldman, LCL]).

18. Riesner argues persuasively that Herod Agrippa's persecution of the church happened early in his reign, in AD 41 or 42. Rainer Riesner, *Paul's Early Period: Chronology, Mission Strategy, Theology*, trans. Douglas W. Stott (Grand Rapids: Eerdmans, 1998), 118–19.

19. Robert E. Osborne, "St. Paul's Silent Years," *JBL* 84 (1965): 60–61. Cf. Hengel and Schwemer, *Paul between Damascus and Antioch*, 158.

20. Mark Wilson, "Cilicia: The First Christian Churches in Anatolia," *TynBul* 54 (2003): 20–24.

21. Hengel and Schwemer, *Paul between Damascus and Antioch*, 157; Wilson, "Cilicia," 27–29; Eckhard J. Schnabel, *Paul and the Early Church*, vol. 2 of *Early Christian Mission*, 2 vols. (Downers Grove, IL: InterVarsity, 2004), 1054–69.

22. Here I follow the description of Paul's opponents in Murray J. Harris, *The Second Epistle to the Corinthians*, NIGTC (Grand Rapids: Eerdmans, 2005), 71–73, 832.

23. Harris, *Second Epistle to the Corinthians*, 729.

24. Harris, *Second Epistle to the Corinthians*, 853.

25. John N. Oswalt, *The Book of Isaiah, Chapters 1–39*, NICOT (Grand Rapids: Eerdmans, 1986), 177.

26. Daniel I. Block, *The Book of Ezekiel, Chapters 1–24*, NICOT (Grand Rapids: Eerdmans, 1997), 4–8; Paul R. House, *Daniel*, TOTC (Downers Grove, IL: IVP Academic, 2018), 2–7.

27. For 1 Enoch 12–16, see George W. E. Nickelsburg, *1 Enoch 1: A Commentary on the Book of 1 Enoch, Chapters 1–36; 81–108*, Hermeneia (Minneapolis: Fortress, 2001), 230–31.

28. Quoted in van der Horst, *Philo's "Flaccus,"* 2–3.

29. Van der Horst, *Philo's "Flaccus,"* 3–4.

30. On this passage as the record of a heavenly ascent, see Alan F. Segal, "Heavenly Ascent in Hellenistic Judaism, Early Christianity and Their Environment," *ANRW* 2.23.2: 1355–56.

31. This cosmology seems to be present in, for example, Neh 9:6 where Nehemiah assumes that God created "the heaven" and "the heaven of heavens with all their host." This would mean that God himself was in the third heaven, a dimension invisible to the unaided eye. Cf. T. Levi 2:6–10; and the discussion of Philip Edgcumbe Hughes, *Paul's Second Epistle to the Corinthians*, New London Commentary (London: Marshall, Morgan & Scott, 1961), 432–34.

32. Harris, *Second Epistle to the Corinthians*, 164–82; cf. William Menzies Alexander, "St. Paul's Infirmity," *ExpTim* 15 (1903–1904): 545–48; Margaret E. Thrall, *The Second Epistle to the Corinthians*, ICC, 2 vols. (Edinburgh: T&T Clark, 1994–2000), 2:808–9, 817–18. The argument of Soon that Paul's thorn was a Satanic angel

inhabiting his flesh is not convincing. Isaac T. Soon, *A Disabled Apostle: Impairment and Disability in the Letters of Paul* (Oxford: Oxford University Press, 2023), 22–28. It is hard to imagine that Paul thought of his union with Christ as compatible with the activity of a demon within his body (1 Cor 6:15–19). The term ἄγγελος in 2 Cor 12:7, then, probably means "messenger" and is metaphorical (cf. Gal 4:14).

CHAPTER 6

1. Kenneth Sperber Gapp, "The Universal Famine under Claudius," *HTR* 28 (1935): 260; Bruce W. Winter, "Acts and Food Shortages," in *The Book of Acts in Its Greco-Roman Setting*, ed. David W. J. Gill and Conrad Gempf, vol. 2 of *The Book of Acts in Its First Century Setting*, ed. Bruce W. Winter, 6 vols. (Grand Rapids: Eerdmans, 1994), 64.

2. Gapp, "Universal Famine," 259. Ramsay had also suggested many years earlier that "in 45 the harvest was probably not good, and provisions grew scarce in the country." See his *St. Paul the Traveller and the Roman Citizen* (London: Hodder & Stoughton, 1896), 51, 68.

3. Adiabene was a small kingdom in what is today northern Iraq. Its king, Izates, and his mother, Helena, were recent converts to Judaism.

4. Winter, "Acts and Food Shortages," 75–76.

5. Winter, "Acts and Food Shortages," 75–76.

6. See, e.g., Ramsay, *St. Paul the Traveller*, 154–55; and Das, *Galatians*, 41.

7. See, e.g., Ramsay, *St. Paul the Traveller*, 48–51; and Das, *Galatians*, 42.

8. See, e.g., Ramsay, *St. Paul the Traveller*, 48–60; and Das, *Galatians*, 41.

9. Das, *Galatians*, 37, 40, 42.

10. J. B. Lightfoot, *Saint Paul's Epistle to the Galatians* (New York: Macmillan, 1896), 127. James D. G. Dunn thinks that Luke was mistaken in including Paul in the famine relief visit, since "Paul's solemn affidavit (Gal. 1.18–21) does not allow room for any intermediate visit by Paul to Jerusalem," but Dunn does not take into account Paul's focus in Galatians on his meetings with the "pillars" of the Jerusalem church, James, Cephas, and John. Dunn, *Beginning from Jerusalem*, vol. 2 of *Christianity in the Making*, 3 vols. (Grand Rapids: Eerdmans, 2009), 376.

11. Craig S. Keener, *Acts: An Exegetical Commentary*, 4 vols. (Grand Rapids: Baker, 2012–2015), 3:2196–97.

12. C. K. Barrett, *A Critical and Exegetical Commentary on the Acts of the Apostles*, ICC, 2 vols. (Edinburgh: T&T Clark, 1994–1998), 1:605; Keener, *Acts*, 2:1993–94; Daniel Marguerat, *Die Apostelgeschichte*, KEK 3 (Göttingen: Vandenhoeck & Ruprecht, 2022), 483.

13. Herod Agrippa I, in a letter to the emperor Gaius in AD 38, says that "not only are the mainlands full of Jewish colonies but also the most highly esteemed of the islands Euboea, Cyprus, Crete" (Philo, *Legat.* 282, trans. F. H. Colson, LCL).

On the Jewish community there, see E. Mary Smallwood, *Jews under Roman Rule*, 412–13; Emil Schürer, *The History of the Jewish People in the Age of Jesus Christ (175 B.C.–A.D. 135)*, rev. and ed. by Geza Vermes et al., 3 vols. (Edinburgh: T&T Clark, 1979), 3.1:68; and Riesner, *Paul's Early Period*, 273.

14. For the boat ride, see Strabo, *Geogr.* 16.2.7, who speaks of traveling upstream from Seleucia to Antioch in a day. The Stanford Geospatial Network Model of the Roman World allows about three quarters of a day for the journey in the opposite direction. For the road, see J. A. Talbert, ed., *Barrington Atlas of the Greek and Roman World* (Princeton, NJ: Princeton University Press, 2002), 67.

15. For the prevailing winds, see the map in Justin Leidwanger, *Roman Seas: A Maritime Archaeology of Eastern Mediterranean Economies* (New York: Oxford University Press, 2020), 143; and for the timing, see the Stanford Geospatial Network Model of the Roman World.

16. Hector William Catling, "Salamis," *OCD*³ 1347.

17. Cf. Barrett, *Acts*, 1:611.

18. Barrett, *Acts*, 1:611.

19. Schnabel, *Paul and the Early Church*, 1082.

20. Duane W. Roller, *A Historical and Topographical Guide to the "Geography" of Strabo* (Cambridge: Cambridge University Press, 2018), 844. I calculated the mileage using Talbert, ed., *Barrington Atlas*, 1, by tracing a direct line from Paphos to Alexandria. The shipping route would have been much longer because of the need to sail south with prevailing winds blowing from the west and northwest. See the map in Leidwanger, *Roman Seas*, 143.

21. Stephen Mitchell, *Anatolia: Land, Men, and Gods in Asia Minor*, 2 vols. (Oxford: Oxford University Press, 1993), 2:6–7; Alanna Nobbs, "Cyprus," in *The Book of Acts in Its Greco-Roman Setting*, ed. David W. J. Gill and Conrad Gempf, vol. 2 of *The Book of Acts in Its First Century Setting*, ed. Bruce W. Winter, 6 vols. (Grand Rapids: Eerdmans, 1994), 282; Rainer Riesner, *Paul's Early Period: Chronology, Mission Strategy, Theology*, trans. Douglas W. Stott (Grand Rapids: Eerdmans, 1998), 139–41; Eckhard J. Schnabel, *Paul and the Early Church*, vol. 2 of *Early Christian Mission*, 2 vols. (Downers Grove, IL: InterVarsity, 2004), 1084.

22. Mitchell, *Anatolia*, 2:6; Nobbs, "Cyprus," 284–87.

23. On court advisors to Roman officials, see Keener, *Acts*, 2:2012–13n319.

24. W. M. Ramsay, *The Bearing of Recent Discovery on the Trustworthiness of the New Testament* (London: Hodder & Stoughton, 1915), 150–52; Ramsay, "Studies in the Roman Province of Galatia," *JRS* 16 (1926): 202–4; Mitchell, *Anatolia*, 2:6–7; Keener, *Acts*, 2:2037–38.

25. Mitchell, *Anatolia*, 2:7; Stephen Mitchell and Marc Waelkens, *Pisidian Antioch: The Site and Its Monuments* (London and Swansea: Duckworth and Classical Press of Wales, 1998), 11–12; Riesner, *Paul's Early Period*, 276; Nobbs, "Cyprus," 287; Keener, *Acts*, 2:2027; Cilliers Breytenbach and Christiane Zimmermann, *Early*

Christianity in Lycaonia and Adjacent Areas: From Paul to Amphilochius of Iconium, AJEC 101/ECAM 2 (Leiden: Brill, 2018), 62.

26. N. P. Milner, "A Roman Bridge at Oinoanda," *Anatolian Studies* 48 (1998): 120; Fatih Onur, "Two Procuratorian Inscriptions from Perge," *Gephyra* 5 (2008): 53–66; Mark Wilson, "The Denouement of Claudian Pamphylia-Lycia and Its Implications for the Audience of Galatians," *NovT* 60 (2018): 337–60.

27. On mid-first-century Perga, see Schnabel, *Paul and the Early Church*, 1122–24; and Keener, *Acts*, 2:2028–30.

28. I have calculated the mileage using Talbert, ed., *Barrington Atlas*, 65.

29. For the route of the Via Sebaste, see Mitchell, *Anatolia*, 1:77; and the map in David H. French, *Roman Roads and Milestones of Asia Minor*, vol. 3, *Milestones*, fasc. 3.2, *Galatia*, Electronic Monograph 2 (Ankara: British Institute at Ankara, 2012), 15; and French, *An Album of Maps*, fasc. 3.9 of *Milestones*, vol. 3 of *Roman Roads and Milestones of Asia Minor*, Electronic Monograph 9 (Ankara: British Institute at Ankara, 2016), 88, 149.

30. Stephen Mitchell, "Via Sebaste," OCD^4 1549. See also Mitchell's *Anatolia*, 1:70 and 2:6.

31. Ramsay, *St. Paul the Traveller*, 90.

32. Ramsay, *St. Paul the Traveller*, 92, 94.

33. Ramsay, *St. Paul the Traveller*, 89–97.

34. See also Theodor Zahn, *Introduction to the New Testament*, 3 vols., trans. John Moore Trout et al., 2nd ed. (New York: Charles Scribner's Sons, 1917), 1:171n2.

35. Murray J. Harris, *The Second Epistle to the Corinthians*, NIGTC (Grand Rapids: Eerdmans, 2005), 172, 851–61.

36. Harris, *Second Epistle to the Corinthians*, 172, 837. Harris dated 2 Corinthians to AD 56 but reckoned Paul's "fourteen years" inclusively. See also E.-B. Allo, *Saint Paul Seconde Épître aux Corinthiens*, 2nd ed., *Ebib* (Paris: Lecoffre, 1937), 321.

37. Allo, *Seconde Épître aux Corinthiens*, 312.

38. Harris, *Second Epistle to the Corinthians*, 172.

39. On this, see Bruce W. Longenecker, "'Until Christ Is Formed in You': Suprahuman Forces and Moral Character in Galatians," *CBQ* 61 (1999): 102.

CHAPTER 7

1. The more precise name distinguished it from another Antioch in Phrygia on the Maeander River (Stephen Mitchell, "Antioch [2]," OCD^4 104).

2. G. Walter Hansen, "Galatia," in *The Book of Acts in Its Greco-Roman Setting*, ed. David W. J. Gill and Conrad Gempf, vol. 2 of *The Book of Acts in Its First Century Setting*, ed. Bruce W. Winter, 6 vols. (Grand Rapids: Eerdmans, 1994), 395.

3. Eckhard J. Schnabel, *Paul and the Early Church*, vol. 2 of *Early Christian Mission*, 2 vols. (Downers Grove, IL: InterVarsity, 2004), 1101.

4. Schnabel, *Paul and the Early Church*, 1102.

5. On the features of Antioch that Paul might have seen in AD 47, see Mitchell, "Antioch," 107; and on the probability of a Greek version of the *Res Gestae* at Pisidian Antioch, see James R. Harrison, *Paul and the Imperial Authorities at Thessalonica and Rome*, WUNT 1.273 (Tübingen: Mohr Siebeck, 2011), 24–25.

6. Harrison, *Paul and the Imperial Authorities*, 25.

7. Robert L. Mowery, "Paul and Caristanius at Pisidian Antioch," *Biblica* 87 (2006): 223–42.

8. David M. Robinson, "Roman Sculptures from Colonia Caesarea (Pisidian Antioch)," *Art Bulletin* 9 (1926): 4–69. See also Richard Gordon, "The Roman Imperial Cult and the Question of Power," in *The Religious History of the Roman Empire*, ed. J. A. North and S. R. F. Price (Oxford: Oxford University Press, 2011), 48.

9. Craig S. Keener, *Acts: An Exegetical Commentary*, 4 vols. (Grand Rapids: Baker, 2012–2015), 1:277–80.

10. Keener, *Acts*, 1:282.

11. Unless otherwise noted, translations of Polybius throughout come from Robin Waterfield, *Polybius: The Histories*, Oxford World Classics (Oxford: Oxford University Press, 2010).

12. Keener, *Acts*, 1:260, 269–70, 282.

13. Τούτου... ἀπὸ τοῦ σπέρματος κατ' ἐπαγγελίαν (Acts 13:23) // προεπηγγείλατο ... ἐκ σπέρματος Δαυὶδ (Rom 1:2–3).

14. Mowery, "Paul and Caristanius," 225.

15. Mowery, "Paul and Caristanius," 238–41.

16. For a stretch of the Via Sebaste between Pisidian Antioch and Iconium, see the photograph in Stephen Mitchell, *Anatolia: Land, Men, and Gods in Asia Minor*, 2 vols. (Oxford: Oxford University Press, 1993), 1:125. There is some dispute about whether Iconium was a Roman colony in this period. Here I follow Stephen Mitchell, "Iconium and Ninica: Two Double Communities in Roman Asia Minor," *Historia: Zeitschrift für Alte Geschichte* 28 (1979): 409–38; and Rainer Riesner, *Paul's Early Period: Chronology, Mission Strategy, Theology*, trans. Douglas W. Stott (Grand Rapids: Eerdmans, 1998), 277n76. I calculated the mileage using Talbert, ed., *Barrington Atlas*, 62, 65, and 66, and a Scalex MapWheel.

17. On the date of *Metamorphoses*, see Frank Justus Miller, *Ovid: Metamorphoses, Books 1–8*, 3rd ed., LCL 42 (Cambridge, MA: Harvard University Press, 1977), xi.

18. Schnabel, *Paul and the Early Church*, 1114.

19. Cf. Keener, *Acts*, 2:2158.

20. Cilliers Breytenbach and Christiane Zimmermann, *Early Christianity in Lycaonia and Adjacent Areas: From Paul to Amphilocius of Iconium*, AJEC 101/ECAM 2 (Leiden: Brill, 2018), 210–11; David H. French, *An Album of Maps*, fasc. 3.9 of *Milestones*, vol. 3 of *Roman Roads and Milestones of Asia Minor*, Electronic Monograph 9 (Ankara: British Institute at Ankara, 2016), 77. I double-checked the mileage figure

using J. A. Talbert, ed., *Barrington Atlas of the Greek and Roman World* (Princeton, NJ: Princeton University Press, 2000), 66.

21. George Ogg, "Derbe," *NTS* 9 (1963): 367–70; Josef Wiesehöfer, "Antiochus (9)," *OCD*⁴ 106; and Arnold Hugh Martin Jones, David Hawkins, and Anthony Spawforth, "Commagene," *OCD*⁴ 358. Ramsay's idea that Derbe lay within the part of Lycaonia under direct Roman rule and that Paul limited his work at this time "to the Roman world, and especially to its great cities" is not correct. W. M. Ramsay, *St. Paul the Traveller and the Roman Citizen* (London: Hodder & Stoughton, 1896), 112.

22. Keener, *Acts*, 2:2179. See also the maps in Mitchell, *Anatolia*, 1:map 3; Talbert, ed., *Barrington Atlas*, 66, 67; and David H. French, *An Album of Maps*, fasc. 3.9 of *Milestones*, vol. 3 of *Roman Roads and Milestones of Asia Minor*, Electronic Monograph 9 (Ankara: British Institute at Ankara, 2016), 155.

23. Keener, *Acts*, 2:2179.

24. On the Jewish persecution of Christians in Pisidian Antioch, Iconium, Lystra, and Derbe, see F. F. Bruce, *The Epistle to the Galatians: A Commentary on the Greek Text*, NIGTC (Grand Rapids: Eerdmans, 1982), 224.

25. Bruce W. Winter, *Divine Honours for the Caesars: The First Christians' Responses* (Grand Rapids: Eerdmans, 2015), 240–44.

26. On this, see Murray J. Harris, *The Second Epistle to the Corinthians*, NIGTC (Grand Rapids: Eerdmans, 2005), 172.

27. Mark Wilson is right to say, however, that if a Christian community did emerge from the preaching of Paul and Barnabas there, it may well have been part of the audience of Paul's later letter to the Galatians. Wilson, "Denouement of Claudian Pamphylia-Lycia and Its Implications for the Audience of Galatians," *NovT* 60 (2018): 341–43, 353–59.

CHAPTER 8

1. Cf. Robert Jewett, "The Agitators and the Galatian Congregation," *NTS* 17 (1971): 198–212; and James D. G. Dunn, *Beginning from Jerusalem*, vol. 2 of *Christianity in the Making*, 3 vols. (Grand Rapids: Eerdmans, 2009), 480–81.

2. On Tiberius Julius Alexander, see E. G. Turner, "Tiberius Ivlivs Alexander," *JRS* 44 (1954): 54–64; and E. Mary Smallwood, *Jews under Roman Rule from Pompey to Diocletian: A Study in Political Relations* (Leiden: Brill, 1981), 258, 262–63.

3. See the discussion in Smallwood, *Jews under Roman Rule*, 153–55.

4. See also James D. G. Dunn, *Beginning from Jerusalem*, vol. 2 of *Christianity in the Making*, 3 vols. (Grand Rapids: Eerdmans, 2009), 480.

5. Rainer Riesner, *Paul's Early Period: Chronology, Mission Strategy, Theology*, trans. Douglas W. Stott (Grand Rapids: Eerdmans, 1998), 101–4, 280–81; Craig S. Keener, *Acts: An Exegetical Commentary*, 4 vols. (Grand Rapids: Baker, 2012–2015), 3:2212–13.

6. Bruce W. Winter, *Divine Honours for the Caesars: The First Christians' Responses* (Grand Rapids: Eerdmans, 2015), 227–28, 243–44.

7. Here I part company with Winter's reading of "make a good showing" (εὐπροσωπῆσαι) in Gal 6:12 as a reference to good legal standing (*Divine Honours for the Caesars*, 244–49). This seems to me to define the word too specifically.

8. J. B. Lightfoot, *Saint Paul's Epistle to the Galatians* (New York: Macmillan, 1896), 102; C. K. Barrett, *A Critical and Exegetical Commentary on the Acts of the Apostles*, ICC, 2 vols. (Edinburgh: T&T Clark, 1994–1998), 2:701.

9. Douglas J. Moo, *Galatians*, BECNT (Grand Rapids: Baker, 2013), 122.

10. Luke's claim that they were "believers" (Acts 15:5) perhaps reflects his knowledge that some of them later changed their position and joined "the whole church" in its affirmation of the council's eventual decision (Acts 15:22).

11. On the law as a blessing in Rabbinic Judaism, see E. P. Sanders, *Paul and Palestinian Judaism: A Comparison of Patterns of Religion* (Philadelphia: Fortress, 1977), 110–11.

12. Cf. Moo, *Galatians*, 231–32.

13. J. L. Nolland, "A Fresh Look at Acts 15.10," *NTS* 27 (1980): 107.

14. Although Nolland argues the case differently (Nolland, "Fresh Look," 109–12), his approach to Acts 15:10 is basically the same.

15. F. F. Bruce, *Paul: Apostle of the Heart Set Free* (Grand Rapids: Eerdmans, 1977), 185.

16. Keener, *Acts*, 3:2263–69.

17. Keener, *Acts*, 3:2275.

18. See, e.g., Ernst Haenchen, *Acts of the Apostles: A Commentary* (Louisville: Westminster John Knox, 1971), 468–72.

19. Cf. Keener, *Acts*, 3:2204

20. Cf. Keener, *Acts*, 3:2278.

21. Theodor Zahn, *Introduction to the New Testament*, 3 vols., trans. John Moore Trout et al., 2nd ed. (New York: Charles Scribner's Sons, 1917), 1:179.

22. Cf. Keener, *Acts*, 3:2203–4.

23. Cf. Lightfoot, *Galatians*, 111; Dunn, *Beginning from Jerusalem*, 470; Keener, *Acts*, 3:2211.

24. Mark A. Seifrid, "Revisiting Antioch: Paul, Cephas, and 'the Ones from James,'" *TLZ* 144 (2019): 1224–35.

25. Cf. Seifrid, "Revisiting Antioch," 1227–30. Titus 1:10 may be an exception to this. See the discussion in Moo, *Galatians*, 147–48.

26. Seifrid, "Revisiting Antioch," 1232. Toward the end of his article ("Revisiting Antioch," 1235), however, Seifrid allows that they may have brought demands: we just don't know.

27. Seifrid, "Revisiting Antioch," 1230–31. The translations here are my own.

28. Lightfoot, *Galatians*, 112.

29. On the importance of Peter's example, see Thomas R. Schreiner, *Galatians*, ZECNT (Grand Rapids: Zondervan, 2010), 139.

30. Dunn, *Beginning from Jerusalem*, 489–94, believes that Paul's silence about the meeting's outcome means that he did not persuade those present, that Peter

prevailed, and that a breach opened up between Paul and the Jerusalem church. This argument from silence, however, does not sufficiently consider the evidence presented below, especially the evidence of Paul's relationship with Silas.

31. See Col 4:10; Acts 5:36–37; 11:22; 12:12.

CHAPTER 9

1. The Jerusalem Council addressed its letter with its "requirements" (Acts 15:28) to believing gentiles not only in Antioch but in Syria and Cilicia also (Acts 15:23). It seems likely that since Paul and Barnabas remained in Antioch for "some days" after their return from the Council, the decrees had already made their way into Syria and Cilicia. If not, Paul and Silas would have introduced them at this point (so Craig S. Keener, *Acts: An Exegetical Commentary*, 4 vols. [Grand Rapids: Baker, 2012–2015], 3:2310), but with the clarifications made necessary by the dispute over their interpretation in Antioch.

2. Luke does not mention Pisidian Antioch in his narration of the actual journey, but since he devoted so much space to the visit of Paul and Barnabas to Pisidian Antioch (Acts 13:14–50) it is likely that he intended his audience to understand that Paul revisited that city also. On this, see Glen L. Thompson and Mark Wilson, "The Route of Paul's Second Journey in Asia Minor: In the Steps of Robert Jewett and Beyond," *TynBul* 67 (2016): 222.

3. For this probable road, see J. A. Talbert, ed., *Barrington Atlas of the Greek and Roman World* (Princeton, NJ: Princeton University Press, 2000), 67. Paul may have traveled this same route a little less than a decade earlier when he went from Jerusalem to Caesarea to Syria and Cilicia (Acts 9:30; Gal 1:21).

4. For these two routes, see Talbert, *Barrington Atlas*, 62, 65, and 66; Cilliers Breytenbach and Christiane Zimmermann, *Early Christianity in Lycaonia and Adjacent Areas: From Paul to Amphilochius of Iconium*, AJEC 101/ECAM 2 (Leiden: Brill, 2018), 34; and the maps in David H. French, *An Album of Maps*, fasc. 3.9 of *Milestones*, vol. 3 of *Roman Roads and Milestones of Asia Minor*, Electronic Monograph 9 (Ankara: British Institute at Ankara, 2016), 77, 88.

5. I arrived at these figures using the map and distance scale in Talbert, *Barrington Atlas*, 66, and measuring with a Scalex MapWheel. I have also relied on the daily distance estimate of fifteen to twenty miles for walking in Rainer Riesner, *Paul's Early Period: Chronology, Mission Strategy, Theology*, trans. Douglas W. Stott (Grand Rapids: Eerdmans, 1998), 311. On ancient walking speeds, see also Glen L. Thompson and Mark Wilson, *In This Way We Came to Rome: With Paul on the Appian Way* (Bellingham, WA: Lexham, 2023), 27. Eckhard J. Schnabel estimates a journey of 150 km (about 93 miles) from Derbe to Lystra. Eckhard J. Schnabel, *Paul and the Early Church*, vol. 2 of *Early Christian Mission*, 2 vols. (Downers Grove, IL: InterVarsity, 2004), 1125.

6. In the Acts of Paul 3.3, Onesiphorus travels from Iconium "on the king's highway toward Lystra" to meet the apostle. Richard I. Pervo, trans., *The Acts of Paul: A New Translation with Introduction and Commentary* (Eugene, OR: Wipf & Stock, 2014), 3. On the Via Sebaste, see Stephen Mitchell, "Via Sebaste," *OCD*⁴ 1549.

7. For the understanding of the relationship between 1 Tim 4:14 and 2 Tim 1:6–7 adopted here, see Gordon D. Fee, *God's Empowering Presence: The Holy Spirit in the Letters of Paul* (Peabody, MA: Hendrickson, 1994), 771–76, 785–89.

8. For this understanding of the verbal sequence here (ᾔδεισαν ... ὅτι ... ὑπῆρχεν), see BDF 170 §330, and C. K. Barrett, *A Critical and Exegetical Commentary on the Acts of the Apostles*, ICC, 2 vols. (Edinburgh: T&T Clark, 1994–1998), 2:761–62. I have used Barrett's translation and added the italics (*Acts*, 2:751).

9. Barrett, *Acts*, 2:761.

10. Ernst Haenchen, *Acts of the Apostles: A Commentary* (Louisville: Westminster John Knox, 1971), 482; Dixon Slingerland, "'The Jews' in the Pauline Portion of Acts," *JAAR* 54 (1986): 309, 311.

11. Michael Gabizon, "The Development of the Matrilineal Principle in Ezra, Jubilees, and Acts," *JSP* 27 (2017): 149.

12. As Gabizon points out ("Matrilineal Principle," 150), this does come up in Neh 10:30 (and, I would add, in 13:23–27).

13. Men marrying foreign women is a concern, however, in Neh 10:30; 13:23–27.

14. Cf. Cilliers Breytenbach, "Probable Reasons for Paul's Unfruitful Missionary Attempts in Asia Minor: A Note on Acts 16:6–7," in *Die Apostelgeschichte und Die Hellenistische Geschichtsschreibung: Festschrift für Eckhard Plümacher zu seinem 65. Geburtstag*, ed. Cilliers Breytenbach and Jens Schröter (Leiden: Brill, 2004), 165.

15. Breytenbach and Zimmermann, *Early Christianity in Lycaonia*, 67–68. On Apamea, see A. H. M. Jones, *Cities of the Eastern Roman Provinces* (Oxford: Oxford University Press, 1937), 71–73.

16. Taking ὤν as an adverbial participle of cause.

17. J. B. Lightfoot, *Saint Paul's Epistle to the Galatians* (New York: Macmillan, 1896), 105.

18. Keener, *Acts*, 3:2796, observes that the Galatians "were among the first to know of" the collection.

19. Strabo calls it Paroreios (*Geogr.* 12.8.13–14). See Thompson and Wilson, "Route of Paul's Second Journey," 223–24. There is learned dispute about whether Luke's phrase τὴν Φρυγίαν καὶ Γαλατικὴν χώραν means "the Phrygian and Galatian region" or, as Barrett, for example, translates it, "Phrygia and Galatian territory" (*Acts*, 2:765; cf. Acts 18:23). If Barrett's translation is correct, then Luke is probably describing a journey north through ethnic Phrygia and ethnic Galatia (the northern part of the Roman province of Galatia). Ample evidence exists, however, that Φρυγία was an ethnic adjective of three terminations in this period and that the term Φρυγίαν here can function as a feminine adjective modifying the term χώραν. If that is the way to take it, the most obvious understanding of the Greek sees both

Φρυγίαν and Γαλατικήν as adjectives in the attributive position, modifying the noun χώραν. See Colin J. Hemer, "The Adjective 'Phrygia,'" *JTS* 27 (1976): 122–26; Hemer, "Phrygia: A Further Note," *JTS* 28 (1977): 99–101; and Hemer, *Book of Acts in the Setting of Hellenistic History*, ed. Conrad H. Gempf (Winona Lake, IN: Eisenbrauns, 1990), 281.

20. See the road labeled "D3" on the map in Thompson and Wilson, "Route of Paul's Second Journey," 244; and the comment of Breytenbach and Zimmerman, *Early Christianity in Lycaonia*, 69 (although they do not follow the geographical route outlined here).

21. Evert van Emde Boas, Albert Rijksbaron, Luuk Huitink, and Mathieu de Bakker say that "Circumstantial participles often express the **cause or motivation** for an action or statement, especially when they **follow the matrix verb**" (emphasis in the original). Emde Boas, Rijksbaron, Huitink, and de Bakker, *The Cambridge Grammar of Classical Greek* (Cambridge: Cambridge University Press, 2019), 627.

22. Ramsay, *St. Paul the Traveller and the Roman Citizen* (London: Hodder & Stoughton, 1896), 195; Thompson and Wilson, "Route of Paul's Second Journey," 227. Barrett, *Acts*, 2:767, dismisses this suggestion but gives no reasons for doing so.

23. See also Keener, *Acts*, 3:2330; and cf. W. P. Bowers, "Paul's Route through Mysia: A Note on Acts 16:8," *JTS* 30 (1979): 508.

24. Ramsay, *St. Paul the Traveller*, 195; Thompson and Wilson, "Route of Paul's Second Journey," 227.

25. See the persuasive argument of Thompson and Wilson, "Route of Paul's Second Journey," 232–37, for this itinerary, despite the lack of archaeological evidence for a road between Ancyra and Hadrianuthera (Bowers, "Paul's Route," 509). During Paul's time "Hadrianuthera" went by a different, unknown name.

26. Ramsay, *St. Paul the Traveller*, 197; BDAG 776, s.v. παρέρχομαι 6; LSJ 1337, s.v. παρέρχομαι 4.

27. Strabo, writing around AD 20, says that Alexandria Troas "today has a Roman settlement and is one of the most reputed of cities" (*Geogr.* 13.1.26). For more on its importance, see Colin J. Hemer, "Alexandria Troas," *TynBul* 26 (1975): 79–112.

28. See the review of the literature and the positions taken by Haenchen (*Acts*, 84–87, 489–91), Barrett (*Acts*, 2:xxv–xxx), and Marguerat (*Apostelgeschichte*, 589–92), and, for the first-person sea journey argument, see Vernon K. Robbins, *Sea Voyages and Beyond: Emerging Strategies in Socio-Rhetorical Interpretation*, Emory Studies in Early Christianity 14 (Dorset, UK: Deo, 2010), 47–81. Further analysis of Luke's use of the first-person plural appears below in appendix 1.

29. On all this, see the detailed and persuasive argument of Keener, *Acts*, 3:2350–63. Cf. Bruce, *Acts*, 307–8. On the first-person plural, see also Arthur Darby Nock, *Essays on Religion and the Ancient World*, 2 vols. (Oxford: Clarendon, 1972), 2:827–28.

30. Hemer, "Alexandria Troas," 92.

CHAPTER 10

1. I calculated the mileage using J. A. Talbert, ed., *Barrington Atlas of the Greek and Roman World* (Princeton, NJ: Princeton University Press, 2000), 51, and a Scalex MapWheel.

2. Yannis Lolos, "Via Egnatia after Egnatius: Imperial Policy and Inter-regional Contacts," *Mediterranean Historical Review* 22 (2007): 273–93.

3. Lolos, "Via Egnatia," 277, 282.

4. Richard S. Ascough, "Civic Pride at Philippi: The Text Critical Problem of Acts 16.12," *NTS* 44 (1998): 94. Strabo, *Geogr.* 7.17.19 says that the Romans divided Macedonia into four parts, "assigning one to Amphipolis, one to Thessalonikeia, one to Pella, and one to the Pelagonians." Duane W. Roller, trans., *The "Geography" of Strabo: An English Translation with Introduction and Notes* (Cambridge: Cambridge University Press, 2014).

5. The others were Dyrrachium and Pella. On this, see Lolos, "Via Egnatia," 278.

6. Emil Schürer, *The History of the Jewish People in the Age of Jesus Christ (175 B.C.–A.D. 135)*, rev. and ed. by Geza Vermes et al., 3 vols. (Edinburgh: T&T Clark, 1979), 2:441n65; and the note of Ralph Marcus in *Jewish Antiquities, Books XII–XIV*, vol. 7 of *Josephus with an English Translation*, trans. Louis H. Feldman, Ralph Marcus, and H. St. J. Thackeray, 9 vols., LCL (London: William Heinemann, 1961), 52–53.

7. Craig S. Keener, *Acts: An Exegetical Commentary*, 4 vols. (Grand Rapids: Baker, 2012–2015), 3:2386–87. Cf. Lolos, "Via Egnatia," 277: "From Amphipolis to Philippi the Egnatia passed north of Mount Pangaion, essentially making a loop in order to avoid the marshy areas, then entered the *pomerium* of the colony of Philippi through a monumental arch and went through the city."

8. Friedrich Gustav Lang, "Neues über Lydia? Zur Deutung von 'Pupurhändlerin' in Apg 16,14," *ZNW* 100 (2009): 29–44. See also Keener, *Acts*, 3:2396–403.

9. Murray J. Harris, *The Second Epistle to the Corinthians*, NIGTC (Grand Rapids: Eerdmans, 2005), 757–63.

10. When Paul's letters mention the history of his relationship with the Philippians, he too focuses on the promising beginning of his original work there (Phil 4:15–16) and the suffering that he experienced at the end (1 Thess 2:2).

11. Something like this seems to have happened a little later with the synagogue in Berea (Acts 17:11–12).

12. Peter Garnsey, "Legal Privilege in the Roman Empire," *Past & Present* 41 (1968): 19; Heike Omerzu, "The Roman Trial against Paul according to Acts 21–26," in *The Last Years of Paul: Essays from the Tarragona Conference, June 2013*, ed. Armand Puig i Tàrrech, John M. G. Barclay, and Jörg Frey, WUNT 1.352 (Tübingen: Mohr Siebeck, 2015), 192. The relevant Roman law appears in *Dig.* 48.6.7–8; *Paul. Sent.* 5.26.1–2.

13. On the normal procedure for dealing with troublemakers of low social stand-

ing, see Ryan S. Schellenberg, *Abject Joy: Paul, Prison, and the Art of Making Do* (New York: Oxford University Press, 2021), 31–38.

14. For the political standing of "magistrates" (στρατηγοί), see BDAG 947–48, s.v. στρατηγός 1.

15. Roman honor had an almost material nature and could be increased or depleted. On this see J. E. Lendon, "Roman Honor," in *The Oxford Handbook of Social Relations in the Roman World*, ed. Michael Peachin (Oxford: Oxford University Press, 2011), 377–403.

16. It may be true, as Schellenberg argues (*Abject Joy*, 72, 74–77), that Paul's relatively low social status (something that his manual labor and frequent imprisonments reveal) made him less vulnerable to feelings of shame, but, as Schellenberg acknowledges, even those of low social standing "had their own sense of dignity, and often guarded it fiercely" (*Abject Joy*, 76).

17. BDAG 1022, s.v. ὑβρίζω. The citation and translation of Aristotle is from this article.

18. 1 Thess 1:1 and 5 imply that Timothy was with Paul and Silas in Thessalonica, although Acts 17:4 and 10 mention only Paul and Silas.

19. Ch. Koukouli-Chrysanthaki, "Amphipolis," in *Brill's Companion to Ancient Macedon: Studies in the Archaeology and History of Macedon, 650 BC–300 AD*, ed. Robin J. Lane Fox (Leiden: Brill, 2011), 430.

20. Thucydides, *P.W.* 102; Strabo, *Geogr.* 7.F15a; and Duane W. Roller, *A Historical and Topographical Guide to the "Geography" of Strabo* (Cambridge: Cambridge University Press, 2018), 408.

21. Keener, *Acts*, 3:2535.

22. P. Adam-Veleni, "Thessalonike," in *Brill's Companion to Ancient Macedon: Studies in the Archaeology and History of Macedon, 650 BC–300 AD*, ed. Robin Lane Fox (Leiden: Brill, 2011), 553. The immediately preceding sentence is also indebted to Adam-Veleni's chapter.

23. On the prominence of the imperial cult, see Holland Lee Hendrix, "Archaeology and Eschatology at Thessalonica," in *The Future of Early Christianity: Essays in Honor of Helmut Koester*, ed. Birger A. Pearson (Minneapolis: Fortress, 1991), 115–17; and James R. Harrison, *Paul and the Imperial Authorities at Thessalonica and Rome*, WUNT 1.273 (Tübingen: Mohr Siebeck, 2019), 55–56.

24. Adam-Veleni, "Thessalonike," 555, 558–59. On the variety of gods, see also David W. J. Gill, "Macedonia," in *The Book of Acts in Its Greco-Roman Setting*, ed. David W. J. Gill and Conrad Gempf, vol. 2 of *The Book of Acts in Its First Century Setting*, ed. Bruce W. Winter, 6 vols. (Grand Rapids: Eerdmans, 1994), 408–9 and 414–15; and Keener, *Acts*, 3:2542.

25. As the imperfect tense of the verb implies. On this, see Abraham J. Malherbe, *The Letters to the Thessalonians*, AB 32B (New York: Doubleday, 2000), 421; Jeffrey A. D. Weima, *1–2 Thessalonians*, BECNT (Grand Rapids: Baker, 2014), 345, 523–24.

26. On the connection between 2 Thess 2:3–12 and Dan 10–12, see Colin Nich-

oll, "Michael, the Restrainer Removed (2 Thess. 2:6–7)," *JTS* 51 (2000): 35–36; and Weima, *1–2 Thessalonians*, 532–33, 576.

27. On this phenomenon generally, see Paula Fredriksen, "How Later Contexts Affect Pauline Content, or: Retrospect Is the Mother of Anachronism," in *Jews and Christians in the First and Second Centuries: How to Write Their History*, ed. Peter J. Tomson and Joshua Schwartz (Leiden: Brill, 2014), 23–24; and for the application of this insight to the context of 1 Thess, see Nijay K. Gupta, "The Thessalonian Believers, Formerly 'Pagans' or 'God-Fearers'? Challenging a Stubborn Consensus," *Neot* 52 (2018): 91–113.

28. Keener, *Acts*, 3:2539n2431, comments that "Luke expects his audience to understand that he sometimes condenses time."

29. Ernst Haenchen, *Acts of the Apostles: A Commentary* (Louisville: Westminster John Knox, 1971), 512.

30. On the prevalence and criticism of these figures in the mid-first-century Roman world, see especially Bruce W. Winter, "The Entries and Ethics of Orators and Paul (1 Thessalonians 2:1–12)," *TynBul* 44 (1993): 55–64; and Winter, *Philo and Paul among the Sophists: Alexandrian and Corinthian Responses to a Julio-Claudian Movement*, 2nd ed. (Grand Rapids: Eerdmans, 2002), 40–79. See also the speech of aggrieved "Philosophy" in Lucian, *Fug.* 12–21, although it is from over a century after Paul and exaggerated for effect. "Every city," says Philosophy, "is filled with such upstarts" (*Fug.* 16 [Harmon, LCL]).

31. See also Abraham J. Malherbe, *Paul and the Thessalonians: The Philosophic Tradition of Pastoral Care* (Philadelphia: Fortress, 1987), 3–4.

32. Harris, *Second Epistle to the Corinthians*, 760.

33. Weima, *1–2 Thessalonians*, 615–16.

34. On the date and character of Jubilees, see the introduction of O. S. Wintermute in *OTP* 1:35–50.

35. Cf. M. J. J. Menken, "Paradise Regained or Still Lost? Eschatology and Disorderly Behaviour in 2 Thessalonians," *NTS* 38 (1992): 277–80, 285–89; G. K. Beale, *1–2 Thessalonians*, IVP New Testament Commentary 13 (Downers Grove, IL: InterVarsity, 2003), 256; and Mark B. Giszczak, "The Rhetoric and Social Practice of Excommunication in 2 Thessalonians 3:6–15," *CBQ* 83 (2021): 111, who believe, however, that the theology of work in 2 Thess 3:6–15 is related to the curse of Gen 3:17–19. Menken ("Paradise Regained or Still Lost?," 278, 280) entertains but rejects the idea that Gen 2:15–16 stands behind the passage, since the pseudonymous "Paul" of the text describes his own exemplary labor as "in toil and hardship," and, to Menken, this seems closer to Gen 3:17–19.

36. Bruce W. Winter, "'If a Man Does Not Wish to Work . . .': A Cultural and Historical Setting for 2 Thessalonians 3:6–16," *TynBul* 40 (1989): 305–9; Malherbe, *Paul and the Thessalonians*, 99–101; Colin R. Nicholl, *From Hope to Despair in Thessalonica: Situating 1 and 2 Thessalonians*, SNTSMS 126 (Cambridge: Cambridge University Press, 2004), 173–75; Giszczak, "Rhetoric and Social Practice," 105–7.

37. Malherbe, *Paul and the Thessalonians*, 99–101; Malherbe, *Letters to the Thessalonians*, 251.

38. Ronald F. Hock, "The Workshop as a Social Setting for Paul's Missionary Preaching," *CBQ* 41 (1979): 442; Jerome Murphy-O'Connor, *St. Paul's Corinth: Texts and Archaeology*, 3rd ed. rev. and exp. (Collegeville, MN: Liturgical Press, 2002), 195–96.

39. Trans. Cora E. Lutz, *Musonius Rufus, "The Roman Socrates,"* Yale Classical Studies 10 (New Haven, CT: Yale University Press, 1947), 81, 83. Cf. Hock, "Workshop," 447.

40. Jerome Murphy-O'Connor, *Paul: A Critical Life* (Oxford: Clarendon, 1996), 86–87.

41. There was probably only one such gift. Paul's puzzling Greek in Phil 4:16 probably means not that the Philippians supported him more than once while he was in Thessalonica but that they supported him in Thessalonica and more than once elsewhere. On this, see Leon Morris, "ΚΑΙ ΑΠΑΞ ΚΑΙ DIS," *NovT* 1 (1956): 208.

42. Many of the relevant inscriptions are from Thessalonica, and at least two of the Thessalonian inscriptions are from the first century. On all this, see G. H. R. Horsley, "Politarchs," *ABD* 5:385–87.

43. Hendrix, "Archaeology and Eschatology," 112–14; Harrison, *Paul and the Imperial Authorities*, 63–65.

44. S. R. F. Price, "Gods and Emperors: The Greek Language of the Roman Imperial Cult," *JHS* 104 (1984): 83.

45. Harrison, *Paul and the Imperial Authorities*, 66–68.

46. D. Clint Burnett, "Imperial Divine Honors in Julio-Claudian Thessalonica and the Thessalonian Correspondence," *JBL* 139 (2020): 579–80, citing *IG* 10.2.1s.1052, an inscription announcing that "Avia Posilla daughter of Aulus" had funded construction of a temple complex in Thessalonica dedicated to the worship of "Imperator Caesar Augustus son of god, Hercules, and the city."

47. Burnett, "Imperial Divine Honors," 580, 584.

48. Burnett, "Imperial Divine Honors," 586–88.

49. F. F. Bruce, *1 and 2 Thessalonians*, WBC 45 (Waco, TX: Word, 1982), xxiv–xxv.

50. Winter (*Divine Honours for the Caesars*, 259) suggests this as a possibility.

51. F. F. Bruce, *The Book of the Acts*, NICNT, rev. ed. (Grand Rapids: Eerdmans, 1986), 326, 327.

52. ἀπορφανισθέντες ἀφ' ὑμῶν. On this expression, see Weima, *1–2 Thessalonians*, 196–97.

53. Cf. C. K. Barrett, *A Critical and Exegetical Commentary on the Acts of the Apostles*, ICC, 2 vols. (Edinburgh: T&T Clark, 1994–1998), 2:817.

54. Talbert, *Barrington Atlas*, 50. Berea is sometimes spelled Beroia or Berroia.

55. Eckhard J. Schnabel, *Paul and the Early Church*, vol. 2 of *Early Christian*

Mission, 2 vols. (Downers Grove, IL: InterVarsity, 2004), 1168; Gill, "Macedonia," 415; Keener, *Acts*, 3:2561.

56. See the roads and possible roads in Talbert, *Barrington Atlas*, 50. Luke says that they left Thessalonica "by night" (διὰ νυκτός). Gill ("Macedonia," 410) and Keener (*Acts*, 3:2561n2633) suggest that Paul and his companions went all the way to Pella on the Via Egnatia before striking out on a southern trajectory.

57. Luke uses the term εὐγενέστεροι to describe them, which probably does not mean in this context "noble" (ESV, NIV) so much as "fair-minded," "receptive," or "open-minded" (REB, NRSV). On this, see F. W. Danker, "Menander and the New Testament," *NTS* 10 (1964): 366–67; and BDAG 404, s.v. εὐγενής 2.

58. The Bereans themselves did not provide this aid since Paul reminds the Philippians in Phil 4:15, "When I left Macedonia, no church entered into partnership with me in giving and receiving, except you only."

CHAPTER 11

1. Alan Herbert Sommerstein, "Aeschylus," *OCD*[4] 26.

2. C. K. Barrett, *A Critical and Exegetical Commentary on the Acts of the Apostles*, ICC, 2 vols. (Edinburgh: T&T Clark, 1994–1998), 2:828–29; Eckhard J. Schnabel, *Paul and the Early Church*, vol. 2 of *Early Christian Mission*, 2 vols. (Downers Grove, IL: InterVarsity, 2004), 1170; Martha C. Nussbaum and Catherine Osborne, "Aristotle," *OCD*[4] 159.

3. Polemon of Ilion in the early second century BC and Pausanias in the second century AD both wrote tourist guides to the city. See Duane W. Roller, *A Historical and Topographical Guide to the "Geography" of Strabo* (Cambridge: Cambridge University Press, 2018), 506.

4. See Pausanias, *Descr.* 1.24.3; and R. E. Wycherley, "St. Paul at Athens," *JTS* 19 (1968): 620.

5. John McRay, *Archaeology and the New Testament* (Grand Rapids: Baker, 1991), 301.

6. Bruce W. Winter, *Divine Honours for the Caesars: The First Christians' Responses* (Grand Rapids: Eerdmans, 2015), 131; Drew W. Strait, "The Wisdom of Solomon, Ruler Cults, and Paul's Polemic against Idols in the Areopagus Speech," *JBL* 136 (2017): 614.

7. *IG* II[2], 3173, trans. Winter, *Divine Honours*, 131.

8. Strait, "Paul's Polemic against Idols," 623.

9. Anna Benjamin and Antony E. Raubitschek, "Arae Augusti," *Hesperia* 28 (1959): 83–85.

10. This seems to be the meaning of παρωξύνετο in Acts 17:16. On this, see Arthur Darby Nock, *Essays on Religion and the Ancient World*, 2 vols. (Oxford: Clarendon, 1972), 2:824.

11. See, e.g., Charles A. Wanamaker, *The Epistles to the Thessalonians*, NIGTC (Grand Rapids: Eerdmans, 1990), 122.

12. It is possible that Silas also arrived since Paul waited for both Timothy and Silas at Athens (Acts 17:15–16), and Paul uses the first-person plural in 1 Thess 3:1 ("When *we* could bear it no longer, *we* were willing to be left behind in Athens alone"). See, e.g., F. F. Bruce, *1 and 2 Thessalonians*, WBC 45 (Waco, TX: Word, 1982), 60. Paul's shift to the first-person singular in 1 Thess 3:5, however, makes it likely that the plural in 1 Thess 3:1 is figurative rather than literal. On this, see Jeffrey Weima, *1–2 Thessalonians*, BECNT (Grand Rapids: Baker, 2014), 207–8.

13. On the meaning of the expression μηκέτι στέγειν, see Philo, *Flacc.* 64, where Philo describes the Jews suffering under the horrors of famine in Alexandria as "unable any longer to endure [μηκέτι στέγειν] their privation."

14. It seems safe to conclude that Luke presents the Areopagus incident as the catalyst for Paul's departure since conflict with important citizens often leads to Paul's departure from a city in Acts. See 13:50–52 (Pisidian Antioch), 14:5–6 (Iconium), 14:20 (Lystra), 16:16–40 (Philippi), 17:5–9 (Thessalonica), 17:13–14 (Berea), 18:12–17 (Corinth), and 19:21–20:1 (Ephesus).

15. See LSJ 1627, s.v. σπερμολόγος.

16. See also Athenaeus, *Deipn.* 3.31.19. On Demosthenes, see George Law Cawkwell, "Demosthenes," *OCD*[4] 439–41.

17. As interpreters have often noticed. See, e.g., Ernst Haenchen, *Acts of the Apostles: A Commentary* (Louisville: Westminster John Knox, 1971), 527; Richard I. Pervo, *Acts: A Commentary*, Hermeneia (Minneapolis: Fortress, 2009), 425; Daniel Marguerat, *Die Apostelgeschichte*, KEK 3 (Göttingen: Vandenhoeck & Ruprecht, 2022), 617.

18. See also Plato, *Apol.* 126b.

19. Luke uses the term twelve times in Luke-Acts, seven of them in a hostile sense. Cf. Haenchen, *Acts*, 527; Pervo, *Acts*, 428. Marguerat (*Apostelgeschichte*, 618) argues against this understanding of the term and for the interpretation of the meeting as an effort simply to find out more about Paul's new beliefs (cf. Acts 17:20–21).

20. Colin J. Hemer, "Paul at Athens: A Topographical Note," *NTS* 20 (1974): 341–50; Craig S. Keener, *Acts: An Exegetical Commentary*, 4 vols. (Grand Rapids: Baker, 2012–2015), 3:2600.

21. E.g., Nock: "I do not for one moment ascribe the speech to Paul . . ." (*Essays on Religion*, 2:824).

22. Haenchen, *Acts*, 529; Carl R. Holladay, *Acts: A Commentary*, NTL (Louisville: Westminster John Knox, 2016), 346.

23. C. K. Barrett, "Paulus als Missionar und Theologe," *ZTK* 86 (1989): 27; Barrett, *Acts* 2:825–26.

24. F. F. Bruce, "Paul and the Athenians," *ExpTim* 88 (1976): 8.

25. Cf. Marguerat (*Apostelgeschichte*, 630–31) who believes Luke constructed the speech but did so in a way that was not incompatible with what can be known of Paul's preaching to unbelieving gentiles in his letters.

26. Barrett, "Paulus als Missionar und Theologe," 27.

27. Bruce, "Paul and the Athenians," 13; Colin J. Hemer, "The Speeches of Acts II: The Areopagus Address," *TynB* 40 (1989): 253.

28. Victor Davis Hanson, "Introduction," in *The Landmark Thucydides: A Comprehensive Guide to the Peloponnesian War*, ed. Robert B. Strassler (New York: Free Press, 1996), xvi.

29. For discussion of this possibility, see Keener (*Acts*, 3:2658), although he believes that Epimenides is the more likely source.

30. Keener, *Acts*, 3:2672.

31. Cf. Homer, *Od.* 11.568–571, although here Minos may simply be acting as a judge among the dead who bring their lawsuits against each other to him. On this, see Robert Garland and John Scheld, "Death, Attitudes Toward," *OCD*[4] 417.

32. Many people did not believe in an afterlife, as the common Latin epitaph "nf f ns nc (non fui, fui, non sum, non curo" demonstrates. It means, in the translation of Mary Beard, John North, and Simon Price, "I wasn't; I was; I'm not; I don't care." See their *Religions of Rome*, 2 vols. (Cambridge: Cambridge University Press, 1998), 2:236.

33. See, e.g., Hans Conzelmann, *Acts of the Apostles*, ed. Eldon J. Epp with Christopher R. Matthews, trans. James Limberg, A. Thomas Kraabel, and Donald J. Juel, Hermeneia (Philadelphia: Fortress, 1987), 146; Bruce, "Paul and the Athenians," 12; F. F. Bruce, *The Book of the Acts*, rev. ed., NICNT (Grand Rapids: Eerdmans, 1988), 343.

34. Henry Chadwick, trans. and ed., *Origen: Contra Celsum* (Cambridge: Cambridge University Press, 1953), 274.

35. Bruce, "Paul and the Athenians," 12; Bruce, *Acts*, 344.

36. On the chronology, see Rainer Riesner, *Paul's Early Period: Chronology, Mission Strategy, Theology*, trans. Douglas W. Stott (Grand Rapids: Eerdmans, 1998), 210.

37. Kevin Clinton, "Eleusis," *OCD*[4] 500.

38. J. G. Frazer, *Pausanias and Other Greek Sketches* (London: Macmillan, 1900), 221. Cf. Roller, *Historical and Topographical Guide*, 497.

39. Jerome Murphy-O'Connor, *St. Paul's Corinth: Texts and Archaeology*, 3rd ed. rev. and exp. (Collegeville, MN: Liturgical Press, 2002), 100. On the timing, see also the calculator on the Stanford Geospatial Network Model of the Roman World (at orbis.stanford.edu).

40. On the date, see Roller, *Historical and Topographical Guide*, 478.

41. On the Lechaeum road, see the quotation and analysis of Plutarch, *Sept. sav. Conv.* 2–3 (146de, 148b) in Murphy-O'Connor, *St. Paul's Corinth*, 106–7. Strabo said that Cenchreae was seventy stadia from Corinth (*Geogr.* 8.6.22), roughly eight miles if one stadion is between 177.7 and 197.3 meters. On the length of the stadion, see Duane W. Roller, *The "Geography" of Strabo: An English Translation with Introduction and Notes* (Cambridge: Cambridge University Press, 2014), 33; and Roller, *Eratosthenes' "Geography"* (Princeton: Princeton University Press, 2010), 271–73.

42. Quoted in Murphy-O'Connor, *St. Paul's Corinth*, 124.
43. Murphy-O'Connor, *St. Paul's Corinth*, 87–89.
44. Quoted in Murphy-O'Connor, *St. Paul's Corinth*, 88.
45. Quoted in Murphy-O'Connor, *St. Paul's Corinth*, 100.
46. Murphy-O'Connor, *St. Paul's Corinth*, 82–83. See also the text and translation in R. A. Kearsley, "Women in Public Life in the Roman East: Iunia Theodora, Claudia Metrodora and Phoebe, Benefactress of Paul," *TynBul* 50 (1999): 203–8.
47. Murphy-O'Connor, *St. Paul's Corinth*, 100 (using the LCL translation of J. W. Cohoon). Dio claims to be describing the experience of Diogenes, the fourth-century BC Cynic philosopher, but Murphy-O'Connor argues that he is speaking of his own experience in the city. See also Bruce W. Winter, *Philo and Paul among the Sophists: Alexandrian and Corinthian Responses to a Julio-Claudian Movement*, 2nd ed. (Grand Rapids: Eerdmans, 2002), 125.
48. Murphy-O'Connor (*St. Paul's Corinth*, 91) believes that this scene in Arrian's *Discourses of Epictetus* is set in Corinth. It is clear from 3.1.34 that this student, at least, was a Corinthian. On the passage generally, see especially Winter, *Philo and Paul*, 113–22.
49. Winter, *Philo and Paul*, 114, 116.
50. On Prisca and Aquila, see Frank Thielman, *Romans*, ZECNT 6 (Grand Rapids: Zondervan, 2016), 712–16.
51. Erich S. Gruen, *Diaspora: Jews amidst Greeks and Romans* (Cambridge, MA: Harvard University Press, 2002), 32–33, 36–41.
52. According to Peter Lampe, "The displacement of 'Chrestus' for 'Christus' by Suetonius produces no difficulty: 'Chrestians' was a popular designation for the Christians." Lampe, *From Paul to Valentinus: Christians at Rome in the First Two Centuries*, ed. Marshall D. Johnson, trans. Michael Steinhauser (Minneapolis: Fortress, 2003), 120.
53. See Harry J. Leon, *The Jews of Ancient Rome*, updated ed. (Peabody, MA: Hendrickson, 1995), 27. Leon comments that if all the Jews had left Rome, tens of thousands of people would have been involved, and Josephus would likely have mentioned the incident. On the public relations motivation of the decree, see Gruen, *Diaspora*, 33: "Like previous moves against astrologers, this [expulsion] served more to express public denunciation than to create a host of exiles."
54. Luke uses the more familiar, diminutive form "Priscilla" (Acts 18:2, 18, 26) rather than Paul's more formal "Prisca" (Rom 16:3; 1 Cor 16:19; 2 Tim 4:19).
55. See the informed and cautious speculation of David G. Horrell, *The Making of Christian Morality: Reading Paul in Ancient and Modern Contexts* (Grand Rapids: Eerdmans, 2019), 46–47; and the more imaginative but plausible description of Murphy-O'Connor, *St. Paul's Corinth*, 194–96.
56. On the materials and result of Paul's labors, see H. Szesnat, "What Did the σκηνοποιός Paul Produce?," *Neotest* 27 (1993): 391–402; and Murphy-O'Connor, *St. Paul's Corinth*, 193–94.

57. Murphy-O'Connor, *St. Paul's Corinth*, 192.
58. Winter, *Philo and Paul*, 113–72.

CHAPTER 12

1. P. J. Parsons, "Background: The Papyrus Letter," *Didactica Classica Gandensia* 20 (1980): separatum, 7–9; Parsons, *City of the Sharp-Nosed Fish: Greek Papyri Beneath the Egyptian Sand Reveal a Long-Lost World* (London: Weidenfeld & Nicolson, 2007), 122–36.
2. P.Oxy. 42.3063, P. J. Parsons, ed. and trans., *The Oxyrhynchus Papyri*, vol. 42, Greco-Roman Memoirs 58 (London: Egypt Exploration Society, 1974), 153–54. The translation is Parsons's.
3. My translation.
4. Parsons, *Oxyrhynchus Papyri*, 42:154, believes that since "the ink and pen look the same" the same scribe wrote these final notations, although in haste. For the position taken here, see Steve Reece, *Paul's Large Letters: Paul's Autographic Subscription in the Light of Ancient Epistolary Conventions*, LNTS 561 (New York: Bloomsbury, 2017), 150. The pen and ink would look the same if Diogenes had taken the pen from the scribe to append these remarks.
5. Trans. Parsons. See the photograph of the letter in Reece, *Paul's Large Letters*, 151.
6. On the parallel between Paul's use of the verb Θαυμάζω here and P.Oxy. 42.3063, line 11, see Richard N. Longenecker, *Galatians*, WBC 41 (Dallas, TX: Word, 1990), 14.
7. In contrast to Paul's signature, Diogenes's letters were about the same size as those of the scribe. On this, see Reece, *Paul's Large Letters*, 150–51.
8. Cf. Reece, *Paul's Large Letters*, 198.
9. Theodor Zahn, *Introduction to the New Testament*, 3 vols., trans. John Moore Trout et al., 2nd ed. (New York: Charles Scribner's Sons, 1917), 1:205–7. Others have also argued that Gal originated in Corinth but place it later in Paul's work there, after 1 and 2 Thess. See, e.g., Johannes Weiss, *Earliest Christianity: A History of the Period A.D. 30–150*, trans. Frederick C. Grant, 2 vols. (New York: Harper, 1959), 1:296; and James D. G. Dunn, *Beginning from Jerusalem*, vol. 2 of *Christianity in the Making*, 3 vols. (Grand Rapids: Eerdmans, 2009), 720–25.
10. Zahn, *Introduction to the New Testament*, 1:205. Cf. Dunn, *Beginning from Jerusalem*, 703–4; Abraham J. Malherbe, *The Letters to the Thessalonians*, AB 32B (New York: Doubleday, 2000), 71–74; Jeffrey A. D. Weima, *1–2 Thessalonians* BECNT (Grand Rapids: Baker, 2014), 38–39.
11. Zahn, *Introduction to the New Testament*, 1:169–71, 197–98, 205–6.
12. "Silas" is the short version of the name "Silvanus," which Paul uses in 1 Thess 1:1 and 2 Thess 1:1.
13. Zahn, *Introduction to the New Testament*, 1:170, 197.

14. On Paul's switch to the first-person singular in 1 Thess 5:27 as a sign that he had taken the pen from the scribe, see especially Weima, *1–2 Thessalonians*, 428–30.

15. Craig S. Keener, *Acts: An Exegetical Commentary*, 4 vols. (Grand Rapids: Baker, 2012–2015), 3:2203.

16. On the meaning of the verb I have translated "intimidating," see BDAG 990 s.v. ταράσσω 2, and, especially, Acts 15:24.

17. Bruce W. Winter, *Divine Honours for the Caesars: The First Christians' Responses* (Grand Rapids: Eerdmans, 2015), 226–28, 243–44.

18. Stephen Mitchell, *Anatolia: Land, Men, and Gods in Asia Minor*, 2 vols. (Oxford: Oxford University Press, 1993), 1:105–7; Winter, *Divine Honours for the Caesars*, 226–27, citing Mitchell.

19. Mitchell, *Anatolia*, 1:107; cf. *Anatolia*, 2:10: "One cannot avoid the impression that the obstacle which stood in the way of the progress of Christianity, and the force which would have drawn new adherents back to conformity with the prevailing paganism, was the public worship of the emperors."

20. Mitchell, *Anatolia*, 2:10.

21. Greeks and Romans often found circumcision offensive, but the Romans tolerated it as a long-standing religious custom of the Jews. See Winter, *Divine Honours for the Caesars*, 228–32.

22. Keener, *Galatians*, 120–21.

23. Dunn calls Galatians "a restatement of Paul's gospel" (*Beginning from Jerusalem*, 725).

24. On the relative length and detail of blessings and curses in these passages, see Martin Noth, *The Laws of the Pentateuch and Other Studies*, trans. D. R. Ap-Thomas (Philadelphia: Fortress, 1966), 122, 129–31.

25. On the possibility that these verses reflect division in Galatia, see the cautious analysis of David A. deSilva, *The Letter to the Galatians*, NICNT (Grand Rapids: Eerdmans, 2018), 452.

26. William Wrede, *Paul*, trans. Edward Lummis (London: Philip Green, 1907), 86–109.

27. Wrede, *Paul*, 122–54.

28. See, e. g., Albert Schweitzer, *The Mysticism of Paul the Apostle*, trans. William Montgomery (New York: Henry Holt, 1931), 220–21; E. P. Sanders, *Paul, the Law, and the Jewish People* (Philadelphia: Fortress, 1983), 17–48; and Douglas A. Campbell, *The Deliverance of God: An Apocalyptic Rereading of Justification in Paul* (Grand Rapids: Eerdmans, 2009), 521, 525, 856–66.

29. Mark T. Finney, "*Servile Supplicium*: Shame and the Deuteronomic Curse—Crucifixion in Its Cultural Context," *BTB* 43 (2013): 127–28.

30. Joseph A. Fitzmyer, "Crucifixion in Ancient Palestine, Qumran Literature, and the New Testament," *CBQ* 40 (1978): 498–507.

31. Finney, "*Servile Supplicium*," 132.

32. This at least seems to be Luke's perspective. See Timothy W. Reardon,

"'Hanging on a Tree': Deuteronomy 21.22–23 and the Rhetoric of Jesus' Crucifixion in Acts 5.12–42," *JSNT* 37 (2015): 420–21.

33. Reardon, "'Hanging on a Tree,'" 415–25.
34. Reardon, "'Hanging on a Tree,'" 416, 419.
35. Cf. Noth, *Laws of the Pentateuch*, 128–31.
36. A. Andrew Das, *Galatians*, Concordia Commentary (Saint Louis: Concordia, 2014), 328.
37. Fitzmyer, "Crucifixion in Ancient Palestine," 509–10.
38. Luke speaks of "hanging him on a tree" (κρεμάσαντες ἐπὶ ξύλου) in Acts 5:30 and 10:39, and Deut 21:22 LXX uses the phrase "if . . . you hang him on a tree" (ἐὰν . . . κρεμάσητε αὐτὸν ἐπὶ ξύλου). On the echo, see Reardon, "'Hanging on a Tree,'" 415. On Roman references to crucifixion, see Finney, "*Servile Supplicium*," 125–27.

CHAPTER 13

1. For this understanding of Paul's difficult Greek in 1 Thess 1:8, see Jeffrey A. D. Weima, *1–2 Thessalonians*, BECNT (Grand Rapids: Baker, 2014), 103–4.
2. D. Clint Burnett, "Imperial Divine Honors in Julio-Claudian Thessalonica and the Thessalonian Correspondence," *JBL* 139 (2020): 586–88.
3. Abraham J. Malherbe offers a plausible argument, based on Paul's use of epistolary conventions in 1 Thess 3:6, 8, and 10, that in addition to responding to information Paul had learned from Timothy, he was probably also responding to a letter from the Thessalonians that Timothy had brought with him. Malherbe, *The Letters to the Thessalonians*, AB 32B (New York: Doubleday, 2000), 75–77, 208–11.
4. The connection between flattery and greed and the need for frankness of speech among true friends were common topics among philosophers in Paul's time. The Epicurean philosopher Philodemus (died c. 40 BC), for example, wrote extensively on both flattery and frankness of speech among friends, and these texts were found in the library of an opulent villa in Herculaneum, destroyed in AD 79 by the eruption of Mount Vesuvius. Similarly, the moral philosopher Plutarch (c. AD 50–120) wrote a long tractate entitled "How to Tell a Flatterer from a Friend." See Clarence E. Glad, "Frank Speech, Flattery, and Friendship in Philodemus," in *Friendship, Flattery, and Frankness of Speech: Studies on Friendship in the New Testament World*, ed. John T. Fitzgerald, Supplements to Novum Testamentum 82 (Leiden: Brill, 1996), 21–59; and Jerome Kemp, "Flattery and Frankness in Horace and Philodemus," *Greece & Rome* 57 (2010): 65–76.
5. Cf. Plutarch's essay, "How to Tell a Flatterer from a Friend," a large portion of which is devoted to the true friend's "frank criticism" (παρρησία). 1 Thess 2:2 uses the verb παρρησιάζομαι to describe the character of Paul's relationship with the Thessalonians.
6. T. J. Deidun, *New Covenant Morality in Paul*, AnBib 89 (Rome: Biblical Insti-

tute Press, 1981), 55–56; Frank Thielman, *Paul and the Law: A Contextual Approach* (Downers Grove, IL: InterVarsity, 1994), 75–77; Weima, *1–2 Thessalonians*, 281–83.

7. N. T. Wright, *The Resurrection of the Son of God*, vol. 3 of *Christian Origins and the Question of God* (Minneapolis: Fortress, 2003), 34; cf. Mary Beard, John North, and Simon Price, *Religions of Rome*, 2 vols. (Cambridge: Cambridge University Press, 1998), 2:236.

8. Wright, *Resurrection of the Son of God*, 32–84.

9. Colin R. Nicholl, *From Hope to Despair in Thessalonica: Situating 1 and 2 Thessalonians*, SNTSMS 126 (Cambridge: Cambridge University Press, 2004), 49–79.

10. See, e.g., Traugott Holtz, *Der erste Brief an die Thessalonicher*, EKK 13, 2nd ed. (Zürich: Benziger, 1990), 203; Nicholl, *From Hope to Despair*, 43–45; Weima, *1–2 Thessalonians*, 319–20, 335.

11. Wright, *Resurrection of the Son of God*, 217–18.

12. N. T. Wright, *Paul and the Faithfulness of God*, vol. 4 of *Christian Origins and the Question of God* (Minneapolis: Fortress, 2013), 1082–85.

13. Nicholl, *From Hope to Despair*, 49–79.

14. See the many examples in Adolf Deissmann, *Light from the Ancient East: The New Testament Illustrated by Recently Discovered Texts of the Greco-Roman World*, trans. Lionel R. M. Strachan, 2nd ed. (London: Hodder & Stoughton, 1911), 372–78. See also MM 407, LSJ 1343, and BDAG 780–81, all s.v. παρουσία.

15. Deissmann, *Light from the Ancient East*, 374–75.

16. Greek text and translation in Arthur S. Hunt and C. C. Edgar, eds., *Official Documents*, vol. 2 of *Select Papyri*, LCL 282 (Cambridge, MA: Harvard University Press, 1934), 76–79. Cf. the discussion in James R. Harrison, *Paul and the Imperial Authorities at Thessalonica and Rome*, WUNT 1.273 (Tübingen: Mohr Siebeck, 2011), 56–57.

17. F. F. Bruce, *1 and 2 Thessalonians*, WBC 45 (Waco, TX: Word, 1982), 102; Harrison, *Paul and the Imperial Authorities*, 60.

18. Weima, *1–2 Thessalonians*, 334.

19. See *RPC* 1.1554. The image is readily available on the website Roman Provincial Coinage based in the Ashmolean Museum, Oxford University. For discussion, see Harrington, *Paul and the Imperial Authorities*, 55; Bruce W. Winter, *Divine Honours for the Caesars: The First Christians' Responses* (Grand Rapids: Eerdmans, 2015), 250; and Burnett, "Imperial Divine Honors," 574–75.

20. Burnett, "Imperial Divine Honors," 571–72, 580, 584.

21. Harrison, *Paul and the Imperial Authorities*, 61–62.

22. See, e.g., William Wrede, *The Authenticity of the Second Letter to the Thessalonians*, trans. Robert Rhea (Eugene, OR: Wipf & Stock, 2017), 14–45; John A. Bailey, "Who Wrote II Thessalonians?," *NTS* 25 (1979): 132–37.

23. Bailey, "Who Wrote II Thessalonians?," 137. Cf. Wrede, *Authenticity of the Second Letter*, 35–45, 64.

24. Wrede, *Authenticity of the Second Letter*, 64; Bailey, "Who Wrote II Thessalonians?," 132–36, 142.

25. Wrede, *Authenticity of the Second Letter*, 72; Bailey, "Who Wrote II Thessalonians?," 137–38 (from whom the quotation is taken).

26. Bailey, "Who Wrote II Thessalonians?," 142–43. Cf. Wrede, *Authenticity of the Second Letter*, 37.

27. Paul Foster, "Who Wrote 2 Thessalonians? A Fresh Look at an Old Problem," *JSNT* 35 (2012): 157; Weima, *1–2 Thessalonians*, 48–49.

28. Foster, "Who Wrote 2 Thessalonians?," 163.

29. Bailey, "Who Wrote II Thessalonians?," 136.

30. Weima, *1–2 Thessalonians*, 51.

31. Cf. Foster, "Who Wrote 2 Thessalonians?," 166.

32. Gordon D. Fee, *The First and Second Letters to the Thessalonians*, NICNT (Grand Rapids: Eerdmans, 2009), 271–77; Weima, *1–2 Thessalonians*, 504–5.

33. Nicholl, *From Hope to Despair*, 131, 142.

34. The relevant clause in 2 Thess 2:2 uses the preposition "through" (διά + the genitive case), not "from" (ἀπό), as in many translations: "whether *through* spirit, *through* speech, or *through* epistle, as *through* us," to give a clunky, word-for-word translation. The NIV (2011) gets this right: "We ask you, brothers and sisters, not to become easily unsettled or alarmed by the teaching allegedly from us—whether by a prophecy or by word of mouth or by letter—asserting that the day of the Lord has already come." See Fee, *Letters to the Thessalonians*, 274–77.

35. Paul's statement, "When I was still with you I told [ἔλεγον] you these things" (2:5) uses the imperfect tense, which here implies repetition (Weima, *1–2 Thessalonians*, 523–24).

36. On the connection to Dan 10–12, see Colin R. Nicholl, "Michael, the Restrainer Removed (2 Thess. 2:6–7)," *JTS* 51 (2000): 35–36; and Weima, *1–2 Thessalonians*, 532–33, 576. On the connection to Jesus's use of Daniel in his eschatological teaching, see W. D. Davies and Dale C. Allison, *The Gospel according to Matthew*, ICC, 3 vols. (London: T&T Clark, 1991–1997), 3:345–46.

37. On the statue, see Erich S. Gruen, *The Construct of Jewish Identity in Hellenistic Judaism* (Berlin: de Gruyter, 2016), 404.

38. Nicholl, *From Hope to Despair*, 171–75; Abraham J. Malherbe, *Paul and the Thessalonians: The Philosophic Tradition of Pastoral Care* (Philadelphia: Fortress, 1987), 95–107; Mark B. Giszczak, "The Rhetoric and Social Practice of Excommunication in 2 Thessalonians 3:6–15," *CBQ* 83 (2021): 96, 105–7, 111–12.

39. Nicholl, *From Hope to Despair*, 155–56.

40. Antiochus IV: 2 Macc 5:15–6:6; Pompey: Josephus, *B.J.* 1.152; *A.J.* 14.71–72; Pilate: Josephus, *B.J.* 2.169–177; *A.J.* 18.55–59; Gaius: Josephus, *A.J.* 18.261. See Craig A. Evans, *Mark 8:27–16:20*, WBC 34B (Grand Rapids: Zondervan, 1988), 318–19; Davies and Allison, *Matthew*, 3:345; and Fritz W. Röcker, *Belial und Katechon: Eine Untersuchung zu 2 Thess 2,1–12 und 1 Thess 4,13–5,11*, WUNT 2.262 (Tübingen: Mohr Siebeck, 2009), 390–98.

41. The participle translated "standing" (ἑστηκότα) is masculine, probably indicating that Jesus conceived of "the abomination" (τὸ βδέλυγμα), which is neuter, as a

person. In Matt 24:15, "standing" (ἑστὸς) is neuter. On this, see Davies and Allison, *Matthew*, 3:346. On the meaning of "an abomination that desolates" in Daniel (9:27 NRSV; cf. 11:31; 12:11), see James A. Montgomery, *The Book of Daniel*, ICC (Edinburgh: T&T Clark, 1927), 388–89. See also the interpretation of the phrase as an altar in 1 Macc 1:54, 59 (cf. 2 Macc 6:2).

42. Nicholl, "Michael," 33–53.

43. E.g., William Neil, *The Epistle of Paul to the Thessalonians* (London: Hodder & Stoughton, 1950), 191–92; Ernest Best, *A Commentary on the First and Second Epistles to the Thessalonians*, HNTC (New York: Harper & Row, 1972), 331, 334–35; M. J. J. Menken, "Paradise Regained or Still Lost? Eschatology and Disorderly Behaviour in 2 Thessalonians," *NTS* 38 (1992): 271–89; G. K. Beale, *1–2 Thessalonians*, InterVarsity New Testament Commentary 13 (Downers Grove, IL: InterVarsity, 2003), 249.

44. Best (*Epistles to the Thessalonians*, 335) had already admitted this cautionary point against the eschatological view, which he favored.

45. Bruce W. Winter, "'If a Man Does Not Wish to Work . . .': A Cultural and Historical Setting for 2 Thessalonians 3:6–16," *TynBul* 40 (1989): 308. Juvenal wrote in the early second century AD.

46. Weima, *1–2 Thessalonians*, 604.

47. Zahn, *Introduction to the New Testament*, 1:233; Malherbe, *Letters to the Thessalonians*, 444.

48. F. F. Bruce, *The Book of the Acts*, rev. ed, NICNT (Grand Rapids: Eerdmans, 1988), 350.

49. On Titius Justus's name, see Bruce, *Acts*, 350; and Craig S. Keener, *Acts: An Exegetical Commentary*, 4 vols. (Grand Rapids: Baker, 2012–2015), 3:2745.

50. On Gallio, see the competing portraits in Murphy-O'Connor, *St. Paul's Corinth*, 161–69; and Bruce W. Winter, "Rehabilitating Gallio and His Judgement in Acts 18:14–15," *TynBul* 57 (2006): 291–308; Winter, *Divine Honours for the Caesars*, 192–93.

51. Murphy-O'Connor, *St. Paul's Corinth*, 164–67; Riesner, *Paul's Early Period*, 202–10. Gallio's term would have lasted one year, probably beginning in July AD 51, and illness probably kept him from finishing it.

52. Bruce W. Winter, "Gallio's Ruling on the Legal Status of Early Christianity," *TynBul* 50 (1999): 222–24; Winter, *Divine Honours for the Caesars*, 193–95; cf. Christos Karakolis, "'Alle schlugen Sosthenes, Gallio aber kümmerte sich nicht darum' (Apg 18.17)," *ZNW* 99 (2008): 245.

53. Winter, "Gallio's Ruling," 223.

54. According to Seneca, Gallio suffered a bout of this illness when he was proconsul of Achaia, and according to Pliny, he suffered an attack after he had served as consul, which would have been several years later during Nero's rule. See Riesner, *Paul's Early Period*, 207. In both cases, he treated the illness with a therapeutic sea voyage.

CHAPTER 14

1. Cf. Bruce W. Winter, *Divine Honours for the Caesar: The First Christians' Responses* (Grand Rapids: Eerdmans, 2015), 195.
2. Carl R. Holladay, *Acts: A Commentary*, NTL (Louisville: Westminster John Knox, 2016), 357.
3. Eliezer Diamond, "An Israelite Self-Offering in the Priestly Code: A New Perspective on the Nazirite," *JQR* 88 (1997): 1–18.
4. Diamond, "Israelite Self-Offering," 2–3.
5. Diamond, "Israelite Self-Offering," 5.
6. Quoted in Diamond, "Israelite Self-Offering," 15.
7. Cf. Kirsopp Lake and Henry J. Cadbury, *English Translation and Commentary*, vol. 4 of *The Beginnings of Christianity, Part I: The Acts of the Apostles*, ed. F. J. Foakes Jackson and Kirsopp Lake (London: Macmillan, 1933), 230. This seems more likely than the idea that Luke used this story to portray Paul as a pious Jew but that Luke did not understand the ritual he describes Paul as observing (Ernst Haenchen, *Acts of the Apostles: A Commentary* [Louisville: Westminster John Knox, 1971], 543–44). In Acts 21:24, Luke shows that he knows Nazirites normally cut their hair in Jerusalem.
8. Friedrich W. Horn, "Paulus, das Nasiräat und die Nasiräer," *NovT* 39 (1997): 120–21.
9. Horn, "Paulus," 120–21.
10. I calculated the length of this journey using the Stanford Geospatial Network Model of the Roman World.
11. I have used J. A. Talbert, ed., *Barrington Atlas of the Greek and Roman World* (Princeton, NJ: Princeton University Press, 2000), 69 and 70 to plot a probable route.
12. James D. G. Dunn, *Beginning from Jerusalem*, vol. 2 of *Christianity in the Making*, 3 vols. (Grand Rapids: Eerdmans, 2009), 754.
13. Luke says that he "greeted" (ἀσπασάμενος) the church and then went down to Antioch, an expression that implies a relatively short visit (cf. Acts 21:7). See BDAG 144, s.v. ἀσπάζομαι 1b. The expression's ambiguity, however, could cover the necessary month.
14. For the date, see E. Mary Smallwood, *Jews under Roman Rule from Pompey to Diocletian: A Study in Political Relations* (Leiden: Brill, 1981), 265.
15. On Cummanus's procuratorship as a "turning-point," see Smallwood, *Jews under Roman Rule*, 263.
16. Martin Goodman, *The Ruling Class of Judaea: The Origins of the Jewish Revolt against Rome, A.D. 66–70* (Cambridge: Cambridge University Press, 1987), 51–66. On Josephus's lack of sympathy with his "bandits," see Goodman, *Ruling Class of Judaea*, 60; and Steve Mason, *Judean War 2: Translation and Commentary*, vol. 1B

of *Flavius Josephus: Translation and Commentary*, ed. Steve Mason (Leiden: Brill, 2008), 39–40n342.

17. Goodman, *Ruling Class of Judaea*, 56–58.
18. Goodman, *Ruling Class of Judaea*, 60–61.
19. Goodman, *Ruling Class of Judaea*, 62–63.
20. Goodman, *Ruling Class of Judaea*, 63. Mishnah Sotah 9:9 includes the sentence, "When Eleazar b. Dinai came (and he was also called Tehinah b. Parishah), they changed his name to Son of the Murderer" (trans. Herbert Danby). Mishnah Kelim 5:10 also refers to him and comments on the kind of oven he used. He was clearly a person of great interest in subsequent decades.
21. Goodman, *Ruling Class of Judaea*, 64–66.
22. On the connection between this famine and brigandage in Judea in the mid-first century, see Richard A. Horsley with John S. Hanson, *Bandits, Prophets, and Messiahs: Popular Movements in the Time of Jesus* (Harrisburg, PA: Trinity Press International, 1999), 67–68. On the connection between the famine (among other factors) and Paul's collection for poor believers in Jerusalem, see Murray J. Harris, *The Second Epistle to the Corinthians*, NIGTC (Grand Rapids: Eerdmans, 2005), 88.
23. Cf. Colin J. Hemer, *The Book of Acts in the Setting of Hellenistic History*, ed. Conrad H. Gempf (Winona Lake, IN: Eisenbrauns, 1990), 257; and Rainer Riesner, *Paul's Early Period: Chronology, Mission Strategy, Theology*, trans. Douglas W. Stott (Grand Rapids: Eerdmans, 1998), 297 (but without reference to the political situation).
24. On the ubiquity of concern for the poor in the Jewish tradition, and on Gal 2:10 as an expression of the desire of the Jerusalem church that Paul teach this concern to the gentiles, see Bruce W. Longenecker, *Remember the Poor: Paul, Poverty, and the Greco-Roman World* (Grand Rapids: Eerdmans, 2010), 108–15, 202–6.
25. On Christians sharing the blessings of Israel that Paul lists in Rom 9:4–5, see N. T. Wright, *Paul and the Faithfulness of God*, vol. 4 of *Christian Origins and the Question of God* (Minneapolis: Fortress, 2013), 2:1012–13.
26. Rounding the figure from the Stanford Geospatial Network Model of the Roman World.
27. Dunn, *Beginning from Jerusalem*, 754–55.
28. Dunn, *Beginning from Jerusalem*, 753–55.
29. Cf. Craig S. Keener, *Acts: An Exegetical Commentary*, 4 vols. (Grand Rapids: Baker, 2012–2015), 3:2796.
30. The translation is from Mark Wilson, "The Geography of Galatia," in *Lexham Geographic Commentary on Acts through Revelation*, Barry J. Beitzel (Bellingham, WA: Lexham, 2019), 490. Cf. the discussion in Stephen Mitchell, *Anatolia: Land, Men, and Gods in Asia Minor*, 2 vols. (Oxford: Oxford University Press, 1993), 2:4; and in Glen L. Thompson and Mark Wilson, "The Route of Paul's Second Journey in Asia Minor: In the Steps of Robert Jewett and Beyond," *TynBul* 67 (2016): 224.
31. The critical word here is καθεξῆς, which F. F. Bruce translates "city by city."

Notes to Pages 174–176

Bruce, *The Book of the Acts*, rev. ed., NICNT (Grand Rapids: Eerdmans, 1988), 356. Others believe that the term refers to Paul traveling successively through first Galatia and then Phrygia, which makes less geographical sense if these churches were all within the southern part of the Roman province of Galatia. See, e.g., Haenchen (*Acts*, 545), and Barrett, who finds it "hard not to agree" with him. See C. K. Barrett, *A Critical and Exegetical Commentary on the Acts of the Apostles*, ICC, 2 vols. (Edinburgh: T&T Clark, 1994–1998), 2:881.

32. On philosophers, see Lucian, *Fug.* 20; and on sophists, see the comments of Bruce W. Winter, *Philo and Paul among the Sophists: Alexandrian and Corinthian Responses to a Julio-Claudian Movement*, 2nd ed. (Grand Rapids: Eerdmans, 2002), 166–67.

33. Anthony C. Thiselton, *The First Epistle to the Corinthians: A Commentary on the Greek Text*, NIGTC (Grand Rapids: Eerdmans, 2000), 1319.

34. Thiselton, *First Epistle to the Corinthians*, 1318.

35. See Talbert, *Barrington Atlas*, 62, 65.

36. Talbert, *Barrington Atlas*, 65.

37. Talbert, *Barrington Atlas*, 62.

38. Jerome Murphy-O'Connor, *St. Paul's Ephesus: Texts and Archaeology* (Collegeville, MN: Michael Glazier, 2008), 37; Mark Wilson, "The 'Upper Regions' and the Route of Paul's Third Journey from Apamea to Ephesus," *Scriptura* 117 (2018): 13. On the ancient route, see the description in Strabo, *Geogr.* 14.2.29; and David H. French, "Pre- and Early-Roman Roads of Asia Minor: The Persian Royal Road," *Iran* 36 (1998): 15–43. Col 2:1 does not disqualify this as Paul's route (e.g., Barrett, *Acts*, 2:893) but would only mean that many Christians in the Lycus Valley were unknown to him. On this, see Ulrich Huttner, *Early Christianity in the Lycus Valley*, trans. David Green, AGJU 85/ECAM 1 (Leiden: Brill, 2013), 123.

39. Luke uses the rare term ἀνωτερικός here, which may mean "upper country" rather than "inland country." According to Wilson ("'Upper Regions,'" 4), Apamea's elevation was 2887 feet above sea level and Ephesus was near sea level, so from the perspective of Ephesus, "upper regions" would be an accurate description of the place from which Paul came.

40. Cf. Harris, *Second Epistle to the Corinthians*, 102.

41. Michael Immendörfer, *Ephesians and Artemis: The Cult of the Great Goddess of Ephesus and the Epistle's Context*, WUNT 2.436 (Tübingen: Mohr Siebeck, 2017), 93.

42. Murphy-O'Connor, *St. Paul's Ephesus*, 27. On the harbor to the north, called Panormos, see Duane W. Roller, *A Historical and Topographical Guide to the "Geography" of Strabo* (Cambridge: Cambridge University Press, 2018), 793; and Talbert, *Barrington Atlas*, 61.

43. Immendörfer, *Ephesians and Artemis*, 85; Murphy-O'Connor, *St. Paul's Ephesus*, 37.

44. Trans. R. Oster and G. H. R. Horsley, ed., *New Documents Illustrating Early*

Christianity, vol. 4, *A Review of the Greek Inscriptions and Papyri Published in 1979* (North Ryde, NSW, Australia: Ancient History Documentary Research Centre, 1987), 75. See also Immendörfer, *Ephesians and Artemis*, 394–95.

45. Murphy-O'Connor, *St. Paul's Ephesus*, 100.

46. On widespread temples, see Murphy-O'Connor, *St. Paul's Ephesus*, 5–6. For νεωκόρος on a coin from Nero's time, see Immendörfer, *Ephesians and Artemis*, 161.

47. Immendörfer, *Ephesians and Artemis*, 124.

48. Murphy-O'Connor, *St. Paul's Ephesus*, 6, 160 (quoting Antipater of Sidon, *Greek Anthology* 9.58).

49. Text in Murphy-O'Connor, *St. Paul's Ephesus*, 116. The "feet" in Pliny's text are Ionian feet, which, according to Murphy-O'Connor, were thirteen inches each (*St. Paul's Ephesus*, 118). The accuracy of Pliny's description is disputed. On the match between it and the archaeology, see Immendörfer, *Ephesus and Artemis*, 128 and 132.

50. Strabo, *Geogr.* 14.1.23; Paul Trebilco, *The Early Christians in Ephesus from Paul to Ignatius* (Grand Rapids: Eerdmans, 2007), 20; Roller, *Historical and Topographical Guide*, 795–96.

51. Murphy-O'Connor, *St. Paul's Ephesus*, 198.

52. Murphy-O'Connor, *St. Paul's Ephesus*, 64 (quoting Dio Chrysostom, *Or.* 31.54–55); Immendörfer, *Ephesus and Artemis*, 141.

53. Murphy-O'Connor, *St. Paul's Ephesus*, 187.

CHAPTER 15

1. Paul Trebilco, *The Early Christians in Ephesus from Paul to Ignatius* (Grand Rapids: Eerdmans, 2007), 126.

2. Cf. Peter Lampe, "Epaenetus," *ABD* 2:532.

3. For the view that they were Christians, see e.g., Bruce, *The Book of the Acts*, rev. ed., NICNT (Grand Rapids: Eerdmans, 1988), 363; Jacob Jervell, *Die Apostelgeschichte*, KEK 3 (Göttingen: Vandenhoeck & Ruprecht, 1998), 475; Carl R. Holladay, *Acts: A Commentary*, NTL (Louisville: Westminster John Knox, 2016), 366; and for the view that they were not Christians, see, e.g., Ben Witherington III, *The Acts of the Apostles: A Socio-Rhetorical Commentary* (Grand Rapids: Eerdmans, 1998), 570–71; Trebilco, *Early Christians in Ephesus*, 127–30; and Craig S. Keener, *Acts: An Exegetical Commentary*, 4 vols. (Grand Rapids: Baker, 2012–2015), 3:2815–20.

4. On the meaning of "tongues" here, see Keener, *Acts*, 3:2822–23.

5. This consistency between Luke and Paul counts against the idea that Luke was creatively retelling a piece of Ephesian lore to bring various similar sects of his own time into the mainstream of Christianity (as in, e.g., Holladay, *Acts*, 367–68).

6. Kirsopp Lake and Henry J. Cadbury, *English Translation and Commentary*, vol. 4 of *The Beginnings of Christianity, Part I: The Acts of the Apostles*, ed. F. J. Foakes Jackson and Kirsopp Lake (London: Macmillan, 1933), 239. On the meaning of the

term "lecture hall" (σχολή), see BDAG 982, and especially the reference in BDAG to Josephus, *C. Ap.* 1.53.

7. James D. G. Dunn, *Beginning from Jerusalem*, vol. 2 of *Christianity in the Making*, 3 vols. (Grand Rapids: Eerdmans, 2009), 768.

8. Paul, too, claims that "signs and wonders" were part of his ministry during this period (2 Cor 12:12; cf. Gal 3:5).

9. Cf. Harris, *Second Corinthians*, 102.

10. Timothy is another possibility, since at some point he traveled from Corinth (Acts 18:5) to join Paul in Ephesus and was with Paul for a time there before Paul sent him back to Corinth (1 Cor 4:17; 16:10; cf. Acts 19:22).

11. Dunn, *Beginning from Jerusalem*, 787.

12. See Helen King, "pornography," OCD^4 1190; Madeleine M. Henry and D. M. Halperin, "prostitution, secular," OCD^4 1227. On the connection between sexual activity and banqueting among the elite, see Bruce W. Winter, *After Paul Left Corinth: The Influence of Secular Ethics and Social Change* (Grand Rapids: Eerdmans, 2001), 82–85, 88.

13. Quoted in Dunn, *Beginning from Jerusalem*, 787n190.

14. On 1 Cor as Paul's response to the influence of Corinth's Roman culture on Corinthian Christians, see Winter, *After Paul Left Corinth*, 27. This influence was probably also the reason for the earlier letter Paul mentions in 1 Cor 5:9.

15. Erastus may be the person of that name that Paul mentions later in Romans as Corinth's "city treasurer" (Rom 16:23).

16. Paul expresses uncertainty in 1 Cor 16:10 about whether Timothy will arrive in Corinth ("If [ἐὰν] Timothy comes, see that he has nothing to fear among you," NRSV).

17. Cf. Murray J. Harris, *The Second Epistle to the Corinthians*, NIGTC (Grand Rapids: Eerdmans, 2005), 103.

18. J. B. Lightfoot, *Biblical Essays* (London: Macmillan, 1893), 276–77.

19. Anthony C. Thiselton, *The First Epistle to the Corinthians: A Commentary on the Greek Text*, NIGTC (Grand Rapids: Eerdmans, 2000), 1332: "It may well be the case." See also Dieter Zeller, *Der erste Brief an die Korinther*, KEK 5 (Göttingen: Vandenhoeck & Ruprecht, 2010), 538.

20. See Rudolf Pesch, *Die Apostelgeschichte*, 2 vols., EKK 5 (Zürich/ Neukirchen-Vluyn: Benziger/Neukirchener Verlag, 1986), 2:176; and Witherington, *Acts*, 589.

21. "Chloe's people" were probably not members of her household, since households were typically identified by their senior male member, even if that person had died. The nature of the report—that the church was split into competing parties, including a "Paul" party—seems to reflect the perspective of outside observers rather than concerned insiders. Cf. Gordon Fee, *The First Epistle to the Corinthians*, NICNT (Grand Rapids: Eerdmans, 1987), 54; Jerome Murphy-O'Connor, *Paul: A Critical Life* (Oxford: Clarendon, 1996), 278; and Thiselton, *First Epistle to the Corinthians*, 121.

22. It is probably Paul who says, "I follow Christ," a confession he wishes would unite the other groups. On this see David E. Garland, *1 Corinthians*, BECNT (Grand Rapids: Baker, 2003), 49–50.

23. Paul's use of the phrase "I hear" in 1 Cor 11:18 probably indicates that he heard about problems at the Lord's Supper from Chloe's people. See Fee, *First Epistle to the Corinthians*, 537n31; as well as C. K. Barrett, *The First Epistle to the Corinthians* (New York: Harper & Row, 1968), 261, who suggests Stephanas, Fortunatus, and Achaicus as other possible sources of this orally delivered information.

24. On the greedy feasting of the wealthy in Corinth, see Winter, *After Paul Left Corinth*, 145, 148, 156–58; and Thiselton, *First Epistle to the Corinthians*, 862–63. On the expectation that wealthy benefactors would eat first in a Corinthian gathering, see James R. Harrison, "Paul and the *Agōnothetai* at Corinth: Engaging the Civic Values of Antiquity," in *Roman Corinth*, vol. 2, *The First Urban Churches*, ed. James R. Harrison and L. L. Welborn, WGRWSup 8 (Atlanta: SBL, 2016), 300.

25. Cephas, and perhaps one or more of the Lord's brothers, seems to have traveled through Corinth (1 Cor 9:5; 15:5, 7, 11).

26. Winter, *After Paul Left Corinth*, 31–43.

27. James R. Harrison, *Paul and the Ancient Celebrity Circuit: The Cross and Moral Transformation*, WUNT 1.430 (Tübingen: Mohr Siebeck, 2019), 309–10, 312–13n67, 325, 327–29. On Greek and Roman clubs generally, see Marcus Niebuhr Tod and Simon Hornblower, "clubs, Greek," *OCD*[4] 337–38; and George Hope Stevenson and Andrew Lintott, "clubs, Roman," *OCD*[4] 338.

28. Harris, *Second Epistle to the Corinthians*, 64, 103.

29. Harris, *Second Epistle to the Corinthians*, 103.

30. For the date, see Valerius Maximus, *Memorable Deeds and Sayings: One Thousand Tales from Ancient Rome*, trans. Henry John Walker (Indianapolis, IN: Hackett, 2004), xiii, xviiin40.

31. Harrison, *Paul and the Ancient Celebrity Circuit*, 19; and for a Corinthian inscription dating to 10 BC encouraging envy of the person honored, see Harrison, *Paul and the Ancient Celebrity Circuit*, 22.

32. MM 679, s.v. φυσιόω. "This vivid image," says L. L. Welborn, "is all too familiar to the student of political history as the caricature of the political windbag, the orator inflated at his success." Welborn, "On the Discord in Corinth: 1 Corinthians 1–4 and Ancient Politics," *JBL* 106 (1987): 88.

33. For the use of inflated bladders as flotation devices in Roman times, see Suetonius, *Jul.* 57: "He covered great distances with incredible speed, making a hundred miles a day in a hired carriage and with little baggage, swimming the rivers which barred his path or crossing them on inflated skins [innixus inflatis utribus], and very often arriving before the messengers sent to announce his coming" (trans. J. C. Rolfe, LCL).

34. Winter, *After Paul Left Corinth*, 145, 148, 156–58; Thiselton, *First Epistle to the Corinthians*, 862–63.

35. For the body as an image for the political functioning of a community, see, e.g., Aristotle, *Pol.* 5.3.35–40, 1302b; Livy 2.33, and, closer to the time of Paul, Valerius Maximus 9.1, and the discussion in Margaret M. Mitchell, *Paul and the Rhetoric of Reconciliation*, HUT 28 (Tübingen: Mohr Siebeck, 1991), 157–64.

36. See Deidun, *New Covenant Morality in Paul*, 12–14; and Frank Thielman, *Paul and the Law: A Contextual Approach* (Downers Grove, IL: InterVarsity, 1999), 87.

37. Winter, *After Paul Left Corinth*, 123–33.

38. Fee, *First Epistle to the Corinthians*, 359–60; Dunn, *Beginning from Jerusalem*, 808.

39. On the biblical allusion here, see the helpfully lucid and reasonable discussion of Joseph A. Fitzmyer, *First Corinthians*, AB 32 (New Haven, CT: Yale University Press, 2008), 569–70.

40. Fee, *First Epistle to the Corinthians*, 744.

41. Garland, *1 Corinthians*, 699–701.

42. On the profoundly biblical nature of Paul's argument through 1 Cor 15, see Wright, *Resurrection of the Son of God*, 320–21, 334–36, and 341.

43. N. T. Wright helpfully recommends the Jerusalem Bible translation of 1 Cor 15:44, "When it is sown it embodies the soul, when it is raised it embodies the spirit. If the soul has its own embodiment, so does the spirit have its own embodiment." Wright, *The Resurrection of the Son of God*, vol. 3 of *Christian Origins and the Question of God* (Minneapolis: Fortress, 2003), 352.

44. Wright: "This is indeed the defeat of death, not a compromise in which death is allowed to have the body while some other aspect of the human being (the soul? the spirit?) goes marching on" (*Resurrection of the Son of God*, 358).

45. So, correctly, Thiselton, *First Epistle to the Corinthians*, 1169–70; Wolfgang Schrage, *Der erste Brief an die Korinther*, 4 vols., EKK 7 (Düsseldorf: Benziger/Neukirchen-Vluyn: Neukirchener Verlag, 1995–2001), 4:7–10; Wright, *Resurrection of the Son of God*, 317, 352.

46. Lightfoot, *Biblical Essays*, 277. Translations differ on this point. For the more usual translation of ἐάν as "if" rather than "when," see, for example, the REB, NRSV, CSB, TOB ("si"), and CEB.

47. Schrage, *Die erste Brief an die Korinther*, 4:437.

48. Cf. Douglas A. Campbell, *Framing Paul: An Epistolary Biography* (Grand Rapids: Eerdmans, 2014), 75: "The collection is in progress, so he will presumably collect money from Macedonia before arriving in Corinth."

49. Some scholars (e.g., Campbell, *Framing Paul*, 74–90) have argued that these plans represent a change from a first set of plans, described in 2 Cor 1:15–16, and 23. Those original plans, perhaps communicated in the previous letter (1 Cor 5:9), involved a twofold visit to Corinth, one on the way from Ephesus to Macedonia and one on the way to Judea after the visit to Macedonia was complete. Paul's announcement in 1 Cor 16:5–9 that he had now decided to visit Corinth only once

after passing through Macedonia led the Corinthians to charge Paul with inconsistency and led Paul to defend himself in 2 Cor 1:12–2:4. Although attractive in its simplicity, this reconstruction has difficulty accounting for the increased specificity of 2 Cor 1:16 ("and have you send me on my way to Judea") compared with 1 Cor 16:6 ("I will stay with you or even spend the winter, so that you may help me on my journey, wherever I go"). Why would Paul not be certain where he was going if he had already decided to go to Judea after leaving Corinth? See Harris, *Second Epistle to the Corinthians*, 62.

50. Zeller, *Der erste Brief an die Korinther*, 534.

CHAPTER 16

1. On Titus's travels, see J. B. Lightfoot, *Biblical Essays* (London: Macmillan, 1893), 276–77.

2. Robert Mackintosh thought that evasion of this responsibility led to Paul's alteration of his travel plans and immediate visit to Corinth. Mackintosh, "The Brief Visit to Corinth," *Expositor*, 7th series, 6 (1908): 228–32.

3. According to the Stanford Geospatial Network Model of the Roman World, this was a journey of 4.7 days, or about 3.5 days according to fig. 4.7 in Justin Leidwanger, *Roman Seas: A Maritime Archaeology of Eastern Mediterranean Economies* (New York: Oxford University Press, 2020), 146.

4. BDAG 604, s.v. λύπη; emphasis in original.

5. Harris, *Second Epistle to the Corinthians*, 59.

6. Victor Paul Furnish, *II Corinthians*, AB 32A (Garden City, NY: Doubleday, 1984), 159. Cf., e.g., C. K. Barrett, *A Commentary on the Second Epistle to the Corinthians* (San Francisco: Harper, 1973), 89; Furnish, *II Corinthians*, 158–64; Paul Barnett, *The Second Epistle to the Corinthians*, NICNT (Grand Rapids: Eerdmans, 1997), 124.

7. Mackintosh, "Brief Visit to Corinth," 228; cf. Harris, *Second Epistle to the Corinthians*, 227.

8. Cf. Harris, *Second Epistle to the Corinthians*, 59, 215, 226–27.

9. Many translations (e.g., RSV, NIV, NRSV, ESV) associate the adverb "again" (πάλιν) with Paul's coming to Corinth rather than with his humiliation, but Paul would have probably used the term in the preceding verse if he had intended to speak of his coming again (Furnish, *II Corinthians*, 562). Cf. Murray J. Harris, *The Second Epistle to the Corinthians*, NIGTC (Grand Rapids: Eerdmans, 2005), 901.

10. On the translation of χάρις here as "benefit," see Harris, *Second Epistle to the Corinthians*, 192–93.

11. On Paul's intention to travel to Macedonia after the painful visit, see also Barrett, *Second Epistle to the Corinthians*, 85–86; Jerome Murphy-O'Connor, *Paul: A Critical Life* (Oxford: Clarendon, 1996), 296.

Notes to Pages 196–198

12. Luke says that Aristarchus was from Thessalonica (in Macedonia), but the only "Gaius" he mentions in the list is from Derbe (in southern Galatia).

13. See the tabulations in Armin D. Baum, "Stylistic Diversity in the *Corpus Ciceronianum* and in the *Corpus Paulinum*: A Comparison and Some Conclusions," *Journal for the Study of Paul and His Letters* 9 (2019): 130–37; and the judgment of Jermo van Nes, *Pauline Language and the Pastoral Epistles: A Study of Linguistic Variation in the "Corpus Paulinum,"* Linguistic Biblical Studies 16 (Leiden: Brill, 2018), 221, on the large number of words that only appear in 1 and 2 Timothy within the Pauline corpus.

14. Martin Dibelius and Hans Conzelmann, *The Pastoral Epistles,* trans. Philip Buttolph and Adela Yarbro, Hermeneia (Philadelphia: Fortress, 1972), 4, 19–20, 24–25. Cf. Jerome D. Quinn and William C. Wacker, *The First and Second Letters to Timothy,* Eerdmans Critical Commentary (Grand Rapids: Eerdmans, 2000), 4–6.

15. Quoted from Dibelius and Conzelmann, *Pastoral Epistles,* 49.

16. James D. G. Dunn, *Neither Jew nor Greek: A Contested Identity,* vol. 3 of *Christianity in the Making* (Grand Rapids: Eerdmans, 2015), 87–88.

17. See, e.g., E. F. Scott, *The Pastoral Epistles,* MNTC (London: Hodder & Stoughton, 1936), xvii; and Dibelius and Conzelmann, *Pastoral Epistles,* 15–16.

18. See, e.g., Scott, *Pastoral Epistles,* xvii; and Dibelius and Conzelmann, *Pastoral Epistles,* 15.

19. Scott, *Pastoral Epistles,* xviii–xix.

20. Preston T. Massey, "Cicero, the Pastoral Epistles, and the Issue of Pseudonymity," *ResQ* 56 (2014): 65–84, comparing *Marius* 24 (*Ad familiars* VII.1) with *Atticus* 75 (IV.3).

21. Andrew W. Pitts, "Style and Pseudonymity in Pauline Scholarship: A Register Based Configuration," in *Paul and Pseudonymity,* ed. Stanley E. Porter and Gregory Fewster, Pauline Studies 8 (Leiden: Brill, 2013), 116–38.

22. Pitts, "Style and Pseudonymity," 143; Stanley E. Porter, *The Pastoral Epistles: A Commentary on the Greek Text* (Grand Rapids: Baker, 2023), 53, 498–500, 703, 856. Philemon might at first look like it too was written to an individual, but Paul and Timothy include "Apphia," "Archippus," and "the church" in Philemon's house in the letter's address (Phlm 2). Pitts and Porter add other contextual factors that might have contributed to the changed register of the Pastorals (e.g., the later period in which they think Paul wrote the letters), but their audience of individuals and, in the case of 1 Tim and Titus, their purpose as administrative letters, are probably sufficient to account for their changed register.

23. See Lyn Kidson, "1 Timothy: An Administrative Letter," *Early Christianity* 5 (2014): 97–116. Kidson's purpose in this article is not to adjudicate the authorship of the letter but only to investigate its genre. Cf. Luke Timothy Johnson, *The Canonical Paul,* vol. 2 of *Interpreting Paul* (Grand Rapids: Eerdmans, 2021), 411–12.

24. This understanding of the implied setting of 1 Timothy resembles in some ways the theory of Jakob van Bruggen, *Die geschichtliche Einordnung der Pastoralbriefe*

(Wuppertal: R. Brockhaus, 1981), 22–30 (summarized in English in van Bruggen, *Paul: Pioneer for Israel's Messiah*, trans. Ed M. van der Maas [Phillipsburg, NJ: P&R Publishing, 2005], 87–94). He too places the letter within Paul's Ephesian ministry and thinks that 1 Tim 1:3 speaks of a journey to Macedonia prior to Paul's final departure from Ephesus in Acts 20:1. Van Bruggen, however, envisions Paul traveling from Ephesus to Macedonia first and then to Corinth (cf. 1 Cor 16:5), rather than from Ephesus to Corinth to Macedonia and back to Ephesus (cf. 2 Cor 1:15–16, 23; 2:1). See *Die geschichtlich Einordung der Pastoralbriefe*, 28. For other similar placements of 1 Timothy, see Karl Wieseler, *Chronologie des apostolischen Zeitalters* (Göttingen: Vandenhoeck und Ruprecht, 1848), 286–315; and Samuel Davidson, *An Introduction to the New Testament*, 3 vols. (London: Samuel Bagster, 1848), 3:3–32. The theory that 1 Timothy belongs to the period covered in Acts 20:1–2 (Luke Timothy Johnson, *The First and Second Letters to Timothy*, AB 35A [New York: Doubleday, 2001], 136–37; Philip H. Towner, *The Letters to Timothy and Titus*, NICNT [Grand Rapids: Eerdmans, 2006], 107) seems unlikely because Timothy was probably with Paul during that time, not back in Ephesus (Rom 16:21; 2 Cor 1:1; Acts 20:4).

25. For discussion of the ambiguous Greek construction here, see Towner, *Letters to Timothy and Titus*, 106.

26. Dibelius and Conzelmann ask, apparently rhetorically, whether Paul's visit from Ephesus to Corinth "was . . . not just an excursion overseas" (*Pastoral Epistles*, 15n5). The answer to Dibelius and Conzelmann's question is "No, probably not." Paul certainly traveled over the Aegean Sea to get from Ephesus to Corinth but then probably continued to Macedonia as he had originally planned.

27. Johnson, *Canonical Paul*, 413.

28. Cf. Lucian, *Podagra* 170, where Lucian imagines "Gout" describing the foolish ways that people try to rid themselves of the disease. Among them is one "mocked by chants imposters sell." Immediately after this line, Gout describes another fool who falls "for the spells of Jews."

29. On the evidence of Josephus and Philo, see Gideon Bohak, *Ancient Jewish Magic: A History* (Cambridge: Cambridge University Press, 2008), 78–79. For the phenomenon of "freelance experts" in religion in the first and second centuries, see especially Heidi Wendt, *At the Temple Gates: The Religion of Freelance Experts in the Roman Empire* (Oxford: Oxford University Press, 2016).

30. On the possible connection between the seven sons of Sceva and Jewish folk beliefs, see Clinton E. Arnold, "Sceva, Solomon, and Shamanism: The Jewish Roots of the Problem at Colossae," *JETS* 55 (2012): 7–26; Arnold, "Initiation, Vision, and Spiritual Power: The Hellenistic Dimensions of the Problem at Colossae," in *Colossians, Hierapolis, and Laodicea*, ed. James R. Harrison and L. L. Welborn, WGRWSup 16, vol. 5 of *The First Urban Churches* (Atlanta: SBL, 2019), 182, 184.

31. For this term, see Wendt, *At the Temple Gates*, 1–39.

32. On these texts, see Albert Pietersma, "Jannes and Jambres," *ABD* 3:638. It is unclear in CD whether the two magicians are Jewish or Egyptian. Pietersma believes

Notes to Pages 201–206

that the pair mentioned in CD are not the Jannes and Jambres of later tradition, although they did give rise to that tradition. See Pietersma, *The Apocryphon of Jannes and Jambres the Magicians*, Religions in the Greco-Roman World 119 (Leiden: Brill, 1994), 23.

33. C. Spicq, *Les Épîtres Pastorales*, 4th ed., 2 vols. (Paris: Lecoffre, 1969), 2:779, 783; and on 2 Tim 3:13, see I. H. Marshall, *The Pastoral Epistles*, ICC (Edinburgh: T&T Clark, 1999), 786: "The use of magic in imitation of Christian miracles (cf. Philo, *Mig.* 83) could well be part of the picture." The reference to Philo describes how the Egyptian magicians imitated the miracles God worked through Aaron to confirm his power to Pharaoh (Exod 7:11–12). On the syncretism of ancient magic, see Hans Dieter Betz, ed., *The Greek Magical Papyri in Translation*, 2nd ed. (Chicago: University of Chicago Press, 1992), xliv–xlviii.

34. I have followed Marshall (*Pastoral Epistles*, 477–80) in my translation of most of the relevant terms.

35. Johnson, *Canonical Paul*, 435–48.

36. Johnson, *First and Second Letters to Timothy*, 167–68 (where Johnson argues for "appropriately" as a translation of νομίμως), 175–76, 182–83.

37. Johnson, *Canonical Paul*, 443–44. Johnson thinks that the reference to the false teachers' concern with money is slander that should not be taken seriously. As we have seen, however, there is ample reason for thinking that Paul's criticism reflects the false teachers' concern with earning a handsome income from their practices.

38. Towner, *Letters to Timothy and Titus*, 48–49.

39. Towner, *Letters to Timothy and Titus*, 258–59, 265.

40. The idea of formal proceedings emerges from the language that Paul uses. First, he speaks of both doing and suffering wrong (2 Cor 7:12), using a word for "violation of human or divine law" (BDAG 20, s.v. ἀδικέω 1a). Second, he mentions the "punishment" of the majority (2:6), using a technical term (ἐπιτιμία) for a judicial penalty (Harris, *Second Epistle to the Corinthians*, 228). Finally, he asks the Corinthians to "reaffirm" their love for the man once he has repented (2:8), again using a word commonly employed in legal contexts to mean "ratify" (BDAG 579, s.v. κυρόω 1; Harris, *Second Epistle to the Corinthians*, 230).

CHAPTER 17

1. Richard E. Oster, "Ephesus as a Religious Center under the Principate, I: Paganism before Constantine," *ANRW* 2.18.3, ed. W. Haase (Berlin: de Gruyter, 1990), 1701.

2. Oster, "Ephesus as a Religious Center," 1701

3. Michael Immendörfer, *Ephesians and Artemis: The Cult of the Great Goddess of Ephesus and the Epistle's Context*, WUNT 2.436 (Tübingen: Mohr Siebeck, 2017), 168.

4. Immendörfer, *Ephesians and Artemis*, 169.

5. Immendörfer, *Ephesians and Artemis*, 158–61.

6. A. N. Sherwin-White, *Roman Society and Roman Law in the New Testament* (Oxford: Oxford University Press, 1963), 90; BDAG 665, s.v. ναός a.

7. The "Asiarchs" seem to have been overseers of sacred athletic contests in the province of Asia. See Steven J. Friesen, "Asiarchs," *ZPE* 126 (1999): 286. At least in the first century AD, there could be more than one Asiarch in a single city such as Ephesus or Tralles (cf. Strabo, *Geogr.* 14.1.42), about thirty miles to the east of Ephesus. On this, see Sherwin-White, *Roman Society and Roman Law*, 90.

8. Sherwin-White, *Roman Society and Roman Law*, 87–88. Cf. Kirsopp Lake and Henry J. Cadbury, *English Translation and Commentary*, vol. 4 of *The Beginnings of Christianity, Part I: The Acts of the Apostles*, ed. F. J. Foakes Jackson and Kirsopp Lake (London: Macmillan, 1933), 252.

9. According to the Stanford Geospatial Network Model of the Roman World. See the similar routes, and the delays that unfavorable winds could create, in Thucydides, *P.W.* 8.99, 101; Josephus, *A.J.* 16.16–20; Pliny, *Ep.* 17a. Thanks to Hemer ("Alexandria Troas," *TynBul* 26 [1975]: 92) for drawing my attention to these texts. On the need to take prevailing winds into account when calculating shipping speeds, see Lionel Casson, "Speed under Sail of Ancient Ships," *TAPA* 82 (1951): 137–38. For wind direction and travel time, see also Justin Leidwanger, *Roman Seas: A Maritime Archaeology of Eastern Mediterranean Economies* (New York: Oxford University Press, 2020), 143 (fig. 4.16) and 146 (fig. 4.17) respectively.

10. Murray J. Harris, *The Second Epistle to the Corinthians*, NIGTC (Grand Rapids: Eerdmans, 2005), 237.

11. Eckhard J. Schnabel, *Paul and the Early Church*, vol. 2 of *Early Christian Mission*, 2 vols. (Downers Grove, IL: InterVarsity, 2004), 1248.

12. Harris, *Second Epistle to the Corinthians*, 238.

13. E.-B. Allo, *Saint Paul Seconde Épître aux Corinthiens*, 2nd ed., Ebib (Paris: Lecoffre, 1937), 12; Harris, *Second Epistle to the Corinthians*, 156, 166, 171.

14. "I sailed first from Alexandria Troas to Lemnos, after happening on a ship setting sail for Thessalonica and agreeing with the captain to set a course first for Lemnos" (ἔπλυσα πρότερον ἀπὸ Τρωάδος Ἀλεξανδρείας εἰς Λῆμνον, ἐπιτυχὼν εἰς Θεσσαλονίκην ἀναγομένου πλοίου, συνθεμένῳ τῷ ναυκλήρῳ παραβάλλειν πρότεραν τῇ Λήμνῳ, my trans.).

15. On the chronology, see Paul Barnett, *The Second Epistle to the Corinthians*, NIGTC (Grand Rapids: Eerdmans, 1997), 369; and Harris, *Second Epistle to the Corinthians*, 104.

16. Barnett, *Second Epistle to the Corinthians*, 368–69.

17. On the desire of some Corinthians to function as Paul's patrons, see, e.g., Barnett (*Second Epistle to the Corinthians*, 513) and L. L. Welborn, "Paul's Caricature of His Chief Rival as a Pompous Parasite in 2 Corinthians 11.20," *JSNT* 32 (2009): 41.

18. Many interpreters believe that the "super-apostles" of 2 Cor 11:5 and 12:11

are identical with the "false apostles" who are the rival apostles in Corinth. See, e.g., Victor Paul Furnish, *II Corinthians*, AB 32A (Garden City, NY: Doubleday, 1984), 502–5; Barnett, *Second Epistle to the Corinthians*, 522–28. I have taken the position of Harris (*Second Epistle to the Corinthians*, 75) and others (e.g., C. K. Barrett, *Essays on Paul* [Philadelphia: Westminster, 1982], 74), however, that the "false apostles" and the "super-apostles" are two separate groups, although I agree with Harris (*Second Epistle to the Corinthians*, 76) that the "false apostles" did not have the backing of the "super-apostles" (as in Barrett, *Essays on Paul*, 80).

19. Robert Mackintosh, "The Brief Visit to Corinth," *Expositor*, 7th series, 6 (1908): 232; Harris, *Second Epistle to the Corinthians*, 70, 880–892.

20. See, e.g., Barrett (*Essays on Paul*, 80), Harris (*Second Epistle to the Corinthians*, 85), and James D. G. Dunn, *Beginning from Jerusalem*, vol. 2 of *Christianity in the Making*, 3 vols. (Grand Rapids: Eerdmans, 2009), 840.

21. C. J. A. Hickling, "The Sequence of Thought in II Corinthians, Chapter Three," *NTS* 21 (1975): 380–95.

22. Lucian was writing about a century after Paul.

23. Eckhard J. Schnabel, *Der Brief des Paulus an die Römer: Kapitel 6–16*, HTA (Witten: Brockhaus, 2016), 825.

24. John N. Collins, "The Mediatorial Aspect of Paul's Role as *Diakonos*," *ABR* 40 (1992): 34–44.

25. Collins, "Mediatorial Aspect," 40. It makes sense, then, that the crowd in Lystra called Barnabas "Zeus" and Paul, the main speaker, "Hermes" (Acts 14:12).

26. Collins, "Mediatorial Aspect," 38.

27. Collins, "Mediatorial Aspect," 38.

28. On the translation "opportunistically" for κατὰ σάρκα, see Furnish, *II Corinthians*, 134. Cf. Harris (*Second Corinthians*, 196) who commends Furnish's translation but prefers "impulsively."

29. Andrew Perriman, "Between Troas and Macedonia: 2 Cor 2:13–14," *ExpTim* 101 (1989–1990): 39–41.

30. Welborn, "Paul's Caricature," 43.

31. Harris, *Second Epistle to the Corinthians*, 729.

32. Barnett, *Second Epistle to the Corinthians*, 562.

CHAPTER 18

1. Jerome Murphy-O'Connor, *Paul: A Critical Life* (Oxford: Clarendon, 1996), 316; Schnabel, *Paul and the Early Church*, 1251; Allan Chapple, "Why Spain? Paul and His Mission Plans," *Journal for the Study of Paul and His Letters* 1 (2011): 211.

2. Similarly, Douglas J. Moo, *The Letter to the Romans*, 2nd ed., NICNT (Grand Rapids: Eerdmans, 2018), 914. Otherwise, Michael Wolter, *Der Brief an die Römer*

(Teilband 2: Röm 9–16), EKK 6.2 (Ostfildern: Patmos; Göttingen: Vandenhoeck & Ruprecht, 2019), 433–34.

3. Frank Thielman, *Romans*, ZECNT 6 (Grand Rapids: Zondervan, 2016), 686.

4. On the theme in Isa, see Paul R. House, *Isaiah*, 2 vols. (Ross-shire: Christian Focus, 2019), 2:433.

5. ἐσχάτη ἱδρυμένη τῆς γῆς. See Chapple, "Why Spain?," 206. Chapple argues that Paul conceived of his plan to go to Spain after reflecting on Isa 49:6 (204–6).

6. As Chapple implies ("Why Spain?," 195–96, 206).

7. Cf. F. F. Bruce, *Paul: Apostle of the Heart Set Free* (Grand Rapids: Eerdmans, 1977), 317, although Bruce probably overemphasizes the use of Latin in Spain. On the languages of Spain in the period, see especially Robert Jewett, *Romans: A Commentary*, Hermeneia (Minneapolis: Fortress, 2007), 76–77. In Gadeira, people probably spoke both Phoenician and Latin. They were Roman citizens (Pliny, *Nat.* 4.119–120), but coins at least through the time of Claudius were minted in the city with Phoenician inscriptions. On the coinage, see J. M. Blazquez, "GADIR (Cádiz) Cáidiz, Spain," *PECS*, 341.

8. Danijel Dzino, *Illyricum in Roman Politics: 239 BC–AD 68* (Cambridge: Cambridge University Press, 2010), 159.

9. On all of this, see Dzino, *Illyricum*, 160–61.

10. Allan Chapple, "Paul and Illyricum," *RTR* 72 (2013): 25.

11. According to the Stanford Geospatial Network Model of the Roman World.

12. Again, using the Stanford Geospatial Network Model of the Roman World. On the Via Egnatia in this area, and on Salona as administrative center, see Dzino, *Illyricum*, 171.

13. See the route plotted by the Stanford Geospatial Network Model of the Roman World.

14. On Salona, see Chapple, "Paul and Illyricum," 26–27; and on the recently constructed road system, see Dzino, *Illyricum*, 170–72.

15. Chapple, "Paul and Illyricum," 32–33. On the level of Romanization in Spain, see Jewett, *Romans*, 75–79.

16. Using the time calculations of the Stanford Geospatial Network Model of the Roman World.

17. See BDAG 318, s.v. Ἑλλάς. The geographer Pausanias, for example, could use the terms "Achaia" and "Greece" basically interchangeably (*Descr.* 7.16.1–10).

18. If Paul wrote 2 Cor from Philippi, then Jason may have joined Paul and Timothy on a stop in Thessalonica as they traveled west along the Via Egnatia toward Illyricum.

19. On the work of a scribe, and on Tertius's work in particular, see Richard N. Longenecker, *Introducing Romans: Critical Issues in Paul's Most Famous Letter* (Grand Rapids: Eerdmans, 2011), 5–10.

20. Many translations take the phrase "in the Lord" (ἐν κυρίῳ) with "I greet you" (ἀσπάζομαι ὑμᾶς) (e.g., NIV, NRSV, ESV), but the analogy with laboring "in

the Lord" in Rom 16:12 and the proximity of "in the Lord" to the verb "wrote" (γράψας) make it more likely that Tertius was speaking of his work in writing the letter as something he did because he was a Christian. On this, see, e.g., the CEB and Thielman, *Romans*, 742n37.

21. Paul's letters to the Colossian Christians and to Philemon were written to churches he had not personally established, but Paul's close friend Epaphras had taught the Colossian Christians the gospel (Col 1:7; cf. Phlm 23). Cf. Michael Wolter, *Der Brief an die Römer (Teilband 1: Röm 1–8)*, EKK 6.1 (Neukirchen-Vluyn: Neukirchener; Ostfildern: Patmos, 2014), 43.

22. Günter Klein, "Paul's Purpose in Writing the Epistle to the Romans," in *The Romans Debate*, ed. Karl P. Donfried, rev. ed. (Peabody, MA: Hendrickson, 1991), 32, 39. Cf. Jewett, *Romans*, 85.

23. Jewett (*Romans*, 79–91) argues that Paul needed the Roman Christians' facility in Latin, their contact with immigrants from Spain, and their connections with Roman bureaucrats who worked in Spain to facilitate his entrance into this new environment. It would be impossible for the Romans to sponsor Paul's mission effectively, however, unless they overcame their own tendency to favor a type of Christianity that was heavily influenced by the Roman system of honor that the "barbarians" in Spain resisted. So, Paul wrote Romans to correct imperialistic tendencies in Roman Christianity but to do so with an eye on the success of his mission to Spain.

24. Wolter, *An die Römer (Teilband 1: Röm 1–8)*, 44–56. Wolter believes Paul learned that Phoebe was going to Rome on a business trip and simply took advantage of this opportunity to send Rom with her.

25. A. J. M. Wedderburn, "Purpose and Occasion of Romans Again," in *The Romans Debate*, rev. ed. (Peabody, MA: Hendrickson, 1991), 199; Moo, *Romans*, 913–14. The verb Paul uses here (φιλοτιμούμενον) refers to having an aspiration (BDAG 1059, s.v. φιλοτιμέομαι), but Paul recognized that aspirations cannot always find fulfillment. He tells the Thessalonian Christians, for example, that they should "aspire [φιλοτιμεῖσθαι] to live quietly" (1 Thess 4:11), but he would have recognized that this was not always possible (1 Thess 2:2).

26. Eckhard J. Schnabel, *Der Brief des Paulus an die Römer: Kapitel 6–16*, HTA (Witten: Brockhaus, 2016), 829.

27. Thielman, *Romans*, 681.

28. Cf. Jewett, *Romans*, 88.

29. On the length of the journey, see Chapple, "Why Spain?," 193–94.

30. BDAG 873, s.v. προπέμπω 2. See also Thielman, *Romans*, 690.

31. Jewett, *Romans*, 88.

32. Peter Lampe, *From Paul to Valentinus: Christians in Rome in the First Two Centuries*, ed. Marshall D. Johnson, trans. Michael Steinhauser (Minneapolis: Fortress, 2003), 9–10.

33. Cf. Acts 18:2, which, however, does not mention Christ. On the expulsion, see Erich S. Gruen, *Diaspora: Jews amidst Greeks and Romans* (Cambridge, MA:

Harvard University Press, 2002), 33. And on the whole issue of "Judaizing Christianity" in Rome, see A. J. M. Wedderburn, *The Reasons for Romans* (Minneapolis: Fortress, 1991), 50–59.

34. See, similarly, Peter Stuhlmacher, "The Purpose of Romans," in *The Romans Debate*, ed. Karl P. Donfried, rev. and exp. ed. (Peabody, MA: Hendrickson, 1991), 236, 238–40; and Wedderburn, *Reasons for Romans*, 123, 134, 139.

35. Within the Hellenized world of Paul, "the Greek" meant any non-Jewish person. See also Rom 2:9–10; 3:9; 10:12 and BDAG 318, s.v."Ἕλλην 2a.

36. Joseph A. Fitzmyer, *Romans*, AB 33 (New York: Doubleday, 1993), 257; Arland J. Hultgren, *Paul's Letter to the Romans: A Commentary* (Grand Rapids: Eerdmans, 2011), 75–76, 609–10. See, similarly, Wolter, *An die Römer (Teilband 1: Röm 1–8)*, 122–23.

37. Frank Thielman, "God's Righteousness as God's Fairness in Romans 1:17: An Ancient Perspective on a Significant Phrase," *JETS* 54 (2011): 41–43; Thielman, *Romans*, 86.

38. Origen, *Commentary on the Epistle to the Romans, Books 1–5*, trans. Thomas P. Scheck, FOC 104 (Washington, DC: Catholic University of America Press, 2001), 87 (1.15). See the discussion in Thielman, *Romans*, 88. Origen's quotation is from Jesus's words in Matt 11:28.

39. The quotation should probably be translated "Whoever is justified through faith shall gain life" (REB; cf. RSV), rather than "The one who is righteous will live by faith" (NRSV; cf. ESV, CEB). On this, see C. E. B. Cranfield, *The Epistle to the Romans*, ICC, 2 vols. (Edinburgh: T & T Clark, 1975–1979), 1:102; Francis Watson, "By Faith (of Christ): An Exegetical Dilemma and Its Scriptural Solution," in *The Faith of Jesus Christ: Exegetical, Biblical, and Theological Studies*, ed. Michael F. Bird and Preston M. Sprinkle (Milton Keynes: Paternoster, 2009), 154–62; Thielman, *Romans*, 84; Moo, *Romans*, 82; and especially Wolter (*An die Römer [Teilband 1: Röm 1–8]*, 127) who points out that this is the most likely meaning of Paul's use of Hab 2:4 in Gal 3:11.

40. See also Wedderburn, *Reasons for Romans*, 122.

41. For Christ as the "place" where atonement happens at God's initiative, see Daniel P. Bailey, "Biblical and Greco-Roman Uses of *Hilastērion* in Romans 3:25 and 4 Maccabees 17:22," in Peter Stuhlmacher, *Biblical Theology of the New Testament*, trans. and ed. Daniel P. Bailey (Grand Rapids: Eerdmans, 2018), 830; and Stephen Hultgren, "*Hilastērion* (Rom. 3:25) and the Union of Divine Justice and Mercy. Part II: Atonement in the Old Testament and in Romans 1–5," *JTS* 70 (2019): 546–99.

42. For the phrase "place of atonement" and for the contribution of Rom 3:4 to this part of Paul's argument, I have relied on Hultgren, "Atonement in the Old Testament," 576.

43. The term appears in Lev 16:2, 13, 14, and 15. ἱλαστήριον is probably a neuter noun describing not a concept ("atonement") but an instrument by which, or place at which, propitiation, expiation, forgiveness, and reconciliation occur (Hultgren, "Atonement in the Old Testament," 561, 563; cf. Bailey, "Biblical and Greco Roman Uses," 830).

44. Stephen Hultgren, "*Hilastērion* (Rom. 3:25) and the Union of Divine Justice and Mercy. Part I: The Convergence of Temple and Martyrdom Theologies," *JTS* 70 (2019): 82–88, esp. 85.

45. Hultgren, "Atonement in the Old Testament," 598.

46. Hultgren, "Convergence of Temple and Martyrdom Theologies," 79–82.

47. Hultgren, "Convergence of Temple and Martyrdom Theologies," 73–88; and Hultgren, "Atonement in the Old Testament," 598–99.

48. Frank Thielman, "Adam's Sin and Jesus' Death in Romans (Romans 5:12–21)," in *Paul's Letter to the Romans: Theological Essays*, ed. Douglas J. Moo, Eckhard J. Schnabel, Thomas R. Schreiner, and Frank Thielman (Peabody, MA: Hendrickson, 2023), 145–54.

49. On this, see Schnabel, *An die Römer: Kapitel 6–16*, 918–20; Wolter, *An die Römer (Teilband 2: Röm 9–16)*, 496–97.

50. Nicholas K. Rauh, *Merchants, Sailors, and Pirates in the Roman World* (Stroud, Gloucestershire, UK: Tempus, 2003), 24–25.

CHAPTER 19

1. Cf. Klaus Haacker, *Die Apostelgeschichte*, THKNT (Stuttgart: Kohlhammer, 2019), 334. Haacker thinks that Paul's knowledge of the plot of Acts 20:3 prompted his comments in Rom 15:31.

2. Ramsay seems to have been the first interpreter to suggest this. W. M. Ramsay, *St. Paul the Traveller and the Roman Citizen* (London: Hodder & Stoughton, 1986), 287. See also, e.g., F. F. Bruce, *The Book of the Acts*, rev. ed., NICNT (Grand Rapids: Eerdmans, 1988), 382; C. K. Barrett, *A Critical and Exegetical Commentary on the Acts of the Apostles*, ICC, 2 vols. (Edinburgh: T&T Clark, 1994–1998), 2:946; and Craig S. Keener, *Acts: An Exegetical Commentary*, 4 vols. (Grand Rapids: Baker, 2012–2015), 3:2952–53.

3. Keener, *Acts*, 3:2952–53.

4. Keener, *Acts*, 3:2953n38.

5. Luke's Greek here poses some difficulty. Some interpreters, such as James Hardy Ropes, *The Text of Acts*, vol. 3 of *The Beginnings of Christianity, Part I: The Acts of the Apostles*, ed. F. J. Foakes Jackson and Kirsopp Lake (London: Macmillan, 1926), 190–91; and Barrett, *Acts*, 2:949, believe that Luke intends to say the group in Acts 20:4 was only "associated with" (συνείπετο) Paul, not that they returned with him through Macedonia. On this view, Luke envisions most of the group sailing to Troas (in Asia) where they waited for Paul, who took a different route through Macedonia and spent the Feast of Unleavened Bread in Philippi (Acts 20:5–6). Cf., e.g., F. F. Bruce, *Paul: The Apostle of the Heart Set Free* (Grand Rapids: Eerdmans, 1977), 340. The Greek term συνέπομαι, however, means "follow along with, accompany" (LSJ 1711, s.v.), and Luke's sudden introduction of himself into the narrative in Acts 20:5 makes it likely that he and the group "were following along with" Paul

when he went to Macedonia and Philippi (my trans.). According to Luke, those who went ahead to Troas (probably only Tychicus and Trophimus) were awaiting "us" there (Acts 20:5). If they were awaiting not only Paul but Luke, they must have been with Luke (and Paul) in Philippi and must have traveled with him there from Corinth.

6. E.g., Joseph A. Fitzmyer, *The Acts of the Apostles*, AB 31 (New Haven, CT: Yale University Press, 1998), 665; Barrett ("perhaps"), *Acts*, 2:949; Daniel Marguerat, *Die Apostelgeschichte*, KEK 3 (Göttingen: Vandenhoeck & Ruprecht, 2022), 688.

7. Ramsay (*St. Paul the Traveller*, 287), similarly, envisions Paul sailing for Macedonia, "where he easily arrived in time to celebrate the Passover in Philippi."

8. Ramsay, *St. Paul the Traveller*, 287.

9. I am largely dependent for my understanding of the Feast of Weeks on E. P. Sanders, *Judaism: Practice and Belief, 63 BCE–66 CE* (London: SCM, 1992), 138–39, 151–54.

10. On this, see especially Keener, *Acts*, 3:2962.

11. Murray J. Harris, *The Second Epistle to the Corinthians*, NIGTC (Grand Rapids: Eerdmans, 2005), 97–98.

12. On Paul's principle of allowing freedom concerning such observances, see Keener, *Acts*, 3:2960.

13. On the probability that Luke's reference to the feast is not simply a time marker but indicates Paul's observance of it, see Jacob Jervell, *Die Apostelgeschichte*, KEK 3 (Göttingen: Vandenhoeck & Ruprecht, 1998), 499; and Keener, *Acts*, 3:2959–60. On the Jewish character of Philippian Christianity at this point, see Haacker, *Apostelgeschichte*, 335.

14. E.g., Kirsopp Lake and Henry J. Cadbury, *English Translation and Commentary*, vol. 4 of *The Beginnings of Christianity, Part I: The Acts of the Apostles*, ed. F. J. Foakes Jackson and Kirsopp Lake (London: Macmillan, 1933), 253.

15. For the suggestion of arranging transportation, see Mark Wilson, "The Lukan *Periplus* of Paul's Third Journey with a Textual Conundrum in Acts 20:15," *AcT* 36 (2016): 232–33; and Glen L. Thompson and Mark Wilson, "Paul's Walk to Assos: A Hodological Inquiry into Its Geography, Archaeology, and Purpose," in *Stones, Bones and the Sacred: Essays on Material Culture and Ancient Religion in Honor of Dennis E. Smith*, ed. Alan H. Cadwallader, Early Christianity and Its Literature 22 (Atlanta: SBL, 2016), 300.

16. E.g., F. F. Bruce, *Paul: Apostle of the Heart Set Free* (Grand Rapids: Eerdmans, 1977), 350; Marguerat, *Apostelgeschichte*, 688.

17. On winds in the eastern Mediterranean, see Lionel Casson, *Ships and Seamanship in the Ancient World*, 2nd ed. (Baltimore: Johns Hopkins University Press, 1995), 272; Nicholas K. Rauh, *Merchants, Sailors, and Pirates in the Roman World* (Stroud, Gloucestershire, UK: Tempus, 2003), 20–32; and Justin Leidwanger, *Roman Seas: A Maritime Archaeology of Eastern Mediterranean Economies* (New York: Oxford University Press, 2020), 31–34 and the chart on 143.

18. Haacker (*Die Apostelgeschichte*, 335) is on the right track here in the main text of his commentary, but he then seems to revert to the contrary wind theory (see also, e.g., Marguerat, *Apostelgeschichte*, 688) in his footnote (335n14).

19. Wilson, "Lukan *Periplus*," 231. For the picture of small coastal vessels making calls at small ports to conduct commerce, see Leidwanger, *Roman Seas*, 154–66.

20. Bruce, *Acts*, 384; cf., e.g., Fitzmyer, *Acts*, 669; Carl R. Holladay, *Acts: A Commentary*, NTL (Louisville: Westminster John Knox, 2016), 391 (who usefully cites Luke 22:19); and Marguerat, *Apostelgeschichte*, 690. Haacker (*Apostelgeschichte*, 336) sees no eucharistic reference here, claiming that it would be odd to observe the Eucharist in the middle of the night. Barrett (*Acts*, 2:950) is also doubtful the Eucharist is in view.

21. N. T. Wright, *Paul: A Biography* (San Francisco: HarperOne, 2018), 344–45.

22. The translation belongs to BDAG 472, s.v. ἱκανός 4b.

23. For the physical construction of these lamps, see BDAG 585, s.v. λαμπάς 2.

24. Barrett (*Acts*, 954) believes "there may be special allusions to the Elijah and Elisha stories." Haenchen (Ernst Haenchen, *Acts of the Apostles: A Commentary* [Louisville: Westminster John Knox, 1971], 585), Keener (*Acts*, 3:2978), and Marguerat (*Apostelgeschichte*, 691) think the influence is clear. The parallels will strike interpreters in different ways, but some careful scholars have found them unimpressive. Lake and Cadbury (*English Translation and Commentary*, 257), for example, thought the parallel with the Elijah story was "far-fetched" and do not even mention the Elisha story.

25. BDAG 377, 959, svv. ἐπιπίπτω 1b; συμπεριλαμβάνω. Xenophon uses the term περιλαμβάνω (without σύν), but this does not alter the meaning significantly.

26. On the young man's dazed condition, see Haacker (*Apostelgeschichte*, 336).

27. Pliny, writing in the first century, comments that "Assos . . . is the same as Apollonia" and then continues to refer to Assos as Apollonia (*Nat.* 32.123).

28. Thompson and Wilson, "Paul's Walk to Assos," 281.

29. For the speed of vessels "when navigating along coasts, islands, and channels," see Leidwanger, *Roman Seas*, 61.

30. Thompson and Wilson, "Paul's Walk to Assos," 271 (map), 279, 281, 282–83, 287–90.

31. Thompson and Wilson, "Paul's Walk to Assos," 279.

32. Thompson and Wilson, "Paul's Walk to Assos," 287.

33. My translation. On the meaning of the term συνέβαλλεν ("met up with") here, see Josephus, *A.J.* 1.219; 2.184; and BDAG 956, s.v. συμβάλλω 4.

34. See John Chrysostom (*Hom. Act.* 43) for the first two suggestions, Lake and Cadbury (*English Translation and Commentary*, 257–58) for the third suggestion, and Thompson and Wilson ("Paul's Walk to Assos," 302–5) for the fourth suggestion.

35. Cf. Eckhard J. Schnabel, "Paul's Missionary Work in the Provinces of Asia and Illyricum," in Barry J. Beitzel, ed., *Lexham Geographic Commentary on Acts through Revelation* (Bellingham, WA: Lexham Press, 2019), 395.

36. Using the speeds and wind directions provided in Leidwanger, *Roman Seas*, 61 and 143.

37. Duane W. Roller, *A Historical and Topographical Guide to the "Geography" of Strabo* (Cambridge: Cambridge University Press, 2018), 773.

38. Roller, *Historical and Topographical Guide*, 773.

39. Following the interpretation of Strabo's comments in Roller, *Historical and Topographical Guide*, 802.

40. The length of a stadion is not entirely clear (Duane W. Roller, trans., *The "Geography" of Strabo: An English Translation with Introduction and Notes* [Cambridge: Cambridge University Press, 2014], 33).

41. According to the Stanford Geospatial Network Model of the Roman World.

42. Wilson, "Lukan *Periplus*," 243–47. If Wilson is right, however, it seems odd that Luke did not simply name the city. For the translations of ἄντικρυς here as "off" or "near," see *CGL* 1:143, s.v. ἄντικρυς 6.

43. Keener, *Acts*, 3:2991–92. Cf. Barrett, *Acts*, 2:959.

44. Keener, *Acts*, 3:2990–91.

45. Using the calculations of the Stanford Geospatial Network Model of the Roman World.

46. John McRay, "Miletus," *ABD* 4:826.

47. McRay, "Miletus," 826; Clyde E. Fant and Mitchell G. Reddish, *A Guide to Biblical Sites in Greece and Turkey* (Oxford: Oxford University Press, 2003), 249.

48. On agricultural production and herding in the area in antiquity, see Alan M. Greaves, *Miletos: A History* (London: Routledge, 2002), 24–32, 136. *P. Cairo Zen.* 59015, from the third century BC, indicates that one ship transported 258 jars and 102 half-jars of oil from both Samos and Miletus to Alexandria. This ship probably picked up oil in Samos and then, like Paul's ship, sailed to Miletus where it picked up more oil. On this papyrus, see Casson, *Ships and Seamanship*, 162n36; and Greaves, *Miletos*, 136.

49. Keener, *Acts*, 3:2991.

50. Not, therefore, to the prophecies of the disciples in Tyre (Acts 21:4) and of Agabus in Caesarea (Acts 21:11) (Holladay, *Acts*, 397) or to the persecutions Paul has experienced "since the beginning of his activity as a preacher of Christ" (seit dem Beginn seiner Aktivität als Prediger Christi") (Marguerat, *Apostelgeschichte*, 703).

51. Cf. William Neil, *The Acts of the Apostles*, NCB (London: Oliphants, 1973), 214; Bruce, *Acts*, 390.

52. Holladay, *Acts*, 394, suggests the messengers to Ephesus may have been the people in the delegation with a connection to Ephesus: Timothy, Aristarchus, Tychicus, and Trophimus (although Tychicus's connection specifically to Ephesus is uncertain).

53. For the route across the gulf to Priene, see Ramsay, *St. Paul the Traveller*, 294. One could not sail directly into Priene, however, as Ramsay imagined. The silting of the Maeander had placed it roughly five miles ("40 stadia") inland already in Stra-

bo's time (*Geogr.* 12.8.17). On this, see John Manuel Cook and Antony Spawforth, "Priene," *OCD*[4] 1209. Ramsay also imagined that the route led from Priene across Mount Mycale, whereas I have followed the hypothetical road marked in J. A. Talbert, ed., *Barrington Atlas of the Greek and Roman World* (Princeton, NJ: Princeton University Press, 2000), 61, and have measured the distances using that map.

54. The term "departure" (ἄφιξιν) in Acts 20:29 is ambiguous, possibly referring to Paul's immediate departure from Asia or to his departure into the next life. On this, see Marguerat (*Apostelgeschichte*, 707n52), who points to the similar ambiguity of the term "departure" (ἔξοδον) in Luke 9:31.

55. For speed, see Leidwanger, *Roman Seas*, 61. The Stanford Geospatial Network Model of the Roman World calculates the trip at 95 kilometers (which is about 51.3 nautical miles) and half a day.

56. For these estimates I mapped a route using both Talbert, ed., *Barrington Atlas of the Greek and Roman World*, map 61, and Google Earth. I used Google Earth to estimate the distance of the route. The Stanford Geospatial Network Model of the Roman World estimates the journey at 119 kilometers (about 64.25 nautical miles) and 0.7 days (about seventeen hours). On navigation by sighting visible landmarks, see James Malcolm Morton, "The Role of the Physical Environment in Ancient Greek Seafaring" (PhD diss., University of Edinburgh, 1988), 166–79.

57. The other harbor was Myra, to the east. On the network of roads and the monument from AD 45 honoring Claudius who "made" (ἐποίησεν) them, see Fatih Onur, "'The Monument of Roads' at Patara," in *Lukka'dan Likya'ya: Sarpedon ve Aziz Nikolaos'un Ülkesi/From Lukka to Lycia: The Country of Sarpedon and St. Nicholas*, ed. H. Işek and E. Dündar, Anadolu Uygarlıkları Serisi 5 (Istanbul: Yapı Kredi Kültür Sanat Yaıyncılık, 2016), 570–77. See also Stephen Mitchell, "Lycia," *OCD*[4] 869.

58. On Phoenicia, see Fitzmyer, *Acts*, 475.

59. I used Google Earth for the distance calculation and took the ship's route past Paphos. The Stanford Geospatial Network Model of the Roman World plots the route from Patara to Tyre through Berytus and places the distance at 800 kilometers (about 432 nautical miles). It calculates the travel time as 4.8 days, which matches almost exactly John Chrysostom's often-cited estimate of five days (*Hom. Act.* 43).

60. For the prevailing winds, see Leidwanger, *Roman Seas*, 143.

61. On top speed under favorable conditions, see Leidwanger, *Roman Seas*, 61; and for nighttime navigation, see Morton, "Ancient Greek Seafaring," 227–29.

62. Lake and Cadbury, *English Translation and Commentary*, 265; Barrett, *Acts* 2:990.

63. I measured the distance using Google Earth and calculated the vessel speed at four knots (see Leidwanger, *Roman Seas*, 61). It is possible that behind Luke's expression "We departed and came to Caesarea" lies a land journey rather than a sea journey, but the sea journey would have been less arduous, and Caesarea would not have been a logical stop for a land journey from Ptolemais to Jerusalem.

CHAPTER 20

1. On the history of the movement, see Martin Hengel, *The Zealots: Investigations into the Jewish Freedom Movement in the Period from Herod I until 70 A.D.*, trans. David Smith (Edinburgh: T&T Clark, 1989), 24–145.

2. Cf. Hengel, *Zealots*, 217.

3. Hengel, *Zealots*, 116–18, 206–24. On Josephus's use of the term "brigand," see Hengel, *Zealots*, 41–46; and Steve Mason, *Judean War 2: Translation and Commentary*, vol. 1b of *Flavius Josephus: Translation and Commentary*, ed. Steve Mason (Leiden: Brill, 2008), 39.

4. Josephus only says that they murdered "their foes," but he also connects them specifically with brigands (*B.J.* 2.254), and the brigands threatened "to kill any who submitted to Roman domination and forcibly to suppress those who voluntarily accepted servitude" (*B.J.* 2.264 [Thackeray, LCL]). See the comments of Mason, *Judean War 2*, 39.

5. On the evocation of Joshua, see E. Mary Smallwood, *The Jews under Roman Rule from Pompey to Diocletian: A Study in Political Relations* (Leiden: Brill, 1981), 275–76.

6. See Hengel, *Zealots*, 114–15.

7. C. K. Barrett, *A Critical and Exegetical Commentary on the Acts of the Apostles*, ICC, 2 vols. (Edinburgh: T&T Clark, 1994–1998), 1001.

8. E.g., Udo Schnelle, *Apostle Paul: His Life and Theology*, trans. M. Eugene Boring (Grand Rapids: Baker, 2005), 361–62; James D. G. Dunn, *Beginning from Jerusalem*, vol. 2 of *Christianity in the Making*, 3 vols. (Grand Rapids: Eerdmans, 2009), 972. Haenchen thinks that the Jerusalem leaders made acceptance of the offering dependent upon Paul's demonstration of loyalty to the Mosaic law. Ernst Haenchen, *Acts of the Apostles: A Commentary* (Louisville: Westminster John Knox, 1971), 613–14.

9. Craig S. Keener, *Acts: An Exegetical Commentary*, 4 vols. (Grand Rapids: Baker, 2012–2015), 3:3115.

10. Cf. Keener, *Acts*, 3:3127.

11. Jacob Jervell (*Die Apostelgeschichte*, KEK 3 [Göttingen: Vandenhoeck & Ruprecht, 1998], 526) sees this as the situation, at least from Luke's perspective.

12. Luke describes the leaders' request to Paul in a compressed way ("take these men and purify yourself along with them") and this has sometimes created confusion among interpreters. It is unclear why the four Nazirites would need purification. Had they contracted corpse impurity (Num 6:9–12)? This is unlikely since, according to Num 6, they would have to start their vow over after the purification ritual, and the vow had to last for at least thirty days (Josephus, *B.J.* 2.313). It is more likely that the vow itself was considered "a vow of purification" (ἡ εὐχὴ τοῦ ἁγνισμοῦ, Num 6:5 [LXX]; cf. 6:21), and Luke was simply indicating that both Paul and they would be involved in purification rituals.

13. Since Paul had lived outside the land of Israel for the last six years, everyone would have assumed that he had contracted corpse impurity. This would only have been confirmed when, in detailing his ministry among the gentiles, he told the story of Eutychus, whom God raised from the dead (Acts 20:7–12; 21:19).

14. Cf., e.g., Friedrich W. Horn, "Paulus, das Nasiräat und die Nasiräer," *NovT* 39 (1997): 134n64.

15. See Josephus, *Ag. Ap.* 2.102–105; *B.J.* 5.190–219; and the carefully researched description of the temple in E. P. Sanders, *Judaism: Practice and Belief: 63 BCE–66 CE* (London: SCM, 1992), 54–69, 308–14. Much of my description follows the account in Sanders.

16. Sanders, *Judaism: Practice and Belief*, 61. See Josephus, *Ag. Ap.* 2.103.

17. Text and translation from Peretz Segal, "The Penalty of the Warning Inscription from the Temple of Jerusalem," *IEJ* 39 (1989): 79. Cf. Josephus, *B.J.* 5.194; 6.125–126; *A.J.* 15.417; Philo, *Legat.* 212; and the comments of Hengel, *Zealots*, 214; and Sanders, *Judaism: Practice and Belief*, 61, 500n39.

18. On the probability of this gallery, see Sanders, *Judaism: Practice and Belief*, 61 (relying on m. Middot 2:5).

19. On the corridor, which is slightly controversial, see Sanders, *Judaism: Practice and Belief*, 500n42.

20. When the mob attacked Paul, Luke says they cried out that Paul had "brought Greeks into the temple and . . . defiled *this* holy place (τὸν ἅγιον τόπον τοῦτον)" (Acts 21:28, emphasis mine). The only place he could have defiled by bringing Greeks into it was the part of the temple beyond the barrier. Josephus calls this area "the holy place" (τὸ ἅγιον, *B.J.* 5.194 [Thackeray, LCL]).

21. On their recognition of Paul, see Keener, *Acts*, 3:3145.

22. According to Segal ("Penalty of the Warning Inscription," 82–83), this was the meaning of the phrase, "will have himself to blame for his subsequent death" in the inscription.

23. On zeal for God's holiness as a reason to execute immediate vengeance on those who violate it without any recourse to the court system, see Philo, *Spec.* 1.53.

24. Segal, "Penalty of the Warning Inscription," 83.

25. Josephus believed that bloodshed in the temple eventually brought down the wrath of God on both temple and city (*A.J.* 20.165–166; cf. *B.J.* 4.201, 215).

26. Sanders, *Judaism: Practice and Belief*, 60.

27. On the effort required, see Sanders, *Judaism: Practice and Belief*, 60.

28. On the tribune, see Brian Rapske, *Paul in Roman Custody*, vol. 3 of *The Book of Acts in Its First Century Setting* (Grand Rapids: Eerdmans, 1994), 144.

29. As Felix had sent the insurrectionist Eleazar to Rome (Josephus, *B.J.* 2.253).

30. Daniel Marguerat, *Die Apostelgeschichte*, KEK 3 (Göttingen: Vandenhoeck & Ruprecht, 2022), 737. Cf. F. F. Bruce, *The Book of the Acts*, NICNT (Grand Rapids: Eerdmans, 1988), 412: "He was . . . surprised when Paul . . . addressed him in an educated Greek voice."

31. Haenchen thinks the tribune's assumption that the Egyptian would not know Greek is implausible because "the Egyptian Jews spoke Greek by preference" (*Acts*, 621). It is not clear how Haenchen knows this. Many Egyptians in the Roman period did not speak Greek. At least in papyri from the second through the fourth centuries AD, some Egyptians needed interpreters to translate their words into Greek when they appeared before local magistrates. On this, see J. A. Crook, *Legal Advocacy in the Roman World* (Ithaca, NY: Cornell University Press, 1995), 62.

32. Luke was still using the first person as late as Acts 21:17–18.

33. Andrea Nicolotti, "The Scourge of Jesus and the Roman Scourge: Historical and Archaeological Evidence," *Journal for the Study of the Historical Jesus* 15 (2017): 2.

34. See the large body of evidence for this and the careful discussion in Rapske, *Paul in Roman Custody*, 47–56. The coin on the book's dust jacket (although from 91–89 BC), and the discussion on pp. 49–50, are particularly relevant.

35. Dunn, *Beginning from Jerusalem*, 969; James D. G. Dunn, *The Acts of the Apostles*, Narrative Commentaries (Valley Forge, PA: Trinity Press International, 1996), 298.

36. Cf. Rapske, *Paul in Roman Custody*, 143.

37. E.g., Bruce, *Acts*, 420; Harry W. Tajra, *The Trial of St. Paul: A Juridical Exegesis of the Second Half of the Acts of the Apostles*, WUNT 2.35 (Tübingen: Mohr Siebeck, 1989), 73; Rapske, *Paul in Roman Custody*, 139, 447.

38. Nicolotti, "Scourge of Jesus," 1–59.

39. Rapske, *Paul in Roman Custody*, 146; Heike Omerzu, "The Roman Trial against Paul according to Acts 21–26," in *The Last Years of Paul: Essays from the Tarragona Conference, June 2013*, ed. Armand Puig i Tàrrech, John M. G. Barclay, and Jörg Frey, WUNT 1.352 (Tübingen: Mohr Siebeck, 2015), 192. The relevant law was the *Lex Iulia de vi publica* (*Dig.* 48.6.7–8; *Paul. Sent.* 5.26.1–2).

40. If Claudius Lysias was afraid because he had put Paul in chains (Acts 22:29), then he must have released him from those chains even before the hearing with the chief priests and the Sanhedrin (22:30). In addition, if Paul's nephew could contact him in the fortress as easily as Luke describes (23:16–17), Paul's conditions of detention must not have been severe. On these considerations, see Rapske, *Paul in Roman Custody*, 146, 148. That Felix will later continue to detain Paul but allow him some freedom and let his friends take care of him (24:23) also supports the idea Paul was already experiencing a less severe detention under Claudius Lysias.

41. See, similarly, Rapske, *Paul in Roman Custody*, 144–45.

42. Commenting on Celer's fate, Mason (*Judean War 2*, 198) says, "Inevitably, the man in such a powerful and visible position (in Jerusalem) faced the constant risk of alienating the people; an incompetent or malevolent tribune could cause great damage," and, it might be added, wind up dead.

43. Martin Goodman, *The Ruling Class of Judaea: The Origins of the Jewish Revolt against Rome, A.D. 66–70* (Cambridge: Cambridge University Press, 1987), 113–16. The Greek term for "sanhedrin" (συνέδριον) basically means a "council" or "meeting,"

and "the sanhedrin" of first-century Judaism seems to have been a gathering of the city's nobility for the purpose of ratifying the desire of some particularly powerful person. On this, see Sanders, *Judaism: Practice and Belief*, 472-88.

44. For resistance to the idea of Luke's historical accuracy on this point, see, e.g., Haenchen, *Acts*, 640; Jervell, *Apostelgeschichte*, 553; Omerzu, "Roman Trial against Paul," 193.

45. I am indebted to Sanders (*Judaism: Practice and Belief*, 485-87) for drawing these passages to my attention. Sanders is making a different point, however, and is not interested in the historical reliability of Acts 22:30–23:10.

46. So, correctly, Bruce, *Acts*, 423: "If he ordered the Sanhedrin to meet, the Sanhedrin met."

47. A. N. Sherwin-White, *Roman Society and Roman Law in the New Testament* (Oxford: Oxford University Press, 1963), 54-55.

48. Omerzu ("Roman Trial against Paul," 194) thinks the incident is a fabrication.

49. Cf. Dunn (*Acts*, 306), who is, however, more cautious about an identification with the *sicarii*.

50. Mason (*Judean War 2*, 188, 374) describes the distance as 3.3 km.

51. B. Bar-Kochva, "Sēron and Cestius Gallus at Beith Ḥoron," *PEQ* (1976): 13.

52. Bar-Kochva, "Sēron and Cestius Gallus," 13-14.

53. See the treatment of both accounts, and especially the translation of Josephus's account, in Bar-Kochva, "Sēron and Cestius Gallus," 15-21.

54. See also Martin Hengel, "The Geography of Palestine in Acts," in *The Book of Acts in Its Palestinian Setting*, ed. Richard Bauckham, vol. 4 of *The Book of Acts in Its First Century Setting* (Grand Rapids: Eerdmans, 1995), 66.

55. See, similarly, Rapske, *Paul in Roman Custody*, 154.

56. Luke prefaces his description of the letter with the statement that Claudius Lysias "wrote a letter to this effect [τύπον]" (Acts 23:25). The use of the word τύπος here probably means that Luke was giving the "purport" of the letter (cf. Let. Aris. 34, ed. and trans. Moses Hadas, *Aristeas to Philocrates [Letter of Aristeas]*, Jewish Apocryphal Literature [New York: Harper, 1951], 113). On the word, see Leonard Goppelt, "τύπος, κτλ.," *TDNT* 8:248. For the preservation of such official documents, see Bruce W. Winter, "The Importance of the *Captatio Benevolentiae* in the Speeches of Tertullus and Paul in Acts 24:1-21," *JTS* 42 (1991): 527-28.

CHAPTER 21

1. Tacitus calls it "the capital . . . of Judea" (*Hist.* 2.78 [Moore, LCL]). Luke and Josephus assume their readers know that the prefects and procurators normally lived there (e.g., *B.J.* 2.171; *A.J.* 18.55, 57; 20.116; Acts 23:23, 33; 25:1, 6). See Emil Schürer, *The History of the Jewish People in the Age of Jesus Christ (175 B.C.–A.D. 135)*, rev. and ed. by Geza Vermes et al., 3 vols. (Edinburgh: T&T Clark, 1979), 1:361; 2:117.

2. H. Keith Beebe, "Caesarea Maritima: Its Strategic and Political Significance to Rome," *JNES* 42 (1983): 204–5.

3. On the date of its construction, see Asher Ovadiah and Rachel Peleg, "The 'Promontory Palace' in Caesarea Maritima and the Northern Palace at Masada," *RB* 116 (2009): 601. Although this building is likely "Herod's praetorium" (Acts 23:35), the identification is not entirely certain. For a cautious acceptance of this identification, see Heike Omerzu, *Der Prozeß des Paulus: Eine exegetische und rechtshistorische Untersuchung der Apostelgeschichte*, BZNW 115 (Berlin: de Gruyter, 2002), 416–18.

4. Joseph Patrich, *Studies in the Archaeology and History of Caesarea Maritima: Caput Judaeae, Metropolis Palaestinae*, AGJU 77 (Leiden: Brill, 2011), 206–10, 240–42. A mosaic in the ruins of the praetorium's southeastern corner from about a century after Paul implies the existence of a prison. On this, see Hannah M. Cotton and Werner Eck, "Governors and Their Personnel on Latin Inscriptions from Caesarea Maritima," *Cathedra: For the History of Eretz Israel and Its Yishuv* 122 (2006): 43–45.

5. Omerzu (*Der Prozeß des Paulus*, 416) mentions the possibility of more than one palace.

6. Brian Rapske, *Paul in Roman Custody*, vol. 3 of *The Book of Acts in Its First Century Setting*, ed. Bruce W. Winter (Grand Rapids: Eerdmans, 1994), 157.

7. Bernard P. Grenfell and Arthur S. Hunt, ed. and trans., *The Oxyrhynchus Papyri*, 85 vols. (London: Egypt Exploration Fund, 1898–2020), 80–81 (P.Oxy. 1.37). On the various possibilities for identifying Theon's role, see J. A. Crook, *Legal Advocacy in the Roman World* (Ithaca, NY: Cornell University Press, 1995), 70.

8. On the possibility that the defendant did have an advocate, since someone named "Theon" pipes up at one point, possibly on her behalf, see Crook, *Legal Advocacy*, 70. This identification seems unlikely, however, since the defendant offers her case directly to the governor in her own words.

9. On his wealth and influence, see Martin Goodman, *Ruling Class of Judaea: The Origins of the Jewish Revolt against Rome, A.D. 66–70* (Cambridge: Cambridge University Press, 1987), 145–46; and James C. VanderKam, *From Joshua to Caiaphas: High Priests after the Exile* (Minneapolis: Fortress, 2004), 458–60.

10. Schürer, *History of the Jewish People*, 1:471–72.

11. Goodman, *Ruling Class of Judea*, 145; VanderKam, *From Joshua to Caiaphas*, 456.

12. Bruce W. Winter, "The Importance of the *Captatio Benevolentiae* in the Speeches of Tertullus and Paul in Acts 24:1–21," *JTS* 42 (1991): 515–16.

13. On the political climate, see Smallwood and Goodman. E. Mary Smallwood, *Jews under Roman Rule from Pompey to Diocletian: A Study in Political Relations* (Leiden: Brill, 1981), 269; Goodman, *Ruling Class of Judaea*, 150–51. Josephus claims that Felix eventually had Jonathan assassinated (Josephus, *A.J.* 20.162–164), although some scholars wonder if this is correct. Goodman (*Ruling Class of Judaea*, 145) argues that Ananias may have been behind Jonathan's murder.

14. Winter, "*Captatio Benevolentiae*," 516.

15. Franz Cumont, "La lettre de Claude aux Alexandrins et les Actes des Apôtres," *RHR* 91 (1925): 4–5; A. N. Sherwin-White, *Roman Society and Roman Law in the New Testament* (Oxford: Oxford University Press, 1963), 51; Winter, "Captatio Benevolentiae," 518.

16. Trans. Barbara Levick, *The Government of the Roman Empire: A Sourcebook*, 2nd ed. (London: Routledge, 2000), 136. The document is dated November 10, AD 41, and its Greek text appears in E. Mary Smallwood, *Documents Illustrating the Principates of Gaius, Claudius, and Nero* (Cambridge: Cambridge University Press, 1967), 99–102. The relevant section is 370.96–99. The word "plague" in Acts translates the Greek term λοιμόν, whereas the term "epidemic" in Claudius's letter translates the term νόσον.

17. Winter ("*Captatio Benevolentiae*," 519) seems to suggest this.

18. Omerzu argues against the idea of verbatim records because of Paul's low social status and Luke's inability to access court records. Heike Omerzu, "The Roman Trial against Paul according to Acts 21–26," in *The Last Years of Paul: Essays from the Tarragona Conference, June 2013*, ed. Armand Puig i Tàrrech, John M. G. Barclay, and Jörg Frey, WUNT 1.352 (Tübingen: Mohr Siebeck, 2015), 193. The social status of the prosecution in Paul's case was, however, extraordinarily high, and the evidence of P.Oxy. 1.37 shows that magistrates sometimes kept nearly verbatim records. The question of whether Luke could access these records seems open.

19. Similarly, Winter, "*Captatio Benevolentiae*," 523.

20. So similarly, Carl R. Holladay, *Acts: A Commentary*, NTL (Louisville: Westminster John Knox, 2016), 449–50. Cf. Ernst Haenchen, *Acts of the Apostles: A Commentary* (Louisville: Westminster John Knox, 1971), 654; Bruce, *Acts*, 443.

21. Some students of Paul's life believe that Paul wrote some or all of his imprisonment letters during this period of confinement in Caesarea. These arguments are persuasive up to a point, but several considerations make them unlikely to be correct. On this, see appendix 2, "The Historical Setting of Paul's Imprisonment Letters."

22. Paul McKechnie, "Judaean Embassies and Cases before Roman Emperors, AD 44–66," *JTS* 56 (2005): 339–61.

23. McKechnie, "Judaean Embassies," 343.

24. Omerzu, *Der Prozeß des Paulus*, 471; cf. Marguerat, *Apostelgeschichte*, 790.

25. See Frank Thielman, "Paul's View of Israel's Misstep in Rom. 32–3: Its Origin and Meaning," *NTS* 64 (2018): 371–76.

26. Kirsopp Lake and Henry J. Cadbury, *English Translation and Commentary*, vol. 4 of *The Beginnings of Christianity, Part I: The Acts of the Apostles*, ed. F. J. Foakes Jackson and Kirsopp Lake (London: Macmillan, 1933), 4:309: "The rendering ['give me up'] does not sufficiently express the sense of granting a favour."

27. For the argument that the phrase "the Jews who killed the Lord Jesus and the prophets and also drove us out" (1 Thess 2:14–15 NIV) refers to the Jewish leadership in Jerusalem, see Thielman, "Paul's View of Israel's Misstep," 371–76.

28. Omerzu, "Roman Trial against Paul," 198.

29. Omerzu, "Roman Trial against Paul," 198. See, e.g., Cassius Dio, *Hist. Rom.* 63.2.3, where in AD 69, under the emperor Galba, an unnamed man appealed his case to the emperor, seemingly before any judgment had been rendered and, it seems, to escape an unjust judge. He failed in his effort because this judge "changed his seat to a high chair and then said: 'Now plead your case before Caesar'" (trans. Earnest Cary, LCL). He then sentenced the man to death.

30. Omerzu, "Roman Trial against Paul," 199–200.

31. Omerzu, "Roman Trial against Paul," 200: Luke was "avoiding casting a negative light on either the Romans or Paul."

32. This was Luke's opinion, at least, and he seems to have been in Caesarea at this time (Acts 27:1).

33. Schürer, *History of the Jewish People*, 1:472, 474.

34. Schürer, *History of the Jewish People*, 1:474–75.

35. Sherwin-White, *Roman Society and Roman Law*, 65; C. K. Barrett, *A Critical and Exegetical Commentary on the Acts of the Apostles*, ICC, 2 vols. (Edinburgh: T&T Clark, 1994–1998), 2:1173–74.

CHAPTER 22

1. Colin J. Hemer cautiously accepts that "the Augustan Cohort" (trans. Fred Baxter) is the same cohort that appears in CIL 3.6687, which describes a certain Quintus Aemilius Secundus who served as a "prefect of *cohors I Augusta*" apparently located in Syria. Hemer, *Book of Acts in the Setting of Hellenistic History*, ed. Conrad H. Gempf (Winona Lake, IN: Eisenbrauns, 1990), 132–33n96. See the text and translation of this inscription in the "Database of Military Inscriptions and Papyri of Early Roman Palestine," §201, under the title "Text Sometimes Related to the Augustan Cohort of Acts 27 (i.e., Cohors Augusta)."

2. Assuming that the ship hugged the coastline.

3. Justin Leidwanger, *Roman Seas: A Maritime Archaeology of Eastern Mediterranean Economies* (New York: Oxford University Press, 2020), 51, 52.

4. Leidwanger (*Roman Seas*, 53) says that three to five crew members were common for small- and medium-sized ships and that ships of one hundred tons might require a dozen crew members.

5. On Sidon as a stopping point, see James Smith, *The Voyage and Shipwreck of St. Paul* (Eugene, OR: Wipf & Stock, 2001; orig. ed. 1880), 64–65.

6. Mark Wilson, "Luke for Landlubbers: The Translation and Interpretation of ὑποπλέω in Acts 27," *AcT* 42 (2022): 361–62. I have calculated the mileage from Cape Kleides to Seleucia ad Calycadnum using both J. A. Talbert, ed., *Barrington Atlas of the Greek and Roman World* (Princeton, NJ: Princeton University Press, 2000), 1; and Google Earth.

7. Wilson, "Luke for Landlubbers," 361–62. For the prevailing wind direction

in this area, see Leidwanger, *Roman Seas*, 143. For prevailing winds in northeastern Cyprus during September and October, see the statistical data at https://www.windfinder.com/windstatistics/rizokarpaso, which gives the wind statistics for Ριζοκάρπασο, a town on the northern part of the Karpas peninsula of Cyprus, about thirteen miles southwest of Cape Kleides.

8. Based on the statistics for September and October at the weather station in Kaş, Turkey, about twenty miles west of Myra as the crow flies. See https://www.windfinder.com/windstatistics/kas.

9. Lionel Casson, *The Ancient Mariners: Seafarers and Sea Fighters of the Mediterranean in Ancient Times*, 2nd ed. (Princeton, NJ: Princeton University Press, 1991), 207–8.

10. On Cnidus, see Leidwanger, *Roman Seas*, 167–69.

11. According to the Stanford Geospatial Network Model of the Roman World.

12. Similarly, Smith judges the wind to have been "west of N. N. W." (*Voyage and Shipwreck of St. Paul*, 75).

13. See the statistical weather chart for the weather station at Μακρύ Γιαλός on the coast of southeastern Crete: https://www.windfinder.com/windstatistics/makrygialos. Cf. Smith, *Voyage and Shipwreck of St. Paul*, 76.

14. On the location of Fair Havens and Lasea, see Smith, *Voyage and Shipwreck of St. Paul*, 82.

15. Hemer, *Book of Acts*, 136.

16. Smith, *Voyage and Shipwreck of St. Paul*, 85. Cf., e.g., Hemer, *Book of Acts*, 136; F. F. Bruce, *The Book of the Acts*, rev. ed., NICNT (Grand Rapids: Eerdmans, 1988), 483.

17. Hemer, *Book of Acts*, 137.

18. Claudius had faced popular unrest because of a lack of grain in Rome "and after this experience he resorted to every possible means to bring grain to Rome, even in the winter season. To the merchants he held out the certainty of profit by assuming the expense of any loss that they might suffer from storms." Suetonius says that these provisions were still in force in his own time (Suetonius, *Claud.* 18–19 [Rolfe, LCL]). Cf. Pliny (*Nat.* 2.47.125) who says that in his time (roughly contemporaneous with Paul) greed kept commercial vessels on the sea even in winter.

19. On Paul's status allowing him a voice, see also Craig S. Keener, *Acts: An Exegetical Commentary*, 4 vols. (Grand Rapids: Baker, 2012–2015), 4:3591–92.

20. On the existence of Christianity on Crete before and apart from the Pauline mission, see Jens Herzer, "Zwischen Mythos und Wahrheit: Neue Perspektiven auf die sogenannten Pastoralbriefe," *NTS* 63 (2017): 443. The seventeenth-century Dutch theologian, philosopher, and statesman Hugo Grotius seems to have been one of the first to argue for a connection between Acts 27:7–8 and Titus 1:5 (*Annotationes in Novum Testamentum*, rev. ed., 9 vols. [Groningen: W. Zuidema, 1826–1834], 7:315). He thought that Christianity had come to Crete when Christians left Jerusalem in response to the persecution following Stephen's murder (Acts 8:1). He then

argued that Paul found out about the state of Christianity on the island during his stop in Fair Havens (Acts 27:7–8) and that Paul left Titus behind on the island to tend to the churches there (Titus 1:5). Everything about this scenario seems plausible except Grotius's dating of Christianity on Crete to the scattering after Stephen's murder. Luke limits that dispersion of believers to Judea and Samaria.

21. For the objection to this scenario that Paul had no time to evangelize the island during this visit, see, e.g., Stephen G. Wilson, *Luke and the Pastoral Epistles* (London: SPCK, 1979), 127; and C. K. Barrett, *A Critical and Exegetical Commentary on the Acts of the Apostles*, 2 vols., ICC (Edinburgh: T&T Clark, 1994–1998), 2:1187. H. J. Holtzmann (*Die Pastoralbriefe* [Leipzig: Wilhelm Engelmann, 1880], 25) objects to the connection Grotius makes between Titus 1:5 and Acts 27:7 (*Annotationes*, 315) with the argument that the letter to Titus presumes Christianity had been on Crete for a long time.

22. On freelance religious experts charging money for their expertise, see Heidi Wendt, *At the Temple Gates: The Religion of Freelance Experts in the Roman Empire* (Oxford: Oxford University Press, 2016), 5.

23. Commentators on Titus (e.g., C. Spicq, *Les Épitres Pastorales*, 4th ed., 2 vols. [Paris: Lecoffre, 1969], 2:691; Martin Dibelius and Hans Conzelmann, *Pastoral Epistles*, Hermeneia, trans. Philip Buttolph and Adela Yarbro [Philadelphia: Fortress, 1972], 153) typically say that the letter portrays Zenas and Apollos as the couriers who took the letter to Crete, but it is equally possible that they were already on Crete and that Paul intends to send them elsewhere.

24. Smith, *Voyage and Shipwreck of St. Paul*, 262. Measurements using Talbert, *Barrington Atlas*, 60, and Google Earth confirm this distance.

25. See the text and translation in Smith, *Voyage and Shipwreck of St. Paul*, 270, and the discussion in Hemer, *Book of Acts*, 140n113.

26. Hemer, *Book of Acts*, 141–42; BDAG 411, s.v. εὐρακύλων.

27. Hemer, *Book of Acts*, 142.

28. Hemer, *Book of Acts*, 143: "The difficulty of bringing in the boat was no doubt due to its being waterlogged."

29. Casson, *Ships and Seamanship*, 91–92, 211n45; Hemer, *Book of Acts*, 143.

30. Smith, *Voyage and Shipwreck of St. Paul*, 111–12; Hemer, *Book of Acts*, 143–44.

31. Smith, *Voyage and Shipwreck of St. Paul*, 116–17.

32. See the illustration from Herculaneum in Smith, *Voyage and Shipwreck of St. Paul*, 135; and the illustration from the late first or early second century in Casson, *Ships and Seamanship*, fig. 150.

33. Smith, *Voyage and Shipwreck of St. Paul*, 133–37. On the rope and pulleys necessary for securing the large rudders, see Casson, *Ships and Seamanship*, 228.

34. Smith, *Voyage and Shipwreck of St. Paul*, 136.

35. On the controlled crash, see Smith, *Voyage and Shipwreck of St. Paul*, 133.

36. Smith, *Voyage and Shipwreck of St. Paul*, 136.

37. I am taking Luke's ambiguous phrase τόπον διθάλασσον to mean "a place

between two seas, the sea behind the ship and the sea in front of the ship." For this interpretation, see Barrett, *Acts*, 2:1212–13.

38. Thomas Ashby and G. McN. Rushforth, "Roman Malta," *JRS* 5 (1915): 24–26.

39. Hemer, *Book of Acts*, 154.

40. Holtzmann (*Die Pastoralbriefe*, 25) believes that Paul's failure to mention his imprisonment prevents the location of Titus in this part of his life. Cf. Van Bruggen, *Die geschichtliche Einordnung der Pastoralbriefe* (Wuppertal: R. Brockhaus, 1981), 35.

41. Paul also plans a year ahead in 1 Cor 16:5–6 where, writing from Ephesus in the winter (16:8–9), he lays out his plans to stay in Corinth the following winter. These plans also changed (2 Cor 1:15–17).

42. See, e.g., I. H. Marshall, *Pastoral Epistles*, ICC (Edinburgh: T&T Clark, 1999), 53–54, 60–63, 79, 92.

43. Holtzmann, *Die Pastoralbriefe*, 203–7. See, similarly, James D. G. Dunn, *Neither Jew nor Greek: A Contested Identity*, vol. 3 of *Christianity in the Making* (Grand Rapids: Eerdmans, 2015), 87–88, 91. Luke Timothy Johnson comments, "Indeed, from F. C. Baur to Walter Bauer, the so-called church order in the three letters to Paul's delegates was regarded as the clinching evidence for their inauthenticity." Johnson, *The Canonical Paul*, vol. 2 of *Interpreting Paul* (Grand Rapids: Eerdmans, 2021), 256.

44. Dibelius and Conzelman, *Pastoral Epistles*, 40–41, 141.

45. T. Christopher Hoklotubbe, "Civilized Christ-Followers among Barbaric Cretans and Superstitious Judeans: Negotiating Ethnic Hierarchies in Titus 1:10 14," *JBL* 140 (2021): 369–90.

46. Stanley E. Porter, *The Pastoral Epistles: A Commentary on the Greek Text* (Grand Rapids: Baker, 2023), 856.

47. Cf. Johnson, *Canonical Paul*, 257.

48. For the argument that the author has merged qualifications for two different offices here, see, e.g., Jerome D. Quinn, *The Letter to Titus*, AB 35 (New York: Doubleday, 1990), 88.

49. On the resemblance between 1 Tim and administrative letters from Egypt during the Ptolemaic and Roman periods, see Lyn Kidson, "1 Timothy: An Administrative Letter," *Early Christianity* 5 (2014): 105–10.

50. Kidson, "1 Timothy: An Administrative Letter," 106–8.

51. E.g., a polite peer-to-peer letter from AD 117 begins, "Aquilius Polion, strategus of the Heracleopolite nome, to his dearest Apollonius, strategus of the Oxyrhynchite nome, greeting. Kindly receive two letters which I have written" (P.Oxy. 9.1189, trans. Arthur S. Hunt, *The Oxyrhynchus Papyri*, part 9 [London: Egypt Exploration Fund, 1912], 208), and a letter of AD 23 from a superior to a subordinate reads, "Apollonios, strategos, to Akous, toparch of Tebtunis, greeting. Send at once to me a supplementary statement of what has been entered [paid], up to date and according to class" (P.Tebt. 2.289, trans. John L. White, *Light from Ancient Letters*, FF [Philadelphia: Fortress, 1986], 116).

52. Kidson ("1 Timothy: An Administrative Letter," 114–15) argues that the use of Paul's example to undergird the letter's advice is more of a philosophical technique than anything found in the brief moral instruction in administrative letters (such as P.Tebt. 1.27). She also argues that this technique is, nevertheless, appropriate in an administrative letter written to an association or society. On an analysis of early Christianity as a scholastic society, beginning with the rabbi Jesus and continuing to the apostle Paul, see E. A. Judge, "The Early Christians as a Scholastic Community," *JRH* 1 (1960): 4–15; and Judge, "The Early Christians as a Scholastic Community: Part II," *JRH* 1 (1961): 125–37.

53. The third-century BC Greek poet Callimachus linked the proverb that "Cretans are always liars" with their claim that they had "built a tomb" for Zeus. That idea is a lie, Callimachus asserts in a prayer to Zeus, "You are forever" (*Hymn. Jov.* 1.8–10 [Clayman, LCL]). Similarly, the satirist Lucian, writing in the second century AD, can prove that whole people groups sometimes lie with the statement that "The Cretans exhibit the tomb of Zeus and are not ashamed of it" (*Philops.* 3 [Harmon, LCL]).

54. Rowan A. Greer, trans., *Theodore of Mopsuestia: Commentary on the Minor Pauline Epistles*, WGRW 26 (Atlanta: SBL, 2010), 753.

55. Polybius, *Hist.* 6.46–47.

56. The line probably comes from Epimenides, a Cretan holy man of the seventh century BC. On Epimenides, see Alan H. Griffiths, "Epimenides," OCD^4 526. Clement of Alexandria in the late second or early third century attributed the quotation to Epimenides (*Strom.* 1.14), as did many other Christian scholars of a later period.

57. For the translation "in harmony with" for πρέπει, see J. N. D. Kelly, *The Pastoral Epistles*, BNTC (Peabody, MA: Hendrickson, 1960), 239.

58. Kelly, *Pastoral Epistles*, 240.

CHAPTER 23

1. Colin J. Hemer, *Book of Acts in the Setting of Hellenistic History*, ed. Conrad H. Gempf (Winona Lake, IN: Eisenbrauns, 1990), 154; C. K. Barrett, *A Critical and Exegetical Commentary on the Acts of the Apostles*, ICC, 2 vols. (Edinburgh: T&T Clark, 1994–1998), 2:1227.

2. Glen L. Thompson and Mark Wilson believe that the date was about a month later, in "early March." They offer both evidence from Pompeii and the argument that large ships with valuable cargoes would have adhered to a conservative sailing schedule. *In This Way We Came to Rome: With Paul on the Appian Way* (Bellingham, WA: Lexham, 2023), 8.

3. On the importance of Puteoli and its cement, which "became the basis of Roman monumental construction," see Duane W. Roller, *A Historical and Topographical Guide to the "Geography" of Strabo* (Cambridge: Cambridge University Press, 2018), 275.

4. Peter Lampe, *From Paul to Valentinus: Christians at Rome in the First Two Centuries*, ed. Marshall D. Johnson, trans. Michael Steinhauser (Minneapolis: Fortress, 2003), 10. On the fertility of the region around Mount Vesuvius, see Strabo, *Geogr.* 5.4.8: "Mount Vesuvius . . . is settled all around with exceedingly attractive fields" (trans. Duane W. Roller, *The "Geography" of Strabo: An English Translation with Introduction and Notes* [Cambridge: Cambridge University Press, 2014]).

5. See Kirsopp Lake and Henry J. Cadbury, *English Translation and Commentary*, vol. 4 of *The Beginnings of Christianity, Part I: The Acts of the Apostles*, ed. F. J. Foakes Jackson and Kirsopp Lake (London: Macmillan, 1933), 344.

6. Roughly following the route plotted from Rhegium to Puteoli by the Stanford Geospatial Network Model of the Roman World.

7. See Lake and Cadbury, *English Translation and Commentary*, 344, who cite Cyril's observation that Alexandrian ships have carvings on either side of their prows.

8. "Voyagers, in a storm, call upon the Dioscuri," said the philosopher Epictetus (*Disc.* 2.19.29 [Oldfather, LCL]). "Storm" here is the Greek word for "winter" (χειμών). The Dioscuri (cf. Acts 28:11) were the twin gods Castor and Pollux. See Lake and Cadbury, *English Translation and Commentary*, 343–44; Robert Parker, "Dioscuri," *OCD*[4] 466; and Craig S. Keener, *Acts: An Exegetical Commentary*, 4 vols. (Grand Rapids: Baker, 2012–2015), 4:3695–99.

9. According to the Stanford Geospatial Network Model of the Roman World.

10. On Syracuse, see G. Voza, "Syracuse," *PECS*, 872.

11. The journey was roughly eighty-three nautical miles. Once again, this figure relies on the calculations of the Stanford Geospatial Network Model of the Roman World. On Rhegium, see Roller (*Historical and Topographical Guide*, 295), who notes that Rhegium was an important point for accessing Sicily from Italy. Presumably, it was also an important point for travel in the opposite direction.

12. They probably did not cover the 208 nautical miles from Rhegium to Puteoli in a single day as, e.g., F. F. Bruce implies. Bruce, *The Book of the Acts*, rev. ed., NICNT (Grand Rapids: Eerdmans, 1988), 501. For the time and distance of this journey in the spring, see the Stanford Geospatial Network Model of the Roman World. Luke says that after waiting for a day in Rhegium, a south wind arose and "We two dayers came [δευτεραῖοι ἤλθομεν] to Puteoli" (Acts 28:13, my clunky translation). On the Greek, see Barrett, *Acts*, 2:1229. Lionel Casson ("Speed under Sail of Ancient Ships," *TAPA* 82 [1951]: 140) and Thompson and Wilson (*In This Way We Came to Rome*, 9–10) put the typical journey from Rhegium to Puteoli at 175 nautical miles and one and a half days, averaging five knots.

13. For this area in the time of Nero, see John H. D'Arms, *Romans on the Bay of Naples: A Social and Cultural Study of the Villas and Their Owners from 150 B.C. to A.D. 400* (Cambridge, MA: Harvard University Press, 1970), 94–99.

14. Lampe, *From Paul to Valentinus*, 9–10.

15. Klaus Haacker comments that Luke's Greek in Acts 28:14 leaves ambiguous who encouraged Paul and his group to stay with the Christians of Puteoli (παρεκλήθημεν παρ' αὐτοῖς ἐπιμεῖναι). It could mean that the centurion Julius en-

couraged the group to stay with the Christians for seven days. Haacker, *Die Apostelgeschichte*, THKNT (Stuttgart: Kohlhammer, 2019), 421.

16. I. Howard Marshall, *The Acts of the Apostles: An Introduction and Commentary*, Tyndale New Testament Commentaries (Grand Rapids: Eerdmans, 1980), 419; Haacker, *Apostelgeschichte*, 421.

17. E.g., Keener, *Acts*, 4:3706; Thompson and Wilson, *In This Way We Came to Rome*, 29–32.

18. On Sinuessa, see Thompson and Wilson, *In This Way We Came to Rome*, 69–73, and on the bridge, see Alan C. Brookes, "Minturnae: The Via Appia Bridge," *American Journal of Archaeology* 78 (1974): 41–48; and Thompson and Wilson, *In This Way We Came to Rome*, 77–78.

19. Thompson and Wilson, *In This Way We Came to Rome*, 80.

20. R. V. Schoder, "Tarracina," *PECS*, 882. Horace, traveling in the opposite direction about a century earlier, speaks of "crawling . . . three miles" as he and his companions "climb up to Anxur, perched on her far-gleaming rocks" (*Sat.* 1.5.25–26 [Fairclough, LCL]). "Anxur" was another name for Tarracina.

21. See the maps in Ferdinando Castagnoli, *Roma Antica: Profilo Urbanistico* (Milan: Jouvence, 1978), 45, Tav. XV and Amanda Claridge, *Rome: An Oxford Archaeological Guide*, 2nd ed. (Oxford: Oxford University Press, 2010), 342.

22. I have calculated the distance using J. A. Talbert, ed., *Barrington Atlas of the Greek and Roman World* (Princeton, NJ: Princeton University Press, 2000), 44.

23. See the notes of H. R. Fairclough in *Horace: Satires, Epistles, and Art of Poetry*, LCL 194 (Cambridge, MA: Harvard University Press, 1929), 62 and 65. Horace was writing in 38 BC (Fairclough, *Horace*, 62). Strabo, writing closer to Paul's time, also mentions the canal: "Most sail on it at night, so they can embark in evening and disembark in the morning, and travel the remainder on the road" (*Geogr.* 5.3.6).

24. Cicero, writing in the first century BC, implies that the Forum of Appia and Three Taverns were common places for stopping along the Appian way and dispatching letters (*Att.* 1.13 and 2.10, 11, 13).

25. Juvenal, *Sat.* 3.62–65: "The Syrian Orontes has for a long time now been polluting the Tiber, bringing with it its language and customs, its slanting strings along with pipers, its native tom-toms too, and the girls who are told to offer themselves for sale at the Circus" (trans. Braund, LCL).

26. On these churches, see Lampe, *From Paul to Valentinus*, 20–21, 41; and on the likelihood that Christians lived in the area around the Porta Capena and the Aventine, see Lampe, *From Paul to Valentinus*, 42–43, and the summary chart, pp. 44–45. Cf. Robert Jewett, *Romans: A Commentary*, Hermeneia (Minneapolis: Fortress, 2007), 62–63.

27. See Haacker, *Apostelgeschichte*, 421n80.

28. Cf. Haacker, *Apostelgeschichte*, 421.

29. Some ancient witnesses to the text of Acts 28:16 seem to identify this official as the στρατοπεδάρχης, a term that may correspond to the "*princeps castrorum*, the

head administrator of the *officium* of the Pretorian Guard." A. N. Sherwin-White, *Roman Society and Roman Law in the New Testament* (Oxford: Oxford University Press, 1963), 110. It is unlikely that these witnesses preserve the actual text of Acts at this point, although they may preserve someone's educated guess in the Latin-speaking part of the empire about the circumstances of Paul's imprisonment (Hemer, *Book of Acts*, 199–200). J. B. Lightfoot thought that the reference was "a genuine tradition, even if it was no part of the original text" (*Saint Paul's Epistle to the Philippians* [London: Macmillan, 1896], 7–8n4). For an argument against Lightfoot on this point, see Michael Flexsenhar III, "The Provenance of Philippians and Why It Matters: Old Questions, New Approaches," *JSNT* 42 (2019): 24–25.

30. For the text, translation, and discussion of this ancient reading of Acts 28:16, see Bruce M. Metzger, *A Textual Commentary on the Greek New Testament*, 2nd ed. (Stuttgart: Deutsche Bibelgesellschaft, 1994), 443.

31. See also Brian Rapske, *Paul in Roman Custody*, vol. 3 of *The Book of Acts in Its First Century Setting*, ed. Bruce W. Winter (Grand Rapids: Eerdmans, 1994), 177. Harry W. Tajra (*The Martyrdom of St. Paul*, WUNT 2.67 [Tübingen: Mohr Siebeck, 1994], 45) doubts this location because no early Christian tradition associates Paul's dwelling with this area.

32. For the location of the Viminal Gate in the present-day geography of Rome, see the helpful map in Amanda Claridge, *Rome: An Oxford Archaeological Guide*, 2nd ed. (Oxford: Oxford University Press, 2010), 392.

33. Claridge, *Rome*, 15; and see the map in Castagnoli, *Roma Antica*, Tav. XV.

34. L. Richardson, Jr., *A New Topographical Dictionary of Ancient Rome* (Baltimore: Johns Hopkins University Press, 1992), 78. For the construction of the city wall around the Viminal Gate to protect against the city's vulnerability from the north, see Strabo, *Geogr.* 5.3.7.

35. Andrea Carandini and Paolo Carafa, eds., *The Atlas of Ancient Rome*, 2 vols., trans. Andrew Campbell Halavais (Princeton, NJ: Princeton University Press, 2017), 1:461.

36. Edward Champlin comments that the dramatic details of Nero's flight from his pursuers are "based certainly on eyewitness accounts" and are "as certain as anything can be in ancient history." Champlin, *Nero* (Cambridge, MA: Harvard University Press, 2003), 4–5.

37. It is also possible that the author was dependent on a form of Acts that included the phrase "outside the barracks." For this understanding of the text, see Richard I. Pervo, *The Acts of Paul: A New Translation with Introduction and Commentary* (Eugene, OR: Wipf & Stock, 2014), 314.

38. Tajra (*Martyrdom of St. Paul*, 45–46) thinks that Paul's lodging was more likely located far to the southwest of the praetorian barracks, close to the banks of the Tiber, and near the ancient church of San Paolo alla Regola. Tradition locates Paul's dwelling there, and that location was both outside the city walls and near ancient barns. See, similarly, Thompson and Wilson, *In This Way We Came to Rome*, 186–87.

39. For its text and translation, see Arthur S. Hunt and C. C. Edgar, eds., *Official Documents*, vol. 2 of *Select Papyri*, LCL 282 (Cambridge, MA: Harvard University Press, 1934), 76–79 (no. 211).

40. Twelve cohorts of a thousand each. On this, see Henry Michael Denne Parker, George Ronald Watson, and Jonathan Coulston, "*cohors*," and Brian Campbell, "praetorians," *OCD*[4] 341, 1204.

41. Flexsenhar, "Provenance of Philippians," 27.

42. Flexsenhar ("Provenance of Philippians," 28) says that Acts never mentions Paul's chains during his time in Rome, and Ryan Schellenberg (*Abject Joy: Paul, Prison, and the Art of Making Do* [New York: Oxford University Press, 2021], 44) implies this, but in Acts 28:20 Luke says Paul referred to the "chain" (ἅλυσιν) he was wearing "because of the hope of Israel."

43. On "the shame of imprisonment and bonds," see Rapske, *Paul in Roman Custody*, 288–91.

44. Eubulus, Pudens, Linus, and Claudia (2 Tim 4:21) were probably local Roman Christians who were supportive of Paul, since Paul attaches their names to "all the brothers and sisters" (NIV) sending greetings from Rome. Paul could say that "Luke alone" was with him (2 Tim 4:11) probably because he was speaking of his special group of coworkers and did not consider the local Roman Christians within that group. On this, see George W. Knight III, *The Pastoral Epistles: A Commentary on the Greek Text*, NIGTC (Grand Rapids: Eerdmans, 1992), 477–78.

45. Andrew Wallace-Hadrill, "*Domus* and *Insulae* in Rome: Families and Housefuls," in *Early Christian Families in Context: An Interdisciplinary Dialogue*, ed. David L. Balch and Carolyn Osiek, Religion, Marriage, and Family (Grand Rapids: Eerdmans, 2003), 10–15.

46. The architectural remains on which Wallace-Hadrill based his analysis date from the early second century and were near the Viminal Gate. On the discovery of this neighborhood, see Wallace-Hadrill, "*Domus* and *Insulae*," 10. The military barracks of the praetorian guard were an easy walk to the northeast. The work of Bradly S. Billings, "From House Church to Tenement Church: Domestic Space and the Development of Early Urban Christianity—the Example of Ephesus," *JTS* 62 (2011): 541–69, seems to confirm Wallace-Hadrill's analysis.

47. Billings, "House Church to Tenement Church," 559.

48. Billings, "House Church to Tenement Church," 559.

49. Billings, "House Church to Tenement Church," 554–55.

50. Harry J. Leon, *The Jews of Ancient Rome*, updated ed. (Peabody, MA: Hendrickson, 1995), 135–37.

51. Billings, "House Church to Tenement Church," 555; relying on the description of OGIS 594–595 in L. Michael White, *Building God's House in the Roman World: Architectural Adaptation among Pagans, Jews, and Christians*, HTS 41, vol. 1 of *The Social Origins of Christian Architecture* (Valley Forge, PA: Trinity Press International, 1996), 32.

52. Billings ("House Church to Tenement Church," 560) argues that "the constant flow of people into a city like Ephesus meant that the means of accommodating them, principally the rental market, would have been, as a consequence, remarkably fluid." The same was probably true of Rome.

53. William L. MacDonald, *The Architecture of the Roman Empire*, rev. ed., 2 vols. (New Haven, CT: Yale University Press, 1982–1986), 2:218–19.

54. MacDonald, *Architecture of the Roman Empire*, 2:213, 219.

55. See the Greek text of both recensions, and the English translation, in Herbert Musurillo, *The Acts of the Christian Martyrs: Introduction, Texts, and Translations* (Oxford: Clarendon, 1972), 44–45, 48–51. Cf. L. Michael White, *Texts and Monuments for the Christian Domus Ecclesiae in Its Environment*, HTS 43, vol. 2 of *The Social Origins of Christian Architecture* (Valley Forge, PA: Trinity Press International, 1997), 42–43.

56. See the depressing description of ancient Roman prison life in Craig S. Wansink, *Chained in Christ: The Experience and Rhetoric of Paul's Imprisonments*, JSNTSup 130 (Sheffield, UK: Sheffield Academic Press, 1996), 27–95.

57. The translation comes from Frank Thielman, *Romans*, ZECNT 6 (Grand Rapids: Zondervan, 2016), 738.

58. On the date of the letter, see Michael W. Holmes's comments in Holmes, trans., *The Apostolic Fathers: Greek Texts and English Translations*, 3rd ed. (Grand Rapids: Eerdmans, 2007), 35–36; and on 1 Clem. 6.1–2 as a reference to Nero's persecution of Christians in Rome, see Oscar Cullman, *Peter: Disciple, Apostle, Martyr*, trans. Floyd V. Filson (Philadelphia: Westminster, 1953), 96.

59. Cullmann, *Peter*, 101; David L. Eastman, "Jealousy, Internal Strife, and the Deaths of Peter and Paul: A Reassessment of *1 Clement*," ZAC 18 (2013): 43–47.

60. Cullmann, *Peter*, 104. Cullmann observes that when Tacitus describes the persecution of Christians under Nero in Rome (*Ann.* 15.44), he "speaks exactly as does Clement of a *multitude ingens*, a 'great multitude'" that suffered. Clement speaks of a πολὺ πλῆθος ("vast multitude"), which suffered "among us" (1 Clem. 6.1), and he was writing from Rome (Salutation). The only persecution during the period in which Clement was writing, says Cullmann, was the persecution of Christians under Nero in Rome.

61. Cullmann, *Peter*, 89–109; Eastman, "Deaths of Peter and Paul," 53; Daniel Marguerat, "On Why Luke Remains Silent about Paul's End (Acts 28.16–31)," in *The Last Years of Paul: Essays from the Tarragona Conference, June 2013*, ed. Armand Puig i Tàrrech, John M. G. Barclay, and Jörg Frey, WUNT 1.352 (Tübingen: Mohr Siebeck, 2015), 331–32.

62. See Rom 16:5, 10, 11, 14, and 15; and the discussion in Lampe (*From Paul to Valentinus*, 359) and Thielman (*Romans*, 705, 708–9).

63. On the evidence that the earliest churches in Rome were small house churches, and for the possibility that this "fractionation" of Christianity in the city contributed to variation in Christian belief, see Lampe, *From Paul to Valentinus*, 359–96. Markus Bockmuehl suggests that perhaps the group still attached to law

observance when Paul wrote Rom 14:1–15:6 had, by the time he wrote Phil, hardened in its opposition to Paul. Bockmuehl, *The Epistle to the Philippians*, BNTC 11 (Peabody, MA: Hendrickson, 1998), 76–78. Cf. Gordon D. Fee, *Paul's Letter to the Philippians*, NICNT (Grand Rapids: Eerdmans, 1995), 121–23.

64. Paul McKechnie, "Jewish Embassies and Cases before Roman Emperors, AD 44–66," *JTS* 56 (2005): 342–49, 361.

65. McKechnie, "Jewish Embassies," 342–44.

66. McKechnie, "Jewish Embassies," 345–49.

67. McKechnie, "Jewish Embassies," 361.

CHAPTER 24

1. Markus Bockmuehl, *The Epistle to the Philippians*, BNTC (Peabody, MA: Hendrickson, 1998), 170.

2. Bockmuehl, *Philippians*, 170.

3. Locating the place from which Paul wrote Philippians is controversial. Some scholars have placed it in Caesarea (see appendix 2) and others in Corinth, but Ephesus is the most common alternative to Rome. Ephesus is a reasonable alternative to Rome for several reasons, but for many scholars the most important reason is the shorter distance between Philippi and Ephesus than between Rome and Ephesus. This shorter distance makes all the traveling back and forth that Paul seems to presume in the letter more plausible. See, e.g., Gerald F. Hawthorne, *Philippians*, rev. and exp. by Ralph P. Martin, WBC 43 (n.p.: Thomas Nelson, 2004), xlii. According to the Stanford Geospatial Network Model of the Roman World, however, a summer journey from Philippi to Rome would take about twenty days, and the return journey would take eighteen days. Several journeys back and forth between the two cities during, say, the first year of Paul's imprisonment, therefore, do not seem unreasonable.

4. Gordon D. Fee, *Paul's Letter to the Philippians*, NICNT (Grand Rapids: Eerdmans, 1995), 107; Bockmuehl, *Philippians*, 81. Cf. Ulrich B. Müller, *Der Brief des Paulus an die Philipper*, THKNT 11/1 (Leipzig: Evangelische Verlagsanstalt, 1993), 48, who observes that in this section of the letter the Philippians would expect Paul to satisfy their curiosity about how he was doing in his imprisonment. Paul, however, focuses not on his own circumstances but on the gospel's progress.

5. On Paul's possible use in Phil of a rhetorical strategy that resembles the Stoic tendency to speak of everything except virtue as "things that are neither good nor bad" (τὰ ἀδιάφορα), see Annalisa Phillips Wilson, "'One Thing': Stoic Discourse and Paul's Reevaluation of His Jewish Credentials in Phil. 3.1–21," *JSNT* 45 (2023): 429–50. Both Paul and the Stoics did not mean that nothing else but their "one thing" mattered but were only relativizing other things in comparison with what really matters.

Notes to Pages 302–306

6. Cf. N. T. Wright, *The Climax of the Covenant: Christ and the Law in Pauline Theology* (Edinburgh: T&T Clark, 1991), 82–90; Richard Bauckham, *Jesus and the God of Israel: God Crucified and Other Studies on the New Testament's Christology of Divine Identity* (Grand Rapids: Eerdmans, 2008), 41–45.

7. Fee (*Philippians*, 261) recognizes the paradigmatic importance of Timothy and Epaphroditus here but correctly notes that this is not the section's only purpose. It also has the mundane purpose of informing the Philippians of Paul's travel plans and of commending the work of Epaphroditus.

8. Martin Hengel, *Crucifixion in the Ancient World and the Folly of the Message of the Cross* (Philadelphia: Fortress, 1977), 89: "To assert that God himself accepted death in the form of a crucified Jewish manual worker from Galilee in order to break the power of death and bring salvation to all men could only seem folly and madness to men of ancient times."

9. See Winter's description of 1 Cor 11:17–34 through the lens of typical Greco-Roman banqueting: Bruce W. Winter, *After Paul Left Corinth: The Influence of Secular Ethics and Social Change* (Grand Rapids: Eerdmans, 2001), 154–58. Winter does not draw the parallel to Phil 3:18–19, but Paul's language there is reminiscent of his disgust in 1 Cor 11:17 and 22 and would be appropriate as a criticism of the kind of behavior Winter describes.

10. See, e.g., Petr Pokorný, *Colossians: A Commentary*, trans. Siegfried S. Schatzmann (Peabody, MA: Hendrickson, 1991), 1–4.

11. Pokorný, *Colossians*, 128–29.

12. Margaret Y. MacDonald, *Colossians and Ephesians*, SP 17 (Collegeville, MN: Liturgical Press, 2000), 8.

13. Maria A. Pascuzzi, "Reconsidering the Authorship of Colossians," *BBR* 23 (2013): 229–30, 235–37.

14. For a discussion of the importance of "register" in sociolinguistic studies of author attribution, see Andrew Pitts, "Style and Pseudonymity in Pauline Scholarship: A Register Based Configuration," in *Paul and Pseudonymity*, ed. Stanley E. Porter and Gregory Fewster, Pauline Studies 8 (Leiden: Brill, 2013), 116–52.

15. Pitts, "Style and Pseudonymity," 119.

16. James D. G. Dunn, *The Epistles to the Colossians and to Philemon: A Commentary on the Greek Text*, NIGTC (Grand Rapids: Eerdmans, 1996), 37–38. Cf. MacDonald (*Colossians and Ephesians*, 184) who does not think Paul wrote the letter but recognizes the challenge that the letter's concluding section presents to this view.

17. Dunn, *Epistles to the Colossians and to Philemon*, 38.

18. Dunn, *Epistles to the Colossians and to Philemon*, 38.

19. F. F. Bruce thought they met in Rome and that Epaphras took Onesimus to Paul. Bruce, *Paul: Apostle of the Heart Set Free* (Grand Rapids: Eerdmans, 1977), 400.

20. Cf. Ulrich Huttner, *Early Christianity in the Lycus Valley*, trans. David Green, AGJU 85/ECAM 1 (Leiden: Brill, 2013), 83, 123.

21. Onesimus was from Colossae (Col 4:9) and Onesimus was Philemon's slave

(Phlm 10–20). Philemon, then, would also have been from Colossae. The evidence that Epaphras was from Colossae is more explicit (Col 4:12). Paul's comment that Philemon owed him "even [his] own self" (Phlm 19) probably means that Paul's proclamation of the gospel was the means of Philemon's conversion.

22. Huttner, *Early Christianity in the Lycus Valley*, 25.

23. Huttner, *Early Christianity in the Lycus Valley*, 84.

24. On Philemon as a businessperson, see Dunn (*Epistles to the Colossians and to Philemon*, 301). On the agricultural fertility of the region in antiquity, see Huttner (*Early Christianity in the Lycus Valley*, 24). On the importance of the textile and leatherworking industries, see Alan H. Cadwallader, *Fragments of Colossae: Sifting through the Traces* (Adelaide, SA: ATF Press, 2015), 110–33. On the milling and metalworking industries and the general economy of the region, see Michael Trainor, "Rome's Market Economy in the Lycus Valley: Soundings from Laodicea and Colossae," in *Colossians, Hierapolis, and Laodicea*, ed. James R. Harrison and L. L. Welborn, WGRWSup 16, vol. 5 of *The First Urban Churches* (Atlanta: SBL, 2019), 298–99.

25. For a survey and careful evaluation of the most common theories, see Jeffrey A. D. Weima, "Onesimus: Still a Runaway Slave," in *Rhetoric, History, and Theology: Interpreting the New Testament*, ed. Todd D. Still and Jason A. Myers (Lanham, MD: Lexington, 2022), 201–30.

26. Weima, "Onesimus," 220.

27. Cf. Sara C. Winter, "Paul's Letter to Philemon," *NTS* 33 (1987): 2; and the review of Winter's thesis in Weima, "Onesimus," 204.

28. Peter Lampe, "Keine 'Sklavenflucht' des Onesimus," *ZNW* 76 (1985): 135–37; Brian Rapske, "The Prisoner Paul in the Eyes of Onesimus," *NTS* 37 (1991): 187–203; Dunn, *Epistles*, 304–5.

29. See *Dig.* 21.1.17.4; Lampe, "Keine 'Sklavenflucht,'" 135; and Rapske, "Prisoner Paul," 196. On the procedure followed in creating the *Digest*, see Tony Honoré, "Justinian's codification," OCD^3 803–4: "Justinian was entitled to amend the previous law as he wished. But the amended texts were 'out of respect for antiquity' attributed to the original authors and books" (804).

30. Winter, "Paul's Letter to Philemon," 3; David W. Pao, *Colossians and Philemon*, ZECNT (Grand Rapids: Eerdmans, 2012), 345–47.

31. For this second point, see R. McL. Wilson, *A Critical and Exegetical Commentary on Colossians and Philemon*, ICC (London: T&T Clark, 2005), 326.

32. Cf. Huttner, *Early Christianity in the Lycus Valley*, 106.

33. Cf. Weima, "Onesimus," 205–6.

34. John M. G. Barclay, "Paul, Philemon and the Dilemma of Christian Slave-Ownership," *NTS* 37 (1991): 164.

35. Weima, "Onesimus," 215–19.

36. Paul normally uses the verb διακονέω, which he uses here, to refer to specifically Christian service (Rom 15:25; 2 Cor 3:3; 8:19–20; 1 Tim 3:10, 13; 2 Tim 1:18). See Wilson, *Colossians and Philemon*, 352–53 (who finds both personal service to Paul and

service to the gospel here); Pao, *Colossians and Philemon*, 390–91; and Peter Müller, *Der Brief an Philemon*, KEK (Göttingen: Vandenhoeck & Ruprecht, 2012), 114–15.

37. I have borrowed a few words here from Frank Thielman, *Ephesians*, BECNT (Grand Rapids: Eerdmans, 2010), 410.

38. For "religious ritual" as a rendering of θρησκεία in Col 2:18, see Clinton E. Arnold, "Sceva, Solomon, and Shamanism: The Jewish Roots of the Problem at Colossae," *JETS* 55 (2012): 21; and LSJ 806, s.v. θρησκεία. The term could have connotations of wrongheaded religious ritual in the first century AD (Philo, *Det.* 21) and at least by the second century could mean "superstition" (MGS 950, s.v. θρησκεία B).

39. Clinton E. Arnold, *The Colossian Syncretism: The Interface between Christianity and Folk Belief at Colossae*, WUNT 2.77 (Tübingen: Mohr Siebeck, 1995), 166–90; Arnold, "Sceva, Solomon, and Shamanism," 11–19.

40. On the date of T. Sol. 18, see Arnold, "Sceva, Solomon, and Shamanism," 11. Elements of T. Sol. 18 resemble 11Q11, columns 1–2, which dates to the mid-first century AD (Arnold, "Sceva, Solomon, and Shamanism," 14).

41. Cf. T. Sol. 18:9, 22, 29, 38.

42. Clinton E. Arnold, "Initiation, Vision, and Spiritual Power: The Hellenistic Dimensions of the Problem at Colossae," in *Colossians, Hierapolis, and Laodicea*, WGRWSup 16, vol. 5 of *The First Urban Churches*, ed. James R. Harrison and L. L. Welborn (Atlanta: SBL, 2019), 175–81. For the relevant inscriptions (the earliest dating from the second century), see Arnold, *Colossian Syncretism*, 110–13; and for the reference to fasting, see Iamblichus, *Myst.* 3.11, also from the second century and quoted in Arnold, "Initiation, Vision, and Spiritual Power," 177.

43. See the discussion in D. S. Russell, *The Method and Message of Jewish Apocalyptic* (London: SCM, 1964), 169–73.

44. For the translation of διάκονος as "courier," see BDAG 230.

45. See, e.g., Dunn, *Epistles to the Colossians and to Philemon*, 88–97.

46. For the interpretation of Col 2:15 adopted here, see J. B. Lightfoot, *Saint Paul's Epistles to the Colossians and to Philemon* (London: Macmillan, 1879), 189–91.

47. The Greek is notoriously difficult, but Douglas J. Moo is right that the reading adopted here solves more problems than the other options. Moo, *The Letters to the Colossians and to Philemon*, PNTC (Grand Rapids: Eerdmans, 2008), 239.

48. Cf. Dunn, *Epistles to the Colossians and to Philemon*, 286. Dunn thinks that Timothy penned Colossians, perhaps at Paul's urging and during his lifetime (38–39).

49. The circulation of a single letter among the churches of Galatia (Gal 1:2) may anticipate this development.

CHAPTER 25

1. Paul seems to have abandoned or postponed his plan to work in Spain after going to Rome (Rom 15:24, 28).

2. Cf. Lewis Johnson, "The Pauline Letters from Caesarea," *ExpTim* 68 (1956): 25; although Johnson sets Philippians, Colossians, Philemon, and Ephesians within Paul's Caesarean imprisonment.

3. Cf. Johnson, "Pauline Letters from Caesarea," 25.

4. Frank Thielman, *Ephesians*, BECNT (Grand Rapids: Eerdmans, 2010), 435–36.

5. These challenges seem to have continued among the Ephesian Christians into the late first and early second centuries. See Rev 2:2–4, 6; and Ignatius, *Eph.* 7, 9, and 16.

6. See, e.g., Andrew T. Lincoln, *Ephesians*, WBC 42 (Dallas: Word, 1990), lxiii, lxxxv–lxxxvi; and, more recently, Christopher S. Atkins, who argues that during a time after Paul's death when the apostle was a controversial figure, 3:4 urges the letter's readers to take the letter itself as the divinely revealed understanding of Paul's theology. Atkins, "Textualizing Pauline Revelation: Self-Referentiality, Reading Practices, and Pseudepigraphy in Ephesians," *HTR* 116 (2023): 24–43.

7. Ernest Best, *A Critical and Exegetical Commentary on Ephesians*, ICC (London: T&T Clark, 1998), 98–101.

8. Thielman, *Ephesians*, 10.

9. See, e.g., the second-century Epistle to the Laodiceans, written as if it comes from "Paul, an apostle not of men and not through man, but through Jesus Christ" but also urging its readers not to "be deceived by the vain talk of some people who tell tales that they may lead you away from the truth of the gospel which is proclaimed by me" (3). This translation is from J. K. Elliott, ed., *The Apocryphal New Testament* (Oxford: Clarendon, 1993), 546.

10. On the importance of expressions of truthfulness in the letter to the issue of authorship, see Harold W. Hoehner, *Ephesians: An Exegetical Commentary* (Grand Rapids: Baker, 2002), 37. See further Thielman, *Ephesians*, 2–3, and the primary and secondary literature mentioned there. For an argument that ancient "forgery" was not necessarily a dishonest practice, see Isaac T. Soon, "Before Deception: The Amoral Nature of Ancient Christian Forgery," *EC* 14 (2023): 429–45.

11. It may also indicate that Paul intended the letter to circulate beyond Ephesus. On this, see Clinton E. Arnold, *Ephesians*, ZECNT (Grand Rapids: Zondervan, 2010), 28–29.

12. Apart from the Pauline corpus, see also 1 Pet 1:3–5, and on benedictory prayers in other Jewish letters, see Thielman, *Ephesians*, 38–39.

13. Thielman, *Ephesians*, 44; David A. deSilva, *Ephesians*, New Cambridge Bible Commentary (Cambridge: Cambridge University Press, 2022), 54.

14. Cf. Thielman, *Ephesians*, 91–92.

15. See, e.g., the image of conquered people cowering at the feet of Roman soldiers in the lower third of the Gemma Augustea: Paul Zanker, *The Power of Images in the Age of Augustus* (Ann Arbor: University of Michigan Press, 1988), 231–32. Augustus sits enthroned next to the goddess Roma above the scene of the conquered enemy. See also the image of Augustus towering over a conquered barbarian who sits

bound at his feet in Christoph Heilig, *The Apostle and the Empire: Paul's Implicit and Explicit Criticism of Rome* (Grand Rapids: Eerdmans, 2022), 75.

16. See Jermo van Nes who argues that in the building boom underway in the first and second centuries, the first readers of Ephesians would have observed temples under construction. Van Nes, "Under Construction: The Building of God's Temple according to Ephesians 2,19–22," in *Paul's Graeco-Roman Context*, ed. Cilliers Breytenbach, BETL 277 (Leuven: Peeters, 2015), 631–44.

17. Thielman, *Ephesians*, 210–12.

18. Thielman, *Ephesians*, 213–17.

19. Thielman, *Ephesians*, 342–51.

20. Peter W. Gosnell, "Ephesians 5:18–20 and Mealtime Propriety," *TynBul* 44 (1993): 363–71. Gosnell observes, "Though special mealtime functions were common among educated urban élite, evidence suggests that convivial gatherings could be popular even for poor country folk. People regularly gathered for meals, which often included drinking, singing and discussion" ("Ephesians 5:18–20," 365).

21. Gosnell, "Ephesians 5:18–20," 371.

22. Thielman, *Ephesians*, 408–10.

23. Jerry Toner, *Popular Culture in Ancient Rome* (Cambridge: Polity, 2009), 2: "Most [nonelite Romans] saw their neighbours as competitors not comrades in the harsh struggle for scarce resources."

24. F. F. Bruce, *Paul: Apostle of the Heart Set Free* (Grand Rapids: Eerdmans, 1977), 424. Bruce explains that the phrase itself belongs to Arthur Samuel Peake. Peake, however, applied the phrase to his own summary of Paul's theology rather to Ephesians. Peake, *The Quintessence of Paulinism* (Manchester, UK: Manchester University Press, 1918).

CHAPTER 26

1. Some commentators believe that the uncertainty Paul expresses here about whether Mark will arrive in Colossae (". . . if he comes to you . . .") reveals some continuing tension between Paul and Mark (e.g., James D. G. Dunn, *The Epistles to the Colossians and to Philemon: A Commentary on the Greek Text*, NIGTC [Grand Rapids: Eerdmans, 1996], 277). It is more likely, however, that it simply reveals the unpredictable nature of ancient travel. Cf. Paul's uncertainty about whether Timothy will arrive in Corinth in 1 Cor 16:10 (ἐὰν δὲ ἔλθῃ Τιμόθεος . . .).

2. On the shame of imprisonment, see Brian Rapske, *Paul in Roman Custody*, vol. 3 of *The Book of Acts in Its First Century Setting*, ed. Bruce W. Winter (Grand Rapids: Eerdmans, 1994), 288–91. Dionysius of Halicarnassus, *Ant. rom.* 13.5–6, provides an example of the connection between imprisonment, shaming, and disgrace in Roman antiquity. Cf. Rapske, *Paul in Roman Custody*, 289.

3. My trans. See BDAG 75, s.v. ἀναψύχω.

4. See Cicero, *Verr.* 1 and 2 (*In C. Verrem Actio Prima* and *Actionis Secundae in C. Verrem*), and the discussion in L. H. G. Greenwood, *Against Caecilius. Against Verres, Part 1*, vol 1 of *Cicero: The Verrine Orations*, 2 vols., LCL 221 (Cambridge, MA: Harvard University Press, 1958), xvi–xvii. Perhaps the procedure these speeches assume is the origin of the comment in C. Spicq, frequently repeated after Spicq, that a judge who could not decide a case based on an *actio prima* held an *actio secunda* to receive more information. Spicq, *Les Épîtres Pastorales*, 2 vols., 4th ed. (Eugene, OR: Wipf & Stock, 2001), 2:818. See also, e.g., J. H. Bernard, *The Pastoral Epistles*, CGTSC (London: C. J. Clay and Sons, 1899), 148.

5. Herbert Musurillo, *The Acts of the Christian Martyrs: Introduction, Texts, and Translations* (Oxford: Clarendon, 1972), 328–29.

6. According to Musurillo, Phileas died under the prefect Clodius Culcianus sometime between 304 and 306. The *Apology of Phileas* in the Bodmer Papyrus XX was penned within a decade of this time. On this, see Musurillo, *Acts of the Christian Martyrs*, xlvi–xlvii. For a somewhat different perspective on the relevance of this document to 2 Tim 4:16, see Harry W. Tajra, *The Martyrdom of St. Paul*, WUNT 2.67 (Tübingen: Mohr Siebeck, 1994), 88–89; and Jerome D. Quinn and William C. Wacker, *The First and Second Letters to Timothy*, Eerdmans Critical Commentary (Grand Rapids: Eerdmans, 2000), 815.

7. Naphtali Lewis and Meyer Reinhold, eds., *Roman Civilization: Selected Readings*, 2 vols. (New York: Columbia University Press, 1951–1955), 2:550. See also Tajra, *Martyrdom of St. Paul*, 87–88.

8. Leanne Bablitz, "Roman Society in the Courtroom," in *The Oxford Handbook of Social Relations in the Roman World*, ed. Michael Peachin (Oxford: Oxford University Press, 2011), 318–20.

9. Bablitz, "Roman Society in the Courtroom," 325. Perhaps Paul had the crowd gathered at his first defense in mind when he said that the "Lord stood by me and strengthened me, so that through me the message might be fully proclaimed and all the Gentiles might hear it" (2 Tim 4:17). Cf. Jens Herzer, "The Mission and the End of Paul between Strategy and Reality: A Response to Rainer Riesner," in *The Last Years of Paul: Essays from the Tarragona Conference, June 2013*, Armand Puig i Tàrrech, John M. G. Barclay, and Jörg Frey, WUNT 1.352 (Tübingen: Mohr Siebeck, 2015), 422–23.

10. Theodor Mommsen, Paul Krueger, and Alan Watson, eds., *The Digest of Justinian*, 4 vols. (Philadelphia: University of Pennsylvania Press, 1985), 2:650, quoting from the third-century AD lawyer Herennius Modestinus (on whom see Tony Honoré, "Herennius Modestinus," *OCD*[4] 667).

11. LSJ 356, s.v. γόης. Cf. Walter Lock, *A Critical and Exegetical Commentary on the Pastoral Epistles*, ICC (Edinburgh: T&T Clark, 1924), 107, 109.

12. Measuring the most likely travel route in J. A. Talbert, ed., *Barrington Atlas of the Greek and Roman World* (Princeton, NJ: Princeton University Press, 2000),

69. On the date of Justin's *1 Apol.*, see A. W. F. Blunt, *The Apologies of Justin Martyr*, Ancient Texts and Translations (Eugene, OR: Wipf & Stock, 2006), xlvii–lii.

13. Trans. Denis Minns and Paul Parvis, *Justin, Philosopher and Martyr: Apologies* (Oxford: Oxford University Press, 2009), 149. See also the slightly more detailed descriptions of Menander in Irenaeus, *Haer.* 1.23.5, and in Eusebius, *Hist. eccl.* 3.26.1–4. Tertullian says that Menander believed "all who partake of his baptism become immortal, incorruptible and instantaneously invested with resurrection-life" and spends several paragraphs mockingly refuting this notion (*An.* 50 [Thelwall, *ANF* 3:227–28]).

14. Bernard (*Pastoral Epistles*, 123–24) believes that "the error of Hymenaeus and Philetus" was not "the outcome of a definite heretical system so much as a private blunder based on misinterpretations of Apostolic doctrine" (expressed in places such as Rom 6:4 and Col 2:12). This judgment, however, does not seem to do justice to the overlap between magic and a realized resurrection in both 2 Timothy and Menander's teachings.

15. On the statue (which was found in the sixteenth century and refers to the Sabine deity Semo Sancus Dius Fidius), see Basil L. Gildersleeve, *The Apologies of Justin Martyr to Which Is Appended the Epistle to Diognetus* (New York: Harper, 1877), 153–54; and Minns and Parvis, *Justin*, 147n7 and 149n1.

16. Martin Dibelius and Hans Conzelmann, *The Pastoral Epistles*, trans. Philip Buttolph and Adela Yarbro, Hermeneia (Philadelphia: Fortress, 1972), 19, 24.

17. Dibelius and Conzelmann, *Pastoral Epistles*, 7–8; Bernhard Heininger, "The Reception of Paul in the First Century: The Deutero- and Trito-Pauline Letters and the Image of Paul in Acts," in *Paul: Life, Setting, Work, Letters*, ed. Oda Wischmeyer, trans. Helen S. Heron and Dieter T. Roth (London: Continuum, 2012), 327.

18. Dibelius and Conzelmann, *Pastoral Epistles*, 127–28.

19. My translation of ὑγιαινούσαις καὶ ἀνόσοις. Dibelius and Conzelmann (*Pastoral Epistles*, 19, 25) mention both examples but believe that the authentic Paul could not have spoken this way.

20. Herzer, "Mission and End of Paul," 422.

21. Quinn and Wacker, *First and Second Letters to Timothy*, 812–13; Philip H. Towner, *The Letters to Timothy and Titus*, NICNT (Grand Rapids: Eerdmans, 2006), 631.

22. Luke Timothy Johnson argues persuasively that 2 Tim is an example of "the personal paraenetic letter," which provides both positive instruction about what to pursue and negative instruction about what to avoid. Johnson, *The First and Second Letters to Timothy*, AB 35A (New York: Doubleday, 2001), 322.

23. For this understanding of 2 Tim 1:6, see, e.g., Lock (*Pastoral Epistles*, 85). Others (e.g., Towner, *Letters to Timothy and Titus*, 459–60) believe 1 Tim 4:14 and 2 Tim 1:6 describe two different events.

24. For the translation of ἀναζωπυρεῖν, see I. H. Marshall, *The Pastoral Epistles*, ICC (Edinburgh: T&T Clark, 1999), 696. The meaning is not that Timothy should

"rekindle" (NRSV) a flame that is snuffed out, or nearly so. Rather, it is that Timothy should add fuel to a flame already burning so that it might burn even more brightly.

25. According to J. E. Lendon, in Roman thinking, honor was "a stable commodity" that could grow, shrink, be given away, and guarded. Lendon, "Roman Honor," in the *Oxford Handbook of Social Relations in the Roman World*, ed. Michael Peachin (Oxford: Oxford University Press, 2011), 389.

26. For the understanding of παραθήκην in 2 Tim 1:12 as a reference to the gospel, see Marshall, *Pastoral Epistles*, 711.

27. For "qualified" as a translation of ἱκανοί here, see the NIV and BDAG 472, s.v. ἱκανός 2.

28. Here I assume that 2 Tim 2:14 points back to the trustworthy people of 2 Tim 2:2 to whom Timothy should entrust the gospel. For this understanding, see, e.g., Knight, *Pastoral Epistles*, 409–10.

29. Michael P. Theophilos, "The Roman Connection: Paul and Mark," in *Paul and Mark: Comparative Essays Part I: Two Authors at the Beginnings of Christianity*, ed. Oda Wischmeyer, David C. Sim, and Ian J. Elmer, BZNW 198 (Berlin: de Gruyter, 2014), 45–72. Theophilos does not think, however, that Mark authored the gospel ("Roman Connection," 56–57).

30. A more detailed argument for this view appears in appendix 2. The view is not uncontroversial. For examples of competing theories, see Rainer Riesner, "Paul's Trial and End according to Second Timothy, *1 Clement*, the Canon Muratori, and the Apocryphal Acts," in *The Last Years of Paul: Essays from the Tarragona Conference, June 2013*, ed. Armand Puig i Tàrrech, John M. G. Barclay, and Jörg Frey, WUNT 1.352 (Tübingen: Mohr Siebeck, 2015), 394–400; and Daniel Marguerat, "On Why Luke Remains Silent about Paul's End (Acts 28.16–31)," in *The Last Years of Paul*, 305–32.

31. C. Kavin Rowe, *World Upside Down: Reading Acts in the Greco-Roman Age* (Oxford: Oxford University Press, 2009), 88–89; David L. Eastman, *Paul the Martyr: The Cult of the Apostle in the Latin West*, WAWSup 4 (Atlanta: Society of Biblical Literature, 2011), 18.

32. Cf. Marguerat, "Why Luke Remains Silent," 331–32.

33. On the importance of this passage in determining Paul's legal position, see Bernardo Santalucia, "Paul's Roman Trial: Legal Procedures Regarding Roman Citizens Convicted of Serious Charges in the First Century CE," in *The Last Years of Paul: Essays from the Tarragona Conference, June 2013*, ed. Armand Puig i Tàrrech, John M. G. Barclay, and Jörg Frey, WUNT 1.352 (Tübingen: Mohr Siebeck, 2015), 223.

34. Santalucia, "Paul's Roman Trial," 225.

35. On the alteration of the charge from temple desecration (Acts 21:28) to attempted temple desecration (24:6), see Heike Omerzu, "The Roman Trial against Paul according to Acts 21–26," in *The Last Years of Paul: Essays from the Tarragona Conference, June 2013*, ed. Armand Puig i Tàrrech, John M. G. Barclay, and Jörg Frey, WUNT 1.352 (Tübingen: Mohr Siebeck, 2015), 191.

36. Cf. Daniel Marguerat, *Die Apostelgeschichte*, KEK 3 (Göttingen: Vandenhoeck & Ruprecht, 2022), 779n20.

37. See the description of the incident in E. Mary Smallwood, *The Jews under Roman Rule from Pompey to Diocletian: A Study in Political Relations* (Leiden: Brill, 1981), 278.

38. Smallwood, *Jews under Roman Rule*, 278.

39. Luke implies that Paul stood before Caesar not only in Acts 27:24 but also in Festus's comment to Herod Agrippa earlier in the narrative that he needed something to write to the "lord" (τῷ κυρίῳ) about Paul (Acts 25:26). On this see Rowe, *World Upside Down*, 85. For a more detailed account of what eventually happened to Paul and the place of his death and burial, see appendix 3.

40. Eastman, *Paul the Martyr*, 31, 43–46, 62–69.

41. Eastman, *Paul the Martyr*, 31, 43–45.

42. On this, see Tajra, *Martyrdom of St. Paul*, 24–26.

43. Gaius (or "Caius"), to whom Eusebius refers here, was probably writing at the end of the second or beginning of the third century. See Tajra, *Martyrdom of St. Paul*, 179. For archaeological evidence that probably points to the location of Paul's ancient "trophy" at the site of the Basilica of Saint Paul Outside the Walls, see Nicola Camerlenghi, *St. Paul's Outside the Walls: A Roman Basilica, from Antiquity to the Modern Era* (Cambridge: Cambridge University Press, 2018), 28–31.

44. By the end of that century, the flood of pilgrims coming to the site required a far larger structure, and work began on rearranging the road system near the church to accommodate it. On the construction of this church in the early fourth century and its reorientation and expansion in the late fourth and early fifth centuries, see Eastman, *Paul the Martyr*, 24–57. The fourth- and fifth-century church tragically burned in 1823.

45. See Camerlenghi, *St. Paul's Outside the Walls*, 26; and Marina Marcelli and Chiara Cicone, "Via Ostiense: Tombe romane presso la Rupe di S. Paolo. Rilievi archeologici e analisi delle strutture (Municipio VIII)," *Bulletino della Commissione Archeologica Comunale di Roma* 120 (2019): 393, 396.

46. On the identification of Paul's memorial with a structure in *opus reticulatum* discovered near the apse of the Basilica of Saint Paul Outside the Walls, see Camerlenghi, *St. Paul's Outside the Walls*, 29–31.

47. Trans. Anthony C. Thiselton, *The First Epistle to the Corinthians: A Commentary on the Greek Text*, NIGTC (Grand Rapids: Eerdmans, 2000), 1258. Cf. Phil 3:21.

APPENDIX 1

1. On the connection between the organization of society (including the home) and the letter's theology of creation, see Luke Timothy Johnson, *The First and Second Letters to Timothy*, AB 35A (New York: Doubleday, 2001), 147–52.

2. One can plausibly read the *Epistles of Anacharsis* in this way. On this, see Patricia A. Rosenmeyer, *Ancient Epistolary Fictions: The Letter in Greek Literature*

(Cambridge: Cambridge University Press, 2001), 211; and Frank Thielman, *Ephesians*, BECNT (Grand Rapids: Baker, 2010), 1. On the whole issue of the morality of ancient forgery, see Isaac T. Soon, "Before Deception: The Amoral Nature of Ancient Christian Forgery," *EC* 14 (2023): 429–45.

3. See, e.g., Bart D. Ehrman, *Forgery and Counterforgery: The Use of Literary Deceit in Early Christian Polemics* (Oxford: Oxford University Press, 2013), 155–237. Cf. Lewis R. Donelson, *Pseudepigraphy and Ethical Argument in the Pastoral Epistles*, HUT 22 (Tübingen: Mohr Siebeck, 1986), 23–66.

4. See the introductory comments of R. G. Bury on the whole corpus and on each of the three letters in R. G. Bury, trans., *Plato: Timaeus, Critias, Cleitophon, Menexenus, Epistles*, LCL 234 (Cambridge: Harvard University Press, 1929), 385–92, 591, 607, 610–13.

5. Bury, *Plato: Epistles*, 608; Donelson, *Pseudepigraphy and Ethical Argument*, 25–27.

6. Bury, *Plato: Epistles*, 611; Donelson, *Pseudepigraphy and Ethical Argument*, 27.

7. Bruce M. Metzger, "Literary Forgeries and Canonical Pseudepigrapha," *JBL* 91 (1972): 10.

8. See J. K. Elliott, *The Apocryphal New Testament* (Oxford: Clarendon, 1993), 535–88.

9. Trans. D. R. Shackleton Bailey, *Cicero's Letters to His Friends*, American Philological Association Classical Resources Series 1 (Atlanta: Scholars Press, 1978), 581.

10. For these two references, I am indebted to Steve Reece, *Paul's Large Letters: Paul's Autographic Subscription in the Light of Ancient Epistolary Conventions*, LNTS 561 (New York: Bloomsbury, 2017), 9n3.

11. Reece, *Paul's Large Letters*, 9.

12. The phrases in quotation marks are from Ehrman, *Forgery and Counterforgery*, 126–27.

13. Again, the phrase in quotation marks is from Ehrman, *Forgery and Counterforgery*, 170.

14. See the comments of John L. White and the letter itself in White, *Light from Ancient Letters*, FF (Philadelphia: Fortress, 1986), 145.

15. Andrew W. Pitts, "Style and Pseudonymity in Pauline Scholarship: A Register Based Configuration," in *Paul and Pseudonymity*, ed. Stanley E. Porter and Gregory Fewster, Pauline Studies 8 (Leiden: Brill, 2013), 119. On the difficulty of knowing how elastic Paul's style was, see Douglas A. Campbell, *Framing Paul: An Epistolary Biography* (Grand Rapids: Eerdmans, 2014), 207–10, 348–49.

16. Pitts, "Style and Pseudonymity," 116–38. See also Stanley E. Porter, *The Pastoral Epistles: A Commentary on the Greek Text* (Grand Rapids: Baker, 2023), 49–52.

17. Pitts, "Style and Pseudonymity," 130–52. Some scholars seem to have grasped intuitively the importance of register in discussions of authorship. See, e.g., Massey ("Cicero, the Pastoral Epistles, and the Issue of Pseudonymity," 65–84), who observes that Cicero could write in exciting or boring ways depending on contextual factors.

18. Jermo van Nes, *Pauline Language and the Pastoral Epistles: A Study of Linguistic Variation in the "Corpus Paulinum,"* Linguistic Biblical Studies 16 (Leiden: Brill, 2018). Van Nes's five categories are words that only occur once in the canonical letters attributed to Paul, the richness of the vocabulary, the absence of indeclinable words, the relationship between clauses, and irregularities in sentence structure.

19. Van Nes, *Pauline Language*, 221–22.

20. Campbell, *Framing Paul*, 201.

21. See, e.g., Ign. *Phld.* 11.2 and Ign. *Smyrn.* 12.1 where Ignatius sends greetings to Troas and commends the letter courier using identical wording (ἀσπάζεται ὑμᾶς ἡ ἀγάπη τῶν ἀδελφῶν τῶν ἐν Τρωάδι ὅθεν καὶ γράφω ὑμῖν διὰ Βούρρου). Cf. Col 4:7–8 and Eph 6:21–22.

22. Campbell, *Framing Paul*, 210–15.

23. Walter Bauer, *Orthodoxy and Heresy in Earliest Christianity* (Philadelphia: Fortress, 1971), 226.

24. Jerome D. Quinn and William C. Wacker, *The Eerdmans Critical Commentary* (Grand Rapids: Eerdmans, 2000), 559.

25. For "counter-propositions" as a translation of *antitheseis*, cf. LSJ 155, s.v. ἀντίθεσις 3.

26. Trans. Roland Teske, *Answer to Faustus, A Manichean*, Part 1, *Books*, Works of Saint Augustine, vol. 20, ed. Boniface Ramsey (Hyde Park, NY: New City Press, 2007), 428–29. Soon argues from this passage that Augustine considered Christian pseudepigraphic works deceptive "because they were not handed down through authoritative channels" ("Before Deception," 443). Augustine's argument, however, seems also to have a rational historical component: if a document has been handed down as genuine to reliable people from the time of its composition, its authorial claim is likely to be trustworthy.

27. See, respectively, Martin Hengel, *Acts and the History of Earliest Christianity* (London: SCM, 1979); and Richard I. Pervo, *Profit with Delight: The Literary Genre of the Acts of the Apostles* (Philadelphia: Fortress, 1987).

28. E.g., Richard I. Pervo, *Acts: A Commentary*, Hermeneia (Minneapolis: Fortress, 2009), 14–20.

29. Darryl W. Palmer, "Acts and the Ancient Historical Monograph," in *The Book of Acts in Its Ancient Literary Setting*, ed. Bruce W. Winter and Andrew D. Clarke, vol. 1 of *The Book of Acts in Its First Century Setting*, ed. Bruce W. Winter (Grand Rapids: Eerdmans, 1993), 1–29.

30. Carey A. Moore, *Judith*, AB 40 (Garden City, NY: Doubleday, 1985), 46.

31. The phrase "Nebuchadnezzar, King of Babylon" occurs in the Old Testament 43 times.

32. Trans. B. P. Reardon, *Chaereas and Callirhoe*, in *Collected Ancient Greek Novels*, ed. B. P. Reardon (Berkeley: University of California Press, 1989), 21.

33. Colin J. Hemer, *Book of Acts in the Setting of Hellenistic History*, ed. Conrad H. Gempf (Winona Lake, IN: Eisenbrauns, 1990), 327–28.

34. Todd Penner, *In Praise of Christian Origins: Stephen and the Hellenists in Lukan Apologetic Historiography*, Emory Studies in Early Christianity 10 (New York: T&T Clark, 2004), 216–17.

35. Trans. Robin Waterfield, *Polybius: The Histories*, Oxford World's Classics (Oxford: Oxford University Press, 2010), 119.

36. A. J. M. Wedderburn, "The 'We'–Passages in Acts: On the Horns of a Dilemma," *ZNW* 93 (2002): 78–98.

37. Eve-Marie Becker, *The Birth of Christian History: Memory and Time from Mark to Luke-Acts*, Anchor Yale Bible Reference Library (New Haven, CT: Yale University Press, 2017), 95.

38. Vernon K. Robbins, *Sea Voyages and Beyond: Emerging Strategies in Socio-Rhetorical Interpretation*, Emory Studies in Early Christianity 14 (Dorset, UK: Deo, 2010), 47–81.

39. Robbins, *Sea Voyages*, 79–81.

40. Robbins, *Sea Voyages*, 80.

41. Robbins, *Sea Voyages*, 91.

42. Wedderburn, "'We'–Passages in Acts," 85.

43. Colin J. Hemer, "First Person Narrative in Acts 27–28," *TynBul* 36 (1985): 79–109; Hemer, *Book of Acts*, 330–32.

44. For the theory that the author of Acts knew Paul's letters, see, e.g., Morton Scott Enslin, "Once Again, Luke and Paul," *ZNW* 61 (1970): 253–71; Ryan S. Schellenberg, "The First Pauline Chronologist? Paul's Itinerary in the Letters and in Acts," *JBL* 134 (2015): 193–213; and Becker, *Birth of Christian History*, 95, 101.

45. Enslin, "Once Again, Luke and Paul," 263.

46. Riesner, *Paul's Early Period*, 88–89.

47. Isaac T. Soon, *A Disabled Apostle: Impairment and Disability in the Letters of Paul* (Oxford: Oxford University Press, 2023), 174.

48. Martin Hengel, *The Pre-Christian Paul*, trans. John Bowden (London: SCM, 1991), 9–10.

49. Murray J. Harris, *The Second Epistle to the Corinthians*, NIGTC (Grand Rapids: Eerdmans, 2005), 761–62.

50. See the discussion in Craig S. Keener, *Acts: An Exegetical Commentary*, 4 vols. (Grand Rapids: Baker, 2012–2015), 3:2740–42.

51. Keener, *Acts*, 3:2570–72.

52. Keener, *Acts*, 3:2570–72, 2740–42.

53. Martin Hengel and Anna Maria Schwemer, *Paul between Damascus and Antioch: The Unknown Years*, trans. John Bowden (Louisville: Westminster John Knox, 1997), 106–13, 386–87.

54. Schellenberg, "Paul's Itinerary," 195–200.

55. Enslin, "Once Again, Luke and Paul," 258; Schellenberg, "Paul's Itinerary," 201.

56. As Schellenberg amply acknowledges ("Paul's Itinerary," 198, 201, 207, 209–10).

57. Schellenberg, "Paul's Itinerary," 209–10.

58. Schellenberg notes the close verbal correspondence between Rom 15:25 and Acts 19:21 and 20:22 regarding Paul's journey to Jerusalem and then to Rome. He also notes the ominous tone that dominates both Paul's narrative of his travel plans in Rom 15:30–31 and the speech of the Lukan Paul in Acts 20:22–23. On Schellenberg's reading, the similarities of both words and mood between these texts indicate Luke's use of Romans to construct his story of Paul's journey from "Greece" to Jerusalem to Rome. The phrase "Now . . . I am going to Jerusalem" (or "to go to Jerusalem") (Νυνὶ [νῦν] δὲ πορεύομαι εἰς Ἰερουσαλὴμ [Rom 15:25; Acts 20:22]/πορεύεσθαι εἰς Ἱεροσόλυμα [Acts 19:21]), however, would be a common way for anyone to speak of going from one city to another. Both this way of speaking and Paul's mood at the time, moreover, could easily have been in Luke's memory if he was with Paul around the time Paul wrote Romans (Acts 20:5–6).

APPENDIX 2

1. See, e.g., in order, Helmut Koester, *History and Literature of Early Christianity*, vol. 2 of *Introduction to the New Testament* (Berlin: de Gruyter, 1982), 130–31; James D. G. Dunn, *Beginning from Jerusalem*, vol. 2 of *Christianity in the Making*, 3 vols. (Grand Rapids: Eerdmans, 2009), 1009–11; Jerome Murphy-O'Connor, *Paul: A Critical Life* (Oxford: Clarendon, 1996), 220–21, 234–39, 257–59; Luke Timothy Johnson, *The Canonical Paul*, vol. 2 of *Interpreting Paul* (Grand Rapids: Eerdmans, 2021), 33–41, 90–92.

2. See, e.g., Ryan S. Schellenberg, *Abject Joy: Paul, Prison, and the Art of Making Do* (New York: Oxford University Press, 2021), 7–8, 26, 45–53.

3. Koester opted for Ephesus (*History and Literature*, 130–31). Michael Flexsenhar believes that Paul was somewhere in Asia, perhaps in the region of Ephesus ("The Provenance of Philippians and Why It Matters: Old Questions, New Approaches," *JSNT* 42 [2019]: 37). Schellenberg thinks it unwise to be more specific than "one of the eastern provinces" (*Abject Joy*, 42–43).

4. E.g., Adolf Deissmann, *Light from the Ancient East*, trans. Lionel R. M. Strachan (Grand Rapids: Baker, 1978), 237; Benjamin W. Robinson, "An Ephesian Imprisonment of Paul," *JBL* 29 (1910): 181–87; Clayton R. Bowen, "Are Paul's Prison Letters from Ephesus?," *AmJT* 24 (1920): 112–35; George S. Duncan, *St. Paul's Ephesian Ministry: A Reconstruction* (New York: Charles Scribner's Sons, 1930); Koester, *History and Literature*, 130–31.

5. Robinson, "Ephesian Imprisonment," 183.

6. Robinson, "Ephesian Imprisonment," 182. (Robinson thinks that Paul wrote Rom 16 to Ephesus and that "Junius" [a man] is the correct reading here rather than "Junia" [a woman].) Cf. Bowen, "Paul's Prison Letters," 115.

7. Bowen, "Paul's Prison Letters," 124.

8. Bowen, "Paul's Prison Letters," 126.

9. Bowen, "Paul's Prison Letters," 122–23.

10. Robinson, "Ephesian Imprisonment," 183–84; Bowen, "Paul's Prison Letters," 123, 125–26, 130–31, 132.

11. Flexsenhar, "Provenance of Philippians," 31–37; Heike Omerzu, "Paul, the *Praetorium* and the Saints from Caesar's Household: Philippians Revisited in Light of Migration Theory," *JSNT* 43 (2021): 453–54; and Cédric Brélaz, "The Provincial Contexts of Paul's Imprisonments: Law Enforcement and Criminal Procedure in the Roman East," *JSNT* 43 (2021): 494–95.

12. Robinson, "Ephesian Imprisonment," 185.

13. Murphy-O'Connor, *Paul*, 359–63.

14. Robinson ("Ephesian Imprisonment," 181–82) thinks that the Acts of Paul is reliable on this point (see Richard I. Pervo, *The Acts of Paul: A New Translation with Introduction and Commentary* [Eugene, OR: Cascade, 2014], 226), but the notion of Paul's Ephesian imprisonment in that text is more likely to be a legend built around 1 Cor 15:32.

15. Ernst Lohmeyer, *Die Briefe an die Philipper, Kolosser und an Philemon*, KEK (Göttingen: Vandenhoeck & Ruprecht, 1961), 40–41; John A. T. Robinson, *Redating the New Testament* (Philadelphia: Westminster, 1976), 59–60.

16. Robinson, *Redating*, 78.

17. Cf. Bo Reicke, "Caesarea, Rome, and the Captivity Epistles," in *Apostolic History and the Gospel: Biblical and Historical Essays Presented to F. F. Bruce*, ed. W. Ward Gasque and Ralph P. Martin (Exeter, UK: Paternoster, 1970), 280. Reicke thought, however, that Paul wrote Philippians later, from Rome.

18. Johnson, "Pauline Letters from Caesarea," 25; Robinson, *Redating*, 78–79.

19. Johnson, "Pauline Letters from Caesarea," 25.

20. Johnson, "Pauline Letters from Caesarea," 25.

21. Robinson, *Redating*, 79–80. Cf. Reicke, "Caesarea, Rome, and the Captivity Epistles," 281, and Lohmeyer (*Briefe an die Philipper*, 14–15), although Reicke seems to have thought that Paul anticipated making this journey as a prisoner, and both thought Paul wrote Colossians and Philemon before Philippians.

22. Robinson, *Redating*, 80.

23. Brian Campbell, "*praetorium*," *OCD*[4] 1204. The relevant sentence in *ILS* 1993 is "nomina speculatorum, qui in praetorio meo militaverunt, item militum, qui in cohortibus novem praetoriis et quattuor urbanis, subieci," which Sandra J. Bingham translates, "I have appended the names of the *speculators* who served in my guard (praetorio), and also of those soldiers who were members of the nine praetorian and four urban cohorts" ("The Praetorian Guard in the Political and Social Life of Julio-Claudian Rome" [PhD diss., University of British Columbia, 1997], 137n43.)

24. See, e.g., Theodor Zahn, *Introduction to the New Testament*, 3 vols., trans. John Moore Trout, William Arnot Mather, Louis Hodous, Edward Strong Worcester, William Hoyt Worrell, Roland Backus Dodge, and Melancthon Williams Jaco-

bus, 2nd ed. (New York: Charles Scribner's Sons, 1917), 1:551; Markus Bockmuehl, *The Epistle to the Philippians*, BNTC (Peabody, MA: Hendrickson, 1998), 75.

25. See Flexsenhar ("Provenance of Philippians," 25–27). On Paul's non-elite social status, see the argument of Schellenberg (*Abject Joy*, 32–33, 54–55, 67) but also the careful qualification of his argument (*Abject Joy*, 76). For the suggestion that the circumstances in which Paul was detained may have more to do with the social position of his accusers than of Paul himself, see Paul McKechnie, "Judean Embassies and Cases before Roman Emperors, AD 44–66," *JTS* 56 (2005): 360.

26. "The whole [ὅλῳ] praetorian guard" is probably hyperbolic. Cf. Rom 1:8 where Paul says that the Roman Christians' faith "is being spread throughout the whole [ὅλῳ] world" (CEB).

27. "While for certain reasons there were more imperial slaves and freedpersons in the imperial capital than anywhere else, they could still be found all over the Mediterranean." Michael Flexsenhar III, *Christians in Caesar's Household: The Emperor's Slaves in the Makings of Christianity*, Inventing Christianity (University Park, PA: Pennsylvania State University Press, 2019), 153n9. For the perspective on Caesar's household I take here, see Udo Schnelle, "Paul's Literary Activity during His Roman Trial," in *The Last Years of Paul: Essays from the Tarragona Conference, June 2013*, ed. Armand Puig i Tàrrech, John M. G. Barclay, and Jörg Frey, WUNT 1.352 (Tübingen: Mohr Siebeck, 2015), 437.

28. The Greek runs Ὀνησίφορ[ος] . . . γενόμενος ἐν Ῥώμῃ σπουδαίως ἐζήτησέν με καὶ εὗρεν.

29. Robinson, *Redating*, 75–76; Bo Reicke, *Re-examining Paul's Letters: The History of the Pauline Correspondence*, ed. David P. Moessner and Ingalisa Reicke (Harrisburg, PA: Trinity Press International, 2001), 115–16.

30. I think Paul wrote Titus on his journey to Rome, perhaps from Malta, and so, from one perspective, it too would be an "imprisonment letter." Paul was, after all, under the watchful eye of Julius the centurion (Acts 27:1, 3, 6, 11, 31, 43). He does not seem to have been in chains, however, during this phase of his judicial confinement and never mentions his confinement in the letter.

31. Cf. Johnson, "Pauline Letters from Caesarea," 25, although in Johnson's scheme Paul's setting is Caesarea.

32. Peter Walker is an exception. He assigns all the prison epistles to a single Roman imprisonment and believes that Paul wrote 2 Tim first. See his essay, "Revisiting the Pastoral Epistles—Part II," *EJT* 21 (2012): 120–32.

33. Cf. the Muratorian Canon §2 (*ANF* 5:603), probably written in the mid-third century, which claims that Paul was released from his Roman imprisonment and traveled to Spain but says nothing further about Paul's fate. On the date of the Muratorian Canon, see Jonathan J. Armstrong, "Victorinus of Pettau as the Author of the Canon Muratori," *VigChr* 62 (2008): 1–34.

34. The reconstruction that follows comes from Gordon D. Fee, *1 and 2 Timothy,*

Titus, Good News Commentary (New York: Harper & Row, 1984), xvii, xviii, xxv, xxxviin6, 244, 250.

35. These questions are based on the objections of, among others, J. E. Huther, *Critical and Exegetical Handbook to the Epistles to Timothy and Titus*, 6th ed., trans. David Hunter (New York: Funk & Wagnalls, 1884), 17–21.

36. On the clarity of the Miletus speech about Paul's fate, see Hans Conzelmann, *Acts of the Apostles*, ed. Eldon J. Epp with Christopher R. Matthews, trans. James Limberg, A. Thomas Kraabel, and Donald H. Juel (Philadelphia: Fortress, 1987), 227–28; and cf. Dunn, *Beginning from Jerusalem*, 1053. On Luke's approach to Paul's death generally, see Daniel Marguerat, "On Why Luke Remains Silent," in Puig i Tàrrech, Barclay, and Frey, *The Last Years of Paul*, 305–32.

37. See, e.g., J. N. D. Kelly, *The Pastoral Epistles*, BNTC (Peabody, MA: Hendrickson, 1960), 9–10.

38. See, e.g., Martin Dibelius and Hans Conzelmann, *The Pastoral Epistles*, Hermeneia, trans. Philip Buttolph and Adela Yarbro (Philadelphia: Fortress, 1972), 126.

39. The theory of Dibelius and Conzelmann (*Pastoral Epistles*, 126–27), which assumes the Pastoral Epistles' pseudonymity, seems at least equally speculative.

40. Jakob van Bruggen, *Die geschichtliche Einordnung der Pastoralbriefe* (Wuppertal: Brockhaus, 1981), 57.

APPENDIX 3

1. The letter says only that it comes from "the church of God that sojourns in Rome," but long-standing tradition assigns it to "Clement," bishop of Rome under the emperor Domitian (Eusebius, *Hist. eccl.* 3.14–16) and, for simplicity, I will follow that tradition. I have used Michael W. Holmes's translation of 1 Clement throughout this discussion.

2. Wolfgang Grünstäudl, "Hidden in Praise," in *The Last Years of Paul: Essays from the Tarragona Conference, June 2013*, ed. Armand Puig i Tàrrech, John M. G. Barclay, and Jörg Frey, WUNT 1.352 (Tübingen: Mohr Siebeck, 2015), 375–89.

3. Edward Champlin, *Nero* (Cambridge, MA: Harvard University Press, 2003), 121–26; L. L. Welborn, "Early Christianity at Rome as Reflected in the So-Called First Epistle of Clement," in *Rome and Ostia*, vol. 6, *The First Urban Churches*, ed. James R. Harrison and L. L. Welborn, WGRWSup 18 (Atlanta: Society of Biblical Literature, 2021), 139–41.

4. Champlin (*Nero*, 122) thinks it likely that Nero intended the Christians' punishments to be sacrifices of expiation to the gods they had offended.

5. Welborn, "Early Christianity at Rome," 143–44.

6. David L. Eastman, "Jealousy, Internal Strife, and the Deaths of Peter and Paul: A Reassessment of *1 Clement*," ZAC 18 (2013): 36; Eastman, *Paul the Martyr: The*

Cult of the Apostle in the Latin West, WAWSup 4 (Atlanta: Society of Biblical Literature, 2011), 19.

7. Eastman (*Paul the Martyr*, 21) dates Gaius (or "Caius") to "the early third century."

8. This, at least, seems to be the implication of Eusebius, *Hist. eccl.* 5.17.3–4. See the interpretation of this passage in Hugh Jackson Lawlor and John Ernest Leonard Oulton, trans., *Eusebius, Bishop of Caesarea: The Ecclesiastical History and the Martyrs of Palestine*, 2 vols. (London: SPCK, 1927–1928), 2:117.

9. Quoted in Eusebius, *Hist. eccl.* 3.31.4 (Lawlor and Oulton).

10. Quoted in Eusebius, *Hist. eccl.* 2.25.7 (Lawlor and Oulton, slightly modified).

11. MGS 2157, s.v. τροπαῖος c. See also Eastman, *Paul the Martyr*, 21–22.

12. On the date of the Acts of Paul, see Richard I. Pervo, *The Acts of Paul: A New Translation with Introduction and Commentary* (Eugene, OR: Cascade, 2014), 70. Tertullian, in *Scorp.* 15, alludes to the story of Paul's martyrdom, and Tertullian wrote *Scorpiace* "in late 203 or early 204" (Timothy D. Barnes, "Tertullian's 'Scorpiace,'" *JTS* 20 [1969]: 131). The story of Paul's martyrdom in the Acts of Paul seems to have circulated separately from the Acts of Paul itself, although whether it circulated separately before or after the composition of the Acts of Paul is not clear.

13. Richard Bauckham, "The *Acts of Paul* as a Sequel to Acts," in *The Book of Acts in Its Ancient Literary Setting*, ed. Bruce W. Winter and Andrew D. Clarke, vol. 1 of *The Book of Acts in Its First Century Setting*, ed. Bruce Winter (Grand Rapids: Eerdmans, 1993), 113–14; cf. Pervo, *Acts of Paul*, 286.

14. Trans. Pervo, *Acts of Paul*, 308.

15. On the complex but basically positive relationship of the Acts of Paul to what Pervo calls "the New Prophecy," see Pervo, *Acts of Paul*, 72, 285.

16. Nicola Camerlenghi, *St. Paul's Outside the Walls: A Roman Basilica, from Antiquity to the Modern Era* (Cambridge: Cambridge University Press, 2018), 28–31. See especially fig. 1.6 with the drawing of the structure in *opus reticulatum* from Virginio Vespignani's sketchbook.

17. On Origen's familiarity with the Acts of Paul, see Pervo, *Acts of Paul*, 44–46.

18. Eusebius did, however, think of the Acts of Paul as "spurious" (ἐν τοῖς νόθοις, *Hist. eccl.* 3.25.4)

19. 1 Clem. says that Peter and Paul bore witness to "the governors" (5.7)

20. Harry W. Tajra, *The Martyrdom of St. Paul*, WUNT 2.67 (Tübingen: Mohr Siebeck, 1994), 20–27.

21. Jens Herzer, "The Mission and the End of Paul between Strategy and Reality: A Response to Rainer Riesner," in *The Last Years of Paul: Essays from the Tarragona Conference, June 2013*, ed. Armand Puig i Tàrrech, John M. G. Barclay, and Jörg Frey, WUNT 1.352 (Tübingen: Mohr Siebeck, 2015), 425.

22. Tajra, *Martyrdom of St. Paul*, 111. Much depends on the translation of τὸ τέρμα in 1 Clem. 5.7. Herzer ("The Mission and the End of Paul," 425), for example, translates the expression as "the turning point of the West," or, less literally, "the border *to* the West" (emphasis in the original).

23. Armstrong, "Victorinus of Pettau," 1–34. For the specific date, see p. 32n102. Pettau is modern-day Ptuj in northeastern Slovenia.

24. Perhaps this common idea forms the basis for the elaborate fantasy about Paul's journey from Rome to Spain and return to Rome found in a single manuscript located in a library in Vercelli, a city in northwest Italy (the so-called *Actus Vercellenses*). The manuscript itself dates from the sixth or seventh century but is probably a translation of a fourth- or fifth-century Greek text (J. K. Elliott, *The Apocryphal New Testament* [Oxford: Clarendon, 1993], 391). It is often thought to be a translation of something Eusebius called "the Acts bearing [Peter's] name" (τῶν ἐπικεκλημένων αὐτοῦ πράξεων, *Hist. eccl.* 3.3.2 [Lake, LCL]), although there is no single extant text of such a work. On all this, see Matthew C. Baldwin, *Whose "Acts of Peter"? Text and Historical Context of the "Actus Vercellenses,"* WUNT 2.196 (Tübingen: Mohr Siebeck, 2005), 1–11.

25. Cf. Lawlor and Oulton (*Eusebius*, 2:73), although they thought the phrase referred to all three Pastoral Epistles. Eusebius's interest seems confined to 2 Timothy.

26. Herzer, "The Mission and the End of Paul," 427.

Bibliography

Adam-Veleni, P. "Thessalonike." Pages 545–62 in *Brill's Companion to Ancient Macedon: Studies in the Archaeology and History of Macedon, 650 BC–300 AD*. Edited by Robin Lane Fox. Leiden: Brill, 2011.

Alexander, William Menzies. "St. Paul's Infirmity." *ExpTim* 15 (1903–1904): 545–48.

Allison, Dale C. "Acts 9:1–9, 22:6–11, 26:12–18: Paul and Ezekiel." *JBL* 135 (2016): 807–26.

Allo, E.-B. *Saint Paul Seconde Épître aux Corinthiens*. 2nd ed. Ebib. Paris: Lecoffre, 1937.

Armstrong, Jonathan J. "Victorinus of Pettau as the Author of the Canon Muratori." *VigChr* 62 (2008): 1–34.

Arnold, Clinton E. *The Colossian Syncretism: The Interface between Christianity and Folk Belief at Colossae*. WUNT 2.77. Tübingen: Mohr Siebeck, 1995.

———. *Ephesians*. ZECNT. Grand Rapids: Zondervan, 2010.

———. "Initiation, Vision, and Spiritual Power: The Hellenistic Dimensions of the Problem at Colossae." Pages 173–86 in *Colossians, Hierapolis, and Laodicea*. WGRWSup 16. Vol. 5 of *The First Urban Churches*. Edited by James R. Harrison and L. L. Welborn. Atlanta: SBL, 2019.

———. "Sceva, Solomon, and Shamanism: The Jewish Roots of the Problem at Colossae." *JETS* 55 (2012): 7–26.

Ascough, Richard S. "Civic Pride at Philippi: The Text Critical Problem of Acts 16.12." *NTS* 44 (1998): 93–103.

Ashby, Thomas, and G. McN. Rushforth. "Roman Malta." *JRS* 5 (1915): 23–80.

Atkins, Christopher S. "Textualizing Pauline Revelation: Self-Referentiality, Reading Practices, and Pseudepigraphy in Ephesians." *HTR* 116 (2023): 24–43.

Bablitz, Leanne. "Roman Society in the Courtroom." Pages 317–34 in *The Oxford Handbook of Social Relations in the Roman World*. Edited by Michael Peachin. Oxford: Oxford University Press, 2011.

Bailey, Daniel P. "Biblical and Greco-Roman Uses of *Hilastērion* in Romans 3:25 and 4 Maccabees 17:22." Pages 824–68 in Peter Stuhlmacher, *Biblical Theology of the New Testament*. Translated and edited by Daniel P. Bailey. Grand Rapids: Eerdmans, 2018.

Bailey, John A. "Who Wrote II Thessalonians?" *NTS* 25 (1979): 131–45.

Baldwin, Matthew C. *Whose "Acts of Peter"? Text and Historical Context of the "Actus Vercellenses."* WUNT 2.196. Tübingen: Mohr Siebeck, 2005.

Barclay, John M. G. "Paul, Philemon and the Dilemma of Christian Slave-Ownership." *NTS* 37 (1991): 161–86.

Bar-Kochva, B. "Sēron and Cestius Gallus at Beith Ḥoron." *PEQ* 108 (1976): 13–21.

Barnes, Timothy D. "Tertullian's 'Scorpiace.'" *JTS* 20 (1969): 105–32.

Barnett, Paul. *The Second Epistle to the Corinthians*. NICNT. Grand Rapids: Eerdmans, 1997.

Barrett, C. K. *A Commentary on the Second Epistle to the Corinthians*. San Francisco: Harper & Row, 1973.

———. *A Critical and Exegetical Commentary on the Acts of the Apostles*. ICC. 2 vols. Edinburgh: T&T Clark, 1994–1998.

———. *Essays on Paul*. Philadelphia: Westminster, 1982.

———. *The First Epistle to the Corinthians*. New York: Harper & Row, 1968.

———. "Paulus als Missionar und Theologe." *ZTK* 86 (1989): 18–32.

Bauckham, Richard. "The *Acts of Paul* as a Sequel to Acts." Pages 105–52 in *The Book of Acts in Its Ancient Literary Setting*. Edited by Bruce W. Winter and Andrew D. Clarke. Vol. 1 of *The Book of Acts in Its First Century Setting*. Edited by Bruce W. Winter. Grand Rapids: Eerdmans, 1993.

———. *Jesus and the Eyewitnesses: The Gospels as Eyewitness Testimony*. Grand Rapids: Eerdmans, 2006.

———. *Jesus and the God of Israel: God Crucified and Other Studies on the New Testament's Christology of Divine Identity*. Grand Rapids: Eerdmans, 2008.

Bauer, Walter. *Orthodoxy and Heresy in Earliest Christianity*. Philadelphia: Fortress, 1971.

Baum, Armin D. "Stylistic Diversity in the *Corpus Ciceronianum* and in the *Corpus Paulinum*: A Comparison and Some Conclusions." *Journal for the Study of Paul and His Letters* 9 (2019): 118–57.

Beale, G. K. *1–2 Thessalonians*. IVP New Testament Commentary 13. Downers Grove, IL: InterVarsity, 2003.

Beard, Mary, John North, and Simon Price. *Religions of Rome*. 2 vols. Cambridge: Cambridge University Press, 1998.

Becker, Eve-Marie. *The Birth of Christian History: Memory and Time from Mark to Luke-Acts*. Anchor Yale Bible Reference Library. New Haven, CT: Yale University Press, 2017.

Beebe, H. Keith. "Caesarea Maritima: Its Strategic and Political Significance to Rome." *JNES* 42 (1983): 195–207.

Benjamin, Anna, and Antony E. Raubitschek. "Arae Augusti." *Hesperia* 28 (1959): 65–85.

Bibliography

Bernard, J. H. *The Pastoral Epistles*. CGTSC. London: C. J. Clay and Sons, 1899.
Best, Ernest. *1 Peter*. NCB. London: Marshall, Morgan & Scott, 1971.
———. *A Commentary on the First and Second Epistles to the Thessalonians*. HNTC. New York: Harper & Row, 1972.
———. *A Critical and Exegetical Commentary on Ephesians*. ICC. London: T&T Clark, 1998.
Betz, Hans Dieter, ed. *The Greek Magical Papyri in Translation*. 2nd ed. Chicago: University of Chicago Press, 1992.
Billings, Bradly S. "From House Church to Tenement Church: Domestic Space and the Development of Early Urban Christianity—the Example of Ephesus." *JTS* 62 (2011): 541–69.
Bingham, Sandra J. "The Praetorian Guard in the Political and Social Life of Julio-Claudian Rome." PhD diss., University of British Columbia, 1997.
Block, Daniel I. *The Book of Ezekiel, Chapters 1–24*. NICOT. Grand Rapids: Eerdmans, 1997.
Blunt, A. W. F. *The Apologies of Justin Martyr*. Ancient Texts and Translations. Eugene, OR: Wipf & Stock, 2006.
Bockmuehl, Markus. *The Epistle to the Philippians*. BNTC 11. Peabody, MA: Hendrickson, 1998.
———. *The Remembered Peter in Ancient Reception and Modern Debate*. WUNT 1.262. Tübingen: Mohr Siebeck, 2010.
Bohak, Gideon. *Ancient Jewish Magic: A History*. Cambridge: Cambridge University Press, 2008.
Böhler, Dieter. "Saul, Saul, warum verfolgst du mich? Zum alttestamentlichen Hintergrund der Damaskusberichte (Apg 9; 22; 26)." *BZ* 61 (2017): 137–47.
Bowen, Clayton R. "Are Paul's Prison Letters from Ephesus?" *AmJT* 24 (1920): 112–35.
Bowers, W. P. "Paul's Route through Mysia: A Note on Acts 16:8." *JTS* 30 (1979): 507–11.
Bowersock, G. W. *Roman Arabia*. Cambridge, MA: Harvard University Press, 1983.
Brélaz, Cédric. "The Provincial Contexts of Paul's Imprisonments: Law Enforcement and Criminal Procedure in the Roman East." *JSNT* 43 (2021): 485–507.
Breytenbach, Cilliers. "Probable Reasons for Paul's Unfruitful Missionary Attempts in Asia Minor: A Note on Acts 16:6–7." Pages 157–69 in *Die Apostelgeschichte und Die Hellenistische Geschichtsschreibung: Festschrift für Eckhard Plümacher zu seinem 65. Geburtstag*. Edited by Cilliers Breytenbach and Jens Schröter. Leiden: Brill, 2004.
Breytenbach, Cilliers, and Christiane Zimmermann. *Early Christianity in Lycaonia and Adjacent Areas: From Paul to Amphilochius of Iconium*. AJEC 101/ECAM 2. Leiden: Brill, 2018.
Brookes, Alan C. "Minturnae: The Via Appia Bridge." *American Journal of Archaeology* 78 (1974): 41–48.

Bruce, F. F. *1 and 2 Thessalonians*. WBC 45. Waco, TX: Word, 1982.
———. *The Book of the Acts*. Rev. ed. NICNT. Grand Rapids: Eerdmans, 1988.
———. *The Epistle to the Galatians: A Commentary on the Greek Text*. NIGTC. Grand Rapids: Eerdmans, 1982.
———. "Paul and the Athenians." *ExpTim* 88 (1976): 8–12.
———. *Paul: Apostle of the Heart Set Free*. Grand Rapids: Eerdmans, 1977.
Bruggen, Jakob van. *Die geschichtliche Einordnung der Pastoralbriefe*. Wuppertal: R. Brockhaus, 1981.
———. *Paul: Pioneer for Israel's Messiah*. Translated by Ed M. van der Maas. Phillipsburg, NJ: P&R Publishing, 2005.
Burchard, Christoph. *Der dreizehnte Zeuge: Traditions- und kompositionsgeschichtliche Untersuchungen zu Lukas' Darstellung der Frühzeit des Paulus*. FRLANT 103. Göttingen: Vandenhoeck & Ruprecht, 1970.
Burnett, D. Clint. "Imperial Divine Honors in Julio-Claudian Thessalonica and the Thessalonian Correspondence." *JBL* 139 (2020): 567–89.
Bury, R. G., trans. *Plato: Timaeus, Critias, Cleitophon, Menexenus, Epistles*. LCL 234. Cambridge: Harvard University Press, 1929.
Cadwallader, Alan H. *Fragments of Colossae: Sifting through the Traces*. Adelaide, SA: ATF Press, 2015.
Camerlenghi, Nicola. *St. Paul's Outside the Walls: A Roman Basilica, from Antiquity to the Modern Era*. Cambridge: Cambridge University Press, 2018.
Campbell, Douglas A. "An Anchor for Pauline Chronology: Paul's Flight from 'The Ethnarch of King Aretas' (2 Corinthians 11:32–33)." *JBL* 121 (2002): 279–302.
———. *The Deliverance of God: An Apocalyptic Rereading of Justification in Paul*. Grand Rapids: Eerdmans, 2009.
———. *Framing Paul: An Epistolary Biography*. Grand Rapids: Eerdmans, 2014.
Carandini, Andrea, and Paolo Carafa, eds. *The Atlas of Ancient Rome*. 2 vols. Translated by Andrew Campbell Halavais. Princeton, NJ: Princeton University Press, 2017.
Casson, Lionel. *The Ancient Mariners: Seafarers and Sea Fighters of the Mediterranean in Ancient Times*. 2nd ed. Princeton, NJ: Princeton University Press, 1991.
———. *Ships and Seamanship in the Ancient World*. 2nd ed. Baltimore: Johns Hopkins University Press: 1995.
———. "Speed under Sail of Ancient Ships." *TAPA* 82 (1951): 136–48.
Castagnoli, Ferdinando. *Roma Antica: Profilo Urbanistico*. Milan: Jouvence, 1978.
Chadwick, Henry, trans. and ed. *Origen: Contra Celsum*. Cambridge: Cambridge University Press, 1953.
Champlin, Edward. *Nero*. Cambridge, MA: Harvard University Press, 2003.
Chapple, Allan. "Paul and Illyricum." *RTR* 72 (2013): 20–35.
———. "Why Spain? Paul and His Mission Plans." *Journal for the Study of Paul and His Letters* 1 (2011): 193–212.

Bibliography

Chesnutt, Randall D. *From Death to Life: Conversion in Joseph and Aseneth*. JSPSup 16. Sheffield: Sheffield Academic Press, 1995.

Claridge, Amanda. *Rome: An Oxford Archaeological Guide*. 2nd ed. Oxford: Oxford University Press, 2010.

Collins, John N. "The Mediatorial Aspect of Paul's Role as *Diakonos*." *ABR* 40 (1992): 34–44.

Conzelmann, Hans. *Acts of the Apostles*. Hermeneia. Edited by Eldon J. Epp with Christopher R. Matthews. Translated by James Limberg, A. Thomas Kraabel, and Donald H. Juel. Philadelphia: Fortress, 1987.

Cotton, Hannah M., and Werner Eck. "Governors and Their Personnel on Latin Inscriptions from Caesarea Maritima." *Cathedra: For the History of Eretz Israel and Its Yishuv* 122 (2006): 31–52.

Cranfield, C. E. B. *The Epistle to the Romans*. ICC. 2 vols. Edinburgh: T & T Clark, 1975–1979.

Crook, J. A. *Legal Advocacy in the Roman World*. Ithaca, NY: Cornell University Press, 1995.

Cullmann, Oscar. *Peter: Disciple, Apostle, Martyr*. Translated by Floyd V. Filson. Philadelphia: Westminster, 1953.

Cumont, Franz. "La lettre de Claude aux Alexandrins et les Actes des Apôtres." *RHR* 91 (1925): 3–6.

Danby, Herbert. *The Mishnah: Translated from the Hebrew with Introduction and Brief Explanatory Notes*. Oxford: Oxford University Press, 1933.

Danker, F. W. "Menander and the New Testament." *NTS* 10 (1964): 365–68.

D'Arms, John H. *Romans on the Bay of Naples: A Social and Cultural Study of the Villas and Their Owners from 150 B.C. to A.D. 400*. Cambridge, MA: Harvard University Press, 1970.

Das, A. Andrew. *Galatians*. Concordia Commentary. Saint Louis: Concordia, 2014.

Davidson, Samuel. *An Introduction to the New Testament*. 3 vols. London: Samuel Bagster, 1848.

Davies, W. D., and Dale C. Allison, *The Gospel according to Matthew*. ICC. 3 vols. London: T&T Clark, 1991–1997.

Deidun, T. J. *New Covenant Morality in Paul*. AnBib 89. Rome: Biblical Institute Press, 1981.

Deissmann, Adolf. *Light from the Ancient East: The New Testament Illustrated by Recently Discovered Texts of the Greco-Roman World*. Translated by Lionel R. M. Strachan. 2nd ed. London: Hodder & Stoughton, 1911.

deSilva, David A. *Ephesians*. New Cambridge Bible Commentary. Cambridge: Cambridge University Press, 2022.

———. *The Letter to the Galatians*. NICNT. Grand Rapids: Eerdmans, 2018.

Diamond, Eliezer. "An Israelite Self-Offering in the Priestly Code: A New Perspective on the Nazirite." *JQR* 88 (1997): 1–18.

Dibelius, Martin, and Hans Conzelmann. *The Pastoral Epistles*. Hermeneia. Translated by Philip Buttolph and Adela Yarbro. Philadelphia: Fortress, 1972.

Donelson, Lewis R. *Pseudepigraphy and Ethical Argument in the Pastoral Epistles*. HUT 22. Tübingen: Mohr Siebeck, 1986.

Downey, Glanville. *A History of Antioch in Syria from Seleucus to the Arab Conquest*. Princeton, NJ: Princeton University Press, 1961.

Duncan, George S. *St. Paul's Ephesian Ministry: A Reconstruction*. New York: Charles Scribner's Sons, 1930.

Dunn, James D. G. *The Acts of the Apostles*. Narrative Commentaries. Valley Forge, PA: Trinity Press International, 1996.

———. *Beginning from Jerusalem*. Vol. 2 of *Christianity in the Making*. 3 vols. Grand Rapids: Eerdmans, 2009.

———. *The Epistles to the Colossians and to Philemon: A Commentary on the Greek Text*. NIGTC. Grand Rapids: Eerdmans, 1996.

———. *Neither Jew nor Greek: A Contested Identity*. Vol. 3 of *Christianity in the Making*. Grand Rapids: Eerdmans, 2015.

Dzino, Danijel. *Illyricum in Roman Politics: 229 BC–AD 68*. Cambridge: Cambridge University Press, 2010.

Eastman, David L. "Jealousy, Internal Strife, and the Deaths of Peter and Paul: A Reassessment of *1 Clement*." *ZAC* 18 (2013): 34–53.

———. *Paul the Martyr: The Cult of the Apostle in the Latin West*. WAWSup 4. Atlanta: Society of Biblical Literature, 2011.

Ehrman, Bart D. *Forgery and Counterforgery: The Use of Literary Deceit in Early Christian Polemics*. Oxford: Oxford University Press, 2013.

Elliott, J. K., ed. *The Apocryphal New Testament*. Oxford: Clarendon, 1993.

Elliott, John H. *1 Peter*. AB 37B. New York: Doubleday, 2000.

Emde Boas, Evert van, Albert Rijksbaron, Luuk Huitink, and Mathieu de Bakker. *The Cambridge Grammar of Classical Greek*. Cambridge: Cambridge University Press, 2019.

Enslin, Morton Scott. "Once Again, Luke and Paul." *ZNW* 61 (1970): 253–71.

Evans, Craig A. *Mark 8:27–16:20*. WBC 34B. Grand Rapids: Zondervan, 1988.

Fairclough, H. R., trans. *Horace: Satires, Epistles, and Art of Poetry*. LCL 194. Cambridge, MA: Harvard University Press, 1929.

Fant, Clyde E., and Mitchell G. Reddish. *A Guide to Biblical Sites in Greece and Turkey*. Oxford: Oxford University Press, 2003.

Fee, Gordon D. *1 and 2 Timothy, Titus*. Good News Commentary. New York: Harper & Row, 1984.

———. *The First and Second Letters to the Thessalonians*. NICNT. Grand Rapids: Eerdmans, 2009.

———. *The First Epistle to the Corinthians*. NICNT. Grand Rapids: Eerdmans, 1987.

———. *God's Empowering Presence: The Holy Spirit in the Letters of Paul*. Peabody, MA: Hendrickson, 1994.

Bibliography

———. *Paul's Letter to the Philippians*. NICNT. Grand Rapids: Eerdmans, 1995.

Feldmeier, Reinhard. *Der erste Brief des Petrus*. THKNT 15/I. Leipzig: Evangelische Verlagsanstalt, 2005.

Finney, Mark T. "*Servile Supplicium*: Shame and the Deuteronomic Curse—Crucifixion in Its Cultural Context." *BTB* 43 (2013): 124–34.

Fitzmyer, Joseph A. *The Acts of the Apostles*. AB 31. New Haven, CT: Yale University Press, 1998.

———. "Crucifixion in Ancient Palestine, Qumran Literature, and the New Testament." *CBQ* 40 (1978): 493–513.

———. *First Corinthians*. AB 32. New Haven, CT: Yale University Press, 2008.

———. *Romans*. AB 33. New York: Doubleday, 1993.

Flexsenhar, Michael, III. *Christians in Caesar's Household: The Emperor's Slaves in the Makings of Christianity*. Inventing Christianity. University Park: Pennsylvania State University Press, 2019.

———. "The Provenance of Philippians and Why It Matters: Old Questions, New Approaches." *JSNT* 42 (2019): 18–45.

Foster, Paul. "Who Wrote 2 Thessalonians? A Fresh Look at an Old Problem." *JSNT* 35 (2012): 150–75.

Frazer, J. G. *Pausanias and Other Greek Sketches*. London: Macmillan, 1900.

Fredriksen, Paula. "How Later Contexts Affect Pauline Content, or: Retrospect Is the Mother of Anachronism." Pages 17–51 in *Jews and Christians in the First and Second Centuries: How to Write Their History*. Edited by Peter J. Tomson and Joshua Schwartz. Leiden: Brill, 2014.

French, David H. *An Album of Maps*. Fasc. 3.9 of *Milestones*. Vol. 3 of *Roman Roads and Milestones of Asia Minor*. Electronic Monograph 9. Ankara: British Institute at Ankara, 2016.

———. *Galatia*. Fasc. 3.2 of *Milestones*. Vol. 3 of *Roman Roads and Milestones of Asia Minor*. Electronic Monograph 2. Ankara: British Institute at Ankara, 2012.

———. "Pre- and Early-Roman Roads of Asia Minor: The Persian Royal Road." *Iran* 36 (1998): 15–43.

Friesen, Steven J. "Asiarchs." *ZPE* 126 (1999): 275–90.

Furnish, Victor Paul. *II Corinthians*, AB 32A. Garden City, NY: Doubleday, 1984.

Gabizon, Michael. "The Development of the Matrilineal Principle in Ezra, *Jubilees*, and Acts." *JSP* 27 (2017): 143–60.

Gapp, Kenneth Sperber. "The Universal Famine under Claudius." *HTR* 28 (1935): 258–65.

Garland, David E. *1 Corinthians*. BECNT. Grand Rapids: Baker, 2003.

Garnsey, Peter. "Legal Privilege in the Roman Empire." *Past & Present* 41 (1968): 3–24.

Gildersleeve, Basil L. *The Apologies of Justin Martyr to Which Is Appended the Epistle to Diognetus*. New York: Harper, 1877.

Gill, David W. J. "Macedonia." Pages 397–417 in *The Book of Acts in Its Greco-Roman*

Setting. Edited by David W. J. Gill and Conrad Gempf. Vol. 2 of *The Book of Acts in Its First Century Setting*. Edited by Bruce W. Winter. 6 vols. Grand Rapids: Eerdmans, 1994.

Gilliard, F. D. "The Problem of the Antisemitic Comma between 1 Thessalonians 2.14 and 15." *NTS* 35 (1989): 481–502.

Giszczak, Mark B. "The Rhetoric and Social Practice of Excommunication in 2 Thessalonians 3:6–15." *CBQ* 83 (2021): 95–114.

Glad, Clarence E. "Frank Speech, Flattery, and Friendship in Philodemus." Pages 21–59 in *Friendship, Flattery, and Frankness of Speech: Studies on Friendship in the New Testament World*. Edited by John T. Fitzgerald. Supplements to Novum Testamentum 82. Leiden: Brill, 1996.

Goodman, Martin. *The Ruling Class of Judaea: The Origins of the Jewish Revolt against Rome, A.D. 66–70*. Cambridge: Cambridge University Press, 1987.

Gordon, Richard. "The Roman Imperial Cult and the Question of Power." Pages 37–70 in *The Religious History of the Roman Empire*. Edited by J. A. North and S. R. F. Price. Oxford: Oxford University Press, 2011.

Gosnell, Peter W. "Ephesians 5:18–20 and Mealtime Propriety." *TynBul* 44 (1993): 363–71.

Greaves, Alan M. *Miletos: A History*. London: Routledge, 2002.

Greenwood, L. H. G. *Against Caecilius. Against Verres, Part 1*. Vol 1 of *Cicero: The Verrine Orations*. 2 vols. LCL 221. Cambridge, MA: Harvard University Press, 1958.

Greer, Rowan A., trans. *Theodore of Mopsuestia: Commentary on the Minor Pauline Epistles*. WGRW 26. Atlanta: Society of Biblical Literature, 2010.

Grenfell, Bernard P., and Arthur S. Hunt, ed. and trans. *The Oxyrhynchus Papyri*. 85 vols. London: Egypt Exploration Fund, 1898–2020.

Grotius, Hugo. *Annotationes in Novum Testamentum*. Rev. ed. 9 vols. Groningen: W. Zuidema, 1826–1834.

Gruen, Erich S. *The Construct of Jewish Identity in Hellenistic Judaism*. Berlin: de Gruyter, 2016.

———. *Diaspora: Jews amidst Greeks and Romans*. Cambridge, MA: Harvard University Press, 2002.

Grünstäudl, Wolfgang. "Hidden in Praise." Pages 375–89 in *The Last Years of Paul: Essays from the Tarragona Conference, June 2013*. Edited by Armand Puig i Tàrrech, John M. G. Barclay, and Jörg Frey. WUNT 1.352. Tübingen: Mohr Siebeck, 2015.

Gundry, Robert H. *Mark: A Commentary on His Apology for the Cross*. Grand Rapids: Eerdmans, 1993.

Gupta, Nijay K. "The Thessalonian Believers, Formerly 'Pagans' or 'God-Fearers'? Challenging a Stubborn Consensus." *Neot* 52 (2018): 91–113.

Haacker, Klaus. *Die Apostelgeschichte*. THKNT. Stuttgart: Kohlhammer, 2019.

Bibliography

Hadas, Moses. *Aristeas to Philocrates [Letter of Aristeas]*. Jewish Apocryphal Literature. New York: Harper, 1951.

Haenchen, Ernst. *Acts of the Apostles: A Commentary*. Louisville: Westminster John Knox, 1971.

Hansen, G. Walter. "Galatia." Pages 377–96 in *The Book of Acts in Its Greco-Roman Setting*, ed. David W. J. Gill and Conrad Gempf. Vol. 2 of *The Book of Acts in Its First Century Setting*, ed. Bruce W. Winter, 6 vols. Grand Rapids: Eerdmans, 1994.

Hanson, Victor Davis. "Introduction." Pages ix–xxiii in *The Landmark Thucydides: A Comprehensive Guide to the Peloponnesian War*. Edited by Robert B. Strassler. New York: Free Press, 1996.

Harrington, Hannah K. "Did the Pharisees Eat Ordinary Food in a State of Ritual Purity?" *JSJ* 26 (1995): 42–54.

Harris, Murray J. *The Second Epistle to the Corinthians*. NIGTC. Grand Rapids: Eerdmans, 2005.

Harrison, James R. "Paul and the *Agōnothetai* at Corinth: Engaging the Civic Values of Antiquity." Pages 271–326 in *Roman Corinth*. Vol. 2 of *The First Urban Churches*. Edited by James R. Jarrison and L. L. Welborn. WGRWSup 8. Atlanta: SBL, 2016.

———. *Paul and the Ancient Celebrity Circuit: The Cross and Moral Transformation*. WUNT 1.430. Tübingen: Mohr Siebeck, 2019.

———. *Paul and the Imperial Authorities at Thessalonica and Rome*. WUNT 1.273. Tübingen: Mohr Siebeck, 2011.

Hawthorne, Gerald F. *Philippians*. Revised and expanded by Ralph P. Martin. WBC 43. n.p.: Thomas Nelson, 2004.

Heilig, Christoph. *The Apostle and the Empire: Paul's Implicit and Explicit Criticism of Rome*. Grand Rapids: Eerdmans, 2022.

Heininger, Bernhard. "The Reception of Paul in the First Century: The Deutero- and Trito-Pauline Letters and the Image of Paul in Acts." Pages 309–38 in *Paul: Life, Setting, Work, Letters*. Edited by Oda Wischmeyer. Translated by Helen S. Heron and Dieter T. Roth. London: Continuum, 2012.

Hemer, Colin J. "The Adjective 'Phrygia.'" *JTS* 27 (1976): 122–26.

———. "Alexandria Troas." *TynBul* 26 (1975): 79–112.

———. *Book of Acts in the Setting of Hellenistic History*. Edited by Conrad H. Gempf. Winona Lake, IN: Eisenbrauns, 1990.

———. "First Person Narrative in Acts 27–28." *TynBul* 36 (1985): 79–109.

———. "Paul at Athens: A Topographical Note." *NTS* 20 (1974): 341–50.

———. "Phrygia: A Further Note." *JTS* 28 (1977): 99–101.

———. "The Speeches of Acts II. The Areopagus Address." *TynBul* 40 (1989): 239–59.

Hendrix, Holland Lee. "Archaeology and Eschatology at Thessalonica." Pages 107–

18 in *The Future of Early Christianity: Essays in Honor of Helmut Koester*. Edited by Birger A. Pearson. Minneapolis: Fortress, 1991.

Hengel, Martin. *Acts and the History of Earliest Christianity*. London: SCM, 1979.

———. *The Atonement: The Origins of the Doctrine in the New Testament*. Translated by John Bowden. Philadelphia: Fortress, 1981.

———. *Crucifixion in the Ancient World and the Folly of the Message of the Cross*. Philadelphia: Fortress, 1977.

———. "The Geography of Palestine in Acts." Pages 27–78 in *The Book of Acts in Its Palestinian Setting*. Edited by Richard Bauckham. Vol. 4 of *The Book of Acts in Its First Century Setting*. Edited by Bruce W. Winter. Grand Rapids: Eerdmans, 1995.

———. "Paul in Arabia." *BBR* 12 (2002): 47–66.

———. *The Pre-Christian Paul*. Translated by John Bowden. London: SCM, 1991.

———. *Saint Peter: The Underestimated Apostle*. Translated by Thomas H. Trapp. Grand Rapids: Eerdmans, 2006.

———. *The Zealots: Investigations into the Jewish Freedom Movement in the Period from Herod I until 70 A.D.* Translated by David Smith. Edinburgh: T&T Clark, 1989.

Hengel, Martin, and Anna Maria Schwemer, *Paul between Damascus and Antioch: The Unknown Years*. Translated by John Bowden. Louisville: Westminster John Knox, 1997.

Hengel, Martin, and Roland Deines. "E. P. Sanders' 'Common Judaism,' Jesus, and the Pharisees." *JTS* 46 (1995): 1–70.

Herzer, Jens. "The Mission and the End of Paul between Strategy and Reality: A Response to Rainer Riesner." Pages 411–31 in *The Last Years of Paul: Essays from the Tarragona Conference, June 2013*. Edited by Armand Puig i Tàrrech, John M. G. Barclay, and Jörg Frey. WUNT 1.352. Tübingen: Mohr Siebeck, 2015.

———. "Zwischen Mythos und Wahrheit: Neue Perspektiven auf die sogenannten Pastoralbriefe." *NTS* 63 (2017): 428–50.

Hickling, C. J. A. "The Sequence of Thought in II Corinthians, Chapter Three." *NTS* 21 (1975): 380–95.

Hock, Ronald F. "The Workshop as a Social Setting for Paul's Missionary Preaching." *CBQ* 41 (1979): 438–50.

Hoehner, Harold W. *Ephesians: An Exegetical Commentary*. Grand Rapids: Baker, 2002.

Hoklotubbe, T. Christopher. "Civilized Christ-Followers among Barbaric Cretans and Superstitious Judeans: Negotiating Ethnic Hierarchies in Titus 1:10–14." *JBL* 140 (2021): 369–90.

Holladay, Carl R. *Acts: A Commentary*. NTL. Louisville: Westminster John Knox, 2016.

Holmes, Michael W., ed. and trans. *The Apostolic Fathers: Greek Texts and English Translations*. 3rd ed. Grand Rapids: Baker, 2007.

Bibliography

Holtz, Traugott. *Der erste Brief an die Thessalonicher*. EKK 13. 2nd ed. Zürich: Benziger, 1990.
Holtzmann, H. J. *Die Pastoralbriefe*. Leipzig: Wilhelm Engelmann, 1880.
Horn, Friedrich W. "Paulus, das Nasiräat und die Nasiräer." *NovT* 39 (1997): 13–28.
Horrell, David G. *The Making of Christian Morality: Reading Paul in Ancient and Modern Contexts*. Grand Rapids: Eerdmans, 2019.
Horsley, G. H. R., ed. *New Documents Illustrating Early Christianity*. Vol. 4, *A Review of the Greek Inscriptions and Papyri Published in 1979*. North Ryde, NSW, Australia: Ancient History Documentary Research Centre, Macquarie University, 1987.
Horsley, Richard A., and John S. Hanson. *Bandits, Prophets, and Messiahs: Popular Movements in the Time of Jesus*. Harrisburg, PA: Trinity Press International, 1999.
Horst, Pieter W. van der. *Philo's "Flaccus": The First Pogrom*. Philo of Alexandria Commentary Series 2. Leiden: Brill, 2003.
House, Paul R. *Daniel*. TOTC. Downers Grove, IL: IVP Academic, 2018.
———. *Isaiah*. 2 vols. Ross-shire: Christian Focus, 2019.
Hughes, Philip Edgcumbe. *Paul's Second Epistle to the Corinthians*. New London Commentary. London: Marshall, Morgan & Scott, 1961.
Hultgren, Arland J. *Paul's Letter to the Romans: A Commentary*. Grand Rapids: Eerdmans, 2011.
Hultgren, Stephen. "*Hilastērion* (Rom. 3:25) and the Union of Divine Justice and Mercy. Part I: The Convergence of Temple and Martyrdom Theologies." *JTS* 70 (2019): 69–109.
———. "*Hilastērion* (Rom. 3:25) and the Union of Divine Justice and Mercy. Part II: Atonement in the Old Testament and in Romans 1–5." *JTS* 70 (2019): 546–99.
Hunt, Arthur S. *The Oxyrhynchus Papyri*. Part 9. London: Egypt Exploration Fund, 1912.
Hunt, Arthur S., and C. C. Edgar, eds. *Official Documents*. Vol. 2 of *Select Papyri*. LCL 282. Cambridge, MA: Harvard University Press, 1934.
Huther, J. E. *Critical and Exegetical Handbook to the Epistles to Timothy and Titus*. 6th ed. Translated by David Hunter. New York: Funk & Wagnalls, 1884.
Huttner, Ulrich. *Early Christianity in the Lycus Valley*. Translated by David Green. AGJU 85/ECAM 1. Leiden: Brill, 2013.
Immendörfer, Michael. *Ephesians and Artemis: The Cult of the Great Goddess of Ephesus and the Epistle's Context*. WUNT 2.436. Tübingen: Mohr Siebeck, 2017.
Instone-Brewer, David. *Feasts and Sabbaths: Passover and Atonement*. Vol. 2A of *Traditions of the Rabbis from the Era of the New Testament*. 6 vols. Grand Rapids: Eerdmans, 2011.
———. *Prayer and Agriculture*. Vol. 1 of *Traditions of the Rabbis from the Era of the New Testament*. 6 vols. Grand Rapids: Eerdmans, 2004.

Jeffreys, Elizabeth, Michael Jeffreys, and Roger Scott. *The Chronicle of John Malalas: A Translation*. Melbourne: Australian Association for Byzantine Studies, 1986.
Jervell, Jacob. *Die Apostelgeschichte*. KEK 3. Göttingen: Vandenhoeck & Ruprecht, 1998.
Jewett, Robert. "The Agitators and the Galatian Congregation." *NTS* 17 (1971): 198–212.
———. *Romans: A Commentary*. Hermeneia. Minneapolis: Fortress, 2007.
Johnson, Lewis. "The Pauline Letters from Caesarea." *ExpTim* 68 (1956): 24–26.
Johnson, Luke Timothy. *The Canonical Paul*. Vol. 2 of *Interpreting Paul*. Grand Rapids: Eerdmans, 2021.
———. *The First and Second Letters to Timothy*. AB 35A. New York: Doubleday, 2001.
Jones, A. H. M. *Cities of the Eastern Roman Provinces*. Oxford: Oxford University Press, 1937.
Jones, Christopher P. *Philostratus: The Life of Apollonius of Tyana*, 2 vols. LCL 16–17. Cambridge, MA: Harvard University Press, 2005.
———. *The Roman World of Dio Chrysostom*. Cambridge, MA: Harvard University Press, 1978.
Judge, E. A. "The Early Christians as a Scholastic Community." *JRH* 1 (1960): 4–15.
———. "The Early Christians as a Scholastic Community: Part II." *JRH* 1 (1961): 125–37.
Karakolis, Christos. "'Alle schlugen Sosthenes, Gallio aber kümmerte sich nicht darum' (Apg 18.17)." *ZNW* 99 (2008): 233–46.
Kearsley, R. A. "Women in Public Life in the Roman East: Iunia Theodora, Claudia Metrodora and Phoebe, Benefactress of Paul." *TynBul* 50 (1999): 189–211.
Keener, Craig S. *Acts: An Exegetical Commentary*. 4 vols. Grand Rapids: Baker, 2012–2015.
———. *Galatians: A Commentary*. Grand Rapids: Baker, 2019.
Kelly, J. N. D. *The Pastoral Epistles*. BNTC. Peabody, MA: Hendrickson, 1960.
Kemp, Jerome. "Flattery and Frankness in Horace and Philodemus." *Greece & Rome* 57 (2010): 65–76.
Kidson, Lyn. "1 Timothy: An Administrative Letter." *Early Christianity* 5 (2014): 97–116.
Kim, Seyoon. *The Origin of Paul's Gospel*. Grand Rapids: Eerdmans, 1982.
———. *Paul and the New Perspective: Second Thoughts on the Origin of Paul's Gospel*. Grand Rapids: Eerdmans, 2002.
Klein, Günter. "Paul's Purpose in Writing the Epistle to the Romans." Pages 29–43 in *The Romans Debate*. Edited by Karl P. Donfried. Rev. and exp. ed. Peabody, MA: Hendrickson, 1991.
Knight, George W., III. *The Pastoral Epistles: A Commentary on the Greek Text*. NIGTC. Grand Rapids: Eerdmans, 1992.

Bibliography

Koester, Helmut. *History and Literature of Early Christianity*. Vol. 2 of *Introduction to the New Testament*. Berlin: de Gruyter, 1982.

Koukouli-Chrysanthaki, Ch. "Amphipolis." Pages 409–36 in *Brill's Companion to Ancient Macedon: Studies in the Archaeology and History of Macedon, 650 BC–300 AD*. Edited by Robin J. Lane Fox. Leiden: Brill, 2011.

Kraemer, Ross Shepard. *When Aseneth Met Joseph: A Late Antique Tale of the Biblical Patriarch and His Egyptian Wife, Reconsidered*. New York: Oxford University Press, 1998.

Lake, Kirsopp, and Henry J. Cadbury. *English Translation and Commentary*. Vol. 4 of *The Beginnings of Christianity, Part I: The Acts of the Apostles*. Edited by F. J. Foakes Jackson and Kirsopp Lake. London: Macmillan, 1933.

Lampe, Peter. *From Paul to Valentinus: Christians at Rome in the First Two Centuries*. Edited by Marshall D. Johnson. Translated by Michael Steinhauser. Minneapolis: Fortress, 2003.

———. "Keine 'Sklavenflucht' des Onesimus." *ZNW* 76 (1985): 135–37.

Lang, Friedrich Gustav. "Neues über Lydia? Zur Deutung von 'Pupurhändlerin' in Apg 16,14." *ZNW* 100 (2009): 29–44.

Lawlor, Hugh Jackson, and John Ernest Leonard Oulton, trans. *Eusebius, Bishop of Caesarea: The Ecclesiastical History and the Martyrs of Palestine*. 2 vols. London: SPCK, 1927–1928.

Légasse, Simon. "Paul's Pre-Christian Career according to Acts." Pages 365–90 in *The Book of Acts in Its Palestinian Setting*. Edited by Richard Bauckham. Vol. 4 of *The Book of Acts in Its First Century Setting*. Edited by Bruce W. Winter. Grand Rapids: Eerdmans, 1995.

Leidwanger, Justin. *Roman Seas: A Maritime Archaeology of Eastern Mediterranean Economies*. New York: Oxford University Press, 2020.

Lendon, J. E. "Roman Honor." Pages 376–403 in *The Oxford Handbook of Social Relations in the Roman World*. Edited by Michael Peachin. Oxford: Oxford University Press, 2011.

Lentz, John Clayton, Jr. *Luke's Portrait of Paul*. SNTSMS 77. Cambridge: Cambridge University Press, 1993.

Leon, Harry J. *The Jews of Ancient Rome*. Updated ed. Peabody, MA: Hendrickson, 1995.

Levick, Barbara. *The Government of the Roman Empire: A Sourcebook*. 2nd ed. London: Routledge: 2000.

Lewis, Naphtali, and Meyer Reinhold, eds. *Roman Civilization: Selected Readings*. 2 vols. New York: Columbia University Press, 1951–1955.

Lightfoot, J. B. *Biblical Essays*. London: Macmillan, 1893.

———. *Saint Paul's Epistles to the Colossians and to Philemon*. London: Macmillan, 1879.

———. *Saint Paul's Epistle to the Galatians*. New York: Macmillan, 1896.

———. *Saint Paul's Epistle to the Philippians*. London: Macmillan, 1896.

Lincoln, Andrew T. *Ephesians*. WBC 42. Dallas: Word, 1990.
Liver, J. "The Half-Shekel Offering in Biblical and Post-Biblical Literature." *HTR* 56 (1963): 173–98.
Lock, Walter. *A Critical and Exegetical Commentary on the Pastoral Epistles*. ICC. Edinburgh: T&T Clark, 1924.
Lohmeyer, Ernst. *Die Briefe an die Philipper, Kolosser und an Philemon*. KEK. Göttingen: Vandenhoeck & Ruprecht, 1961.
Lolos, Yannis. "Via Egnatia after Egnatius: Imperial Policy and Inter-regional Contacts." *Mediterranean Historical Review* 22 (2007): 273–93.
Longenecker, Bruce W. *Remember the Poor: Paul, Poverty, and the Greco-Roman World*. Grand Rapids: Eerdmans, 2010.
———. "'Until Christ Is Formed in You': Suprahuman Forces and Moral Character in Galatians." *CBQ* 61 (1999): 92–108.
Longenecker, Richard N. *Galatians*. WBC 41. Dallas, TX: Word, 1990.
———. *Introducing Romans: Critical Issues in Paul's Most Famous Letter*. Grand Rapids: Eerdmans, 2011.
Lüdemann, Gerd. *Early Christianity according to the Traditions in Acts*. Minneapolis: Fortress, 1989.
Lutz, Cora E. *Musonius Rufus, "The Roman Socrates."* Yale Classical Studies 10. New Haven, CT: Yale University Press, 1947.
MacDonald, Margaret Y. *Colossians and Ephesians*. SP 17. Collegeville, MN: Liturgical Press, 2000.
MacDonald, William L. *The Architecture of the Roman Empire*. Rev. ed. 2 vols. New Haven, CT: Yale University Press, 1982–1986.
Mackintosh, Robert. "The Brief Visit to Corinth." *Expositor*, 7th series, 6 (1908): 226–34.
Malherbe, Abraham J. *The Letters to the Thessalonians*. AB 32B. New York: Doubleday, 2000.
———. *Paul and the Thessalonians: The Philosophic Tradition of Pastoral Care*. Philadelphia: Fortress, 1987.
Marcelli, Marina, and Chiara Cicone. "Via Ostiense: Tombe romane presso la Rupe di S. Paolo. Rilievi archeologici e analisi delle strutture (Municipio VIII)." *Bulletino della Commissione Archeologica Comunale di Roma* 120 (2019): 393–97.
Marcus, Joel. *Mark 1–8*. AB 27. New York: Doubleday, 2000.
Marcus, Ralph. *Jewish Antiquities, Books XII–XIV*. Vol. 7 of *Josephus with an English Translation*. Translated by Louis H. Feldman, Ralph Marcus, and H. St. J. Thackeray. 9 vols. LCL. London: William Heinemann, 1961.
Marguerat, Daniel. *Die Apostelgeschichte*. KEK 3. Göttingen: Vandenhoeck & Ruprecht, 2022.
———. "On Why Luke Remains Silent about Paul's End (Acts 28.16–31)." Pages 305–32 in *The Last Years of Paul: Essays from the Tarragona Conference, June*

2013. Edited by Armand Puig i Tàrrech, John M. G. Barclay, and Jörg Frey. WUNT 1.352. Tübingen: Mohr Siebeck, 2015.

Marshall, I. Howard. *The Acts of the Apostles: An Introduction and Commentary*. Tyndale New Testament Commentaries. Grand Rapids: Eerdmans, 1980.

———. *The Pastoral Epistles*. ICC. Edinburgh: T&T Clark, 1999.

Mason, Steve. *Judean War 2: Translation and Commentary*. Vol. 1B of *Flavius Josephus: Translation and Commentary*. Edited by Steve Mason. Leiden: Brill, 2008.

Massey, Preston T. "Cicero, the Pastoral Epistles, and the Issue of Pseudonymity." *ResQ* 56 (2014): 65–84.

McConville, J. G. *Deuteronomy*. Apollos Old Testament Commentaries. Downers Grove, IL: InterVarsity, 2002.

McKechnie, Paul. "Judaean Embassies and Cases before Roman Emperors, AD 44–66." *JTS* 56 (2005): 339–61.

McRay, John. *Archaeology and the New Testament*. Grand Rapids: Baker, 1991.

Menken, M. J. J. "Paradise Regained or Still Lost? Eschatology and Disorderly Behaviour in 2 Thessalonians." *NTS* 38 (1992): 271–89.

Metzger, Bruce M. "Literary Forgeries and Canonical Pseudepigrapha." *JBL* 91 (1972): 3–24.

———. *A Textual Commentary on the Greek New Testament*. 2nd ed. Stuttgart: Deutsche Bibelgesellschaft, 1994.

Millar, Fergus. *The Roman Near East 31 BC–AD 337*. Cambridge, MA: Harvard University Press, 1993.

Miller, Frank Justus. *Ovid: Metamorphoses, Books 1–8*. 3rd ed. LCL 42. Cambridge, MA: Harvard University Press, 1977.

Milner, N. P. "A Roman Bridge at Oinoanda." *Anatolian Studies* 48 (1998): 117–24.

Minns, Denis, and Paul Parvis. *Justin, Philosopher and Martyr: Apologies*. Oxford: Oxford University Press, 2009.

Mitchell, Margaret M. *Paul and the Rhetoric of Reconciliation*. HUT 28. Tübingen: Mohr Siebeck, 1991.

Mitchell, Stephen. *Anatolia: Land, Men, and Gods in Asia Minor*. 2 vols. Oxford: Oxford University Press, 1993.

———. "Iconium and Ninica: Two Double Communities in Roman Asia Minor." *Historia: Zeitschrift für Alte Geschichte* 28 (1979): 409–38.

Mitchell, Stephen, and Marc Waelkens. *Pisidian Antioch: The Site and Its Monuments*. London and Swansea: Duckworth and Classical Press of Wales, 1998.

Mommsen, Theodor, Paul Krueger, and Alan Watson, eds. *The Digest of Justinian*. 4 vols. Philadelphia: University of Pennsylvania Press, 1985.

Montgomery, James A. *The Book of Daniel*. ICC. Edinburgh: T&T Clark, 1927.

Moo, Douglas J. *Galatians*. BECNT. Grand Rapids: Baker, 2013.

———. *The Letter to the Romans*. 2nd ed. NICNT. Grand Rapids: Eerdmans, 2018.

———. *The Letters to the Colossians and to Philemon*. PNTC. Grand Rapids: Eerdmans, 2008.
Moore, Carey A. *Judith*. AB 40. Garden City, NY: Doubleday, 1985.
Mørkholm, Otto. "Antiochus IV." Pages 278–91 in *The Hellenistic Age*. Edited by W. D. Davies and Louis Finkelstein. Vol. 2 of *The Cambridge History of Judaism*. 8 vols. Cambridge: Cambridge University Press, 1990.
Morris, Leon. "ΚΑΙ ΑΠΑΞ ΚΑΙ ΔΙΣ." *NovT* 1 (1956): 205–8.
Morton, James Malcolm. "The Role of the Physical Environment in Ancient Greek Seafaring." PhD diss., University of Edinburgh, 1988.
Mowery, Robert L. "Paul and Caristanius at Pisidian Antioch." *Biblica* 87 (2006): 223–42.
Müller, Peter. *Der Brief an Philemon*. KEK. Göttingen: Vandenhoeck & Ruprecht, 2012.
Müller, Ulrich B. *Der Brief des Paulus an die Philipper*. THKNT 11/1. Leipzig: Evangelische Verlagsanstalt, 1993.
Munck, Johannes. *Paul and the Salvation of Mankind*. Translated by Frank Clarke. Atlanta: John Knox, 1977.
Murphy-O'Connor, Jerome. *Paul: A Critical Life*. Oxford: Clarendon, 1996.
———. *St. Paul's Corinth: Texts and Archaeology*. 3rd ed. rev. and exp. Collegeville, MN: Liturgical Press, 2002.
———. *St. Paul's Ephesus: Texts and Archaeology*. Collegeville, MN: Michael Glazier, 2008.
Musurillo, Herbert. *The Acts of the Christian Martyrs: Introduction, Texts, and Translations*. Oxford: Clarendon, 1972.
Neil, William. *The Acts of the Apostles*. NCB. London: Oliphants, 1973.
———. *The Epistle of Paul to the Thessalonians*. London: Hodder & Stoughton, 1950.
Nes, Jermo van. *Pauline Language and the Pastoral Epistles: A Study of Linguistic Variation in the "Corpus Paulinum."* Linguistic Biblical Studies 16. Leiden: Brill, 2018.
———. "Under Construction: The Building of God's Temple according to Ephesians 2,19–22." Pages 631–44 in *Paul's Graeco-Roman Context*, edited by Cilliers Breytenbach. BETL 277. Leuven: Peeters, 2015.
Nicholl, Colin R. *From Hope to Despair in Thessalonica: Situating 1 and 2 Thessalonians*. SNTSMS 126. Cambridge: Cambridge University Press, 2004.
———. "Michael, the Restrainer Removed (2 Thess. 2:6–7)." *JTS* 51 (2000): 27–53.
Nickelsburg, George W. E. *1 Enoch 1: A Commentary on the Book of 1 Enoch, Chapters 1–36; 81–108*. Hermeneia. Minneapolis: Fortress, 2001.
Nicolotti, Andrea. "The Scourge of Jesus and the Roman Scourge: Historical and Archaeological Evidence." *Journal for the Study of the Historical Jesus* 15 (2017): 1–59.
Nobbs, Alanna. "Cyprus." Pages 279–89 in *The Book of Acts in Its Greco-Roman Setting*. Edited by David W. J. Gill and Conrad Gempf. Vol. 2 of *The Book of*

Bibliography

Acts in Its First Century Setting. Edited by Bruce W. Winter. 6 vols. Grand Rapids: Eerdmans, 1994.
Nock, Arthur Darby. *Essays on Religion and the Ancient World*. 2 vols. Oxford: Clarendon, 1972.
Nolland, J. L. "A Fresh Look at Acts 15.10." *NTS* 27 (1980): 105–15.
Noth, Martin. *The Laws of the Pentateuch and Other Studies*. Translated by D. R. Ap-Thomas. Philadelphia: Fortress, 1966.
Ogg, George. "Derbe." *NTS* 9 (1963): 367–70.
Omerzu, Heike. *Der Prozeß des Paulus: Eine exegetische und rechtshistorische Untersuchung der Apostelgeschichte*. BZNW 115. Berlin: de Gruyter, 2002.
———. "Paul, the *Praetorium* and the Saints from Caesar's Household: Philippians Revisited in Light of Migration Theory." *JSNT* 43 (2021): 450–67.
———. "The Roman Trial against Paul according to Acts 21–26." Pages 187–200 in *The Last Years of Paul: Essays from the Tarragona Conference, June 2013*. Edited by Armand Puig i Tàrrech, John M. G. Barclay, and Jörg Frey. WUNT 1.352. Tübingen: Mohr Siebeck, 2015.
Onur, Fatih. "'The Monument of Roads' at Patara." Pages 570–77 in *Lukka'dan Likya'ya: Sarpedon ve Aziz Nikolaos'un Ülkesi/From Lukka to Lycia: The Country of Sarpedon and St. Nicholas*. Edited by H. Işek and E. Dündar. Anadolu Uygarlıkları Series 5. Istanbul: Yapı Kredi Kültür Sanat Yaıyncılık, 2016.
———. "Two Procuratorian Inscriptions from Perge." *Gephyra* 5 (2008): 53–66.
Origen. *Commentary on the Epistle to the Romans, Books 1–5*. Translated by Thomas P. Scheck. FOC 104. Washington, DC: Catholic University of America Press, 2001.
Osborne, Robert E. "St. Paul's Silent Years." *JBL* 84 (1965): 59–65.
Oster, Richard E. "Ephesus as a Religious Center under the Principate, I: Paganism before Constantine." *ANRW* 18.3:1661–1728. Part 2, *Principat*, 18.3. Edited by W. Haase. Berlin: de Gruyter, 1990.
Oswalt, John N. *The Book of Isaiah, Chapters 1–39*. NICOT. Grand Rapids: Eerdmans, 1986.
Ovadiah, Asher, and Rachel Peleg. "The 'Promontory Palace' in Caesarea Maritima and the Northern Palace at Masada." *RB* 116 (2009): 598–611.
Palmer, Darryl W. "Acts and the Ancient Historical Monograph." Pages 1–29 in *The Book of Acts in Its Ancient Literary Setting*. Edited by Bruce W. Winter and Andrew D. Clarke. Vol. 1 of *The Book of Acts in Its First Century Setting*. Edited by Bruce W. Winter. Grand Rapids: Eerdmans, 1993.
Pao, David W. *Colossians and Philemon*. ZECNT. Grand Rapids: Eerdmans, 2012.
Parsons, P. J. "Background: The Papyrus Letter." *Didactica Classica Gandensia* 20 (1980): 3–19.
———. *City of the Sharp-Nosed Fish: Greek Papyri beneath the Egyptian Sand Reveal a Long-Lost World*. London: Weidenfeld & Nicolson, 2007.
———, ed. and trans. *The Oxyrhynchus Papyri*. Vol. 42. Greco-Roman Memoirs 58. London: Egypt Exploration Society, 1974.

Pascuzzi, Maria A. "Reconsidering the Authorship of Colossians." *BBR* 23 (2013): 223–45.
Patrich, Joseph. *Studies in the Archaeology and History of Caesarea Maritima: Caput Judaeae, Metropolis Palaestinae*. AGJU 77. Leiden: Brill, 2011.
Peake, Arthur Samuel. *The Quintessence of Paulinism*. Manchester, UK: Manchester University Press, 1918.
Penner, Todd. *In Praise of Christian Origins: Stephen and the Hellenists in Lukan Apologetic Historiography*. Emory Studies in Early Christianity 10. New York: T&T Clark, 2004.
Perriman, Andrew. "Between Troas and Macedonia: 2 Cor 2:13–14." *ExpTim* 101 (1989–1990): 39–41.
Pervo, Richard I. *Acts: A Commentary*. Hermeneia. Minneapolis: Fortress, 2009.
———. *The Acts of Paul: A New Translation with Introduction and Commentary*. Eugene, OR: Wipf & Stock, 2014.
———. *Profit with Delight: The Literary Genre of the Acts of the Apostles*. Philadelphia: Fortress, 1987.
Pesch, Rudolf. *Die Apostelgeschichte*. 2 vols. EKK 5. Zürich/ Neukirchen-Vluyn: Benziger/Neukirchener Verlag, 1986.
Pietersma, Albert. *The Apocryphon of Jannes and Jambres the Magicians*. Religions in the Greco-Roman World 119. Leiden: Brill, 1994.
Pitts, Andrew W. "Style and Pseudonymity in Pauline Scholarship: A Register Based Configuration." Pages 113–152 in *Paul and Pseudonymity*. Edited by Stanley E. Porter and Gregory Fewster. Pauline Studies 8. Leiden: Brill, 2013.
Pokorný, Petr. *Colossians: A Commentary*. Translated by Siegfried S. Schatzmann. Peabody, MA: Hendrickson, 1991.
Porter, Stanley E. *The Pastoral Epistles: A Commentary on the Greek Text*. Grand Rapids: Baker, 2023.
———. *When Paul Met Jesus: How an Idea Got Lost in History*. Cambridge: Cambridge University Press, 2016.
Price, S. R. F. "Gods and Emperors: The Greek Language of the Roman Imperial Cult." *JHS* 104 (1984): 79–95.
Quinn, Jerome D. *The Letter to Titus*. AB 35. New York: Doubleday, 1990.
Quinn, Jerome D., and William C. Wacker. *The First and Second Letters to Timothy*. Eerdmans Critical Commentary. Grand Rapids: Eerdmans, 2000.
Ramsay, W. M. *The Bearing of Recent Discovery on the Trustworthiness of the New Testament*. London: Hodder & Stoughton, 1915.
———. *The Cities of St. Paul: Their Influence on His Life and Thought*. London: Hodder & Stoughton, 1907.
———. "Studies in the Roman Province of Galatia." *JRS* 16 (1926): 172–205.
———. *St. Paul the Traveller and the Roman Citizen*. London: Hodder & Stoughton, 1896.

Bibliography

Rapske, Brian. *Paul in Roman Custody*. Vol. 3 of *The Book of Acts in Its First Century Setting*. Edited by Bruce W. Winter. Grand Rapids: Eerdmans, 1994.

———. "The Prisoner Paul in the Eyes of Onesimus." *NTS* 37 (1991): 187–203.

Rauh, Nicholas K. *Merchants, Sailors, and Pirates in the Roman World*. Stroud, Gloucestershire, UK: Tempus, 2003.

Reardon, B. P., trans. *Chaereas and Callirhoe*. Pages 17–124 in *Collected Ancient Greek Novels*. Edited by B. P. Reardon. Berkeley: University of California Press, 1989.

Reardon, Timothy W. "'Hanging on a Tree': Deuteronomy 21.22–23 and the Rhetoric of Jesus' Crucifixion in Acts 5.12–42." *JSNT* 37 (2015): 407–31.

Reece, Steve. *Paul's Large Letters: Paul's Autographic Subscription in the Light of Ancient Epistolary Conventions*. LNTS 561. New York: Bloomsbury, 2017.

Reicke, Bo. "Caesarea, Rome, and the Captivity Epistles." Pages 277–86 in W. Ward Gasque and Ralph P. Martin. *Apostolic History and the Gospel: Biblical and Historical Essays Presented to F. F. Bruce*. Exeter, UK: Paternoster, 1970.

———. *Re-examining Paul's Letters: The History of the Pauline Correspondence*. Edited by David P. Moessner and Ingalisa Reicke. Harrisburg, PA: Trinity Press International, 2001.

Richardson, L., Jr. *A New Topographical Dictionary of Ancient Rome*. Baltimore: Johns Hopkins University Press, 1992.

Riesner, Rainer. *Paul's Early Period: Chronology, Mission Strategy, Theology*. Translated by Douglas W. Stott. Grand Rapids: Eerdmans, 1998.

———. "Paul's Trial and End according to Second Timothy, *1 Clement*, the Canon Muratori, and the Apocryphal Acts." Pages 391–409 in *The Last Years of Paul: Essays from the Tarragona Conference, June 2013*. Edited by Armand Puig i Tàrrech, John M. G. Barclay, and Jörg Frey. WUNT 1.352. Tübingen: Mohr Siebeck, 2015.

Robbins, Vernon K. *Sea Voyages and Beyond: Emerging Strategies in Socio-Rhetorical Interpretation*. Emory Studies in Early Christianity 14. Dorset, UK: Deo, 2010.

Robinson, Benjamin W. "An Ephesian Imprisonment of Paul." *JBL* 29 (1910): 181–89.

Robinson, David M. "Roman Sculptures from Colonia Caesarea (Pisidian Antioch)." *Art Bulletin* 9 (1926): 4–69.

Robinson, John A. T. *Redating the New Testament*. Philadelphia: Westminster, 1976.

Röcker, Fritz W. *Belial und Katechon: Eine Untersuchung zu 2 Thess 2,1–12 und 1 Thess 4,13–5,11*. WUNT 2.262. Tübingen: Mohr Siebeck, 2009.

Roller, Duane W. *The "Geography" of Strabo: An English Translation with Introduction and Notes*. Cambridge: Cambridge University Press, 2014.

———. *A Historical and Topographical Guide to the "Geography" of Strabo*. Cambridge: Cambridge University Press, 2018.

Ropes, James Hardy. *The Text of Acts*. Vol. 3 of *The Beginnings of Christianity, Part I:*

The Acts of the Apostles. Edited by F. J. Foakes Jackson and Kirsopp Lake. London: Macmillan, 1926.

Rosenmeyer, Patricia A. *Ancient Epistolary Fictions: The Letter in Greek Literature*. Cambridge: Cambridge University Press, 2001.

Rowe, C. Kavin. *World Upside Down: Reading Acts in the Greco-Roman Age*. Oxford: Oxford University Press, 2009.

Russell, D. S. *The Method and Message of Jewish Apocalyptic*. London: SCM, 1964.

Safrai, S., and M. Stern, eds. *The Jewish People in the First Century: Historical Geography, Political History, Social, Cultural and Religious Life and Institutions*. Philadelphia: Fortress, 1974.

Sanders, E. P. *Jesus and Judaism*. Philadelphia: Fortress, 1985.

———. *Judaism: Practice and Belief, 63 BCE–66 CE*. London: SCM, 1992.

———. *Paul and Palestinian Judaism: A Comparison of Patterns of Religion*. Philadelphia: Fortress, 1977.

———. *Paul, the Law, and the Jewish People*. Philadelphia: Fortress, 1983.

Sandnes, Karl Olav. *Paul—One of the Prophets? A Contribution to the Apostle's Self-Understanding*. WUNT 2.43. Tübingen: J. C. B. Mohr, 1991.

———. "Prophet-Like Apostle: A Note on the 'Radical New Perspective' in Pauline Studies." *Biblica* 96 (2015): 550–64.

Santalucia, Bernardo. "Paul's Roman Trial: Legal Procedures regarding Roman Citizens Convicted of Serious Charges in the First Century CE." Pages 213–30 in *The Last Years of Paul: Essays from the Tarragona Conference, June 2013*. Edited by Armand Puig i Tàrrech, John M. G. Barclay, and Jörg Frey. WUNT 1.352. Tübingen: Mohr Siebeck, 2015.

Sayar, Mustafa H. "Römische Straßen und Meilensteine im Ebenen Kilikien." Pages 147–65 in *Roman Roads: New Evidence—New Perspectives*. Edited by Anna Kolb. Berlin: de Gruyter, 2019.

Schaper, Joachim. "The Pharisees." Pages 402–27 in *The Early Roman Period, Part 2*. Edited by William Horbury, W. D. Davies, and John Sturdy. Vol. 3 of *The Cambridge History of Judaism*. Edited by W. D. Davies and Louis Finkelstein. Cambridge: Cambridge University Press, 1999.

Scheck, Thomas P., trans. *Origen, Commentary on the Epistle to the Romans: Books 1–5*. FOC 104. Washington, DC: Catholic University of America Press, 2001.

Schellenberg, Ryan S. *Abject Joy: Paul, Prison, and the Art of Making Do*. New York: Oxford University Press, 2021.

———. "The First Pauline Chronologist? Paul's Itinerary in the Letters and in Acts." *JBL* 134 (2015): 193–213.

Schnabel, Eckhard J. *Der Brief des Paulus an die Römer: Kapitel 6–16*. HTA. Witten: Brockhaus, 2016.

———. *Paul and the Early Church*. Vol. 2 of *Early Christian Mission*. 2 vols. Downers Grove, IL: InterVarsity, 2004.

Bibliography

———. "Paul's Missionary Work in the Provinces of Asia and Illyricum." Pages 385–97 in *Lexham Geographic Commentary on Acts through Revelation*. Edited by Barry J. Beitzel. Bellingham, WA: Lexham, 2019.

Schnelle, Udo. *Apostle Paul: His Life and Theology*. Translated by M. Eugene Boring. Grand Rapids: Baker, 2005.

———. "Paul's Literary Activity during His Roman Trial." Pages 433–51 in *The Last Years of Paul: Essays from the Tarragona Conference, June 2013*. Edited by Armand Puig i Tàrrech, John M. G. Barclay, and Jörg Frey. WUNT 1.352. Tübingen: Mohr Siebeck, 2015.

Schrage, Wolfgang. *Der erste Brief an die Korinther*. 4 vols. EKK 7. Düsseldorf: Benziger/Neukirchen-Vluyn: Neukirchener Verlag, 1995–2001.

Schreiner, Thomas R. *Galatians*. ZECNT. Grand Rapids: Zondervan, 2010.

Schürer, Emil. *The History of the Jewish People in the Age of Jesus Christ (175 B.C.–A.D. 135)*. Revised and edited by Geza Vermes et al. 3 vols. Edinburgh: T&T Clark, 1973.

Schwartz, Daniel R. *2 Maccabees*. CEJL. Berlin: de Gruyter, 2008.

Schweitzer, Albert. *The Mysticism of Paul the Apostle*. Translated by William Montgomery. New York: Henry Holt, 1931.

Scott, E. F. *The Pastoral Epistles*. MNTC. London: Hodder & Stoughton, 1936.

Segal, Alan F. "Heavenly Ascent in Hellenistic Judaism, Early Christianity and Their Environment." *ANRW* 23.2: 1333–1394. Part 2, *Principat*, 23.2. Edited by H. Temporini and W. Haase. Berlin: de Gruyter, 1980.

Segal, Peretz. "The Penalty of the Warning Inscription from the Temple of Jerusalem." *IEJ* 39 (1989): 79–84.

Seifrid, Mark A. "Revisiting Antioch: Paul, Cephas, and 'the Ones from James.'" *TLZ* 144 (2019): 1224–35.

Seland, Torrey. "Saul of Tarsus and Early Zealotism: Reading Gal 1,13–14 in Light of Philo's Writings." *Biblica* 83 (2002): 449–71.

Selwyn, Edward Gordon. *The First Epistle of St. Peter*. 2nd ed. London: Macmillan, 1947.

Shackleton Bailey, D. R. *Cicero's Letters to His Friends*. American Philological Association Classical Resources Series 1. Atlanta: Scholars Press, 1978.

Sherwin-White, A. N. *Roman Society and Roman Law in the New Testament*. Oxford: Oxford University Press, 1963.

Slingerland, Dixon. "'The Jews' in the Pauline Portion of Acts." *JAAR* 54 (1986): 305–22.

Smallwood, E. Mary. *Documents Illustrating the Principates of Gaius, Claudius, and Nero*. Cambridge: Cambridge University Press, 1967.

———. *The Jews under Roman Rule from Pompey to Diocletian: A Study in Political Relations*. Leiden: Brill, 1981.

Smith, James. *The Voyage and Shipwreck of St. Paul*. Eugene, OR: Wipf & Stock, 2001.

Soon, Isaac T. *A Disabled Apostle: Impairment and Disability in the Letters of Paul.* Oxford: Oxford University Press, 2023.

———. "Before Deception: The Amoral Nature of Ancient Christian Forgery." *EC* 14 (2023): 429–45.

Spicq, C. *Les Épîtres Pastorales.* 4th ed. 2 vols. Paris: Lecoffre, 1969.

Stanton, Graham N. *Jesus and the Gospel.* Cambridge: Cambridge University Press, 2004.

Stillwell, Richard, William L. MacDonald, and Marian Holland McAllister, eds. *The Princeton Encyclopedia of Classical Sites.* Princeton, NJ: Princeton University Press, 1976.

Strait, Drew W. "The Wisdom of Solomon, Ruler Cults, and Paul's Polemic against Idols in the Areopagus Speech." *JBL* 136 (2017): 609–32.

Stuhlmacher, Peter. "The Purpose of Romans." Pages 231–42 in *The Romans Debate.* Edited by Karl P. Donfried. Rev. and exp. ed. Peabody, MA: Hendrickson, 1991.

Swete, Henry Barclay. *The Gospel according to St. Mark.* London: Macmillan, 1898.

Szesnat, H. "What Did the σκηνοποιός Paul Produce?" *Neot* 27 (1993): 391–402.

Tajra, Harry W. *The Martyrdom of St. Paul.* WUNT 2.67. Tübingen: Mohr Siebeck, 1994.

———. *The Trial of St. Paul: A Juridical Exegesis of the Second Half of the Acts of the Apostles.* WUNT 2.35. Tübingen: Mohr Siebeck, 1989.

Talbert, J. A., ed. *Barrington Atlas of the Greek and Roman World.* Princeton, NJ: Princeton University Press, 2000.

Taylor, Jane. *Petra and the Lost Kingdom of the Nabataeans.* Cambridge, MA: Harvard University Press, 2002.

Taylor, Justin. "The Ethnarch of King Aretas at Damascus: A Note on 2 Cor 11:32–33." *RB* 99 (1992): 719–28.

Teske, Roland, trans. *Answer to Faustus, A Manichean.* Vol. 20 of *Books.* Part 1 of *The Works of Saint Augustine.* Edited by Boniface Ramsey. Hyde Park, NY: New City Press, 2007.

Theophilos, Michael P. "The Roman Connection: Paul and Mark." Pages 45–72 in *Paul and Mark: Comparative Essays, Part I: Two Authors at the Beginnings of Christianity.* Edited by Oda Wischmeyer, David C. Sim, and Ian J. Elmer. BZNW 198. Berlin: de Gruyter, 2014.

Thielman, Frank. "Adam's Sin and Jesus' Death in Romans (Romans 5:12–21)." Pages 145–54 in *Paul's Letter to the Romans: Theological Essays.* Edited by Douglas J. Moo, Eckhard J. Schnabel, Thomas R. Schreiner, and Frank Thielman. Peabody, MA: Hendrickson, 2023.

———. *Ephesians.* BECNT. Grand Rapids: Eerdmans, 2010.

———. "God's Righteousness as God's Fairness in Romans 1:17: An Ancient Perspective on a Significant Phrase." *JETS* 54 (2011): 35–48.

---. *Paul and the Law: A Contextual Approach*. Downers Grove, IL: InterVarsity, 1994.

---. "Paul's View of Israel's Misstep in Rom 9.32–3: Its Origin and Meaning." *NTS* 64 (2018): 362–77.

---. *Romans*. ZECNT. Grand Rapids: Zondervan, 2016.

Thiselton, Anthony C. *The First Epistle to the Corinthians: A Commentary on the Greek Text*. NIGTC. Grand Rapids: Eerdmans, 2000.

Thompson, Glen L., and Mark Wilson. *In This Way We Came to Rome: With Paul on the Appian Way*. Bellingham, WA: Lexham, 2023.

---. "Paul's Walk to Assos: A Hodological Inquiry into Its Geography, Archaeology, and Purpose." Pages 269–313 in *Stones, Bones and the Sacred: Essays on Material Culture and Ancient Religion in Honor of Dennis E. Smith*. Edited by Alan H. Cadwallader. Early Christianity and Its Literature 22. Atlanta: SBL, 2016.

---. "The Route of Paul's Second Journey in Asia Minor: In the Steps of Robert Jewett and Beyond." *TynBul* 67 (2016): 217–46.

Thrall, Margaret E. *The Second Epistle to the Corinthians*. ICC. 2 vols. Edinburgh: T&T Clark, 1994–2000.

Toner, Jerry. *Popular Culture in Ancient Rome*. Cambridge: Polity, 2009.

Towner, Philip H. *The Letters to Timothy and Titus*. NICNT. Grand Rapids: Eerdmans, 2006.

Trainor, Michael. "Rome's Market Economy in the Lycus Valley: Soundings from Laodicea and Colossae." Pages 293–324 in *Colossians, Hierapolis, and Laodicea*. James R. Harrison and L. L. Welborn. WGRWSup 16. Vol. 5 of *The First Urban Churches*. Atlanta: SBL, 2019.

Trebilco, Paul. *The Early Christians in Ephesus from Paul to Ignatius*. Grand Rapids: Eerdmans, 2007.

Turner, E. G. "Tiberius Ivlivs Alexander." *JRS* 44 (1954): 54–64.

VanderKam, James C. *From Joshua to Caiaphas: High Priests after the Exile*. Minneapolis: Fortress, 2004.

Walker, Henry John, trans. *Valerius Maximus, Memorable Deeds and Sayings: One Thousand Tales from Ancient Rome*. Indianapolis, IN: Hackett, 2004.

Walker, Peter. "Revisiting the Pastoral Epistles—Part II." *EJT* 21 (2012): 120–32.

Wallace-Hadrill, Andrew. "*Domus* and *Insulae* in Rome: Families and Housefuls." Pages 3–18 in *Early Christian Families in Context: An Interdisciplinary Dialogue*. Edited by David L. Balch and Carolyn Osiek. Religion, Marriage, and Family. Grand Rapids: Eerdmans, 2003.

Wanamaker, Charles A. *The Epistles to the Thessalonians*. NIGTC. Grand Rapids: Eerdmans, 1990.

Wansink, Craig S. *Chained in Christ: The Experience and Rhetoric of Paul's Imprisonments*. JSNTSup 130. Sheffield, UK: Sheffield Academic Press, 1996.

Waterfield, Robin, trans. *Polybius: The Histories*. Oxford World's Classics. Oxford: Oxford University Press, 2010.
Watson, Francis. "By Faith (of Christ): An Exegetical Dilemma and Its Scriptural Solution." Pages 147–63 in *The Faith of Jesus Christ: Exegetical, Biblical, and Theological Studies*. Edited by Michael F. Bird and Preston M. Sprinkle. Milton Keynes: Paternoster, 2009.
Wedderburn, A. J. M. "Purpose and Occasion of Romans Again." Pages 195–202 in *The Romans Debate*. Edited by Karl P. Donfried. Rev. and exp. ed. Peabody, MA: Hendrickson, 1991.
———. *The Reasons for Romans*. Minneapolis: Fortress, 1991.
———. "The 'We'–Passages in Acts: On the Horns of a Dilemma." *ZNW* 93 (2002): 78–98.
Weima, Jeffrey A. D. *1–2 Thessalonians*. BECNT. Grand Rapids: Baker, 2014.
———. "Onesimus: Still a Runaway Slave." Pages 201–30 in *Rhetoric, History, and Theology: Interpreting the New Testament*. Edited by Todd D. Still and Jason A. Myers. Lanham, MD: Lexington, 2022.
Weiss, Johannes. *Earliest Christianity: A History of the Period A.D. 30–150*. Translated by Frederick C. Grant. 2 vols. New York: Harper, 1959.
Welborn, L. L. "Early Christianity at Rome as Reflected in the So-Called First Epistle of Clement." Pages 137–200 in *Rome and Ostia*. Vol. 6 of *The First Urban Churches*. Edited by James R. Harrison and L. L. Welborn. WGRW Supplement Series 18. Atlanta: SBL, 2021.
———. "On the Discord in Corinth: 1 Corinthians 1–4 and Ancient Politics." *JBL* 106 (1987): 85–111.
———. "Paul's Caricature of His Chief Rival as a Pompous Parasite in 2 Corinthians 11.20." *JSNT* 32 (2009): 39–56.
Welles, C. Bradford. "Hellenistic Tarsus." *Mélanges de l'Université Saint Joseph* 38 (1962): 43–75.
Wendt, Heidi. *At the Temple Gates: The Religion of Freelance Experts in the Roman Empire*. Oxford: Oxford University Press, 2016.
Wenham, David. *Paul: Follower of Jesus or Founder of Christianity?* Grand Rapids: Eerdmans, 1995.
White, John L. *Light from Ancient Letters*. FF. Philadelphia: Fortress, 1986.
White, L. Michael. *Building God's House in the Roman World: Architectural Adaptation among Pagans, Jews, and Christians*. HTS 41. Vol. 1 of *The Social Origins of Christian Architecture*. Valley Forge, PA: Trinity Press International, 1996.
———. *Texts and Monuments for the Christian Domus Ecclesiae in Its Environment*. HTS 43. Vol. 2 of *The Social Origins of Christian Architecture*. Valley Forge, PA: Trinity Press International, 1997.
Wieseler, Karl. *Chronologie des apostolischen Zeitalters*. Göttingen: Vandenhoeck & Ruprecht, 1848.
Williamson, H. G. M. *Ezra, Nehemiah*. WBC 16. Nashville: Thomas Nelson, 1985.

Wilson, Annalisa Phillips. "'One Thing': Stoic Discourse and Paul's Reevaluation of His Jewish Credentials in Phil. 3.1–21." *JSNT* 45 (2023): 429–50.
Wilson, Mark. "Cilicia: The First Christian Churches in Anatolia." *TynBul* 54 (2003): 15–30.
———. "The Denouement of Claudian Pamphylia-Lycia and Its Implications for the Audience of Galatians." *NovT* 60 (2018): 337–60.
———. "The Geography of Galatia." Pages 438–93 in *Lexham Geographic Commentary on Acts through Revelation*. Edited by Barry J. Beitzel. Bellingham, WA: Lexham, 2019.
———. "The Lukan *Periplus* of Paul's Third Journey with a Textual Conundrum in Acts 20:15." *AcT* 36 (2016): 229–54.
———. "Luke for Landlubbers: The Translation and Interpretation of ὑποπλέω in Acts 27." *AcT* 42 (2022): 343–66.
———. "The 'Upper Regions' and the Route of Paul's Third Journey from Apamea to Ephesus." *Scriptura* 117 (2018): 1–21.
Wilson, R. McL. *A Critical and Exegetical Commentary on Colossians and Philemon*. ICC. London: T&T Clark, 2005.
Wilson, Stephen G. *Luke and the Pastoral Epistles*. London: SPCK, 1979.
Windisch, Hans. "Die Christusepiphanie vor Damaskus und ihre religionsgeschichtlichen Parellelen." *ZNW* 31 (1932): 1–23.
Winter, Bruce W. "Acts and Food Shortages." Pages 59–78 in *The Book of Acts in Its Greco-Roman Setting*. Edited by David W. J. Gill and Conrad Gempf. Vol. 2 of *The Book of Acts in Its First Century Setting*. Edited by Bruce W. Winter. 6 vols. Grand Rapids: Eerdmans, 1994.
———. *After Paul Left Corinth: The Influence of Secular Ethics and Social Change*. Grand Rapids: Eerdmans, 2001.
———. *Divine Honours for the Caesars: The First Christians' Responses*. Grand Rapids: Eerdmans, 2015.
———. "The Entries and Ethics of Orators and Paul (1 Thessalonians 2:1–12)." *TynBul* 44 (1993): 55–74.
———. "Gallio's Ruling on the Legal Status of Early Christianity." *TynBul* 50 (1999): 213–24.
———. "'If a Man Does Not Wish to Work . . .': A Cultural and Historical Setting for 2 Thessalonians 3:6–16." *TynBul* 40 (1989): 303–15.
———. "The Importance of the *Captatio Benevolentiae* in the Speeches of Tertullus and Paul in Acts 24:1–21." *JTS* 42 (1991): 505–31.
———. *Philo and Paul among the Sophists: Alexandrian and Corinthian Responses to a Julio-Claudian Movement*. 2nd ed. Grand Rapids: Eerdmans, 2002.
———. "Rehabilitating Gallio and His Judgement in Acts 18:14–15." *TynBul* 57 (2006): 291–308.
Winter, Sara C. "Paul's Letter to Philemon." *NTS* 33 (1987): 1–15.

Witherington, Ben, III. *The Acts of the Apostles: A Socio-Rhetorical Commentary.* Grand Rapids: Eerdmans, 1998.

Wolter, Michael. *Der Brief an die Römer (Teilband 1: Röm 1–8).* EKK 6.1. Neukirchen-Vluyn/Ostfildern: Neukirchener/Patmos, 2014.

———. *Der Brief an die Römer (Teilband 2: Röm 9–16).* EKK 6.2. Ostfildern: Patmos; Göttingen: Vandenhoeck & Ruprecht, 2019.

Wrede, William. *The Authenticity of the Second Letter to the Thessalonians.* Translated by Robert Rhea. Eugene, OR: Wipf & Stock, 2017.

———. *Paul.* Translated by Edward Lummis. London: Philip Green, 1907.

Wright, N. T. *The Climax of the Covenant: Christ and the Law in Pauline Theology.* Edinburgh: T&T Clark, 1991.

———. *Paul: A Biography.* San Francisco: HarperOne, 2018.

———. *Paul and the Faithfulness of God.* Vol. 4 of *Christian Origins and the Question of God.* Minneapolis: Fortress, 2013.

———. *The Resurrection of the Son of God.* Vol. 3 of *Christian Origins and the Question of God.* Minneapolis: Fortress, 2003.

Wycherley, R. E. "St. Paul at Athens." *JTS* 19 (1968): 619–21.

Zahn, Theodor. *Introduction to the New Testament.* 3 vols. Translated by John Moore Trout, William Arnot Mather, Louis Hodous, Edward Strong Worcester, William Hoyt Worrell, Roland Backus Dodge, and Melancthon Williams Jacobus. 2nd ed. New York: Charles Scribner's Sons, 1917.

Zanker, Paul. *The Power of Images in the Age of Augustus.* Ann Arbor: University of Michigan Press, 1988.

Zeller, Dieter. *Der erste Brief an die Korinther.* KEK 5. Göttingen: Vandenhoeck & Ruprecht, 2010.

Index of Authors

Adam-Veleni, P., 392n22, 392n24
Alexander, William Menzies, 381n32
Allison, Dale C., 374n17, 375n19, 375n20, 403n36, 403n40, 403–4n41
Allo, E.-B., 384n36, 384n37, 416n13
Ap-Thomas, D. R., 400n24
Armstrong, Jonathan J., 378n17, 457–58n33, 460n23
Arnold, Clinton E., 310, 414n30, 445n37, 445n39, 445n40, 445n42, 446n11
Ascough, Richard S., 391n4
Ashby, Thomas, 434n38
Atkins, Christopher S., 446n6

Bablitz, Leanne, 448n8, 448n9
Bailey, Daniel P., 420n41, 420n43
Bailey, John A., 402n22, 402n23, 402n24, 403n25, 403n26
Bakker, Mathieu de, 390n21
Balch, David L., 440n45
Baldwin, Matthew C., 460n24
Barclay, John M. G., 391n12, 428n39, 431n18, 441n61, 444n34, 448n9, 450n30, 450n33, 450n35, 457n27, 458n2, 458n36, 459n21
Bar-Kochva, B., 429n51, 429n52, 429n53
Barnes, Timothy D., 459n12

Barnett, Paul, 412n6, 416n15, 416n16, 416n17, 416–17n18, 417n32
Barrett, C. K., 375n1, 377n27, 382n12, 382n18, 383n17, 387n8, 389n8, 389n9, 389n19, 390n28, 394n53, 395n2, 396n23, 397n26, 406–7nn31, 407n38, 410n23, 412n6, 412n11, 416–17n18, 417n20, 421n2, 421n5, 422n6, 423n20, 423n24, 424n43, 426n7, 432n35, 434n21, 434n37, 436n1, 437n12
Bauckham, Richard, 41, 44, 373n41, 377n6, 378n7, 378n9, 378n10, 378n12, 378n16, 378n18, 378n19, 429n54, 443n6, 459n13
Bauer, Walter, 453n23
Baum, Armin D., 413n13
Baxter, Fred, 432n1
Beale, G. K., 393n35, 404n43
Beard, Mary, 397n32, 402n7
Becker, Eve-Marie, 454n37, 454n44
Beebe, H. Keith, 430n2
Beitzel, Barry J., 406n30, 423n35
Benjamin, Anna, 395n9
Bernard, J. H., 448n4, 449n14
Best, Ernest, 379n30, 404n43, 404n44, 446n7
Betz, Hans Dieter, 415n33
Billings, Bradly S., 293, 440n46,

INDEX OF AUTHORS

440n47, 440n48, 440n49, 440n51, 441n52
Bingham, Sandra J., 456n23
Bird, Michael F., 420n39
Blazquez, J. M., 418n7
Block, Daniel I., 381n26
Blunt, A. W. F., 448–49n12
Bockmuehl, Markus, 378n15, 441n63, 442n1, 442n2, 442n4, 457n24
Bohak, Gideon, 414n29
Böhler, Dieter, 375n21
Boring, M. Eugene, 426n8
Bowden, John, 372n10, 374n10, 375n2, 378n24, 379n32, 380n12, 454n53
Bowen, Clayton R., 455n4, 455–56n6, 456n7, 456n8, 456n9, 456n10
Bowers, W. P., 390n23
Bowersock, G., 33–34, 376n15, 376n16, 377n25, 377n26
Brélaz, Cédric, 456n11
Breytenbach, Cilliers, 383n25, 385n20, 388n4, 389n14, 389n15, 390n20, 447n16
Brookes, Alan C., 438n18
Bruce, F. F., 322, 386n24, 387n15, 390n29, 394n49, 394n51, 396n12, 396n24, 397n27, 397n33, 397n35, 402n17, 404n48, 404n49, 406n31, 408n3, 418n7, 421n2, 421n5, 422n16, 423n20, 424n51, 427n30, 428n37, 429n46, 431n20, 437n12, 443n19, 447n24
Bruggen, Jakob van, 413n24, 435n40, 458n40
Burchard, Christoph, 374n4
Burnett, D. Clint, 125, 394n46, 394n47, 394n48, 401n2, 402n19, 402n20
Bury, R. G., 425n6, 452n4, 452n5
Buttolph, Philip, 413n14, 434n23, 449n16, 458n38

Cadbury, Henry J., 375n3, 405n7, 408n6, 416n8, 422n14, 423n24, 423n34, 425n62, 431n26, 437n5, 437n7, 437n8
Cadwallader, Alan H., 422n15, 444n24
Camerlenghi, Nicola, 367, 451n43, 451n45, 451n46, 459n16
Campbell, Brian, 440n40, 456n23
Campbell, Douglas A., 373n44, 376–77n24, 377n26, 400n28, 411n48, 411n49, 452n15, 453n20, 453n22
Carafa, Paolo, 439n35
Carandini, Andrea, 439n35
Cary, Earnest, 432n29
Casson, Lionel, 416n9, 422n17, 424n48, 433n9, 434n32, 434n33
Castagnoli, Ferdinando, 438n21, 439n33
Catling, Hector William, 383n16
Cawkwell, George Law, 396n16
Chadwick, Henry, 397n34
Champlin, Edward, 439n36, 458n3, 458n4
Chapple, Allan, 417n1, 418n5, 418n6, 418n10, 418n14, 418n15, 419n29
Chesnutt, Randall D., 374n5
Chilton, Bruce, 371n1, 372n19
Cicone, Chiara, 451n45
Claridge, Amanda, 438n21, 439n32, 439n33
Clarke, Andrew D., 453n29, 459n13
Clarke, Frank, 374n2
Clinton, Kevin, 397n37
Cohoon, J. W., 398n47
Collins, John N., 214, 417n24, 417n25, 417n26, 417n27
Colson, F. H., 382n13
Conzelmann, Hans, 397n33, 413n14, 413n15, 413n18, 413n19, 414n26, 434n23, 435n44, 449n16, 449n17, 449n18, 449n19, 458n36, 458n38, 458n39
Cook, John Manuel, 424–25n53
Cotton, Hannah M., 430n4

Index of Authors

Coulston, Jonathan, 440n40
Cranfield, C. E. B., 420n39
Crook, J. A., 428n31, 430n7, 430n8
Cullmann, Oscar, 379n32, 441n58, 441n59, 441n60, 441n61
Cumont, Franz, 431n15

Danby, Herbert, 371n1, 406n20
Danker, F. W., 395n57
D'Arms, John H., 437n13
Das, A. Andrew, 376n14, 376n24, 379n38, 382n6, 382n7, 382n8, 382n9, 401n36
Davidson, Samuel, 413–14n24
Davies, W. D., 372n13, 380n7, 403n36, 403n40, 403-4n41
Deidun, T. J., 401n6, 411n36
Deines, Roland, 372n21
Deissmann, Adolf, 402n14, 402n15, 455n4
deSilva, David A., 400n25, 446n13
Diamond, Eliezer, 168, 405n3, 405n4, 405n5, 405n6
Dibelius, Martin, 413n14, 413n15, 413n18, 413n19, 414n26, 434n23, 435n44, 449n16, 449n17, 449n18, 449n19, 458n38, 458n39
Dodge, Roland Backus, 456n24
Donelson, Lewis R., 425n6, 452n3, 452n5
Donfried, Karl P., 419n22, 420n34
Downey, Glanville, 380n9
Duncan, George S., 455n4
Dündar, E., 425n57
Dunn, James D. G., 169–70, 172, 181, 373n33, 379n31, 382n10, 386n1, 386n4, 387n23, 387n30, 399n9, 400n23, 405n12, 406n27, 406n28, 409n7, 409n11, 409n13, 411n38, 413n16, 417n20, 426n8, 428n35, 429n49, 435n43, 443n16, 443n17, 443n18, 444n28, 445n45, 445n48, 447n1, 455n1, 458n36

Dzino, Danijel, 418n8, 418n9, 418n12, 418n14

Eastman, David L., 334, 441n59, 441n61, 450n31, 451n40, 451n41, 451n44, 458n6, 459n7, 459n11
Eck, Werner, 430n4
Edgar, C. C., 402n16, 440n39
Ehrman, Bart D., 452n3, 452n12, 452n13
Elliott, J. K., 446n9, 452n8, 460n24
Elliott, John H., 378n28, 379n30
Elmer, Ian J., 450n29
Emde Boas, Evert van, 390n21
Enslin, Morton Scott, 454n44, 454n45, 454n55
Epp, Eldon J., 397n33, 458n36
Evans, Craig A., 403n40

Fairclough, H. R., 438n23
Fant, Clyde E., 424n47
Fee, Gordon D., 389n7, 403n32, 403n34, 409n21, 411n38, 411n40, 441–42n63, 442n4, 443n7, 457–58n34
Feldman, Louis H., 391n6
Feldmeier, Reinhard, 379n29
Fewster, Gregory, 413n21, 443n14, 452n15
Filson, Floyd V., 379n32, 441n58
Finkelstein, Louis, 372n13, 380n7
Finney, Mark T., 400n29, 400n31, 401n38
Fitzgerald, John T., 401n4
Fitzmyer, Joseph A., 379n34, 400n30, 401n37, 411n39, 420n36, 422n6, 423n20, 425n58
Flexsenhar, Michael, III, 357–58, 438–39n29, 440n41, 440n42, 455n3, 456n11, 457n25, 457n27
Foster, Paul, 403n27, 403n28, 403n31
Fox, Robin J. Lane, 392n19, 392n22
Frazer, James G., 136, 397n38

INDEX OF AUTHORS

Fredriksen, Paula, 393n27
French, David H., 379n42, 384n29, 385n20, 386n22, 388n4, 407n38
Frey, Jörg, 391n12, 428n39, 431n18, 441n61, 448n9, 450n30, 450n33, 450n35, 457n27, 458n2, 458n36, 459n21
Friesen, Steven J., 416n7
Furnish, Victor Paul, 412n6, 412n9, 416–17n18, 417n28

Gabizon, Michael, 389n11, 389n12
Gapp, Kenneth Sperber, 382n1, 382n2
Garland, David E., 397n31, 410n22, 411n41
Garnsey, Peter, 391n12
Gasque, W. Ward, 456n17
Gempf, Conrad, 382n1, 383n21, 384n2, 389–90n19, 392n24, 406n23, 432n1, 454n33
Gildersleeve, Basil L., 449n15
Gill, David W. J., 382n1, 383n21, 384n2, 392n24, 394–95n55, 395n56
Gilliard, F. D., 379n35
Giszczak, Mark B., 393n35, 393n36, 403n38
Glad, Clarence E., 401n4
Goodman, Martin, 171, 405n16, 406n17, 406n18, 406n19, 406n20, 406n21, 428n43, 430n9, 430n11, 430n13
Goppelt, Leonard, 429n56
Gordon, Richard, 385n8
Gosnell, Peter W., 447n20, 447n21
Grant, Frederick C., 399n9
Greaves, Alan M., 424n48
Green, David, 407n38, 443n20
Greenwood, L. H. G., 448n4
Greer, Rowan A., 436n54
Grenfell, Bernard P., 430n7
Griffiths, Alan H., 436n56
Grotius, Hugo, 433–34n20, 434n21

Gruen, Erich S., 380n10, 398n51, 398n54, 403n37, 419n33
Grünstäudl, Wolfgang, 364, 458n2
Gundry, Robert H., 378n19
Gupta, Nijay K., 393n27

Haacker, Klaus, 421n1, 422n13, 423n18, 423n20, 423n26, 437n15, 438n27, 438n28
Haase, W., 415n1
Hacham, Noah, 375n4
Hadas, Moses, 429n56
Haenchen, Ernst, 377n27, 387n18, 389n10, 390n28, 393n29, 396n17, 396n19, 396n22, 405n7, 406–7n31, 423n24, 426n8, 428n31, 429n44, 431n20
Halavais, Andrew Campbell, 439n35
Halperin, D. M., 409n12
Hansen, G. Walter, 384n2
Hanson, John S., 406n22
Hanson, Victor Davis, 133, 397n28
Harrington, Hannah K., 372n21, 402n19
Harris, Murray J., 77, 208, 351, 381n22, 381n23, 381n24, 381n32, 384n35, 384n36, 384n38, 386n26, 391n9, 393n32, 406n22, 407n40, 409n9, 409n17, 410n28, 410n29, 411–12n49, 412n5, 412n7, 412n8, 412n9, 412n10, 415n40, 416n10, 416n12, 416n13, 416n15, 416–17n18, 417n19, 417n20, 417n28, 417n31, 422n11, 454n49
Harrison, James R., 79, 125, 185, 385n5, 385n6, 392n23, 394n43, 394n45, 402n16, 402n17, 402n21, 410n24, 410n27, 410n31, 414n30, 444n24, 445n42, 458n3
Hawkins, David, 386n21
Hawthorne, Gerald F., 442n3
Heilig, Christoph, 446–47n15
Heininger, Bernhard, 449n17

Index of Authors

Hemer, Colin J., 346, 348, 389–90n19, 390n27, 390n30, 396n20, 397n27, 406n23, 416n9, 432n1, 433n15, 433n16, 433n17, 434n25, 434n26, 434n27, 434n28, 434n29, 434n30, 435n39, 436n1, 438–39n29, 453n33, 454n43
Hendrix, Holland Lee, 392n23, 394n43
Hengel, Martin, 372n10, 372n12, 372n21, 373n31, 374n10, 375n2, 375n3, 375n22, 375n23, 376n11, 376n12, 376n13, 376n17, 376n18, 376n23, 378n18, 378n19, 378n24, 379n32, 380n12, 381n16, 381n19, 381n21, 426n1, 426n2, 426n3, 426n6, 427n17, 429n54, 443n8, 453n27, 454n48, 454n53
Henry, Madeleine M., 409n12
Heron, Helen S., 449n17
Herzer, Jens, 433n20, 448n9, 449n20, 459n21, 459n22, 460n26
Hickling, C. J. A., 417n21
Hock, Ronald F., 394n38, 394n39
Hodous, Louis, 456n24
Hoehner, Harold W., 446n10
Hoklotubbe, T. Christopher, 435n45
Holladay, Carl R., 396n22, 405n2, 408n3, 408n5, 423n20, 424n50, 424n52, 431n20
Holmes, Michael W., 378n7, 378n10, 441n58, 458n1
Holtz, Traugott, 402n10
Holtzmann, H. J., 434n21, 435n40, 435n43
Honoré, Tony, 444n29, 448n10
Horbury, William, 372n13
Horn, Friedrich W., 405n8, 405n9, 427n14
Hornblower, Simon, 410n27
Horrell, David G., 398n55
Horsley, G. H. R., 394n42, 407n44
Horsley, Richard A., 406n22

Horst, Pieter W. van der, 380n6, 381n28, 381n29
House, Paul R., 381n26, 418n4
Hughes, Philip Edgcumbe, 381n31
Huitink, Luuk, 390n21
Hultgren, Arland J., 420n36
Hultgren, Stephen, 231, 420n41, 420n42, 420n43, 421n44, 421n45, 421n46, 421n47
Hunt, Arthur S., 402n16, 430n7, 435n51, 440n39
Hunter, David, 458n35
Huther, J. E., 458n35
Huttner, Ulrich, 306, 443n20, 444n22, 444n23, 444n24, 444n32

Immendörfer, Michael, 407n41, 407n43, 407–8n44, 408n46, 408n49, 408n52, 415n3, 416n4, 416n5
Instone-Brewer, David, 372n20, 372n22, 372n28
Işek, H., 425n57

Jackson, F. J. Foakes, 375n3, 405n7, 408n6, 416n8, 421n5, 422n14, 431n26, 437n5
Jacobus, Melancthon Williams, 456–57n24
Jeffreys, Elizabeth, 380n9
Jeffreys, Michael, 380n9
Jervell, Jacob, 408n3, 422n13, 426n11, 429n44
Jewett, Robert, 227, 375n5, 375n7, 386n1, 418n7, 418n15, 419n22, 419n23, 419n28, 419n31, 438n26
Johnson, Lewis, 446n2, 446n3, 456n18, 456n19, 456n20, 457n31
Johnson, Luke Timothy, 202, 413n23, 413–14n24, 414n27, 415n35, 415n36, 415n37, 435n43, 435n47, 449n22, 451n47, 455n1

INDEX OF AUTHORS

Johnson, Marshall D., 398n53, 419n32, 437n4
Jones, A. H. M., 386n21, 389n15
Jones, Christopher P., 371n8, 380n15
Judge, E. A., 435–36n52
Juel, Donald H., 397n33, 458n36

Karakolis, Christos, 404n52
Kearsley, R. A., 398n46
Keener, Craig S., 118, 371n2, 374n6, 375n4, 375–76n8, 377n1, 379n34, 382n11, 382n12, 383n23, 383n25, 384n27, 385n9, 385n10, 385n12, 385n19, 386n5, 386n22, 386n23, 387n16, 387n17, 387n19, 387n20, 387n22, 387n23, 388n1, 389n18, 390n23, 390n29, 391n7, 391n8, 392n21, 392n24, 393n28, 394–95n55, 395n56, 396n20, 397n29, 397n30, 400n15, 400n22, 404n49, 406n29, 408n3, 408n4, 421n2, 421n3, 421n4, 422n10, 422n12, 422n13, 424n43, 424n44, 424n49, 426n9, 426n10, 427n21, 433n19, 437n8, 438n17, 454n50, 454n51, 454n52
Kelly, J. N. D., 435n58, 436n57, 458n37
Kemp, Jerome, 401n4
Kidson, Lyn, 413n23, 435n49, 435n50, 436n52
Kim, Seyoon, 374n3, 374n10, 376n9
King, Helen, 409n12
Klein, Günter, 419n22
Knight, George W., III, 440n44, 450n28
Koester, Helmut, 455n1, 455n3, 455n4
Kolb, Anna, 379–80n42
Koukouli-Chrysanthaki, Ch., 392n19
Kraabel, A. Thomas, 397n33, 458n36
Kraemer, Ross Shepard, 374n5
Krueger, Paul, 448n10

Lake, Kirsopp, 375n3, 405n7, 408n6, 416n8, 421n5, 422n14, 423n24, 423n34, 425n62, 431n26, 437n5, 437n7, 437n8
Lampe, Peter, 227, 398n52, 408n2, 419n32, 437n4, 437n14, 438n26, 441n62, 444n28, 444n29
Lang, Friedrich Gustav, 391n8
Lawlor, Hugh Jackson, 459n8, 460n25
Légasse, Simon, 373n41
Leidwanger, Justin, 383n15, 383n20, 412n3, 416n9, 422n17, 423n19, 423n29, 424n36, 425n55, 425n60, 425n61, 425n63, 432n3, 432n4, 433n7, 433n10
Lendon, J. E., 392n15, 450n25
Lentz, John Clayton, Jr., 371n9, 372n11
Leon, Harry J., 398n54, 440n50
Levick, Barbara, 431n16
Lewis, Naphtali, 448n7
Lightfoot, J. B., 109, 382n10, 387n8, 387n23, 387n28, 389n17, 409n18, 411n46, 412n1, 438–39n29, 445n46
Limberg, James, 397n33, 458n36
Lincoln, Andrew T., 446n6
Lintott, Andrew, 410n27
Liver, J., 372n16
Lock, Walter, 448n11, 449n23
Lohmeyer, Ernst, 456n15, 456n21
Lolos, Yannis, 391n2, 391n3, 391n5, 391n7
Longenecker, Bruce W., 384n39, 406n24
Longenecker, Richard N., 399n6, 418n19
Lüdemann, Gerd, 379n33
Lummis, Edward, 400n26
Lutz, Cora E., 394n39

Maas, Ed M. van der, 413–14n24
MacDonald, Margaret Y., 443n12, 443n16
MacDonald, William L., 441n53, 441n54

Index of Authors

Mackintosh, Robert, 412n2, 412n7, 417n19
Malherbe, Abraham J., 392n25, 393n31, 393n36, 394n37, 399n10, 401n3, 403n38, 404n47
Marcelli, Marina, 451n45
Marcus, Joel, 372n18, 372n27
Marcus, Ralph, 391n6
Marguerat, Daniel, 382n12, 390n28, 396n17, 396n19, 396n25, 422n6, 423n18, 423n20, 423n24, 424n50, 425n54, 427n30, 431n24, 441n61, 450n30, 450n32, 450n36, 458n36
Marshall, I. Howard, 415n33, 415n34, 435n42, 438n16, 449n24, 450n26
Martin, Ralph P., 442n3, 456n17
Mason, Steve, 405n16, 426n3, 426n4, 428n42, 429n50
Massey, Preston T., 413n20, 452n17
Mather, William Arnot, 456n24
Matthews, Christopher R., 397n33, 458n36
McConville, J. G., 378n22
McKechnie, Paul, 298, 431n22, 431n23, 442n64, 442n65, 442n66, 442n67, 457n25
McRay, John, 395n5, 424n46, 424n47
Menken, M. J. J., 393n35, 404n43
Metzger, Bruce M., 340, 439n30, 452n7
Millar, Fergus, 376n10, 377n26
Miller, Frank Justus, 385n17
Milner, N. P., 384n26
Minns, Denis, 449n13, 449n15
Mitchell, Margaret M., 411n35
Mitchell, Stephen, 147, 383n21, 383n22, 383n24, 383n25, 384n1, 384n29, 384n30, 385n5, 385n16, 386n22, 389n6, 400n18, 400n19, 400n20, 406n30, 425n57
Moessner, David P., 457n29
Mommsen, Theodor, 448n10
Montgomery, James A., 400n28, 403–4n41
Montgomery, William, 400n28
Moo, Douglas J., 376n14, 387n9, 387n12, 387n25, 417n2, 419n25, 420n39, 421n48, 445n47
Moore, Carey A., 453n30
Mørkholm, Otto, 380n7, 380n8
Morris, Leon, 394n41
Morton, James Malcolm, 425n56, 425n61
Mowery, Robert L., 385n7, 385n14, 385n15
Müller, Peter, 444–45n36
Müller, Ulrich B., 442n4
Munck, Johannes, 374n2, 374n3
Murphy-O'Connor, Jerome, 177, 371n2, 377n2, 394n38, 394n40, 397n39, 397n41, 398n42, 398n43, 398n44, 398n45, 398n46, 398n47, 398n48, 398n55, 398n56, 399n57, 404n50, 404n51, 407n38, 407n42, 407n43, 408n45, 408n46, 408n48, 408n49, 408n51, 408n52, 408n53, 409n21, 412n11, 417n1, 455n1, 456n13
Musurillo, Herbert, 441n55, 448n6, 448n45
Myers, Jason A., 444n25

Neil, William, 404n43, 424n51
Nes, Jermo van, 343, 413n13, 447n16, 453n18, 453n19
Nicholl, Colin R., 392–93n26, 402n9, 402n10, 402n13, 403n33, 403n36, 403n38, 403n39, 404n42
Nickelsburg, George W. E., 381n27
Nicolotti, Andrea, 258, 428n33, 428n38
Nobbs, Alanna, 383n21, 383n22, 383n25
Nock, Arthur Darby, 390n29, 395n10, 396n21
Nolland, J. L., 387n13, 387n14
North, J. A., 385n8
North, John, 397n32, 402n7

INDEX OF AUTHORS

Noth, Martin, 400n24, 401n35
Nussbaum, Martha C., 395n2

Ogg, George, 386n21
Omerzu, Heike, 269, 391n12, 428n39, 429n44, 429n48, 430n3, 430n5, 431n18, 431n24, 431n28, 432n29, 432n30, 432n31, 450n35, 456n11
Onur, Fatih, 384n26, 425n57
Osborne, Catherine, 395n2
Osborne, Robert E., 381n19
Osiek, Carolyn, 440n45
Oster, Richard E., 407n44, 415n1, 415n2
Oswalt, John N., 381n25
Oulton, John Ernest Leonard, 459n8, 460n25
Ovadiah, Asher, 430n3

Palmer, Darryl W., 453n29
Pao, David W., 444n30, 444–45n36
Parker, Henry Michael Denne, 440n40
Parker, Robert, 437n8
Parsons, P. J., 399n1, 399n2, 399n4, 399n5
Parvis, Paul, 449n13, 449n15
Pascuzzi, Maria A., 443n13
Patrich, Joseph, 430n4
Peachin, Michael, 392n15, 448n8, 450n25
Peake, Arthur Samuel, 447n24
Pearson, Birger A., 392n23
Peleg, Rachel, 430n3
Penner, Todd, 454n34
Perriman, Andrew, 417n29
Pervo, Richard I., 374n4, 389n6, 396n17, 396n19, 439n37, 453n27, 453n28, 456n14, 459n12, 459n13, 459n14, 459n15, 459n17
Pesch, Rudolf, 409n20
Pietersma, Albert, 414n32
Pitts, Andrew W., 413n21, 413n22, 443n14, 443n15, 452n15, 452n16, 452n17
Pokorný, Petr, 443n10, 443n11
Porter, Stanley E., 374n16, 413n21, 413n22, 435n46, 443n14, 452n15, 452n16
Price, Simon, 397n32, 402n7
Price, S. R. F., 385n8, 394n44
Puig i Tàrrech, Armand, 391n12, 428n39, 431n18, 441n61, 448n9, 450n30, 450n33, 450n35, 457n27, 458n2, 458n36, 459n21

Quinn, Jerome D., 343–44, 413n14, 435n48, 448n6, 449n21, 453n24

Ramsay, W. M., 76–77, 371n5, 380n13, 380n14, 382n2, 382n6, 382n7, 382n8, 383n24, 384n31, 384n32, 384n33, 386n21, 390n22, 390n24, 390n26, 421n2, 422n7, 422n8, 424n53
Ramsey, Boniface, 453n26
Rapske, Brian, 264, 427n28, 428n34, 428n36, 428n37, 428n39, 428n40, 428n41, 429n55, 430n6, 439n31, 440n43, 444n28, 444n29, 447n2
Raubitschek, Antony E., 395n9
Rauh, Nicholas K., 421n50, 422n17
Reardon, B. P., 401n38, 453n32
Reardon, Timothy W., 400n32, 401n33, 401n34
Reddish, Mitchell G., 424n47
Reece, Steve, 342, 399n4, 399n5, 399n7, 399n8, 452n10, 452n11
Reicke, Bo, 358, 456n17, 456n21, 457n29
Reicke, Ingalisa, 457n29
Reinhold, Meyer, 448n7
Rhea, Robert, 402n22
Richardson, L., Jr., 439n34
Riesner, Rainer, 371n3, 376n23, 379n38, 381n18, 382–83n13, 383n21, 383n25, 385n16, 386n5, 388n5, 397n36,

494

404n51, 404n54, 406n23, 450n30, 454n46
Rijksbaron, Albert, 390n21
Robbins, Vernon K., 390n28, 454n38, 454n39, 454n40, 454n41
Robinson, Benjamin W., 455n4, 455n5, 455n6, 456n10, 456n12, 456n14
Robinson, David M., 385n8
Robinson, John A. T., 358, 456n15, 456n16, 456n18, 456n21, 456n22, 457n29
Röcker, Fritz W., 403n40
Rolfe, J. C., 410n33
Roller, Duane W., 240, 371n4, 383n20, 391n4, 392n20, 395n3, 397n38, 397n40, 397n41, 407n42, 408n50, 424n37, 424n38, 424n39, 424n40, 436n3, 437n4, 437n11
Ropes, James Hardy, 421n5
Rosenmeyer, Patricia A., 451n2
Roth, Dieter T., 449n17
Rowe, C. Kavin, 450n31
Rushforth, G. McN., 435n38
Russell, D. S., 445n43

Safrai, S., 380n1
Sanders, E. P., 255, 372n26, 387n11, 400n28, 422n9, 427n15, 427n16, 427n17, 427n19, 427n26, 427n27, 428n18, 428–29n43, 429n45
Sandnes, Karl Olav, 374n12, 374n13, 374n14, 374n15
Santalucia, Bernardo, 450n33, 450n34
Sayar, Mustafa H., 379n42
Schaper, Joachim, 372n13, 372n14, 372n17, 372n23, 372n24, 372n25
Schatzmann, Siegfried S., 443n10
Scheck, Thomas P., 420n38
Scheld, John, 397n31
Schellenberg, Ryan S., 391–92n13, 392n16, 440n42, 454n44, 454n54, 454n56, 454n57, 455n2, 455n58
Schnabel, Eckhard J., 381n21, 383n19, 383n21, 384n3, 384n27, 385n4, 385n18, 388n5, 394n55, 395n2, 416n11, 417n1, 417n23, 419n26, 421n48, 421n49, 423n35
Schnelle, Udo, 426n8, 457n27
Schrage, Wolfgang, 411n45, 411n47
Schreiner, Thomas R., 387n29, 421n48
Schroder, R. V., 438n20
Schröter, Jens, 389n14
Schürer, Emil, 376n22, 382–83n13, 391n6, 429n1, 430n10, 432n33, 432n34
Schwartz, Daniel R., 374n7
Schwartz, Joshua, 393n27
Schweitzer, Albert, 400n28
Schwemer, Anna Maria, 374n10, 375n2, 375n3, 375n22, 375n23, 376n11, 376n12, 376n13, 376n23, 379n32, 380n12, 381n16, 381n19, 381n21, 454n53
Scott, E. F., 413n17, 413n19
Scott, Roger, 380n9
Segal, Alan F., 381n30
Segal, Peretz, 427n17, 427n22, 427n24
Seifrid, Mark A., 100, 387n24, 387n25, 387n26, 387n27
Seland, Torrey, 373n33, 373n34, 373n35, 373n36
Selwyn, Edward Gordon, 48, 378n26
Shackleton Bailey, D. R., 185, 288, 343, 452n9
Sherwin-White, A. N., 270, 416n6, 416n7, 416n8, 429n47, 431n15, 432n35, 438–39n29
Sim, David C., 450n29
Slingerland, Dixon, 389n10
Smallwood, E. Mary, 333–34, 380n2, 380n3, 380n4, 380n5, 380n11, 382–83n13, 386n2, 386n3, 405n14, 405n15, 426n5, 430n13, 431n16, 451n37, 451n38
Smith, David, 426n1
Smith, James, 275, 432n5, 433n11,

433n12, 433n13, 433n14, 433n16,
  433n46, 434n24, 434n25, 434n30,
  434n31, 434n32, 434n33, 434n35,
  434n36
Sommerstein, Alan Herbert, 395n1
Soon, Isaac T., 377n30, 381–82n32,
  446n10, 452n2
Sooner, 454n47
Spawforth, Anthony, 386n21,
  424–25n53
Spicq, C., 415n33, 434n23, 448n4
Sprinkle, Preston M., 420n39
Stanton, Graham N., 378n15
Steinhauser, Michael, 398n53, 419n32,
  437n4
Stern, M., 380n1
Stevenson, George Hope, 410n27
Still, Todd D., 444n25
Stott, Douglas W., 371n3, 376n23,
  379n38, 381n18, 383n21, 385n16,
  386n5, 388n5, 397n36, 406n23
Strachan, Lionel R. M., 402n14, 455n4
Strait, Drew W., 395n6, 395n8
Strassler, Robert B., 397n28
Stuhlmacher, Peter, 420n34, 420n41
Sturdy, John, 372n13
Swete, Henry Barclay, 378n17, 378n20
Szesnat, H., 398n56

Tajra, Harry W., 428n37, 439n31,
  439n38, 448n6, 448n7, 451n42,
  451n43, 459n20, 459n22
Talbert, J. A., 373n42, 379n39, 379n42,
  383n14, 383n20, 384n28, 385n16,
  385–86n20, 386n22, 387n5, 388n3,
  388n4, 391n1, 394n54, 395n56,
  405n11, 407n35, 407n36, 407n37,
  407n42, 424–25n53, 425n56, 432n6,
  438n22, 448n12
Taylor, Jane, 376n19, 376n20, 376n21
Taylor, Justin, 376n22, 376–77n24,
  377n25, 377n29
Teske, Roland, 453n26

Thackeray, H. St. J., 248, 391n6
Theophilos, Michael P., 450n29
Thielman, Frank, 375n6, 377n28,
  379n36, 379n37, 398n50, 401–2n6,
  411n36, 418n3, 418–19n20, 419n27,
  419n30, 420n37, 420n38, 420n39,
  421n48, 431n25, 431n27, 441n57,
  441n62, 445n37, 446n4, 446n8,
  446n10, 446n12, 446n13, 446n14,
  447n17, 447n18, 447n19, 447n22,
  452n2
Thiselton, Anthony C., 407n33,
  407n34, 409n19, 409n21, 410n24,
  410n34, 411n45, 451n47
Thompson, Glen L., 239, 388n2, 388n5,
  389n19, 390n20, 390n22, 390n25,
  406n30, 422n15, 423n28, 423n30,
  423n31, 423n32, 423n34, 436n2,
  437n12, 438n17, 438n18, 438n19,
  439n38
Thrall, Margaret E., 381n32
Tod, Marcus Niebuhr, 410n27
Tomson, Peter J., 393n27
Toner, Jerry, 447n23
Towner, Philip H., 413–14n24, 414n25,
  415n38, 415n39, 449n21
Trainor, Michael, 444n24
Trapp, Thomas H., 378n18
Trebilco, Paul, 408n1, 408n3, 408n50
Trout, John Moore, 384n34, 387n21,
  399n9, 456n24
Turner, E. G., 386n2

VanderKam, James C., 430n9, 430n11
Vermes, Geza, 376n22, 382–83n13,
  391n6, 429n1
Voza, G., 437n10

Wacker, William C., 343–44, 413n14,
  448n6, 449n21, 453n24
Waelkens, Marc, 383n25
Walker, Henry John, 410n30
Walker, Peter, 457n32

Index of Authors

Wallace-Hadrill, Andrew, 293, 440n45, 440n46
Wanamaker, Charles A., 396n11
Wansink, Craig S., 441n56
Waterfield, Robin, 385n11, 454n35
Watson, Alan, 448n10
Watson, Francis, 420n39
Watson, George Ronald, 440n40
Wedderburn, A. J. M., 348, 419n25, 419–20n33, 420n34, 420n40, 454n36, 454n42
Weima, Jeffrey A. D., 308, 392n25, 393n33, 394n52, 396n12, 399n10, 400n14, 401n1, 401–2n6, 402n10, 402n18, 403n27, 403n30, 403n32, 403n35, 403n36, 404n46, 444n25, 444n26, 444n33, 444n35
Weiss, Johannes, 399n9
Welborn, L. L., 410n24, 410n32, 414n30, 416n17, 417n30, 444n24, 445n42, 458n3, 458n5
Welles, C. Bradford, 371n6, 371n7, 371n8, 371n9
Wendt, Heidi, 414n29, 414n31, 434n22
Wenham, David, 377n3, 377n4, 377n5
White, John L., 435n51, 452n14
White, L. Michael, 440n51, 441n55
Wiesehöfer, Josef, 386n21
Wieseler, Karl, 413–14n24
Williamson, H. G. M., 372n15, 372n16
Wilson, Annalisa Phillips, 442n5
Wilson, Mark, 239, 379n40, 381n20, 381n21, 384n26, 386n27, 388n2, 388n5, 389n19, 390n20, 390n22, 390n25, 406n30, 407n38, 407n39, 422n15, 423n19, 423n28, 423n30, 423n31, 423n32, 423n34, 424n42, 432n6, 432n7, 436n2, 437n12, 438n17, 438n18, 438n19, 439n38
Wilson, R. McL., 444n31, 444n36
Wilson, Stephen G., 434n21

Windisch, Hans, 374n8, 374n9
Winter, Bruce W., 373n41, 382n1, 382n4, 382n5, 383n21, 384n2, 386n6, 386n25, 387n7, 392n24, 393n30, 393n36, 394n50, 395n6, 395n7, 398n46, 398n47, 398n48, 399n58, 400n17, 400n18, 400n21, 402n19, 404n45, 404n50, 404n52, 404n53, 405n1, 407n32, 409n12, 409n14, 410n24, 410n26, 410n34, 411n37, 429n56, 430n6, 430n12, 430n14, 431n15, 431n17, 431n19, 439n31, 443n9, 444n30, 447n2, 453n29, 459n13
Winter, Sara C., 444n27
Wintermute, O. S., 393n34
Wischmeyer, Oda, 449n17, 450n29
Witherington, Ben, III, 408n3, 409n20
Wolter, Michael, 417n2, 419n21, 419n24, 420n36, 420n39, 421n49
Worcester, Edward Strong, 456n24
Worrell, William Hoyt, 456n24
Wrede, William, 151, 400n26, 400n27, 402n22, 402n23, 402n24, 403n25, 403n26
Wright, N. T., 238, 402n7, 402n8, 402n11, 402n12, 406n25, 411n42, 411n43, 411n44, 411n45, 423n21, 443n6
Wycherley, R. E., 395n4

Yarbro, Adela, 413n14, 434n23, 449n16, 458n38

Zahn, Theodor, 145–46, 384n34, 387n21, 399n9, 399n10, 399n11, 399n13, 404n47, 456n24
Zanker, Paul, 446n15
Zeller, Dieter, 409n19, 412n50
Zimmermann, Christiane, 383n25, 385n20, 388n4, 389n15, 390n20

Index of Subjects

Achaia, 135, 145, 155, 165–66, 173, 179, 181–82, 193, 213, 223, 232
Achaicus, 183–84
Agabus, 69, 246, 332
Alexander (false teacher in Ephesus), 325–26
Alexander of Abonoteichus, 233–34
Alexandria: Claudius's edict, 57–58, 60, 265; violent uprising of Greeks against the Jewish population, 54–58, 64
Amphipolis, 114–15, 118
Ananias, 16, 26, 31, 257, 260, 264–66, 333
Anatolian mission, 84, 103, 104–12
Annas, 14
Antioch. *See* Pisidian Antioch; Syrian Antioch
Antiochus III of Syria, 159
Antiochus IV Epiphanes, 55, 56, 67, 89, 90
Antonia Fortress, 255–56, 258–60, 297, 298
Apamea, 109, 110–11, 175
Apion, 57
Apollonia, 110–11, 114, 118, 175, 239
Apollonius, 58
Apollos, 179, 181–84, 276–77, 281, 300
Arabia: Nabatean kingdom, 27, 33–37;

Paul's proclamation of the gospel, 27, 33–37, 50
Aretas IV, King, 27, 34–37
Aristarchus, 196, 204, 207, 209, 223, 271–73, 292, 293–94
Aristobulus II, 341
Artemas, 273, 281, 285
Artemis cult and temple (Ephesus), 176, 206–7
Aseneth's conversion, 18–19
Assos, 239–40. *See also* Apollonia
Athens: the city, 128–29; Paul's hearing before the Areopagus council and his speech on idolatry, 130–35, 158; Paul's marketplace evangelism, 129, 131; Paul's second missionary journey, 127, 128–35; Timothy's arrival, 130
Augustus (Caesar Augustus), 3, 60, 79, 124–25, 129, 160, 221

Barnabas: bringing Paul to Antioch, 53, 68–69; end of first missionary journey and disagreement with Paul, 103, 104; famine relief to Christians in Judea, 69–72; mission with Paul in Cyprus, 49–50, 72–75, 115; mission with Paul in southern Galatia, 75–78, 79–87; and the multiethnic church in Antioch, 53, 67–69, 88–103; and

Index of Subjects

Paul's post-conversion return to Jerusalem, 49–50
Basilica of Saint Paul Outside the Walls (Rome), 334–35, 363, 367
Berea, 126–27, 128–29, 156, 192, 210, 352
Bithynia, 87, 111
"brigands and impostors," 247–48

Caesarea-by-the-Sea: church of, 245–46, 263, 332; city of, 263, 267; competing claims of Syrian and Jewish inhabitants, 267; new procurator Festus, 267–70, 271; and Paul's imprisonment letters, 354–58; Paul's palace imprisonment, 263–70; Paul's transfer under military escort, 261–62; Paul under custody of Felix, 263–67. *See also* Paul's imprisonment
Caiaphas, 14
Capua, 286, 288
Caristanius (C. Caristanius Fronto Caisianus Iullus), 79, 83
Celer, 259
Cenchreae, 137, 166, 167–68, 169, 179, 217, 223, 232
Chairas, 342
Chariton's *Chaereas and Callirhoe*, 345
Chios, 208, 240–41
Chloe, 183
Cilicia: Cilicia Tracheia, 274; Jewish community and civil unrest during Paul's ministry, 58–62; Paul's birth in Tarsus, 2–3; Paul's first missionary journey, 52, 53–66, 67–69
circumcision controversy: false teachers and, 102, 104, 146–48; Jerusalem church leaders meeting with Paul and Barnabas, 92–102, 107, 109–10; Jerusalem Council's decree, 97–102, 104, 107, 110, 146; Jewish Christians' suspicion that Paul and Barnabas were accommodating to gentiles, 89–92; Mosaic law and, 88–89, 92, 94, 95–97, 110; and Paul's first missionary journey in Syrian Antioch, 88–103; and Paul's letter to the Galatians, 91–96, 100, 146–48; Peter and, 95–97, 99–102; Timothy's circumcision, 106–10
Circus Maximus, 114, 288, 289
Claros, oracle at, 311
Claudius, 53–54, 79, 166, 247, 265, 268, 297; edict expelling Jews from Rome, 139, 227; edict to the Alexandrians, 57–58, 60, 265; and the Jewish character of the Roman church, 227; triple-arched gateway and temple in Pisidian Antioch, 79, 83, 147
Claudius Lysias, 256–62
Cnidus, 273, 274, 361
collection for Jerusalem, 169–72, 174–75, 183, 210, 217–18, 223, 226, 232, 235, 251; the delegation in Philippi, 236–37; the delegation sailing from Assos to Miletus, 240–41; the delegation's return to Jerusalem, 232, 233–46; the delegation's travel to Troas, 236–39; delivery to Jerusalem church leaders, 248–49, 251
Colossae: Christian community, 175, 305–6, 310–13, 326; false teachers in, 310–13, 326
Colossians, letter to, 304–5, 310–13, 314–15, 326, 353–62; authorship question, 304–5; writing style and vocabulary, 304–5
Commagene, 86
Corinth: Christians' growing opposition and disillusionment with Paul, 184–85, 193–94, 204, 210–12, 218; city, location, and philosopher-teachers, 136–38; divisions in the church, 183; the early church in, 140–42; opposition to Paul from Jewish leaders (and Gallio's ruling), 164–66; Paul, Silas, and Timothy

reunited in, 156; Paul's announcement of his plans to return to, 191–92, 194; Paul's departure after Gallio's ruling, 166; Paul's receiving distressing news about the Christian community, 181–92, 193–96, 204–5, 207–19; and Paul's second missionary journey, 136–42, 143–54, 168; Paul's second visit to confront the church in disarray, 194–96, 211; Paul's third visit to, 223; Paul's work with Prisca and Aquila, 138–41, 146, 155; sexual immorality in the church, 183, 188, 191, 194; and Titus, 193, 205, 207–10, 213, 217, 223; writing letters to Thessalonica, 145–46, 156–63; writing letter to the Galatians, 143–54

Corinthians, first letter to the, 181–83, 185–92, 213–19; emphasizing the Corinthians' identity as people of God, 188–91; on idolatry, 189; instruction on sexual behavior, 181–82, 188–89; on life after death and bodily resurrection, 189–91; on pride and its theological antidote, 185–87

Corinthians, second letter to the, 155, 196, 204–5, 207–8, 210–19, 220; Paul's description of his vision of paradise, 62–65, 218–19; Paul's role as God's mediator, 214–19; Titus's report on the Corinthians' response to, 210–12

Cornelius (centurion), 88, 96, 101

Council of Nicaea (AD 325), 62

Crescens, 292

Crete: Fair Havens, 273, 275–77; false teachers on, 276–77, 283–85; Paul's administrative instructions for the churches, 283–85; and Paul's letter to Titus, 273, 281–85, 314; prisoner Paul's journey south and shelter on, 274–77

Crispus, 165

Cumae, 288, 289
Cumanus (Ventidius Cumanus), 170, 247, 259, 261, 265, 297
Cynic philosophers, 121, 131
Cyprus: mission of Paul, Barnabas, and John Mark, 49–50, 72–76, 115; and prisoner Paul's turbulent journey west from Caesarea to Rome, 273–74

Dalmatia, 222
Damascus, 31–33; Paul's escape from the Jewish authorities, 16, 35–37, 38, 349; Paul's proclamation of the gospel, 31–33, 50; pre-Christian Paul's journey from Jerusalem to, 15–16; Roman rule, 35–36; synagogues, 32
Day of Atonement, 230–31, 254, 275
Derbe, 86, 87, 93, 105–6, 145, 148, 173
Domitian, emperor, 288
Dora, 57–58, 60–61, 89
Drusilla, 266–67

Egyptian, the, 248, 256, 266
Eleazar, son of Deinaeus, 171
Eleusis, 136
Elymas the magician, 74–75, 83, 93
Enoch, visionary experience of, 63–64
Epaenetus, 179
Epaphras, 175, 292, 299, 304–6, 308, 310, 312, 316, 326
Epaphroditus, 292, 299–304
Ephesians, letter to the, 305, 314–22, 353–62; authorship question, 316–17; instructions on living a way of life consistent with the church's mission and God's love, 320–22; Paul on his intercession for the Ephesians, 318; praise to God, 317–18; the setting and general nature of, 316–17; three examples of God's gracious power, 319–20; writing style and vocabulary, 305, 316
Ephesus: Apollos and the Christian community, 179, 181–84, 276–77, 281, 300;

Index of Subjects

Artemis cult and temple, 176, 206–7; the city, 175–77; Demetrius's demonstration against Paul, 206–7; false teachers in, 198, 199–203, 243–44, 316, 323, 325–26; and first administrative letter to Timothy, 196–204, 242–43, 323, 325–26; origins and growth of the Christian community, 178–81; Paul's challenges and opposition in, 195–204, 242–44, 332; Paul's fight from prison against discouragement in, 314–22; and Paul's imprisonment letters, 354–58; Paul's meeting in Miletus with Ephesian church elders, 242–44; Paul's third missionary journey, 169, 175–77, 178–92, 193–205, 206–7; Paul's work in the tentmaking workshop, 179; Prisca and Aquila's missionary work, 169, 178–80

Epicurean philosophers, 131

Erastus, 182–83, 191–92, 193, 354, 360, 361

Eunice (mother of Timothy), 106–9

Euodia, 116, 300, 304, 342

Eutychus, 238–39

evidence for Paul, 337–52; authorship of first administrative letter to Timothy, 197–98, 282, 327–28, 344; authorship of letter to the Colossians, 304–5; authorship of letter to the Ephesians, 316–17; authorship of letter to Titus, 281–82, 327–28, 344; authorship of second letter to the Thessalonians, 160–62, 338, 341, 342, 344; authorship of second letter to Timothy, 327–28, 344; authorship of the Pauline letters, 337–45; the historical value of Acts, 345–52, 353; and literary forgeries in the ancient world, 338–44

Fadus (Cuspius Fadus), 268, 297
Fair Havens (Crete), 273, 275–77
false teachers, 146–51; attacks on Paul's qualifications and integrity, 148, 149; and circumcision controversy, 102, 104, 146–48; on Crete, 276–77, 283–85; denying table fellowship to gentiles, 147; in Ephesus, 198, 199–203, 243–44, 316, 323, 325–26; first letter to Timothy on, 198, 199–203, 323, 325–26; and magicians, 76, 200–201, 310–12, 323, 326–27; Paul's concerns during his house arrest in Rome, 310–13, 323, 325–27, 330; and Paul's letter to the Colossians, 310–13, 326; and Paul's letter to the Galatians, 87, 98–99, 146–51; second letter to Timothy on, 323, 326–27, 330

Feast of Unleavened Bread, 234–36
Feast of Weeks (Pentecost), 235–36, 254
Felix, procurator, 247–48, 256, 259–62, 263–67, 297–98, 333; Paul's imprisonment under custody of, 263–67
Festus, procurator, 166, 267–70, 271, 281, 298, 314, 333
Flaccus, 54–55, 56
Florus, 259–60
Fortunatus, 183–84
Forum of Appia, 288–89

Gadeira, 221
Gaius, emperor, 53, 54, 56–57, 60; order to erect statue of Zeus in the Jerusalem temple, 56–57, 89–90, 162, 163
Gaius (Paul's Macedonian traveling companion), 196, 204, 207, 209, 223
Gaius Verres (governor of Sicily), 324
Galatia: Derbe, 86; expulsion of Paul and Barnabas, 82–83; false teachers in, 87, 98–99, 146–51; Iconium, 83; imperial cult in, 147–48; Lystra, 83–87; Paul's first missionary journey with Barnabas, 75–78, 79–87; Paul's stoning in Lystra, 61–62, 85–86, 109; Paul's synagogue sermon in Antioch, 80–83; Pisidian Antioch, 75–78, 79–83

INDEX OF SUBJECTS

Galatians, letter to the, 143–54; on Christ's substitutionary death, 151–54; on the circumcision controversy, 91–96, 100, 146–48; date of writing, 145–46; on false teachers distorting the gospel, 87, 98–99, 146–51; on justification through faith, 151–52; and letter writing in the Roman East at Paul's time, 143–45; Paul's arguments in defense of the gospel, 149–50; Paul's arguments on Jewish scriptures, Mosaic law, and the meaning of Christ's death, 149–51; Paul's defense of his integrity, 148, 149; as summary of Paul's long-standing theological convictions, 151–54
Gallio (L. Iunius Gallio Annaeanus), ruling of, 165–66, 167
Gamaliel, Rabbi, 1, 4, 7, 12
Germanicus (proconsul), 159
Gnaeus Cornelius (consul), 159
Gnostic Christians, 197

Heliodorus legend, 19–20
Hermes, 84, 128, 214
Herod Agrippa I, 3, 4, 49, 53–54, 57, 60, 70, 72, 90
Herod Agrippa II, 265, 270, 297–98, 314, 333
Herod Antipas, 9, 34
Herod the Great, 34, 263–64, 267
Hierapolis, 40, 175, 306
Hippocrates, 344
Hymenaeus, 325–26, 330

Iconium, 75, 83, 85–87, 90, 93, 104–7, 109–10, 127, 145, 148, 173
Illyricum, 199, 214, 219, 220–23, 337; divided city of, 221–22; Paul's journey and traveling companions, 222–23
imperial cult, 60, 118, 125, 147–48, 156
imprisonment letters, 292, 353–62; Colossians, 304–5, 310–13, 314–15, 326, 353–62; Ephesians, 305, 314–22, 353–62; on false teachers, 310–13, 323, 326–27, 330; historical setting of, 353–62; Laodicea, 313, 353, 355, 359, 362; order of, 358–62; Philemon, 292, 305, 306, 307–9, 314, 353–62; Philippians, 295, 300–304, 314, 353–62; second letter to Timothy, 315, 327–31, 343, 344, 353–62; writing styles and vocabulary, 304–5, 316, 327–28, 343
Isaiah's suffering servant, 21–22, 25–26, 43, 44, 46–47, 82, 221
Ishmael son of Phabi, 333–34

James the brother of Jesus, 15, 38, 49, 70–72, 91, 93, 94, 97–103, 170, 218, 249, 250, 252
Jannes and Jambres (magicians), 326
Jason, 120, 124, 125–26, 223
Jerusalem: "brigands and impostors" in, 247–48; church leadership's plan for Paul to undergo purification to enter the temple, 250–52; delivering the collection, 248–49, 251; Gaius's statue of Zeus in the temple, 56–57, 89–90, 162, 163; Jewish-Christian community's opposition to Paul's teaching, 50–52, 249–52; Judeans' plot against Paul, 233–34; Paul brought up as Pharisee in, 4–12; Paul mobbed and arrested in the temple, 252–62, 333; Paul's collection for Christians, 169–72, 174–75, 183, 210, 217–18, 223, 226, 232, 235, 251; Paul's early journey to Damascus from, 15–16; Paul's fifteen-day stay with Peter (Cephas), 38–40, 43–49; Paul's final meeting with the church leadership, 248–52; Paul's final visit, 233–46, 247–62; Paul's "first defense" and trial before church leaders, 295,

315, 324–25, 332–34, 369–70; Paul's first post-conversion return, 38–52; Paul's second post-conversion visit, 70–72; Paul's temple vision, 50
Jerusalem Council, 53, 97–102, 104, 109–10, 146, 148, 152, 154, 167, 249; decree and dietary restrictions, 98, 101; decree and idolatry, 97–98; decree on circumcision, 97–102, 104, 107, 110, 146
Jerusalem temple: Antiochus IV Epiphanes and, 55; church leadership's plan for Paul to undergo purification rite to enter, 250–52; conflicts between Jesus and Pharisees on, 10–12; Gaius's statue of Zeus, 56–57, 89–90, 162, 163; layout of Herod's Temple, 253–55; Nero and, 333–34; Paul's arrest for temple defilement, 252–62, 333; Paul's detention in the Antonia Fortress, 255–56, 258–60; Paul's temple vision, 50; Pharisees and, 5, 10–12
Jewish revolt (AD 66–70), 58
John Malalas (sixth-century chronographer), 56
John Mark, 49–50, 72–77, 91, 103, 104, 292; assistance to Barnabas and Paul during mission to Cyprus, 49–50, 72–76, 115; departure from the mission, 76–77, 88; help to Paul while under house arrest in Rome, 292, 331
John the Baptist, 96, 179–80
Jonathan (high priest), 265, 267
Joseph and Aseneth (ancient historical novel), 18–19
Jubilees, book of, 108–9, 122
Judas (emissary from the Jerusalem church), 99
Judas the Galilean, 90–91
Judea: Barnabas and Paul's famine relief visit to, 69–72; the Judeans' plot against Paul, 233–34; Nabatean kingdom's relationship with Jews of, 34. *See also* Caesarea-by-the-Sea
Judith, book of, 345
Julius (centurion), 271, 273–74, 276–77, 281, 286, 287, 288
Julius Caesar, 3, 159–60
Junia Theodora, 137, 342

Laodicea, 175, 306, 313; Paul's imprisonment letter to, 313, 353, 355, 359, 362
Lesbos, 208, 240, 271
letter writing in the Roman East, 143–45
literary forgeries in the ancient world, 338–44; Plato's letters, 339–40, 341; scholarly evidence on the disputed Pauline letters, 338–44. *See also* evidence for Paul
Lucian of Samosata, 233–34
Luke: account of Paul's conversion, 17, 18–21, 24–26, 27–28, 349; account of Paul's synagogue sermon in Pisidian Antioch, 80–83; first-person-plural narrative of Macedonia mission, 112–13, 117; help to Paul while under house arrest in Rome, 292, 293–94; mission to Philippi, 114–17; and Paul's journey as prisoner from Caesarea to Rome, 271–73
Lycia, 137, 245, 274
Lydia, 115–16, 118
Lystra: Paul and Barnabas's mission in, 83–87; Paul's healing of a lame man, 84; Paul's stoning in, 61–62, 85–86, 109; Timothy and his mother, 84, 106–9

Macedonia mission, 112–13, 114–27; Luke's first-person-plural narrative, 112–13, 117; Paul, Silas, and Timothy flee to Berea, 126–27; Paul's third missionary journey, 207–10; Philippi

INDEX OF SUBJECTS

mission of Paul, Silas, Timothy, and Luke, 114–17; Thessalonica mission of Paul, Silas, and Timothy, 117–26
magicians: Elymas the magician, 74–75, 83, 93; false teachers, 76, 200–201, 310–12, 323, 326–27; Jannes and Jambres, 326; Jewish magicians and folk religion, 200–201
Malta: the island and its people, 280–81; Paul's post-shipwreck winter of hospitality on, 280–85, 286–87; travel to Rome after three-month stay in, 286–87; writing letter to Titus in, 273, 281–85, 314
Marcion's *Antitheses*, 343–44
Megara, 136
Menander, 326–27
Miletus, 240–42, 273, 275; city of, 242; Paul's important meeting with Ephesian church elders, 242–44; temple of Apollo Delphinios (Apollo the Dolphin God), 242
Mithridates IV, King of Pontus, 159
Mitylene, island of Lesbos, 240–41
Mnason, 246, 248–49
Muratorian Canon, 368–69, 457n33
Musonius Rufus, 123
Myra, 263, 273–74
Mysia, 111–12, 271

Nabatean kingdom of Arabia, 27, 33–37; deities of, 34–35, 36; Paul's proclamation of the gospel to, 27, 33–37, 50; Paul's trouble with authorities under King Aretas IV, 27, 34–37; relationship with Jews of Judea, 34
Nazirite vow, 167–68, 170, 250–52
Neapolis, 113, 114, 209, 236–37, 331
Nero, 74, 289, 297–98; coins, 229; confirmation of Felix as governor of Judea, 247, 248; and the Jerusalem temple, 333–34; legal environment in court at the time of Paul's imprisonment, 297–98; persecution of Christians (AD 64), 296–97; and the praetorian barracks in Rome, 290; replacement of Felix with Festus, 267
Nicodemus, 9
Nicolaus of Antioch, 68

Onesimus: help to Paul while under house arrest in Rome, 292, 299; and Paul's letter to Philemon, 292, 305, 307–10; visiting Paul during his two years in Rome, 292, 299, 304–10, 316
Onesiphorus, 292, 324, 329, 331

Paphos (Cyprus), 73–74
Papias, bishop of Hierapolis, 40–43, 44; *Exposition of the Logia of the Lord*, 40–43
Patara, 241, 245
Paul, pre-Christian, 1–16; birth and early education in Tarsus, 1–4; journey from Jerusalem to Damascus, 15–16; as Pharisee, 4–16; zealous persecution of the early church, 1, 12–16, 18, 29–30, 44–45
Paul's conversion, 17–26, 349; account in Galatians, 20–23, 349; and Aseneth's conversion, 18–19; commission to preach the gospel to the gentiles, 21–22, 25–26, 30–31, 50, 221; immediate aftermath, 27–28; Luke's account, 17, 18–21, 24–26, 27–28, 349; and new understanding of the relationship between sin and Mosaic law, 29–30; as personal transformation, 22–25, 30–31, 32–33, 45, 215–16; as prophetic call, 21–22, 25–26; and story of Heliodorus in 2 Maccabees, 19–20; as a surprise, 17–18, 20–21
Paul, post-conversion: fifteen-day stay with Peter (Cephas) in Jerusalem, 38–40, 43–49; first return to Jerusalem, 38–52; fleeing Damascus to escape

Index of Subjects

arrest, 16, 35–37, 38, 349; immediate aftermath, 27–28; Jerusalem Jewish-Christian community's opposition to Paul, 50–52; Jerusalem temple vision, 50; learning of Jesus's life and teaching, 38–40; learning the role of Jesus's death in the forgiveness of sins, 33; learning the significance of Christ's death/crucifixion, 43–49; meeting James, 38, 49; new understanding of God's concern for all people, 30–31; new understanding of the relationship between sin and Mosaic law, 29–30; period of repentance, 28–31; proclamation of the gospel in Arabia, 27, 33–37, 50; proclamation of the gospel to Jewish Christians in Damascus, 31–33, 50; second visit to Jerusalem, 70–72

Paul's first missionary journey, 53–66, 67–78, 79–87, 88–103; attacks and stonings, 61–62, 85–86, 109; circumcision controversy in Syrian Antioch, 88–103; context of political turmoil and civil unrest in Alexandria, 54–62, 64; famine relief in Judea, 69–72; Jewish Christians' suspicion of Paul and Barnabas, 82–83, 89–92; Lystra, 61–62, 83–87, 109; map and routes, 72, 73, 75, 86–87; ministry to the gentiles, 59–62, 81–83, 89–92; mission to Cyprus with Barnabas and John Mark, 49–50, 72–78, 115; Paul's recurring illness ("thorn in the flesh"), 65–66, 76–77; Paul's vision of paradise, 62–65, 218–19; Peter and the incident at Antioch, 99–103, 349–50; Pisidian Antioch, 75–78, 79–83; to southern Galatia with Barnabas, 75–78, 79–87; synagogue sermon and expulsion from Pisidian Antioch, 80–83; Syrian and Cilician ministry, 52, 53–66, 67–69; Syrian Antioch, 52, 53–54, 67–72, 88–103

Paul's second missionary journey, 104–13, 114–27, 128–42, 143–54, 155–66; Anatolian mission, 84, 103, 104–12; Athens, 127, 128–35; Berea, 126–27; directed to Troas by the Holy Spirit, 110–12, 208; Gallio's ruling and departure from Corinth, 164–66; hearing before Athens' Areopagus council and Paul's speech on idolatry, 130–35, 158; the interval in Corinth, 136–42, 143–54, 168; Macedonian mission, 112–13, 114–27; map and routes, 104–6, 110–12, 113, 114, 117–18, 126–27, 136; Paul's recurring illness ("thorn in the flesh"), 130; Philippi, 114–17; Silas and, 103, 104–6, 110–12, 156; Thessalonica, 117–26; Timothy and the Anatolian mission, 84, 106–12; writing letters to Thessalonian Christians, 145–46, 156–63; writing letter to the Galatian Christians, 143–54

Paul's third missionary journey, 167–77, 178–92, 193–205, 206–19, 220–32; collection for Jerusalem Christians, 169–72, 174–75, 183, 210, 217–18, 223, 226, 232, 235, 251; difficult journey to Macedonia, 207–10; distressing news about the Corinthian Christians, 181–92, 193–96, 204–5, 207–19; Ephesus, 169, 175–77, 178–92, 193–205, 206–7; Illyricum, 214, 219, 220–23; letter to the Roman Christians, 223–32, 233, 294–95, 297; map and routes, 169, 173–74, 175; Paul's recurring illness ("thorn in the flesh"), 208–9; plans to return to Corinth, 191–92, 194; second visit to Corinth to confront the church in disarray, 194–96, 211; sending Timothy and coworkers to Macedonia and Achaia, 182–83, 191–92, 193, 194; travel from Ephesus to Syrian Antioch, 169, 172; Troas, 208–9, 215, 236–39; visiting Jerusalem to confer with the church leaders, 169–72; visiting Syrian Antioch, 172–73; writing first administrative letter to Timothy, 196–204, 242–43; writing first letter to the Corinthians, 181–83, 185–92, 213–19; writing second letter to the Corinthians, 155, 196, 204–5, 207–8, 210–19, 220

Paul's final visit to Jerusalem, 233–46, 247–62; "brigands and impostors" in Jerusalem, 247–48; changed itinerary and symbolism of his arrival in the Jewish calendar, 234–36; the collection delegation's travel to Troas, 236–39; delivering the collection to church leaders, 248–49, 251; the important meeting in Miletus with Ephesian church elders, 242–44; the Judeans' plot against Paul, 233–34; last leg of journey from Caesarea, 246; meeting with the church leadership, 248–52; mobbed and arrested in the temple, 252–62, 333; Paul's bad reputation among Jewish Christians, 249–52; plan for Paul to undergo purification rite to enter the temple, 250–52; return with the collection delegation, 232, 233–46; sailing from Assos to Miletus, 240–41; solo walk to Assos, 239–40. *See also* Paul's arrest in the Jerusalem temple; Paul's imprisonment

Paul's arrest in the Jerusalem temple, 252–62, 333; detention in the Antonia Fortress, 255–56, 258–60; the layout of Herod's Temple, 253–55; news of the plot against Paul's life, 260–61; Paul mistaken for the Egyptian, 256; Paul's hearing before the Sanhedrin, 259–60; Paul's transfer to Caesarea under military escort, 261–62. *See also* Paul's imprisonment

Paul's imprisonment, 263–70, 271–85, 286–98, 299–313, 314–22, 323–35; appeal to Caesar as Roman citizen, 269–70; under custody of Felix, 263–67; the difficult voyage to Myra, 273–74; and new procurator Festus in Caesarea, 267–70, 271; palace imprisonment in Caesarea-by-the-Sea, 263–70; Paul's travel entourage, 271–73; the slow journey south and shelter on Crete, 274–77; storm and shipwreck, 277–80, 286; transfer to Caesarea under military escort, 261–62; travel to Rome, 271–85, 286–87; turbulent journey west from Caesarea to Rome, 271–85, 286–87; winter of hospitality on Malta, 280–85, 286–87; writing letter to Titus, 273, 281–85, 314. *See also* imprisonment letters; Paul under house arrest in Rome

Paul under house arrest in Rome, 286–98, 299–313, 314–22, 323–35; arrival and welcome from Roman Christians, 288–89, 297; concerns about false teaching, 310–13, 323, 325–27, 330; continuing his work, 291–94; "first defense" and trial before Jerusalem leaders, 295, 315, 324–25, 332–34, 369–70; help from network of coworkers, 292–94, 299; the legal environment in Nero's court, 297–98; lodging in the vicinity of the praetorian barracks, 290–91, 293; opposition from some Roman Christians, 294–98; receiving visitors, 299–313; writing final letter to Timothy, 315, 323–32, 353–62; writing letter to Colossae, 304–5, 310–13, 314–15, 326, 353–62; writing letter to Laodicea, 313, 353, 355, 359, 362; writing letter to Philemon, 292, 305, 306, 307–9, 314, 353–62; writing letter to the Ephesians, 305, 314–22, 353–62; writing letter to the Philippians, 295, 300–304, 314, 353–62

Paul's death in Rome, 332–35, 363–70; Clement on, 296–97, 363–70; dating, 368–70; execution by beheading, 334, 366–68; "first defense" and trial before Jerusalem leaders, 295, 315, 324–25, 332–34, 369–70; place of burial, 334–35; where and how Paul died, 334, 363–68

Perga, 75–77, 87, 88, 104, 110, 130

Peter (Cephas): and the circumcision controversy in Syrian Antioch, 95–97, 99–102; the incident at Antioch, 99–103, 349–50; and Mark's Gospel, 41–43, 44–45; and Paul's fifteen-day stay in Jerusalem, 38–40, 43–49

Petronius, 57–58, 60–61

Pharisees, 4–16; and "brigands and impostors" in Jerusalem, 247; interpretation of Mosaic law, 4–12, 247; Jesus and, 7, 8–12, 43; Paul as, 4–16

Phileas, bishop of Thmuis and ruler of Alexandria, 324

Philemon, 175, 305, 306; Paul's letter to, 292, 305, 306, 307–9, 314, 353–62

Philetus, 326, 330

Philippi: the city/colony, 114–15; Epaphroditus and gift from, 299–304; Lydia and women who supported Paul's work, 115–16, 118; mission of Paul, Silas, Timothy, and Luke, 114–17; Paul and delegates spending the Feast of the Unleavened Bread in, 236–37; Paul and Silas's arrest and beatings by magistrates, 116–17, 209–10

Philippians, letter to the, 295, 300–304, 314, 353–62; on adherence to Mosaic law, 303; warning against distortions of Roman culture, 303–4

Philip V of Macedonia, 159

Phoebe, 137, 166, 223, 342

Phoenicia, 92, 241, 245

Phoenix (Crete), 276, 277

Phrygian Galatia, 110–12, 175. *See also* Galatia

Pisidian Antioch, 75–78, 79–83; Claudius's triple-arched gateway and temple, 79, 83, 147; Paul and Barnabas's mission, 75–78, 79–83; Paul's synagogue sermon and expulsion, 80–83; temple of Augustus, 79, 147

Plancus (L. Munatius Plancus), 341

Pompey, 3, 35, 163, 197

Pontius Pilate, 32, 154, 163

Poppaea (Nero's wife), 298

Porta Capena, 114, 288–89, 293

Prisca and Aquila: missionary work in Ephesus, 169, 178–80; tentmaking in Corinth, 138–41, 146, 166, 331

Ptolemais, 245

Publius, 280–81

Puteoli, 227, 276, 286–87, 293

Quadratus (Ummidius Quadratus), 170, 265, 297

Rhegium, 287

Rhodes, 244–45, 274

Romans, letter to the, 223–32, 233, 294–95, 297; Paul's definition of the gospel as the revelation of "the righteousness of God," 228–32; Paul's "principle of noninterference," 224–25; Paul's reasons for writing, 224–25, 228; Paul's "spiritual gift" to the Roman church, 225–26

Rome: the established church and its origins, 224–27; Jewish character of Roman Christianity, 227–28, 294–95, 297; opposition to Paul from some Christians, 294–98; Paul's death in, 332–35, 363–70; and Paul's imprisonment letters, 354–58; Paul's lodging in vicinity of the praetorian barracks, 290–91, 293; Paul's two years under house arrest, 286–98, 299–313,

314–22, 323–35; prisoner Paul's turbulent journey west from Caesarea to, 271–85, 286–87; Roman Christians' warm welcome of Paul, 288–89, 297
Rufus, 331–32, 342

Sadducees, 6
Salamis (Cyprus), 73
Sallust's *War with Catiline*, 345–46
Salona, 222–23
Samos, 241
Sanhedrin, 259–60, 268
Sceva, 200, 311
Seleucia, 52, 73, 105
Sergius Paulus, 74–77, 91, 93
sicarii (assassins), 90, 248, 260–61
Silas: arrest and beating by Philippi magistrates, 116–17, 209–10; fleeing to Berea, 126–27; mission to Philippi, 114–17; mission to Thessalonica, 117–26; and Paul's first missionary journey, 87, 99; and Paul's second missionary journey, 103, 104–6, 110–12, 156
Simon (false teacher), 327
Socrates, 128, 129, 131
Solomon, King, 310
Sosipater, 232
Spain, Paul's mission to, 221–27, 236
Stephanas, 183–84, 185
Stephen, 29, 50–52, 58; death of, 1–2, 12, 14, 23–24, 50–51, 52
Stoics, 3, 131, 134
Syntyche, 116, 300, 304, 342
Syracuse, 287
Syrian Antioch, 52, 53–54, 67–72, 88–103; Barnabas and Paul and the multiethnic church, 53, 67–69, 88–103; circumcision controversy, 88–103; local resistance to the multiethnic church, 88–103; origins of the church in, 67–69; and Paul's early ministry in Syria and Cilicia, 52, 53–54; Paul's third missionary journey and meetings with the church, 172–73; Peter and the incident at Antioch, 99–103, 349–50; timing of Paul's year in, 53–54

Tarsus: the city, 3; Paul's birth and early education in, 1–4; Paul's escape from Jerusalem to, 52, 53; and Paul's second missionary journey, 104–5. *See also* Cilicia
temple of Apollo Delphinios (Apollo the Dolphin God), 242
temple of Apollo Smintheus (Apollo the Mouse God), 239
temple of Artemis in Ephesus, 176, 206–7
Tertius, 223, 232
Tertullus the advocate, 265–66, 333
Thessalonians, letters to, 145–46, 156–63; first letter, 145, 156–60; instructions about the necessity of work, 164; Paul's corrections of misunderstandings about death, the afterlife, and the coming "day of the Lord," 157–60, 162–64; Paul's defense of his character, 156–58; political implications of Paul's teaching on the second coming, 158–60; second letter, 160–66, 338, 341, 342, 344
Thessalonica: the city, 118; the hasty departure of Paul, Silas, and Timothy, 123–27, 129; imperial cult in, 118, 124–25, 156; "Jason" and the Christian community in, 120, 124, 125–26, 223; Jewish accusations against Paul's ideas, 123–26; mission of Paul, Silas, and Timothy, 117–26; Paul's instructions about the necessity of work, 164; Paul's labor/work with his hands, 120–23; Paul's multiethnic outreach, 118–20; Paul's second missionary journey and anxiety for the commu-

Index of Subjects

nity, 129–30; Timothy's "good news" about the community, 156, 157
Tiberius, emperor, 35, 74, 139, 159, 221–22, 290
Tiberius Julius Alexander, 69, 90–91, 96
Timothy, 156, 323–31; accompanying Paul with the collection to Jerusalem, 232; arrival in Athens, 130; circumcision, 106–10; help to Paul while under house arrest in Rome, 292, 293–94; missing from Paul's letter to the Ephesians, 314–15; mother, 84, 106–9; and Paul's Anatolian mission, 84, 106–12; and Paul's letter to the Philippians, 302; and prisoner Paul's journey from Caesarea to Rome, 273; sent to Macedonia and Achaia, 182–83, 191–92, 193, 194
Timothy, first administrative letter to, 196–204, 242–43, 325; authorship, 197–98, 282, 327–28; and the Ephesian churches, 196–204, 242–43, 325; on false teachers in Ephesus, 198, 199–203, 323, 325–26; style of, 197–98, 282, 343
Timothy, second letter to, 315, 323, 327–31, 343, 344, 353–62; authorship, 327–28, 344; on false teachers, 323, 326–27, 330; vocabulary and style, 327–28, 343
Titius Justus, 165
Titus: giving Paul troubling news about the Corinthian Christians, 193, 205, 207–10, 213, 217, 223; help to Paul while under house arrest in Rome, 292; missionary work in Dalmatia, 222; and Paul's meeting with Jerusalem church leaders over circumcision, 93–94, 107, 109–10; sent to Macedonia and Achaia, 182–83, 191–92, 193, 194. *See also* Titus, letter to

Titus, emperor, 58, 333
Titus, letter to: authorship, 281–82, 327–28, 344; and Christianity on Crete, 276–77; dating, 282; Paul's administrative instructions for Cretan churches, 283–85; written during three-month stay on Malta, 273, 281–85, 314
Troas: the collection delegation's travel to, 236–39; Paul's group directed by the Spirit to, 110–12, 208; Paul's near-death experience in, 65, 77; Paul's third missionary journey, 208–9, 215, 236–39
Trophimus, 236–37, 241, 243, 255, 273, 275
Tychicus, 236–37, 243, 271–73, 281, 292, 305, 341; help to Paul while under house arrest in Rome, 292; and prisoner Paul's journey west from Caesarea to Rome, 271–73; sent with Paul's letters, 315, 316, 323, 331, 355, 356, 359, 362
Tyre, 172, 232, 234, 245, 293, 332

Vespasian, emperor, 58, 74, 214–15
Via Appia, 114, 286, 288–89
Via Domitiana, 288
Via Egnatia, 114, 115, 117–18, 126, 219, 222, 236
Via Laurentina, 334
Via Ostiensis, 334, 335
Via Sebaste, 75, 83, 87, 105, 109, 110, 175
Via Tauri, 105

work and manual labor in the Greco-Roman world, 120–23, 164

Zeus, 31–32, 34–35, 55, 84, 134–35, 162, 214, 283–84; Antiochus IV Epiphanes and the Jerusalem temple, 55; Gaius and the Jerusalem temple, 56–57, 89–90, 162, 163

Index of Scripture and Other Ancient Sources

Old Testament

Genesis
1:26–27	188
2–3	65
2:8	150
2:15–16	122, 164, 393n35
2:15–23	150
2:18–25	188
2:21–22	188
2:24	39, 97, 188
3:8	65
3:8a	150
3:17–19	189, 393n35
3:19	190
5:24	63
6:2	63
9:4	97
12:2–3	95
15:6	149
17:4–6	95
17:4–8	89
17:5	231
17:10–11	89
17:13–14	89
18:18	149
34:25	63
34:30	108
40:19	45, 152
41:45	19
41:50	19
46:20	19
48:14	198

Exodus
4–11	248
7:11	326
7:11–12	415n33
7:22	326
13:21–22	189
14:19–31	189
16:18	172
17:6	189
30:11–17	372n16

Leviticus
6:8–9	5
6:12–13	5
7:19–21	168
10:9	168
16:2	420n43
16:13	420n43
16:14	420n43
16:15	420n43
16:17	230–31
16:29–30	231
17:10–14	97
18:1–30	157, 188
18:5	150
18:8	188
20:26	188
23:16	235
26:11–12	65
26:14–39	150

Numbers
6:1–21	167
6:2	168
6:3–4	168
6:5	168, 426n12
6:6–12	168
6:9–12	426n12
6:13–17	168
6:15	250
6:18	168, 250
6:21	426n12
14:21–45	189
18:12–16	235
19:11–13	250
28:26	235

Deuteronomy
6:4	189
10:17–19	171
13:5	153, 165
16:10	235

Index of Scripture and Other Ancient Sources

18:18	248
21:22	154, 401n38
21:22–23	45, 152, 154, 165
21:23	45, 47, 81, 150, 152, 153
24:10–22	171
27:9–28:68	153
27:26	45, 94, 150, 153
28:15–68	150
28:48	96

Joshua
8:29	152
10:26	152

Ruth
3:10	2

1 Samuel
9:1–2	349
20:31	2
22–26	25

2 Samuel
7:12–13	23
12:15–16	29

1 Kings
4:29–34	310
12:21	2
17:21–22	238

2 Kings
4:32–35	238
24–25	345

1 Chronicles
19:10	2

Ezra
9–10	108
9:1–2	108
10:3	108
10:44	108

Nehemiah
8:1	4
8:2	4
8:4	4
8:9	4
8:13	4
9–10	4–5
9:6	381n31
9:31	5
9:38–10:39	5
10:30	389n12, 389n13
10:31	5
10:32–33	5
10:34	5
13:15–18	5
13:23–27	389n12, 389n13

Esther
5:14	45, 152
6:4	152

Psalms
8:6	318
22	42
32:1–2a	31
98:2–3	229
104:24	312
110	29
110:1	24, 32, 318
130:3	96
130:8	96
143:2	102
143:2 [142:2 LXX]	150
146:5–9	171

Proverbs
3:19	312
8:22–31	312
26:5	62, 218

Isaiah
6:1–7	63
6:5–6	22
9:6–7	23
10:1–4	171
11:1	81
11:1–10	23
25:6–8	335
25:8	191
27:9	231
29:13–14	10
42	26
42:6–7	25
42:10	221
42:16	25
49	26
49:1	21, 22, 82
49:1–5	82
49:1–6	21–22, 82
49:1–7	26
49:2–6	21
49:3	22
49:5	82
49:6	21, 82, 221, 418n5
51:5	229
52:13–53:12	221
52:15	186, 221
53:4–6	221
53:4–12	46
53:5	46
53:6	46
53:7	43, 46
53:9	44, 46
53:12	44, 45, 46–47
57:19	379n34
59:14–15	322
59:17	322

INDEX OF SCRIPTURE AND OTHER ANCIENT SOURCES

64:3–4	186
65:16	186
66:20	235

Jeremiah

1	26
1:5	22, 25
1:6	22
1:8	25
1:19	25
3:16	186
7:5–7	171
23:5–6	23
31:33	231

Ezekiel

1–3	26
1:4–28	63
1:27–28	24
1:28	24, 374–75n18
2:1	24
34:27	96
36:27	157
37:6	157
37:14	157
37:25–28	65
44:21	168

Daniel

7	29
7:9–10	63
7:13	32
7:13–14	43, 63
8:26	63
9:27	119, 162, 403–4n41
10–12	119, 162, 392–93n26, 403n36
10:13	163
11:21	119, 163
11:31	119, 162, 403–4n41
12:1	163
12:2–3	162
12:7	63
12:9	63
12:11	119, 162, 403–4n41

Joel

1:13–14	29

Amos

3:7–8	22
7:14–15	22

Habakkuk

2:4	150, 229–30, 420n39

NEW TESTAMENT

Matthew

5:1	8
9:11	7
10:10	39
10:10–11	120
11:28	420n38
11:29	96
12:6	11
16:64–66	24
19:5–6	39
19:6	39
21:12–13	11
21:42	29
22:41–46	24
23:2	8
23:3	9
23:23	7, 8, 10
23:23a	9
23:23b	9
23:25–26	7
24:2	11
24:9–22	39
24:15	119, 162, 403–4n41
24:15–31	162
24:21	162
24:24	119
24:29–31	119
24:30–31	39
24:31	162
24:36–44	119
24:43–44	39
25:1	238
25:3–4	238
25:7–8	238
26:60–61	12
26:61	12
26:63–66	14
27:39–40	165
27:40	12
27:62–66	14
28:1	237

Mark

1:16	38, 42
1:16–17	44
1:17	42
1:22	14
1:31	214
2:5–7	43
2:10	43
2:15	9
2:16	7
2:17	9
2:24	43
2:28	43
3:2	43
3:6	10, 14, 43, 165
3:16–17	42
3:21	38
3:31–35	38

Index of Scripture and Other Ancient Sources

5:37	42	14:60–61	43, 46	11:42	7, 8, 10		
6:10	120	14:61–64	14	12:39	39		
7:3	6	14:62–64	24, 43	13:14	10		
7:3–4	7	14:66–72	42	13:31	9		
7:3–4a	7	14:68	44	14:1	9		
7:4b	7	14:70	44	15:1–32	10		
7:5	6	14:71	44	15:2	9		
7:6–7	10	14:72	44	17:8	214		
7:7	7	15:16–20	43	18:32	246		
7:9–13	10	15:21	331	19:45–46	11		
7:15	10	15:29	12	20:17	29		
7:18	10	15:29–30	44	20:41–44	24		
7:21–22	9	15:31–32	44	21:6	11		
8:29	42	16:2	237	21:24	11		
9:2	42	16:7	42, 44	21:27	39		
9:35	8			22:19–20	33		
10:7–9	39	**Luke**		22:27	214		
10:9	39	1:1	113, 346	22:66–71	361		
10:45	33, 44, 46, 47	1:1–2	348	22:67–71	14, 32		
11:15–18	11	1:1–4	348	22:69–71	24		
12:10–11	29	1:2	346	23:1–5	361		
12:35–36	23	1:3	346	23:2	32, 153, 165		
12:35–37	24	1:6	96	23:4	361		
12:36	32	2:22–24	96	23:6–12	361		
12:41–43	8	2:27	96	23:14	153, 165		
13:2	11	2:39	96	23:14–15	361		
13:3	42	2:41	96	23:22	361		
13:9–20	39	4:20–21	8	24:1	237		
13:14	119, 162, 163	4:41	181				
13:14–27	162	5:3	8	**John**			
13:19	162	5:29	9	1:19	11		
13:26–27	39	5:30	7	1:24	11		
13:27	162	5:32	9	2:13–16	11		
14:24	44, 46, 47	7:36	9	2:16	11		
14:27–28	44	9:4	120	2:19	11		
14:29	44	9:31	425n54	2:20	11		
14:33	42	10:7	39, 120	3:1–2	9		
14:37	44	10:40	214	5:18	10, 165		
14:50	44	11:37	9	6:14	248		
14:55	261	11:39	7	7:3–5	38		
14:57–58	12	11:41	10	7:40	248		
14:58	12, 165						

513

INDEX OF SCRIPTURE AND OTHER ANCIENT SOURCES

7:50–52	9	6:1	2	9:11	2, 28
11:47–48	11	6:2–3	109	9:13–14	28
11:47–50	14	6:5	40, 68, 365	9:14	261
19:7	14	6:6	198	9:15	20, 26
19:30	9	6:8–10	50	9:17	198
19:31	153	6:8–7:1	51	9:17–19	26
		6:9	58	9:19–22	225
Acts		6:9–14	16	9:19b	26, 31
1:1	346	6:11–12	58	9:20	16, 32, 59
1:3	2	6:12–7:1	14	9:21	261
1:8	332	6:14	11, 12	9:22	32, 112, 349
2:11	34, 276	6:54–60	51	9:23	36, 276, 349, 351
2:33–36	32	7:1	16	9:23–24	36
2:38	33	7:54–60	50	9:23–25	16
2:39	379n34	7:55–56	14, 29, 32	9:25	349, 377n30
2:41	34	7:56	23	9:26	26, 38, 71
2:47	2	7:58	1, 12, 16	9:26–27	49
3:1–10	211	7:58–13:9	349	9:27	68, 350, 377n1
3:18	119	8:1	12, 14, 16, 73,	9:28	214
4:3	2		377n1, 433n20	9:29	16, 50, 226
4:5	2, 261	8:3	68	9:29–30	246
4:5–6	14	8:4–8	365	9:30	2, 52, 104, 388n3
4:13	211	8:14	68	10:2	101
4:16–17	14	8:14–17	106	10:24	263
4:16–18	261	8:26–40	365	10:34–35	88
4:36	49, 68, 73	8:30–35	119	10:39	47, 153, 154,
4:36–37	350	8:40	246		401n38
5:17–18	261	9	26	10:40	153
5:27–28	261	9:1	14, 17, 32, 261	10:43	33, 153
5:28	14	9:1–2	20, 216	10:44	263
5:30	47, 153, 154,	9:2	15, 16, 32	10:45	100
	401n38	9:3	17, 24, 349	10:45–47	88
5:30–31	32	9:3–6	19	10:47–48	263
5:31	33, 153	9:4	24, 25, 27,	11–12	71
5:31a	154		374–75n18	11:2–3	88
5:31b	154	9:4–5	20	11:18	88
5:33	261	9:5	28	11:19	73, 75
5:34	4, 7	9:6	20	11:19–20	73
5:34–39	9	9:7	27	11:19–21	68
5:36–37	388n31	9:8	28	11:22	68, 100, 388n31
5:38–39	7	9:8–9	20	11:23	68
5:42	2	9:9	28	11:24	68, 350
		9:10–19	20	11:25–26	53, 104

514

Index of Scripture and Other Ancient Sources

11:25–26a	69	13:27	81	14:25–26	88
11:26	225	13:28–29	81	14:27	91
11:26b	68, 69	13:29	47, 154	14:27a	88
11:27	53	13:29–37	81	14:27b	88
11:27–28	73, 246	13:30	154	15:1	88, 91, 98, 102, 104, 146, 148
11:27–30	53, 71	13:31	81	15:1–2	71
11:28	69	13:38	33	15:2	71, 91, 92
11:28–29	70	13:38–39	81	15:3–4	91
11:29	70	13:38–40	154	15:4	71, 92
11:30	70, 71	13:42–43	82	15:5	9, 71, 91, 92, 387n10
12:1	53, 70	13:43	83		
12:1–11	72	13:44	82	15:6	71, 91, 92, 94
12:1–19	268	13:45	82, 109, 124	15:7	94
12:3	60	13:46	84	15:10	96, 387n14
12:12	43, 49, 72, 88, 388n31	13:47	21, 26	15:11	96–97
		13:48	83	15:12	94, 97, 148
12:19	53	13:48–49	82	15:13	99
12:20–25	53, 70	13:50	83, 90, 109, 147	15:15	102
12:21–20:1	396n14	13:50–52	396n14	15:19–20	97
12:25	49, 70, 71, 72, 88	13:52	83	15:19–21	92
13–19	62	14:1	73, 83, 115, 126	15:20	101, 146
13:1	69, 70, 111	14:2	83, 109	15:22	103, 387n10
13:1–2	73	14:3	83	15:22–23	71
13:1–3	350	14:5	109, 147	15:23	62, 91, 98, 148, 388n1
13:2	88	14:5–6	83, 396n14		
13:4–14:23	53	14:8–10	84	15:24	91, 92, 98, 99, 147, 400n16
13:5	49, 73, 115, 126	14:11	84		
13:6–7	74	14:12	417n25	15:27	103
13:6–12	200	14:15	85	15:28	388n1
13:7	74	14:15–17	84	15:28–29	148
13:8–12	74	14:17	85	15:29	97, 101, 146
13:13	75, 76, 88	14:19	61, 85, 109, 127, 147	15:30	97, 98
13:13–14	130			15:32	103, 111
13:13–14a	87	14:20	396n14	15:32–33	99
13:13b	103	14:20a	85	15:33	103
13:14	73, 80, 115, 126	14:20b	86	15:34–40	172
13:14–50	388n2	14:21	86	15:35–36	99
13:14–14:28	173	14:21–22	83	15:36	103
13:15	80	14:21–23	87	15:36–39a	103
13:16–41	80	14:22	147	15:36–20:16	352
13:16b–41	81	14:23	107, 124, 198	15:37	50
13:22–23	81	14:24–28	53	15:38	76
13:23	385n13	14:25	75, 77, 87, 110		

INDEX OF SCRIPTURE AND OTHER ANCIENT SOURCES

15:39	50, 350	16:25–27	116	17:27–28	134
15:39–40	103	16:30–34	116	17:28	134
15:39–18:18a	350	16:35	117	17:29–30	135
15:40	103, 350	16:37	61, 116, 117	17:29–31	133
15:40–16:5	167	16:37–38	3	17:30	132
15:41	62	16:37–39	257	17:31	134–35
15:41–16:1	174	17:1	73, 117, 126	17:32	135, 158, 190
16:1	84, 87, 106	17:2	118	17:32–34	133
16:1–2	145	17:3	118, 124	17:34	135
16:1–3	174, 350	17:4	103, 119, 392n18	18:1	136
16:3	107	17:5	124	18:2	138, 139, 226, 398n54, 419n33
16:4	71, 97, 98, 110, 146	17:5–6	125–26		
16:6	109, 110–11, 112, 173, 208	17:5–7	223	18:2–3	155
		17:5–9	120, 350, 396n14	18:2–4	73
16:6–7	87	17:6	120, 124	18:3	123, 179
16:6–8	175	17:6–7	156	18:3–4	139
16:7	111	17:7	124, 160	18:4	140, 155
16:8	112	17:8–9	210	18:5	103, 115, 120, 145, 156, 350, 351, 409n10
16:8–11	208	17:10	73, 103, 126, 162		
16:9	112, 278	17:11	126		
16:10	112, 113, 237	17:11–12	391n11	18:5–6	165
16:10–17	120, 346, 347	17:12	127	18:6	168
16:11	113	17:13	127, 210	18:6–7	165
16:11–12	209, 237	17:13–14	396n14	18:7	165
16:12	114–15	17:14	126, 156	18:8	165
16:12–13	115	17:14–15	127, 350, 351	18:9–10	165, 278
16:13	115, 126, 236	17:15	127	18:11	143, 276
16:14–15	115	17:15–16	396n12	18:12	168
16:15	115	17:16	128–29, 351, 395n10	18:12–13	166, 233
16:16	116			18:12–17	396n14
16:16–24	168	17:16–21	120	18:14	166
16:16–39	103	17:17	73	18:14–16	269
16:16–40	300, 396n14	17:17–18	129	18:15	166
16:18	115	17:18	131	18:17	131
16:18–19	116	17:19	131	18:18	143, 166, 167, 250, 398n54
16:19	131	17:20–21	396n19		
16:19–21	116	17:22	128	18:18–19	139
16:19–34	350	17:22–31	131–32	18:19	73, 169, 178
16:20–21	115	17:23	129, 133	18:19–20	178
16:21	117, 303	17:24	134	18:19–21	169, 356
16:22	61	17:24–26	134	18:21	179
16:22–24	116	17:26	134	18:22	169, 246, 247, 250

516

18:23	172, 173, 174, 389n19	20–28	361	20:21	244
		20:1–2	77, 199, 413–14n24	20:22	455n58
18:24	184			20:22–23	243, 244, 455n58
18:24–27	225	20:2	213, 276, 351		
18:25	179	20:2–3	213, 223	20:23	240, 242, 245, 258
18:26	139, 178, 398n54	20:2–6	352		
18:26–27	169	20:2a	199	20:24	244
18:27	179	20:3	36, 232, 421n1	20:24–25	360
18:28	184	20:3a	233	20:25	242, 243, 332
19:1	175, 179	20:3b	234	20:27	243
19:1–2	179	20:3b–6	234	20:28	244
19:1–7	179	20:4	171, 196, 209, 223, 232, 236, 271, 273, 281, 352, 413–14n24, 421n5	20:28–30	243
19:1–20:1	356			20:29	243, 244, 425n54
19:4–5	180				
19:6	106, 180			20:29–30	243, 316
19:8	73, 179, 180			20:31	181, 244, 276, 316
19:9	180–81, 203, 316	20:4–6	267, 356		
19:9–10	254	20:5	236, 271, 421–22n5	20:33	244
19:10	181, 276, 316			20:33–35	122, 243
19:11	181	20:5–6	117, 421n5, 455n58	20:33–36	179
19:11–20	181			20:34–35	244
19:12	179, 181	20:5–15	346, 347	20:36–38	244
19:13–14	200	20:6	234, 236, 237, 361	20:38	243, 332, 360
19:13–20	311			21:1	244
19:18–21	356	20:6–12	77, 112, 360	21:1–2	241
19:21	192, 205, 258, 354, 455n58	20:7	208, 237, 238	21:1–18	346, 347
		20:7–12	427n13	21:2	245
19:22	182, 183, 193, 354, 409n10	20:9	238	21:3	232, 245
		20:11	238	21:4	245, 332, 361, 424n50
19:23–38	316	20:12	239		
19:24	206	20:13	239, 240	21:6	245
19:26	206, 254	20:14	239, 240	21:7	245, 405n7
19:26–27	207, 356	20:14–15	208	21:8	245, 263, 365
19:29	196, 204, 207, 209, 223, 271	20:15	240, 241	21:8–9	40
		20:16	234, 238, 241	21:8–16	267
19:30–31	207	20:16–17	199	21:9	365
19:31	356	20:17	198, 242	21:10	69
19:33–35	356	20:18–21	243	21:10–12	332
19:35	176, 207	20:18b–21	243–44	21:10a	246
19:39	207	20:18b–35	243	21:10b–11	246
19:40	207	20:19	36, 244, 254	21:11	361, 424n50
19:41	207	20:20	180, 244	21:13	246, 258, 361

INDEX OF SCRIPTURE AND OTHER ANCIENT SOURCES

21:13–14	332	22:6	17, 24	23:23	429n1
21:15	246	22:6–7	20	23:25	429n56
21:16	246, 263	22:6–10	19	23:25–30	262
21:17–18	249, 428n32	22:6–11	257	23:26	256
21:17–19	103	22:7	24, 25, 27, 374–75n18	23:26–30	260
21:18	99			23:29	260, 269, 361
21:19	427n13	22:8	24, 28	23:30	268
21:19–20	249	22:9	28	23:33	429n1
21:20–21	91	22:10	20	23:33–24:23	361
21:20–22	226	22:11	20, 28	23:33–27:1	356
21:20b	249	22:12	16, 31	23:35	262, 263, 356, 357
21:20b–21	249	22:12–14	257	24:1	166, 333
21:21	297	22:12–16	20	24:2–5	265
21:22	250	22:15	20, 26, 257	24:4	80
21:23–24	250	22:17–21	50, 278	24:5	250, 265
21:24	405n7	22:18	50	24:5–6	166, 333
21:25	97, 101, 146	22:20	12	24:6	265, 450n35
21:26	252	22:21	50, 257, 375n23	24:6–9	266
21:27	252, 254	22:22	255, 257	24:10	266
21:27–28	255	22:24	257	24:11	266
21:28	257, 427n20, 450n35	22:25	3, 324	24:14	250
		22:25–26	116	24:14–16	266
21:29	255, 273, 275, 356, 361	22:28	3	24:17	249, 266
		22:29	116, 428n40	24:18	252
21:30	255, 259	22:30	428n40	24:19	266
21:31	255	22:30–23:10	361, 429n45	24:21	266
21:31–32	255, 256			24:22	266
21:33	256	23:1–2	260	24:23	264, 267, 428n40
21:36	255, 256, 257	23:6	4, 9, 330	24:24	266
21:37–38	256	23:6–9	260	24:26	267
21:38	256	23:7	260	24:27	267
21:39	2, 3	23:9	9, 361	24:29	266
21:39–40	256	23:9–10	260	25:1	429n1
22	26	23:11	258, 264, 278	25:1–2	267
22:1	257	23:12–15	268	25:2–3	268
22:1–21	15	23:12–22	260	25:3	269
22:3	1, 2, 4, 14, 15, 247	23:16	248	25:5	268
22:3–5	257	23:16–17	428n40	25:6	429n1
22:4	15	23:17–18	2	25:6–26:32	361
22:4–5	20	23:19	2	25:7–8	270
22:5	14, 15	23:19–21	268	25:9	268, 269
22:5–6	17	23:19–22	2	25:11	269

Index of Scripture and Other Ancient Sources

25:11–12	269, 357	27:2–3	271	28:3–5	280
25:15	268	27:3	273, 276, 287,	28:4	280
25:16	268, 325		457n30	28:6	280
25:18	166	27:4	274	28:7	280
25:18–19	269, 361	27:4–5	274	28:8–9	281
25:19	166	27:5	273, 274	28:10	281
25:22	270	27:5–6	263	28:11	280, 286, 287,
25:23	264, 270	27:6	274, 457n30		437n8
25:24	268	27:7	273, 274, 361,	28:12	287
25:25	269, 314, 361		434n21	28:13	286, 287, 437n12
25:26	270, 451n39	27:7–8	434n20	28:13–14	226, 276
26:3	270	27:8	273, 275	28:14	287, 437n15
26:4	4	27:8a	275	28:14–16	276
26:5	4, 6, 13, 247	27:9–10	275	28:15	289, 297
26:9–11	20	27:10	276	28:16	289, 291, 438n29,
26:10	14	27:11	457n30		439n30
26:11	15	27:11–12	276	28:17	73, 291
26:12	17	27:12	276	28:17–20	291
26:12–18	19	27:16	278	28:19	357
26:13	17, 24	27:17a	278	28:20	291, 440n42
26:13–15	20	27:17b	278	28:23	290
26:14	15, 24, 25, 28,	27:18–19	278	28:24	291
	374–75n18	27:20	278	28:30	291
26:15	28	27:21	276	28:30–31	291, 332, 370
26:16	24	27:21–26	278	28:31	332
26:16–18	20, 25	27:23	278		
26:17	29, 375n8	27:23–24	280	**Romans**	
26:17–18	26, 30, 31, 50,	27:24	278, 334, 367,	1:1	24
	59		451n39	1:1–5	32
26:18	33, 35, 47	27:28	279	1:1–6	24
26:20	26, 270	27:29–30	279	1:2–3	81, 385n13
26:22–23	270	27:31	457n30	1:3	25, 32, 39
26:23	119	27:31–32	279	1:4	378n21
26:24	3, 270	27:33–35	279	1:5	225, 338
26:28	270	27:36–38	279	1:8	224, 225, 457n26
26:31	314, 361	27:37	274	1:9–15	192
26:32	270, 281, 357, 361	27:40	279	1:11	225
27:1	270, 271, 432n32,	27:41	280, 286	1:11–12	224
	457n30	27:43	457n30	1:12	226
27:1–28:16	346, 347,	27:43–44	280	1:13	225, 227
	348	28:1–2	280	1:14	84
27:2	267, 271, 356	28:2	280		

INDEX OF SCRIPTURE AND OTHER ANCIENT SOURCES

1:15	228	4:25	81, 231	11:26–27	231
1:16	73	5:3–4	66	12:1	232
1:16–17	228	5:6–8	221	12:1–15:7	225
1:17	228, 230	5:12	231	12:3	225, 232
1:18–32	132	5:17	231	12:5	304
1:19–20	85	5:18	231	12:9	309
2:1	230	5:20	30, 297	12:14	232
2:3	230	5:21	231	12:16	232
2:4	85	6:1	228, 249, 295	12:17–21	232
2:6–11	308	6:1–14	30, 46	13:1–10	307
2:9–10	420n35	6:2b	48	13:8–10	232, 309
2:11	229, 321	6:3	304	13:13	98
2:12	230	6:4	449n14	14:1	232
2:13	230	6:4–11	24	14:1–15:6	441–42n63
2:14–16	132	6:5	304	14:1–15:13	226
2:15	328	6:11	48	14:2–3	227, 295
2:17	230	6:12	231	14:3	110, 226
2:18	230	6:14	231	14:3a	101
2:20	230	6:15	228, 249, 295	14:3b	102
2:20–22	230	6:17	46	14:5	252
2:25–29	230	6:17–18	48	14:5–6	110, 227, 252
3:1	227	7:5	30	14:5–9	236
3:4	420n42	7:6	30, 297	14:5a	295
3:5	228	7:10–11	30	14:10	102, 110
3:8	228, 249, 294	7:12	30	14:11	82
3:9	420n35	8:1–6	231	14:13	102, 110
3:9–20	231	8:12–13	231	14:13–23	98
3:20	230	8:28	66	14:14	98, 251, 295
3:21	228, 229	8:31–39	66	14:15	98
3:21–26	221, 230	8:34	24	14:19	98
3:22	228	9:3	67	14:20	295
3:23	231	9:4–5	172, 406n25	14:20–21	110
3:24	230	9:6	231	15:1	232
3:25	85, 133, 228	9:30–33	29	15:1–2	98
3:25–26	230	10:2	15, 29	15:5–6	252
3:26	228, 230, 231	10:3	228	15:5–7	102
3:29–30	308	10:12	308, 420n35	15:7	226, 232, 295
3:31	228	11:1	4, 231	15:8–9	82
4:1–8	81, 231	11:5	231	15:8–12	172
4:6–8	31	11:13	227, 338	15:11–12	81
4:11	110, 252	11:13–16	82	15:14	224
4:12	100	11:16	235	15:15	225
4:17	231	11:25–27	82	15:15–16	224, 225, 338

Index of Scripture and Other Ancient Sources

15:16	225, 236, 255	16:11	227, 441n62	2:9	186
15:18–21	236	16:11a	224	3:1–3	195
15:19	199, 214, 219, 337, 351	16:12	418–19n20	3:2	141
		16:12–13	224	3:4	182
15:19–20	220	16:13	331, 342	3:6	142
15:20	224–25	16:14	441n62	3:7	142
15:20–21	34	16:15	441n62	3:9	142, 187, 300
15:21	221	16:17	295	3:10	142, 187
15:22–29	370	16:18	295	3:11	187
15:22–32	224	16:21	223, 232, 273, 300, 338, 413–14n24	3:16–17	187
15:23–24	192			3:21	186
15:24	222, 224, 226, 236, 281, 354, 368, 445n1	16:22	223	3:22	99
		16:23	223, 361, 409n15	4:3–5	184, 194
				4:6	185
15:25	183, 444n36, 455n58	**1 Corinthians**		4:7	186
		1:2	188	4:9–13	338
15:25–28	338	1:10–12	183	4:10–12	140
15:26	171, 232	1:12	99, 102, 182	4:11	179
15:26–27	226, 235	1:14	165, 223	4:12	120
15:27	70, 103, 110, 172, 338	1:14–16	139	4:17	107, 182, 183, 195, 338, 409n10
		1:17	184, 211		
15:28	224, 281, 354, 368, 445n1	1:18	186, 211	4:18	185, 192, 194
		1:18–2:5	132	4:18–19	181, 205
15:30	226	1:19	103	4:19	185, 192, 194
15:30–31	455n58	1:20	184, 211	4:20	194
15:30–31a	233	1:22–25	303	4:21	194, 211
15:30–32	224	1:23	59, 165, 186	5–6	181
15:31	240, 242, 421n1	1:26	185	5:1	183, 188
15:31a	226	1:26–28	186	5:1–2	186
15:31b	226	1:26–29	141, 308	5:1–5	194
16:1	213, 342	1:29	186	5:1–13	98, 182
16:1–2	137, 166, 223	1:30	186	5:2	183
16:3	227, 300, 354, 398n54	1:31	186	5:7	39
		2:1	184, 211	5:7–8	235
16:3–4	224	2:1–2	133	5:9	182, 183, 409n14, 411n49
16:3–5	139, 179, 338	2:1–5	141		
16:3–16	223	2:2	59, 165, 211	6:1	183
16:5	224, 235, 441n62	2:2–3	165	6:3	183, 191
16:6	227	2:3	186	6:7–8	183
16:7	227, 342, 354	2:3–4	184, 211	6:10	191
16:8	224	2:4	186	6:12	183, 186, 187, 194
16:9–10a	224	2:8	39, 59, 81	6:12–20	98, 186
16:10	441n62			6:12–21	182

6:13–14	191	10:17	235	12:26	172		
6:13–17	188	10:19–21	98	12:28	187		
6:15–16	183	10:20–22	189	12:30	187		
6:15–19	381–82n32	10:23	186, 187	13:1	187		
6:16	39, 97	10:23–11:1	189	13:1–14:1	187		
7:1	183–84	10:25	98	13:8	187		
7:1–40	184, 188	10:25–27	98	14:1–25	187		
7:10	39	10:25–30	98	14:1–40	187		
7:18	107	10:31–32	67	14:4–6	180		
7:18–19	251	10:31–33	98	14:22	180		
7:25	184	10:31–11:1	252	14:23–25	140		
8:1	184, 187	10:32	102, 141	14:39	180		
8:1–11:1	184	11:2	184	15:1	184		
8:4	189	11:2–16	184	15:1–11	190		
8:4–6	98	11:5	189	15:1–58	184		
8:5–6	59	11:7–12	188	15:3	33, 45, 48, 119, 190		
8:7–13	189	11:13	189	15:3–4	39, 81, 119		
8:8	98, 251	11:17	184, 443n9	15:3–5	38		
8:9	187	11:17–34	191, 237, 303, 443n9	15:3–11	38, 59		
8:10	98, 186, 187, 189			15:4–7	39		
9:1–2	211	11:18	410n23	15:5	102–3, 152, 410n25		
9:2	184	11:18–19	183				
9:4–5	120	11:20	235	15:5–8	81		
9:5	99, 102, 410n25	11:20–22	186	15:7	38, 103, 410n25		
9:6	120, 172	11:21–22	183	15:8–9	337		
9:11–12	211	11:22	443n9	15:9	15, 18, 45		
9:14	39, 120	11:23	39	15:9–10	319, 338		
9:15	120, 211	11:23–26	235	15:9–10a	45		
9:16	22, 37	11:24–25	33, 39	15:9–11	184		
9:16–17	18, 106, 117	11:25	141	15:10	18		
9:18	120, 155, 211	11:33–34	183	15:10b	45		
9:19–23	98	11:34	192	15:11	410n25		
9:20	109	12:1	184	15:12	190		
9:20–23	252	12:1–14:40	184	15:12–13	190		
9:23	335	12:2	188	15:16–19	191		
10:1	189	12:8–10	180	15:17	190		
10:1–13	189	12:10	187	15:18	190		
10:1–22	98	12:12	304	15:20	191, 335		
10:7	97	12:13	309	15:21–22	189, 190		
10:12	189	12:14–16	187	15:23–28	190		
10:14	189	12:21	187	15:25–49	189		
10:14–22	97	12:25	235	15:29	190		

15:29–32	335	16:17	183	2:12–16	215
15:30–32	191	16:19	139, 169, 180, 338, 398n54	2:13	77, 208, 238, 338, 351
15:32	193, 195, 196, 354, 456n14	16:21	341	2:13–14	205
15:32–34	191			2:14	338
15:35	190	**2 Corinthians**		2:17	212, 216, 217, 302
15:42–44	59, 135, 335	1:1	107, 182, 223, 413–14n24	3:1	211, 212
15:44	411n43			3:1–6	215
15:45	190	1:3–5	317	3:3	444n36
15:45–49	190	1:8	209	3:4–18	212
15:47	24, 190	1:8–9	77, 209	3:7–18	215
15:50	191	1:8–10	354	3:14–16	30
15:51–53	191	1:10	209	4:1	216
15:54	191	1:11	209	4:1–2	302
15:54–55	190, 335	1:12	212	4:2	122, 211, 212, 216
15:54–57	191	1:12–2:4	411–12n49	4:4	23
15:56	30, 190	1:13	211	4:4–6	26
16:1	110, 174, 184	1:15	194, 196	4:5–6	20
16:1–4	184, 191, 338	1:15–16	194, 411n49, 413–14n24	4:6	23
16:2	70, 140, 237, 251			4:7–12	216
16:2–4	174	1:15–17	211, 435n41	4:8–12	338
16:3	194, 251	1:16	198, 199, 226, 411–12n49	4:10	211, 212
16:3–4	171			4:10–11	216
16:4	192, 251	1:17	204, 211, 212, 215	4:14	216
16:5	192, 194, 413–14n24	1:19	156, 350, 351	4:18	212
		1:23	195, 199, 204, 211, 413–14n24	5:1	216
16:5–6	195, 435n41			5:4	216, 335
16:5–9	337, 411–12n49	1:24	215	5:6	216
16:6	192, 196, 211, 226, 411–12n49	2:1	194, 199, 204, 413–14n24	5:9	335
				5:10	216
16:8	169	2:3–4	211, 215	5:11	216
16:8–9	192, 338, 435n41	2:4	204–5, 211, 216	5:12	24, 193, 211, 212, 216, 217
16:9	65, 181, 193, 195, 196	2:5–11	195		
		2:6	217, 415n40	5:13	212
16:10	107, 192, 194, 409n10, 409n16, 447n1	2:6–7	210	5:14	24, 216
		2:7	210	5:14–15	211, 212
		2:8	415n40	5:15	217
16:10–11	182	2:9	204–5	5:16	23
16:11	193, 195	2:12	112, 205, 208, 337, 351	5:17	24, 65, 216, 335
16:12	181, 182, 184			5:18	214
16:15	135, 235	2:12–13	77, 199, 207, 209, 236, 238	5:19	216
16:15–16	185			5:21	39, 46, 81

523

6:2	82, 216	8:18–19	217	11:5	211, 218, 416n18
6:3–10	217	8:19	174, 194, 217,	11:5–12	243
6:4	211		223	11:6	62, 211, 217
6:5	140, 354	8:19–20	183, 444n36	11:7	155, 217
6:8	217, 249	8:19–21	171, 251	11:7–10	212
6:12	213	8:20	217	11:7–11	211
7:2	212, 213	8:20–21	212, 217	11:7–12	217
7:4	210	8:21	174, 251	11:7–15	276
7:5	77, 199, 208, 337,	8:22	213	11:8–9	115, 120, 156,
	347, 351	8:22–23	217		209
7:5–7	238	8:22–24	223	11:9	122, 155, 351
7:6–7	338	8:23	205, 338	11:11	216
7:6–13a	217	9:1	183, 217	11:12	211
7:7	210	9:2	182, 193, 210	11:13	218
7:8	208	9:3	213, 217, 219	11:13–15	302
7:9	204	9:3–5	219, 223	11:14–15	218
7:11	210	9:4	204	11:16–18	218
7:12	204–5, 415n40	9:5	174, 213	11:18	211
7:13	210, 213	9:7	70, 175	11:20	62, 218
7:13b–15	217	9:11–14	304	11:20–22	211
7:14	195, 205, 208,	9:12	171, 217	11:21	218
	210	9:12–13	183	11:21b–33	218
7:15	210, 213	9:13	217, 249	11:22	4, 211, 212
7:16–9:15	217	9:13–14	175	11:22–23	62, 218, 303
8:1–5	70, 304	10:1	211	11:23	140, 215, 218,
8:1–9:15	338	10:2	213		354
8:2	210	10:8	216	11:23–25	338
8:3–5	210	10:9	211	11:23–27	61
8:4	183, 217	10:9–10	211	11:24	36
8:5	210	10:10	184, 211, 217,	11:25	85, 117
8:6	182, 193, 205, 338		243	11:25–27	106
8:7	216	10:12	211	11:26	136
8:8–9	70	10:12–13	62	11:27	120, 140, 155, 168
8:9	338	10:13–14	220	11:28	155, 168
8:10	182, 193	10:14	243	11:28–29	130
8:11–15	70	10:15	220	11:29	155
8:13–15	172	10:15–16	222, 223	11:30	218
8:16	338	10:15–18	62	11:32	16, 349
8:16–17	213	10:16	220	11:32–33	35, 37, 338, 349
8:16–18	223	10:18	211	11:33	377n30
8:16–24	213, 219	11:1	218	12:1	62
8:18	213	11:4	212	12:1–4	62

Reference	Pages	Reference	Pages	Reference	Pages
12:1–6	218	1:2	87, 445n49	2:2–3	149
12:2	209	1:4	144	2:2–5	71
12:2–3	63, 77	1:6	87, 91, 95, 110, 144	2:3	67, 91, 92, 109
12:2–4	63	1:7	92, 146	2:3–4	92
12:4	219	1:8–9	144	2:3–5	107, 146
12:7	63, 76, 130, 219, 381–82n32	1:10	91, 148, 243	2:4	94, 95, 102
		1:10–2:14	148	2:5	94, 148
12:7–9	209	1:11–12	152	2:6	148, 152, 321
12:7a	65	1:11–17	20, 149	2:6–9	91–92, 152
12:7b	65	1:11–24	148	2:6–10	92, 149, 170
12:8	77	1:11–2:14	149	2:7–9	97
12:8–9	65	1:12	20, 23, 26	2:7–10	148
12:9	37	1:12–16	337	2:9	38, 71, 148, 218
12:10	61, 65, 66, 219	1:13	15, 20, 21, 29	2:10	70–71, 110, 171, 249, 406n24
12:11	211, 218, 416n18	1:13–14	12, 14, 18, 45		
12:11–12	218	1:13–17	21	2:11–13	211
12:11b–12	211	1:14	12, 13, 18, 23, 29	2:11–14	99, 104, 146, 251
12:12	338, 409n8	1:15	24, 82		
12:13	217	1:15–16	18, 22	2:11–15	99–100
12:13–14	122	1:15–17	21, 26	2:12	100–101, 147
12:13–18	212	1:15–18	33	2:12–13	147
12:14	120, 199, 213, 223	1:16	20, 23, 26, 31, 32, 50, 58, 59, 149	2:13	101, 172, 349
				2:13–14	152
12:14–15	122, 223	1:16–17	50	2:14	102, 148, 149
12:15	216	1:16–18	376n14	2:14–15	102
12:16	212, 217	1:16–2:10	337	2:15	67, 152
12:17–18	243, 244, 251	1:17	35, 349	2:15–16	49, 146, 150, 152
12:18	182, 193	1:17–18	16, 26, 351		
12:19	216	1:18	38, 43, 49, 71, 349	2:15–21	149
12:20	193, 213			2:16	102
12:20–21	195	1:18–19	49, 68, 71, 149	2:18	151
12:21	182, 193, 194, 196, 223	1:18–21	382n10	2:19b–20	45, 48
		1:18–2:10	70	2:20	24, 47
13:1	199, 213, 223	1:19	38	2:21	95, 151
13:1–4	223	1:21	52, 59, 104, 379n38, 388n3	3:1	59, 81, 133, 144, 154
13:2	193, 194–95			3:4	87
13:2–3	213	1:23	17, 23, 45, 58, 149	3:5	83, 409n8
13:9–11	216	1:24	82	3:6	149
13:10	213	2:1	70, 71	3:6–9	149
		2:1–2	152	3:8	149
Galatians		2:1–10	53, 91, 99, 338	3:9	149
1:1	148	2:2	70, 91, 92, 94	3:10	45, 153

3:10–13	150, 153, 154, 165	5:14	102	2:3	321
3:11	420n39	5:15	102, 151	2:4–6	319
3:11a	94	5:19–21	151	2:5–6	305, 322
3:11b–12	94	5:26	148, 151	2:10	319, 321
3:13	45, 47, 48, 81, 94–95, 152	6:2	102	2:11–12	319
		6:6	87, 120, 124	2:11–13	172
3:14	95, 150	6:6–7	282	2:11–22	172, 319
3:15–4:7	87	6:10a	308	2:13–18	319
3:18	95	6:10b	308	2:14–17	321
3:19	150	6:11	144, 146, 161–62, 341–42	2:19–22	319
3:22	149, 150			2:22	320
3:24–25	150	6:12	147, 387n7	3:1	317
3:26–28	309	6:12a	91	3:1–10	375n24
3:26–29	95, 150	6:12b	91	3:1–13	319
3:27–29	149	6:13	91	3:2	316, 317
4:1–3	95	6:15	24, 65, 144, 150, 251	3:3	375n24
4:4	39			3:3–7	317
4:4–5	95	6:17	62, 148, 243	3:4	446n6
4:8–9	149			3:6	375n24
4:9	151	**Ephesians**		3:8	319
4:9–11	148	1:1	316, 355	3:9	375n24
4:10	147, 148	1:3–7	318	3:9–10	320
4:13	76, 130, 208	1:3–14	318	3:13	316, 317, 338
4:13–14	78	1:3–23	305	3:14–21	320
4:14	78, 381–82n32	1:8–10	318	4:1	317
4:16	243	1:9–10	315	4:1–2	320
4:16–19	148	1:11–12	318	4:3	320
4:17	147	1:13–14	318	4:7–11	320
4:19	144	1:15	316	4:7–16	320
4:20	144, 148	1:15–16	318	4:8–10	322
4:21	91, 148	1:17–23	318	4:12	305
4:21–31	87	1:18–23	318	4:12–16	320
4:29	87, 90, 147	1:20	24	4:14	316, 326, 338
5:1	96	1:20–21	318	4:15	317
5:2	107, 147	1:20–23	322	4:15–16	305
5:2–3	144	1:21	315	4:17	338
5:2–4	151	1:22	318	4:17–24	98
5:4	95, 148	2:1	321	4:17–5:2	321
5:10	92, 146	2:1–3	319	4:20–21	316
5:11	108, 109, 148, 243	2:1–10	30	4:21	316, 317
5:12	146	2:1–3:13	319	4:25	317
				4:28	122

5:2	309	1:17	295	2:30	300
5:3–14	98	1:18	302	3:1	303
5:5	315	1:18–19	360	3:2–16	303
5:5–6	321, 326	1:20	314, 358	3:3	303
5:6	316, 338	1:21	24, 335	3:4–6	303
5:11–12	321	1:24–26	360	3:4–9	31
5:14	321	1:25	301, 358	3:5	349
5:15–20	321	1:25–26	314	3:5–6	4, 12, 13, 247
5:21	321	1:26	354	3:6	14, 18, 30, 45
5:22–33	321	1:26–27	354	3:6a	29
5:25–33	321	1:27–28	300	3:6b	29
5:31	39	1:27–30	302	3:7–9	22, 303
6:1–4	321	1:28–30	300	3:8	23
6:5–8	321	1:30	116	3:9	31, 230, 303
6:9	308, 309, 310, 321	2:1–30	302	3:12	18
6:10–20	322	2:2	300	3:17	301
6:14	317	2:2–3	302	3:18	303
6:14–20	322	2:5	300, 302	3:18–19	303, 443n9
6:18b–20	317	2:6	302	3:20–21	59, 304, 335
6:19	315	2:7	302	3:21	24, 451n47
6:20	291, 315	2:8	302	4:2	300
6:21	273, 292, 315	2:9–11	302	4:2–3	116, 304, 342
6:21–22	281, 292, 315, 355, 359, 453n21	2:12–16	302	4:4–9	304
		2:14	300	4:9	301
		2:15	300	4:10–20	301, 304
		2:17	331	4:11–13	304
Philippians		2:19	107, 273, 331, 356	4:15	118, 395n58
1:1	107, 198, 273, 282, 292, 300, 314, 350, 360	2:19–22	195	4:15–16	115, 124, 138, 209, 337, 391n10
		2:19–23	338		
		2:19–24	292	4:16	120, 350, 394n41
1:5	301	2:19–30	302, 354	4:17–18	304
1:7	291, 301	2:20	107, 127, 328	4:18	299
1:10	301, 302	2:22	107, 328, 350	4:22	353, 357
1:12	301, 355	2:22–23	107		
1:12–14	66	2:23	331	**Colossians**	
1:12–18	302	2:23–24	314, 354, 359	1:1	107, 273, 292, 314, 360
1:12–18a	302	2:24	354, 358, 360		
1:13	291, 338, 353, 356, 357	2:25	299	1:2	305
		2:25–30	292, 299	1:3–14	305
1:13–17	291	2:26	300	1:5–7	312
1:14	295	2:26–27	300	1:6–8	175
1:15	295, 303, 332	2:27	300		

527

INDEX OF SCRIPTURE AND OTHER ANCIENT SOURCES

1:7	292, 306, 419n21	4:11	100	2:14–16	51–52, 268
1:7–8	292	4:12	175, 292, 359, 443–44n21	2:14–17	130
1:9–14	312			2:15	51–52, 269
1:15–20	312	4:14	358, 359	2:15–16	52
1:18	304	4:16	313, 340, 353, 355, 359	2:17	123, 124, 126, 157, 162, 350
1:21–22	312			2:18	77, 130
1:23	312	4:17	305, 359	2:19	130
2:1	306, 407n38	4:18	291, 342	3:1	123, 130, 133, 145, 168, 350, 351, 396n12
2:4	310, 326				
2:8	310, 312, 326	**1 Thessalonians**			
2:8–23	305	1:1	103, 107, 350, 392n18, 399n12	3:1–2	130
2:12	449n14			3:1–3	77, 350, 351
2:12–13	304	1:3	284	3:1–5	156, 157
2:12–15	313	1:5	85, 157, 392n18	3:2	107, 156
2:15	310, 445n46	1:6	130	3:4–5	130
2:16	310	1:7–8	337	3:5	123, 130, 396n12
2:16–23	313, 326	1:7–10	155	3:6	107, 145, 156, 157, 401n3
2:18	310, 311, 445n38	1:8	401n1		
2:19	304	1:8–9	145	3:7	168
2:20	310	1:9	85, 119, 125	3:8	401n3
2:21	310	1:9–10	59, 98, 124, 133	3:8–9	123
2:23	310, 312, 313, 326	1:9b–10	156	3:10	124, 156, 162, 401n3
3:1	24, 30	1:10	119, 158		
3:1–3	304	2:1–12	157	3:12	123
3:1–4:6	313	2:2	116, 117, 157, 168, 300, 337, 350, 391n10, 401n5, 419n25	4:2	124
3:5	98			4:2–8	98, 182
3:9–11	309			4:4–5	157
3:14	309			4:6	124, 133
3:25	321	2:3	157	4:7	157
4:1	308	2:4	157	4:8	157
4:3	306	2:5	157	4:11	163, 419n25
4:7	273, 292	2:6	157	4:11–12	163, 164
4:7–8	292, 359, 453n21	2:7–8	157	4:12	123, 164
4:7–9	281, 307, 356	2:8	123	4:13	162
4:9	175, 292, 315, 359, 443–44n21	2:9	120, 138, 140, 157, 168	4:13–18	60, 157, 190
				4:15–17	158
4:10	49, 172, 271, 292, 356, 358, 359, 388n31	2:10	157	4:16	124, 130, 160, 162
		2:11	123, 157		
		2:12	158		
4:10–14	305	2:14	51	4:16–17	39
4:10a	323	2:14–15	36, 39, 59, 349, 431n27	5:1–2	124
4:10b	323			5:1–3	158

5:1–11	160	3:6	163, 164	3:2	203
5:2	119	3:6–9	122	3:4	201
5:2–3	160	3:6–15	161, 163, 338,	3:7	203
5:2–4	39		393n35	3:8–13	282
5:2–10	119	3:7–8	120	3:10	203, 444n36
5:3	125, 156, 161	3:7–10	164	3:13	444n36
5:4	161	3:8	138, 140, 168	3:14	197, 198, 203, 360
5:5	158	3:9	120, 155	3:15	199, 201, 203
5:8	158	3:10	122, 163, 164	4:1–2	325
5:8–9	160	3:13	122	4:1–3	316, 325
5:9	158	3:14	164	4:1–5	338
5:12–13	124, 282	3:15	164	4:2	200, 203, 326
5:14	163	3:17	146, 161, 341, 342	4:3	199, 201, 202, 203
5:19–20	180			4:7	199, 201, 325
5:19–21	162	**1 Timothy**		4:12	203, 338
5:27	146, 161, 400n14	1:2	338	4:13	197, 198
		1:3	107, 196, 197,	4:14	107, 197, 329,
2 Thessalonians			198, 338, 360,		389n7, 449n23
1:1	103, 107, 350,		413–14n24	5:1–6:2	338
	399n12	1:3–4	242, 316	5:3	202
1:3–4	163	1:3–5	196	5:4	202
1:4	162	1:4	199, 201, 203, 325	5:8	202
1:5–12	163	1:5	197, 202, 327	5:9	282
1:10	119	1:6	199	5:11	282
2:1–12	160, 161, 338	1:6–7	242	5:13	201, 202, 316
2:2	119, 161, 162, 341,	1:7	199, 201, 202	5:16	202
	342, 403n34	1:8	202	5:17–22	197
2:2–3	162	1:9–11	202	5:18	39, 120
2:3	119	1:10	197, 201, 327	5:22	243
2:3–4	39	1:12–17	18	5:23	341
2:3–12	119, 344,	1:13	15, 45, 202	6:3	197, 201
	392–93n26	1:18	338	6:3–5	242
2:4	163	1:19	197, 203, 326	6:3–10	316
2:5	119, 162, 403n35	1:20	325	6:4	199
2:6–7	163	2:1–3:13	338	6:4–5	203, 325
2:7	163	2:2	203	6:5	199, 200, 201, 203,
2:8	164	2:4	203		244
2:9	163	2:8–15	201	6:10	200, 244, 276
2:13	163, 235	2:9–15	197	6:11	203
2:14–15	377n28	2:15	197	6:20	199, 242, 343–44
3:1–2a	165	3:1–13	197, 201, 243, 344	6:20–21	325
				6:21	198

529

2 Timothy

Verse	Pages
1:2	328
1:3	327
1:3–7	338
1:4	324, 328
1:5	84, 106, 329
1:6	329, 449n23
1:6–7	106, 329, 389n7
1:8	291, 329
1:9	329
1:12	291, 329, 450n26
1:13	327
1:14	329
1:15	315, 323, 324, 329
1:16	291, 292, 331
1:16–17	358
1:16–18	324
1:17	355, 358
1:17–18	329
1:18	323, 329, 331, 338, 444n36
2:1	329, 338
2:2	330, 450n28
2:8	330
2:8–9	330
2:9	291
2:12	329
2:14	330, 450n28
2:16	326, 330
2:16–18	330
2:17	323
2:17–18	326
2:18	330
2:19	326
2:22	326, 338
2:23	326, 330
2:25	330
3:5	330
3:6	326
3:6–7	338
3:8	201, 326
3:10–11	86, 338
3:10–15	330
3:11	109
3:12	330
3:13	201, 326, 415n33
3:14–15	330
3:15	84, 338
3:16	330
3:17	330
4	370
4:2	330
4:3	326, 327
4:3–5	330
4:6	331, 369
4:6–8a	315
4:6–18	369
4:7	331
4:8	329
4:8a	331
4:8b	331
4:9	107, 324, 328, 362
4:9–12	292
4:9–21	362
4:10	222, 324, 362
4:10–11	358
4:10–13	341
4:11	172, 292, 323, 324, 332, 356, 362, 369, 440n44
4:12	273, 292, 315, 323, 331, 338, 356, 362
4:13	315, 328, 356, 360, 362
4:13–14	328
4:13–15	331
4:15	328
4:16	295, 315, 324, 325, 332–33, 369, 448n6
4:17	369, 448n9
4:18	329
4:19	323, 324, 331, 398n54
4:20	273, 275, 360, 362
4:21	107, 324, 328, 331, 362, 440n44
4:22	198, 328

Titus

Verse	Pages
1:1	283
1:2–3	283
1:4	92
1:5	273, 276, 282, 338, 360, 433n20, 434n21
1:5–9	338
1:7	282
1:9	327
1:10	276, 283, 387n25
1:10–14	282
1:11	276, 282, 284, 338
1:12	276, 283–84
1:14	284
1:14–15	276–77
1:15	327
1:16	276
2:1–10	282, 338
2:2	284
2:3–5	284
2:4	284
2:4–5	284
2:5	284
2:6	284
2:6–8	284
2:8	284
2:9–10	284
2:10	284
2:11–12	285
2:14	285
3:1–2	282, 285
3:2	360
3:3	285
3:4–7	285
3:8	276

Index of Scripture and Other Ancient Sources

3:9	276, 284	2:24	47, 48	1:62–63	89
3:9–10	284	5:13	43, 49, 72, 99, 331	2:24–27	13
3:11	276			2:29–41	89
3:12	273, 281, 314	**Jude**		2:46–47	89
3:13	226, 276, 281	12	237	2:50	13
3:14	276			2:54	13
3:15	198, 282	**Revelation**		3:13–26	261
		2:2–4	446n5	3:49–53	168
Philemon		2:6	446n5	5:48	112
1	107, 175, 273, 292, 305, 306, 314, 338, 359, 360	2:7	65		
		2:14	97	**2 Maccabees**	
		2:20	97	3:12	19
1–2	306	21:3–4	65	3:25–36	20
2	305, 306, 413n22	22:2	65	5:15–6:6	403n40
7	175, 306			5:17–20	11
8–9	307	**Deuterocanoni-**		6:1–7:42	55
9	309	**cal Works**		6:2	55, 162, 403–4n41
10	175, 291, 292, 308, 309	**Tobit**		**Old Testament**	
10–20	443–44n21	11:9	238	**Apocrypha and**	
12	308, 354	11:13	238	**Pseudepigrapha**	
13	291, 292, 309				
15	307	**Judith**		**1 Enoch**	
16	309	1:1	345	12–16	64, 381n27
17	175, 306, 308, 309	12:7	115	14:8	63
17–18	309			14:16	63
18	308	**Wisdom**		14:19–20	63
19	175, 443–44n21	7:17	310		
22	306, 314, 354, 357, 358, 360	7:20	310	**4 Ezra**	
		7:26	312	5:20	311
23	175, 292, 338, 419n21	9:1–2	312	6:31	311
				6:35	311
23–24	292, 305, 359	**1 Maccabees**		9:23–26	311
24	172, 271, 292, 323, 358	1:11	89	14:37–48	312
		1:41–50	55	14:42	312
		1:43	89		
1 Peter		1:48	89	**Joseph and Aseneth**	
1:3–5	446n12	1:54	55, 403–4n41	6–13	19
2:22	46	1:59	403–4n41	14:2–17	19
2:22–25	46	1:60–61	89	14:8	19

Jubilees

3:15	122, 164
30:7	108
30:17	108
30:17–18	108
34:12	231
34:18–19	231

Letter to Aristeas

34	429n56

Psalms of Solomon

17:21	23

Testament of Levi

2:3	64
2:3–10	63
2:6–10	381n31

Testament of Simeon

2:13	29
3:4	29

Testament of Solomon

18	445n40
18:1–2	310
18:3	310
18:4–42	310
18:5	310
18:8	311
18:9	445n41
18:15	311
18:22	445n41
18:29	445n41
18:38	445n41

Dead Sea Scrolls

4Q19

XXVI 9–10	231

4Q169

3–4 I, 7–8	153

11Q11

columns 1–2	445n40

11Q19

LXIV 6–13	153

CD

5	200–201
17b–19	200–201

Ancient Jewish Writers

Josephus

Against Apion (Ag. Ap.)

1.53	408–9n6
2.39	67
2.73	57
2.102–105	427n15
2.103	427n16

Jewish Antiquities (A.J.)

1.38	122, 164
1.219	423n33
2.138	270
2.184	423n33
3.249	235
3.252	235
3.262	250
12.106	115
13.288	6
13.294	6
13.296	6
13.297	6
13.298	6
13.380	153
13.401–402	6
14.29	35
14.71–72	403n40
14.117	35
14.258	115
15.417	427n17
16.16–20	416n9
17.41	6
17.185	264
17.328	227, 287
18.4	13
18.4–7	247
18.8	13
18.15	6
18.23	13, 247
18.55	429n1
18.55–59	403n40
18.57	429n1
18.116–119	180
18.237	380n1
18.252	380n1
18.257–258	57
18.261	403n40
18.273–309	57
18.297–298	381n16
19.283–285	60
19.285	57
19.290	57
19.299–311	57
19.300	57
19.301	381n17
19.303–311	61
19.306	58, 61
19.311	61
19.350–351	380n1
19.351	53
20.4–10	90
20.6–14	297
20.13	268
20.23–25	90
20.51	69
20.100	90
20.100–101	69
20.102	90

20.105–136	259	2.220	266	*Life (Vita)*	
20.116	429n1	2.223–246	259	3.15	348
20.118–136	297	2.228–231	261	16	298
20.120	170	2.232–246	297	191	6, 247
20.123	170	2.237	170		
20.131	265	2.238	170	**Philo**	
20.135–136	265	2.243	265		
20.139	109	2.245	265	*Against Flaccus (Flacc.)*	
20.141–143	266	2.253	427n29	26	54
20.141–144	266	2.254	426n4	27–30	380n5
20.142	200	2.254–255	248	36–40	54
20.160	247	2.258	248	41–43	55
20.161	261	2.259	248	45	55
20.162	265	2.263	256	46	56
20.162–164	267, 430n13	2.264	426n4	47	56
		2.266–270	267	64	396n13
20.163–164	261	2.302	259	95–96	55
20.165	261	2.309–313	168	103	380n5
20.165–166	427n25	2.313	170, 426n12	*Allegorical Interpretation (Leg.)*	
20.167–168	248	2.318	259		
20.173–178	267	2.546–550	261		
20.182	267	2.559–561	32	23.155	293
20.192	333	2.561	349, 373n43	*On the Creation of the World (Opif.)*	
20.193	333	3.354	214		
20.195	298, 334	3.399–408	74		
20.199	6	3.626	215	105	2
20.200	250, 268, 373n40	4.201	427n25	*On the Embassy to Gaius (Legat.)*	
		4.215	427n25		
20.203	373n40	5.190–219	427n15	134	55
20.206–207	260	5.194	427n17, 427n20	179	54, 380n5
				188	56
Jewish War (B.J.)		5.243–244	256	200–202	57
1.110	6	6.125–126	427n17	212	427n17
1.137	341	6.126	254, 256, 259	265	56
1.152	403n40	6.128	333	275–333	57, 381n16
1.663	264	7.43	67	281	380n13
2.104	227, 287	7.43–44	67	282	382n13
2.118	90	7.45	68	346	56
2.162	6	7.100	289		
2.166	7	7.253–258	90	*On the Life of Abraham (Abr.)*	
2.169–177	403n40	7.255	90		
2.171	429n1	7.368	349, 373n43	275	328

533

On the Migration of Abraham (Mig.)

83	415n33

On the Special Laws (Spec.)

1.53	427n23
1.55	13
1.56	13
1.248	168
2.253	13
3.1–6	64
3.3	64
3.5	64
3.100–101	200
4.48–50	200

That the Worse Attacks the Better (Det.)

21	445n38

Rabbinic Works

m. Demai

2:3a	7

m. Hagigah

2:7	8

m. Kelim

5:10	406n20

m. Middot

2:5	427n18

m. Sanhedrin

9:6	255

m. Shabbat

14:3–4	10

m. Sotah

9:9	171, 406n20
9:15	371n1

Early Christian Writings

1 Clement

4.1–13	296
5.1	296, 364
5.2	363
5.4	99
5.4–5	364
5.5	332, 366
5.5–6.1	296
5.6	364
5.6–7	368
5.7	364, 459n19, 459n22
6.1	99, 364, 370, 441n60
6.1–2	296, 441n58
6.2	364
31.2	368
40.5	372n30
44.1–3	296
50.6	368

Clement of Alexandria

Miscellanies (Strom.)

1.14	436n56

Eusebius

Ecclesiastical History (Hist. eccl.)

2.14.6–15.2	331
2.22	359
2.22.2	369
2.22.4	369
2.22.5	369
2.22.6	369, 370
2.22.8	367
2.25.4–5	367
2.25.5	367
2.25.7	334, 459n9
2.25.8	365
3.3.2	460n24
3.3.5	367
3.14–16	458n1
3.25.4	459n18
3.26.1–4	449n13
3.31.1	367
3.31.3	378n8
3.31.4	459n9
3.31.9	40
3.39.1	377n6
3.39.3–4	378n11
3.39.15	49, 378n11
4.23.11	365
5.17.3–4	459n8
6.20.3	365

Gospel of Thomas

71	165

Ignatius of Antioch

To the Ephesians (Eph.)

7	446n5
9	446n5
16	446n5

To the Magnesians (Magn.)

4	327

To the Philadelphians (Phld.)

11.2	453n21

To the Smyrnaeans (Smyrn.)

12.1	453n21

Index of Scripture and Other Ancient Sources

Irenaeus

Against Heresies (Adv. Haer.)
1.23.5	449n13
1.24.2	197
3.10.5	42

John Chrysostom

Homilies on the Acts of the Apostles (Hom. Act.)
43	423n34, 425n59

Justin Martyr

1 Apology
26.2	327
26.4	326–27
56.1	327

Dialogue with Trypho (Dial.)
100.4	42
101.3	42
102.5	42
103.6	42
103.8	42
104.1	42
105.1	42
105.5	42
105.6	42
106.4	42
107.1	42

Muratorian Canon
§ 2	368–69, 457n33

Origen

Against Celsus (Cels.)
5.14	135

Ecclesiastical History (Hist. eccl.)
3.1.3	367

Papias

Exposition of the Logia of the Lord
Prologue	40–42

Tertullian

Against Marcion (Marc.)
4.2.5	42

Antidote for the Scorpion's Sting (Scorp.)
15	367, 459n12

The Soul (An.)
50	449n13

GRECO-ROMAN LITERATURE

Aelius Aristides

Orations (Orat.)
46.22	137

Aeneas Tacticus

Poliorcetica
29.6–8	377n30

Aeschylus

Agamemnon (Ag.)
1624	373n39

Eumenides (Eum.)
644–651	135

Prometheus Bound (Prom.)
942	214

Aratus

Phaenomena (Phaen.)
2–4	134
5	134
5–13	134

Aristotle

Politics (Pol.)
5.3.35–40, 1302b	411n35

Rhetoric (Rhet.)
2.2	117

Arrian

Epicteti dissertationes (Epict. diss.)
3.1.1	138
3.1.14–15	138
3.1.34	398n48
3.1.42	138

Athenaeus

Deipnosophistae (Deipn.)
3.31.19	396n16

Callimachus

Hymns (Hymn.)
1.2	134
1.8–10	436n53

Cassius Dio

Roman History (Hist. Rom.)
47.31.3	3
63.2.3	432n29

INDEX OF SCRIPTURE AND OTHER ANCIENT SOURCES

Chion of Heraclea

Epistulae
4.2 — 348

Cicero

Epistulae ad Atticum (Att.)
1.13 — 438n24
2.10 — 438n24
2.11 — 438n24
2.13 — 438n24
5.20.6 [letter 113] — 185
8.16.2 — 159

Epistulae ad familiares (Fam.)
3.8 — 3
7.25 — 343
10.21 — 341

In Pisonem (Pis.)
36.89 — 352

In Verrum (Verr.)
1 — 448n4
2 — 448n4
2.5.65 — 258

Pro Caelio (Cael.)
20.48 — 182

Pro Rabirio Perduellionis (Rab. Perd.)
4.13 — 154

Demosthenes

On the Crown (Cor.)
127 — 131

Digest of Roman Law (Dig.)
21.1.17.4 — 444n29
22.3.2 — 324
22.5.2 — 325
48.6.7–8 — 391n12, 428n39
48.24.1 — 334
48.24.3 — 334

Dio Chrysostom

Orations (Or.)
5.5–11 — 278
6 — 136
8.5 — 137
31.54–55 — 408n52
32.9 — 121, 131
32.10–11 — 121
32.11 — 121
34.8 — 3

Diodorus Siculus

Library of History (Bib. hist.)
15.7.1 — 95
15.36.2 — 95
15.36.2a — 95

Dionysius of Halicarnassus

Roman Antiquities (Ant. rom.)
13.5–6 — 447n2

Epictetus

Diatribai (Diatr.)
1.11.28 — 327

Discourses (Disc.)
2.19.29 — 437n8

Euripides

Bacchanals (Bacch.)
794–795 — 373n39

Galen

Simple Medicines (Simpl. Med.)
9 — 209

Homer

Odyssey (Od.)
11.568–571 — 397n31

Horace

Satires (Sat.)
1.5.3–24 — 288

Iamblichus

On the Mysteries (Myst.)
3.11 — 445n42

Juvenal

Satires (Sat.)
3.10–16 — 289
3.58–125 — 289
3.62–65 — 438n25
5.1–2 — 164
6.542–547 — 200

Livy

History of Rome
2.33 — 411n35

Lucian

Alexander the False Prophet (Alex.)

5	200
22	200
23	200
56–57	233–34

Charon (Char.)

1	214

Lexiphanes

6.10	377n30

The Lover of Lies (Philops.)

3	436n53

Podagra

170	414n28

The Runaways (Fug.)

12–21	393n30
16	393n30
20	407n32

Salaried Posts in Great Houses (Merc. cond.)

3	212

A True Story (Ver. hist.)

1.2	347
1.4	347

Ovid

Metamorphoses (Metam.)

8.618–724	84

Pausanias

Description of Greece (Descr.)

1.1.4	134

1.14.5	128
1.24.3	128, 395n4
4.31.8	176
7.16.1–10	418n17

Philostratus

Life of Apollonius

6.34.2	58

Pindar

Pythian Odes (Pyth.)

2.89–96	373n39

Plato

Apology (Apol.)

126b	396n18
358b	340
360a	340
363b	340
363b–c	340
363e	340

Letters

9	339–40
12	339–40
13	339–40

Pliny the Elder

Natural History (Nat.)

2.5.27	135, 190
2.47.122	286
2.47.125	433n18
2.232	311
4.10	137
4.119–120	418n7
5.10	69
28.7.36	78
30.2.11	200, 201
31.33	166
32.123	423n27
36.21.95–96	176

Pliny the Younger

Epistulae (Ep.)

2.14	325
4.16	80
17a	416n9

Plutarch

Septem sapientium convivium (Sept. sav. Conv.)

2–3 (146de, 148b)	397n41

Polybius

Histories (Hist.)

2.56.10	347
4.2.1–3	347
5.26.8	289
5.43.3	289
6.46–47	436n55
12.4c.4–5	347
12.25a	80
12.25a.5	243
12.25a–b	80
12.27.4–6	347
12.27–28	41
18.48.4	159

Pseudo-Plato

Epistulae (Ep.)

13 361A	341

Quintilian

Institutio oratoria (Inst.)

12.5–6	325

Sallust

War with Catiline (Bell. Cat.)

3.2	346
4.3–4	346

Seneca

Epistulae morales (Ep.)

51.11	287
77.3	286
88.40	57
101.14	154
104.1	166

De tranquillitate animi (Tranq.)

3.4	327, 328

Sophocles

Ajax (Aj.)

944	96

Fragments of Unknown Plays

591	96

Statius

Silvae (Silv.)

4.3.32–37	288

Strabo

Geography (Geogr.)

3.1.8	221
5.3.6	438n23
5.3.7	439n34
5.4.6	286
5.4.8	437n4

7.17.19	391n4
7.F15a	392n20
8.6.20	136–37
8.6.22	397n41
8.6.23	136
9.1.4	136
12.4.4–6	111
12.8.1–2	111
12.8.13–14	389n19
12.8.14	79
12.8.17	424–25n53
13.1.26	390n27
13.2.2	240
14.1–23	408n50
14.1–42	416n7
14.1.15	241
14.1.35	240–41
14.2.5	245
14.2.29	407n38
14.5.1	2
14.5.10	379n41
14.5.12	3
14.5.13	3
14.5.14	3
14.5.20	379n41
14.6.3	74
16.2.7	52, 383n14
16.2.8	379n42
16.2.22	273
16.4.21	34

Suetonius

Divus Claudius (Claud.)

18–19	433n18
25.3	258
25.4	139, 227, 357

Divus Julius (Jul.)

57	410n33

Nero

36.1	74
48.2–3	290

Tiberius (Tib.)

14.4	74

Tacitus

Annales (Ann.)

2.54	311
2.59	159
4.2	290
12.54	267
15.38	289
15.44	289, 296, 364, 441n60

Historiae (Hist.)

2.278	429n1
5.9	267

Thucydides

History of the Peloponnesian War (P.W.)

1.22.1	80, 243
6.27	128–29
8.99	416n9
102	392n20

Valerius Maximus

8.9	185–86
8.10	186
8.14.5	185
9.1	411n35

Vergil

Aeneid (Aen.)

6.432–433	134
6.566–569	134

Index of Scripture and Other Ancient Sources

Xenophon

Anabasis (Anab.)
7.4.10   238

Memorabilia (Mem.)
1.1.1   131
1.10   129

PAPYRI

P. Cairo Zen.
59015   424n48

P.Oxy.
1.37   430n7, 431n18
9.1189   435n51
42.154   399n4
42.3063   399n2
42.3063, line 11   399n6

P.Tebt.
1.27   435–36n52
2.289   435n51